PERSIA AND THE GREEKS

To

the Greeks of 1940

PERSIA AND THE GREEKS

the Defence of the West, c. 546–478 B.C.

A. R. BURN

Second Edition
With a Postscript by
D. M. LEWIS

Stanford University Press
Stanford, California
1984

Stanford University Press
Stanford, California

Originating publisher of the Second Edition:
Gerald Duckworth & Co. Ltd, London
Second Edition first published in the U.S.A. by
Stanford University Press in 1984

Printed in Great Britain

ISBN 0-8047-1235-2

LC 83-40516

Contents

Maps

Preface to the First Edition

In this volume the writer concludes a program of work undertaken many years ago, attempting to produce a readable account of the early age of Greece, from the age of the Trojan War (in *Minoans, Philistines and Greeks*, 1930) and the late prehistoric (in *The World of Hesiod*, 1936, both long out of print,[1] and the former largely out of date), through *The Lyric Age of Greece* (1960), to the eve of the rise of the Athenian Empire. The rise of Greek civilisation was described in the last-named book; in the present work we begin with that of the Persians, one of the great imperial peoples of history, who deserve more sympathetic treatment than, from our inevitably and rightly phil-Hellenic point of view, they have sometimes received. The Persian Wars themselves, too, embrace much more than the great culminating episode of Xerxes' invasion, which Thucydides dismissed as 'settled by two battles at sea and two on land'. He would have been more just if he had compared that, not to the whole length of the Peloponnesian War, but to the one episode of the Sicilian expedition. The Persian wars too, together with the simultaneous struggle against Persia's allies, the Phoenicians, were a prolonged though intermittent series of campaigns, ranging in time from Cyrus' conquest of Ionia in 546 to Kimon's last campaign in Cyprus in 450, and in space extending throughout the whole length of the Mediterranean. To trace the course and connections of these campaigns, together with the rise, just in time to be the decisive factor, of the democracy of Athens and of its sea-power, is a task the more worth attempting for the fact that it has not been the subject of a full-length study since that of Grundy, published in 1899.

The author is greatly indebted to the Director and Faculty of the Institute for Advanced Study at Princeton for electing him to membership for 1961–2, and thus enabling him to complete the work under

[1] Reprinted, respectively, by Dawson, London, 1968, and B. Blom, New York, 1966.

ideal conditions, and to the University of Glasgow for granting him leave of absence; also to A. Alföldi, B. D. Meritt, M. H. Jameson, A. E. Raubitschek, Homer Thompson, William Wallace and A. G. Woodhead for much stimulating discussion and many references, especially to recent periodical literature; and not least to his wife for her skilled and untiring assistance in proof-reading and the preparation of the index.

Spelling of proper names is as in *The Lyric Age of Greece*; usually in the Greek manner, though some familiar names, such as Cyrus, Aeschylus, Delphi, are given in their familiar forms.

Princeton – Glasgow A. R. BURN
April – August, 1962

Preface to the Second Edition

TWENTY-TWO years, as Mr Lewis says in the Postscript to this new impression, is a long time in the development of our studies nowadays, and it is an honour to be asked for a reprint of a book written so long ago. Ideally, especially in view of the important new discoveries discussed in the Postscript, it should have been a new edition, rewritten in parts, to take account of those discoveries, and also of my own and others' further exploration of the battlefields; especially of the positive discoveries made by E. Vanderpool and E. Mastrokostas at Marathon (see now pp. 606–7. This I did not feel I could undertake, being committed to the completion of an unpublished work begun long ago, and too old to have a reasonable prospect of finishing both. I am therefore the more grateful to the publishers for accepting the project of the present volume, and to Mr Lewis, one of the most learned and acute of workers now in the field and, above all things, candid friend and critic, for drawing attention to what most needs updating. Readers who are new to the subject may be recommended to read the Postscript first and take careful note of its separate index before turning, if they choose, to the main text. The pages of my text most affected are 287ff., with the multiplication of the known *ostraka* of Athens, and 323–5, 333–6, on the prosopography of the Persian nobility and military high command (see especially Lewis on the likely family connexions of Gergis, p. 323, and Artabazos, p. 324, important later). As to battlefield topography, it can be an enthralling out-of-door study; but I do not think that the progress made in it by Vanderpool's, W. K. Pritchett's and other studies seriously affect our picture of the strategy and tactics of the campaigns. My last views are to be found in *Greece and the Eastern Mediterranean* (Studies presented to F. Schachermeyr, De Gruyter, Berlin & New York, 1977). Works on which I feel that I should express a personal opinion include Hignett, *Xerxes' Invasion* (OUP, 1963), to which my reaction is one of hearty agreement on the literary sources and disagreement on the usefulness of field studies (see my review in *CR*, 1964); and, from 1983, J. M. Cook's *Persian Empire* (London, Dent), references to which would, in a regular new edition, replace many of those to A. T. Olmstead's *Persian Empire* of 1948, the author of which unfortunately did not live to see his book through the press. The latest article on a still controversial topic is N. G. L. Hammond's on the Troizen Decree (*JHS*, 1982), which, dating it in 481 B.C., attractively explains at least some problems.

Oxford, 1983 A. R. BURN

Abbreviations

Ab. Berl. Akad.	*Abhandlungen der Berliner Akademie*
Ael. Ar.	Aelius Aristides
Aelian *V.H.*	*Varia Historia*
Aesch. *Pers.*	Aeschylus, *Persians*
Agath.	Agathias
AJA	*American Journal of Archaeology*
AJP	*American Journal of Philology*
AJSL	*American Journal of Semitic Languages*
Amm.	Ammianus Marcellinus
Anab.	(Xenophon) *Anabasis*
Anat. Stud.	*Anatolian Studies*
Andok.	Andokides
A.P. (*Anth. Pal.*)	*Anthologia Palatina*
ap.	*apud*
Ar. Boi.	Aristophanes of Boiotia
Ar. *Pol.*	Aristotle, *Politics*
Ar. *Eth. N.*	Aristotle, *Nicomachean Ethics*
Arch. Mitt. aus Iran	*Archäologische Mitteilungen aus Iran*
Aristoph.	Aristophanes
Ath.	Athenaios
Ath. Mitt.	*Mitteilungen des deutschen Instituts in Athen*
Ath. P.	*Athenaion Politeia*
ATL	*Athenian Tribute Lists*
Bab. Hist. Texts	(S. Smith) *Babylonian Historical Texts*
BCH	*Bulletin de Correspondance Hellénique*
Beloch, *GG*	*Griechische Geschichte*
Ber.	Berosos
B.I.	*Behistun Inscription*
BM	British Museum
B.S.A.	*Annual of the British School at Athens*
Bury, *HG*	*History of Greece*
Busolt, *GG*	*Griechische Geschichte*
CAH	*Cambridge Ancient History*
Clem. Alex. *Strom.*	Clement of Alexandria, *Stromateis*
Clinton, *FH*	*Fasti Hellenici*
Com. Fr.	*Comic Fragments*
CQ	*Classical Quarterly*
CR	*Classical Review*
D.B.	Darius, Behistun Inscription
D.H. (Dion. Hal.)	Dionysios of Halikarnassos
Dittenberger, *SIG*[3]	*Sylloge Inscriptionum Graecarum*, edn. 3
D.L.	Diogenes Laertios
DN	Darius, Naksh-i-Rustem Inscr.
D.S.	Diodorus Siculus
Dunbabin, *WG*	*Western Greeks*
E.B. (*Enc. Brit.*)	*Encyclopaedia Britannica*
Eph.	Ephoros

Et. Mag.	*Etymologicum Magnum*
Eur.	Euripides
Euseb.	Eusebios
FGH	(Jacoby) *Fragmente der griechischen Historiker*
FH	(Clinton) *Fasti Hellenici*
FHG	(Müller) *Fragmenta Historicorum Graecorum*
GdA	(Meyer) *Geschichte des Altertums*
Gesch. Aeg.	(Wiedemann) *Geschichte Aegyptens*
GG	*Griechische Geschichte*
GHI	*Greek Historical Inscriptions*
Grundy, *GPW*	*The Great Persian War*
H.	Herodotos
Hammond, *HG*	*History of Greece*
Harp.	Harpokration (*Lexicon of the Attic Orators*)
Head, *HN*	*Historia Nummorum*
Her. Pont.	Herakleides Pontikos
Hes. *Theog.*	Hesiod, *Theogony*
Hes. *WD*	Hesiod, *Works and Days*
Hesp.	*Hesperia*
Hesych.	Hesychios
Hiller, *H. Gr. Ep.*	*Historische griechische Epigramme*
How & Wells, *Comm. on H.*	*Commentary on Herodotus*
IG	*Inscriptiones Graecae*
ILN	*Illustrated London News*
Isokr. *Paneg.*	Isokrates, *Panegyric*
J or Jac.	Jacoby
Jacoby, *FGH*	*Fragmente der griechischen Historiker*
JEA	*Journal of Egyptian Archaeology*
JHS	*Journal of Hellenic Studies*
JNES	*Journal of Near Eastern Studies*
Jos.	Josephus
JRGS	*Journal of the Royal Geographical Society*
JRS	*Journal of Roman Studies*
Ktes.	Ktesias
L.A. (or *Lyric Age*)	(Burn) *The Lyric Age of Greece*
LAAA	*Liverpool Annals of Archaeology & Anthropology*
LXX	The Septuagint
Meyer, *GdA*	*Geschichte des Altertums*
Mon. Ant.	*Monumenti antichi pubblicati per cura della Reale Accademia dei Lincei*
Müller, *FHG*	*Fragmenta Historicorum Graecorum*
Nem.	(Pindar) *Nemean Odes*
Nep.	Cornelius Nepos
O.	Olmstead, *Persian Empire*
OCT	*Oxford Classical Texts*
Od.	(Homer) *Odyssey*
Ol.	(Pindar) *Olympian Odes*
Olmstead, *P.E.*	*Persian Empire*
OLZ	*Orientalische Literaturzeitung*
Pareti, *Stud. sic. ed it.*	*Studi siciliani ed italioti*
Paus.	Pausanias

P.E.	(Olmstead) *Persian Empire*
Pl. *NH*	Pliny, *Natural History*
Plut.	Plutarch
Plut. *Ar.*	Plutarch, *Aristeides*
Plut. *Kim.*	Plutarch, *Kimon*
Plut. *Mal. Hdt.* (or *MH*)	Plutarch, *De Malignitate Herodoti*
Plut. *Mor.*	Plutarch, *Moralia*
Plut. *Them.*	Plutarch, *Themistokles*
Poly.	Polyainos
Polyb.	Polybios
Pritchard, *Texts*	*Ancient Near Eastern Texts*
ps.-Skylax	pseudo-Skylax
ps.-Xen. *Pol. Ath.*	pseudo-Xenophon, *Politeia Athenaion*
Ptol. *Geog.*	Ptolemy, *Geography*
PW	Pauly-Wissowa, *Realencyclopädie*
Pyth.	(Pindar) *Pythian Ode*
q.	quoted, or quoting
Rev. des Ét. anc.	*Revue des Études anciennes*
Riv. di fil.	*Rivista di filologia*
Sandys	Sir J. E. Sandys, *Pindar* (Loeb edition)
SB	*Sitzungsberichte*
S.B.	Stephanos Byzantinos
SEG	*Supplementum Epigraphicum Graecum*
Servius *ad Aen.*	on Vergil, Aeneid (with reference)
*SIG*³	see Dittenberger
Smith, *Texts*	*Babylonian Historical Texts*
Steph. Byz.	Stephanos Byzantinos
Stes.	Stesichoros
Str.	Strabo
s.v.	*sub voce*
Tac.	Tacitus
TAPA	*Transactions of the American Philological Association*
Theog.	Theognis
Thk.	Thucydides
Tod, *GHI*	*Greek Historical Inscriptions*
Val. Max.	Valerius Maximus
VH	(Aelian) *Varia Historia*
v.l.	*varia lectio*
WG	(Dunbabin) *Western Greeks*
Wilamowitz, *Ar. und Ath.*	*Aristotel und Athen*
Xen.	Xenophon
Xen. *Anab.*	Xenophon, *Anabasis*
Xen. *Cyr.* or *Cyrop.*	Xenophon, *Cyropaedia*
Xen. *Hell.*	Xenophon, *Hellenika*
Xen. *Mem.*	Xenophon, *Memorabilia*
Xen. *Oik.*	Xenophon, *Oikonomikos*
X.P.	Xerxes, Persepolis Inscriptions
Zeitschr. für Ag. Spr. u. Altertumskunde	*Zeitschrift für Ägyptische Sprach- und Altertumskunde*
ZfN	*Zeitschrift für Numismatik*

Corrigenda

p. 3, n. 3, line 2 *for* Myers *read* Myres
p. 6, para 2, line 10 *for* Pampeluna *read* Saragossa
p. 85, n. 17, line 2 *for* creen *read* screen
p. 203, para 2, line 5 *for* hand *read* hands
p. 248, line 1 of note *for* Suad *read* Suda
p. 428, para 2, line 2 *for* of *read* to
p. 573, col. 2 *add* Epilykos, 564
p. 584, s.v. Teisandros *delete* (3), 564

Introduction:

Herodotos and Other Sources

THE age of the Persian Wars, from the time of Cyrus – the point at which Herodotos, after a preface on the kings of Lydia, starts his history – is the first fully historic period in Greece and therefore in any part of Europe. This statement may appear at first sight shocking to anyone brought up on the tradition that Historic Times in Greece begin with the First Olympiad, 776; yet it is a fact, that the whole period from then until the late sixth century is not fully historic but 'proto-historic'; an age on which we have indeed some information from Greek historians, beginning with the computed dates and sometimes foundation-stories of colonies, and from which there survive some written texts, those of the surviving remains of Greek poetry; but the historians are not contemporary, and the contemporary texts were not written to help historians.

Greek historical writing begins in the last years of the sixth century, contemporarily with the work of the first Ionian 'natural philosophers', and perhaps, like that work, inspired in part by contact with the east, where lists of kings had been kept and the myths describing origins written down already for many centuries. The *locus classicus* for us on the first Greek historians, important for the circumstances in which Herodotos worked, and for the question, what evidence was available to later writers, is in the essay *On Thucydides* of Dionysios of Halikarnassos (ch. 5).

Among 'many ancient historians living before the Peloponnesian War', Dionysios lists

Eugeon of Samos	Hekataios of Miletos
Deïochos of Prokonnesos	Akousilaos of Argos
Eudemos of Paros	Charon of Lampsakos
Demokles of Phygela [in Karia]	Melesagoras of Chalkedon

> and to these he adds 'living a little before the Peloponnesian War, and overlapping the time of Thucydides',
>
> | | |
> |---|---|
> | Hellanikos of Lesbos | Xenomedes of Chios |
> | Damastes of Sigeion | Xanthos of Lydia |
>
> and many others. All these followed a similar plan in their choice of subject and did not differ much, one from another, in scope (*dynamis*). They wrote up the histories, some of Greek and some of non-Greek regions, not connecting them together but giving separately those of the different peoples and cities, and all with one and the same aim, namely to publish the records (*mnēmai*) preserved locally among the peoples and cities, whether in sacred or civil archives,[1] and make them generally available, just as they found them, without either additions or omissions; including some myths believed from ancient times and sensational tales of disaster,[2] which seem very childish to the modern reader. They all used much the same language (apart from differences of dialect): a style lucid, colloquial, pure and terse, appropriate to their subject-matter, and with no addition of artificial ornament; in spite of which, their works possess a kind of freshness and charm (some of them more than others) which has led to their preservation down to the present day. But Herodotos of Halikarnassos, who was born a little before the Persian and lived into the time of the Peloponnesian War, chose a larger and more splendid theme, not the history of one city or people,

– but, to paraphrase Dionysios' next lines, that of the whole Near East from Gyges to the invasion of Xerxes.

Some of Dionysios' dozen primitives were no doubt among those who, as Thucydides tells us (i, 97, 2), had written on the Persian Wars. The aim 'to publish the archives' sounds, like much in ancient Greece, curiously modern, and the loss of these 'primitives', as of most of early Greek literature, is greatly to be regretted; unfortunately the Roman and Byzantine periods, much addicted to the cult of artistic Greek and Latin prose composition ('rhetoric'), were less kind to them than the Hellenistic. As a motive for the sudden outbreak of historical writing in eastern Greece, we may guess that the Greeks, like Darius the Persian, as appears from his *Res Gestae*, and like the Romans in the third century B.C., were impressed by the discovery that such chronicles existed among their eastern neighbours. We notice that only

[1] *εἴ τ᾽ἐν ἱεροῖς εἴ τ᾽ ἐν βεβήλοις ἀποκείμεναι γραφαί.*
[2] *θεατρικαί τινες περιπέτειαι.*

one of the twelve comes from west of the Aegean: Akousilaos of Argos, whose researches may have facilitated Hellanikos' publication of the list of Priestesses of Hera at Argos as part of his chronological work, and whose own work may have had a political motive: to prove from sanctified traditions the rightful claims of Argos, now defeated by Sparta, to seniority among the Dorians. All the easterners, we notice, must have written under foreign domination, that of Persia or, later, of Athens; a domination which gave them periods of peace and security, but also cut them off from the major excitements of politics. The urge had not yet touched Athens or Corinth, much less Sparta; there, men were still too busy making their own history. The Athenian antiquarianism of the *Atthidográphoi*, a matter of research into temple records, old laws and the historical information to be gleaned from poems (very much like what Dionysios says of the primitives), begins only at the end of the fifth century, when Athens herself had fallen upon evil days. History represents an attempt to answer the question, 'How did things get like this?' – and the question is often stimulated by a sense that the world has gone wrong.

The above is of importance for the question of the sources available to Herodotos, who far outweighs all the other sources that we have for the Persian Wars, and of how far his successors were in a position to improve on his work, a task frequently attempted.

Herodotos, it appears, then, is *not* strictly the Father of History; certainly not its 'onlie begetter'; but he is the first great artist or architect of history, the scale of whose edifice dwarfed all that had been done before. A born story-teller in a nation of story-tellers, he often retails stories for their own sake, without pedantically caring overmuch whether they are strictly relevant or necessary; but in his first sentence, as it were on the title-page to his book, he states the question which may well have been present with him since his youth in Halikarnassos, in a city troubled by strife between leading Greek families (including his own) and a half-Karian dynasty, and between Persia and Athens:

HERODOTOS OF HALIKARNASSOS, his RESEARCHES,[3] here set down, that the deeds of men may not be forgotten in time, and that

[3] *Historia;* the word to which he gave for ever after the special meaning of History. For this sentence, 'dressed' in the manner of a 17th-century title-page, see J. L. Myers, *Herodotus, Father of History*, p. 67.

the great and noble exploits both of Greeks and foreigners may not lose their fame; and more especially, the causes of the War that took place between them.

On the causes of the Persian War he does not, in fact, reveal any very profound thought;[4] one of the chief points in which he himself is still primitive is that he does not probe for historical causes deeper than the desires of principal actors. But he does show, in his first paragraphs, how in his time, and more than before as the result of the rise of the Persian Empire, opposing an organized 'Barbary' to a Greek world increasingly conscious of its unity, there had arisen a conception of a deep cleavage between men living on opposite sides of the Mediterranean;[5] a conception fraught with long-lasting and tragic consequences, even after the age-long union of the Mediterranean world under Rome. What he does do is to tell a candid and for that reason all the more inspiring story of the Greeks' defence of their freedom against a mighty and (at least in its original intention) beneficent empire; shedding incidentally, while using the setting of the stage as his excuse, a flood of light upon the affairs of men throughout the whole near eastern world in his time.

His other chief weakness, and a serious one in the circumstances, is that he seems to be totally without military experience. Born a subject of Xerxes (in 484 according to Greek chronography),[6] and living later under the Athenian peace in the Aegean, he may never, unless late in his active life, at Thouria, have had occasion even to drill with spear and shield. Certainly he had no such experience as the Athenian general, Thucydides. This is particularly unfortunate in view of the fact that, while he must have talked with hundreds of men who had fought in the great war, and who, like the old men in Aristophanes, were very ready to talk about it, he came upon the scene as a historian too late to know the men, middle-aged in 480, who had held the chief commands (cf. p. 441, below). This did not prevent him from hearing detailed accounts of all that went on in the councils of war, since Greek

[4] For a recent discussion of this, cf. G. Nenci, *Introduzione alle guerre persiane e altri saggi* (Pisa, 1958), pp. 13–212.

[5] i, 1–4; taken up again at the very end of the work, in ix, 116.

[6] Gellius, *Attic Nights*, xv, 23; perhaps an instance of placing a man's unknown birthdate 40 years before some important event in his life, taken as marking his *floruit;* in this case H.'s migration to Thouria: How and Wells, *Commentary*, I, p. 2, after Diels in *Rhein. Mus.* XXXI (1876).

gossip invariably 'knows everything'; but it did leave him unable to evaluate it, and to see what appears to every modern critic to be the truth, that what he heard was what young soldiers had believed about the high command thirty or forty years before, exacerbated in the light of subsequent quarrels between the former allies. No one, unfortunately, who held a command in 480–79 wrote his memoirs or talked to a historian. As we have seen, our list of early historians includes no name from any of the cities which took part in the defence of Greece; and Plutarch, a very learned man, who desired to criticise Herodotos, not least for what he said about Greek commanders, might have been expected to find such material if there had been any. What Plutarch did find in the way of independent material on the Persian Wars is an important subject, to which we must return.

Pioneer as he is, moreover, Herodotos did not appreciate, as Thucydides did,[7] the fact that 'what really happened' usually appears deceptively clear when we have only one witness, and that the historian ought deliberately to give himself the trouble of seeking different accounts, cross-examining witnesses when possible, and considering how any discrepancies are most likely to have arisen. On the other hand, he is extremely honest. An admirer of Athens, he does not shrink from giving his opinion that Athens saved Greece (vii, 139; see p. 348), at a time when that opinion had become widely unpopular, and though he could have avoided making it so explicit. He praises democracy, though not uncritical of it (v, 78; cf. 96, 2); he often admits ignorance of a fact, and when variant accounts come his way, he records them, and does not suppress the fact in the interests of giving a clear story (e.g. vi, 14, 1; 115, 121, 124, recording an allegation which he does not himself accept; viii, 94, recording that other Greeks did not accept an Athenian story). And even the situation that left him without military experience was not without its advantages. If he had been a citizen of imperial Athens and immersed in its affairs, he would hardly have found the time to travel widely, as he did, in the Persian Empire; and hardly could any Athenian of the time have been the unattached human being that Herodotos was.

When we seek opportunities to check Herodotos' accuracy, we are for the most part baffled by the sheer lack of other material; some attempts which have been made to 'control' him by means of other

[7] Cf. Thk. i, 22, 2f.

Greek material are discussed in the text and notes of this book, and will be summarised here. Strangely enough, the best 'control' that we have is Persian: the text of some of the inscriptions of Darius and Xerxes themselves; inscriptions which Herodotos could not read; for some mistakes which he makes about the spelling and meaning of Persian names (vi. 98; cf. commentaries) or the gender of the god Mithra (i, 131) make it clear that he did not know the language. Yet his list of the six Persian nobles who helped Darius to gain the throne, compared with Darius' own *res gestae* at Behistun, shows only one mistake, and that an explicable one; and his list of the satrapies corresponds closely with the lists, given in several inscriptions, of the lands over which the Great King ruled (below, pp. 94, 109ff). Likewise, though less surprisingly, his list of the Greeks who fought at Salamis and Plataia corresponds closely with the Spartan list of the 31 states which 'fought in the war', given on the Serpent Column which now stands in Constantine's Hippodrome (pp. 382f, 441f, 523f, 544). His Egyptology may be wild, but with that we are not concerned. Where we can test him on the history of his special subject, he comes out well. It is reasonable therefore to trust him also where we cannot test him, *for 'public facts'*; such facts as those about the movements of armies or about what was publicly said, e.g. by Themistokles to the army or the Assembly (e.g. pp. 455, 469). On the other hand, anything which he alleges to have been said in secret, as in councils of war, must be suspected of being derived by way of oral tradition from camp gossip (it is usually quite silly enough) and treated with mistrust or at least reserve.

Tradition is a great corrupter. It may preserve important facts, though even then the preservation may take the form of seizing on one important or merely picturesque fact and embroidering it. Einhard tells us that Hrodland, Count of the Breton Marches, was killed by the Basques in an attack on the rearguard of Charlemagne's army returning from Spain; three hundred years later, Roland is the hero of a mighty epic, falling after tremendous slaughter before a huge host of Saracens, and avenged by the destruction of all the hosts of Babylon by his lord (who a few weeks earlier, with Roland to help him, had been unable to capture Pampeluna). Why Roland became the hero of the great poem, we may perhaps guess when we remember what was Roland's most famous attribute: a horn; and what was famous about the horn: that, at the crisis of his fortunes, he refused to blow it. Did the real Count Hrodland refuse to call for help and stop the main column in a defile, for an attack by these barbarians? If so, for his gallantry and pride he paid with his life. This is exactly the kind of thing that seizes the imagination of mankind; but it constitutes a warning against expecting popular tradition to preserve reliable history for long periods. One aspect of the literary interest of the earliest Greek historians is that they caught the tradition of the Persian war period before it had passed through many generations of 'improvement' in oral saga or story; and in two cases in particular, the stories of the fate of Croesus and of Harmodios and Aristogeiton, both commemorated both in poetry and prose and in works of art, we have the opportunity to see a legend in process of growth within a couple of generations after the event.[8] What we owe to Herodotos may be well seen in his account of Leonidas' last fight; his story, probably correct, that in his last battle Leonidas *attacked* the enemy, had become after a hundred years of patriotic commemoration at Sparta a tale, recorded probably by Ephoros and eagerly followed by Plutarch as well as by Diodoros, of the Spartans penetrating to the very tent of Xerxes in a night attack on the Persian camp (pp. 416f); a similar though slighter development than that of the poetic from the prose account of the fight at Roncesvalles.

It is idle, then, to think of correcting Herodotos out of later oral tradition, as represented particularly by the fourth-century Attic orators; though they may preserve a few independent facts, which we may try to distinguish from patriotic fiction. In considering how far we can get behind Herodotos, or supplement or correct him from other sources, we must ask first what written sources Herodotos may have used, and second, what other sources were available to the later writers whose accounts we have.

Plutarch's essay *On the Meanness of Herodotos* (*De Malignitate Herodoti* in its customary Latin title, cited hereinafter as *MH*), though it sheds more light on the human weaknesses of its author than of his bugbear, performs a great service in showing us something of the sources available. In particular, he quotes verbatim two brief extracts from Charon, which are important as giving a glimpse of the 'clear and succinct style', praised by Dionysios, of one of those early historians,

[8] Croesus, below, p. 42, n. 9; Harmodios, in my *Lyric Age of Greece*, pp. 320–22.

whose works (as may be seen in Jacoby's or Müller's collection of the fragments) are so quoted all too seldom.

On the capture of Paktyas (below, pp. 45f; Plut. *MH* 20):

> Charon of Lampsakos, an older writer . . . says simply (I quote verbally): 'And Paktyas, when he heard of the advance of the Persian army, fled, first to Mytilene and then to Chios; and he fell into Cyrus' hands.'

On the Athenian march on Sardis (pp. 200f; *MH* 24):

> Charon of Lampsakos says simply (I quote verbally): 'The Athenians sailed with twenty triremes to help the Ionians, and marched on Sardis and took it, all except the royal citadel; and having done this they returned to Miletos.'

Here Herodotos says 'to Ephesos', adding that they suffered a defeat before regaining their ships. Plutarch objects that Charon does not mention a defeat, and complains, in the earlier passage, that Herodotos adds that Paktyas was betrayed, through the timorousness of the Greek islanders. But in view, precisely, of Charon's extreme succinctness, it is obvious that Plutarch here makes a classic misuse of the *argumentum ex silentio*, jumping from the fact 'X does not mention Y' to the conclusion 'X knows nothing of it'. Plutarch makes a better point, and does convict Herodotos' Athenian informants of 'meanness' when they alleged that the Corinthians took no part in the Battle of Salamis (an allegation on which Herodotos himself, it must be remembered, casts doubt). Plutarch here cites the genuinely contemporary and documentary evidence of the epitaph on the Corinthian dead, buried in the island (p. 444); as well as the significant names of the Corinthian admiral's children, which may have been preserved on family monuments. Plutarch is clearly *searching* for sticks with which to beat Herodotos; which creates a certain presumption, though less than certainty, that when he does not produce any, it is because he has found none. He says of the alleged branding of the Thebans taken prisoner at Thermopylai, that 'no one before Herodotos knows anything of it' (*MH* 33). Presumably there were, as Thucydides says (above, p. 2), earlier histories of the campaign of 480; but if they were as brief as Charon's work they would hardly have gone into details about the circumstances in which prisoners were taken; and if there had existed an account detailed enough to be significant, we should have expected Plutarch to quote it as he quotes Charon earlier.

Herodotos no doubt used written sources when he could get them. He cites Hekataios of Miletos, the father of Mediterranean geography, in order to criticise him for the lack of depth in his chronological perspective (ii, 143) and again as an authority on mythical origins (vi, 137), and may be indebted to him for other facts, which he saw no reason to doubt (cf. How and Wells, *Comm.* I, pp. 22ff); and he may well have derived his chronological framework for the history of western Asia from his younger contemporary, Hellanikos, a scholar interested in systematic chronology as Herodotos was not.[9] He did not use Xanthos for the history of Lydia; for Nikolaos of Damascus, who does purport to have used him, differs in most details; but he may have used Charon for the history of the Ionian Revolt, in which Charon's city of Lampsakos was involved. It is precisely here that we find the history of the middle years of that six-years war, between the more detailed accounts of its beginning and end, represented by a few lines of annals so terse and dry as to leave us in some doubt about the distribution of the campaigns over the years.[10] But we have no trace of the existence of any *detailed* account of the invasions of Greece earlier than that of Herodotos himself. If he used any earlier written account, it has perished without trace. Most probably, then, Herodotos did his own collecting of raw material, straight from old men who had taken part in the war when they were young. There certainly seems to be no room for a 'forerunner' such as has sometimes been postulated, to whom we are to attribute almost everything that is sound in Herodotos' own narrative.[11]

[9] M. Miller, cited in *Lyric Age*, p. 407; cf. her article in *Klio*, forthcoming (1962?).

[10] v, 116f, 122f; all assigned to one year (cf. 116, 122, 2), that immediately after the raid on Sardis. This is accepted by, e.g., Macan, *Comm. on H. iv–vi*; but at the cost of being left with no campaigns at all to put into the next two years. I would sooner believe that H. was misled by the brevity of his source.

[11] Cf., e.g., Ernst Obst, *Der Feldzug des Xerxes*, Beiheft to *Klio*, 1914 (the sole published book of one of those who were brilliant young men in that year), pp. 27ff. I do not deny the existence of any *Vorlage*; Thucydides makes it certain that there were such; but I believe that any that existed on the invasions of Greece were more like Charon than like Herodotos. Nor can I share Obst's sanguine confidence that he can, by careful reading, distinguish exactly what in, say, the account of Thermopylai (Obst, pp. 101–113) is from the *Vorlage*, and *brauchbar*, and what is not. Obst was representative of his age, and gives us the quintessence of the methods of 19th-century *Quellenkritik*. – I would here refer with approval to the remarks of Arnold Gomme in his *Thucydides*, I, pp. 81ff. on the *Quellenkritik* applied to Plutarch.

Next, we have to ask what independent material was available to the later writers, out of whom some moderns have tried to correct or supplement Herodotos. None of them names any writer who can be convincingly identified with the author of the supposed major *Vorlage*; and this, at least in Plutarch, is surprising if any such existed. But they did have access to some contemporary material, useful within limits, in the shape of war-memorial inscriptions like that on the Corinthians, quoted by Plutarch (fragments of several have been discovered by archaeologists, cf., e.g., pp. 255, 444), and other *poems*. We still have, in Aeschylus' *Persians*, a source of major importance on the Battle of Salamis, and can derive occasional hints from the poems of Pindar and Bakchylides. Plutarch adds to these a reference to the part played by the Corinthians at Plataia from an elegy by Simonides (p. 537), and an attack on Themistokles, interesting because strictly contemporary, by Timokreon of Ialysos (p. 468n). Herodotos, though he quotes the Thermopylai memorial-epigrams, makes less use of poetic material than the later writers; probably because, in the presence of a living, oral tradition, he did not feel that he needed it. Thucydides, some 13 years younger than Herodotos, was *in Athens* before him. Diodoros, whose main and perhaps sole source on Greece proper in the fifth century was the popular, readable and 'romantic' work of the fourth-century Ephoros, has some details, important if genuine, and which there is no positive reason to doubt, on the order of battle of the fleets at Salamis (pp. 458f). Ephoros might have derived these from one of the dry and factual pre-Herodoteans. His accounts of Thermopylai and Plataia are useless, but that of Salamis seems valuable; and here it is interesting to notice that Polybios, who did have military experience, while he severely criticises Ephoros' accounts of land battles (referring to Leuktra and Mantineia (362), and implying, it is interesting to see, the use of a plan drawn to scale), does opine that he 'seems to understand naval tactics'.[12] (Or is it too uncharitable to suspect that Ephoros *knew he did not* understand the technicalities of naval warfare, and consequently followed his sources, instead of romancing?) But for the most part, Ephoros' account of Xerxes' invasion (where the full text of Diodoros begins again after a long break) is consistent with Herodotos, only, it seems, rationalising, sometimes heightening the effect (cf., e.g., p. 424, n. 2), and turning broken

[12] Polyb. xii, 25.

into round numbers. It seems as though he used Herodotos, freely after his manner, rather than as if he and Herodotos both used a great but lost and totally unknown predecessor (as per Obst, *loc. cit.*). Except on Salamis, there is nothing to be gained by trying to improve on Herodotos out of Diodoros.

Even less is to be gained, though the attempt has so often been made that his name must appear repeatedly in our pages (e.g. pp. 94, 379n), by trying to improve on Herodotos out of the early fourth-century work of Ktēsias. Ktēsias of Knidos, a physician, who claimed to have tended Artaxerxes II when wounded by his brother in the battle of Kunaxa, is said, after being captured by the Persians in that action, to have remained for seventeen years Artaxerxes' court doctor.[13] He availed himself of his opportunities to write a work or works on Persia down to his own time, which was used by Plutarch for his *Artaxerxes*, by Strabo in his *Geography*, and by Diodoros. In addition to their citations of his work, we have a brief epitome of it by the Byzantine Bishop Photios, who remarks in his preface that Ktesias constantly wrote controversially against Herodotos, calling him a liar and a mere story-teller. Among the nineteenth-century scholars, with whom Herodotos' reputation sank low, Ktesias inspired high hopes as a possible corrective; but the decipherment of the Old Persian inscriptions reversed the trend. It ought, indeed, to have reversed it more decisively; for the name of Ktesias still lurks with distressing frequency in the footnotes of modern works on the Persian Wars. For events nearer his own time he may have his uses; for the earlier period, only a desperate and needless effort to find an alternative to Herodotos can account for, while it does not excuse, the continued trailing of this ancient red herring. That he puts the battle of Plataia between Thermopylai and Salamis, has Mardonios slain by the wrath of heaven in the storm which saved Delphi, and has Delphi itself sacked by an army under a eunuch named Matakas after the return of Xerxes to Asia and the death of Mardonios, is not more repugnant to Herodotos' story than to *a priori* probability; but if that were all, it would be a duty not to let our ideas of *a priori* probability lead us to neglect ancient evidence. But that is not all. The decipherment of Darius' *res gestae* at Behistun, which, with the lists of peoples, confirms the soundness (not the infallibility) of Herodotos' information on Persia, revealed the unsoundness of that of Ktesias, for all his

[13] D.S. ii, 32, 4; cf. Xen. *Anab.* i, 8, 26ff.

opportunities (cf. p. 94). Where Herodotos gets only one name among the Six Conspirators wrong, and even there inserts that of another henchman of Darius, Ktesias gets only one right, while in two cases he gives the names of sons of the men named by Darius; and when we notice that the name he does get right, Hydarnes, was also the name of a son of Hydarnes the friend of Darius, it begins to look as if the (oral?) information, on which Ktesias based his attempt to improve on Herodotos, was only right by chance even here.

But further, Ktesias is not only a victim of inaccurate information. He was also responsible for the introduction into western learning of the monster called the Martichora (a good Persian word, meaning man-eater, which, corrupted into *mantichora,* passed by way of Aristotle, Pliny and Aelian into the mediaeval bestiary). It was, according to Aristotle's account (in *Hist. Animal.* ii, 1; 501a), of the size of a lion, and had two rows of teeth in each jaw (others say three). It had a lion's claws, but a face and ears like a man. Its voice was as of a trumpet; it could run as fast as a deer; it shot stings out of the end of its tail, and, as its name implied, it ate men. Aelian, who gives the fullest account (*Nat. Hist.* iv, 21), even adds the size of the missile stings; they were about a foot long. Aristotle, it should be added for his credit, prefaces his account with 'if one may believe Ktesias'; Aelian reveals the reason why he nevertheless provisionally accepted the account: 'Ktesias says that he saw this creature in Persia; for one was sent from India as a present to the king.' The difference from Herodotos, who introduced the Phoenix into the west (after Hekataios, according to Porphyry[14]), is summed up in the contrast between this lie and Herodotos' scrupulous confession (ii, 73) 'I myself have not seen this bird, except in a picture'. In short, Ktesias reveals himself as reckless of truth and concerned only to make an impression; and even when he does tell us a detail which might be true, it is always well to remember the martichora.

However, the confidence with which Ktesias gave his information, and the fact that he undoubtedly had unique opportunities for collecting it, impressed the ancient writers who followed him. How much he may have contaminated the references which we have to later Persian history, e.g. in Plutarch's *Artaxerxes* or in Diodoros, we are not here called upon to determine; but it is of importance for Plutarch's

[14] In Euseb. *Preparation of the Gospel,* x, 3.

account of the Battle of Salamis, which is largely independent of that of Herodotos, that one of Plutarch's direct sources for his *Themistokles*, Phanias (Phainias in the dialect of his native Lesbos), appears to have been dependent on Ktesias! (See note on pp. 474f.) Once more it appears that attempts to supplement and even more to 'correct' Herodotos out of the later sources have to be made with extreme caution and treated with reserve.

Almost all our good information on the Persian invasions of Greece, then, it appears most probable, comes from the living memories of those who took part, collected by Herodotos and by Thucydides, whose scattered references to the Persian Wars are important, and quite as authoritative as Herodotos' own. Herodotos had interviewed men who were on the Persian as well as on the Greek side; he names, for instance, Thersandros of Orchomenos (p. 511) and Dikaios, an Athenian exile (p. 448): both, we notice, on cases of prescience; Herodotos is interested in what would nowadays be called supernormal phenomena, quoting oracles extensively, digressing to reject a sceptical view of them (viii, 77) and devoting several pages of his last book (ix, 33–7, 92–5) to the biographies of three different seers. On normal facts, which he saw no reason for anyone to doubt, he does not name his sources; but his information, for instance, on Dāmarātos, the exiled king of Sparta, may have come from his family, domiciled after the war in the Troad (p. 394n). One would dearly like to know who were the 'learned Persians' to whom he refers at the beginning of his work, and who had views on Greek legends; but we are left to guess. One is pretty certainly that Zōpyros, son of one of Xerxes' marshals and great-grandson of one of the men who placed Darius on the throne, who 'came over to the Greeks' (iii, 160, cf. 153), after his father's rebellion and death.[15] Others may have stood near one or other of two Persian generals who survived the war with undamaged reputations, Hydarnes and Artabazos. Both were afterwards given western commands which became hereditary 'marcher lordships' (pp. 321, 324); they were the ancestors, respectively, of the famous Tissaphernes and Pharnabazos of the end of the century. To one of their courts may have belonged that Ostānes (p. 69), said to have given the Greeks

[15] Cf. J. Wells, 'The Persian Friends of Herodotos' in *JHS* XXVII, reprinted in his *Studies in Herodotus*.

their first knowledge of the name of the prophet Zoroaster, whom Herodotos does *not* mention, but Xanthos may have; and Persian gentlemen directly concerned in gaining an intimate knowledge of Greek affairs, as these Persians certainly did, might well have been willing to talk with a Greek so well informed as Herodotos.

But Herodotos and Thucydides in their published works certainly did not exhaust the Athenian tradition. As we have seen, every old man in Aristophanes had his memories of the Great War. Even, in the *Lysistrata*, they can remember the siege of the Acropolis, which was a hundred years ago! (Cf. p. 182.) It had become a tradition of the comic stage, that 'Old men remember'. In an age still with few books, this oral tradition was important. The *telling* of old stories was much more important than now, and the young were dependent on the old for much of what is now dispensed both by books and by the cinema and television. The folk-memory of Athens' finest hours was very much alive a century later; and, as Raubitschek stresses (*TAPA* XCI, p. 178), it was not dependent on Herodotos. How much of what we are told, incidentally to patriotic oratory, by the fourth-century orators (cf. pp. 352, 384, etc.), depends on books (for if there were any much earlier Athenian histories, we do not hear of them), and how much, *as they themselves say* (it may not be a pure convention), on oral tradition, is a matter on which different views are taken; but the tradition was reinforced, as we have seen, by contemporary monuments and other poems.

Nevertheless, as Thucydides knew, and reminds us *à propos* of the Harmodios affair (above, p. 7), the popular tradition did tend continuously to 'improve' the stories. Derived from the oratorical tradition by Plutarch and the popular lecturers of the Roman period, such as Dion Chrysostom and Aelius Aristides,[16] we find 'improved' versions of what, for instance, Aristeides the Just said to Themistokles and *vice versa* (pp. 454f and n) which differ widely from Herodotos. Without claiming verbal inspiration for Herodotos, there is no doubt which should be preferred; and the fact should serve to keep us reminded, how little store Greeks set by precise accuracy of quotation. To repeat the general sense of what was said, and even to make it more effective according to one's own lights, was standard procedure.

This brings us finally to the most important and currently the most

[16] On them, see Macan, *Hdt. VII–IX*, Part II, pp. 101ff.

vexed and debated question regarding the Athenian oratorical tradition. Orators, from the middle of the fourth century onwards, and not earlier (but *perhaps only because we do not have earlier specimens of this kind of literature*), cite decrees of the people of this heroic age, such as that proposed by Miltiades before Marathon or by Themistokles before Salamis (pp. 241, 364ff), as well as other documents, such as the Oath of the Greek allies before Plataia (pp. 512f) and the treaty with Persia which brought the war to an end in 449 (p. 563); and the last two are specified, 'among others' not named, by the learned and non-Athenian historian Theopompos as forgeries, 'with which the people of Athens deceive the Greeks' (cf. pp. 373f, 563). Fourth-century Athens had texts of these disputed documents set up in public, on stone; that of the Oath is extant, as set up by a fourth-century priest of the war-god at Acharnai; and the question of authenticity has been brought into the first rank of importance by the discovery in 1959 of a somewhat later copy of such a text of Themistokles' mobilisation-decree, made for a memorial set up at Troizen.

Now long, prose inscriptions, recording *psephismata*, 'decrees', executive decisions, were not set up at Athens in the early fifth century. Public inscriptions, indeed, of any kind are rare before the reforms of 461. Then they become much commoner, but still for the most part record *covenants* (treaties with independent cities; charters according specified rights to colonists or dependents) or the handling of *sacred* funds; continuing, in fact, the traditions respectively of the earlier Salamis (colonisation) decree and the archaic bronze fragment naming the sixth-century treasurers of Athena. Even the famous Athenian 'Tribute-Lists' are really the records of the 60ths paid to the Goddess. Nor is it likely that even the now famous Themistokles Decree was set up immediately after the war as part of a memorial.[17] It was not the style of the time; we have fragments of a number of war-memorial inscriptions of that time; all are short, and most of them in elegiac verse. We have not a single fragment of any such bulky inscription as an Athenian public record of the mobilisation-order of 480 must have been. If, then, these decrees were continuously preserved, they must have been preserved in archives. We know all too little about the archives of fifth-century Athens, but what we do hear suggests that there were no central state archives before the foundation of the

[17] As suggested by H. Berve in *Sitzungsb. der Bayer. Akad.*, 1961 (3), p. 7.

Mētrōōn at the end of the century.[18] Previously, different offices kept such papers or tablets ('whitened boards', which were presumably re-whitewashed and re-used when the record was no longer wanted) as they required. As to whether 'dead files' were preserved, we have no evidence either way; but we should require positive evidence for believing that they were, rather than that they were not. Mr A. G. Woodhead suggests[19] as a possibility that, in the more record-conscious age of the late fifth century, when the Metroön was founded (and when, one might add, the generation that remembered the invasion was passing away, in the persons of old men like Sophocles), an attempt was made to 'restore' the texts of some famous and historic decrees, such as may often have been cited in oratory in the fifth century as in the fourth, from memory if no written records of them existed; a view perhaps preferable to that suggested tentatively in the text below (p. 375). If that was the history of the patriotically-cited 'documents' of which we hear from our later orators, we can understand Theopompos' denunciation, which, so far as we know, went unanswered in antiquity.

This does not mean that Theopompos' 'forgeries' are totally without historic importance. They represent what fourth-century Athens believed about its fifth-century history, and thus rank in authority along with Diodoros, where he uses Ephoros, or with Isokrates or Demosthenes. But, as is argued in more detail below (pp. 366ff, 513ff), it appears optimistic to believe that we have in them anything that, in modern history, would be recognized as an 'original document'.[20]

The general attitude adopted in this book, therefore, may be described as conservative; I have more confidence in Herodotos' statements of 'public fact' than had some 'elder statesmen' of Herodotean studies of a generation ago, such as Bury and Munro. Going back to the early works in which they argued their views, one is salutarily

[18] On the Mētrōōn, cf. H. A. Thompson in *Hesperia* VI (1937, when its precise location and architectural history had just been worked out), pp. 203ff; on the archives, U. Kahrstedt in *Klio* XXXI (1938), pp. 25ff; esp. 28ff, on the state of things before the Metroön was founded, adjacent to the new Bouleuterion; a state of things which, with the multiplication of written documents, was becoming intolerable.

[19] In a lecture at Princeton, Feb. 20, 1962; I owe him thanks also for much discussion of this whole subject.

[20] The author here wishes to note that Professors Meritt, Jameson and Raubitschek remain more sanguine as to the chances of Themistokles' original mobilisation-orders having survived until the fourth century, and to commend to the reader any future contributions to the debate.

reminded that those great scholars too were brilliant *young* men once, and remained humanly fallible; and it is sobering to realise that Macan, a humane and attractive scholar, had a Hibernian fluency which at times might have been curbed with positive advantage, and would have done better to pause on occasion before identifying minor characters who bear the same name (pp. 334ff); or that Grundy, the father of modern Persian War topography, like Herodotos himself, did not go over the mountains (pp. 410, 520n). On Munro, 'distinguished', as a modern scholar remarks, 'for knowing much better than Herodotos what really happened',[21] it may be worth while to remark that his studies on the Persian invasions in *JHS* XIX, XXII and XXIV appear to me much better than his chapters in the *Cambridge Ancient History*, over twenty years later, in which the mixture seems to have become over-cooked. On the other hand, I cannot share the neo-fundamentalism of Mr Hammond, whose apparent belief in the parity of all ancient sources leads him, for instance, to quote without warning, in a book intended for students, as a chronological authority, a date-chart which in an adjacent paragraph assigns several pre-Socratics and Socrates himself all to one and the same epoch (p. 128, n. 4); or to use the extremely unreliable compiler Aristodemos as though he deserved as much confidence as Herodotos (p. 437, n. 32). At the same time, my debt to Mr Hammond for several topographical and other details is acknowledged below (e.g. pp. 248, n. 24; 456, n. 12); as also the manifold debts which any modern writer on this subject must owe to the above-named scholars, with whatever reserve one may treat them; to the three great Germans, the encyclopaedic Busolt, the brilliant Meyer, the sceptical and erratic but always stimulating Beloch; to the older British writers, Grote and Clinton, interesting for the question how the sources looked to intelligent men innocent of the theories and criticism of the last hundred years; and to modern articles too numerous to list in one place, especially the topographical studies of W. K. Pritchett.

[21] Professor J. R. Grant, 'Leonidas' Last Stand', in *The Phoenix*, XV (1961); an interesting study, though I am not convinced by his conclusions.

Part I

The Rise of Persia

Chapter I

Babylon and the Medes

COMFORT ye, comfort ye my people, saith your God. Speak, to comfort Jerusalem; for her humiliation is completed, her sin is pardoned; she hath received at the Lord's hand double for all her sins.' [1]

So begin the poems of the 'great Anonymous' of the mid-sixth century among the Jews of the Captivity in Babylon, whose works were later 'bound up' with those of Isaiah and passed under his name. For two hundred years, from Amos to the 'Second Isaiah', the Hebrew prophets cast the light of passionate feeling upon a time of troubles in the Near East, illuminating the scene known to us also from the good but tendentious history of the Old Testament, the bragging monuments of conquerors, and the precisely dated Babylonian business documents which give precision to our chronology. They show us something of the anguish of the small peoples under the heel of Assyria and Babylon; they remind us too that what Assyria broke up was not a paradise. The resistance of the Hebrew kingdoms themselves was weakened by the results of social injustice. No longer was every man a warrior; even under the good King Hezekiah, as Sennacherib's annals show us, the defence of Jerusalem depended largely upon Arab mercenaries.

Thus Isaiah (about 700):

> Woe unto you who join house to house, who join estate to estate to deprive your neighbour. Will you dwell all alone upon the earth?
>
> Woe to the mighty men, the wine-bibbers, the powerful men who mingle strong drink; who find in favour of the godless for bribes, and set aside the just plea of the just man. Therefore, as the dry corn-stalks are burned off and consumed by the fire, so . . . their bloom

[1] Isaiah xl, 1 (LXX). The Greek of the Septuagint, translated from a text much older than the mediaeval Masoretic, appears from the evidence of the 'Dead Sea' scroll of Isaiah to preserve a text sometimes, at least, closer to the original.

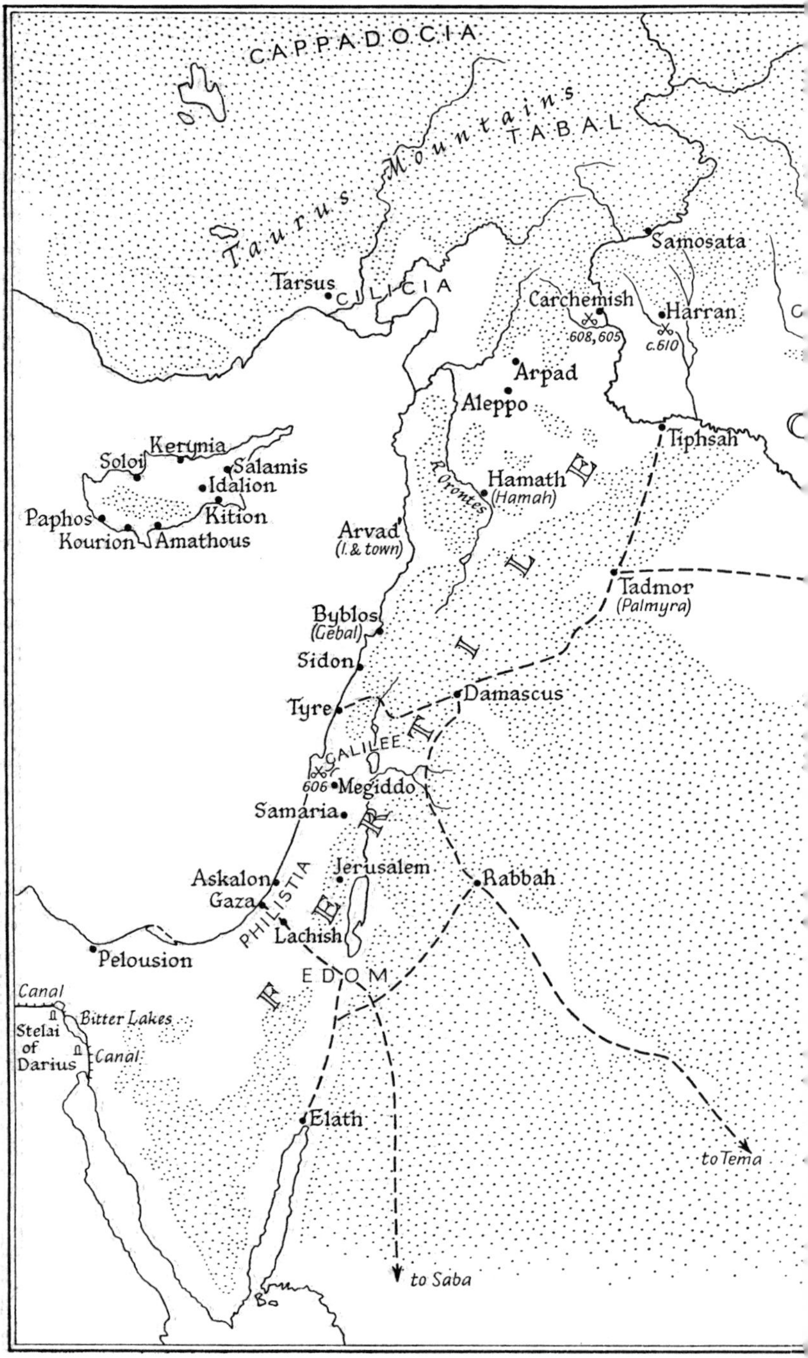
CAPPADOCIA
Taurus Mountains
TABAL
Samosata
Tarsus
CILICIA
Carchemish
608, 605
Harran
c. 610
Arpad
Aleppo
Tiphsah
Kerynia
Soloi
Salamis
Idalion
Paphos
Kition
Kourion
Amathous
Hamath
(Hamah)
R. Orontes
Arvad
(I. & town)
Tadmor
(Palmyra)
Byblos
(Gebal)
Sidon
Tyre
Damascus
GALILEE
606
Megiddo
Samaria
Jerusalem
Askalon
Gaza
Rabbah
PHILISTIA
Lachish
Pelousion
EDOM
FERTILE
Canal
Bitter Lakes
Stelai of Darius
Canal
Elath
to Tema
to Saba

The Fertil

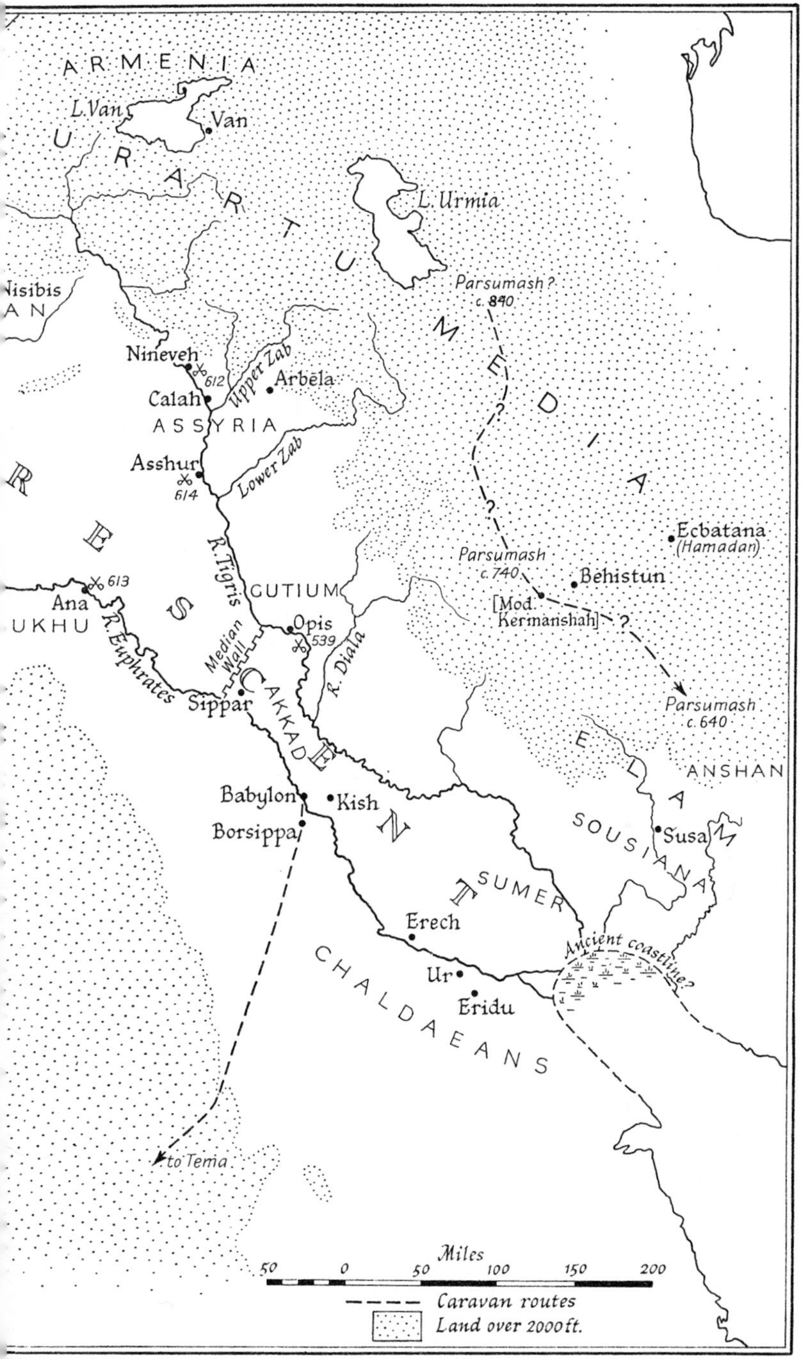
ARMENIA
L.Van
Van
URARTU
L.Urmia
Nisibis
Parsumash?
c. 840
MEDIA
Nineveh
612
Upper Zab
Arbela
Calah
ASSYRIA
Asshur
614
Lower Zab
R.Tigris
Ecbatana
(Hamadan)
Parsumash
c.740
Behistun
GUTIUM
613
Ana
UKHU
R. Euphrates
Opis
539
Median Wall
[Mod. Kermanshah]
R. Diala
Sippar
AKKAD
Parsumash
c.640
ELAM
ANSHAN
Babylon
Kish
Borsippa
SOUSIANA
Susa
SUMER
Erech
Ancient coastline?
Ur
Eridu
CHALDAEANS
to Tema
Miles
50 0 50 100 150 200
Caravan routes
Land over 2000ft.

rescent

> shall go up as dust; for they rejected the law of the Lord, . . . and the Lord Sabaoth was greatly angered against his people . . .
>
> Therefore will he raise up a standard to the nations afar, and will whistle them up from the ends of the earth; and see! they come swiftly. They shall not be weary nor hungry nor drowsy, nor sleep; they shall not undo their girdles, nor their shoe-straps break. Their arrows are sharp and their bows are strung. Their horses' hoofs are like hard stone, their chariot-wheels like a storm. They rage like lions, they are upon us like lions' whelps. He shall lay hold of the prey, and shall roar like a beast, and cast it aside, and there shall be none to deliver them. He shall roar over them in that day as with the voice of a storm at sea; and men shall look toward the land, and lo! grim darkness in their perplexity.[2]

One is reminded of the tremendous reliefs of the Assyrian kings and their galloping horse-archers, as they may still be seen in the reliefs from Nineveh. This was the world of the great Hebrew prophets; it requires an effort to remember that there was not always trouble everywhere, and that even then there were many years in many places when there was peace locally and the sun shone and the rain fell in season, and harvests were gathered with rejoicing and thanksgiving to the gods. But the prophets remind us, too, of what a too narrowly classical approach can let us forget: that the Persian peace that came with Cyrus the Great came as a blessing and even a liberation to Jews and other broken peoples; a blessing which the Persians, a great people whose kings believed in their mission to impose peace and law, would fain have imposed upon the Greeks, who were unbroken, though they broke themselves afterwards. As it was, the Persians did much damage to Greece. This is the tragedy of the Persian Wars.

The Assyrian army marked a formidable advance in military efficiency upon anything seen before it, with its organized regiments of every arm, specialised for every function; its heavy cavalry and light cavalry, mounted on improved breeds of horses and gradually rendering the chariot obsolescent; its archers and armoured spearmen, trained to act in combination; its sappers, protected by conical helmets and heavy coats, who moved up under covering fire of arrows to ply pick and crowbar (even in such clothing) against city walls; and the great armoured vehicles, through whose open, conical 'snouts' swung the

[2] Isaiah ix, 8, 22ff (LXX).

massive battering rams. All this was part of the heritage which the Persians took over. More constructively, the Assyrian empire was also the first to organize real provincial government under Assyrian officers, reporting regularly to the king, whereas the Eighteenth-Dynasty Pharaohs, for example, had relied (to their cost) upon local dynasts, with the Pharaoh, were he not an Akhnaton, marching out at intervals to exact tribute and obeisance.

But Assyria, long invincible, earned hatred by her remorseless cruelty and exhausted her manpower in unceasing campaigns. Syrians and Egyptians were among her least formidable victims. The civilised highlanders of Urartu (Ararat), skilled metal-workers, were worn down only in long struggles; and their weakening eased the coming of northern hordes: Gimirrai and Skutha, Kimmerians, against whom Sargon the captor of Samaria fell in battle, and Scythians from beyond the Caucasus. The Medes of the north-east, when first harried by Assyria, were tribal barbarians, known vaguely to the civilised world as the Umman-Manda; forty-five chiefs of the Medes paid tribute to Sargon in 713.[3] But they drew together under pressure; there was one chief, Daiukku, at this time, important enough not only to be named by Sargon, but to be deported to Hamath in Syria (Hamah). He probably died there, and whatever dreams he had been dreaming and commending to his fellow-tribesmen might seem to have died with him; but his name was not forgotten among his people. By the time of Herodotos, the details recounted about him were almost wholly legendary; but the legend put him in his correct place in social development; he is Herodotos' Deiokes, the wise village elder who introduced kingship among the Medes.[4] More ominous, the Medes learned from the Assyrians the arts of war; Kyaxares, called by Herodotos the son of Phraortes the son of Deiokes (though, as he lived till 584, this is hardly possible), was said to have organized his army in the first regular, drilled units seen in Media (Herodotos (i, 103) says 'in Asia'!).

Babylonia too, though its tradesmen and peasants were not fighting men, was continually restive under Assyrian rule; there were repeated revolts, one of the most serious a 'brothers' war', when Shamash-shum-ukin, whom his brother Asshur-bani-pal had made king of Babylon, took up arms against him; and the tough and organized kingdom of

[3] Date acc. to Meyer, *GdA* III (1937), p. 40.

[4] H. i, 96ff.

Elam supported Babylon as a buffer against Asshur. Asshur-bani-pal followed up the overthrow of his brother with an invasion of Elam, now itself troubled by civil war; but in spite of this the Elamites fought with determination. Almost every corner of Elam was devastated, and the kingdom destroyed; but the Assyrians also had lost heavily before the campaigns ended, about 639.

Then comes an ominous entry in Asshur-bani-pal's records. 'After the victorious weapons of Asshur had overcome and destroyed all Elam' . . . [fear came upon the nations round about]. 'The fear of My Majesty overwhelmed them, and they sent their messengers to win friendship and peace with costly presents. They enquired after the well-being of My Majesty; they kissed my feet and besought my lordship.' And then comes a mention of the first King Cyrus the Persian, the grandfather of Cyrus the Great. 'Kurash, king of the land of Parsuwash, heard of the mighty victory that I had won over Elam, with the help of Asshur and Bel and Nebo, the great gods, my lords; how that I had overwhelmed Elam like a flood. He sent Arukku, his eldest son, with tribute to Nineveh my residence, to do homage, and implored my lordship.' [5]

This is not the first extant mention of the Persian name. Already Shalmaneser III (858–824) mentions a 'land of Parsumash' or Parsuwash, but it appears to be on the borders of Armenia, south-east of Lake Urmia. Later it appears to be round the headwaters of the Diala, west of modern Kermanshah (*c.* 744); and men of Parsuwash and Anzan (or Anshan, which we shall meet again), a dependent princedom of Elam, fought among the allies of Elam and Babylon against Sennacherib in the great battle of Khalule about 681. We seem to see them as a tribal people, moving south-east parallel to the mountain ranges of western Iran, till they reach their historic home in the high valleys of Persis, the modern Fars. Their arrival there and the emergence of a settled monarchy may have taken place in the time of Teïspes, father of the first Cyrus and son of Akhaimenes, the earliest recorded ancestor of the great royal line.

Teïspes had two sons; besides Cyrus another, Ariaramnes, is now known not only from the later pedigree of Darius the Great but perhaps from a document, a gold tablet said to have been found at the

[5] Weidner, in *Archiv für Orientforschung*, VII (1931–2); cf. Campbell Thompson and Mallowan in *LAAA* XX (1933).

Median capital, Ecbatana (Hamadan). He mentions his brother 'the great king, king of the city of Anshan' but to himself he gives the title 'great king, king of kings, king of Persia'. 'King of kings' presumably marks the emergence of a centralised monarchy, supreme over other Persian petty chiefs; Ariaramnes is apparently the senior brother. He continues: 'This land of Persia which I hold, which has good horses and good men, Ahura Mazda the Great God granted to me; by the favour of Ahura Mazda I am king of this land; may Ahura Mazda bring me aid.' [6]

But for all these proud titles, the might of Persia was a small thing in the world as yet. It was the Medes, their kindred, who had not moved from their home in recent centuries, who grew great as Assyria weakened. Under Phraortes (Fravartish), the father of Kyaxares, they are said to have forced the Persians to accept their overlordship; and Ariaramnes' tablet probably came to Ecbatana as tribute or spoil. Media's progress was interrupted by a catastrophic raid or migration of the nomad Scyths, some of whom rode on far to the south-west, we are told, even to Askalon; Pharaoh Psamatik himself bought them off with gifts; but they suffered from sickness in the hot lands, and when the storm passed, Kyaxares the son of Phraortes methodically set about re-establishing his position, breaking the power of those Scyths who tried to settle as lords in Media by making their leaders drunk at a banquet and massacring them.[7] Then he and Nabopolassar the Chaldee, leader of yet another revolt of Babylonia, closed in from north and south upon the Assyrian homeland.

Our evidence, though Babylonian, scarcely disguises the fact that the Medes did the most effective fighting. The Babylonians regarded their allies with some horror. They sacked temples throughout Assyria, and even in cities 'within the territory of Akkad, which had been hostile and not come to the help of the King of Akkad'. (Thus the priestly chroniclers, who, in their 'Byzantine' manner, regularly give countries their ancient, 'classical' names.) This is evidence of how far south the Medes penetrated. The king of Babylon let his hair grow and slept on the ground in penance. The Assyrians, at bay, struck back

[6] Herzfeld, in *Arch. Mitt. aus Iran*, II, pp. 117ff. But R. G. Kent (*Old Persian Grammar*) would date the lettering about 400 B.C.

[7] H. i, 103–6. I do not understand why Olmstead (*Persian Empire*, p. 32, n. 87) says that there is 'absolutely no evidence' for the raid into Syria. H. *may* be wrong, but his evidence on this time and region is quite as good as much that O. accepts without question.

desperately, sometimes with success; they never fought better than in these campaigns, their 1814. But their armies dwindled and dwindled. Asshur, the ancient capital, was carried by assault in 614, and over its ruins Nabopolassar, who, we are told, had 'come too late for the battle', swore oaths of friendship with Kyaxares. His son, Nebuchadrezzar, married a Median princess, for whom he later built the famous 'Hanging Gardens' and conveyed water to them, to comfort her homesickness out of sight of her hills. Kyaxares returned home and in the campaign of 613 did not appear, perhaps through some unknown trouble in the north-east, and without the Medes the Babylonians fared ill; the Sukhu on the middle Euphrates came into the field against them (feeling that the Chaldaean was growing too strong?) and from before Ana in their territory the Assyrians drove Nabopolassar back in retreat. But in 612 the Medes returned. They came down the east bank of the Tigris to join Nabopolassar, who evidently did not venture to advance without them; and after months of fighting, including three pitched battles, great Nineveh fell.[8]

This is the 'crowning mercy' celebrated in the fierce verses of the Hebrew Nahum (if this is indeed a name, and if we should not, with some translators, take the heading as a title, 'The Vision of Comfort'):

The Burden of Nineveh

> The sledge-hammer is come up against thee! Guard the ramparts, watch the way, gird up thy loins, put forth all thy strength! . . . The shields of his heroes are red, his warriors are in scarlet; the steel of his chariots gleams, the spears are brandished. . . . They haste to the wall of the city; the mantlets are set up. The gates of the canals are opened [perhaps meaning that defensive moats are drained]; the palace crumbles.
>
> Woe to the bloody city! There is nought but plunder within her. The crack of the whip; the noise of rattling wheels; horses prancing, chariots jolting, horsemen charging; flashing swords, glittering spears; a multitude of slain, a mass of dead bodies; there is no end to the corpses; men stumble over the corpses.

[8] Account of the campaigns in C. J. Gadd, *The Newly Discovered Babylonian Chronicle* (British Museum) and *The Fall of Nineveh* (both 1923); tr. A. L. Oppenheim, in Pritchard, *Ancient Near-Eastern Texts*, pp. 303–5. Sacking of temples by the Medes, the Nabonidus Inscription in Istanbul, ii (Pritchard, p. 309). Nebuchadrezzar's wife and the Hanging Gardens, Berosos, in Josephus, *Against Apion*, 19. – The Medes themselves had no temples and, like the Jews, no images of the gods; and having been harried by the Assyrians of old, they may have acquired a Hebrew outlook on the 'gods of the heathen'.

Take the spoil of silver, take the spoil of gold! There is no end to the treasure, the wealth of all manner of fine furniture.

She is empty and void and waste; hearts melt, knees knock together, anguish is in all loins, faces are twitching with fear.

Where is the den of the lions, the feeding place of the young lions, where the lion and the lioness walked, and none made them afraid? The lion tore for his whelps and killed for his lionesses; he filled his caves with prey and his dens with ravin.

The den is clearly Nineveh itself; but the imagery may also have been suggested by the actual park of captive lions which the kings of Assyria had kept for hunting. The poet turns to remember Assyria's cruelty in the sack of Egyptian Thebes fifty years before:

Art thou better than No-Amon, that stood among the canals, with the waters round her?—whose rampart was the Nile, and her wall the waters? Ethiopia was her strength, Put and Libya her helpers. Yet she too was carried away, she went into captivity; *her* infants too were dashed in pieces at the head of every street, and they cast lots for her honourable men, and her great men were bound in chains.

Thy shepherds slumber, O king of Assyria; thy nobles are at rest; thy people are scattered upon the mountains and there is no man to gather them. There is no healing of thy hurt; thy wound is grievous. All that hear the tale of thee clap their hands over thee; for upon whom has not thy wickedness passed continually?[9]

By the autumn of 610, the allies had cleared the great western bend of the Euphrates, where Asshur-uballit, the last prince of Assyria and high-priest at Harran, held out for a time, hoping for Egyptian support. An Egyptian army with the Assyrian remnants recaptured Carchemish on the Euphrates in 609; but they failed before Harran, and their success was brief. Jeremiah has a famous prophecy 'Of Egypt: concerning the army of Pharaoh Necho, which Nebuchadrezzar king of Babylon smote in the fourth year of Jehoiakim, king of Judah' (605):

Who is this that riseth up like the Nile, as the rivers swell in flood? The waters of Egypt shall rise as a river; he said: 'I will go up, I will cover the earth and destroy the dwellers therein.'

[9] Nahum ii, 1–4, 6; iii, 1–3; ii, 8–12; iii, 8–10, 18, 19 (end); version from RV, RM, and E. W. Hamond, *The Seventh and Sixth Century Prophets*. The LXX seem to have been baffled by the difficulties of parts of this poem.

> Mount your horses, make ready the chariots; go forth, warriors of Ethiopia and armoured Libyans; ride, Lydians, bend your bows.
>
> Why are they dismayed, why retreating? Because their mighty men are cut down, they fled headlong, not turning back. . . . Let not the swift flee, nor the mighty man save himself; in the north, by the river Euphrates, they stumbled and fell.[10]

The Pharaoh who had smitten Josiah in the pass of Megiddo fled, hotly pursued, and 'came not any more out of his land; for the king of Babylon had taken, from the brook of Egypt to the river Euphrates, all that pertained to the king of Egypt'.[11]

But neither the destruction of Asshur nor the humiliation of Egypt brought peace to the small nations of Syria. Jeremiah saw the truth: that Babylon under its desert-edge Chaldaean kings was now far the strongest power locally, and that submission was the only possible policy. Jeremiah, himself a countryman, was concerned for the sufferings of country people; but clever men at Jerusalem could not resist the temptation to play balance-of-power politics. They could not believe that the near and imposing Egypt was really so weak, and they were irked by the prospect of Chaldaean lordship and one of its consequences: that Nebuchadrezzar would levy tribute on the profits of that transit trade between the north (now the Mediterranean, especially) and the Red Sea lands of Arabia Felix, a source of wealth in Israel at many periods, from long before Solomon to long after Herod. The inevitable result was war again, and the 'Babylonian Captivity' (589). The Temple, palace and 'every great house' were methodically sacked and pillaged. Some seventy selected leaders of the war party were executed after the surrender, and 4600, according to the detailed figures given by Jeremiah's editor – almost the whole governing class, bourgeoisie and craftsmen of Jerusalem – were removed to Babylonia in three separate deportations. Jeremiah and others of the peace party were released, and one of them, Gedaliah, was left as governor, shortly to be murdered by some of the diehards who had kept up resistance in the country districts and evaded capture; and we are expressly told that the peasantry of the land was not removed. The fortunes of the exiles, including the intelligentsia, one may fairly say, of Judah, 'by the waters of Babylon', were to be seminal for later history.[12]

[10] Jeremiah xlvi, 2–4, 7–9, 5, 6; RV and LXX.
[11] 2 Kings xxiv, 7.
[12] Jeremiah xxxix, xl, lii; 2 Kings xxv; Psalm cxxxvii.

After the battle of Carchemish the allies parted company, evidently by agreement, and Kyaxares turned to his own programme of expansion in the north-west. How much Iranian migration into the lands devastated by Assyrian, Kimmerian and Scythian raids there had already been, we do not know. Herodotos (vii, 73) makes the Armenians 'colonists of the Phrygians', from the west, speakers of an Aryan language perhaps not distantly related to Iranian; but there was certainly much immigration from the east too. It may have been Kyaxares who made a final end of the much-tried Kingdom of Urartu.[13] The name of its people, 'Khaldians', disappears from the interior and, like those of the Tibarēnoi and Moschoi (Tubal and Meshech), both once widespread, survives in Greek times only in a narrow area between the northern mountains and the Black Sea.[14] In place of these and of the ancient Hittites appear, west of Armenia, the Iranian-speaking Cappadocians (Katpatuka), partly mingling with the older peoples,[15] partly driving them to the coast, much as the Turks were to do long afterwards at the expense of Christian 'Roum'.

Further west, Kyaxares ran into stiff opposition: that of the Lydian kingdom under its military dynasty, the House of the Hawk, come to power in the crisis of the Kimmerian raids and long accustomed to furnish mercenaries to Egypt. The veteran Alyattes held Kyaxares to a draw in six stubborn campaigns, culminating in the battle interrupted by an eclipse, which Thales the Milesian, perhaps from some knowledge of Babylonian astronomy, had predicted as due during the year (585 or 582).[16] Both sides were ready for peace; Kyaxares, who died not long after, may have been already a sick man; and through the mediation of Nebuchadrezzar[17] and of Syennesis, king of Cilicia (the

[13] So Sayce, in *CAH* III, p. 183.

[14] Strabo xi, 497, xii, 548f, 555; his statement that 'Chaldaioi' is the 'modern name' of the ancient, metal-working Chalybes (549) clinches the identification.

[15] Cf. H. vii, 72, on their arms.

[16] 585, Pliny, *NH* ii, 12/53; 584, with textual variations, Euseb. Arm., Jerome: the eclipse of May 28th, 585, is accepted in most modern books, but Beloch (*GG* I, ii, 354f) points out that, though all but total, it would have begun in Cappadocia only about three-quarters of an hour before sundown; he therefore prefers that of Sept. 21st, 582, nine-tenths total and beginning about 9.0 a.m. O. Neugebauer (*The Exact Sciences in Antiquity*, 1962 edn., pp. 109–19, 142f) doubts the whole story, showing that Bab. astronomy was as yet in no condition to make any such predictions. They may have made little more than a lucky guess.

[17] H. i, 73f. – For Nebuchadrezzar, H. writes 'Labynetos', an ancient corruption for Nabynetos, i.e. Nabuna'id (see below). Nabuna'id was not king until 556; but he was an important official with North Syrian connections, and possibly was Nebuchadrezzar's plenipotentiary.

first known to us of a line of dynasts bearing this name or title), a treaty was arranged. The river Halys was agreed as the frontier, and Aryēnis, daughter of Alyattes, was given in marriage to Astyages, Kyaxares' son.

Modern writers have sometimes suggested that the neutral powers intervened through fear of the Medes, 'to save Lydia'; but there is no positive evidence of this. Kyaxares, so far from his home base, had shown few signs of being able to overcome Lydia, and if Nebuchadrezzar had been chiefly concerned over the growth of Median power, he might have preferred to let the struggle continue. More probably the kings, who were well aware of the revenue-producing possibilities of tolls on trade, were concerned to free the channels of the trade with Lydia, which the war in Cappadocia was interrupting: a trade in western tin and 'Babylonitish' textiles (there is direct archaeological evidence even for the latter; the rosettes and other filling-ornament on Corinthian and Ionian pottery copy the embroidery as well as the jewelry shown on the sculptured robes of Assyrian kings); a trade, too, in Taurus silver and Lydian gold, which had just prompted the Lydian middle-men to the invention of coinage.[18] Nevertheless, Median power was a subject of anxiety; one of the major works probably of Nebuchadrezzar's later years was the great line of brick fortifications covering Babylonia from Tigris to Euphrates known as the Median Wall, which Xenophon and the Ten Thousand were to see, centuries later. He also heavily fortified Babylon itself.[19] Jeremiah, or the author of a prophecy preserved among his, already foretells vengeance upon Babylon by Median hands,

> for out of the north there cometh up a nation against her, which shall make her land desolate, and none shall dwell therein.
>
> Thus saith the Lord of hosts, the God of Israel: Behold, I will punish the king of Babylon and his land, as I have punished the king of Assyria . . .
>
> Behold, a people cometh from the north; a great nation and many kings, from the ends of the earth, with bow and short sword. They are fierce and shall not pity. Their shout shall echo as the sea, they ride upon horses, prepared for war like a fire, against thee, O daughter of Babylon . . .

[18] See, more fully, *Lyric Age*, pp. 61, 86f (ornament); 91, 177f (coins).

[19] *Anabasis* i, 7, 15; ii, 4, 12 (Median Wall); Babylon, Berosos *ap.* Jos. *Against Apion*, i, 19.

> Make ready the arrows, fill the quivers; for the Lord hath stirred up the spirit of the King of the Medes, because his wrath is against Babylon, to destroy her.[20]

But the time was not yet; Babylon was not devastated and, so far as the King of the Medes was concerned, the prophecy was unfulfilled. Among the great powers after the Halys treaty there appears to have been peace for over thirty years, which deserves to be remembered to their credit. Many exiled Jews grew rich and influential in Babylon (the background of the historical romances of Daniel and Esther); and the desolation of the Temple cried in vain.

Nebuchadrezzar, since the north and east were closed to him, developed his power in the west; his Chaldaean ancestors were a desert people, and Berosos' statement (*loc. cit.*) that he conquered 'Arabia' has some basis in fact. He was unable to take the island fortress of Tyre, and that he ever entered Egypt remains at least unconfirmed; but he does seem to have repulsed some piece of aggression by Egypt, supported by Greek mercenaries, on their common frontier.[21] Nebuchadrezzar lived till 562, and his dynasty did not long outlive him. His son, Awēl-Marduk (the Evil-Merodach recorded to have mitigated the captivity of Jehoiachin, ex-king of Judah[22]), was murdered after two years by his sister's husband, who reigned till 556, and died leaving the throne to a youthful son, Labashi-Marduk; and Labashi-Marduk, after only a few months, was overthrown by a conspiracy of his courtiers and tortured to death (or 'clubbed to death'). Official history assures us that he was of bad character, but what he had done to earn such hatred does not appear.[23]

Nabonidus (Nabuna'id), the nominee, it seems, of the conspirators, claims to be 'the real executor' of the wills of Nebuchadrezzar and his son-in-law; which is against the theory that this palace revolution marked a reaction of the native Babylonians against the Chaldees. He was himself, in fact, if not a Chaldaean, certainly a western provincial nobleman. His mother had been priestess of the great temple of Sin, the moon-god, at Harran, sacked by the 'Umman-Manda' in 610, and

[20] Jeremiah l, li (= LXX, xxvii, xxviii); 3; 41f; 11.

[21] D. J. Wiseman, *Chronicles of Chaldaean Kings*, pp. 94f.

[22] 2 Kings xxv, 27ff.

[23] Nabonidus Stele in Istanbul, iv–v (Pritchard, *Texts* (cf. n. 8 above), p. 309); Berosos, *loc. cit.*; B.'s figures for lengths of reign are confirmed by the dates on contemporary business documents (cf. Parker and Dubberstein, *Babylonian Chronology*, p. 10). 'Clubbed to death', Gadd in *Anatolian Studies*, VIII, p. 70, n. 2.

his most heartfelt desire, as well as hers – she was still alive and vigorous – was to see it restored. He was already an elderly man; his mother died in 547, aged 104 (perhaps his age, as in some Roman palace-revolutions, was a recommendation); but like her, he proved to be durable and full of vigour, and it was only violence which brought his reign to an end after seventeen years.

What we do discover from documents of the time is that there were tensions in Babylon, and that these were, at least in part, of an ecclesiastical character. Nabonidus accuses some earlier rulers of installing an 'incorrect' or 'inappropriate' image in the temple of Ishtar of Erech; and shortly we find the clergy of Babylon bringing exactly the same kind of complaint against him.[24] The degree of priority to be accorded to the re-building of a distant temple of the Moon-god was only one among the subjects over which an acute coolness arose. As a reaction to clerical hostility, Nabonidus, after celebrating the New Year Festival of 555 and 'taking the hands of Bel' at the beginning of his reign, went off to the west, where he killed in battle the king of Tema (the biblical Teman) and made this western Arabian oasis his headquarters until his eleventh year (545); he also secured other western oases (e.g. the biblical Dedan) perhaps even as far south as Medina, thus controlling the spice-trade caravan routes to the Hejaz. At Tema he is said to have built himself a city 'like Babylon'. Meanwhile some work of restoration proceeded at Harran, perhaps initially by permission of the Medes, for there is no evidence that they were dislodged from Harran before the revolt of Cyrus in 550. Three inscriptions of Nabonidus at Harran, recently discovered, give some valuable chronological information, incidentally to a biography of the king's mother, whose piety and penitential mourning for the devastation of the temple are described by her in the first person; they also condemn in the frankest terms the disloyalty of his Babylonian subjects, and confirm beyond doubt the facts of the king's long residence at Tema and the westward extension of his empire.[25] Meanwhile at Babylon the Chronicle records year after year 'The king was in Tema; the crown prince, his officials and his army were in Akkad; the king

[24] Nabonidus Stele, iii; cf. the (hostile) *Verse Account of N.* (Pritchard, *Texts*, pp. 313–14).

[25] See Dr D. S. Rice (the discoverer) in *ILN*, 21 Sept. 1957; detailed account of the inscrs. with translation and commentary by C. J. Gadd in *Anatolian Studies*, VIII (1958), pp. 35–92.

did not come to Babylon for the month Nisan', i.e. for the royal New Year ceremonies. The crown prince was Belshazzar, 'Belshazzar the King' of the book of Daniel. To his efficiency and his army, no doubt of loyal westerners, we may attribute the fact that seditious feelings did not break out in rebellion.

CHAPTER II

The Coming of Cyrus

NABONIDUS, we are not surprised to find, was a dreamer of dreams. One such, reported at length by the king in a document from Babylon, records how

> At the beginning of my reign, the gods revealed a dream to me: Marduk, the great lord, and Sin, the light of heaven and earth, stood on either side. Marduk said to me 'Nabuna'id, King of Babylon, carry up bricks with thy horses and chariots and restore E-Khul-Khul' [the Temple of Joy; the name of the temple at Harran]. 'Make Sin, the great lord, to dwell in his abode.' Fearfully I spoke to the lord of the gods, saying, 'O Marduk, . . . the Umman-Manda surrounds it and he is exceeding strong.' Then Marduk said to me 'The Umman-Manda of whom thou speakest is no more; neither he nor his land nor the kings who march with him. With the coming of the third year, the gods have caused Cyrus to march against him, Cyrus the king of Anshan, his petty vassal, with his small army. He has overthrown the far-flung Umman-Manda; he has captured Ishtuwigu, king of the Umman-Manda, and led him captive to his own land.
>
> [Then] . . . I was seized with anxiety and my countenance was troubled. I set my far-flung armies in motion, from Gaza on the border of Egypt, from the Upper Sea which is beyond Euphrates to the Lower Sea. The kings, the princes, the governors and my far-flung armies, which Sin, Shamash and Ishtar my lords entrusted to me, came to restore E-Khul-Khul . . . the temple which is in Harran, which Asshur-bani-pal, king of Assyria, son of Esarhaddon king of Assyria, a prince who was before me, had restored. In the proper month, on a propitious day, I laid the foundation.[1]

Though the revolt of Cyrus is here spoken of in the past tense, scholars have commonly believed that the events lay still in the future,

[1] S. Langdon, *Die Neubabylonischen Königsinschriften* (Leipzig, 1912), Nabonidus, no. 1; S. Smith, *Babylonian Historical Texts*, pp. 44f.

as they certainly did if Nabonidus is honest in referring the dream to the beginning of his reign. If so, 'the preterites used are the *perfectum propheticum*' (S. Smith). Religious fanatic as the king was, it is not impossible that he may, as Smith suggests, have consulted some oracle which sent answers in dreams, and made alliance as a result with the king of Anshan. If so, the march of his western army from Gaza to Syria was admirably adapted, from his ally's point of view, to divert the Median king's attention and some of his troops to the west, until Cyrus was ready to revolt openly two years later.

During the thirty years of the long peace we have little news from Iran. Astyages continued to reign over Media; probably, his western frontiers being delimited by treaty and by marriage-alliances, he turned east and established his overlordship over the thinly spread Iranian and pre-Aryan populations as far east as Bactria. Certainly, when the curtain of our ignorance is raised again, all these lands form part of the Iranian empire, and continue to do so until the time of Alexander. But it would seem that there was solider, more intensive growth in the subordinate kingdom of Persia, enlarged by the incorporation of Sousiana, the old kingdom of Elam, war-ravaged in the seventh century by Assyria, but a land of ancient and settled civilisation. That there was also a considerable measure of political fusion with the Elamite remnants, no doubt multiplying again in two generations of peace, is shown by the fact that Cyrus the Great set up inscriptions with versions in Elamite as well as in his own language.

Cyrus I left his throne to a son, Cambyses; Arukku, his eldest son, who had borne his tribute to Asshur-bani-pal, is not heard of again; he may well, it has been suggested, have been detained as a hostage and died in Assyria. This first Cambyses in turn was the father of Cyrus II, who came to the throne in 559. Meanwhile, in the other, more easterly Achaemenid kingdom, Ariaramnes was followed by his son Arsāmes, who was still living, an old man, in 521; but he and his son Hystaspes were then no longer kings. It looks as though at some time unknown, perhaps early in the reign of Cyrus II, Arsāmes was constrained to accept an honourable but subordinate position in face of the superior resources and powerful personality of the king of Anshan.[2]

[2] Pedigree in Darīus' Behistun Inscription, i, 2, of which this is the generally accepted interpretation; Weidner, in *Archiv für Orientforschung*, VII (1932), pp. 1ff. on Arsāmes, cf,

Cyrus' mother is said to have been Mandane, a daughter of Astyages, married to Cambyses in yet another dynastic alliance; but he had no love or respect for his suzerain. Nabonidus' dream suggests that he had come to an understanding with Babylon as early as 555. Herodotos' story of his youth, like Xenophon's historical novel about him, contains too much of romance to be used for details, even when these are plausible; but in the sixth year of Nabonidus, 550, we have the brief, contemporary Babylonian account of the first of Cyrus' great conquests. There may have been references to earlier phases of his rebellion in the preceding years, but for these the Chronicle is fragmentary. Now we read:

> [King Ishtuwigu] marched against Cyrus, King of Anshan [to battle.] Ishtuwigu's troops mutinied and he was captured, and they gave him up to Cyrus. Cyrus [marched] against the country Agamtanu (Ecbatana); [he seized] the royal residence; he carried off the silver, gold and chattels of the land of Agamtanu and brought them to Anshan.[3]

Nabonidus had secured Harran, and, though still on bad terms with his subjects, was able ultimately to fulfil his dream of the restoration of E-Khul-Khul. At about this time, too, one of his Harran inscriptions records a general peace with the peoples with whom he had had trouble. 'In that year' (it is not clear which), there was prosperity and summer rain through the favour of Sin. 'At the word of Sin also Ishtar, lady of battle, without whom war and peace exist not nor a weapon is forged, [she crossed?] her hands over them, and the king[s?] . . . of Egypt, the city of the Medes, the land of the Arabs and all the kings who were hostile sent messengers before me.'

It has been suggested that the unusual and curiously vague expression 'city of the Medes' may date from 'immediately after the victory of Cyrus, who had perhaps not secured or assumed his official titles'.[4]

Herodotos adds to the tale of diplomatic exchanges at this time the name of Croesus of Lydia, who had alliances with both Egypt and

---

Herzfeld, *A New Inscription of Xerxes* (Chicago Univ., Oriental Institute, 1932), § 3 (p. 4). H. (vii, 11) has the pedigree in a garbled form, making the two royal lines into one. The reference in Olmstead, *Persian Empire*, p. 214, n. 1, to *Archiv für O.* IV is a slip for *Arch. Mitt. aus Iran*, IV (1932).

[3] *Nabonidus Chronicle*, ii; Sidney Smith, *Babylonian Historical Texts*, p. 115; Pritchard, *Texts*, p. 305; H. i, 127ff. Cf. Polyainos, vii, 6, 1 and 9.

[4] Gadd, in *Anatolian Studies*, VIII, pp. 59 (text), 77 (commentary).

Babylon. After consulting Greek oracles, with a view to reinforcing his army from among the armoured Hellenes, the best infantry in the world, he also sent presents and made a treaty with 'the most powerful of the Greeks', who, he found, were the Spartans. But Croesus made no treaty with Cyrus. He was married to Astyages' sister, which gave him a *casus belli* against the usurper; also it seemed a good opportunity, while Media was in confusion, to secure the land of Cappadocia, for which his father had contended in vain, and to cut out the tolls levied by Iranian middle-men. The story that the Delphic Oracle, of whose clairvoyance Croesus had gained a high opinion, also spurred him on with the prophecy, 'Croesus crossing the Halys will destroy a mighty empire', could be quite true.[5]

So Croesus crossed the Halys, probably in 547, the ninth year of Nabonidus, helped in the operation, so a Greek story told, by Thales of Miletos, who directed engineering works for dividing the river into two fordable streams (turning some of the water back into an old bed?). Such hydraulic operations were in the Babylonian manner, and Thales, as his astronomical lore shows, knew something of Babylonian science. Herodotos disbelieves the story ('*I* think he crossed by the existing bridge'); Herodotos himself had crossed that bridge in his time, but we do not know if he had good reason for thinking that it was there a century earlier. Croesus took the strong fortress of Pteria (no longer held by a Median garrison?), and encamped in Cappadocia, rounding up for the slave-market the local peasantry, innocent victims, as Herodotos remarks.[6] No doubt he intended to people his new frontier district with a reliable population. But he did not know Cyrus.

Cyrus must have had long forewarning of Croesus' preparations. He had a long way to come to the rescue; 1200 miles as the road wound from Persia, and fully 800 from Media; but he wasted no time. Before the snow was off the passes, his troops were mustering; and in the ninth year of Nabonidus (547), in the month Nisan, which is the month of the spring equinox, he 'crossed the Tigris below Arbēla'. This route would take him through Assyria, past the ruins of Nineveh, past Nisibis and north of Harran, which is Carrhae, past Samosata; names famous in the wars of Rome. This was the route followed later by the royal road described by Herodotos; from Tigris to Euphrates it followed the steppe country of the desert edge; there would still be

[5] H. i, 46, 53, 56, 70, 77.

[6] H. i, 75–6.

water for an army to be found in April, in water-holes and in wadis cut by streams flowing from the northern mountains. Starting so early, Cyrus was also by this route avoiding the danger of late spring storms in the high valleys of Armenia. From Arbela to north of Harran, the route also ran hard by the Babylonian frontier, and no doubt hearts in the south beat faster; it is probably to this more than academic interest in his route that we owe our one essential detail of it: 'below Arbela'.[7] But the hurricane moved on to the west; it was not bound for Babylonia this year.

It was therefore still quite early in the summer when Cyrus reached the scene of what were to be epoch-making operations in Cappadocia; but there was no early decision. Croesus was an experienced commander; Cyrus a great one. Neither would engage at a disadvantage, nor fall easily into a trap; and the season seems to have been far advanced before, at last, the expected and mutually desired battle took place; a bloody, stubborn, indecisive affair, according to Herodotos, ending only when it was too dark to see. We have no tactical account of it Xenophon's is romance; but we know how the combatants were equipped. Croesus' best infantry were the armoured Ionians from his subject cities (Cyrus had in the previous year sent emissaries to try to subvert them – perhaps in trading vessels from Syria) and Lydians armed in like manner; but his main striking force was that of the Lydian cavalry with their long spears. On the other side, almost all Medes and Persians carried bow and short sword; infantry came from the agricultural peoples, cavalry especially from the pastoral nomads, the Dahai, Mardians, Sagartians. Whether Cyrus yet had any armoured 'regulars' like the later Immortals, we do not know; Astyages' former army may have supplied some. Between two such forces, the battle must have been curiously like those between Turks and Christians in the same part of the world. What we do know is that Cyrus acquired a very salutary respect for the Lydian lancers.[8]

[7] Cf. Xen. *Cyrus* iii, 4, 41, where C. at this juncture marches close to 'the wall of Babylon' – a mistake for the frontier or 'Median' wall (cf. p. 54, below).

[8] H. i, 76, 4; armament, Lydian cavalry, 79, 3, infantry, vii, 74, 1; Iranian infantry, vii, 61, 1, 62, 1, 64, 1; cavalry, 84–86, 1. It must here be remarked, since it is often denied, that ancient spear-armed cavalry, though stirrupless, could charge with violence, wielding their spears, as many Greek works of art show us, 'overarm'; not, of course, 'lance in rest' like mediaeval knights with their elaborate saddles and girths. Xenophon tells, reporting the incident purely for its military interest, of an advanced-guard encounter in Phrygia in 396, in which 'all the Greeks who struck their man broke their spears; but the Persians, with their *palta* [short spears, which could be thrown] of cornel-wood,

On the morning after the battle, Cyrus' army kept close and made no move; and Croesus for his part felt his troops in no condition to attack the archers in position behind their wall of shields stuck in the ground. Cyrus' army, we are told, was far the larger; this may be true, but we could believe it more implicitly if it were not that the enemy's army always is. Croesus, in any case, satisfied that he had fought the enemy to a standstill, determined to call off the campaign, raise larger forces during the winter, from Sparta, from Egypt with its thousands of Greek and other mercenaries, and to appeal to Nabonidus to take up arms. Without more ado, he marched for home.

Then Cyrus showed his genius, and his hold over his troops. He gave Croesus just long enough start to let his demobilisation for the winter get well under way, and marched after him, moving so fast that he arrived unheralded before Sardis; as Herodotos vividly says, 'his own messenger'. Croesus had to fight again with his Lydians alone. His one chance was an irresistible cavalry charge; but against this also Cyrus sprang a surprise. The Persian transport was largely camel-borne; and it had been noticed, probably during the summer's operations, that the Lydian horses, which had never seen camels, would shy off at the sight and smell of these beasts. On the advice, Herodotos says, of Harpagus, the Median general who had deserted Astyages, Cyrus caused his men to advance behind a long line of the unladen camels. The Lydian cavalry-charge broke down in a chaos of rearing and unmanageable horses; and though the Lydians fought well on foot, outnumbered as they were, there could be only one end. They fled, and Croesus withdrew with his guards into his citadel.

Croesus had written to his allies to assemble at Sardis in the spring, 'in five months' time' (so it was now late October; Cyrus had not hesitated to commit his highlanders to a campaign in the cold autumn of Anatolia). Other messengers were now sent off in hot haste, with a cry for immediate relief. Yet the position did not seem hopeless. The precipitous-sided citadel of Sardis was reckoned impregnable. It is still an impressive sight, though there is no longer much room on top; the soft, geologically recent deposits of which it is formed are weathering rapidly away. If Cyrus' army, so far from home, were efficiently

---

quickly killed twelve troopers and two horses; and the Greek horse gave way' (*Hellenika*, iii, 4, 15). The Greek spears were badly shown up, but we are not told that anyone fell off from the shock of impact.

harassed from without, the blockade might become impossible. But there was no long blockade. Cyrus' men were accustomed to mountains; and Cyrus sent out a proclamation to his host, promising a handsome reward to the first man over the wall. After fourteen days, says the story, an accident revealed a feasible route up the most precipitous side of the stronghold. A Lydian soldier dropped his helmet over the edge, and climbed down and recovered it. He did not escape the eyes of a watcher, Hyroiades the Mardian. This part of the wall was almost ungarrisoned; it was, men said, the only part where the ancient king Mēles omitted to carry round the lion that his concubine brought forth, when prophets said that if the monster were borne round the walls, Sardis would never be taken. Hyroiades led a party of his comrades on the climb; and, as so often in history, an 'impregnable' position fell to daring and initiative.

As to what happened to Croesus, there was clearly a rich growth of legend. The earliest Greek account of his fate seems to have been that he burnt himself in his palace when all was lost. All the world knows Herodotos' story that Cyrus intended to burn Croesus alive, and then repented, out of curiosity on hearing him call upon the name of Solon, the sage who had once warned him to call no man happy till he was dead; but that Cyrus would have been too late to quench the pyre, had not Apollo, in answer to Croesus' prayer, then sent a miraculous storm of rain which extinguished it. Croesus then appears in Herodotos, who is followed by the later historians, as accompanying Cyrus and his son after him, an honoured captive to whom Cyrus is more than once indebted for wise advice. The story is almost impossible, since it would have been contrary, it seems, to the Iranian religion (whether or not Cyrus knew anything of the teaching of the prophet Zoroaster, on whom see chap. IV) to pollute the divine fire by burning a body in it.[9]

Babylonian chronicles must have mentioned this campaign, but not,

[9] This seems to be a case where, as in that of Harmodios and Aristogeiton (cf. *Lyric Age*, pp. 320–2), we can see something of the growth of a Greek saga. Our earliest evidence is that of the painting on the Louvre amphora by Myson, not long after 500, where Croesus, robed, garlanded and sceptre in hand, sits on an ornamental chair on top of a pyre, pouring a libation, while an attendant (named in writing Euthümos, 'Cheerful') sprinkles holy water with twigs on the ground beside it (rather than lights the pyre, which is already blazing); cf. A. H. Smith in *JHS* XVIII, pp. 267f, fig. 1; Furtwängler-Reichhold, *Gr. Vasenm.*, pl. 113; Olmstead, *Persian Empire*, pl. vii. Bakchylides, *Epinikion* iii (for Hieron, 468 B.C.), tells in detail how Croesus determined not to outlive his happiness, and caused the pyre to be lit amid the shrieks of his daughters; but Zeus sent rain and quenched it,

apparently, in any of the portions which we have. (The reading 'Lu[dia]', under the year 547, though attractive, is now denounced by specialists as impossible. We are thrown back upon Herodotus, to our no great disadvantage.) On matters concerning his native Greek Asia Minor he is well informed. Cyrus did not stay there long; but the stay he did make was fateful.[10]

Before returning to the east, Cyrus had his first direct contact with the Greeks. The Aiolic and Ionian cities hastily sent envoys, offering to submit as tributaries on the same terms as to Croesus: but Cyrus made it clear that, since they had rejected his invitation to revolt from Lydia before the campaign, the conditions would now be stiffer. 'There was a man', he said, according to one of Herodotos' charming stories (i, 141), 'who piped to the fish in the sea, hoping thus to get them to come out; but when this did not work, he took a net and hauled out a great draft of them; and when he saw them flopping about, he said "You need not dance now, since you would not dance out when I piped to you."'

With the powerful Miletos, at the end of the Maiandros (Meander, Menderes) valley route, Cyrus did deign to renew Croesus' treaty, thus astutely splitting any Greek resistance at the outset. The other Ionians sent delegates to their customary meeting-place, Paniōnion, at the sanctuary of Poseidon Helikōnios by Cape Mykale, opposite Samos.[11] (We shall hear of other delegate-conferences there, pp. 147, 210, etc.; but this step towards unity fell far short of the creation of a federal state.) Their decision was to appeal for help to Sparta, and an embassy was sent in haste, led by Pythermos of Phokaia, the city

---

and Apollo carried off the aged king to the land of his worshippers, the Hyperboreans. Croesus, for his piety, is thus numbered among those delivered from ordinary death (like Harmodios, according to the song); Greek imagination shrank from the idea that one so great and so generous to the gods had really suffered an awful fate. Of this legend, Herodotos then gives a rationalised version (as of Attis and the Boar, earlier in his Croesus story, i, 34–45; the presentation of this episode looks very much as though it were derived from a drama). His version (i, 86ff, cf. i, 207, 211, iii, 34ff, etc.), that Croesus' life was spared, was then followed by all later writers, with their own variations: D.S. ix, excerpt 34 Dindorf (from Ephoros?), Xen. *Cyrop.* vii, 2, 5ff, Ktesias vii (epit.), Nikolaos (*FHG* 90 F 68). For Croesus' generosity, *philophron areta*, cf. Pindar, *Pyth.* i, 94, also for Hieron, 470 B.C.; C. was evidently then a type of the good despot in the Syracusan circle.

Meyer (*GdA* III (1937), p. 184f) combines Bakchylides and H.: C. tried to immolate himself, but was rescued and given a principality near Ecbatana; this last from the worthless evidence of Ktesias, whose 'Barene' is perhaps nothing but a rationalisation of the Hyperboreans (so Olmstead, *P.E.*, p. 40).

[10] See S. Smith, *Bab. Hist. Texts*, Pl. xii.

[11] H. i, 141, cf. 148.

named by a later writer as at this time the leading sea-power of the Greek world.[12] The Spartans prudently declined to commit their forces, but sent an embassy of their own in a light warship, chiefly, Herodotos opines, to gather information on Cyrus' strength and the state of Ionia. They did also, however, venture on a diplomatic *démarche*. Landing at Phokaia, the envoys visited Cyrus at Sardis and delivered a warning to him to abstain from any hostile act against Greek cities, since 'the Spartans would not tolerate it'. There was a short silence. Then Cyrus turned to the Greeks who were with him.

'Who *are* the Spartans?' asked Cyrus.

Herodotos continues (i, 153) with a characteristic and significant passage:

> . . . And while enquiring, he said to the Spartan herald: 'I was never yet afraid of men who have an appointed place in the middle of their city in which to meet and deceive each other on oath; and if I have good health, it will not be the Ionians' troubles they will be talking about, but their own.' This saying of Cyrus was a hit at all the Greeks, because they have established markets in which to buy and sell; for the Persians have not the custom of marketing; the market is completely non-existent in their country.

Whether or not Cyrus said it, Herodotos lays his finger upon an essential point: the economic basis of the 'temperamental incompatibility' between the Greek and Persian social systems. That of the Persians was socially aristocratic, politically feudal, and economically based on a food-producing peasantry. It was at a stage of development out of which the more progressive parts of the Greek world had been passing in recent centuries. The Persian nobleman's contempt for the trader might have been paralleled in the Homeric age, and even later among Dorian aristocrats of the stamp of Theognis;[13] as it happened, there were probably plenty of men among the 'peers' of Sparta herself who shared such sentiments. But Greek civilisation by this time was dependent upon trade for its whole character; even the Spartan aristocracy was to some extent parasitic upon it. How much of good there was in the Greek way of life, and how dependent it was upon its

[12] H. i, 152; D.S. excerpt *ap*. Euseb. (the 'Thalassocracy List').
[13] e.g. *Od.* viii, 159ff; Theog. 183ff, 679, etc.

economic basis, was something beyond the Persians' ken; and much blood and many tears were to flow in consequence.

Cyrus started for home, leaving a Persian named Tabalos as governor of Sardis and one Paktyas, a Lydian, as finance-officer 'to bring in the gold of Croesus and of the other Lydians. He allotted the Ionians no very high priority; for he was concerned over Babylon and the Bactrians and Sakai and Egypt, countries against which he was proposing to conduct campaigns in person, while sending another general against Ionia.' Thus Herodotos quietly corrects the perspective of his Greek audience. However, Cyrus had not got far on the road when he was overtaken by the news that Lydia was in revolt. Paktyas, too implicitly trusted, decamped with the treasure to the coast, where he set about hiring mercenaries. He then marched on Sardis and besieged Tabalos in the citadel. Cyrus had to detach a force, under a Mede named Mazares, with orders to disarm the Lydians, sell as slaves all armed rebels, and bring back Paktyas alive. Mazares duly relieved Sardis, and chased Paktyas to the coast, where he took refuge at Kyme. Mazares demanded his extradition, and the Kymaian assembly was inclined to give him up. Herodotos here tells the charming story of how, when the oracle of Branchidai supported this course, Aristodikos, a leading citizen of Kyme, persuaded the people to send him to consult the oracle again. The interpreters of the oracle repeated the same advice; whereupon Aristodikos proceeded to pull out the nests of the sparrows which had 'found them an house where they might lay their young' in corners of the temple building. Then a voice was heard from the sanctuary saying 'Villain, how dare you? Will you take and slay my suppliants from the Temple?' 'Lord,' said Aristodikos, 'but do you bid the men of Kyme surrender *their* suppliant?' And the voice came again, 'Yes, I do, that you may perish the quicker for this impiety, and not again come to consult my oracle about surrendering suppliants.' Then the men of Kyme shipped Paktyas across the sea to the greater safety of Lesbos. Here Mazares, without ships, could only offer bribes; but the Lesbians soon showed signs of accepting them. The men of Kyme then rescued him from Mytilene, and put him over to Chios; but the Chians, no less corruptible, agreed to surrender him in return for the coast land of Atarneus (opposite Lesbos; the Lesbians must have regretted not being quicker to conclude their bargain); and Paktyas was torn from sanctuary in the temple of Athene Poliouchos at Chios and handed over. His fate is not recorded; nor is that of the stout-hearted Aristodikos of Kyme.[14]

Mazares disarmed the Lydians, and their military spirit was soon a thing of the past; it died with the overthrow of their equestrian aristocracy. He also set about the subjugation of Ionia. He harried the plain of the Maiandros down to the frontier of friendly Miletos, and sold as slaves the population of the small city of Priēne, Miletos' neighbour; then he fell sick and died. His successor in command was another Mede, the trusty Harpagos, who cleared the northern river-valley route to the coast, that of the Hermos, and attacked Phokaia. The Phokaians had recently built a great, solid masonry wall round their city, paying for it with silver supplied by their friend in Spain, Arganthōnios, king of Tartessos and lord of its mines; but as Harpagos' siege-mound rose implacably they saw that it would soon be useless. They asked for an armistice. Harpagos professed that he would be satisfied with a purely formal surrender, 'the demolition of one bastion and the dedication of one house'. The Phokaians asked for twenty-four hours to consider this; and Harpagos, though he professed to know quite well what were their real intentions, called off his troops for so long. The Phokaians launched all their ships, put their families and valuables on board, and stripped their temples of everything but the wall paintings and bronze or stone statues; and so, sailed over to Chios. There they made a proposal to purchase from Chios the Oinoussai, the 'Wine Islands' (modern Psara and Antipsara), off Chios' north coast; but the Chians decided that the Phokaians would be too formidable neighbours, and refused to have them. Then the Phokaians took the heroic resolve to sail to the western Mediterranean and join their colonists in Corsica, at the city of Alalia, founded twenty years before (cf. p. 153). Before going, they made a vicious swoop back upon Phokaia, and cut to pieces the garrison that Harpagos had left there. They also cast a great lump of iron into the sea, and swore an oath never to return to Phokaia till that iron came up again. 'But in spite of this, as they set off for Corsica, more than half of them were overcome by homesickness and pity for their city and their familiar places, and they broke their oath and sailed back to Phokaia.'[15] We are not told what sort of reception they expected from the Persians; but fifty years

[14] H. i, 153–61 [15] *ib.* 163–5.

later there was still a shrunken city of Phokaia on the old site (H. vi, 8, 2).

The other Ionians met again at the Paniōnion, and Bias of Priene, the celebrated sage (who must have escaped from the sack of his city), recommended that they should all follow the Phokaians' example and migrate to Sardinia, where there were still no Greek or (probably) Phoenician colonies; but they could not bring themselves to do it. Only the Teians, when the mound was actually laid against their walls, sailed off on the shorter journey to Abdēra (not far enough, in fact, to save them from Persian domination for long), and there made good their footing with difficulty against the warlike natives. The rest could think of no better policy than the habitual reaction of ancient Greeks to invasion: to defend their walls. This, says Herodotos, they did manfully; but Harpagos with his siege-mounds and archers had his own way with them all.[16] Afterwards (the entire process probably took a few years), with Aiolic and Ionian levies reinforcing his army, he subdued the south-west, the warlike hillmen of Karia and Lykia and the Dorians of Halikarnassos and Knidos on their peninsulas. The Knidians made an attempt to 'make themselves an island' by means of a canal, but found cutting the hard, splintering rock difficult and dangerous. After many had suffered eye injuries, they consulted Delphi; and the oracle, like nearly all Greek oracles nearly all the time in dealing with Persia, recommended resignation and submission.[17] So far, 'the Mede' had not found Greek resistance at all difficult to deal with.

[16] *ib.* 168–70; cf. 162, 2.

[17] *ib.* 171, 1; 174–6.

Chapter III

Great Babylon is Fallen

CYRUS, meanwhile, was carrying all before him in the east. The campaigns in Bactria and against the Sakai, consolidating his empire in Iran, *may* be among those to be placed in the six years between the conquest of Lydia and that of Babylon; but the Babylonian Chronicle for these years is lost, save for fragments, and Herodotos omits all details.[1] Whether he conquered Syria and so encircled Sumer and Akkad before closing in upon them (which might be a reason for the fact that Nabonidus returned to Babylon) or whether he left them to be gathered in as the fruits of decisive victory is uncertain; the latter seems the more likely, since it appears that Nabonidus was able to complete his dearest enterprise, the restoration of his father's and mother's temple at Harran, only after her death, which took place in the same year as the fall of Lydia.[2] However, by 540 he was ready for the matador thrust against Babylonia. There may already have been hostilities against Babylonia's territories east of the Tigris; the fragments of the Chronicle mention Elam in 546, the Tigris in 540, and fighting apparently near that river;[3] but it is only in 539 that detailed history is available again.

[1] i, 177; cf. 153, 4.

[2] *Nabonidus Chronicle*, col. ii, line 13 (Smith, p. 113; Pritchard, p. 306); date of completion of the works of Harran, Gadd in *Anat. Studies*, VIII, inscr. H. 2, coll. ii (pp. 61–3); conclusions, p. 75. – The 'Syria' mentioned by H. (i, 72, in the early stages of the Lydian campaign; cf. Smith, p. 102) is not to the point; it is not our Syria, but Cappadocia. Greeks used the term 'Syrian' (a mere corruption of 'Assyrian') very loosely; at first for all inhabitants of the old Assyrian Empire; cf. the use in Xenophon's *Cyrus*; also Hekataios, in Steph. Byz. *s.v.* Teiria (on the Black Sea); then they distinguished the Cappadocians as 'White Syrians', e.g. Strabo, xii, 542, 544; xvi, 737; and if Berosos said that Cyrus conquered 'all the rest of Asia' before attacking Babylon (Jos. *Against Apion*, i, 20), he may have meant 'all except the Babylonian Empire'.

[3] Olmstead, *Persian Empire*, p. 45, seems to build too much on this fragmentary foundation in ascribing the revolt of Gobryas (see below) definitely to 546; and Xenophon, who makes Croesus the generalissimo of a huge allied army and describes, in great detail, only one battle with him, with the advance on Babylon following immediately (*Cyrus*, Books vi, vii), is again too clearly romantic to be used, though he did have some genuine materials at his disposal.

'In the seventeenth year' (of Nabonidus), we read in the Chronicle, 'Nebo came from Borsippa to meet Bel; . . . the king entered the Temple . . . a great plenty of wine among the soldiery.[4] . . . Bel went out in procession; the New Year Festival was celebrated with proper ritual.'

But Babylon was still full of disloyalty. It was probably inevitable that, in such a society, there should be tension between Babylonians proper on the one side – the rich merchants and bankers and especially the great temple corporations; civilised men, and many of them intelligent, but now 'blinkered' in their thinking by the tradition of ages – and on the other the Chaldaeans or westerners who provided the military class, such as it was, and consequently exercised secular power. Nebuchadrezzar, by his vigour, his dazzling victories and the long reign in which he became established as a 'father-figure', had gained universal respect; more than one Babylonian nationalist pretender in the following decades was to adopt his name and claim to be his descendant; but Nabonidus, with his devotion to the western god whom he would fain have made head of the divine state, had personally added a ground of dislike which accentuated the country's military weakness. In the west, there are some grounds for thinking, he had made considerable use of Jews in the furtherance of his policies, granting lands to them in colonies in the oases of the northern Hedjaz, and employing (if we may trust the evidence of a Qumran Aramaic document which deals with his sojourn at Tema) a Jewish soothsayer, perhaps from among the exiles in Babylon.[5] One is reminded of the later Jewish story of Daniel. But in that story too we find the king offending the religious loyalty of his Jewish liegemen by his demands for worship for a god of his own; and though the king, in that much later historical romance, is called Nebuchadrezzar, it is a curious fact that not only is he Belshazzar's father, and not only does his character recall Nabonidus, but even the biblical story of his madness looks like an echo of a temporary mental breakdown alleged to have befallen the latter.[6] It seems as though the Hebrew writer, like Xenophon, was acquainted with some genuine historical traditions.

[4] Line 7, tr. Smith (p. 117). Belshazzar's feast?! But the reading is uncertain; cf. Pritchard, p. 306.

[5] Gadd in *Anat. Studies*, VIII, pp. 87f; quoting, on the Jewish '*devin*', J. T. Milik in *Rev. Biblique*, LXIII (1956), pp. 407ff. That he was from Babylon, however, is a conjectural restoration of a gap in the text.

[6] Described as a consequence of his religious enormities in the hostile 'Verse Account of Nabonidus' (probably published under Cyrus), end of col. i; S. Smith, *Texts*, pp. 87f;

Nabonidus was very much in earnest, we see, about his religion. In this, to do him justice, he was very typical of the spirit of his age, that extraordinary Axis Age which witnessed a quickening of religious and philosophical thought all through the civilised world from Greece to China. But it was not in him to foster anything really new and creative.[7] All that he produced was discontent, by his partisanship of his own favourite among the ancient gods, while new movements toward a higher religion went on, beyond his ken, among the Jews and Iranians who were his close neighbours. The writing was on the wall; Nabonidus and Belshazzar were weighed in the balances and found wanting; the days of the older world were numbered and Babylon was divided indeed.[8]

This is the historical context of the prophesyings or verse pamphlets of the 'Second Isaiah'. Written in a highly personal and characteristic style, not unworthy of the great predecessor under whose name they pass, and whose works the unnamed author probably knew and loved, they are among the most splendid political (as well as religious) poetry ever penned. 'Comfort ye, comfort ye my people, saith God.... Comfort Jerusalem, for her humiliation is completed.'

At once the poet feels humbled before the greatness of the opportunity: 'A voice said "Cry out!" And I said "What shall I cry? All flesh is grass, and all the glory of men as the flower of the meadow. The grass withereth, the flowers fall, but the word of our God abideth for ever." '[9]

The reply comes immediately:

> Thou that tellest good tidings to Sion, go up upon a high mountain; thou that tellest good tidings to Jerusalem, lift up thy voice with strength. Lift up your voices, do not fear. [This sentence in the plural.] Say to the cities of Judah, Behold your God! Behold the Lord, the Lord cometh with power....
>
> Who hath measured the waters in the hollow of his hand, and the heaven with his span, and all the earth in his grasp? ... And Lebanon is not sufficient to burn, nor all its beasts for a full offering.[10]

Pritchard, *Texts*, p. 313. Smith suggests (p. 46) that there is even a discrete reference to this affliction in Nabonidus' own account of the dream which directed him to advance upon Harran, the Abu Hamma Inscription (translated *ib.* pp. 44f).

[7] Cf. discussion in *The Lyric Age of Greece*, pp. 327ff.

[8] Daniel, v. It would be easy, but is scarcely necessary in a romance, to rationalise and say that what Belshazzar really read was a seditious wall-scribble by one of the numerous disaffected.

[9] xl, 1f, 6ff (LXX).

[10] *ib.* 9f, 12, 16.

Early in the collection (though we can have no certainty that all these broadsheets have been collected in strict order), the poet is concerned with 'the islands'. Will they accept the new order?

> Be made new before me, islands, for the rulers shall change. Let them come near and speak together; then let them report decision. Who has raised up justice from the east, who has called it to follow him where he goes? He shall give us a foe of the nations, and he shall drive out kings; he shall give their swords to the earth, and as the blown chaff their bows. He shall pursue them and pass through in peace. Who has wrought and done these things? . . . I, God, the first; and unto the future I AM.
>
> . . . I raised up him of the North and him of the East; they shall be called by my name. Let the Rulers come; and as the potter his clay, as the potter tramples his clay, so shall you be trampled.[11]

'The man of the North, the man of the East' is clearly Cyrus. Dr Sidney Smith suggests that this early oracle belongs to the time of the campaign against Croesus.[12] Later the poet dares to be much more explicit. God addresses Israel:

> Thus saith the Lord, thy liberator and he that formed thee from the womb; I am the Lord who maketh all things; I spread forth the heavens alone, and made fast the earth. Who else shall scatter the signs of the mediums and the soothsayers, turning cunning men back and making their counsel folly? . . . He that saith to Jerusalem, Thou shalt be inhabited, and to the cities of Edom, Ye shall be built; and he will restore her desolate places; who saith to the deep, Be dry, and I will dry up thy springs; who biddeth Cyrus be wise, and he shall perform all my pleasure; who saith to Jerusalem, Thou shalt be built, and I will lay the foundations of my holy house.
>
> Thus saith the Lord unto Cyrus, my Anointed, whose right hand I have grasped, that the nations shall obey him, and I will break the strength of Kings: I will open gates before thee, and cities shall not be shut up. I will go before thee and level mountains; I will shatter gates of bronze, and smash bars of iron, and will give thee the hidden treasures of darkness; I will open to thee unseen places; that thou mayest know that I am the Lord, the God who calleth thee by thy name, the God of Israel. [And later in the same chapter:] I have raised him up to reign as a king with justice, and all his ways are

[11] xli, 1-4, 25 (LXX).

[12] *Isaiah, Chapters XL–LV* (1944; Schweich Lectures, 1940), pp. 49f.

straight; he shall build up my city, and shall turn again the captivity of my people, not for ransom nor for reward, saith the Lord of Hosts.[13]

Here the whole passage is a paean for the coming attack on Babylon. The 'mediums', literally 'belly-speakers', and soothsayers are the famous soothsayers of Babylon; and Edom also (altered in later texts to 'Judah') had suffered under the heel of Nabonidus. The 'treasures of darkness' are the treasures of the vaults of Babylon. Most astonishing is the address to Cyrus, twice named, as 'My Anointed', in Hebrew 'my Messiah', in the Latin Vulgate 'Christo meo' (as in the Greek) Was it not shocking to Jews even then? – for the Lord's Anointed should have been a Davidic king. Dr Sidney Smith suggests that it *was* shocking, and that perhaps after the victory the prophet was seized by his enemies, probably in Palestine, and put to death; Chapter LIII, the famous 'Suffering Servant' poem, may then be a lamentation for his death.[14] But this was still in the future.

Striking, too, is the extent to which the prophet uses words, here and elsewhere, which might be expected to appeal to Persians. The repeated reference to Justice and 'the just' or 'the righteous one' reminds us of the Persian word *arta*, 'the right', frequent in their royal inscriptions and a common element in Persian names. Compare also the end of the address to Cyrus (xlv, 4ff.):

> For my servant Jacob's sake and Israel my chosen, I will call thee by name and receive thee, though thou knewest me not.
> For I the Lord am God, and there is no other. I am he that formed the light and created darkness, he that createth peace and maketh evil; I the Lord am the God who maketh all these things.
> Let the heavens above rejoice, and let the clouds rain down righteousness . . .

'The terms', says Sidney Smith, 'can be justified within the sphere of Hebrew religion.' But 'the equivalence light-weal as against darkness-evil . . . point[s] very strongly to the language being adapted to suit Cyrus' own religious beliefs.' These, he adds, must have included the myth of Ahura-Mazda (who is Light and the Good) and Ahriman

[13] xliv, 24 to xlv, 3 (LXX).
[14] *Isaiah XL–LV*, pp. 73–5; cf. 70f, where it is suggested that L, 5f refers to earlier persecution for the same reason.

(darkness, evil and the father of lies), both issuing from the god of Time, Zervan.[15] (This suggestion, however, must be treated with reserve. The idea of identifying Yahweh, lord of history, with Zervan is certainly an attractive one; but Zervan does not appear in what seem to specialists to be the oldest Iranian religious texts. The chronology of Persian religious development is a very difficult study, and it is believed by many of those competent to judge that this monotheistic concept dates only from the Sassanid period, centuries after the Christian era.) However, it does seem as though the address to Cyrus must have been intended for translation as well as for circulation to Jews; as propaganda addressed *to* Cyrus as well as for him. So confident is the poet that it seems as though Cyrus' agents must have been in contact with nationalist Jews, as well as (we shall see) with other dissidents in Babylonia, and as though they had made definite promises that the exiles would be allowed to return home; and whatever the state of Persian religion in Cyrus' time (a question to which we shall return in the next chapter), it is a striking and important fact that its ethical content, as well as its eschewing of 'graven images', had aroused hopes of a new and better age in the Hebrew prophet.

In 539, the decisive campaign took place. In the spring, the royal New Year Festival was duly performed at Babylon; but in the high summer, in spite of the exhausting heat of a season 'when nothing is done unless urgently necessary',[16] things had become so serious that the great images of the gods from the outlying cities were being brought into Babylon for safety. The religious Nabonidus knew of the sacrileges committed in earlier wars by the infidel Umman-Manda, and wished to avert the worst; but disaffected priests were quick to represent this as another piece of the king's heretical eccentricity.[17] The Hebrew prophet seizes the opportunity for some characteristic mockery of the 'graven images':

> Bel is fallen, broken is Nebo! Their statues are upon the beasts and upon the cattle. Take them away, tied up, a burden to the weary beast, exhausted and hungry; it has no strength left. They have no power to deliver themselves from war, but themselves are led captive.[18]

[15] *op. cit.* pp. 58–9.
[16] Smith, *op. cit.* p. 46.
[17] *Nabonidus Chronicle*, iii, 9–11; Smith, *Texts*, p. 117; Pritchard, p. 306.
[18] xlvi, 1f.

The images from northern Sippar and from Borsippa, indeed, never reached Babylon. Were they captured on the way?

Historians have known, since the Babylonian records became available, that the Greek accounts of a siege and dramatic capture of the city of Babylon are unhistorical. However, Herodotos is not merely romancing. There was sharp fighting, but it took place not in a defence of the city wall, but of *the wall of Babylonia, the country*; that is the 'Median Wall' that Nebuchadrezzar had built in the north, from

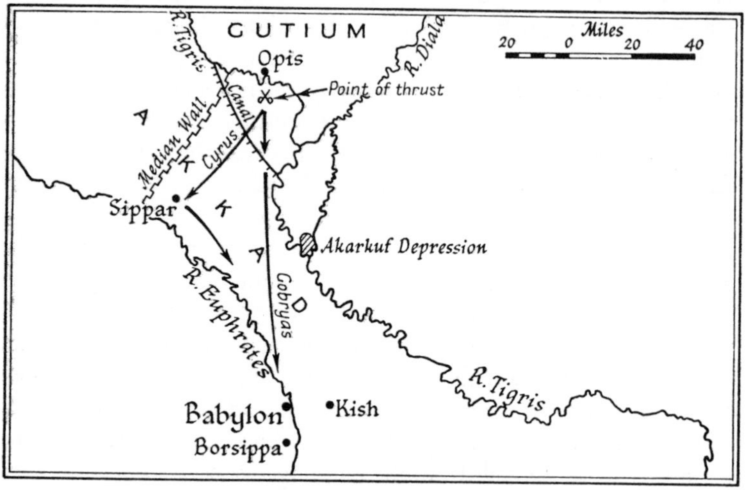

Cyrus conquers Babylon

Tigris to Euphrates, with its right and left flanks supported by the fortress cities of Opis and Sippar. This must also be the 'wall of Babylon' past which Xenophon's Cyrus (iii, 4, 41) marches on his way to the campaign against Croesus. Herodotos tells of great engineering works of Cyrus to get his army across the Gyndes, a tributary of the Tigris, by dividing its waters among many channels, an operation taking months, and again to divert the Euphrates where it flowed under the water-gate of the city; also of how the Babylonians gave battle before their walls, but were driven back within them.[19] His only mistake, it seems, is that he thinks of the wrong wall, and hence this charming detail that 'the city' (*sic*) was so huge that when the enemy had got in,

[19] H. i, 189ff; cf. Xen. *Cyrus*, vii, 5, 8ff.

the citizens did not know it and, as it was a festal season, went on feasting. 'The river that can be drained', says Sidney Smith, 'is the Tigris; this is possible owing to the Aqarquf depression. The place where Cyrus broke into the fortifications was Opis.'[20] Here, after those vast engineering operations which, Herodotos says, had occupied the whole of the previous year, Cyrus crossed the shrunken Tigris, and the whole of Babylonia's Maginot line was taken in reverse. 'In the month Tesri' (October), says the Chronicle, 'Cyrus did battle at Opis on the Tigris against the troops of Akkad.' One battle broke the Babylonian king's paid army; and there was no popular resistance anywhere. Indeed, on one reading of the text, Akkad broke out into open revolt, and Nabonidus' last military achievement was some slaughter of rebels.[21] There was already in Cyrus' army a high-ranking Babylonian officer, Ugbaru or Gubaru, governor of Gutium, the province east of the middle Tigris, with the troops of his province; how long since he had made his surrender, we do not know. He is the Gobryas of Xenophon, who according to his romance had deserted to Cyrus from the 'Assyrians', like Harpagus from Astyages, in revenge for a grievous wrong.[22] Cyrus now, with his usual tact and capacity for trusting men and receiving loyal service from the conquered, sent Gobryas with his native troops south to occupy the country, while he in person cleared up the broken front. 'On the 14th of Teshri, Sippar' (at the other end of the line) 'was taken without a battle; Nabonidus fled. On the 16th, Ugbaru, governor of Gutium, and the troops of Cyrus entered Babylon without a battle'; and when Nabonidus in flight entered his capital, he found it already in the enemy's hands and was captured.

The Chronicle continues, emphasising the peaceful and orderly character of the occupation: 'Until the end of the month, the shields of Gutium surrounded the gates of Esagila' (the huge temple of Bel-Marduk, which Herodotos was to see 'still there in my time'); 'but no one carried arms in Esagila or the temples, and no appointed ceremony

[20] S. Smith, *Isaiah XL–LV*, p. 46.

[21] So, A. L. Oppenheim in Pritchard, *loc. cit.*; Campbell Thompson in *CAH* III, p. 224; *aliter*, Smith, *Texts*, p. 117, *Isaiah XL–LV*, p. 46.

[22] V. Scheil in *Rev. d'Assyriologie*, XI (1914); C. F. Lehmann in *Klio*, II, 341ff. A similar name, Gaubaruva, also existed in Persian (cf. below, p. 94), and the confusion of homonyms is easy; but Gubaru, apparently an elderly man (he died soon after, see below), may be identical with an officer who had held a command in southern Babylonia some twenty years before (Scheil, *op. cit.* p. 166; G. B. Gray in *CAH* IV, p. 12).

was omitted.' Business also was 'as usual', and by the month's end (October 26th by our calendar) documents were already being dated in the Accession Year of Cyrus, King of the Lands.[23] On the third day of Arahshamnu (Oct. 29), Cyrus made his ceremonial entry. 'Green twigs were spread before him; peace was declared. Cyrus to all Babylon sent greetings. Ugbaru his governor appointed governors in Babylon'; i.e. the invaluable Gobryas, now Satrap of Babylonia, was set to overhaul appointments; enough documents survive to show us that, both at administrative and at clerical levels, most officials kept their posts. Only eight days after Cyrus' ceremonial entry, Gobryas died; it sounds like a stroke. He had held power in Babylon for less than a month; but, as we know well in our time, the first month after the Occupation is the most important. Retrospectively, Gobryas must be judged to have served his country, as well as Cyrus, by smoothing the transition. The elderly man from Gutium is perhaps, though his name is given wrongly, in the mind of the later Jewish writer when he tells us that, on the Persian conquest, 'Darius the Mede received the kingdom, being about threescore and two years old'.[24]

Meanwhile the process of restoring to their native cities the divine images which had been taken to Babylon during the emergency went on for months; and Cyrus, in his first official year as king of Babylon (538), issued a decree permitting Jewish exiles to return to Jerusalem and rebuild their temple, and to reclaim the sacred vessels taken therefrom, which had been preserved in Babylonian temple-treasuries.[25]

To earnest 'Zionists' the immediate result was probably disappointing. Few of the exiles, it seems, chose to leave the fleshpots of Babylon for the hazards of recolonisation in the land of their grandfathers under Sheshbazzar, the governor appointed by Cyrus. The movements led by Ezra and Nehemiah came in the fifth century (and why *just* then we do

[23] Olmstead, *P.E.*, p. 50.
[24] Daniel v, 31.
[25] Ezra i, 1ff, and (especially) vi, 3ff, in the Aramaic passage where there is reference to later complaints by the neighbouring people that a restored Israel would be a menace, a counterclaim by the Jews that their city-state had a charter from Cyrus, and consequent search in the methodically kept Persian archives at Ecbatana. – The Books of Ezra and Nehemiah in the Hebrew version, it has often been pointed out, are a collection of historical sources rather than a finished book. Personal memoirs from the fifth century related in the first person, letters and decrees, some of them not in Hebrew but in the kindred Aramaic which was the international language of the Persian Empire (these include Cyrus' Decree), are laid side by side, with a minimum of editing. The result is one of the most reliable historical sections of the O.T., and the chance of the Cyrus Decree being a forgery appears to be slight. The LXX Greek version, on the other hand, seems to have suffered from much more drastic editing.

not know); and they were faced by many difficulties; human nature, they found, had not changed with the revolution. But this belongs to the later history of Judaism. For the present all was joy, and the unnamed poet has his day of triumph. Outside the main block of the Cyrus-prophecies, but in its spirit, the great Chapter LX of our 'Isaiah' prophesies a glory at least partly mundane:

> Shine, shine, Jerusalem; for thy light is come, and the glory of YAHWEH is risen upon thee; for behold, darkness shall cover the earth and thick darkness the gentiles; but upon thee shall YAHWEH shine, and his glory shall be seen upon thee. And kings shall walk in thy light, and nations in thy brightness.
>
> Lift up thine eyes, look round, and see thy children assembled; all thy sons are come from afar, and thy daughters carried on their shoulders. Then thou shalt see and tremble, and be transported at heart, that the wealth of the sea is turned to thee, and of nations and peoples. Great caravans of camels shall come to thee; the camels of Midian and Gaipha; all they of Saba shall come bringing gold and frankincense, and shall tell the good news of the salvation of YAHWEH. . . . For me have the Isles waited, and the ships of Tarshish first, to bring thy sons from far, and their silver and their gold with them.[26]

These fine lines have been sacred to many as a prophecy of another Messiah; but their *prima facie* meaning in the time in which they were written is that, with the abolition of frontiers and the breaking of the Babylonian monopoly, commercial opportunities of unexampled richness would be offered to the crossroad land of Palestine between Arabia and the Mediterranean.

Of the coming fate of Babylon he speaks with vindictive harshness:

> Down! Sit in the dust, virgin daughter of Babylon! . . . Never more shall it be thine to be called soft and luxurious. Take the quern, grind flour, take off thy veil! . . .

Even so, he was less embittered than the author of the famous Psalm 137:

> O daughter of Babylon, that art to be destroyed, happy shall he be that rewardeth thee as thou hast served us:
>
> Happy shall he be that taketh *thy* little ones and dasheth them upon the stones.

[26] lx 1–6, 9 (LXX).

But these horrible though understandable wishes were not to be fulfilled. Cyrus had many adherents in Babylon, from Gobryas downwards, other than the Jews, and he had no intention of destroying a civilisation that was to bring him more wealth than any other part of his dominions. In the spring of 538 his son Cambyses was installed as king of Babylon and went through the historic New Year ritual.[27] Cambyses did homage to Bel and Nebo; his father, we see, was no dogmatic monotheist, but he avoided carrying out in person the acts of penance and the ritual of public though temporary humiliation of the king, which were part of the ancient ceremony. And willing propagandists for Cyrus were soon at work. The 'Verse Account' of Nabonidus tells the story of his reign in a hostile manner, and celebrates Cyrus as a liberator almost as enthusiastically as the 'Second Isaiah'; especially his release of the gods whom Nabonidus had concentrated in Babylon, to return with joy to their homes. The preserved part of the text ends:

> [To the inhabitants of] Babylon a heart is given now;
> [They are like prisoners when] the prisons are opened;
> [Liberty is restored to] those who were surrounded by oppression;
> [All rejoice] to look upon him as king![28]

In the cuneiform text on the Cyrus Cylinder, a similar picture is given. Nabonidus was heretical; he changed the details of worship. He was also an oppressor, 'exhausting the people with forced labour'; i.e. he is to be given no credit for his works on the restoration of temples; only the labour is emphasised. But Bel-Marduk 'cast his eye over all countries, seeking for a righteous ruler . . . Then he called by name Cyrus, King of Anshan, and pronounced him ruler of the lands.' (Even the language, here and elsewhere, is reminiscent of the Second Isaiah.) And Cyrus treated justly 'the black-headed people' whom Marduk had made him to conquer. 'Black-headed people' was a traditional term for the people of Babylonia, giving grounds for the intriguing question whether there had already been rulers who were not black-headed? The heretical behaviour of Nabonidus, the restora-

[27] *Chronicle*, iii, 24ff (the last lines of continuous text); Smith, p. 118; Pritchard, p. 306, end.

[28] Restoration and trn. by A. L. Oppenheim in Pritchard, *Texts*, p. 315. For the humiliation of the king, cf. the ritual text, tr. A. Sachs, *ib.* p. 334; F. Thureau-Dangin, *Rituels accadiens* (Paris, 1921), pp. 127–54.

tion of the right worship of the gods by Cyrus, the peaceful and disciplined character of the Occupation are here again emphasised. Finally the conqueror speaks in his own person:

> I am Cyrus, King of the world, the Great King, the legitimate king, King of Babylon, King of Sumer and Akkad, King of the four corners of the earth' [son of Cyrus the son of Cambyses the son of Teispes] 'of a family which has always exercised kingship; whose rule Bel and Nebo love.' Cyrus commends himself to the gods, together with 'Cambyses my son, the offspring of my loins', and his army. 'All the kings of the whole world, from the upper to the lower sea, those who sit in throne-rooms, those who live in other . . ., all the kings of the west dwelling in tents' [the Midian and Kedar of the Hebrew poet] 'brought their heavy tribute and kissed my feet.' And Cyrus restored sanctuaries and houses [war damage?] and gave peace to Babylon.[29]

Cyrus lived until 530, but we have little more 'news' of him. We see only that many things *have been* done, *before* the curtain rises again. Darīus' Behistun Inscription takes for granted the organization of the empire, before the events of 522–0, in about twenty vast provinces, each under a governor whose title, *Khshathrapavan* (Satrap), is literally translated Protector of the Kingdom.[30] There were Greeks in two of these; Lydia included Ionia, and Phrygia, in north-west Asia Minor, 'Those upon the Sea', the Sea of Marmara and its straits and the adjacent Black Sea coast; the *parathalassioi andres* of Herodotos.[31] Syria, called by the Persians 'Beyond the River' (Euphrates), had within it the city kings of the Phoenicians and on its borders the Syennesis dynasty of Cilicia, preserving their titles as vassals, and providing the first nucleus of imperial sea-power. The title 'King of Kings', borne thereafter by the Achaemenids, was no empty one; though within the Iranian area, as in most of the empire, local kingships were suppressed in favour of Satraps. The aged Arsāmes, son of King Ariaramnes, of the formerly senior Achaemenid house, was still alive, but apparently in retirement, and his son Hystaspes held, and was apparently content with, the great central satrapy of Parthia and Hyrcania (cf. pp. 100–2). In the Greek cities on the coast of Asia Minor, citizens approved by the Satraps were recognised as governors. With the

[29] See Oppenheim in Pritchard, pp. 315–16; Olmstead, *P.E.*, pp. 52ff.
[30] Lehmann-Haupt in *PW*, *s.v.* Satrap. [31] v, 25.

might of the overlord behind them, they were in a position to dominate or dispense with councils or assemblies; the Greeks called them, in their own language, tyrants.[32] Many independent Greek cities at the time were under the personal government of such dictators, often popular leaders, such as was Peisistratos at Athens, and there is no reason to believe that the eastern Greeks immediately resented the change to Persian overlordship from that of Lydia. There was tribute to pay, but on the other hand trade-routes inland were secure. Greek oracles, in particular, like the Hebrew and the Babylonian religious authorities, strongly approved of the Persian Peace, which facilitated the movement of their visitors; and we have evidence to this effect from one temple of Apollo, probably at Magnesia on the Maiandros, which Darīus found recorded in his archives as having won favour by having 'spoken all truth to the Persians' in the time of his predecessors.[33]

At home, Cyrus concerned himself with the beautifying of the first Persian imperial city, his residence since the days before his war with Astyages.[34] The place was called by the Greeks Pasargadai, which was also the name, Herodotos says (i, 125), of one of the Persian tribes; but one writer gives the name as Persagada (with MS variations), and another interprets it as meaning 'Camp of the Persians'. It is therefore an attractive suggestion that 'the true name was something like Parsagard', which would be a name of the same form as later Sassanian Darabgerd and Dastagerd and Armenian Tigranocerta. 'In actual fact', adds Olmstead, 'the ruins of the settlement suggest a typical Aryan camp, for no trace of a wall can be detected.' [35] The houses are represented chiefly by small column-bases of stone, which must be supposed to have supported wooden posts or pillars. Here, however, Cyrus also provided himself with a palace, with a great audience-hall over sixty yards long, its façade adorned with sculptured orthostats in the Assyrian manner: priests driving a bull to sacrifice on either side of the door, and guardian demons with human bodies but an eagle's head and

[32] H. iv, 138; v, 37; etc.

[33] The 'Gadates Inscription'; Tod, *GHI*, no. 10; a text of Roman imperial date, ostensibly (and probably, despite Beloch, *GG* (1924) I, i, p. 41; II, ii, 154f) re-copying an old and worn one; see p. 114, n. 45.

[34] So later tradition says, e.g. Nikolaos (J 90 F 66, §§ 41ff.), perhaps from Ktesias; Polyainos vii, 6, 1 and 9.

[35] *P.E.*, p. 60, and more fully in *AJSL* LV, p. 394, n. 8. 'Persagada' etc., Curtius, v, 6, 10 (and C.'s sources embodied, as Tarn has shown, some material from Greek soldiers who had served in Persia); trn. 'Camp of the P.' Anaximenes of Lampsakos (who also accompanied Alexander), *ap.* S.B. *s.v.*; J. 72 F 19.

claws. Around it spread a wide, walled park or 'paradise' (one of the few words which the garden-loving ancient Persians have bequeathed to modern languages), with a ceremonial main entrance through a pillared gateway with lodges, guarded by huge winged bulls, again showing Assyrian influence. Above the gate was the inscription, in Persian, Akkadian and Elamite: 'I am Cyrus, the King, the Achaemenian.' [36]

The place is over 6000 feet above sea-level, and chill in winter; but here Cyrus had spent his early years, and here he built his tomb. With Babylonia at his disposal, his decision to stay here was clearly deliberate, and it is probably commemorated in the charming piece of saga with which Herodotos, very characteristically, chooses to end his history. Artembāres, a Persian nobleman, is said to have taken the lead, and gained the hearty approval of the Persians, with the proposal that, as rulers of all south-west Asia, they should choose a pleasanter country and migrate to it; and they laid it before the king. Cyrus, we read, 'did not think it a good idea'. 'Do so if you wish,' he said; 'but if you do, be ready to find yourselves no longer governors but governed; for soft lands breed soft men; it does not happen that the same land brings forth wonderful crops and good fighting men'. 'And the Persians saw the point of that', says Herodotos, 'and got up and withdrew, realising that Cyrus was right; and they chose to be lords of an empire, living in a rough land, rather than to be cultivators of a plain and subjects of others.' [37]

Cyrus' last campaign, known to us only from Herodotos and inferior and later accounts, was on his north-eastern frontier, the immemorial battleground of cultivators and nomads, Iran and Turan. His antagonists were the Massagetai, who, says Herodotos, 'use gold and bronze for all purposes . . . but have no iron or silver'. Their culture was otherwise 'like that of the Scythians'. Their ruler was a queen, Tomyris; and in invading her country, the old king was killed.[38] His men recovered his body and brought it back to lie in the simple tomb which he had prepared.[39] There was no trouble over the succession. The royal house was revered among the Persians and Cambyses, king of Babylon

[36] Olmstead, *P.E.*, pp. 61ff; pl. ix [and now D. Stronach in *Iran*, Vol. I, 1963].
[37] H. ix, 122.
[38] H. i, 201, 205, 211–16.
[39] Arrian, *Alexander*, vi, 29 (from Aristoboulos, who inspected the tomb after a report of looting).

(as it were a 'King of the Romans' under a mediaeval Emperor), had long since been his father's colleague and heir-apparent. By September 530, Babylonian business-men were dating documents in the accession-year of the new reign.

CHAPTER IV

The Iranian Religion

WHEREVER he went, Cyrus had found collaborators: Babylonian priests; Miletos and the oracle of Branchidai; the unnamed Hebrew who hailed him as the Lord's Anointed; many Medes, against their own king. To Jews and Babylonians he brought religious freedom; to the trading cities, peace and open roads. Phoenicia and Cilicia did not resist, and kept their local self-government; in Lydia, disarmed after one brief rebellion, Sardis continued to flourish, and Lydian military spirit disappeared overnight.

Some of this may be put down to Cyrus' powerful character, evidently also a character of great charm. The Persians remembered him as 'a father', a gentle ruler, very different from his despotic son.[1] Some, too, may be put down to the errors of Persia's opponents. Astyages is said to have been cruel. Babylon especially, under the doctrinaire Nabonidus, had interfered too much. But much, too, must be attributed to the fact that Persian rule, if stern, was just and constructive. Persian governors had a sense of responsibility for the economic well-being of their people. Darius commends 'his servant Gadatas' for introducing fruit-trees from 'beyond the Euphrates' (translating the Persian name of the province of Syria?) into Asia Minor.[2] If this was self-interest, it was also enlightened. But it was also in accord with the teaching of the Iranian religion, as reformed under the influence of the prophet Zoroaster. In the ethics of this religion, attention to agriculture (quaintly, to our ears; not merely attention to duty in general) figures as a cardinal virtue; and servants of the Achaemenid Empire acted on this principle. A duty of the soldier and nobleman was to protect agriculture; and at the very end of the empire we find the principle being practised, even imprudently. In face of Alexander's invasion, Memnon of Rhodes, the Greek professional soldier in Persian service, advised

[1] H. iii, 89, 3.

[2] *GHI* (1969), no. 12 (cf. p. 114, n. 45).

the western satraps not to give battle but to withdraw, 'scorching the earth' and using their numerous cavalry to deny supplies to the enemy. But Arsites, Satrap of Hellespontine Phrygia, in whose province the operation was taking place, rejected this advice with indignation. 'I', he said, 'will not stand by and see one farm burnt, of those which the King has committed into my hands.' [3] So they gave battle, and met with disaster.

Persian noblemen, whatever Greek propaganda, not unmixed with envy, might say about their luxury, never lost their toughness. Cyrus the younger, admired by the Athenian Xenophon, also came to a perfect understanding with the Spartan Lysander; and one of the things which impressed Lysander (according to Xenophon, who knew Cyrus personally and at least men of Lysander's circle) was that Cyrus looked after his own orchard at Sardis, and had even planted many of the trees in it with his own hands. He told Lysander with pride that, when in good health, he never sat down to dinner without having really sweated over some exercise, warlike or peaceful.[4] Xenophon also recounts, as an eye-witness, a revealing incident from the same Cyrus' famous March Up-Country. In Mesopotamia his wagon-train, its beasts weak and reduced in number from the desert marches behind them, had to negotiate a wadi with sticky clay bottom.

> Cyrus stood looking down, with his chief nobles about him, and sent Glous and Pigres with some of the native troops to help get the wagons out. But then, as they seemed to be taking a long time about it, as though in anger he ordered the leading Persian officers of his own staff to go and help and get those wagons moving. Then one really did see something of his discipline. They threw off their purple cloaks, each one just where he was standing, and shot down the bank – and it was very steep – as if they were running a race, dressed as they were in their rich tunics and embroidered trousers, and some of them wearing necklaces and bracelets as well. They rushed straight into the mud in all this finery and, in less time than one would have thought possible, they simply lifted the wagons out.[5]

Such were at least some Persian aristocrats, after a century and a half of empire; and the men who served the first Cyrus were presumably

[3] Arrian, *Campaigns of Alexander*, i, 12.
[4] Xen. *Oikonomikos*, iv, 10ff.
[5] *Anab.* i, 5, 7ff.

not less so. Herodotos (i, 131ff), some fifty years before Xenophon, gives our earliest account of Persian customs:

> This is what I know about Persian customs.
>
> It is not their custom to make cult-statues or temples or altars; indeed, they think those who do this foolish, because, as I think, they do not believe the gods to be anthropomorphic as the Greeks do. Their custom is to go up on to the highest hilltops to offer sacrifice to Zeus; and 'Zeus' they call the whole circle of the heavens. They also sacrifice to the Sun and Moon and Earth and Fire and Water and the Winds. These are the only deities to whom they have offered sacrifice from of old; but they have learned more recently from the Assyrians [i.e. Babylonians] and Arabs, to sacrifice also to [Aphrodite] the Heavenly. (Aphrodite's name in Assyrian is Mylitta; in Arabic, Alilat, and in Persian, Mitra.)

Here Herodotos has either suffered a lapse of memory, or got his notes mixed. Mithras, masculine, later so famous in the Roman world, was a very ancient Aryan sun-god, popular, as Plutarch later correctly says,[6] as Mesites, the Mediator (Guardian of Oaths; perhaps also Mediator between a rather remote High God and mankind). The Persian 'Aphrodite', a nature-goddess and mother-figure, was named Anaïtis, a name correctly given by later Greek writers; and she also was old Iranian, though no doubt under the Achaemenid Empire men's idea of her came to owe something to the Semitic Queen of Heaven, Ishtar. The other foreign names quoted for her seem to be correct: Mylitta, probably Belit, 'Lady', the feminine of Bel, 'the Lord'; Alilat, Al-Ila, 'the God', plus, again, the Semitic feminine termination *-t*.[7]

Herodotos continues (after mentioning various other details of Greek ritual which the Persians did not have): 'And the sacrificer is not allowed to pray for benefits for himself alone; but he prays that it may be well with all the Persians, and with the King.' Afterwards, before the sacrificial feast, 'a Magian, who is standing by, sings a hymn; its subject, they say, is drawn from the mythology. Without the presence of a Magian, no sacrifice may be performed.' The Magi, who have been mentioned earlier (H. i, 101) as a tribe of the Medes, here make their

[6] *On Isis and Osiris*, 46; the whole passage (= *Moralia*, 369D–370C) is important.

[7] Anaïtis, e.g. Strabo xi, 512, xii, 559, xv, 733; her worship was familiar to him in Cappadocia, in his native Asia Minor. Both she and Mithras figure repeatedly in the Persian *Avesta* (much later, in the form in which we have it); see below, pp. 77f.

appearance as the priestly tribe, the Levites of Media. Later (i, 140) they appear again, in connection with burial customs:

> Thus far I can attest from personal knowledge; but there is also something told rather as a secret and not openly, about their disposal of the dead: which is that the body of a Persian is not buried until it has been torn by a bird or dog. The Magi, I know for certain, do observe this custom, for they do it quite openly. The Persians, however, cover the body over with wax, and then inhume. The Magi have many customs which distinguish them not only from the rest of mankind but even from the priests of Egypt; for *they* make it a point of holiness to kill no living thing, except in sacrifice; but the Magi slay with their own hands every species except man and the dog, and do this as zealously as if they were scoring points in a game, killing indiscriminately ants and snakes and all other creatures, creeping and winged.

Now these religious customs, both those which strike us (with our Jewish tradition) as enlightened and those which strike us as odd or repulsive, alike show Herodotos as describing the external features of a religion which is essentially that known also from the *Avesta* (old Persian *ābastā*, 'The Law'); the body of old Persian religious literature still preserved by the Parsees.[8]

This literature, considerable in bulk though it is, is explicitly said in one of the later books to embody only surviving fragments of a far larger *corpus*, most of which was destroyed by the malice of 'Iskender Rumi' – 'Alexander the Roman', i.e. Alexander the Great.[9] It consists, moreover, as it stands, partly of books of regulations, of more than

[8] Translated in *Sacred Books of the East*, ed. Max Müller, vols. IV, XXIII (= *The Zend-Avesta*, Part I, Part II), by James Darmesteter; vol. XXXI (*Z.-A.*, Part III), by L. H. Mills; cf. also vols. V, XVIII, XXIV, XXXVII, XLVII, *Pahlavi Texts*, tr. E. W. West. Mills' version of the *Yasna* (which includes the Gāthās) is', says Professor Zaehner (*Zoroastrianism*, Weidenfeld & Nicolson, 1961, p. 339), 'wholly out of date . . . Darmesteter . . . still useful.' I have therefore used for the *Yasna* the versions of K. F. Geldner (*Die Zoroastrische Religion*, Tübingen, 1911) and J. Duchesne-Guillemin (*Zoroastre*, Paris, 1949). The title *Zend-Avesta* is, as Darmesteter says, 'a very improper designation', since Zend is not a language, but a word meaning 'commentary or explanation'. The phrase 'Avesta *and* Zend' appears in the Pahlavi (later literary Persian) religious literature, in the sense of 'The Law and its Commentary'; *op. cit.*, Part I, p. xxx, n. 1.

[9] Darmesteter, *loc. cit.* (= Introduction to the *Vendidad* [better, *Videvdat*] or Law-Book), p. xxxii. Such a destruction is out of character for the historical Alexander, who treated the Persians with so much respect (even wearing the 'Median' dress) as to incur disfavour with his own Macedonians. He has been blamed, like Cromwell, for loss, much of which was due to ages of neglect rather than to the violence of enemies.

Pharisaean minuteness, aimed at ensuring ritual purity, and partly, especially the older parts, of service books, a collection of hymns, including much mythological material, such as Herodotos shows the Magi chanting in his own day. There are no such ancient Parsee historical books as are contained in our Bible; and one may imagine the limitations that would be imposed upon a Chinese scholar, if he had to reconstruct the history of Christianity and Judaism from their legal, prophetic and devotional literature. Further, western linguistic studies of old Persian, especially on the language of the *Gāthās*, a group of 'prophecies' (in the Old Testament sense) which are the most primitive part of the Avestan literature, still leave room for doubts and disagreements among specialists in that field, of whom the present writer is not one.[10]

The religion of the Avesta is a dualism, in which a good Spirit or God, called and addressed as Ahura-Mazda (later Ormuzd, cf. Greek Oromazdes), is opposed by an evil spirit or devil, Angra-Mainyu, later Ahriman, a form already known to Aristotle.[11] The whole cosmos is involved in this war, and most wild beasts and 'creeping things upon the earth' are zealously to be destroyed by the faithful as the creatures of the Evil One. The 'corn-carrying ants' (as Herodotos mentions), along with snakes, frogs, flies and earthworms, are specified in this connection, and killing large numbers of them is a possible penance for a grievous sin.[12] One the other hand, some species useful to man are explicitly under the protection of Ahura-Mazda. Among such are the horned cattle and the dog and, more unexpectedly, the hedgehog, called 'the dog with the prickly back and the long, thin muzzle', which, because 'from midnight to morning it kills thousands of the creatures of the Evil One', receives honorary canine rank.[13]

In like manner, Herodotos refers to the subject of the most famous

[10] The latest authoritative discussion in English is that of Zaehner (see n. 8 above), 1961. Cf. the French translation and comments of Professor J. Duchesne-Guillemin, *Zoroastre* (Paris, 1949), and the cautionary observations of A. C. Bouquet in *Sacred Books of the World* (1954). The widely divergent views of the prophet taken by such established orientalists as Professor H. S. Nyberg (*Religionen des alten Iran*, Leipzig, 1938) and E. Herzfeld (*Zoroaster and his World*, Princeton, 1947, and O.U.P.) are fiercely and cogently demolished by Professor W. B. Henning (*Zoroaster*: Ratanbai Katrak Lectures at Oxford, 1949; O.U.P., 1951), partly reprinted in Zaehner, pp. 349ff. The attractive account of Olmstead (*P.E.*, 94ff) secures simplicity by ignoring difficulties.

[11] [Plato?] *Alkibiades* I, 122A (Oromazes); Ar. *On Philosophy* (q. by D.L., *Lives of the Philosophers*, Introduction, vi, 8): Oromasdes = Zeus, Areimanios = Hades.

[12] e.g. *Vendidad*, Fargard xiv; Darmesteter, Part I, pp. 166f.

[13] *ib.* xiii, pp. 152f.

of all provisions of the Avestan law, when he tells us that Persians, especially the Magi, do not bury their dead 'till the body has been torn by beast or bird'. Perhaps, indeed, he understates, for the later law lays down that *no* body should be committed either to earth or fire, lest it defile the sacred elements. Corpses should be laid out in a place reserved (a place surrounded by a built wall is best, 'if [those concerned] can afford it') there to be devoured by the ravens or vultures. So it is done by the Parsees at the present day, and such was the law under the Sassanid Empire (third to seventh centuries of our era), under which the Avestan religion was most elaborately developed and its law codified. Codified and elaborated it was, indeed, to fantastic lengths, with punishments of hundreds of stripes, such as it is difficult to think that anyone even dreamed of enforcing, for every offence against sexual or other ritual purity. The common people, one fancies, must have groaned under the yoke and the threats of hell of the state-supported clergy, until the storm of Islam came as the proverbial 'breath of fresh air'. In Herodotos' time the Median priestly Magi, whose services seem to have been accepted by Cyrus,[14] already held, to judge by Herodotos' account of Persian practices, substantially their later views; but Persia was not yet priest-ridden as it became under the Sassanids. Cremation was eschewed, 'for the Persians consider fire to be a god . . . and therefore that it is not right to commit a corpse to it'.[15] But inhumation was practised, as we have seen, by the Achaemenian Persians, including their kings; the contamination of the earth, also sacred, being probably considered sufficiently avoided by the practice of covering the corpse in wax.

Now in all their observances, from the war on ants to the attention to agriculture practised by Persian princes and noblemen, the Persians of the Avesta held themselves to be obeying the commands of God as revealed to the prophet Zarathustra.[16] Zoroastres, as the Greeks called him, is not mentioned in Herodotos either by name or by way of allusion to any recent, notable reformer; his name first appears in Greek in the (pseudo-?) Platonic *First Alkibiades* (n. 11 above). Who, then,

[14] Xenophon, *Cyrus*, viii, 1, 23f, explicitly says so. For this and other passages of X. bearing on Persian religion, cf. C. Clemen, *Fontes Hist. Religionis Persicae*, pp. 16–22. His evidence is, of course, better for his own time than for that of Cyrus the Great.

[15] H. iii, 16.

[16] On agriculture, see *Vendidad*, Fargard iii; Darmesteter, I, pp. 22–31.

was Zarathustra, when did he live, and for what teachings did he gain renown?

To these questions, as we have seen (n. 10), learned specialists have given divergent answers. As in some religious controversies nearer home, the sources, to which all parties alike appeal, do not suffice to enforce agreement upon all points, and it is sound sometimes to confess: We do not know. He had lived, according to some Greek writers, quoted by Pliny and Diogenes, in the remotest past, at dates equivalent to more than 6000 B.C.[17] From the time of Alexander's conquest, Greek writers gained access to oriental records, and their scholarship, though not infallible, is not to be despised, as we can now see by comparison with the fragments of ancient records known at first hand. But what the very remote dates imply is that the Magi, who were the Hellenistic Greeks' sources of information, and whose own scholarship was not historical, simply made their own religion and its prophet coeval with the foundation of the world. Between the time of Ostānes (n. 17), who in 480 may have put the prophet '600 years ago', and the later and longer estimates, *may* have intervened the invention of the Magian theory of a 'world-year' of 12,000 solar years, from the Creation to the 'end of the aeon' and a Last Judgment. To put the prophet 'in the beginning', or sometimes after the first three millennia, would be in accordance with the concept of him in most of the Avestan literature; here he becomes a superhuman personage, the one revealer of God's will to man; the angels longed for his birth and all creation rejoiced at it; he 'laughed on the day of his birth'; his life is threatened in infancy by the wicked Durasobo, 'the Herod of the story'; his temptation by the evil one at the outset of his ministry is a cosmic event, like that of Gautama Buddha; the corresponding Christian stories are modest and realistic by comparison.[18] Zoroaster, moreover, is to triumph again over the evil one at the end of our aeon, through his son Saoshyant, who is

[17] Pliny *NH* xxx, 1ff; Eudoxos, who formed a high opinion of Z.'s 'philosophy', put him 6000 years before the death of Plato, as did Aristotle. Pliny, *ib.* 2, 8, mentions one Ostānes, said to have accompanied Xerxes to Greece and to have been the first to interest Greek writers in the prophet. O. could thus have been the authority of Xanthos the Lydian (cited by D.L., *Lives*, Introduction, 2), said to have given the more modest date of 600 years before Xerxes' invasion (Clemen, *Fontes*, pp. 41ff, 74f).

[18] Birth, *Farvardin Yast* (a hymn-sequence to the Fravashis, the Parsee 'church triumphant' or spirits of the saints), §§ 88–94; Darmesteter, *Avesta*, II, pp. 201f. Laughter, Pliny, *NH* vii, 16/72. Threatened and tempted at birth, *Vendidad*, Fargard xix (Darm. I, pp. 204ff, 218); *Dinkard*, vii, 3 (West, *Pahlavi Texts*, V, = *Sacred Books of the East*, XLVII, pp. 35ff). Summary in A. V. Williams-Jackson, *Zoroaster*, chap. iii.

yet to be miraculously born. So strong is the mythic element that Darmesteter himself, whose Introduction to his translation is still classic, inclined to the view that Zarathustra was originally a god, only later 'rationalised' into a heroic man.[19] Few if any later scholars have followed him here, however, for reasons which will appear.

There is another chronology of the prophet, preserved in Parsee literature, though of a date much later than the Greco-Roman writers above mentioned. The *Bundahishn*, a mediaeval work (and also older sources, according to the great Mohammedan scientist Al-Beruni, who used the *Bundahishn*, *inter alia*), put the 'coming' (birth?) of Zarathustra in the tenth instead of the fourth millennium of the world-year, and in fact (by implication only, in the actual text of the *Bundahishn*), 258 years before Alexander, who is correctly said to have reigned for 14 years. 258 + 14 + 323 B.C., the date of the death of Alexander, gives us 595 as the date of the birth *or* beginning of the Mission of Zarathustra. The source, with its millennarian context, does not inspire much confidence; but it does give the fourteen years (not quite complete) of Alexander correctly; there *may* have survived some historical reckoning of years since the prophet in some part of Iran, though if so it is curious that it never reached the Greeks whose statements have come down to us; and this date has found favour with good modern authorities.[20] It would agree well enough with the tradition that a famous cypress, planted by Zarathustra at Kishmar in Khorassān (Bactria) to commemorate the conversion of King Gushtasp, was 1450 years old when cut down by order of Mutawakkil, the tenth Abbasid Caliph, in the year of the Hejira 232 (A.D. 846). 1450 solar years before 846 = 605 B.C. (since there is no 'year zero'); if we should first subtract the 232 Mohammedan *lunar* years (= 224 sun-years) we get a date eight years later: 597.[21]

One line of approach to the attempt to link Zoroaster with historically known characters we must firmly reject. The King Gushtasp converted by Zoroaster in Bactria is *not* to be identified with Vishtaspa or

[19] *Avesta*, I, p. lxxix.

[20] e.g. E. Herzfeld in *Oriental Studies in honour of Cursetji Erachji Pavry* (1933); W. B. Henning, *Zoroaster*, pp. 35ff; Clément Huart, *La Perse Antique*, pp. 207ff; Zaehner, *Zoroastrianism*, p. 33 and nn. Earliest source, perhaps Theodore bar Konai (7th cent., Christian), see Zaehner, *Zurvan*, p. 441.

[21] *Dabistan*, tr. Shea and Troyer, i, 306–9; q. by A. V. W. Jackson, *Zoroaster*, pp. 163f. thence by Lehmann-Haupt, *Wann lebte Zarathustra?* in *Oriental Studies in honour of C. E. Pavry*, pp. 265ff.

Hystaspes, the son of Arsāmes the Achaemenid and father of Darius I. If we had no account of Gushtasp's family, the identification would be a plausible and attractive guess; but we do have references to several members thereof, in the *Gāthās*, that group of 'prophesyings' in a more archaic dialect than the rest of the Avesta, which seems to give, at least in part, the words of the prophet himself; and there is no correspondence at any point. The father of Darius was son of Arsāmes, of the Achaemenid house, ruling Hyrcania as satrap; the patron of Zoroaster is son of Aurvat-aspa or Lohrasp, ruling Bactria as *kavi* or petty king. Gushtasp has numerous sons, none of whose names bear any resemblance to that of Darius; and while he has a wife Hutaosa (Atossa), the Atossa of Herodotos and Aeschylus is not the wife of Hystaspes, but of Darius himself.[22] Ammianus Marcellinus of Antioch, whose knowledge of the Persians was not negligible, is the first western writer to make the identification; but the Byzantine Agathias, author of several well-informed pages on Persian religion and customs, rightly insists that there is no evidence for it.[23]

Not much reliance, then, can be placed even upon such chronological sources as we have. But, if the evidence for a sixth-century date for Zarathustra is weak, it gains at least some slight reinforcement from a sociological consideration. This is that the seventh and sixth centuries, the *Achsenzeit* in Karl Jaspers' expression, formed a period in which, through the whole length of the civilised zone, men turned to the formation of the first philosophies and the reformation of religion: in Judaea and Greece, in China and India; only *not* in those regions where, as in Egypt and Babylonia, priestly corporations of the previous period had retained their influence. Nor, it need hardly be said, did the activities of the great thinkers of this age proceed in a vacuum; their coincidence in time, with no evidence or likelihood of any of these regions having been influenced by any other, was due, it seems probable, to the circumstances of an age of economic change and expansion, and its political concomitant, power-politics and war. Widening horizons, the enforced adaptation of ancient customs to a changing world, even accompanying developments in the use and potentialities of language itself, provided an audience (though by no means coextensive with the whole of any society) ready to receive and transmit new

[22] Jackson, *op. cit.* pp. 69ff; Henning, *op. cit.* 24f; Geldner in *Enc. Brit.*[11], XXVIII, p. 1041a–b.

[23] Amm. xxiii, 6, 32; Agath. ii, 24; Clemen, *Fontes*, pp. 84, 101.

thought, and the possibility of communicating it; and war and oppression were among the forces which stimulated sensitive men in many regions to undertake it.[24]

I would therefore be disposed to accept the views of those specialists who place Zoroaster in the sixth century or at its beginning; those who place him much earlier, e.g. *ca.* 1000 B.C., are placing him in a prehistoric period, of whose circumstances indeed we know nothing, but in which it seems unlikely that the tribal life of still migrant Iranians can have provided the social preconditions for such a religious development. I would emphasise, for *such* a development. That there may have been development of some kind we are in no position to deny; indeed, the appearance, it seems, of the title Ahura-Mazda, 'the Wise Lord', Zoroaster's name for the High God, in an Assyrian list of native and foreign deities under Asshur-bani-pal, and of its derivative Mazdaka as the name of a Median chief before 700, is significant; but significant of what? We cannot say precisely; and it certainly does not follow that Zoroaster, who need not have invented the name *de toutes pièces*, had already done his work.[25]

That Zoroaster was a man, no faded godling, there seems no reason to doubt. His name is a human name, compounded with *-ushtra*, 'camel', as are so many Persian and Greek names with *aspa* or *hippos*, horse; though many scholars do not commit themselves to an elucidation of the earlier syllables (prominent in Greek by-forms of the name, Zaratas, Zarades). Olmstead explains it as 'with golden camels', and adds, 'his father was Pourushaspa, "With Grey Horses", and his mother Dughdhova, "Who Has Milked White Cows". . . . His race was Spitama, the "White".'[26] But it is the text of the *Gathas*, which 'alone within the Avesta make claim to be the *ipsissima verba* of the prophet',[27] that especially establishes both his humanity and the genuineness of these 'prophesyings' themselves. They are as personal as the writings of Jeremiah or of Hesiod. They contain many proper names, especially

[24] Cf. *Lyric Age*, pp. 3ff, 327ff.

[25] See, in *Oriental Studies in honour of C. E. Pavry*, the contributions of E. Herzfeld (*The Traditional Date of Z.*), R. G. Kent (*The Name Ahuramazda*), C. F. Lehmann-Haupt (*Wann lebte Z.?*) and A. T. Olmstead (*Ahura Mazda in Assyrian*). Of these scholars, Kent remained in favour of a date about 1000; the other three favoured the sixth century, as do Henning (cf. n. 20, above) and Zaehner. Meyer, *GdA* III (1937), p. 97, still says 'spätestens etwa um 1000 v. Chr.' (as in *E.B.*[11], XXI, 205b).

[26] *Persian Empire*, p. 94; discussion in his article in *Review of Religion*, IV (1939), which I have not seen.

[27] Geldner in *Enc. Brit.*[11], XXVIII, 1040b.

those of his kindred and the circle of his patron, the king Gushtasp or Vishtaspa, and none of these is in the least redolent of mythology. They belong to concrete situations, and to our ignorance of these is due, in part, their obscurity; they are emphatically not a model of a forger's idea of what the founder of a religion *ought* to leave in writing. The archaic language, *not* identical with the Old Persian of the early Achaemenid inscriptions (so perhaps eastern Iranian, the dialect of Bactria, where Vishtaspa is said to have reigned), is also, as we have seen, still imperfectly known; but something can still be made of them. There are, after all, not a few obscurities and not a few differences between translations, in the text of the Psalms.[28]

From these personal utterances, elucidated in part by later scriptures, we can draw the picture of a man of perhaps chieftainly but not very powerful family, distressed by the sufferings of men and cattle at the hands of other men. Zoroaster's people are settled people, farmers; that, he and his disciples assume throughout, is the right way to live. They suffer from the raids of nomad herdsmen, as men and cattle were long to suffer on that Bactrian frontier of Iran and Turan. Dahai or Daoi, a Persian appellation for the nomads, which the Greeks took for a proper name, appears to mean simply 'enemies' or 'robbers'.[29] Not for nothing did the young Zarathustra become convinced that the 'human predicament' imposes a choice between two ways of life, and that its setting is that of a war; such was the setting of his own life. The same interplay of ideas of the natural and the supernatural pervades the development of the Iranian national saga; to take one among many instances, the fiend Frangrasyan, a figure of ancient myth, becomes already in the later *Avesta* 'the Turanian murderer' (the Afrasiab of the *Shah Namah*), slain by 'the uniter of the Aryan nations' Husravah, Kai Khosru.[30] Meyer comments that in Judaism, in origin a religion of the desert-edge, the parts are naturally reversed, and the primordial murder is that of Abel, the herdsman, by Cain the cultivator of the soil.[31]

There were two ways of life, and they were at enmity. There were

[28] Translations, e.g.: Greek (LXX); Latin (Vulgate – and St Jerome was a good scholar); Latin authorised by Pius XII in 1945; English, Great Bible (as in the Book of Common Prayer); AV; RSV; R. A. Knox. Cf., e.g., Ps. lxviii (Latin lxvii) or cxli (Lat. cxl).

[29] E. Meyer in *Enc. Brit.*[11], XXI, 202d. The name, first in H. i, 125.

[30] *Yasht* ix, 18, 21; cf. v, 41; and Darmesteter's notes, *Avesta*, II, pp. 64, 114.

[31] *GdA* III (1937), p. 101, n. 1.

also two kinds of gods in the Aryan pantheon that the young Zarathustra must have known: the nature-gods or sky-gods, *daevas* (*cf. divi, dei, theoi*), and the gods of human ways and law. 'At the head of the latter stand the closely connected pair, Varuna, god of the Oath, and Mithras, god of Treaties; it is they who have established the reign of law, *Arta*' [32] – a fine Persian word, common among the elements of their proper names, and already found in western Asia, along with the names of these same gods, among the bronze-age Aryans of Mitanni.[33] 'To Zoroaster, these moral powers are the only true gods; the *daevas* are the powers of Falsehood [*druj*], phantasms whose worship leads to sin and ruin.' [34] In India, where the same names (including Indra the storm-god, also known in Mitanni) appear in the bronze-age polytheism of the Vedas, the subsequent development is different, and it is the *asuras* who become the malignant powers. The contrast is not merely verbal or a matter of semantics. The main development of religion in India is towards acquiescence; it is mystical, pessimistic, world-renouncing; whereas in Iran (in a more bracing physical climate), the Persian celebrated his birthday, and took pride in the number of his children,[35] and Zoroaster's message is that man can and must work with God.

It was not without trouble that the prophet either reached his conclusions or gained a hearing. The tradition tells how as a young man he used to withdraw to the mountains to meditate. Up there among the rocks and the huge trees of the primaeval forest, as to Moses at the Burning Bush, Reality (I AM) seemed to glow through the things of sense. 'Good Thought came to me', he says; and he personifies Good Thought as a Holy Spirit sent from God. And the practical conclusion from his illumination is the same as for Moses: You must go back to the people, and tell them that which they do not want to hear.

The feeling that drove him was, it seems, also the same: the pain of his world. In what many have conjectured to be his earliest surviving utterance, the 'Soul of the Cattle' cries to God:

' "For whom did you create me? And by whom did you fashion me? Upon me comes the assault of wrath and of violent power, . . . of

[32] Meyer, *ib.* p. 99.
[33] Cf. S. A. Cook in *CAH* II, pp. 400f.
[34] Meyer, *ib.*; cf. nn.
[35] H. i, 133, 136; cf. Meyer, *loc. cit.* p. 104; *EB*[11], XXI, 205d.

arrogance and robbery. No other herder have I than you; teach me to find good pasture." '

'Then he who made the kine asked Justice' [Asa, = Arta]. God asks His Justice or His Righteousness, which is both treated as an attribute of God and also personified and even invoked in worship, what steps Justice has taken to appoint a guardian for the 'Soul of the Kine'. Justice answers: There was not a man to be found who had power to smite the spoilers but was himself without hate. Then, it seems, Zarathustra speaks in his own person: 'That is why both I and the soul of the kine are making our supplication.'

'Then the Lord, the Creator, who knows [. . .?] by his wisdom, spoke:' [No such chieftain has been found] . . . ' "Therefore *thee* have I named, for the tillers of the ground. . . . This man has been found for me alone, who has heard our commands: Zarathustra Spitama. . . . Therefore will I give him the [authority?] of a speaker." '

'But the soul of the kine lamented: "So I have in my distress a powerless lord; the voice of a feeble and weak-hearted man, whereas I desire one who is mighty." '

But Zarathustra prays for grace to accept and carry out his mission; a mission, it thus appears, to preach righteousness, and end the rule of violence.[36] Like many other prophets, he feels himself unworthy of his mission, but with prayer, though full of fear, he embarks on it.

Opposition appears at once. 'The Enemy has ever fought with me; . . . he is most powerful. . . . O Mazda, aid me; obtain for me with thy Good Thoughts his defeat.' There seems to have been fighting, which has not gone well.[37] In another place the prophet is near despair. 'To what land to turn? Whither shall I go? Kinsman and friend turn from me; none is found, to conciliate, to give to me; still less the false-believing chiefs of the land.

'This I know, Mazda, why I am powerless: [because?] my flocks are diminished and my followers are few. Therefore I cry to thee: Lord, look upon it.' [38] It seems from the later tradition that he left his home, a prophet without honour in his own country (perhaps Media), and

[36] *Yasna* xxix.

[37] *Yasna* xlix; cf. xliv, 15. (It must be noted that the *Gāthās* are not arranged in chronological order, but according to their metres.)

[38] *Yasna* xlvi, 1–2.

that it is in north-eastern Bactria that he converts and receives protection from the Kavi Gushtasp, repeatedly mentioned in the *Gāthās* with honour and gratitude, and from other powerful helpers.

Elsewhere we may perhaps see something of the development of his religious thought. He looks back with thankfulness to the meditations in which illumination first came to him:

'... I will regard Thee as holy and mighty, O Wise Lord, if by thy hand, that holds the lot of false and true believers, if through thy Fire's flame, the power of Good Thought comes to me.'[39] Good Thought, Vohu Mana, like Arta, is one of the personified spirits, emanating from the deity, later systematised as the six great Amesha Spenta or good angels.

> Thee I conceived as holy, O Wise Lord, when thy Good Thought appeared to me and asked me: 'Who art thou? And whose is thine allegiance? ...'
>
> Then I answered: 'Zarathustra am I; to the false believers a forthright enemy, but to the righteous a mighty help and joy. ...
>
> Thee I conceived as holy, O Wise Lord, when thy Good Thought appeared to me. ... A difficult thing it seemed to me, to spread thy faith among men, to do that which Thou didst say was best.[40]

In another place he presents his questioning:

> This I ask, O Lord; tell me truly: How shall I complete the praise of one like Thee? Yet, such as Thou art, tell me as a friend, even such as I am. ...
>
> This I ask, O Lord; tell me truly: Who by generation was the first father of Righteous Order? Who gave the sun and stars their way? Who established the waxing and waning of the moon? ... Who established the earth beneath, and the heavens above, that they do not fall? ... Who, O Wise One, is the creator of good thoughts?[41]

Gradually his thoughts clarify:

> Therefore as the First did I conceive of Thee, O Wise Lord; as the one to be adored with the mind in the creation, as the Father of the Good Mind within us. ...

[39] *Yasna* xliii, 4.

[40] *Yasna* xliii, 7, 8, 11. The whole passage expresses, as Zaehner says, 'an intensely personal experience of the reality of God's goodness' (*Zoroastrianism*, p. 45).

[41] *Yasna* xliv, 1, 3, 4.

> [Thy Spirit] chose the husbandman, the thrifty toiler in the fields, as a holy master. . . Never, O Wise One, shall the thieving nomad share the good creed.[42]

Gradually he works out and proclaims the essential elements of his dualistic system, all of which can be found in or at least justified from the *Gāthās* (though, as usual in such cases, the possibility that these have suffered interpolation cannot be *dis*proved). The good and evil spirits,[43] the destined victory of the good (not always easy to distinguish from his hoped-for victory in the wars of his day and place), a last judgment, heaven and hell,[44] all are to be found; later Zoroastrianism elaborates them *ad nauseam*. One absence we note, however: the name of Angra Mainyu, the Evil One, later furnished with a hierarchy of his own parallel to the Amesha Spentas or 'angels' – Angra Mainyu is scarcely, perhaps not at all, to be traced in Zarathustra's own utterances. The evil principle to him is *Druj*, 'The Lie',[45] the false; evil seems to be negative, almost as in the ex-Manichaean St Augustine. His thought seems, indeed, to have been quite remarkably abstract and intellectual; even the heaven and hell of his later followers, the final states of reward and punishment, may have been, as some of his modern exponents have thought, to him states of mind, to which the good and the wicked come as the result of confirmation in their ways.[46]

It would not therefore be surprising if, after Zoroaster's death, there was a certain back-sliding; the reappearance of some elements of ancient polytheism, such as Mithras the Mediator and Anaïtis the mother-goddess (in Bactria especially associated, it seems, with the river Oxus), prominent in the fifth century though unknown to the *Gāthās*. *Haoma* (the *soma* of India), the local brand of alcohol, considered divine in early Iran as in most proto-historic societies, but spurned by the prophet (*Yasna* xlviii, 10), resumes its place in ritual; and Strabo, in the time of Augustus, even records a joint worship of Anaïtis with Ōmanos,[47] Zarathustra's Vohumana or Good Thought,

[42] *Yasna* xxxi, 8ff.

[43] *Yasna* xxx, 3, 4; xlv, esp. 2, 11.

[44] *Yasna* xlvi, 10–13; li, 13; cf. Zaehner, *Zoroastrianism*, 56f.

[45] e.g. *Yasna* xliv, 13; xlviii, 1; li, 14; cf. Geldner in *EB*[11], XXVIII, p. 1042b.

[46] Cf., e.g., *Yasna* li, 15ff; Zaehner, *loc. cit.* (n. 44). On the other hand, this view is not compatible with *Y.* xliv, 18 ('O Lord, tell me truly! How shall I obtain Thy Righteous Order's prize, ten mares with a stallion, and the camel?') – if, as Meyer believed (*GdA* III, p. 106), this charmingly naïve petition refers to the rewards due to the faithful in a peasant heaven.

[47] Str. xi, 512.

in Cappadocia. One great name of the primitive Aryan pantheon never reappears, however: Varuna (Ouranos?) the sky-god and the guardian of *arta*, once famous from Vedic India to bronze-age Mitanni. The reason is probably that even before the time of Zarathustra, in the Assyrian age (cf. p. 72 above), his holy name had gone out of general use, replaced by the appellation of Ahura-Mazda, the Wise Lord; for he is surely the high god whom Persians worshipped, as Herodotos tells us (p. 65), 'calling the whole circle of the heavens Zeus'.

Other features, too, of later Iranian religion appear, as we have seen, in Herodotos' account. To those mentioned above we may add that they would not defile a river by spitting, urinating or washing their hands in it, 'for they revere rivers greatly'.[48] Xenophon, or the author of the appendix that forms the last chapter of his *Cyrus*, notes that they would not spit, 'nor would they eat or drink during a journey, nor be seen performing the necessities that arise therefrom'.[49] The Persian passion for hunting, too, emphasised in the same chapter (§ 12), may well have been encouraged by the fact that to destroy wild animals was deemed pleasing to God, like the war on ants and snakes and the like, equally passionately waged by the Magi; but finer, and of great significance for the early success of their empire, was that devotion to truth and abhorrence of lying which Herodotos mentions in one of his most famous phrases. The whole of Persian education, says he, might be summed up as learning to ride and to shoot with the bow, and to speak the truth.[50]

The Persian gentleman of the great days was thus encouraged by his religion to be manly, honourable, athletic and courageous; devoted to hunting and the promotion and protection of agriculture; contemptuous of trade, and shunning debt, which 'led to lying';[51] dignified in his manners, even a little prudish. Under the temptations of power and wealth, the standards were not maintained, as Xenophon says, and also Herodotos before him. They were great borrowers of foreign customs,

[48] H. i, 138. The same scruple prevented Vologeses, king of Parthia and himself a priest, from crossing the sea to pay a state visit to Nero, lest, as he explained, he should have to 'defile the sea by spitting or the other needs of nature': Pliny, *NH* xxx, 2, 6/16; Tacitus, *Annals* xv, 24.

[49] viii, 8, §§ 8, 11. Valckenaer pointed out that the picture of Persian degeneration from the standards of Cyrus' day in this chapter is inconsistent with present-tense praises of the Persians elsewhere in the work. It may however still have been added by X. himself, for political reasons, and in any case seems certainly to date from before Alexander's conquests.

[50] i, 136.

[51] *ib.* 138, 1; cf. 153, 1 (above, p. 44).

Herodotos notes, especially luxuries; and they had also picked up homosexuality from the Greeks.[52] By the excessive ritualism and scrupulousness of the Magi they were untrammelled; and they differed also, as we have seen, in burial customs. These differences have been much discussed, and explained as belonging to the customs of different periods or, almost inevitably, as arising from difference of race.[53] It may be suggested that it is at least as likely that the differences are those between the outlook of a professional clergy and a military aristocracy. Legalism and an obsession with ritual purity are among the occupational diseases which, in many ages, have beset the professional religious. If some of the meticulous regulations of the *Avesta*, e.g. those on the disposal of nail-parings, beard-clippings, etc., remind one of worldwide and presumably very ancient superstitions which appear in the practice of magic (a pseudo-science which the Magi were unjustly supposed to have invented), it must be remembered also that these worldwide superstitions *are* worldwide because they fit in with universal tendencies of human psychology.[54] They can therefore crop up again after disappearing (not eradicated, but driven underground) and visibly do so whenever the soil of society is fertile for them. A professional priesthood, and especially a hereditary priesthood, such as the Magi provided in the persons of the *Athravans* ('fire-tenders', Greek *pyraithoi*, as they called themselves; 'Magi', the name of the tribe, being hardly found in the *Avesta*), may develop superstition elaborately, since scrupulousness may easily come to be counted for righteousness and so

[52] *ib.* 135.

[53] Thus the Magian priestly tribe is sometimes said to have been 'probably pre-Aryan'. There is no evidence for this theory; and Zarathustra himself may well have been a Magian, especially if he came from Rhagai in Media (cf. Jackson, *Zoroaster the Prophet*, App. IV, pp. 202ff). The syllogism seems to be: (1) The Magi were a priestly caste addicted to ritualism and religious legalism. (2) Priestcraft is an un-Aryan activity. (3) Therefore the Magi were not Aryans – a conclusion likely to commend itself to a 19th-century professor with a Lutheran upbringing. There is, it may be noted, no room for similar assertions about the Brahmans.

[54] See the very interesting essay of Edwyn Bevan, *Dirt*, in his *Hellenism and Christianity* (London, Allen & Unwin, 1921), which, though not concerned with the religion of the Magi, sheds a flood of light on the character of their obsessions. On nail-parings, hair, etc., see the *Vendidad*, Fargard xvii (Darmesteter, *Avesta*, I (*SBE* IV), pp. 185–9); for the universality of superstitions on this subject, cf. my *World of Hesiod*, pp. 49–51, 85 (and chap. III, 'The Psychology of Magic', generally). Magic attributed to the Magi without question, the name having become established, see Pliny, *NH* xxx, 1ff; but better authorities knew that this was false: Aristotle 'in his *Magikos*' and Deinon, author of a book on Persia, agreed, according to Diogenes (see the good and learned treatment of the Magi in his introduction, § 8), that magic in the vulgar sense (*τὴν γοητικὴν μάγειαν*) was unknown to them.

be a road to eminence. Peasants, also, much at the mercy of uncontrollable natural forces, are liable to it; but military aristocrats, accustomed to get their way by successful self-reliance, are much less so. Hence the absence of religiosity, and indeed of any deep religious feeling, in Homer, whereas in the farmer Hesiod superstition is, by the standards of Greek literature, prominent. Hence among the Bantu,

> Livingstone was struck by the absence of idols among the Bechuanas and Caffres [the Bantu 'master tribes of the Zambesi area' as he elsewhere calls them] whilst they were present everywhere among the [subject] negro Balondas, and he points out the extreme dread of spirits and medicines among the latter, while so much superstition was unknown among the former. The Makololo upbraided the Makalaka for being superstitious, and reproached them with turning back from an enterprise if a certain bird called to them, saying that it was unlucky.[55]

In Persia, it was not until the Sassanid period that the Magian priests were able to set the tone of society. Under the Achaemenids, it might have been so. There was, as we shall shortly see, a conflict decided by force of arms between a Magian and a military party; and the Kshatriyas, if we may borrow the Indian term, beat the Brahmans. This result contributed to a certain laxity, which has often been noted, in the Mazdaean religion of the Achaemenids; notably, to a certain amount of syncretism with Babylonian religion and astrology, and to the survival in full prominence of Mithras and Anaïtis, which, to judge by the *Gāthās*, would not have won the approval of Zarathustra. Nevertheless, the great Darius and his supporters were, according to their lights, deeply religious. God had given them their position. God had given them the duty to subdue the world and impose settled life and His order; *pacisque imponere morem; parcere subiectis et debellare superbos*. Zarathustra before his death (killed, according to late tradition, at the age of 77, in a raid of the Turanians upon Bactra[56]) had established and delivered to his disciples a doctrine, that men (and kings among them) must work with God for the establishment of His Righteous Order, which Persian imperialism was to find very congenial.

[55] Ridgeway, *Early Age of Greece*, vol. II, p. 422, citing Livingstone, *Missionary Travels and Researches in South Africa*, p. 272 (cf. 158, 281, 286).
[56] Jackson, *Zoroaster the Prophet*, chap. X.

CHAPTER V

From Cambyses to Darius

CAMBYSES the son of Cyrus succeeded his father and reigned for seven years and five months (late 530 to early 522). He conquered Egypt and consolidated Persia's sea-power in the Levant.[1] King of Babylon under his father, he lacked neither administative experience nor the conqueror's drive; yet the traditional account of him is unfavourable.

For this there is more than one reason. Tyrannical indeed he may well have been. The inevitable comparisons, too, with a father so spectacular and so well beloved as Cyrus were enough to make any ruler sensitive. There were stories of Cambyses asking those nearest him what men said of him, and taking a critical answer badly; the criticism in question was that he drank heavily.[2] By way of reaction, he may have aspired to elevate the monarchy higher above the Persian nobility. He married two of his sisters, Atossa and one called by Ktesias Roxāne, whom he is said, in a probably untrue atrocity story, to have killed in a rage, by kicking her when pregnant.[3] Whatever the truth of this, he left no child by these or any other women, and this, in a society in which men prided themselves on the numbers of their sons only less than on military prowess (p. 74, above), must have exacerbated his lack of his father's easy self-confidence. Weak he was certainly not; in him the Persians felt that they had a stern master, unlike the beloved Cyrus who had been as a father to them;[4] and the practice of sister-marriage, if established as a custom, as among the Pharaohs and the kings of Elam, would naturally have set a gulf, unbridged by kinship, between the king and his nobles. Unready as yet to flout the 'law of the

[1] The latter achievement is emphasised in H. iii, 34, 4. [2] *ib.* 34f.

[3] *ib.* 31f; A. named, 68, 4, etc.; Roxāne, Ktes. (Photios' *Epitome*) 12; but K.'s unreliability is shown most conspicuously by his capacity for getting names wrong, cf. below, p. 94. The same story was told of Nero.

[4] H. iii, 89, 3.

Medes and Persians' unceremoniously, Cambyses is said to have consulted his jurists on this matter: the 'Royal Judges', who held office for life unless convicted of misconduct. There was indeed no precedent; but the judges, fearful of offending the king, reported that they had found another principle recorded, That the king may do as he pleases.[5] One would like to know what the original context was.

Over and above this, tradition represented Cambyses as of unsound mind and at the end of his reign definitely mad. Some said he was epileptic. Herodotos does not commit himself on this, pointing out that the story of his insanity comes from hostile Egyptian sources, and of his alleged epilepsy reporting 'It is said that Cambyses suffered from birth from the grave sickness which some call the Sacred Disease.' He shows his usual good sense, and incidentally foreshadows a famous judgment of the great Hippokrates, who denied that the so-called Sacred Sickness was more specially sacred than any other.[6] Cambyses *may* have been unstable; he may have been epileptic; he may have committed atrocities, though some of the stories told against him are suspect, if not definitely untrue. But not least significant among the facts concerning his reputation (like those of some of the traditionally bad Roman Emperors) are the facts that his life ended in mysterious circumstances; that his death was followed by civil wars and a dynastic revolution; and that his great successor, under whom the tradition took shape and, at least in part, was officially promulgated, was, to say the least, not interested in glorifying his memory.

By September 530, merchants of Babylon were dating documents by the years of Cambyses 'King of Babylon, King of the Lands'. The former title had long been his; the latter had been reserved to himself by Cyrus, and its assumption by Cambyses implies that the news of Cyrus' death had arrived.[7] We hear nothing from Herodotos, here our sole detailed source, on the early years of the reign; he was interested in the Mediterranean, and we may infer that, after the death of his father, the new king's first concern was, necessarily, to curb the Massagetai and make good the frontier of Iran and Turan. But by 526 at latest preparations were in train for the next great enterprise in the

[5] H. iii, 31, 5.
[6] *ib.* 29, 1; 30, 1; 33; cf. Hipp. *On the Sacred Disease*, 1.
[7] Olmstead, *P.E.*, p. 87; W. H. Dubberstein, 'The Chronology of Cyrus and Cambyses', in *AJSL* LV (1938).

west, the conquest of Egypt. A quarrel was picked, it is said, by a demand for a daughter of the old Pharaoh Amasis to join the Persian king's harem, a demand which Amasis, 'knowing that she would be a concubine rather than a wife', i.e. that compliance would be equivalent to acknowledgement of Persian overlordship, felt compelled to evade. He is said to have tried to deceive Cambyses by sending a daughter of his dethroned predecessor Hophra instead; but, since Pharaoh Hophra had been dead for forty years, this is the most unconvincing detail of the story.[8]

Old Amasis, a soldier himself, had regarded Persia realistically. The grand alliance had gone down ignominiously; further prospects of resistance were not bright, but he did what he could. A natural line, at which Persia might perhaps be content to stop if there were resistance beyond, was that of the coast and the Sinai Desert. If the sea were held, the desert might prove impassable. Amasis had long since secured Cyprus, taking tribute (probably light, for he needed their good will) from its city-kings, and making full use of the prestige of Egyptian culture. Most of the elaborate statues, some still bearing traces of their original gay paint, of Cypriote royal or aristocratic worshippers wearing the Egyptian kilt and sometimes the serpent crown, must be dated to his time. Further afield he made dedications to Athena of Lindos in Rhodes, 'two statues of stone and a linen corselet, which is well worth seeing', and to Hera of Samos 'two portraits of himself in wood, which were placed in the great temple and were still there down to my time, behind the doors'. (They had perhaps been moved to a less conspicuous position during the Persian occupation.) 'The dedications to Samos were in connection with his friendship with Polykrates the son of Aiakes', adds Herodotos; the pirate king who had made himself for a space, since the fall of mainland Ionia, the chief power in he central Aegean.[9]

These arrangements lasted exactly until Persia was ready. When the eastern colossus moved, the frail island curtain collapsed at a touch, the city-kings going over in a body to the side which already

[8] H. iii, 1.

[9] H. ii, 182. Cypriote statues, cf. Myres, *Handbook to the Cesnola Collection* in the Metropolitan Museum, New York; Dikaios, *Guide to the Cyprus Museum*; recent finds from Kouklia (Old Paphos) at Ktima. Details of further dedications by A. at Lindos, from writers cited in the *Lindos Temple-Chronicle* (ed. Blinkenberg), xxix. History of Polykrates, see *Lyric Age*, pp. 314ff.

controlled the sea-power of Phoenicia. Cypriotes (the Greeks, that is, as well as the Phoenicians of Kition) sent their squadrons, as in the days of the Assyrians, to join the fleet preparing against Egypt; and Polykrates did the same, though his squadron never arrived; the prominent Samians whom he had placed in charge of it (because, it was said, he thought them dangerous at home) turned against him and sailed back from Karpathos to make an unsuccessful attack on him.[10] Amasis was fortunate not least in the hour of his death, on the eve of the invasion (winter, 526–5).

The Persians could thus, if necessary, have circumvented the Sinai Desert by moving troops by sea. The usefulness of the Bay of Acre, with some shelter from Mount Carmel, became familiar to them in several later Egyptian revolts; but we have no positive evidence that Cambyses used it.[11] The sea was still an unfamiliar element; and in fact the Persians solved the problem of getting their troops across the desert successfully. A highland people, they never repeated the conquests of Nabonidus in Arabia, just as the Semites had never anticipated theirs in Asia Minor, and in Herodotos' time certain 'trading places on the coast between Kadytis [Gaza] and Ienysos' (somewhere near later Rhinokoloura, el-Arish) actually 'belong to the Arabian king', no doubt the king of the Nabataeans; but the Persians concluded a treaty with the reigning sheik, and vast caravans of camels carrying water-skins met the army at the desert-edge.[12]

Meanwhile in Egypt all was far from well. Phanes of Halikarnassos, an officer of Amasis' mercenaries, falling foul of his master, had deserted apparently even before the invasion was imminent, and fled to Cambyses, bringing him valuable information about the desert and the importance of getting help from the Arabs;[13] and Uzahor-resenet, Warden of the temple of Neith at Saïs and admiral of the Egyptian fleet or some part of it, was probably already foreseeing defeat and considering his course of action.[14] He afterwards made himself very useful to the Persians under two kings. The position was like that of Babylon before the invasion of Cyrus. The regular army was not

[10] H. iii, 19; 44.
[11] Str. xvi, 758, says only 'the Persians used to use it'.
[12] H. iii, 4ff; cf. 91, 1; 97, 5.
[13] *ib.* 4.
[14] The Udjahorresne of Olmstead, *P.E.*, pp. 88–91, 113, 143f; on him, cf. Hall in *CAH* III, pp. 311–14; G. B. Gray, *ib.* IV, pp. 18–25. His inscription at Saïs giving an *apologia pro vita sua* is almost the only source of evidence on these events outside Herodotos; the later Greek and Roman writers (full references in Olmstead, pp. 88–9 nn) add nothing of any value.

negligible. Apart from the Greeks and Karians, many of them of families long domiciled in the country, it included the forces called by Herodotos Hermotybies (perhaps 'spearmen') and Kalasiries, *Khalshere*, 'Young Syrians', a name derived ultimately from Syrian mercenaries of the XIXth Dynasty.[15] Whether or not they were largely of Libyan or other foreign descent, they were so thoroughly domiciled that Herodotos got the impression that they were natives; but at the same time they were so thoroughly distinguished from the mass of the population that he took them (mistakenly) for a caste. Egyptian society was deeply class-divided, and the Pharaoh, for all his sacred position, was so far from being the beloved of his people that Amasis is recorded to have transferred the Greeks and Karians from 'The Camps' at Daphnai (near the modern canal zone) to Memphis 'for his protection against the Egyptians'.[16]

With these troops Psamatik III, a six-months king, gave battle before Pelousion. Polyainos speaks, highly unconvincingly, of siege-operations. The mercenaries were full of fight; indeed, knowing that Phanes was in the hostile army, they are said to have slain his children in front of their lines and drunk their blood mixed with wine, the more firmly to pledge themselves to receive no quarter. In any case finally there was a pitched battle, hard-fought and bloody; Herodotos saw the bones of the dead still littering the desert two generations later; but the end of it was that the Egyptians and mercenaries were worsted and 'fled in complete disorder'.[17] Pelousion fell. The victors followed up by land and water, unopposed; for not only is there no mention of the Egyptian war-fleet, which in Xerxes' invasion of Greece was still formidable, but it is a fair inference from Uzahor-resenet's inscription that he omitted to give any orders to the fleet which would have brought it into action, and that his ceremonial reception of Cambyses in his 'see' of Saïs belongs to this point, i.e. that he surrendered the town. Psamatik and his army were driven into Memphis, and the Persian command entrusted a ship of Mytilene, a city with old commercial connections with Egypt, with the task of conveying in a Persian herald to demand surrender on terms. But the Egyptians,

[15] H. ii, 164ff; Hall, *op. cit.* p. 308, after Möller in *Zeitschr. für Äg. Spr. u. Altertumskunde*, 1920.

[16] H. ii, 154.

[17] H. iii, 11f. Polyainos' story (vii, 9) that C. used beasts sacred to the Egyptians as a creen against missiles from the walls is a typically romantic embellishment.

militarily impotent, were still fanatical. They swarmed down upon the ship as she lay at the wharf, and massacred the whole crew along with the herald. There was, therefore, a siege; and when it ended in surrender, 2000 Egyptians, including the king's son, are said to have been put to death; ten for each member of the ship's company. Psamatik was compelled to witness the humiliation of his people; but thereafter he was humanely treated, as were, Herodotos points out, other royal princes captured by the Persians, including the sons of some later Egyptian rebels. But he could not let affairs of state alone; he plotted rebellion, and being detected is said to have committed suicide.[18]

Cambyses set himself to consolidate his position and to subdue the adjacent countries. He intended, no doubt, nothing less than a conquest of Africa, of whose extent (like Alexander later in India) he had no idea. The project of subduing Carthage had to be given up, in view of the unwillingness of his Phoenician sailors, the core of his navy, to sail against their own kindred; but Cyrene and Barka, a city at this time no less powerful than Cyrene itself, made their submission, as did the Libyan tribes inland. West of the Thebaïd, 'the City of Oasis' (the ancient name of the oasis of Kharga), where there was a strange, inland Greek colony of Samians 'of the Aischrionian tribe', was occupied; and there would seem to have been little need for Cambyses to send troops (let alone an army of 50,000 men!) to secure the Siva oasis, sacred then as now, where stood the oracular temple of Zeus Ammon. Yet this is what he is said to have done; and the army is further said to have been overwhelmed by sandstorms and perished to a man.[19] It is far from impossible that some Persian expeditions, probably little more than reconnaissances in force, may have met with disaster in the Sahara; but it is at this point that our accounts of Cambyses become accounts of a megalomaniac tyrant, in which, as in the Roman accounts of Caligula or Nero, it is hard to distinguish any foundation of fact from the superstructure of malicious exaggeration.

Similar disaster is said to have overtaken a major expedition led by Cambyses in person against the Ethiopians. He is said to have marched 'without making any provisions of supplies, nor taking thought that he was preparing an expedition to the ends of the earth' (a startling

[18] H. iii, 13–15.

[19] Carthage, *ib.* 19; Cyrenaica, 13; Oasis (Kharga) and Ammon, 26. Importance of Barka, cf. *Lyric Age*, p. 140.

contrast to his careful and adequate preparations before crossing the desert of Sinai), with the result that his troops ran short of food, ate their baggage animals and finally resorted to cannibalism. The whole story is, at the least, wildly exaggerated. The Persian army does not thereafter appear crippled by its losses, though no doubt there may have been hardships on the march, and even loss of life; and the Long-Lived Ethiopians themselves, against whom the expedition is supposed to have been directed, are a fabulous people whose name and epithet is derived from Homer, and of whose civilisation Herodotos gives an unusually fabulous account.[20] What is true is that Cambyses did subdue at least a part of the real Ethiopia (Nubia) beyond the First Cataract, as appears from surveys of the Persian Empire which Herodotos quotes elsewhere; its revenues included 'gifts' from 'the Ethiopians on the borders of Egypt, whom Cambyses conquered',[21] and their warriors are described in his list of fighting men of the empire, whether or not Xerxes really took them to Greece: 'They were dressed in leopard-skins and lion-skins, and had bows made from the mid-rib of the palm-leaf, fully six feet long, and short arrows of reed, with heads of sharp stone, the kind they also use for cutting seal-stones; and they had spears with heads of gazelle-horn, sharpened like a lance, and knotted clubs.'[22] These stone-age warriors, however, represent only some of the outlying and least civilised former subjects of the Nubian monarchy, which itself possessed a not inconsiderable culture and degree of organization, derived from that of Pharaonic Egypt. This kingdom remained unconquered. Cambyses probably penetrated a long way up the Nile. There was a place called 'Cambyses' Depôt', Kambysou Tamieion, in Roman times, near the Third Cataract,[23] though the possibility that the name, which must have been taken over by the Greeks from a native source, may really have represented something other than Cambyses' name, cannot be excluded. Strabo indeed says Cambyses reached Meroe, not far from Khartoum, whither the capital had been transferred from the more northerly Napata; but when he adds that the city was named after a sister and/or wife of Cambyses, who died there, one is constrained to suspect that his source is late and

[20] iii, 20ff; the expedition, 25.
[21] *ib.* 97.
[22] vii, 69.
[23] Ptolemy's *Geography*, iv, 7, 16; cf. Pliny, *NH* vi, 35/181 ('Cambusis'); (*not* in Strabo, as stated in *CAH* IV, p. 21).

romantic.[24] There is, moreover, an Ethiopic inscription from Meroe in which King Nastesenen claims to have routed 'the man K-m-b-s-u-d-n', who had led against him a well-appointed expedition by land and water, and to have captured all his supplies. It is tempting to identify this invader's name with that of Cambyses, and to suppose that, even if only by raiding his communications, it was Nastesenen who reduced the Persian army to sore straits; but some authorities believe Nastesenen to have reigned much later. If, however, K-m-b-s-u-d-n is not Cambyses he is not identified.[25] In any case, Cambyses extended his power permanently beyond the First Cataract, and Elephantine long continued to be held for Persia by a military colony of Jews. These Jews, whose ancestors had been there since Saïte times (perhaps descended from the diehards who fled into Egypt in the time of Jeremiah), had a temple of Yahu (Yahweh), but worshipped other gods also; their religion, known in part from papyri found at the place, gives a glimpse of an earlier and pre-Deuteronomic form of Judaism reminiscent of that of the Samaritans.[26]

In like manner dispute rages over the proceedings of Cambyses in Egypt. He is said to have abused the mummified corpse of Amasis and then burnt it, outraging the feelings of his own 'fire-worshipping' Persians as well as of Egyptians,[27] and later, on his return from the south, to have sent for the young sacred bull, lately recognised as the incarnation of Apis by the traditional distinguishing marks, and stabbed it in the thigh with his dagger, laughing the while at such animal 'gods' of flesh and blood; to have driven from his presence with whips the priests who had brought it, and threatened death to any persons found celebrating this incarnation. So 'the rejoicing of the Egyptians was stopped, and the wounded Apis lay in its temple dying. . . . And when it died of its wound, the priests buried it, secretly from Cambyses.' [28]

This, says one modern scholar, is false; for the sacred bull died 'in his

[24] Str. xvii, 790.

[25] Identified by Lehmann-Haupt in *PW* X (1919), *s.v.* Kambyses; criticised by Reisner in *Harvard African Studies*, II. G. B. Gray in *CAH* IV, p. 21n, inclines to follow Reisner; H. R. Hall, *ib.* III, p. 312, to keep the identification.

[26] Van Hoonacker, *Une communauté judéo-araméenne à Éléphantine* (1915); A. Vincent, *La religion des Judéo-Araméens d'Éléphantine* (1937); A. E. Cowley, *Aramaic Papyri of the Fifth Century* (Oxford, 1923; texts, trn. and notes) or *Jewish Documents of the Time of Ezra* (London, S.P.C.K., 1919; trn. and brief notes only).

[27] H. iii, 16, 2.

[28] *ib.* 29.

sixth year [524], while Cambyses was absent on his Ethiopian expedition', and 'the next Apis bull, born in the fifth year of Cambyses, survived to the fourth year of Darius'.[29] On the other hand it is argued that the 'sixth year' is later, Cambyses' last, and that this 'does not contradict the story, as we are expressly told that the bull did not die at once'.[30] But this seems to be special pleading. The Apis which died under Cambyses was, moreover, buried with great magnificence, in a vast grey granite sarcophagus, with an inscription recording that it was made to the order of Cambyses himself, with his name and royal cartouche as Pharaoh Mestiu-Re or Re-mesuti, 'Born of Re'. It is difficult to imagine that this was done secretly 'to disguise the cruel death of the last Apis', though the attempt has been made;[31] the birth of the next Apis is then supposed to have been ante-dated deliberately, for the same reason.

Cambyses certainly did treat several Egyptian temples and cults with great severity; whether these proceedings were the eccentricities of a madman or the calculated severities of a conqueror bent on stamping out a revolt, there is no doubt about the fact, for which we have, *inter alia*, the disinterested evidence of the Jews of Elephantine; they mention a widespread destruction of temples merely in passing, *à propos* of the fact that the Persians had spared theirs.[32] Cambyses' madness and most of his acts of tyranny are placed by Herodotos after his baffled return from Ethiopia, where he felt resentment at the rejoicings of Egyptian festivals. We do not know when Psamatik was put to death; Herodotos *relates* it immediately after the conquest, but this would hardly be the best moment at which to start planning a rebellion. It *may* be that the absence of the king and most of his Persian regiments, leaving the Greeks, we are told, to garrison Lower Egypt,[33] as Greeks had done for two centuries, encouraged thoughts of a possible rebellion, in which the priests, rallying to the dethroned Pharaoh, would be natural leaders. On the other hand, *before* going up the Nile, Cambyses appears to have taken steps to placate the Egyptians. A papyrus, the so-called Demotic Chronicle, describes how he reduced the dues

[29] Olmstead, *P.E.*, pp. 89–90.

[30] Hall in *CAH* III, p. 312. There was great confusion in Egyptian dating by regnal years after Cambyses' conquest; see Parker in *AJSL* LVIII (1941), 285ff; cf. M. Miller in *Klio*, XXXVII (1959), p. 31.

[31] By A. Wiedemann (*Gesch. Aeg.*, 229); see How and Wells, *Comm. on Hdt. ad loc.*

[32] Cowley, *Aramaic Papyri*, no. 30 (trn., p. 113); *Documents*, pp. 72–3.

[33] H. iii, 25, 2.

payable in silver and in kind to many of the temples, requiring the priests (in good Iranian fashion) to raise more of their own necessities from their own lands;[34] a measure calculated to please the people, but not the priests, accustomed to idleness. And especially, as we have already seen, he took steps to have himself crowned as Pharaoh, as legitimate king of Egypt, just as his father had done in Babylon. The collaborator Uzahor-resenet made himself useful as an adviser on the formalities, preparing the king's official style, and incidentally using his opportunities to secure preferential treatment for his own temple and city of Saïs. The hypothesis of a rebellious movement about 524–3 would account both for Cambyses' long sojourn in Egypt, and for the contrast between the evidence of a conciliatory policy and his visitations upon the temples.

But the sands were running out for Cambyses himself. 'While he tarried in Egypt, there rebelled against him two men of the Magi, brothers, one of whom Cambyses had left in charge of his household.' Thus Herodotos (iii, 61). He is in agreement with the *Res Gestae* of Darius, the official history of the period, many copies of which were no doubt circulated to the empire (fragments of the text have been found written in Aramaic on papyrus),[35] but of which the master-copy was and remains the great rock inscription, first copied by Sir Henry Rawlinson, at Behistun:[36]

> Thus says Darius the King: . . . After Cambyses went to Egypt, the people became hostile. Thereafter there was great deceit in the land, both in Persia and in Media and in the other provinces. . . . There arose a Magian, by name Gaumata. . . . On the fourteenth day of the month Viyakhna [March 11th, 522] he rose up. He deceived the people, saying 'I am Bardiya, son of Cyrus, brother of Cambyses.' Then all the people became estranged from Cambyses and went over to him, both Persia and Media and the other provinces. On the ninth day of the month Garmapada he seized the kingdom; thereafter Cambyses died his [destined?] death.[37]

[34] Olmstead, *P.E.*, p. 91, from Spiegelberg, *Die sogenannte demotische Chronik.*

[35] See, e.g., Tolman in *AJP* XXXII, pp. 444f.

[36] Trn. by L. W. King and R. C. Thomson, London, British Museum, 1907; R. G. Kent, *Old Persian*, New Haven, Conn., 2nd ed., 1953.

[37] *D.B.* i, 11. Usually translated (e.g. King and Thomson, Kent) 'died by his own hand'; but it is not clear that the phrase *uvāmaršiyuš amariyatā*, 'died his [own] death', means this. Cf. Meyer, *GdA* III (1937), p. 192; C. F. Lehmann-Haupt in *PW*, *s.v.* Kambyses, and in *Essays in honour of C. E. Pavry*, p. 279 (after W. Schulze, 'Der Tod des K.', in *Sitzb. d. Berl. Akad.*, 1912).

By midsummer, that is, the process was complete. Already on April 14th a document had been dated in Babylon in the accession-year of King Bardiya.[38] By July 1st almost all the empire acknowledged him ('he seized the kingdom'), and he had the zealous support of the powerful Magi, especially the minister whom Cambyses had left 'in charge of his house'. The new government immediately proclaimed a peace policy, to the joy of a war-weary world; there were to be no expeditions and no war-taxes for three years.[39] There was also some destroying of temples; Darius later says (*D.B.* i, 14) 'The temples which Gaumata the Magian destroyed, I rebuilt'. This has caused perplexity to some, who, in enthusiasm for Darius' later constructive achievements, have taken his doubtless sincere expressions of gratitude to Ahura-Mazda as evidence that he was a zealous Zoroastrian. His enemies, it is felt, should then be a corrupt and reactionary, pre-Zoroastrian, perhaps even pre-Aryan, priesthood. In fact Darius, as we shall see (pp. 117ff), was *not* an orthodox Zoroastrian, not a Catholic as it were, but a compromiser. Many difficulties disappear if we take the view that this peace party and clerical party,[40] which seized power in Cambyses' absence, represented also the most thoroughgoing Zoroastrianism of the age, characterised both by its love of peace and its disapproval of the older worships and of 'temples made with hands'.

These things were done in the name of King Bardiya, the younger son of Cyrus; the Mardos of Aeschylus, a form soon assimilated to Smerdis, an early Greek personal name.[41] According to Darius' official history, which Herodotos follows on this point, the new king was an impostor, a brother of Cambyses' faithless Magian minister; and as the pseudo-Smerdis he has figured in almost all books, ancient and modern. But is the official account to be followed so implicitly? In our day and age, we should have learned, surely, to apply criticism to official accounts as well as unofficial; and not least to what a successful revolutionary government says about its defeated enemies. If it has been judged by government necessary to kill someone, it is also necessary, for the sake of public opinion, to damn his memory. Roman history is particularly rich in examples; so is that of the Stalin era.

Let us examine the evidence.

[38] Dates from Olmstead, *P.E.*, p. 92f.
[39] H. iii, 67.
[40] Cf. the view of G. Rawlinson (*Herodotus*, II, pp. 454ff).
[41] e.g. Ar. *Politics*, 1311b. 'Mardos', Aesch. *Pers.* 774.

> Thus says Darius the King [*D.B.* i, 10, at the beginning of his narrative]: . . . Cambyses had a brother named Bardiya, born of the same mother and father. Cambyses slew this Bardiya . . . [but] it was not known to the people that Bardiya was slain. Then Cambyses went to Egypt [and subsequently, as we have seen, Gaumāta the Magian 'deceived the people' and impersonated Bardiya]. There was not a man, Persian nor Mede nor any of our family, who could deprive that Gaumāta the Magian of his power. The people feared him for his tyranny; the many who had known Bardiya formerly, he would slay,[42] for this reason 'that they may not know me, that I am not Bardiya the son of Cyrus.' No one dared to say anything against that Bardiya until I came. Then I prayed to Ahura-Mazda. Ahura-Mazda brought me aid.

The chief oddity in this is the presumption that the king's brother and heir-presumptive could disappear without anyone certainly knowing that he was dead; though in a state the size of the Persian Empire it can hardly be called impossible.

Herodotos' account is a saga; but a saga derived from well-informed Persian sources, men whose beliefs were based on the official account, though they differed about some details and added others. According to him (iii, 30), the true 'Smerdis' was killed by an emissary sent from Egypt *after* the conquest, Cambyses having dreamed that he saw Smerdis sitting on the royal throne, 'and his head touched the heavens'. Accounts were given of how the murder was accomplished, differing in every detail. Later, when heralds arrived in Syria from the new government, ordering the army (now on the march home) to obey the new king, everyone believed that they came from 'Smerdis' the son of Cyrus, including Cambyses himself, who supposed that his emissary had betrayed him. It is further added that the new king bore a strong facial resemblance to the true Smerdis, and moreover that, by a remarkable coincidence, Smerdis actually was his name.[43] Altogether, there is much to be said for Beloch's and Olmstead's bold theory, that it really was Bardiya, the son of Cyrus, who rebelled successfully against his brother with the support of the Magi,[44] afterwards to be

[42] Optative; cf. Kent, *O.P.* p. 120.

[43] H. iii, 61f.

[44] Olmstead, *P.E.*, p. 109 and, more fully, in *AJSL* LV (1938), 'Darius and his Behistun Inscription'; anticipated by Beloch, *GG*^{2} II, i, p. 4n. O. ought not to have claimed, however, that 'contemporary Aeschylus' makes Mardos a legitimate monarch. In his list of kings of the Medes and Persians, 'a son of Cyrus fourth commanded the host, and fifth

damned as an impostor by the victorious military reaction. Strabo, though it is unlikely that he had any independent information, seems to put the matter in its right perspective, when he says simply that Cambyses 'was overthrown by the Magi' (xvii, 736).

Cambyses died in mysterious circumstances. All accounts of his death differ; none is worth much. That of Herodotos (iii, 62–6), than which we have none better, says that, convinced at last, after re-examining the herald and the murderer of his brother, that he was confronted by an impostor, he was mounting his horse to march against him, when the guard of his scabbard fell off and the point of the short sword entered his thigh, 'just where he himself had wounded the Apis'. The wound gangrened, and he died of it, after confessing the murder to the nobles with him and adjuring them, 'especially the Achaemenids who were present, not to endure that the Empire should fall back into the hands of the Medes'. But the nobles, for the moment, made no move, still believing that it was Bardiya who had seized the kingdom and that Cambyses had lied. No one says that Cambyses was murdered by his officers; but even this possibility cannot be excluded.

Herodotos continues (68–79), with many exciting and romantic details, to the effect that it was only after seven months that suspicion developed among a few Persian nobles that the new king *was* an impostor, and finally proof was obtained. The length of the reign is correctly given (March to September, 522). A conspiracy was then formed by six great nobles, joined at the last moment by the impetuous young Darius, son of the Achaemenid Hystaspes and lately a guardsman in Egypt.[45] He insisted on instant action before anything should leak out. Darius himself only says (continuing the passage quoted, p. 92): 'Ahura-Mazda brought me aid. On the tenth day of the month Bagayadi [Sept. 29th], I slew that Gaumāta the Magian and his chief associates, [at] a stronghold . . . [in] the land of Nisaya in Media; I deprived him of the kingdom; by the will of Ahura-Mazda, I became king.'

Later (*B*. iv, 68) Darius gives the names of the six Persians who were with him when he slew Gaumāta. Herodotos also gives a list of

---

reigned Mardos, a disgrace to his country and ancient throne, whom noble Artaphrenes slew by guile'. After all, the speaker (*Persians*, 773–6) is the ghost of Darius himself!

[45] D. in Egypt, H. iii, 139.

them, which is a testimony to the reality (though not the infallibility) of his knowledge of Persian affairs. They are as follows:

Darius (*B.* iv, 68)		Herodotos, iii, 70
Vindafarna	the son of Vayaspara	Intaphernes
Utana	„ „ „ Thukra	Otanes (s. of Pharnaspes, iii, 68)
Gaubaruva	„ „ „ Marduniya	Gobryas (*father* of the later Mardonios, vi, 43, etc.)
Vidarna	„ „ „ Bagabigna	Hydarnes
Bagabuksha	„ „ „ Datuhya	Megabyxos
Ardumanish	„ „ „ Vahauka	Aspathines

Herodotos gets only one name wrong, the last in our list (unlike the egregious Ktesias, who gets only one right, 'Idernes'); and even this seems to be due to a confusion with the name of Aspachana, the 'quiver-bearer' of Darius, named by him in another inscription, that of Naksh-i-Rustem. 'You who shall be king herafter, preserve well the families of these men,' adds Darius; and indeed, the members of these great houses (except that of Intaphernes, who perished in disgrace not long after) were to play a conspicuous part in the history of subsequent generations.[46]

It was a true counter-revolution, led by the heads of great families of the Persian aristocracy; just how revolutionary is shown by the fact that the new king set up by the conspiracy was Darius, an Achaemenid indeed, of the older branch which had been overshadowed by the house of Cyrus, but a comparatively young man, whose father and grandfather were both alive. This fact is particularly stressed by his son Xerxes, whose own accession was due not to primogeniture, but to selection.[47] Herodotos even insists, in two famous passages,[48] that the conspirators, before establishing Darius as king, and with the despotism of Cambyses fresh in their memories (H. 80, 2), debated among themselves what kind of constitution to set up. The speeches, indeed, in which he makes Otanes propose democracy and Megabyxos oligarchy, while Darius wins the support of the other four for adherence to the monarchical system, draw on Greek political experience, and are interesting chiefly as a Herodotean dialogue on politics; and Herodotos has come in for much ridicule for his *naïveté*, or accusations (to quote

[46] *D.B.* iv. 69; Aspathines, *DNd* (Kent, p. 140); Intaphernes, H. iii, 118.
[47] Herzfeld, *A New Inscr. of X.* (Chicago, 1932); § 3. Kent, p. 150 (*XPf*).
[48] iii, 80ff; cf. vi, 43, 5.

one) of 'amazing mendacity'. Yet the more we come to know of ancient manners and customs, the more reason we find to respect Herodotos as an honest and clear-sighted reporter; and absolute monarchy, we now know, is *not* a primitively universal form of government; rather, it comes in (as among the Hebrews) in warlike times, with the need for a strong executive. The Persians were not many generations removed from tribal life, in which the people have some control over their executive; and it is rash, when Herodotos categorically affirms it, to deny that the leaders of a revolutionary conspiracy at least considered the idea of placing ultimate power in the hands either of some Persian aristocratic élite or of the people, that is (as in Macedonia) the body of warriors.

Herodotos imagines the slaying of the Magian king to have taken place at Sousa, which, as the inscription shows us, is erroneous; but it was no doubt especially in the Persian area that there at once followed, he tells us (iii, 79), a pogrom against the Magi: 'had not night supervened, they would have left not one living'. He adds even that the anniversary of this day was remembered and celebrated, a celebration during which the Magi kept out of sight.

Well indeed might the native Persians celebrate the victory of the Seven Men, Persians all, as Darius carefully says, a victory which restored their privileged position, won within living memory. But other peoples were not so happy. The death of the seven-months king was mourned by 'all the peoples of Asia, except the Persians themselves'. They had no desire to see the revocation of their relief from war-tax and service, and further, no intention of submitting tamely to it. Even in Persia, with tales of usurpation and imposture in the air, personal ambitions stirred. Since the common ancestor of Cambyses and Darius was four generations back, were there no other Achaemenids as near to the line of Cyrus as Darius was?[49] Within a few months there was revolt in every corner of the empire, and the thirty-year-old leader needed all his strength and ability in the throes of a desperate counter-revolutionary war.

[49] A question shrewdly asked by Aymard, in *Peuples et Civilisations; Histoire générale*, I, p. 695.

Chapter VI

Darius the Great

In the course of a twelvemonth – autumn, 522, to 521 – Darius and his friends fought nineteen battles and killed or led captive nine kings.[1] After that, his troubles were not at an end; there remained the elimination of the western viceroys, who had enjoyed too well their *de facto* independent power. But the campaigns of the first year were fought in the heart of the empire, in Babylonia, Media, Persia itself, Sousiana and central Iran. One marvels at first sight (and Darius intended us to marvel) that either he or the unity of the empire survived. He survived through his own cool and ruthless determination; through his trust that God, whom he continually honours in his narrative, would not allow him to fail in the mission that he had undertaken – but it is fair to remember that many of the defeated must have trusted in God also – and with the help of good friends and a few important satraps: his father Hystaspes in Parthia and Hyrcania, Vivana in Arachosia to the south-east, and Dadarshish in the north-east, in Bactria. Also, he commanded throughout the best body of troops in the empire, the war-hardened 'regular' army that Cambyses had led to Egypt. Exiguous in numbers, as Darius says, his forces were united and never wavered; while among his opponents there was no combination. Two successive self-styled Nebuchadrezzars in Babylon had nothing in common with a Mede claiming descent from Kyaxares, nor he in turn with a party in Persia which held to the house of Cyrus, under yet another leader who claimed to be the legitimate King Bardiya.

Rebellion must have been brewing in Babylonia as soon as ever it was clear that the conquerors had come to blows among themselves. By October 3, only four days after Darius had slain his rival, documents begin to be dated in the reign of 'Nebuchadrezzar the son of Nabu-

[1] Summary in the *Res Gestae*, *D.B.* iv, 2ff.

naid'; Nidintu-Bel, an elderly man, as Darius' artist depicts him among the defeated rulers, with a deeply lined face, old enough to win credence for his claim.[2] Leaving Media, Darius hastened against him.

'The army of Nidintu-Bel held the Tigris', says Darius. 'There was also a flotilla.' But the river would have been low, before the greater rains, and Darius must have found an unguarded reach.

> Then I placed my army on floats of skins. Some I made to be borne on camels, for some I brought horses. Ahura-Mazda brought me aid. By His will we crossed the Tigris. There the army of Nidintu-Bel I smote utterly.... I marched on Babylon. Before I reached it, at Zāzāna on the Euphrates, Nidintu-Bel met me with his army [Dec. 18th].... By the will of Ahura-Mazda, I smote that army; the enemy was driven into the river; the water carried them away.... Nidintu-Bel with a few horsemen fled to Babylon.... Thereafter I took Babylon; I captured Nidintu-Bel at Babylon and put him to death.[3]

Already on the 22nd documents were being dated 'in the beginning of the reign of Darius'.

But the idea of revolt was spreading. In Elam (Sousiana) there had already been one revolt, at the same time as that of Babylon, but when a royal officer arrived, supported by the news that Darius had killed the 'false Bardiya' and was marching south, the rebels collapsed and handed over their leader for execution. Soon things were more serious: 'While I was in Babylonia, these are the provinces that rebelled against me: Persia, Sousiana, Media, Assyria, Parthia, Margiana, Sattagydia, the Saka' (or eastern nomads). The last three surrounded Bactria, and pinned down the forces of the loyal Dadarshish, though he held his own, defeating Frada the Margian leader on December 9th.[4] There was another revolt in Sousiana, this time under a Persian, though he took the name of Umannish, i.e. of an Elamite hero of the Assyrian wars, Khumbanigash; and, separated by this from Darius in Babylonia, Vahyazdata, another Persian, seized the throne in Persia itself, as 'Bardiya, son of Cyrus', and dispatched troops eastward against the loyal Vivana in Arachosia. Vivana repulsed him from before the fortress of Kapishakani on December 29th.[5] One is, indeed, at liberty to

[2] Olmstead, *P.E.*, p. 112; dates after Parker and Dubberstein, *Babylonian Chronology*.
[3] *D.B.* i, 18 – ii, 1. I abridge the style of the monument, omitting some of its repetitions.
[4] *D.B.* iii, 3. – Darius deals with these campaigns in geographical order, from west to east.
[5] *ib.* iii, 10.

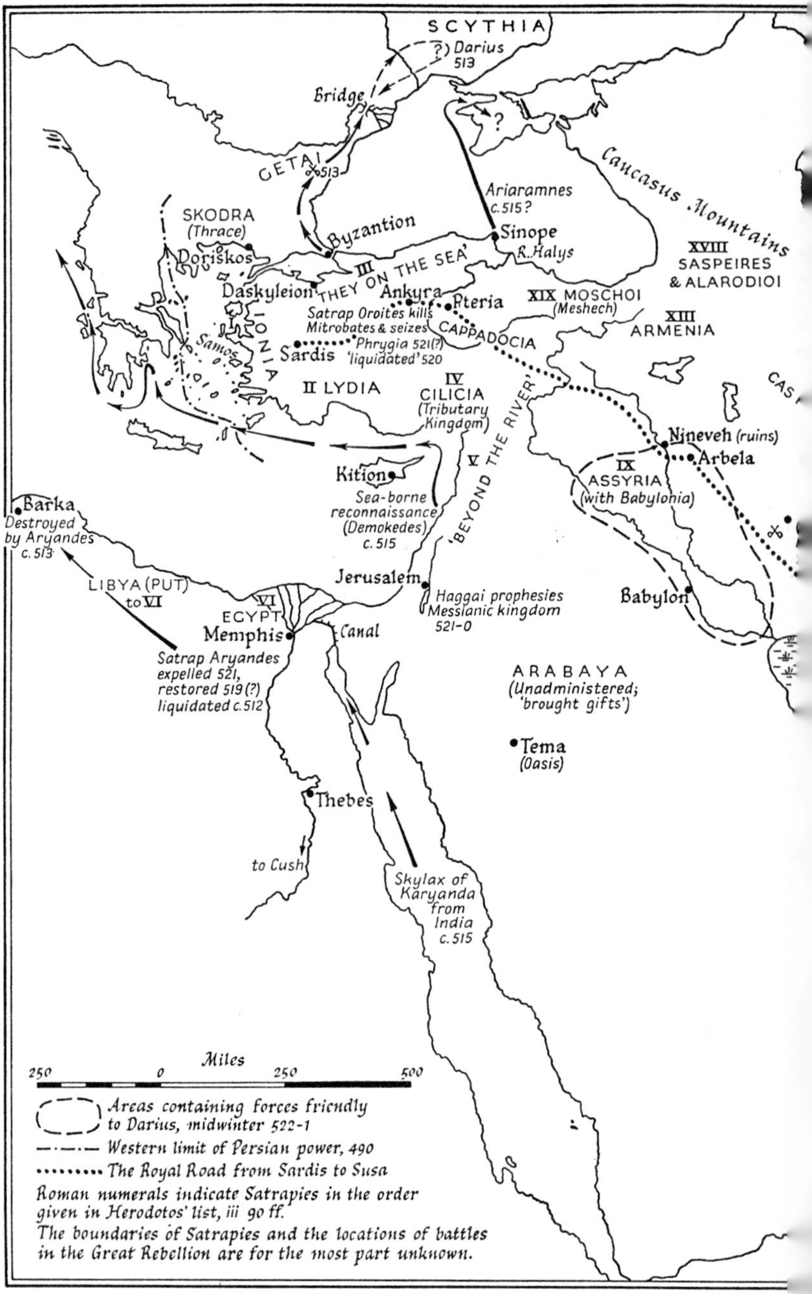
SCYTHIA
(?) Darius 513
Bridge
GETAI
513
Ariaramnes c.515?
Caucasus Mountains
SKODRA (Thrace)
Byzantion
Sinope
R. Halys
Doriskos
XVIII SASPEIRES & ALARODIOI
III
'THEY ON THE SEA'
Daskyleion
Ankyra
Pteria
XIX MOSCHOI (Meshech)
Satrap Oroites kills Mitrobates & seizes Phrygia 521(?) 'liquidated' 520
CAPPADOCIA
XIII ARMENIA
Samos
IONIA
Sardis
II LYDIA
IV CILICIA (Tributary Kingdom)
'BEYOND THE RIVER'
Nineveh (ruins)
Arbela
V
Kition
IX ASSYRIA (with Babylonia)
Sea-borne reconnaissance (Demokedes) c.515
Barka
Destroyed by Aryandes c.513
Jerusalem
LIBYA (PUT) to VI
VI EGYPT
Haggai prophesies Messianic kingdom 521-0
Babylon
Memphis
Canal
Satrap Aryandes expelled 521, restored 519(?) liquidated c.512
ARABAYA (Unadministered; 'brought gifts')
Tema (Oasis)
Thebes
to Cush
Skylax of Karyanda from India c.515
Miles
250 0 250 500
Areas containing forces friendly to Darius, midwinter 522-1
Western limit of Persian power, 490
The Royal Road from Sardis to Susa
Roman numerals indicate Satrapies in the order given in Herodotos' list, iii 90 ff.
The boundaries of Satrapies and the locations of battles in the Great Rebellion are for the most part unknown.

The Persian Empire: the Gr

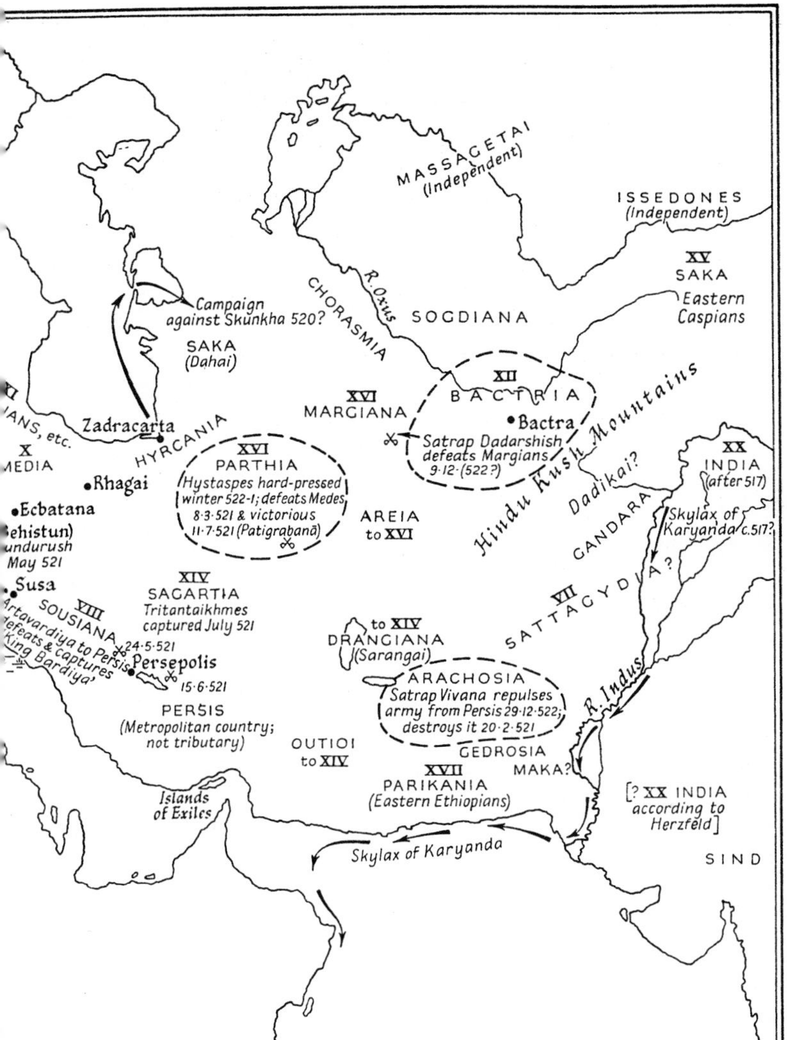
MASSAGETAI
(Independent)
ISSEDONES
(Independent)
XV
SAKA
Eastern
Caspians
R. Oxus
CHORASMIA
SOGDIANA
Campaign
against Skunkha 520?
SAKA
(Dahai)
XII
BACTRIA
Bactra
Hindu Kush Mountains
XVI
MARGIANA
Satrap Dadarshish
defeats Margians
9·12·(522?)
Zadracarta
HYRCANIA
X
MEDIA
XVI
PARTHIA
Hystaspes hard-pressed
winter 522-1; defeats Medes
8·3·521 & victorious
11·7·521 (Patigrabanā)
Rhagai
Ecbatana
AREIA
to XVI
Dadikai?
XX
INDIA
(after 517)
GANDARA
Skylax of
Karyanda c.517?
XIV
SAGARTIA
Tritantaikhmes
captured July 521
Susa
VIII
SOUSIANA
24·5·521
Persepolis
15·6·521
VII
SATTAGYDIA?
to XIV
DRANGIANA
(Sarangai)
ARACHOSIA
Satrap Vivana repulses
army from Persis 29·12·522;
destroys it 20·2·521
R. Indus
PERSIS
(Metropolitan country;
not tributary)
OUTIOI
to XIV
GEDROSIA
MAKA?
XVII
PARIKANIA
(Eastern Ethiopians)
[? XX INDIA
according to
Herzfeld]
Islands
of Exiles
Skylax of Karyanda
SIND

ebellion and the Work of Darius

wonder how far Dadarshish and Vivana, these great military chiefs, really were at this early date in any sort of understanding with Darius, and how far they were merely fighting for their own hands against local rivals, only to profess their loyalty to him when he broke through to the east.

But it was the revolt of Media, the only one in this whole series to be mentioned by Herodotos,[6] which was by far the most formidable. It broke out as soon as ever Darius appeared to be tied down by the revolt of Babylon. Fravartish (Phraortes?) 'of the seed of Kyaxares' was proclaimed king under the name of Khshathrita, a hero of Median legend. All Media accepted him; so did Armenia to the west and Parthia and Hyrcania to the east, where Darius' father Hystaspes was unable to hold the position.[7] All the old Median empire was ablaze, and Median troops advanced south into Assyria, where they threatened the rear of Darius in Babylonia.

It was the Alexander-like speed of Darius' own operations that saved him then. The decisive victory of Zāzāna on the 18th December enabled him to detach a force under a general named Vaumisa, which on the last day of the year checked the Medes in Assyria and drove them back some distance. A second small column under Hydarnes (he of the Seven?) advanced directly upon Media; it crossed the frontier, and claimed a victory at Marush; but Hydarnes was in no position to advance on Ecbatana, and remained encamped at Kampada (near Kermanshah?) until Darius was able to join him in the spring.[8] The front was thus held until Darius was able to leave Babylon early in February.

Darius advanced first into Sousiana, where once more the rebellion collapsed quickly. 'King Umannish' was captured and executed.[9] Then Darius again divided his forces. Against Persia, 'Says Darius the King: Then I sent forth the Persian and Median army that was with me. A Persian named Artavardiya, my servant, I made chief of them. The rest of the Persian army went with me to Media.'[10]

Median regiments of Darius' regular army, it appears, were mostly sent against Persia, for obvious reasons, and Persians against Media. The swift fall of Babylon and Darius' aggressive moves had early repercussions further east; it looks as though the opposition there, both

[6] i, 130, 2; iii, 126.
[7] *D.B.* ii, 16.
[8] *ib.* ii, 6 (Hydarnes), 10 (Vaumisa).
[9] *ib.* ii, 4.
[10] *ib.* iii, 6.

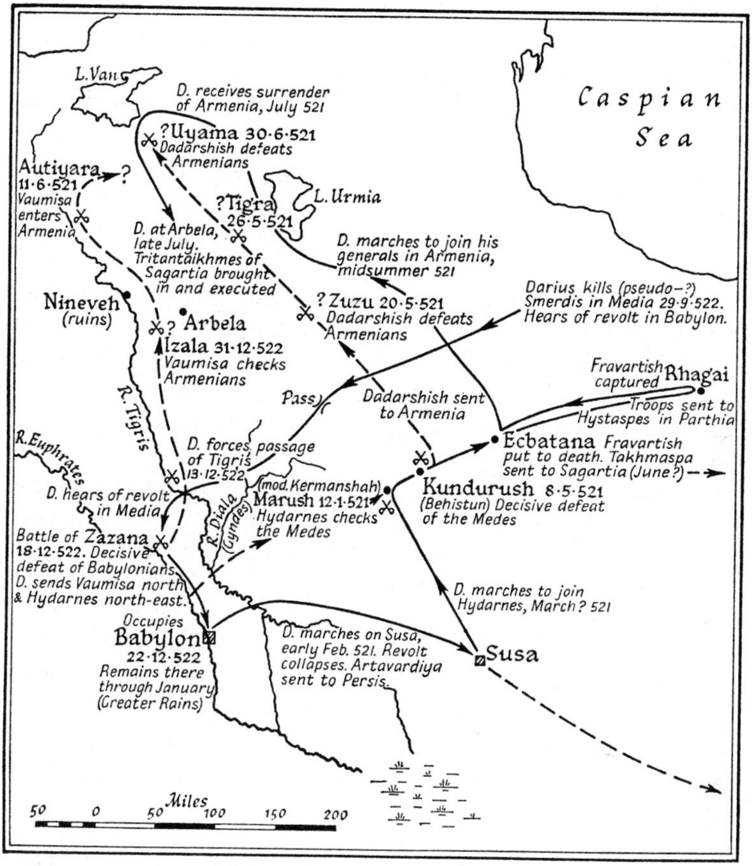

The Campaigns of Darius, 522–1

in north and south, was weakened by the recall of troops to the main front. Vivana in Arachosia was able to take the offensive. On the 20th February he shattered the enemy army in his province, and its general fled to a local fortress, where he was afterwards captured and executed with his chief officers;[11] and fifteen days later Hystaspes defeated the Medes in Parthia,[12] though all was still far from well there. The rest of March and April passed with little to report; perhaps the swelling of torrents with snow from the spring thaw made movement difficult;

[11] *ib.* iii, 12f.

[12] *ib.* ii, 16.

but in May the decisive offensive opened on all fronts. Darius with Hydarnes advanced from Kampada upon Ecbatana, and on the 8th of May utterly defeated Fravartish in the plain of Kundurush, under the crags where later the great Behistun Inscription was to dominate this decisive battlefield. Fravartish fled from Ecbatana to Raga, hotly pursued, by the same route where, nearly two centuries later, another Darius was to be pursued by Alexander. Near Raga, 'Fravartish was captured and brought to me. I cut off his nose and ears and tongue, and put out his eyes. In my gates he was kept bound; all the people saw him. After that, I impaled him on a pole at Ecbatana; and his chief associates, them I flayed within the fortress of Ecbatana.'[13]

Sixteen days after Kundurush, Artavardiya in Persia defeated 'King Bardiya'.[14] The worst of the crisis was now over; but 'mopping-up' operations continued for months, and were often tough. Probably from Ecbatana (though, owing to the geographical arrangement of the *res gestae*, it is not clear), an Iranian officer from Armenia, a second Dadarshish, was sent to pacify his native province; but he found the work hard. He is credited with a victory on May 20th, another at 'the fort Tigra' on the 30th and a third at 'the fort Uyama' at the end of June; while on June 11th Vaumisa in Assyria (p. 100, above) won a second victory in the northern (Tiyari) mountains, and entered Armenia. But Oroites, the satrap left by Cyrus in Lydia, sent no aid (Darius paid him out for that later); he was engaged, or had been, in private warfare with Mitrobates, satrap of Phrygia and the Hellespontine region, whom he killed;[15] and resistance in the Armenian mountains remained so obstinate that Darius, who had advanced to Raga, perhaps with the idea of joining hands with his father, sent a detachment to join him, and himself turned west. At his coming, the Armenians seem to have laid down their arms without further fighting; and by late July, returning towards the centre of the empire, he halted at Arbēla.[16]

Here he was met by news of victory in the east. His father, reinforced, had crushed the opposition in Parthia (Battle of Patigrabanā, July 11th).[17] Artavardiya in Persia, four days later, finally defeated 'King Bardiya' in the district of Paishiyāuvādā, the same Persian district in which the first claimant to the name of the son of Cyrus had

[13] *D.B.* ii, 12f. [14] *ib.* iii, 6f. [15] H. iii, 126; cf. 120.
[16] *D.B.* ii, 7–11; Olmstead, *P.E.*, pp. 114f. [17] *ib.* iii, 1f.

first raised his standard, only sixteen months before. The pretender and his chief adherents were impaled in Persia.[18] And at Arbela too there was delivered to Darius another claimant to descent from Kyaxares, Chithrantakhma (Tritantaikhmes), who had proclaimed himself king among the horse-riding Sagartians in central Iran, now captured by a Median officer in the service of Darius. Of his treatment, Darius records the same grisly details as of Fravartish, ending 'all the people saw him; after that, I impaled him at Arbela'.[19]

Even now there was not an end of all fighting. In Babylonia and in Sousiana, lands which had seen Darius come in haste and depart in haste for the grim northern war, people were slow to believe in the reality of his victory. Babylon rose yet again under yet another 'Nebuchadrezzar', one Arkha, an Armenian (of the pre-Iranian stratum, by his looks), by whom a document is dated on September 21st; but it was no longer necessary for Darius himself to take the field. Intaphernes, one of the Seven, captured him and the city on November 27th, and he and his chief supporters were, as usual, impaled.[20] No longer lasted the third revolt in Sousiana; it was suppressed by Gobryas, probably of the Seven (but the name is a common one); it is dated only by the fact that it is recorded in the last column of the Behistun Inscription, which was inscribed after the rest, and after what was evidently meant to be a peroration of the *res gestae*.[21]

This was the last flicker of trouble in the interior of the empire. The record of the third Sousian revolt is followed by another brief thanksgiving to Ahura-Mazda, evidently meant to make a tidy end to the text; but, like Charlemagne at the end of the *Chanson de Roland*, Darius at once found that a distant frontier demanded his attention. Another addition follows, recording a campaign against the Saka, including a sea-crossing. The Persian text is damaged, and in the adjacent Babylonian and Sousian versions the paragraph does not occur, since there was no room left on the rock, where these versions end hard up against the Persian text; but it appears most probable that this campaign was fought soon after 520, against the 'Pointed-Hat Saka' east of the Caspian. The mention of a sea-crossing naturally makes it tempting to see here an account of Darius' famous Scythian expedition, prominent

[18] *ib.* iii, 7f.
[19] *ib.* ii, 14.
[20] *ib.* iii, 14f; date in Olmstead, *P.E.*, p. 115, from Parker and Dubberstein (see n. 2).
[21] v, 1.

in Herodotos, dated in the later Greek tradition about 513 (pp. 128ff, below); but it seems rather likely that the addition to the Behistun Inscription, though later than the main text, is not much later. The 'Saka beyond the Sea', i.e. the Scythians known to the Greeks and probably also the equestrian Getai and Odrysai south of the Danube, appear only in the last of Darius' lists of peoples subject to him, on his funerary monument at Naksh-i-Rustem, recorded among western peoples; at Behistun, only Saka, unspecified, are mentioned among the rebels, coming at the end of the list after eastern peoples, and there they appear also, a few years later, in the list of the king's subjects at his palace at Persepolis. At Naksh-i-Rustem, 'Amyrgian Saka' and Pointed-Hat Saka are distinguished, coming after Gandara and India, and separated from the western 'Saka beyond the Sea'. It seems best therefore to suppose that the sea crossed was the Caspian, perhaps in order to spring a trap upon the elusive nomads by landing troops north of them. The expression 'pointed-hat-wearing' (*[khauda]m tigram barataya*) is, indeed, probably to be found in the inscription, formerly translated as a reference to a crossing of the river Tigris, which has little sense here.[22] A late Greek writer has some references to these eastern wars, including one to the capture alive of a whole Saka division of 10,000 men, whose clothes are then used to deceive another division; also a story of Darius' army in danger from shortage of water on the steppe. The stories are too full of romance to carry much weight; yet there is a hint that they embody some Hellenistic scholarship as well as invention, in the name given to one of the three Saka kings, Amorges; the name clearly preserves that of the Amyrgian Saka, assimilated (like 'Smerdis') to a name familiar in Ionia.[23] Darius appears, then, to have 'taught a lesson' to the nomads of the eastern steppe, among whom he claims to have taken many prisoners, including Skunkha, a hostile king. He was proud enough of the success, won where Cyrus had failed, to have the figure of his prisoner added at the end of the file of nine bound and captive kings (making ten, including the prostrate Gaumata who lies under his feet), and even to have a portion of the text cut away to make room for Skunkha's characteristic and three-foot-high, no doubt royal, pointed head-dress.

[22] *B.I.* v. 3; 'Tigris', King and Thompson, p. 81. The view here taken is that of Kent, p. 134, Olmstead, *P.E.*, p. 141. Many others, including Meyer (*GdA* IV, p. 108 – still in the 1939 edn.), have taken the reference to be to D.'s European expedition.

[23] Polyainos, vii, 11, 6; vii, 12.

In the west, the Sousian version of the Behistun Inscription adds to the list of rebellions 'while I was in Babylon' the name of Egypt; but if this is correct, we have no official account of the re-conquest. There is, however, again a possible allusion to it in Polyainos, who speaks of a rebellion against 'the oppression of the satrap Aryandes'; of how Darius crossed the desert, like Cambyses, with Arab guides; and of how he disarmed hostility by his generous respect for the worship of Apis.[24] Uzahor-resenet, the great collaborator, refers in his *apologia* to an absence from Egypt, after which he was sent back 'while His Majesty King Darius was in Elam' (Sousiana), his journey being officially 'facilitated', for the special purpose of restoring the great Saïte School of Medicine. Olmstead suggests that he had been driven out in the rebellion against Aryandes; that Darius reconquered Egypt in a campaign beginning in the winter of 519–18; and that, while in the west, he incidentally regulated the affairs of Palestine, where the 'prophesyings' of Haggai and Zechariah, 'in the second year of Darius', show that the 'shaking of all nations' had raised Messianic hopes:

> I will shake all nations; and the chosen things of all nations shall come; and I will fill this house with glory, saith the Lord of Hosts. The silver is mine, and the gold is mine, saith the Lord of Hosts. The latter glory of this house shall be greater than the former, saith the Lord of Hosts . . .
>
> Speak to Zerubbabel, Governor of Judah, saying 'I shake the heavens and the earth; and I will overthrow the thrones of kings, and destroy the power of the kings of the gentiles; I will overthrow chariots and riders; and horses and riders shall come down, every one with the sword, against his brother. In that day, saith the Lord of Hosts, I will take thee, Zerubbabel, son of Salathiel, my servant, and will set thee as a signet; for I have chosen thee, saith the Lord of Hosts.'[25]

This campaign, if it took place, was certainly one of Darius' 'lightning' operations; for he was certainly back in the centre of his empire by the end of 518, and *writing* to Aryandes to provide for a codification of the laws of Egypt down to the end of the reign of Amasis, and for a

[24] Poly. vii, 11, 7.

[25] Haggai, ii, 6ff, 21ff RV, LXX; dates, i, 1, ii, 1, ii, 20; cf. Zech. i–vi; Olmstead, *P.E.*, pp. 135ff (cf. Cameron in *JNES* II pp. 309ff). That Zerubbabel 'presumably was summoned to account and executed as a rebel, for his name disappears from our sources' (O. *ib.* p. 142) seems, however, to be presuming much from silence.

copy of the code to be sent to the king for his files.[26] This was typical of Darius' throughness and attention to detail; but it is rather surprising that he should not have made the arrangement while he was in Egypt if he had been there at all. On the whole, 'it is probable that what is referred to' in the Sousian version (if the name of Egypt there is not simply a mistake, as Meyer thought) 'is the failure of Aryandes the satrap of Egypt to lend Darius any active support'.[27] Darius later had occasion to put him to death, but the date of this is uncertain. Aryandes had been a distinguished man in his generation; left as satrap of Egypt by Cambyses, he had secured Persia's hold on Libya, receiving its surrender and sacking Barka, where the king of Cyrene who had made his submission to Persia was assassinated by an opposition faction. He is said by Herodotos to have given offence finally by coining silver of special purity, in rivalry with Darius' own *darics* of specially pure gold. This story is not convincing in itself, and moreover is not supported by any finds of 'Aryandic' coins, although the purest metal, 'driven out' of circulation by baser, always tends to be hoarded. This part of his offence perhaps really consisted in melting down imperial coin, in order to make a profit by selling it as bullion, such as Egypt still used, weighing its silver with the scales.[28] If there is any truth in this story, it must in any case refer to a time when Darius and his coinage had become well established. Herodotos dates it after Darius' great Balkan and Scythian expedition of about 513.[29]

On the other hand, Darius lost no time in dealing with the satrap who is explicitly said to have omitted to help him, Oroites of Lydia. He had probably dreamed, like others after the death of Cambyses, of independent power, and, as we saw, had compassed the death of the neighbouring satrap Mitrobates, his son and other Persians, no doubt Mitrobates' supporters, and even an official messenger from Darius himself, whom he caused to be privily waylaid on the road back. 'Darius . . . decided not to send an army against him, as things were still unsettled . . . and Oroites' power was reported to be considerable; he had a bodyguard of 1000 Persians, and the provinces of Lydia, Ionia

[26] Olmstead, p. 142, after Spiegelberg, *Die sogenannte demotische Chronik*, pp. 30ff. Diodoros (i, 95) also mentions this codification by Amasis and by D. after him.

[27] G. B. Gray in *CAH* IV, p. 181.

[28] J. G. Milne in *JEA* XXIV (1938), pp. 245ff. On Aryandes, H. iv, 166; war with Barka, *ib.* pp. 165–7, 200ff. On the background (and the importance of Barka since Cyrene was weakened by a defeat by the natives), cf. *Lyric Age*, pp. 136–43.

[29] iv, 166; cf. 145.

and Phrygia.' Several Persian officers, however, volunteered for the mission to eliminate him; and one Bagaios, drawing the lot to make the first attempt, set out for Sardis with a budget of dispatches, carefully drafted, we are told, by himself and sealed with the royal seal. Coming before the satrap, he delivered one dispatch after another, dealing with more or less indifferent matters, to the Secretary in attendance (a member of the royal clerical staff), while he himself carefully noted the demeanour of the guards.

> And when he saw that they treated the letters with great respect, and their contents with even more, he put in another, of which the text was: 'Persians, King Darius forbids you to serve as guardsmen to Oroites.' And when they heard this, they laid down their spears before him. Then, when he saw them obedient to the written order, Bagaios was emboldened to hand to the Secretary the final letter, which read: 'King Darius to the Persians in Sardis gives orders to kill Oroites.' And at this the guardsmen drew their short swords, and killed him on the spot.[30]

One is reminded of the details of Tiberius' method of 'sounding' the Senate when getting rid of Seianus. Thus perished Oroites, whose most famous exploit had been the arrest, by treachery, and execution of Polykrates, the spectacular and piratical sea-king of Samos.[31]

So Darius was king,

> and all the dwellers in Asia were subject to him, except the Arabs. . . . The Arabs were never reduced to absolute subjection by the Persians, but became their allies when they gave Cambyses passage into Egypt; for against their will the Persians would never have got into that country. Darius now contracted marriages with the first ladies of Persia; he married two daughters of Cyrus, Atossa and Artystōne (Atossa had already been married to her brother Cambyses and again to the Magian king; Artystōne was a virgin). He also married Parmys, a daughter of Smerdis the son of Cyrus, and the daughter of Otanes,

said in Herodotos' story to have been the leader in the conspiracy against the Magian; the daughter, whose name is Hellenised as Phaidymiē, had then made sure, at the risk of her life, that the reigning king

[30] H. iii, 127f. [31] *ib.* 120–5.

was not the true Bardiya. Otanes had then stood aside from being a candidate for election as king by the other conspirators, on the understanding that he and his house should be subject to no man; 'and to this day this house remains the one free family of the Persians, obeying to the extent of its own free will, while not transgressing the laws of the Persians'. The family was probably of Achaemenid descent; for Phaidymiē also had already been married to Cambyses. It is also said to have been agreed by the conspirators that the king should thereafter marry only from among their descendants, the Seven Houses. Thus Herodotos; actually, all the Seven Houses were probably already the leading families of the Persian nobility; but it is evident that the new king, raised to power by force of arms with the support of the chief Persian nobles and the regular army, now sought in every way by dynastic marriages to assert the legitimacy and continuity of the monarchy in his house.[32]

Darius' next concern was for the consolidation and organization of the empire, and this he carried out with a thoroughness and an attention to detail which gave south-western Asia nearly two hundred years of seldom-broken peace, and which mark him off from among mere conquerors who are that and no more. In particular, he was well aware of the importance of economic matters; an awareness that gained him no honour from his ungrateful fellow-Persians. Their opinion of the matter was summed up in the famous saying that 'Cyrus was a father, Cambyses a master, and Darius a shop-keeper'.[33] It was characteristic of him to inaugurate the first Persian coinage, at a time when the use of coins was still far from universal in the Near East; Babylon, Phoenicia, Egypt, in the hundred-odd years since invention of coinage in Lydia, had not adopted it for themselves, nor had all even of the Greek trading cities yet struck their own. Now, in Darius' empire, his golden *darics* with the device of the running archer – a *crowned* archer, so it represents the Great King himself, armed and swift – circulated wherever trade was considerable, and did away with the need for use of the scales when the king paid his armies. Armed and swift: this was the image of the king to be borne in the memory of millions who never saw the king or his likeness otherwise. As the Roman emperors knew well, coinage, apart from its usefulness, could be a potent instrument of propaganda.

Also, and most important, the financier-king regulated the taxes of

[32] H. iii, 88; cf. 68f, 83f.

[33] *ib.* 89 (cf. p. 81, above).

the empire and laid down clearly the amount that each province had to pay. The remission of Cyrus' and Cambyses' war-levies had roused the enthusiasm of the peoples for the Magian or pro-Magian king, and kindled resistance to the return of the military party. Now, it is not certain that taxes were reduced; in fact, when continued for generations, it will appear that Darius' taxes were too heavy. Gold was increasingly withdrawn from circulation (though more was at the same time being mined) into an unhealthily vast hoard in the royal treasury. But at least they were regular. Herodotos gives, apparently from a first-rate Persian source (perhaps that Zōpyros, son of the great general Megabyxos, whom he mentions as fleeing to Greece after his father's rebellion[34]), an account of the organization of the empire into twenty satrapies, with the amounts which they paid; the outline of a statistical account, which shows us at least the relative wealth of the different regions of the empire.[35]

The great vice-royalties called Satrapies (from Satrap, *Khshathrapavan*, 'Protector of the Kingdom' [36]) dated, some of them at least, from the time of Cyrus; they figure already both in Herodotos' and Darius' own accounts of his early struggles. Darius increased their number, both by conquest and by some subdivision; but many of them remained vast. Darius himself, in successive inscriptions, also gives lists of *the peoples over whom he ruled.* Most of the names in them appear in Herodotos' list of satrapies, though Darius also (for example) repeatedly includes the Arabs, who according to the Greek did not pay tribute and were self-governing. On the Behistun Inscription (i, 6) we have a list from the beginning of the reign, containing twenty-three names, including that of Persia, which stands first. Eight names cover the Semitic or non-Iranian west: Sousiana, Babylon, Assyria, Arabia, Egypt, 'They of the Sea' (the Black Sea coast to the Hellespont), Sfarda (Sardis, i.e. Lydia), Ionia. The Syria of our geographies is not represented; that great tract, with its varied peoples and cultures, was to the Persians not yet even a 'geographical expression', administratively it was still joined to Babylonia. A contract of 520 names one Ushtani[37] (Gk. Hystānes or Ostanes) as satrap of Babylonia and 'Beyond-the River', Abar-Nahara, a huge satrapy of the entire 'Fertile Crescent', which Darius was too good an administrator to leave long undivided.

[34] iii, 160; Ktesias xvii (epit. § 43).
[35] *ib.* 90–5.
[36] Lehmann-Haupt in *PW*, *s.v.*
[37] Olmstead, p. 115 n. 34.

Three names – Media, Armenia, Cappadocia – next cover the north-west of the Iranian world, and eleven names the east: Parthia, Drangiana (the Sarangai of Herodotos), Aria, Bactria, Sogdiana, Chorasmia, Gandara (eastern Afghanistan), the Saka, Sattagydia (from *sata-gaus*, the people of the Hundred Oxen?), Arachosia and the Maka (probably in south-eastern Iran, the later Mekran; perhaps the Mükoi of Herodotos, iii, 93; vii, 68).

Later inscriptions make some additions. At Naksh-i-Rustem, at the end of Darius' reign, there are twenty-nine names. The eastern Saka are distinguished into Amyrgian Saka and Pointed-Hat Saka, and there are additions in the west. Darius' conquests in Europe (pp. 130ff) are represented by Skudra (Thrace and Macedonia) and the 'Saka beyond the Sea', Scythians or perhaps only the horse-riding Getai and Odrysai. Put and Cush, names known from the Old Testament, appear, representing the Libyans to the west and 'Ethiopians' to the south, 'beyond Egypt', and Karka represents Karia.[38] In the palace inscription, Persepolis *e*, Sagartia is mentioned, but does not appear again; perhaps this thinly populated area was re-incorporated in Media. But the greatest achievement of Darius in the east is represented by the appearance, first, it seems, in the list in the Egyptian version of his 'Suez Canal' inscriptions and thereafter on all monuments, of the name of India: the territory, now entirely within Pakistan, as far as the great river Sindhu, our Indus.[39]

In Herodotos' list of the twenty satrapies with the tribute which they paid, all the more important names can be identified in our Persian sources; which is significant among the abundant evidence of the soundness of his information and methods. But his list differs in important respects; e.g. Cappadocia and Arachosia do not appear (they do not give their names to satrapies), and some other names which figure in the Persian lists are grouped together: as Gandara and Sattagydia in his Seventh satrapy, Sagartia and Sarangia (Drangiana) with lands south to the Persian Gulf in his Fourteenth, and no less than four names, Parthia, Chorasmia, Sogdiana and Aria, in his Sixteenth. Dis-

[38] Olmstead, p. 158; R. G. Kent in *JNES* II (1943), p. 306 n. 20, after W. Eilers in *OLZ* XXXVIII.

[39] Herzfeld suggested placing Darius' Hindush in Sind and the Sattagush in the Punjab. On the Hamadan Tablets, see Herzfeld, *Altpersische Inschriften*, pp. 18f; but cf. Buck in *Language*, III (1927), pp. 1ff. On the lists generally, see Kent (as n. 38, above), 'Old Persian Texts, IV: The Lists of Provinces'; and on the Egyptian 'Canal' lists, G. G. Cameron in the same vol., pp. 307ff.

counting the possibility that the historian, just where he professes to speak with the greatest precision, is totally unreliable, it appears clear that *either* the boundaries of taxation districts were different from those of governorships – which is improbable; we know that satraps were directly concerned with revenue[40] – *or* the Persian monumental lists are *not* lists of the administrative satrapies, as modern scholars have often assumed, but simply of the chief *peoples and lands* over which the Great King ruled.

Herodotos says that the satrapies which he lists were those organized by Darius; and, though naturally boundaries shifted from time to time, it seems unlikely that there had been, before he wrote, such drastic reorganization as Olmstead supposed. Certainly, from the early years of Xerxes (within living memory when Herodotos wrote), there exists a list of the peoples of his empire differing in no essentials from those of his father.[41]

Herodotos gives us therefore our best approximation to a statistical survey of the empire; a very valuable document, especially if taken in conjunction with the list of contingents in the army of Xerxes (which also is *not* strictly a satrapy-list). The information given by both can be best presented in tabular form, as it will be found appended at the end of this chapter.

The satraps wielded power over vast areas, though the royal assent had to be obtained for major decisions; even, for example, for a minor war of conquest which was in accord with general imperial policy.[42] Darius established a courier service to speed necessary communications. Routes were defined, no doubt following already ancient caravan trails; one, described by Herodotos, ran from Sardis to Sousa, 'Shushan the Palace', the old capital of the kings of Anshan, in an estimated ninety days for an ordinary traveller moving at about eighteen miles (150 Greek *stadia*) a day: 'There are official staging-posts all along it with excellent rest-houses, and the whole route goes through safe and inhabited country.' There was a bridge at the river Halys, 'with gates, which everyone must pass through before crossing the river, and a large military post thereby'; so the place could function as a passport-control. There were other guard-posts at the deep gorge of the Cilician Gates,

[40] e.g. Xen. *Oik.* iv, 11; H. vi, 42 (Artaphernes' taxation-survey of Ionia); Thk. viii, 5, 5 (Tissaphernes held responsible for levying these taxes by Darius II).

[41] Xerxes, Persepolis *h*; Kent, *loc. cit.*

[42] e.g. H. v, 31, 4 (Artaphernes and the Cyclades); contrast Aryandes!

at the Amanus Pass where one left Cilicia, and after the Euphrates ferry, somewhere in 'Armenia', which must have been skirted, keeping along the foot of the hills. Other ferries crossed the Tigris and its eastern tributaries (later there was a bridge over at least one of these). Most of the route is that trodden by Alexander's army in 333 and 331. 'Three months' journey from the sea' sounded to Greeks of Darius' time like outer space; but the king's messages took much less time than that. 'There is nothing mortal that goes faster than these messengers; so well have the Persians organized the matter. They say that at every day's journey along the whole route' (that is, presumably, the day's journey for a foot-passenger) 'there are horses and men stationed, whom neither snow nor rain nor heat nor darkness checks from completing their allotted course at the utmost speed. One galloper passes the message to another, and he to a third, and so on, as in the torch-races which the Greeks run in honour of the Fire-God.' [43]

Another 'royal road', also followed by Alexander, led from Ecbatana north-east to Bactria; and no doubt the routes to Egypt and India had received similar attention. There was no great mileage of paved or metalled roads; the Assyrians, over shorter distances, had done more in that line; but the trails were made fit for a galloping horse, 'the crooked places straight and the rough places plain'. Perhaps from the self-same generation, a poem in the Confucian *Book of Odes* gives a glimpse of a similar King's Courier in China: sweat on the slackened reins; a piebald horse galloping; a messenger, with question or news or rescript, looking only forward, pressing on night or day, thundering past, receding into the distance.

Even so, it might take weeks to hear serious news, especially if the king himself were on a distant frontier. It was in such circumstances, when Darius was beyond the Danube, that Aryandes, satrap of Egypt, despatched without permission his expedition to Cyrenaica, against dissident elements in the city of Barka. The expedition was a success; nevertheless, Darius shortly felt that Aryandes was growing too independent (above, p. 106). There were indeed a few checks on the satrap's local power. Military commands were sometimes separated from the administrative;[44] Datis the Mede in the Marathon expedition (pp. 236 ff),

[43] The Road, H. v, 52f, cf. 49f; bridge at the Halys, i, 75; at the northern Zab, Q. Curtius iv, 16, 8f; couriers, H. viii, 98.

[44] Xenophon (*Oik.* iv, 9) says systematically; but in his time this was certainly untrue.

Megabates in that of 499 (pp. 195ff) are examples; though the latter, himself an Achaemenid, was, we are told, selected by the satrap, who was his cousin and the king's half-brother. In Xerxes' mobilisation in 481, the troops of six satrapies from Ionia to the Caucasus appear in ten separate contingents under different commanders (pp. 121–6). Further, the Secretary attached to a satrap, who appears prominently in the story of Oroites (an appointment, therefore, dating from before Darius' reorganization), was a 'Royal Secretary' (p. 107), evidently a member of a regular service. Aramaic, not Persian, was the usual diplomatic language of the empire and, as an Aramaic inscription at Taxila shows, was not confined to the west of it. Persian had only recently been written at all; a Persian nobleman's education 'in nothing else but to ride and to shoot and to tell the truth' (p. 78) does not seem to leave much room for literary studies. It is likely, indeed, that Darius himself and all his chief nobles were illiterate, 'it was written and read to me', he says of his Behistun Inscription; but the Scribes, all or most of them drawn from the old civilised peoples, had behind them a tradition of orderly business correspondence and filing reaching back for many centuries; and the kings knew well how to use secretaries. Darius is credited with an order (though perhaps not in the picturesque form given by Herodotos, v, 95; vi, 94) to 'bring forward' the question of Athens regularly; and the king in the *Book of Esther* (vi, 1; romance, but well informed), finding himself sleepless at night, sends for a scribe to bring and read him some files.

In the last resort, however, there was only one safeguard: the traditional and strong loyalty of Persians to their king; and only one way of governing: that the king himself must work hard. Xenophon's Socrates (see n. 44) depicts him (though it is an idealised picture) as constantly occupied with the inspection, in person or through trusted officers (the 'King's Eye' of Aristophanes' *Acharnians*), of both the military efficiency and the attention to economic affairs of the governors in all parts of the empire. Only so, in the long run, could the traditional loyalty of powerful and distant governors be held; and when some later kings neglected business, falling victims to the manifold opportunities for luxury and sensuality which their position afforded, it was not held. The last century of the empire's history is largely a history of revolts.

But Darius did attend to business. One of the documents which show him doing so is the famous Gadates Inscription: a letter of Darius addressed to a governor in Ionia, set up, in an Ionic translation, by the priests of a sanctuary of Apollo near Magnesia, as a charter of their immunity granted by the Great King. Long afterwards, under the Roman Empire, when the original was growing faint after the lapse of centuries, a new copy was set up; the spelling is largely adapted to the Greek *koine* of the time, but traces of the Ionic survive both in spelling and idiom. That it is a later forgery has been argued; but if so, it is remarkable in its resemblance to the style of Darius' Persian inscriptions (which would hardly have been known to later Greeks) and in its introduction of matter irrelevant to the local priestly interests:

> King of Kings Darius, son of Hystaspes, to his servant [in Greek, 'slave'] Gadates thus says:
>
> I hear that you are not in all things obeying my orders; for in that you are cultivating my land, introducing food-crops from beyond Euphrates [Syria, Abar-Nahara?] into lower Asia, I commend your policy, and for this great credit will be given to you in the house of the King. But in that you are causing my intention on behalf of the gods to be forgotten, I shall give you, if you do not change your course, cause to know that I am angered; for you have levied tribute from the sacred gardeners of Apollo, and ordered them to dig unhallowed soil, not knowing my feeling towards the god, who spoke all truth to the Persians, and——[45]

Here the stone is broken off. Alike in its manifestation of the Persian zeal for agriculture, in its reference to the systematic recording of good service,[46] and in its uninhibited disregard of the feelings of the officer thus rebuked 'in the hearing of the men', to whom the Secretary must have been ordered to communicate the message, it seems typical of Darius. Darius appears unconcerned to foster the prestige of his governor. Cyrus, according to Xenophon,[47] had advised his satraps to 'imitate him' in the splendour of their courts; but Darius had seen the dangers that might arise from over-mighty subjects. He was concerned for the prestige of government, but of one man only, the king.

[45] Dittenberger, *SIG*³, 22; *GHI* (1969), no. 12; rejected (characteristically) by Beloch as 'eine plumpe Fälschung im Interesse der Kirche', *GG* I, i, p. 41 (detailed argument in II' ii, pp. 154f); defended on grounds of style and of the traces of old Ionic by Nachmanson, *HGI* no. 10. For 'forcing the priests to dig unhallowed ground', compare Cambyses, dealing with Egyptian priests, p. 90.

[46] Cf. Esther vi, 1ff; H. viii, 85; Thk. i, 129 (with the same phrase, 'in my house').

[47] *Cyrus*, viii, 6, 11ff.

One of the most far-reaching of all Darius' economic projects was the attempt to foster the commercial use of the southern seas.

Far back in the Bronze Age sailors had already ventured on these waters; African and Indian archaeology will probably show us more of this. The apparent but still mysterious signs of contact between the civilisations of Sumer and the Indus region may be due to contact by sea. Later Egyptian expeditions to 'Punt' (Somaliland?) are well known, especially through the pictorial record of that of Queen Hatshepsut. Pharaoh Necho had attempted in vain to extend to the Red Sea (the 'Arabian Gulf' of the Greeks) a canal, driven eastward from the Nile already under the Middle Kingdom to irrigate the Wadi Tumilat.[48] Darius, who may, as Cameron says, have passed through the wadi on his way to Egypt, now completed the enterprise, and erected five great stelae of red granite to testify to his success. Trilingual cuneiform inscriptions (as at Behistun) give the text: 'Says Darius the King: I am a Persian. From Persia I conquered Egypt. I ordered that this canal be dug from the river which is called Nile, which flows in Egypt, to the sea which goes from Persia. Then the canal was dug as I commanded, and ships sailed from Egypt through this canal to Persia, according to my will.' In the Egyptian text, which was fuller, 'twenty-four ships with tribute for Persia' appear; and the curt statement of conquest was delicately replaced by a representation of the Two Niles (the Earthly and the Heavenly Nile) 'binding the lands', with the inscription 'I have given you all the lands, all the Fenkhu [Phoenicians], all the bows . . . all the peoples of the isles.' There follows a list of subject peoples, twenty-four in number, among which, appropriately to the geographical setting, 'Cush and Put', Ethiopia and Libya, figure alongside Egypt. (It does not, surely, follow, as Olmstead has it, that each had a satrap of its own.) Also on the list, making its first appearance in a western document, is India.[49]

The appearance of India at this point in Darius' annals is appropriate. Significantly, Herodotos mentions the canal (whose completion by Darius he has already *narrated* in his book on Egypt) twice again in

[48] O., pp. 145ff. It seems now less likely the canal was really driven through to the Red Sea by Seti I (as per How and Wells, *Comm. on H.* ii, p. 158). On Necho's effort, completed by Darius, see H., *ib.*; cf. iv, 42.

[49] O. pp. 145–7, 149; Weissbach, *Keilinschr. der Achäm.* (Dar. Suez *c*, trn., p. 105); R. G. Kent, 'Old Persian Texts, I: the Darius Suez *c* Inscription', in *JNES* I (1942); Scheil in *Bull. de l'Inst. français du Caire*, XXX (1931).

Book iv (39, 42), in his fascinating section on the limits of the known world and their exploration; for eastern exploration and the canal, though he does not appear to realise it, had a common significance in the attempt (taken up again by Alexander and the Ptolemies) to increase the use of sea-transport in the Indian Ocean. They may well have come into Herodotos' ken together, perhaps through Zopyros, whose family touches the story of western exploration in this same section (43, 2). Herodotos, however, credits Darius not with economic and strategic foresight, but with the same wide-eyed and childlike curiosity that was a part of his own genius:

'Darius wished to know about that Indian river which is the only other river in the world to produce crocodiles' [*sc.*, other than the Nile; the Niger, reached by Libyan explorers, having been identified with the Nile's upper reaches[50]]. 'About this river he wished to know where it came out into the sea; so he sent ships, manned by men whom he trusted to report truly, among others Skylax, a man of Karyanda' [in Karia, and quite near Halikarnassos. It is not stated that Skylax commanded the expedition]. 'They started from the city of Kaspatyros' [better, Kaspapyros;[51] at or near Kabul?] 'and the land of the Paktües, and sailed downstream towards the dawn and the sunrise to the sea; and thence by sea, sailing west, in the thirtieth month they reached the place from which the Egyptian king [Pharaoh Necho] sent off the Phoenicians, whom I mentioned earlier [chap. 42] to sail round Africa.'[52]

A problem is presented by the facts that the Indus does not flow east, and the Kabul river, in which the explorers might be supposed to have started 'in the land of the Paktües' (Pakhtun, Pathans), is said to be too swift for navigation. Taking this in connection with the length of the voyage, thirty months, and the fact that there are no crocodiles in the Indus today, Myres suggested that Skylax' 'Indian river' was actually the Ganges.[53] But Herodotos is quite capable of getting a point of the compass wrong through a preconception (he does so even at Thermopylai, where he had himself been[54]). There may have been 'muggers' then where there are none now; and we do not know what time-

[50] H. ii, 32f.

[51] Kaspapyros, Hekataios *ap*. Steph. Byz., *s.v.*; Kapyros, Hdt. iv, 44, ms R; Kastapyros, S V; Kaspatyros, A B C P (assimilated to the well-known words Kaspia, Tyros?). But at iii, 102, all mss have Kaspatyros.

[52] H. iv, 44.

[53] *Geog. Journal*, 1896; *Herodotos, Father of History*, pp. 39f.

[54] vii, 176.

consuming relations, friendly or hostile, the expedition may have had with peoples *en route*. Evidence is lacking that the Persians (any more than Alexander) ever reached the Ganges; whereas they certainly did have a province of 'Hindush', and an Indus expedition (but hardly a Ganges expedition) could be reasonably described as 'starting from Kaspapyros' in Gandara. That the fleet ultimately reached Suez, and not only the Persian Gulf, suggests that, like the Hellenistic explorer Hippalos starting in the reverse direction, Skylax' party was borne by the monsoon; but also, that Darius had given instructions to that effect, being interested, as his canal shows, in the enormous possibilities of profit from trade, as in the days of Solomon, between the remotest known east and the Mediterranean.[55]

So Darius prospered. He established the rule of law, adopting as his own the great body of Babylonian case-law already codified long before by Hammurabi and applied by the Assyrians. The Iranian word for 'legal decision', *dat*, appears already, early in his reign, in a Babylonian legal document, in the phrase 'according to the king's *dat* they shall make good',[56] as later in Hebrew, repeatedly in the books of Ezra and Esther. He started the building of great palaces at Sousa, whose name in Persian meant 'the lilies'[57] – the Persians were great lovers of natural beauty – and Persepolis. He ordered the restoration of the Egyptian medical school, the 'House of Life', at Saïs, as Uzahor-resenet tells us, and employed (like Cyrus before him, according to Herodotos) Egyptian doctors at his court.[58] In all his inscriptions he piously gives thanks to God:

'Says Darius the King: For this reason Ahura-Mazda helped me, and the other gods who are: because I was not wicked, nor a liar, nor tyrannical, neither I nor my family. I walked according to right and justice. Neither to [high nor low?] have I done violence.'[59]

The phraseology raises the question of Darius' religion. Was he a Zoroastrian? (Cf. pp. 80, 91, above.) One phrase in particular casts doubt upon the supposition; the phrase 'Ahura-Mazda *and the other gods who are*'. Not only is a tendency to polytheism explicit, though not emphasised, but the word for 'gods', *baga*, does not appear in this sense

[55] References for the earlier phases in *Lyric Age*, pp. 44f, 130f.
[56] O., p. 119 (and ff, on the whole subject).
[57] Ath. xii, 514, from Aristoboulos.
[58] H. iii, 129; cf. 1.
[59] *D.B.* 63 (= col. iv, 13).

in the *Avesta.* The absence of the name of Zarathustra from this and from all Darius' pious expressions is *not* a serious objection, and does not show that Darius 'knew nothing of him', as it is all too easy to say; we should not expect the Emperor Constantine to render thanksgiving to St Paul, nor a Caliph to Muhammad, nor early Protestants to Luther or Calvin. The absence of any mention of the prophet's name in Herodotos is more significant; but all that it really suggests is that he had not yet been elevated to the rank of a divine Saviour, as in the later *Avesta,* and therefore that he probably did *not* belong already to the remote past. *Drauga,* cognate with Gathic *druj,* 'the Lie', is indeed emphasised, and has impressed many as a Zoroastrian expression; but in the context (see p. 90 above), it seems simply to denote political 'deceit'. As Duchesne-Guillemin says, 'drauga ne désigne pas, comme dans les gâthâ, le principe et la caractéristique de tout acte contraire à la justice. La doctrine gâthique est ignorée'.[60] The same applies to Darius' use of the word *khshathra* (Gathic *khshassa*), 'lordship', which in his inscriptions means simply 'empire', without any of the Gathas' religious overtones. Darius, again, uses the term *magu,* 'Magi', for 'priests' (as in Herodotos), and not *athravan,* 'fire-tenders', which the *Avesta* and apparently the Magi themselves used; and under Darius the name of *baga Mithra,* the god Mithras, still figured in the calendar, as it figures among Persian gods in Herodotos.

No, Darius was a worshipper indeed of Ahura-Mazda, but no strict Zoroastrian. The 'high-church' Zoroastrian doctrine was probably preserved rather by the Magi themselves, the defeated clerical or peace party, to regain influence with the kings (already quite noticeably under Xerxes[61]) as the memory of the great civil war receded. Under Artaxerxes I, 'Zoroastrian' names for the months were adopted. Modern readers have been impressed both by the great constructive works of Darius and by the attractive characteristics of Zarathustra and his religion. The desire to associate the two follows naturally; but it does not appear to be gratified by a close study of the evidence.[62]

Darius, indeed, as a conqueror, restorer and organiser, bears com-

[60] *Zoroastre,* p. 122 (and cf. the whole section, 120ff, 'Darius était-il Zoroastrien?'). Zaehner, *Zoroastrianism,* p. 157, agrees, but still finds 'the religion of Darius . . . very closely akin to that of Zoroaster'.

[61] Duchesne-Guillemin, *op. cit.* pp. 125ff, 'Xerxès et son zoroastrisme'; Zaehner, p. 159.

[62] The present writer formerly adopted the theory of Darius the good Zoroastrian promptly and with enthusiasm, and came over slowly and unwillingly to the contrary view.

parison with Augustus; and, like Augustus, he had waded through slaughter to a throne. Gentle he was not; even when firmly in power, the 'business king' remained stern and terrible; capable, indeed, of a cruelty which was alien to the Roman world (except, of course, when dealing with refractory slaves). Herodotos tells a story of how, when Darius, with the empire now firmly organised, was planning new conquests, a Persian named Oiobazos, who had three sons serving in the army, asked as a favour that one might be left at home. Darius said quietly, 'as though to a friend making a modest request, "They shall all stay." Oiobazos was overjoyed, thinking his sons were exempted from military service; but Darius ordered their commanding officers to put to death all Oiobazos' sons. So they were left behind then and there, dead; and Darius marched to Chalcedon on the Bosporos, where a bridge of boats had been laid across the strait', to cross into Europe.[63]

The story might not be true; but it is an early tradition of how Darius was considered capable of behaving. In any case, we have Darius' own word for the events of the beginning of his reign, including what we might willingly forget: the ravaged faces of Phraortes and Tritantaikhmes, pinioned to await a horrible death, 'in the gates' at Ecbatana and Arbela, until 'all the people had seen them' and Darius gave the order.

[63] H. iv, 84f.

ADDITIONAL NOTE TO CHAPTER VI

THE PERSIAN EMPIRE ACCORDING TO HERODOTUS

Herodotos' lists of Darius' satrapies and Xerxes' military and naval contingents add flesh and blood to the skeleton provided by the royal inscriptions, which are (it should hardly be necessary to say) not administrative documents but 'propagandist' proclamations of the royal power. The chief importance of the Persian lists to the historian is, indeed, that they confirm the reality (which is by no means to say the infallibility) of Herodotos' information. There are indeed some probably accidental omissions in his satrapy-list, including, most curiously, the name of his own kinsmen the Dorians of Asia, whose submission to Cyrus has been recorded in Book i, 174, and whose contingent appears in the fleet in vii, 93. One might well suspect an early textual omission of *kai Dorieon* between *kai Aioleon* and *kai Karon*. In satrapy XVI, too, *Hyrkanoi* (mentioned in the army-list and in iii, 117) should probably be added to the four other well-known names. On a different footing is the curious absence of the name Arachosia, Arachōtoi (Pers. *Harauvatish*), which is in all the Persian lists but nowhere in Herodotos at all. For some reason unknown, his source must have used a different name for this country (wholly or largely in modern Beluchistan; cf. Strabo, 513). It must have been either included in satrapy XVII or on the borders of this and VII. One might speculate as to whether a bungled spelling or copying of this name underlies that of the mysterious Aparüitai in satrapy VII (H. iii, 91, and not found again in any writer[1]); but there still remains the mystery of their absence from the army-list.

In the following table, in the list of all the peoples named in the satrapy-list, I have given one or occasionally two names of countries in each satrapy, in capitals, which might serve as a convenient 'short title' for the satrapy.

The known Persian lists, now five in number, are to be found

[1] But cf. the Parüētai of Ptolemy, in Arachosia (*Geog.* vi, 20), and the Apartaei of Pliny (*NH* vi, 8/21); the latter are north of the Caucasus, a long way from Arachosia; but cf. the widely separated Kaspioi of H. himself, in satrapies XI and XV.

most conveniently and completely translated and discussed in R. G. Kent's article, 'Old Persian Texts: IV', in *JNES* II (1943), and the Egyptian ('Suez') list in G. G. Cameron's 'Darius, Egypt and the "Lands beyond the Sea"', in the same volume, immediately following the above.

The last two columns in the Table show the distribution, by satrapies according to the list in H. iii, of the infantry contingents under named commanders, mounted troops and ships, recorded in the list of Xerxes' armament in Book vii. That the list of infantry commanders is not to be regarded as equivalent to a list of satraps seems to emerge clearly from close study. Some of the commanders are satraps, commanding the troops of their provinces: Akhaimenes, the king's brother, commands the fleet from his satrapy of Egypt (vii, 97, cf. 7), and his cousin, Artaphernes II, Satrap of Lydia, the contingent from Lydia and Mysia in his province. But the Lasonioi and Kabalioi (or Kabēleës) also assigned to this satrapy in iii, 90, are brigaded separately, together with the Milyai, the mountain 'aborigines' of Lykia (H. i, 173). A separate satrapy of these mountain peoples *could* have been formed since the time of Darius; but the difficulties are worse in the case of the Phrygians and Armenians (the 21st division), whose homelands do not seem even to have been contiguous, with Cappadocia and Paphlagonia lying between. The Thracians of Asia (Thünoi and Bithünoi, i, 28) never appear at any other time as a satrapy, though their fighting men were important enough to fill a separate contingent, the 23rd. The two Caucasus satrapies (XVIII and XIX), north of Armenia, account, with their borderlands, for five contingents; nos. II and III (Lydia and Phrygia respectively, with their neighbours) for four, and parts of two more; but there is never a hint later (e.g. in Xenophon) of so many satrapies. Further east, the vast though not rich satrapy of northern Iran (XVI), rated at 300 talents, produces four contingents. Its famous peoples, the Parthians, Chorasmians, Arians, Sogdians, are named separately in all the Persian lists. There seems no reason for Herodotos or his source to have alleged that they formed but one satrapy unless, administratively, under Darius, they did; and if we accept the authenticity of the Greek list and of all the Persian lists *as lists of satrapies*, we have to suppose that Darius momentarily combined them, only, almost immediately, to change his mind; and then that this very short-lived arrangement was nevertheless the one preserved in memory or in a document to be reported to the historian. The much richer satrapy south of this, paying 600 talents – a sum exceeded only by 'India', Babylonia and Egypt – produces three infantry contingents, plus the 8000 'cowboy' cavalry of Sagartia, armed with lassoos; and one of the infantry formations, the last on the list (29), is that of 'the deported people' from the islands in the Persian Gulf. (One is reminded of the German 999 Division of 1944, formed from convicts.) It seems unlikely that they had a satrap of their own.

My conclusion is that the Persian military organization was *not* (as is held, e.g., by Olmstead, *P.E.*, pp. 239–45) identical with the administrative, though, since both were based on natural, ethnic divisions, they bore a considerable resemblance. One might compare the organization of the British army of recent times, in which, generally, each county had an infantry regiment, and each infantry 'line' regiment a county; but some counties were combined to recruit a regiment (e.g. the 'Oxford and Bucks.'), and some large counties, such as Yorkshire and Lancashire, had more regiments than one.

THE PERSIAN EMPIRE ACCORDING TO HERODOTOS

THE SATRAPIES

Serial no. and amt. of tribute (H. iii, 90ff)	Names of peoples (H., *ib.*)	Persian equivalents	Infantry contingents (order in H. vii, 62ff)	Cavalry (H. vii, 84ff), numbers of ships (89ff)
I T. 400	IONIA	Yauna	—	100
	Magnētes in Asia		—	
	Aiolians in Asia		—	60
	Karians	Karka	—	70
	Lykians		—	50
	Milyai		24 (with II, below)	
	Pamphylians		—	30
[Omitted, H. iii:	Dorians in Asia]		—	30
II T. 500	Mysians		} 22	
	LYDIA	Sfarda (= Sardis)		
	Lasonioi		} 24 (with Milyai, see I)	
	Kabalioi			
III T. 360	Hellespont	'They of the Sea'	—	100
	PHRYGIA		21 (with Armenioi, XIII)	
	Thracians in Asia		23	
	Paphlagones		19 (with Matiēnoi, XVIII)	
	Mariandünoi		} 20	
	'Syrians' (Gk. name of Kappadokai, H. i, 72)	Katpatuka		

Serial no. and amt. of tribute (H. iii, 90ff)		Names of peoples (H., *ib.*)	Persian equivalents	Infantry contingents (order in H. vii, 62ff)	Cavalry (H. vii, 84ff), numbers of ships (89ff)
IV	T. 500 'and 360 white horses'	CILICIA (Kilikes)		—	100
V	T. 350	'from Posideion to Egypt', i.e. [SYRIA]	Abar-Nahara (= 'Beyond-the-River')		
		Phoenicia		—	300
		Cyprus		—	150
VI	T. 700, + cost of army of occupation	EGYPT	Mudraya	—	200
		Libyans	Putaya	18	Chariots
VII	T. 170	SATTAGYDIA and GANDARA	Thatagush Gadāra	—	
		Dadikai	}	11	
		Aparütai	[Harauvatish?]	—	
VIII	T. 300	SOUSIANA	Uvja (= Elam)		
		Kissians		3	Cavalry
IX	T. 1000 'and 500 eunuchs'	BABYLONIA and ASSYRIA	Babirush } Athura	5	
X	T. 450	MEDIA 'Parikanoi' (= Paraitakēnoi?)	Mada	2	Cavalry and marines

XI	T. 200	KASPIA	(?) Akaufaciya	(12? – cf. XV)	
		Pausikai	(= 'Mountaineers', cf.	—	
		Pantimathoi	Xerxes, Persepolis *h.*)	—	
		Dareitai		—	
XII	T. 360	BAKTRIA	Baktrish	6 (with XV)	Cavalry
XIII	T. 400	Paktües		13	
		ARMENIA	Armina	21 (with Phryges, III)	
XIV	T. 600	SAGARTIA and	Asagarta	—	8000 cavalry
		SARANGIA [Drangiana]	Zaranka	14	
		Outioi		} 15	
		Mükoi			
		'Anaspastoi' [tribesmen deported to Persian Gulf Is.]		29	
XV	T. 250	SAKAI Amyrgioi	Saka Haumavarga	6 (with XII)	Cavalry and marines
		Kaspioi		(12? – cf. XI)	Cavalry
XVI	T. 300	PARTHIA	Parthava	} 9	
		Chorasmioi	Uvarazmiya		
		Sogdoi	Suguda	10	
		Arioi	Araiva	8	
[H. iii, 117 adds:		Hyrkanoi]	Varkana	4	
XVII	T. 400	PARIKANIA		16	Cavalry
		Ethiopians of Asia		7 (with XX)	
XVIII	T. 200	Matiēnoi	(?) 'Mountaineers', cf. XI	19 (with Paphlagones, III)	
		Saspeires		} 28	
		ALARODIA			

Serial no. and amt. of tribute (H. iii, 90ff)	Names of peoples (H., *ib.*)	Persian equivalents	Infantry contingents (order in H. vii, 62ff)	Cavalry (H. vii, 84ff), numbers of ships (89ff)
XIX T. 300	Moschoi TIBARĒNE		} 25	
	Makrōnes Mossünoikoi		} 26	
	Mãres		27 (with Kolchoi, see below)	
XX T. 1000 of gold dust	'INDIA'	Hindush	7 (with XVII, cf. H. vii, 70)	Cavalry, chariots
To these must be added:				
Metropolitan country (iii, 97; vii, 61, 83f, 96, 1):				
(Untaxed)	PERSIA	Parsa	1	Cavalry and marines
		in addition to the 10,000, horse and foot, 'Immortals' or Guard Division.		
Later conquests in Europe (iii, 96; vii, 95, 185):				
Tribute, unspecified	THRACE and MACEDONIA	Skudra	Troops, unspecified	Greek ships, 120
	Cyclades		—	,, ,, 17
Unadministered frontier areas (iii, 97, and army-list):				
'Gifts'	Kolchis and Caucasus		27 (with Mãres, XIX)	
,,	Ethiopians of the Egyptian frontier	Kushiya	} 17	
,,	Arabs	Arabaya	} 17	Camel corps

Of the gifts, H. says: 'The Ethiopians on the borders of Egypt, whom Cambyses conquered, brought every second year (and still do) two quart-measures of unrefined gold, and 200 trunks of ebony and five Ethiopian boys and twenty big elephant tusks; and the Kolchians and their neighbours, as far as mount Caucasus (this is the limit of the Persian empire) . . . every four years, 100 boys and 100 maidens.' [One is reminded of the fate of Circassians under the Turks.] 'And the Arabians brought 1000 talents of frankincense every year.'

Chapter VII

The Persians enter Europe

It is the natural tendency of all conquerors (as Thucydides' Athenians said at Mēlos) to extend their conquests as far as they can. Most men love power for its own sake, and in any man who has attained a position of great power against opposition – any man who, therefore, 'has what it takes' to do such a thing – the desire to extend that power may be taken for granted. The desires to build, to construct, to tidy things up, or to direct other people for their own good (the manifestation of a paternal instinct) are often supposed to be put forward as mere rationalisations of the lust for power; but this is often probably unfair. The passion to construct or arrange, equally normal in *homo faber* and found often in the most disinterested forms, as in artists and poets, is, rather, found *along with* the lust for power quite as normally as without it. The man who enjoys exercising power, even ruthlessly, while alleging like Darius that he is doing God service, is not always a hypocrite.

Greed is *not* usually an important ingredient in a conqueror's character. The famous conqueror inevitably possesses or controls, before he is in mid-career, the means to luxury, beyond the most gargantuan powers of consumption. Moreover, the great man of action, even the 'great bad man', is often personally austere. But avarice may be a very important motive in the 'average, sensual' *poor* men, who 'jump on the band-wagon' and form a conqueror's armies; which is why the thesis of the importance of economic, material motives is not controverted by insistence on the idealism or personal austerity of a leader. Alexander reminded his soldiers precisely of the revolution which he and his father before him had wrought *in their standards of* life.[1]

It required therefore no curtain-lecture from Atossa to fire Darius with the project of extending his power beyond the Aegean, nor yet

[1] Arrian, vii, 9 (the speech at Opis).

the motive, imputed by Herodotos, of avenging the Scythian raids into Asia more than a hundred years before, to make him turn his attention next, after subduing the Punjab, to the north coasts of the Black Sea.[2] Nor was he, at least primarily, in search of a frontier, either defensible – for that, the coast would have done very well – or ethnic, though with the eastern Greeks subdued and the western free, an Ionian revolt might no doubt have led him in any case to seek that in the end. There is a charming conversation, reported by Plutarch, between Pyrrhos, before he attacked the Romans, and his Greek diplomatist Kineas, which sums up in little the psychology of a conqueror:

'If God gives us victory over the Romans,' said Kineas, 'what use shall we make of our victory?' 'We shall win all Italy,' said Pyrrhos; 'and then Sicily, rich, populous, and at present in anarchy, is simply stretching out her hands for a conqueror.' 'True,' said Kineas, 'but is that all?' 'God grant us victory,' said Pyrrhos, 'and we will use this as the prelude to an ambitious enterprise.' And he pointed out that Carthage had proved very vulnerable to an invader (Agathokles) with fewer resources than his. 'And if we could win those lands,' he went on, 'none of our present enemies [in Greece] could stand against us.' 'No,' said Kineas; 'clearly then we could recapture Macedonia and be supreme in Greece. But what then?' 'Then,' said Pyrrhos, smiling, 'we will have peace and sit at our ease and drink and be merry together.' 'Well,' said Kineas, 'is there anything to prevent our drinking and taking our ease *now*, without all this bloodshed, and without taking (and giving others) so much trouble?' Pyrrhos had nothing to say in answer to this, and was rather annoyed; but he could not bear to lay aside his ambitions.[3]

In India, Darius had drawn rein at the arid country east of the Sutlej. A highland people, the Persians, as we have seen, did not like hot sandy deserts, and had even withdrawn from the attempt to tax and administer those parts of Arabia which had been subject to Babylon. Darius had now visited successively the north-east, south-west (perhaps) and south-east frontiers of his empire. The north-west remained, and thither he proceeded with a great army, in or not long before 513.[4]

[2] H. iii, 134; iv, 1. [3] Plut. *Pyrrhos* 14 (abridged).

[4] The *Capitoline Annals* (*IG* XIV, 1297; a date-chart in Gk., at Rome, of the same type as the *Parian Marble*, and ending in A.D. 18) gives a date 12 years after Cambyses' conquest of Egypt; but dates the latter 523/2 ('540 years ago'), and the *Skythika* '528 years ago', 511/10 B.C.; but at the same epoch as the murder of Hipparchos (probably 514). Hammond (*GH*, p. 179) relies too implicitly on such rubbishy evidence. However, we may say certainly after the conquest of Samos (517?), and long enough before the fall of

Samos, where the island lordship of Polykrates had been held together for a time by his secretary Maiandrios, had by now fallen to the Persians. A possible date is given by the List of Sea-Powers, which makes a sea-power of Samos end in 517. Otanes, he who according to Herodotos had organized the Conspiracy of the Seven and thereafter eschewed any desire to be king, had been sent by Darius to Asia Minor with an army; and by a sudden attack he seized the island, and installed as vassal ruler, Syloson, the brother of Polykrates whom Polykrates had driven into exile. Maiandrios, who on the death of Polykrates had proposed, we are told, the restoration of a free state, but found it too dangerous to lay down his power (so that 'desiring to be the most righteous of men, he was not able'), offered no resistance, and retired to Sparta; a brother of his, Lykarētos, entered the Persian service, and was afterwards governor of Lemnos; but some fighting broke out after the surrender, and led to a massacre.[5] Lesbos and Chios accepted Persian overlordship, and Darius was able to summon the fleets of all Asian Greece to support him in his enterprise on the Black Sea. Mandrokles, one of the skilful engineers of Samos, superintended the construction of the bridge of boats across the narrows of the Bosporus, by which the great host crossed without endless ferrying, and was well paid for his work. Herodotos saw at Samos a painting, which Mandrokles set up in the great Temple of Hera in proud commemoration, showing the bridge, and King Darius sitting in state, while the army marched over. Characteristically, Darius first took ship up the straits on a sight-seeing trip, 'to see the ocean'. He also commemorated the crossing, as he had commemorated the construction of his Suez canal, by setting up two monuments, with inscriptions in Greek and cuneiform; but these the historian did not see, save for one stone 'covered with Assyrian writing'; for in a later generation the men of Byzantion demolished them and 'taking them into the city, used them for building the altar for Artemis Orthosia'.[6] It is not beyond the bounds of possibility that they, or some parts of them, may yet be found by archaeologists among the foundations of later Constantinople.

Hippias at Athens for him to marry his daughter to the son of Hippoklos of Lampsakos because of the 'influence with Darius' which Hippoklos then acquired (p. 133). 'About 516', Cary in *CAH* IV, 212; 'bald nach 515', Meyer *GdA* III (1937), 737; 513, O.147.

[5] H. iii, 139–49. 'Thalassocracy-List' from Diodoros in Eusebios (ed. Schoene, I, p. 225); date 517 by working back from Xerxes' invasion; 513 Eus. *Canones*, ed. Schoene, II, p. 98; cf. Myres in *JHS* XXVII; M. Miller in *Historia*, forthcoming; Lykaretos, cf. H. v, 27.

[6] iv, 87, 2; and, on the whole episode, 85–9 *passim*.

Herodotos prefaces the Samian story with a charming incident, characteristic of his strength and weakness: his greatness as a storyteller and reporter, and his lack of any but the most primitive ideas on historical causation. Syloson, years before when in exile, had been, like many other Greeks, traders, soldiers and tourists, as he says (iii, 139), in Egypt at the time of Cambyses' invasion. 'He was shopping in the market at Memphis, wearing a red cloak; and Darius, who was serving as a guardsman of Cambyses and was not yet a man of any great account, coveted that cloak, and went up to him and offered to buy it. Syloson, seeing that he wanted it very badly, said, by inspiration, "I am not selling this for any money; but I will give it to you, if you simply must have it." . . . Syloson thought that his good nature had meant a dead loss; but later . . . when Darius had become king . . . he went up to Sousa and sat down at the portals of the palace, and said that he was a benefactor of the King.' And this was why Darius sent Otanes to take Samos for him. From this time on, we shall continually find Herodotos telling of Greeks, usually exiles, influencing Persian policy: Dēmokēdes the doctor, the family of Peisistratos, the Aleuadai of Larisa, Dāmarātos of Sparta. Their presence at Persian headquarters need not be doubted; their alleged influence is clearly saga, not history. To the Persians, these exiles or defectors were pawns in the game; sources of intelligence, and sometimes potentially useful agents for subversion and for the government of conquered states. The stories of their conversations with and sage advice to kings and generals may in some cases very well go back to what they themselves related of their interviews, but this does not make them first-class historical material; it is only to be expected that unsuccessful men would, even in their own conscious memory, embellish the story of how they influenced history in their little hour, when they had speech with the great.

Darius marched north through Thrace, subduing the tribes; those of the south-east submitted without fighting; the Getai, whose territory reached to the Danube, 'the most warlike and righteous of the Thracians', who held a belief in immortality, gave battle and 'were immediately subdued'.[7] At a pass leading west into the central Balkans – the headwaters of the river Tearos, which drained into the Hebros – he is said to have set up another inscription, though whether it really

[7] H. iv, 93. For Thracian and Scythian religion and customs, see *Lyric Age*, pp. 96f, 122–7, 366ff.

celebrated the merits of the drinking water may be doubted.[8] But he was not concerned with the west immediately, but to explore and if possible secure the coasts of the Black Sea. Not content with what Greeks could tell him (if they would), he had already, if we may trust one of the more probable-sounding passages of the unreliable Ktesias, had a reconnaissance carried out by Persians. Ariaramnes, satrap of Cappadocia, crossed the Pontos with a light squadron (thirty fifty-oared galleys) 'to take prisoners, both men and women', no doubt for interrogation; and among those secured was a brother of the Scythian king, found languishing under arrest, having incurred disfavour.[9] Not unnaturally the Scythian king sent a strong protest, which Darius is said to have answered uncompromisingly. . . . But in any case Darius was, like any great king of his age, unashamedly bent on honourable aggression, and the precise *casus belli* alleged is of little importance.

From the Bosporus the Ionian naval allies sailed north, under orders to meet the army at the Danube. What information Darius had, on which to base directions for a rendezvous, we do not know; but there were probably Greeks versed in the Pontic trade, who had sailed the river and could agree on and guide the king to a suitable crossing-point, clear of the delta. Arriving first (for the fleet could move much faster than the army could march, especially with some opposition) the Greeks made a pontoon-bridge of their ships, on which the army marched over and disappeared into the steppe, leaving the Greeks on guard at the crossing.[10]

About the campaign north of the Danube, it must be confessed that we know nothing. Seasoned soldier as Darius was, and no doubt informed as to the size of the Pontos, we may acquit him of lunatic ideas, such as that he might march right round the sea and return by the Caucasus; it is therefore unlikely that he proposed, as Herodotos says, to dismantle his bridge and take the soldiers from the fleet with him, and needed to be dissuaded from this course by Koes, commander of the squadron from Mytilene; nor is it likely that he told the Greeks they might go home after sixty days if he had not reappeared; though the statement that he did reappear after somewhat over sixty days may be true. Herodotos conducts him on a baffled march all over the Ukraine (much too far for the time allotted), bringing into his story all the

[8] H. iv, 90ff.
[9] Photios' *Epitome*, § 16f (p. 38b Bekker).
[10] H. iv, 89, 97f.

tribes of south Russia,[11] about which he had collected a considerable amount of information (half the long fourth book in our texts). It looks very much as though Greeks of Pontos, whom he may have questioned, being unwilling (in characteristic Greek style) to say that they knew nothing, had provided him with a romance, which Herodotos, who unlike most Greeks had probably had no occasion to see any military service, was not able to criticise. One concrete detail is included: that Darius built eight forts about seven miles apart at the furthest point of his penetration, 'of which the ruins were still there in my time'.[12] Since, however, these forts are said to have been on the banks of the river Oaros, east of the Don, which both armies are said to have crossed (without details as to the method of crossing a river not much less formidable than the Danube), it seems scarcely possible that they were the work of an expedition from the west. If they really existed and were really Persian, it is more likely that they were founded (to protect coastal agriculturists against raids from the steppe?) by some sea-borne expedition like that of Ariaramnes.

The romance gives quite a vivid account of Scythian tactics: avoiding battle with the powerful invading army, blocking up wells and destroying pasture; and of the inability of the Persians, mostly on foot, to bring their mounted enemies to bay. But Darius had encountered similar nomads in the Sakai of his eastern marches, and had somehow managed, as he tells us, to capture the chief, Skunkha, and many thousands of his people. If he really hoped to strike a weakening blow at the European nomads, he must have had some plan; hoping perhaps to 'fetch a compass' north of them and drive them towards the sea. Whatever plan he did have, it was a failure. Not only do all our sources say so, but (what is of more significance, in view of the weakness of our sources) subsequent events bear out their statements. The sources say, perhaps truly, that he narrowly escaped total disaster, getting out with the loss of a rear division, or abandoning his sick and wounded.[13] He certainly suffered some temporary loss of prestige.

[11] H. iv, 118–36.

[12] *ib.* 124.

[13] Sick and wounded left to keep fires burning when D. marches out, telling them that he means to fall on the enemy, H. iv, 135f; bridge towed away before the last tenth of the army could cross, lest the enemy should cross too, Ktes. 17 (p. 38b, Photios), which sounds like romance. Justin (ii, 5) follows Ktesias; Strabo (vii, 305) believes that D. operated only west of the Dniester, where, after nearly perishing from thirst on the steppe, he realised his mistake and turned back just in time; but it is unlikely that S. had

Back at the Danube bridge, the Ionians waited. Here, among the Greeks, we come back to a definite though not infallible tradition, derived from men who were there. The sixty days, which Darius had given as the probable limit of his absence, passed, and there was no word from him. No messenger could get through the hostile country. Then there appeared, not Persians but Scythians in force, with the report that Darius was on the run; let them no longer be afraid, 'but sail away as free men, giving thanks to heaven and the Scythians; and as for your master that was, we will deal with him to such purpose that he will never invade any country again'. There was, no doubt, excitement in the camp, and some feeling that to leave the Persians stranded in Scythia would be a good thing to do; but that Miltiades of Athens, lord of the Gallipoli Peninsula and its cities, only newly made subject, openly proposed demolishing the bridge in a council of the commanders 'as Herodotos says' has often been doubted. The proposal, if made, could not have been kept a secret; every Greek ruler had enemies, and among those present was Hippoklos, tyrant of Lampsakos, with which city Miltiades' family in the Chersonese had a long-standing feud. If it was made, clearly it was not from the Scythians that Miltiades had to flee for his life soon afterwards, as Herodotos himself says later, but from the wrath of Darius, and he can hardly have returned to his principality in the next fifteen years. In any case the assembled Greek tyrants, who as Darius' governors in their respective cities felt that the king was their support against rising democratic sentiment, succeeded in restraining any mutinous movement; and Darius, after a moment of anxiety when he arrived in darkness on the north bank and found that the bridge had been towed away from that side 'for fear of the Scythians', was able to cross to safety with his sorely tried army.[14]

any independent tradition; rather, he gives a sensible 'reconstruction' such as a modern writer might. Cf. Meyer's notes, *GdA* IV, i (1939), pp. 106–7.

[14] H. iv, 133, 136–42; on Miltiades, 137, and cf. vi, 40, where the chronology is difficult and must be either mistaken or corrupt in the mss. H. must be wrong on one point or the other. *Either* (1) M. made no such daring proposal, but pretended that he had when he wished to gain favour at Athens twenty years later (a view as old as Thirlwall, *Hist. of Greece*, II, chap. xiv and app. ii, p. 486, and favoured by Meyer (*loc. cit.* p. 108n), Berve, *Miltiades* (*Hermes*, Einzelschrift, 1937), pp. 40f, and others); *or* (2) M. really fled from the Persians, not the Scyths as H. says, and must have returned to his principality only at the time of the Ionian revolt; as is assumed, e.g., by Cary in *CAH* IV, p. 214, and argued with cogency and ingenuity by Grote (vol. IV, long note on pp. 368f) and Wade-Gery, *Essays in Gk. Hist.*, pp. 158ff (reprinted from *JHS* LXXI). One ancient writer alone says that M. fled from the Persians after the Scythian expedition: Nepos (*Miltiades*, 3), who, as

'Darius returned through Thrace, and came to Sestos in the Chersonese, whence he crossed over in his ships to Asia, leaving as general in Europe Megabazos', one of his most trusted officers, with a large army.[15] Megabazos subdued the Samian colony of Perinthos, which, in spite of a previous disaster at the hands of the Paiones, stubbornly refused to submit until it was forced to; then he turned westwards, 'bringing under the King's peace every city and tribe of the region; for Darius' directive to him was "to conquer Thrace".' The region actually affected was the north Aegean coast and its hinterland; and here, apparently in not more than one campaign (for he is said to have returned to Asia with his prisoners before Darius returned to Sousa), Megabazos had reached the frontier of Macedonia, and received the symbolic 'earth and water', tokens of formal submission, from King Amyntas.[16]

Herodotos has a story that the king's son Alexander massacred the Persian ambassadors and all their suite, when they became insolent to Macedonian ladies after dinner, and hushed up the matter by giving a large bribe and the hand of his sister Gügaie in marriage, to Boubares, the officer sent to enquire what had become of them. This looks like an invention by Alexander himself, later on, when the Persians had been repulsed and he wished to conciliate the Greeks. The marriage, and also the fact that Alexander himself took part, perforce, in Xerxes' invasion, were 'public' facts that could not be denied; but his explanation was successfully 'sold' to Herodotos and his (Athenian?) informants. This is the Alexander, who also entered for the Olympic Games (200 yards), surviving an appeal against him as not being a Greek by claiming that his house, the Argeadai, were descended from early kings of Argos, and according to Herodotos 'ran a dead heat with the winner'; though, as his name is not in our list of winners, derived from Hippias of Elis, either this is wrong too, or else he was beaten in a deciding race.[17]

Megabazos' time was too short to let him penetrate far to the northwest; he did not personally enter Macedonia. Probably his furthest

---

Grote says, 'may be substantially right', but this little work is such a muddle (e.g. confusing M. with his namesake and predecessor, and making the Battle of Marathon follow immediately after the bridge episode), that I feel very strongly that if Nepos *is* right it is only by accident. Cf. pp. 218–20, below.

[15] H. iv, 143f. [16] H. v, 1; 18, 1.

[17] *ib.* 18–21; the massacre story doubted by commentators, cf. Macan, etc., *ad.*

point was near its borders, at Lake Prasias, where he 'tried', says Herodotos, presumably unsuccessfully, to force the surrender of a tribe of lake-dwellers. Their village was built 'on tall piles in the middle of the lake, with one narrow way in; . . . and their law is that every man who marries a wife must fetch from Mount Orbēlos and plant three piles; and each man marries several wives. . . . They tether their small children by the leg, lest they should fall off; and they feed fish to their horses and beasts of burden.' There was a great plenty of fish in the lake, which they used to catch in basketwork traps, let down through a trapdoor belonging to each man's hut. Megabazos did, however, conquer the horse-riding Paiones east of this point; they mustered to meet him on the coast road, but Megabazos, with guides from Thrace, thrust a column over an inland pass and seized their villages in the Strymon basin in rear of the fighting men. Several thousands of them were deported to Phrygia, by special order of Darius, we are told, who had been impressed by the industry of a Paionian woman whom he had seen in Asia. Two young Paionians, aspiring to become chiefs under Persian overlordship, attended his camp at Sardis, and caused their sister to be seen by him finely dressed and leading a horse to water, with a pitcher on her head, leading the horse with the crook of her arm, and spinning flax as she went. Darius was more impressed than they had intended, and decided that he must 'import' those people.[18]

Darius meanwhile had been rewarding faithful service. Koes, the admiral from Mytilene, was made at his own request 'tyrant' of his city; Histiaios, already tyrant of Miletos, who was credited with having taken the lead in holding the Ionians to their allegiance during the crisis, asked and was granted the lands of Myrkinos on the Ēdōnian coast, at the limit of the territory since pacified by Megabazos. He promptly sailed there and set about colonising; but Megabazos, when he reached the area overland, was impressed with its strategic and economic potentialities; its wealth in silver-mines and fine timber, and its already considerable population both of natives and Greeks. When he returned with his army and the Paionian captives, he suggested to the king that in such a place a man as enterprising as Histiaios might found a principality too powerful for the empire's convenience. Darius took the suggestion seriously, sent for Histiaios for 'important consultations', and on the pretext of taking him as a confidential

[18] *ib.* 12–16.

adviser carried him off to gilded captivity at Sousa.[19] Miletos was left under the government of his deputy, Aristagoras, his cousin and brother-in-law.[20]

All this time Byzantion, whose tyrant Ariston had served with his contingent in the Danube, and Kalchādōn (Chalcedon), which is not mentioned in Herodotos' list of commanders (the city was therefore probably charged with guarding the bridge over the Bosporos), had apparently been in revolt; and Kalchadon is said to have planned to destroy the Bosporos bridge, and to have demolished Darius' monument.[21] Darius now planned retribution. The situation accounts for Darius having returned to Sardis by boat across the Dardanelles, and confirms the tradition that his Scythian campaign had been a fiasco. The fact that he was apparently not in a position to fall upon the Bosporus cities at once suggests, further, that Megabazos' army left in Europe included the bulk of the troops who had come back from Scythia, rather than, as Ktesias says, a tenth of them. Darius returns to show himself safe and sound at his base, and leaves the army to show, by a powerful offensive in Thrace, that its strength was unbroken. The Bosporos cities could wait. Megabazos' army was now brought back to the straits. The Paionian country could not be garrisoned, so the Paiones, or all of them that could be rounded up, were brought back too; and Histiaios was lured from his north-western colony and not allowed to return.

Darius himself now returned to Sousa, taking Histiaios with him, and leaving 'safe' men in charge in the north-west. His own brother Artaphernes became satrap at Sardis, and another Otanes, son of Sisamnes, a 'royal judge', who had been put to death by Cambyses for alleged reception of bribes, was appointed 'military commander of the sea-coast men'. 'Sea-coast men' sounds like a translation of the already known Persian title of the great satrapy of northern Asia Minor, whose administrative capital was at Daskyleion; since Otanes is not given the title of satrap, he was probably subordinate in political matters to the royal prince Artaphernes. Otanes had a way of settling himself into his chair of office, which gave rise, it has been suggested, to the Greek story that Cambyses had that chair lined with the skin of the occupant's deceased father, and had then appointed Otanes in his father's place, and told him not to forget what he was sitting on. 'This Otanes, then,

[19] H. v. 11; 23f. [20] *ib.* 30, 2. [21] Ktesias, epit. Phot. 17.

who sat on that chair, now succeeded to Megabazos' command. He took Byzantion and Kalchadon, and also Antandros and Lampōnion [in the Troad] and with a fleet from Lesbos he took Lemnos and Imbros, both then still inhabited by Pelasgians. The Lemnians put up a stiff fight, but were finally defeated and suffered severely. Over the remnants of them the Persians installed as governor Lykarētos, the brother of Maiandrios who had been lord of Samos.' Otanes also probably campaigned in eastern Thrace (but there is a break in the sense; some words seem to have dropped out of Herodotos' text). It continues: 'he enslaved and conquered everyone, accusing some of failing to send contingents against the Scythians, and some of harassing Darius' army on its return. These were his achievements during his command.'[22]

Thus Persian power was established and prestige restored on both sides of the straits. For the rest, the forward policy in Europe was for the moment suspended; and for a few years there was peace.[23]

Darius, early in his reign, also took steps to inform himself more accurately about the western Mediterranean, its peoples, islands, cities and the political situation. Hitherto, all information on this great region reaching the Middle East had been mediated by the sea-peoples, of whom the most important were the Greeks and Phoenicians. The Greeks were great romancers, and the Phoenicians were adept at concealing information which might be useful to a competitor. Darius was now in a position to insist that Asian coast-dwellers, of both races, should do his bidding; and one of the things which he did was to require them to conduct and guide Persian officers, who would bring back reliable reports.

Herodotus tells a famous and revealing story of the doctor, Dēmokēdes, who after many earlier adventures had treated Darius himself and his queen. Born at Krotōn in south Italy, whose medical school was becoming famous, and having there received training, Demokedes failed to get on well with his father (presumably also a doctor), and set out to seek his fortune in old Greece. He went first to Aigina, where he so rapidly achieved fame, 'in spite of his lack of instruments', that in his second year there the government 'retained' him for a fee of a talent (6000 drachmas). In the next year Athens, under the sons of Peisistratos,

[22] H. v, 25ff. On Otanes, cf. Myres, *Herodotus, Father of History*, p. 174.
[23] *ib.* 28, 1.

out-bid Aigina and secured him for 10,000, and in the next Polykrates of Samos, the richest prince in the Aegean, out-bid Athens with 12,000. Thus Demokedes was in the retinue of Polykrates when he went to the mainland and was captured by Oroites; and among the slaves of Oroites he was next transported to the court of Darius. Here he is said to have languished unrecognised 'in rags and in fetters', till an opportunity arose. Darius, 'springing from his horse while out hunting', made a bad landing and dislocated an ankle. He had Egyptian doctors at his court; but on this occasion they completely failed to reduce the dislocation and, resorting to violent efforts, made matters worse. A Persian who had been at Oroites' court then remembered the reputation of Demokedes; and he, with much less violence, succeeded. Later he cured the queen Atossa of an ulcer in the breast, and through her good offices is said to have gained the favour of being sent on a visit to Greece, accompanied by fifteen Persian officers, sailing in two Sidonian ships of war accompanied by a supply-ship.

These officers conducted a leisurely reconnaissance of Greece, 'viewing the coasts and making notes, until they had seen most of the important places', and then proceeded to Italy. Here, however, they ran into trouble. At Taranto, nearest of the great western cities, Demokedes, no longer with seas between him and his home, 'jumped the ship'; and to cover his escape, he prompted Aristophilidas, king of Taranto (one of the few well-authenticated instances of lawful monarchy in a Greek colony),[24] to object to the Persians' activities as espionage and arrest the ships. They were finally released, and followed Demokedes to his home at Kroton, where they tried to arrest him in the market-place as 'a runaway slave of their King'. But a crowd collected and delivered him, refusing to be intimidated by threats of Darius' vengeance. The Krotonians also seized the store-ship and its contents, which Demokedes claimed to be his, 'as a present from the King for his father and brethren'. Thus crippled, the Persians started for home, only to lose both their remaining ships, wrecked somewhere near the 'heel' of Italy. The seas and weather in the straits of Otranto, where two wider seas and their weather-systems meet, can be very treacherous. The survivors were captured by the natives and held as slaves, until one Gillos, an exile from Taranto, persuaded the Iapygians that they would find it worth while to let them go home. Gillos accompanied them, and

[24] Taras, like Cyrene, it may be noted, was a colony of Sparta.

Darius 'was ready to give him any reward he asked'. The natives presumably received a suitable ransom, but for himself Gillos asked only to be restored to his home; this, he thought, could be achieved by diplomacy, through the good offices of Knidos, which had close ties with Taranto. The king duly gave the word, and his lieges the Knidians transmitted it; but the men of Taranto, alas, remained obdurate. The detail is interesting evidence on the extent and the limits of Persian prestige in the west towards the end of the century.[25] The whole story is also a good example of Herodotos' use of the oral 'saga' that was his chief source of material. He no doubt heard the story in south Italy, where Demokedes will have ended his days. That Darius sent fifteen officers with three ships to reconnoitre the coasts of Greece and make notes is no doubt true; this was probably not the only such intelligence mission. What happened in the market-places of Taranto and Kroton was 'public' fact, known to hundreds immediately. But it is also typical of the Father of History and of his saga-material, the purveyors of which always liked to 'know all the answers', that a sufficient reason for sending the mission is that the queen had promised a boon to her Greek doctor (Demokedes tells the story in such a manner as to enhance his own importance), and that we are supposed to know just what the queen said to the king in their bed-chamber.

With this, we pass to the state of the Greek world at the time of the rise of Persia.

[25] H. iii, 125, 129–38.

Part II

Greece on the Eve

Chapter VIII

Carthage, Etruria and the Western Greeks

What Darius found out about the state of the Mediterranean world will have included the fact that an intermittent war was in progress between Greek and Phoenician colonists, and that in it the Phoenicians for the most part had the support of the local peoples, of whom the most civilized and best organized were the Etruscans.

The Phoenicians (Chna, 'Canaanites', in their own language, a word variously interpreted as 'Purple-Dyers' or, better, Lowlanders) were one of the least numerous peoples ever to make a great mark in history. From their small and tightly packed strongholds on the Syrian coast (Tyre, Sidon, Byblos (Gebal, Jebail), Arvad (Ruad island), and Beirut, still unimportant) they expanded to Cyprus, where they held Kition (biblical Chittim, mod. Larnaka), called by them simply Karti-Hadasti, 'New Town', and then far afield to north Africa, with a more famous Karti-Hadasti, Carthage, and to Tarshish, Tartessos, in southern Spain. Most of their colonies were tiny, mere trading posts or 'factories'. Everywhere they relied on good relations with native peoples, maintained by honest trading, as in the 'silent trade' which they had succeeded in developing with timid aborigines on a 'gold coast' somewhere in West Africa. Here the Carthaginians would 'unload their cargo and lay it out near the tidemark, and then get back into their ships and make smoke. And at sight of the smoke, the natives come down to the sea, and lay out gold in exchange for the goods, and retire from the goods. Then the Carthaginians land and look at it, and if they think there is enough gold, they take it and go; but if not, they embark in their boats again and wait; and the natives come and add more gold, until they satisfy them. And neither side, they say, cheats' [adds Herodotos with surprise]; 'for neither do the Carthaginians touch the gold before it equals the price of their wares, nor do the natives touch the goods till the Carthaginians have taken the gold.'[1]

In face of the outpouring of Greek peasant colonists to east Sicily around 700, the Phoenicians withdrew. As in North America in another age, 'homesteaders' replaced both the 'Indian' and the 'Indian-trader'. Earlier, says Thucydides, the Phoenicians had settled 'all round Sicily, occupying headlands and off-shore islands for the sake of trade with the Sikels'.[2] Since no traces of these settlements have been found, this statement has been widely doubted; but now that the minute size of most early Phoenician trading-posts is appreciated (some of them were no more than camps), it seems safer at least to suspend judgment.[3] 'When the Greeks came in by sea in large numbers,' he continues, 'they abandoned most of these and concentrated at Motye and Soloeis and Panormos [Palermo], near the Elymoi, relying on their alliance with the Elymoi, and because this part of Sicily is divided by the shortest sea-crossing from Carthage.' The Elymoi, a civilised people who had reached western Sicily probably by sea in the early Iron Age, held the walled cities of Eryx and Egesta; Thucydides explains them, as Greeks explained most non-Greek city-dwelling populations in the Mediterranean, as descendants of 'fugitives from Troy'.[4]

Here, then, as in Cyprus, where the Greeks could never capture Kition, Phoenician policy was to hold fast to what was absolutely necessary for trade with an 'interior'; and on this basis, a state of permanent war did not develop immediately. The same is true of Etruria. It is unsound to say, with late Greek writers, followed by some good moderns, that beyond Messina 'Tyrrhenian pirates rivalled Phoenician "swindlers" in sea-wolf hostility' or, of Etruria, that 'this armed injustice turned with utter frightfulness upon everything Greek that carried oars and a sail'.[5] Carthage imported vast quantities of Greek pottery, especially Corinthian; showing indeed, in the general enthusiasm for things Greek, little discrimination, and contributing to the commercial success that was to lead Corinthian producers down the rake's progress of mass-production. Etruria, showing the while much finer taste, became steeped in Greek influence throughout every side

[1] H. iv, 196. [2] Thk. vi, 2, 6.
[3] Cf. *Lyric Age*, pp. 46f and n.
[4] vi, 2, 3; archaeological confirmation, it should be said, is here too lacking, and Bernabo Brea doubts the tradition (*Sicily before the Greeks*, p. 176).
[5] J. L. Myres in *CAH* III, p. 671 (after Ephoros, *ap.* Str. vi, 267).

of material culture, and in her own not inconsiderable art Greek religious mythology provided many favourite subjects. The Chalkidian alphabet of Cumae was adopted and, as adapted by the Etruscans and transmitted to Rome, became the somewhat defective instrument which we still use today. Merchants of Sybaris grew rich as middlemen in Milesian–Etruscan trade;[6] and probably by the same route travelled the wares of that great Ionian comic artist whose works, from the place where most of them, including the longest-known, were found, have become known as the Caeretan hydriai. Caere, in earlier times called Agylla, was that city which, we are told, 'enjoyed a high reputation among the Greeks for courage and justice; for it abstained from piracy although very powerful, and set up at Delphi the building called the Treasury of the Agyllaians'.[7] The more nearly contemporary Herodotos (i, 167) confirms that Agylla was still in touch with Delphi even in the warlike times of the late sixth century.

All this is not to say that there were no cases of piracy or swindling. Undoubtedly there must have been both, and it is not at all likely that the Greeks were behind in them. The way Greeks behaved to each other in home waters should be sufficient warning against supposing that in the west they left the initiative in private aggression to foreigners.[8] Also, there was a feeling in some quarters that robbery of non-Greeks was more virtuous. Nor, on the other hand, did the later worsening of relations lead to a cessation of trade; nor should we expect it to. The commercial relations between Christendom and the Mohammedan world, actually stimulated by the Crusades, form a suggestive parallel. But there does seem to have been a worsening of relations. In the early seventh century, contacts were growing closer; the worst human hazard to shipping was probably casual piracy, on which the state authorities, with an eye to legitimate trade, probably frowned, like the men of Ithaca on Eupeithes when he raided friendly people.[9] In the sixth century, there was war.

That a state of war did develop, moreover, seems to have been due to the aggression of the Greeks, who moved in on areas where the

[6] Ath. xii, 519 (from Timaios); cf. H. vi, 21.

[7] Str. v, 220.

[8] Cf. Thk. i, 5 (with ref. to Homer, esp. *Od.* iii, 71–4); Xen. *Anab.* vi, 1, 7f; 'Law of Solon' in *Digest*, xlvii, 22, 4; best evidence of all, probably the 5th-cent. inscr. from Galaxidhi in London (*BMI* 953+; Tod, *GHI*, no. 34); *Lyric Age*, p. 32; on the whole subject, H. A. Ormerod, *Piracy in the Ancient World*, early chapters.

[9] *Odyssey*, xvi, 424ff.

Phoenicians were already established, without more inhibitions than were manifested by the Chosen People towards the inland Canaanites, or later by Christian Europeans in other parts of the world. In the late seventh century, Greeks from the cities long established in eastern Sicily moved out – Dorians in the south, Chalkidians in the north – probably almost simultaneously, into the western half of the island, founding Selinous and Himera respectively, not on the nearest convenient sites still unoccupied, but, on both coasts, as far west as was possible without immediate collision with Phoenicians and Elymoi.[10] The Greeks had probably just discovered Tartessos in southern Spain, with its rich silver-mines, through the voyage of Kōlaios the Samian,[11] and it has been suggested that the fine coins of Himera, the first struck in the west, were coined from Spanish silver. Newcomers to the west, the Ionians of Phokaia, made their appearance in these waters in the same generation. 'These Phokaians were the first Greeks to make long sea-voyages' [the first *deliberately*, unlike Kolaios, who was blown out of his course, to strike across the open sea?] 'and it was they who revealed the Adriatic[12] and Etruria and Iberia and Tartessos; and,' adds Herodotos ominously, 'they made their voyages not in round [merchant] ships but in fifty-oared galleys', ships of war.[13] Etruria had in fact been known to the Greeks since the foundation of Cumae over a century earlier, and Tartessos is said to have been first discovered by Kolaios; but we must presumably understand the word 'revealed' in the sense of 'thoroughly explored'. There was clearly no doubt about the aggressiveness of the Phokaians, and when they crowned their explorations by the foundation of Marseilles, we hear for the first time (in our fragmentary tradition) of open war: 'The Phokaians, when they founded Massalia, defeated the Carthaginians at sea.'[14] That the Carthaginians here, for the first recorded time, gave battle indicates that they had something important at stake; probably the hither end of the short land-passage to the Atlantic, important for the tin trade.[15]

[10] Thk. vi, 5; Diodoros xiii, 59 and 62; for the chronology, see *Lyric Age*, pp. 143f, n.41.
[11] H. iv, 152.
[12] i.e. the *northern* Adriatic, named from the Etruscan colony of Atria, near the Po delta (Livy v, 33, 8; Str. v, 214).
[13] H. i, 163, 1.
[14] Thk. i, 13, 6 (not 'used to beat', as the imperfect is sometimes rendered; the tense is used also of simple past events, cf. the use of the same verb and tense thrice in Thk. 105, 1, 2).
[15] Cf. D.S. v, 22.

The defeat was serious. In the following generations Massalia's daughter colonies spread down the east coast of Spain: Rhode and Emporiai (Rosas and Ampurias, where late-sixth-century pottery has been found), on the Costa Brava; 'three small cities' near the mouth of the Sucro (mod. Jucar, in Valentia province), of which the most important was Hemeroskopeion, 'the Watchtower', with a temple of Ephesian Artemis, and far to the south Mainake, the westernmost settlement of any Greeks, near modern Malaga.[16] Arganthōnios, the 'Silver Man', the proverbially long-lived king of Tartessos (Tarshish), welcomed the Greeks with open arms[17] (for 'Tyrians', before the rise of Carthage, are said to have made conquests in Spain[18]). The whole Phoenician metal-trade with Tarshish was being imperilled.

Nor did the Greek menace stop there; there were Greeks too who planned to seize the westernmost cape of Sicily. In 580 tr. Pentathlos, a Herakleid nobleman of Knidos, with an expedition from his native city and from Rhodes (both are well known to have had other dealings in the west) seized Lilybaion, completely commanding the Bay of Motye. Their fellow-Dorians of Selinous, pushing north across the island, were already at war with Egesta. The situation for the non-Greeks was critical; the Elymites and Phoenicians in concert put forth a supreme effort, and won a decisive victory. Pentathlos was killed with many of his men, and the remainder, finding the colony untenable, elected new leaders, Gorgos, Thestor and Epithersidas, kinsmen of Pentathlos, and found a new home in the Lipari Islands. Here they founded a unique and interesting Greek communist state (later modified into a system of state leases for land, falling in every twenty years – the Greek revolutionary demand for 'a redistribution of the land' was thus 'written into' the constitution), which held its own against many Etruscan 'piratical raids' (probably by no means unprovoked), and made 'many fine dedications' from its spoils to Apollo at Delphi.[19]

Better fortune than that of Pentathlos attended, about the same time, the colonisation of Akragas, half-way between Gela and Selinous, by

[16] Str. iii, 156, 159f; cf. *Lyric Age*, pp. 147f; Schulten, *Tartessos*, pp. 44ff; Rhys Carpenter, *The Greeks in Spain*, pp. 19ff.

[17] H. i, 163, 2.

[18] Str. v, 158.

[19] Principal source, D.S. v, 9; Pausanias (x, 11, 3) adds the name of an earlier authority, Antiochos of Syracuse. Piracy *by* L. (in 396 B.C.), D.S. xiv, 93, Livy v, 28; trophies, Dittenberger, *SIG*³, no. 14, Paus. x, 16, 7, *A.P.* vii, 650a (cf. *Lyric Age*, pp. 150, 154). 'Knidian colonists', Thk. iii, 88.

The Wars with Carthage and Etruria
(for Sicily, see p. 299)

the Rhodian and Cretan colonists of the former town with reinforcements from Rhodes itself.[20] Lying east of Selinous, it was not, like Pentathlos' venture, a dagger at the throat of non-Greek Sicily; but it soon became the most powerful Greek city west of Syracuse, and while Selinous, after Pentathlos' disaster, forswore aggression, Akragas extended its boundaries at the expense of the Sikans until they marched with those of Himera.

These conquests were carried out under the rule of a tyrant, the redoubtable Phalaris, who reigned traditionally from 571, ten years after the foundation of the city, till 555. Almost every fact alleged about him is disputed; many, indeed, are certainly false, from Eusebios' alternative dates—652–625, before the city was founded according to Thucydides—to the late-antique forgery of his alleged Letters, believed genuine by many until their exposure by Bentley. Nevertheless, an account can be given of him which is fairly reliable.

Aristotle describes him as a tyrant of the older type, who made himself despot while holding high office, not by demagogy. The learned though uncritical Polyainos adds some details: he was in charge of the building of the temple of Zeus Polieus on the high citadel (as he might well be, in the early years of the colony); he used his position to collect slaves, guards and materials there; he obtained permission to barricade the citadel on the pretext that material was being stolen, armed his slaves and seized the city during the women's festival of the Thesmophoria, when men would be off the streets.[21] He then becomes the typical bad tyrant, famous for roasting his enemies alive in a bronze bull. This story, sensational enough to be fabulous, is in fact the earliest attested detail that we have about him, appearing in Pindar.[22] There was, moreover, a bull-cult in Rhodes, a cult of Zeus on Mount Atabyrios, a name which reappears at Akragas, giving a title to the citadel itself.[23] Dunbabin plausibly suggested that the atrocity stories 'may have originated in a grim jest. Phalaris' enemies said that he and his bull portended ill to the city; he said that if that was so he would make the bull roar with their cries.' [24] Malicious legend did the rest.

[20] Thk. vi, 4; *Lyric Age*, pp. 149f; Dunbabin, *WG* 305ff. Rhodians, cf. Pindar, *Ol.* ii and scholia.

[21] Ar. *Pol.* 1310b; Polyainos, v, 1.

[22] *Pyth.* i, 95f.

[23] Polybios ix, 27; scholl. on Pindar, *Ol.* vii (written for Diagoras of Rhodes), 160ff; Steph. Byz. *s.v.* Atabyron (*sic*), quoting Timaios for an Atabyrion in Sicily. Cf. Dunbabin, *WG* 311 and nn.

[24] *WG* 321.

In any case, Phalaris certainly did not 'slaughter most of the men', as Polyainos said; for he was in a position to carry out a vigorous foreign policy. Two forts ascribed to him bestrode the river Himeras, the city's frontier with Gela; Dunbabin suggests that he may have been a champion of the younger city's independence.[25] If so, it may fairly be added, he was probably also a champion (though himself a prominent man, like most tyrants before their usurpation) of the *populace* of Akragas against the aristocracy of both cities; this would account for his having both strong support and bitter enemies. He extended his city's territory inland, conquering with force, skill and treachery the Sikans under a chief named Teutos of Uessa;[26] and (a remarkable story, but it is one of those mentioned by Aristotle[27]) he is said to have been called in, to be general of their forces, by the Greeks of Himera, against the advice of the aged poet Stesichoros, who told in warning the fable of the Horse and the Stag. The horse, unable to make head against a stag, which was driving it off its pasture, called in a Man as its ally, and found, after the stag had been driven away, that it had got itself a master. Himera may have found its position precarious since Pentathlos' disaster; but it may also be that here too Phalaris, like many tyrants in old Greece, was regarded as a friend of the commons against an aristocracy.

Phalaris thus consolidated Greek power in western Sicily, hitherto represented for some fifty years by Himera and Selinous as rather isolated outposts. During his time, too, Phokaia had established a supporting colony, a half-way house on the long sea passage from the straits to Marseilles, by the occupation of Alalia in Corsica about 565.[28] In Africa itself the Greeks of Barka (the most powerful of the Greek cities of Cyrenaica in the middle of the sixth century, when Cyrene had been crippled by a defeat by the Libyans) were pressing westward into the Syrtes and are said to have defeated the Carthaginians at sea.[29] Piracy based on Lipara and Alalia was in a position to make the routes to Etruria unsafe. Greeks were already casting greedy eyes upon Sardinia.[30] From Libya in a vast crescent through the islands to Mainake in Spain (p. 147), the Greeks were excluding the Phoenicians from more and more of the sources of metals and precious raw materials, on which their life as a trading people depended. There was no planned strategy,

[25] D.S xix, 108; *WG* 317.
[26] Polyainos, v, 1, 3f.
[27] *Rhetoric*, ii, 20 (1393b).
[28] H. i, 165.
[29] Servius, *ad Aen.* iv, 42.
[30] H. i, 1, 170 (advice of Bias, c. 546); cf. v, 106, 124.

but that made little difference; Greeks desired what the Phoenicians and the indigenous peoples had. Even without central direction the movements of an expanding people can manifest the same resemblance to planned aggression, searching out every weakness, as the movement of wind or water.[31]

Also, the Greek advance was not totally unplanned. 'Wise men' like Bias, who pointed to Sardinia, oracles like that which directed the Phokaians to 'colonise Kyrnos' (Corsica),[32] represented the views of well-informed men in the home country. The legends, found already in the poems of Stesichoros of Himera,[33] which localised episodes in the adventures of Herakles in Spain and western Sicily, represented an invitation to Herakleids like Pentathlos to claim their forefather's heritage; and a little later, if not already, there was an oracle threatening intrusion on the very homeland of Carthage and Utica themselves. The attached legend said that Jason and the Argonauts had left a bronze tripod in the care of the sea-god Triton on the coast of this part of Libya, and it was prophesied that when a descendant of one of the Argonauts should recover that tripod, then it was fated that a hundred Greek cities should be established round the Tritonian Lake. (The 'lake', *limnē*, was perhaps at this time a 'sea-loch', the Gulf of Gabes, though later it was identified with the Shatt el Jerid, inland.) 'And when the Libyan natives heard of this, they hid the tripod.' [34] Another oracle more specifically said that Spartans were to colonise the island of Phla in the 'lake',[35] which in this context might be the fertile island of Jerba. These *unfulfilled* prophecies, it has often been pointed out, show that even oracles connected with successfully established colonies are not always to be dismissed as inventions *post eventum*. They represent the 'inspirations' of men who had clear ideas about where, guided by 'manifest destiny', Greek colonists ought to go.

The Greeks were planning, then, if they were not stopped, nothing less than the conquest of the whole western Mediterranean. About the middle of the century the western Phoenicians passed from apprehension to a determination that systematic resistance must be organised. In this organisation, the lead was taken by Carthage. The smaller neighbouring 'Liby-Phoenician' cities, of which the most important

[31] Cf. the remarks of Tolstoi on the relative unimportance of planning in great movements (whether or not he exaggerates it) in the concluding chapters of *War and Peace*.

[32] H. 167, 4.

[33] Stes. *ap.* Str. iii, 148; cf. Pherekydes, *ib.* 150.

[34] H. iv. 179.

[35] *ib.* 178.

was Utica, were brought into her alliance; not always willingly, it seems probable, any more than the Greek cities were always willing to accept the leadership of Athens or Sparta; but the need was pressing. Then, 'in the time of Cyrus' (559–529), as a late writer says (no doubt rightly, though it is not clear that he had more evidence than we have[36]) a fateful step was taken when, for the first time, a Carthaginian army landed in Sicily.

This army was under a general, already distinguished in the wars in Africa, named Malchus or something similar.[37] He is said to have operated 'long successfully'[38] and to have 'conquered part of Sicily'; but against whom he campaigned we are not told. He may have been engaged largely in forcing the Elymoi and the local Phoenicians to accept Carthaginian protection. He may also have imposed peace upon Selinous, whose stately temples and great school of sculpture begin to rise in the following decades, peace and a position as *entrepôt* in trade with Carthage perhaps providing the foundation of her prosperity. There is an undated story of how one Theron, son of Miltiades, made himself tyrant there after a defeat by the Carthaginians, when the dead of Selinous had been left unburied on the field. Theron volunteered to cremate the bodies where they lay, if given a contingent of 300 slaves equipped for wood-cutting; he then returned with them at night, and being admitted without question made himself master of the sleeping city.[39] It is obvious that such a stratagem could have offered no hope of lasting success unless, like most Greek tyrants, Theron enjoyed considerable support, presumably that of the less privileged classes. As to the date, all we can say with certainty is that in 480 Selinous was among the allies of Carthage (p. 479).

It is also a tempting speculation, and has had some popularity, that 'Malchus' fought against Phalaris of Akragas, and that it was against him that the men of Himera called in the great tyrant. Certainly the hostile tradition about Phalaris might have suppressed the fact (if it was

[36] Orosius, iv, 6. O. *may* at this point have looked up the full text of Pompeius Trogus; but it is noticeable that as a rule, after citing as his authorities 'Trogus and Justin', he uses only Justin's epitome of Trogus, quoting verbally except where he introduces a few original falsifications designed to emphasise the desired atmosphere of gloom. Justin, our only other source on the rise of Carthage, without giving dates, gives the impression that it took place within two generations ending in 480 B.C. (xviii, 7–xix, 2).

[37] Maleum, Malei, Justin xviii, 7, mss; Mazeum, Mazeus, Orosius; 'Malchus' conj. Voss. The fact that it *is* a conjecture, however attractive, seems in some danger of being forgotten.

[38] *diu feliciter*, Justin; *diu infeliciter*, Orosius!

[39] Polyainos, i, 28, 2.

a fact) that Phalaris had done anything so creditable in the eyes of later Greek patriotism as to fight against Carthage. But Phalaris is said to have been overthrown and killed in a revolution at Akragas about 555, and it seems rather likely that the Carthaginian campaigns were after 550.

After subduing part of Sicily, 'Malchus' and his army were next ordered to Sardinia; and the occasion for this was probably the sharpening of the western crisis as a direct result of Cyrus' conquest of Ionia. The western Greeks were reinforced by many irreconcilables, landless, bellicose and frustrated. It was well for Carthage that the population of Ionia did not take Bias' advice to migrate to Sardinia in a body. As it was, nearly half the population of Phokaia arrived to reinforce Alalia in Corsica. 'They lived there together with the previous colonists for five years' (545–40 or a little later) 'and built temples. But as they raided and plundered all their neighbours, the Etruscans and Carthaginians made common cause and launched an expedition against them of sixty ships from each.' [40] The navy of Alalia is said to have numbered only sixty ships all told; but the allies, as an invasion-fleet, were probably hampered, either through having a convoy to guard or through carrying many soldiers and their supplies (as Greeks often did[41]) aboard some of the ships of war. As they approached, the Greeks, under Kreontiades of Phokaia,[42] came boldly out and fell upon them before they could come to land.

After fighting of extreme ferocity, the allies drew off. They had captured a number of ships and made a considerable haul of prisoners; but they were far from their base in Italy,[43] and they had suffered so severely that they withdrew baffled. But, says Herodotos, 'for the Phokaians it was a Kadmeian victory' (an allusion to the Children of the Dragon's Teeth, who fought till nearly all were killed). Only twenty ships, and these no longer battleworthy, with bent and broken rams, limped back into harbour. Rather than wait for a renewed attack, they evacuated Alalia and withdrew to Rhegion. They were bewildered at their plight, since the Delphic oracle itself had bidden them 'stablish' (which could also mean 'colonise') Kyrnos, the Greek name for Corsica; but at Rhegion a man of Poseidonia produced the kind of explanation customary in such cases. There was a hero named

[40] H. i, 166, 1.
[41] e.g. Thk. i, 116; vi, 43; viii, 62.
[42] Antiochos of Syracuse, *ap*. Str. vi, 252.
[43] Cf. Thk. vi, 34, 4 (Hermokrates on this difficulty for an invasion-fleet).

Kyrnos, and it was a shrine for him that the God had really meant them to establish in their new home. Thus fortified, they proceeded to colonise Velia (Elea or Hüéle as the Greeks, who had difficulty with the initial W-sound, called it), a day's journey south of Poseidonia, which no doubt was glad to have Greek neighbours; Elea, soon to be famous as the home of the great philosopher Parmenides.

The fate of a large batch of the Greek prisoners, who fell into the hands of the Etruscans of Agylla (the later Caere), was to be massacred, stoned to death there by the infuriated populace. These long phil-Hellenic people, who had a reputation among the Greeks for 'courage and justice' and who had themselves 'refrained from piracy, though they were very powerful',[44] had evidently been stung to a hysteria of rage by the Phokaians' depredations. After the massacre, their consciences were uneasy, and a superstition grew up that every man or beast that passed the place where the bodies had lain became deformed or went mad. They consulted Delphi, where they may already have built their 'treasury',[45] and received instructions to offer sacrifices and hold funeral games in honour of the spirits of the murdered men. This they were still doing a hundred years later, in the time of Herodotos; 'they offer great sacrifices, and hold athletic contests and horse-races';[46] a striking piece of evidence on the Hellenisation of the culture of Etruria.

This latest Greek adventure had thus brought the Etruscan cities into line with Carthage. The battle of Alalia is the first exploit of an Etruscan fleet of which we hear. It was not the last. The allies determined to secure the islands permanently. Corsica fell to the Etruscans' share, and though it is unlikely that they conquered the mountainous interior, it was reckoned an Etruscan possession in the fifth century.[47]

Meanwhile Carthage turned her attention to Sardinia, where some early Phoenician settlements probably already existed.[48] It may well have been after the battle of Alalia that 'Malchus' and his army were ordered thither from Sicily.

But the Sardinians, a people, like the Elymoi, perhaps of eastern sea-raider origins, proved no easy victims. Their armour and archery (attested by many of their fine bronze statuettes, now attributed to the Iron Age) and their skill in building the famous round towers of the island,

[44] Str. v, 220; cf. above, p. 145.
[45] Str., *ib.*
[46] H. i, 167.
[47] D.S. xi, 88.
[48] Albright in *AJA* LIV (1950); (but cf., *contra*, Rhys Carpenter in *AJA* LXII).

the *nuraghe*, made them formidable.[49] The Carthaginian army suffered heavy losses, and is then said to have been 'exiled' – perhaps meaning that the general and his war-weary troops wished to withdraw from the island and were forbidden by the home government. Against that government therefore 'Malchus' now turned his arms. A grim story was told of the fate of his son Carthalo, who had been sent to carry tithes of the spoils of Sicily to the temples of Tyre, and returned to find his father besieging Carthage. Carthalo insisted successfully on being allowed to enter the city to complete his pious mission; he returned a few days later, wearing his priestly robes, and perhaps tried to mediate; in any case he refused to join the rebellion, and so infuriated his father that he crucified him before the city. A few days later the general took Carthage, and justified his conduct before a mass-meeting of the citizens. He contented himself with putting to death ten of his chief enemies,[50] and did not seize despotic power; with the almost inevitable result that he was accused not long afterwards of plotting to do so, and put to death. We cannot, on the evidence, tell how just the grievances of the general or his army were; but it appears that the pattern of later Carthaginian history was taking shape.

Mago, the next commander-in-chief (*shophet*, Latin *suffetus*, the word translated 'Judge' in our Old Testament), was an important figure, described as founder of the Carthaginian empire and military system; by which we should probably understand the system of mercenary armies of warlike Libyans and Europeans, which for centuries made up for the deficiencies of the Phoenicians' own manpower. When Carthage herself henceforth puts a citizen infantry division into the field (a heavy-armed phalanx armed in the Greek manner[51]) it is a sign of financial stringency or of a major crisis. The Phoenicians, townsmen and traders, were not themselves soldiers by choice; but they produced, generation after generation, officers capable of recruiting and organising barbarians into a formidable army, applying to war the skill in gaining the confidence and respect of outland peoples which Phoenicians had built up through centuries of exploration and trade. To such an army, or to its cadre of officers, Mago was credited with having imparted

[49] M. Pallottino, *La Sardegna nuragica* (Rome, 1950); G. Pesce and G. Lilliu, *Sculture della Sardegna nuragica* (Venice, 1949).
[50] Justin xviii, 7, 16f; improved by Orosius (*loc. cit.*) to 'interfectis plurimis senatorum'!
[51] e.g. Plut. *Timoleon*, 27f.

its own special *êthos* and morale.[52] So Carthage came to have its military families, some of them great families, like that of Mago himself and that of Hamilcar Barca, Barak, 'the Lightning', later; families which inevitably had political as well as military importance, and might be regarded with jealousy by the ordinary run of Carthaginian capitalists, suspicious that they might aim at supreme power. In the fifth century the constitution was overhauled with a view to securing the combination of a strong military command with civilian control, and the inner Council of a Hundred (really 104) was established, with judicial functions, especially that of receiving an account of the actions of generals after their campaigns. Military officers were held in honour, and must have been conspicuous in society when they appeared in their decorations; we hear that 'they have the right to wear as many armlets as they have served campaigns'.[53] In case of disputes between the Suffetes (whom Aristotle calls 'elective kings') and the Council, questions were referred to a citizen assembly, in which real debates took place and any speaker might 'oppose the motion'; poverty was alleviated by the recruitment of poor men for the increasing number of Carthaginian colonies; and a stability was achieved to which Aristotle, writing when the city's power was at its height, gives measured praise.[54]

It was not without reason that the Carthaginian republic took its precautions; for the House of Mago had indeed achieved an almost royal position. Mago was succeeded by his son Hasdrubal, eleven times Shophet and hero of four victorious wars. Under him an attempt was made to discontinue the tribute or rent to the Libyans for the territory of Carthage itself, which had been paid ever since the peaceful and mercantile beginnings of the colony; but, perhaps because the north Africans proved now as ever difficult to bring to battle and defeat decisively, it was given up, to be successfully renewed only in the next century. Even in Hasdrubal's time, the merchant city found it more economical to continue the payment than to become involved in an endless guerrilla war. The arduous campaigns in Sardinia were renewed, and here Hasdrubal, after some successes, was at last mortally wounded, to be buried at Carthage with great ceremony amid scenes

[52] So I would understand Trogus (Justin xix, 1, 1): 'cum primus omnium, ordinata disciplina militari, imperium Poenorum condidisset, viresque civitatis non minus bellandi arte quam virtute firmasset . . .'

[53] Justin xix, 2, 5; decorations, Ar. *Politics*, 1324b.

[54] *Politics*, 1272b–73b.

of unprecedented public mourning.[55] This is said to have taken place during the reign of Darius in Persia, and just before the western campaigns of Dorieus of Sparta, of which more hereafter.

In Spain, the earliest Carthaginian conquests are even more completely undated; but probably they too should be assigned to the days of Mago and Hasdrubal. The ancient Tyrian colony of Gaddir, 'the Walled Place' [56] (Greek Gadeira, Latin Gades, modern Cadiz), was brought under Carthaginian protection, perhaps unwillingly, and 'a great part of the land' conquered.[57] The Kingdom of Tartessos appears no more in history, and Avienus confuses its capital with Gades itself. Mainake, the westernmost outpost of Massalia, was also wiped off the map so thoroughly that it was sometimes confused with its Phoenician successor Malaga (not on the same site); yet its ruins remained, 'still preserving the appearance of a Greek town', whereas Malaga *looked* Phoenician (perhaps less orderly?).[58] The Greeks were pushed back permanently; the detailed knowledge of the west shown by Hekataios of Miletos (*c.* 500 B.C.) and other Ionian writers contrasts with the vagueness of Herodotos (though he had lived in Italy) fifty years later. For him, the Danube 'rises among the Kelts and [near] the city of Pyrēne' (nowhere else mentioned, but probably a real place, from which the Massaliotes will have named the 'Pyrenaean Mountains'); and 'the Kelts are outside the Pillars of Herakles and neighbours of the Kynesioi, who are the furthest west of men'.[59]

Further up the coast, however, Massalia held her own; her sea-power proved still a match for that of Carthage, and the Etruscans were not interested in Spain (and still less, presumably, in building up a Phoenician monopoly throughout the west). We might have expected Carthage to build up a vast navy, employing barbarian oarsmen; but evidently her purse was not long enough to induce enough barbarians to submit for long periods to such a severe and unattractive discipline. That barbarians *could* be trained as oarsmen was shown by Greek

[55] Justin xix, 1, 3ff. [56] Avienus, *Ora Maritima*, 267ff.

[57] Justin xliv (the book on Spain), 5, 2f. A siege of Gades, Vitruvius x, 19. J. goes straight on, with a 'postea quoque', to the campaigns of Hamilcar Barca; but as he goes from prehistoric times to Augustus in a paragraph (as in an encyclopaedia article), he may well be skipping uncharted centuries. (Schulten, *Tartessos*, 46, is probably right; I withdraw my doubts in *Lyric Age*, p. 148, n. 65.)

[58] Str. iii, 156.

[59] H. ii, 33; contrast the numerous western names cited from Hekataios by Steph. Byz. and the detailed though 'dated' knowledge of Avienus, for whose Ionian sources see his ll. 41ff.

Herakleia in Bithynia; but she was in a position to coerce her hill-men.[60] Massalia held her own in a war, undated, 'arising out of the seizure of some fishing-boats'[61] (probably Greek); the statement suggests that this was after zones of activity had been delimited by treaty. Massalia's southern limit in Spain long remained, it appears, at Hēmeroskopeion, 'the Watch-Tower', well identified as the splendid, thousand-foot 'pillar rock' of the Punta de Ifach, nine miles south of the Cabo del Nao, a stronghold that figured later in Sertorius' wars. Upon it the Phokaians had built a shrine of their Ephesian Artemis, a goddess much venerated in Massalia and her daughter colonies, whence the neighbouring settlement came to be called Artemision, later Latinised as Dianium.[62]

It may have been off this Artemision that a battle was fought early in the fifth century, in which Herakleides of Mylasa in Karia, known to Herodotos as the organiser of a famous ambush on land in the Ionian Revolt (p. 206), proposed tactics which the Massaliotes were to remember centuries later. 'The Phoenicians' (we read in a papyrus fragment of a work on the campaigns of Hannibal) 'when they meet an enemy fleet face to face, have the practice of bearing down as though to ram head on, but then do not ram immediately but row on through the enemy line and turn and ram the opposing ships on the now exposed quarter.' The manœuvre takes for granted superior speed, skill, and the expectation that the enemy would be taken by surprise, hesitate, lose way and probably be caught trying to turn round, a performance which the ancient 'long ship', 110 feet in length, could not carry out in an instant. 'Now the Massaliotes' (the papyrus continues after a short gap) 'had read in history about the battle off Artemision fought by Herakleides of Mylasa, one of the most resourceful captains of his time; and accordingly they gave orders for a first line abreast to be followed by a second at appropriate intervals, the ships of which, as soon as those of the enemy passed through the line in front, should attack them while

[60] Ar. *Politics*, 1327b (*addendum* to refs. in *Lyric Age*, p. 120, n. 65); position of the Mariandünoi, Str. xii, 542.

[61] Justin xliii, 5.

[62] Rhys Carpenter, *The Greeks in Spain*, pp. 19ff, 117ff; Str. iii, 159 adds that there were three small settlements of the Massaliotes hereabout, and this may have led to the name being later transferred to Denia, north of the Cape, giving rise to prolonged scholarly disputes; cf. Schulten, *Avienus*, comm. *ad v.* 476; A. Berthelot, *Avienus* (Paris, 1934), p. 106. Rhys Carpenter, p. 22, cites large quantities of late RF Attic pottery at Ifach, as well as Hellenistic and native. Eph. Artemis at Massalia, cf. Str. iv, 179.

still passing' (and presumably without room to manœuvre). 'This was what Herakleides had done long before, and been the architect of victory.'[63] It cannot be proved that the reference is *not* to the famous battle off the Euboian Artemision (pp. 400ff); but that was hardly a victory; there is nothing about Herakleides there in Herodotos; and 'it is extremely unlikely that the Massaliotes, or Sosylus either, knew more than Herodotus about the operations'.[64] Herakleides, when all was lost in Ionia, had probably sailed to the west like many others (including the admiral Dionysios of Phokaia, p. 214), and suggested to the Massaliotes these tactics, which they remembered *out of their own history*, when engaged once more against the same foe.

It may be noted that the Carthaginians apparently did not, in either of these battles, enjoy superiority in numbers; otherwise the Massaliotes could not have shortened their front line by detaching ships for a second, without exposing themselves to being outflanked; *periplous*, the attack in flank, being, as the classical Athenian navy knew so well, even more deadly as well as more obvious than the daring *diekplous* or 'sailing through'. On land, Carthage might deploy masses of hired barbarians; at sea, her sailors were limited in numbers and relied on their skill.

So the war with Massalia ended probably in a treaty soon after 490, a treaty delimiting waters prohibited to Greek shipping (as the fishing-boat episode suggests), as in the treaties which Carthage also concluded with early Rome (below, pp. 165f). Massalia held the coast as far as the Artemision, where the 'three settlements' supported each other, while the first outpost of Carthage was 80 miles to the south-west: Massia, an old native stronghold with 'Cyclopean' walls, once the easternmost fortress of the Kingdom of Tartessos,[65] and later refounded by Hamilcar Barca as new Carthage, Cartagena.

While Carthage was founding her empire in the west, the Etruscans, scarcely more united than the Greeks,[66] but potentially formidable, were extending their boundaries in Italy. Their great territorial expansion to Bologna and thence to the Adriatic and the plains of the Po

[63] Sosylos of Sparta, Hannibal's Greek tutor (D.S. xxvi, 4; Nepos, *Hannibal*, 13); Wilcken in *Hermes* XLI (1906); Bilabel, *Klein. Historikerfr. auf. Pap.*, no. 10.; *FGH* 176 F 1.

[64] Munro in *CAH* IV, p. 289.

[65] Avienus, 449–63.

[66] 'A rather loose confederation of quasi-independent city-states' – J. B. Ward-Perkins in *Harvard Studies in Cl. Phil.* LXIV (1959), p. 17; cf. von Vacano, *The Etruscans* (Eng. trn., 1960), pp. 38f, 48f, 139.

seems to have begun only about the end of the century;[67] their first recorded aggression outside their traditional area, like that of Carthage, represents an attempt to drive back the Greeks or at least (as was successfully done) to stem their advance. The evidence for Greek cities, before this date, north-west of Cumae, at Satricum on the Volscian coast, at Amunclae near Fundi, and at Pisae (Pisa) in the north is tenuous, though Pais accepted it.[68] That there were such is not in itself improbable; and the presence of numerous sixth-century Greek *traders* is undoubted; apart from the Greek pottery on Etruscan sites and the Greek influence on Etruscan art, armament (the Greek panoply, as at Carthage) and the introduction of the Chalkidian alphabet, we find an intimate Etruscan knowledge of Greek legends, shown by the recognisable names of gods and heroes (not only Apollo and Herakles but, for example, Meleagros and Atalanta) on works of art.[69] Some of these Greeks may well have settled permanently in the country, like that Dēmaratos, a merchant (and, we are assured, a Bakchiad nobleman) of Corinth, said in a widely reported legend to have risen to power at Tarquinii and to have been an ancestor of the Tarquinian kings of Rome.[70] If there were Chalkidians, as Justin says,[71] at Falerii, Nola and Abella, they were probably merchants of Cumae. A specifically Phokaian element in this penetration is attested, if it were necessary, by a coin-hoard from Volterra: 65 silver pieces from Greek Asia Minor, prominent among which are coins of Phokaia and of her eastern colony, Lampsakos.[72] They *might* have come through a Phokaian colony at Pisa; but, if there ever was one, it suffered for the sins of the men of Alalia and disappeared without trace. After Alalia, as we have seen, and soon after, we may guess, the Etruscans secured Corsica; and other Etruscans were pushing south. The Etruscan dynasty of the Tarquins held Rome and its crossing of the Tiber; and Etruscans pushed along the Liris valley even into Campania. Greek Cumae would be a rich prize, if it could

[67] Date of Etruscan Bologna, Pallottino, *The Etruscans* (Eng. trn. 1955), p. 92; MacIver, *The Etruscans*, pp. 133ff. Dion. Hal. (vii, 3) is wide of the mark in speaking of the aggressors further south as already driven *from* the Adriatic by the Gauls.

[68] *Italia antica*, II, 295–307, 331f; for Pisa, cf. Justin xx, 1, 11; the context, a list of legendary foundations, does not inspire confidence; nor does Strabo's derivation (v, 222) from a 'Trojan War' colony from Pisa in Elis.

[69] Cf. Beazley, 'The World of the Etruscan Mirror', in *JHS* LXIX.

[70] D.H. iii, 46; Livy i, 34; Polyb. vi, 2; etc.; Blakeway in *JRS* XXV (1935).

[71] xx, 1, 13 (cf. also Strabo, 243, 245f, on early Kymaian expansion).

[72] In the Florence museum; cf. R. A. L. Fell, *Etruria and Rome*, p. 36.

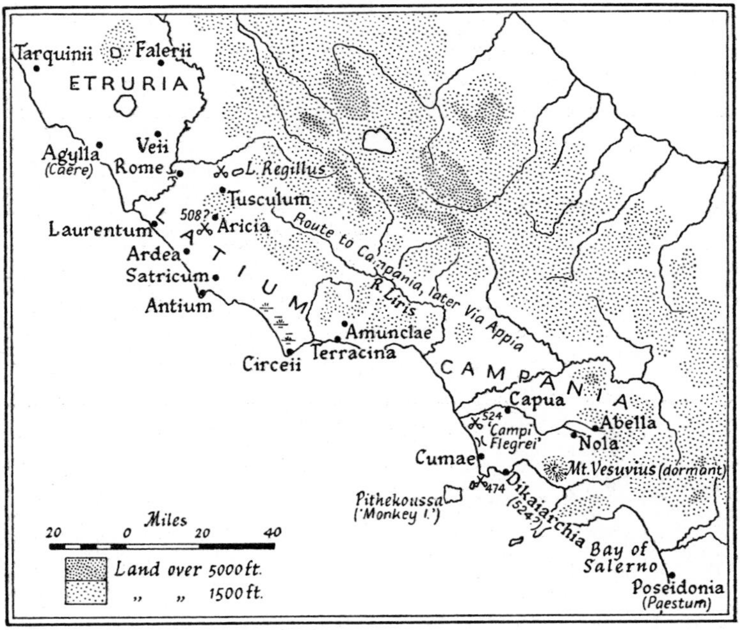

Greeks, Latins and Etruscans

be won; and in 524 by ancient computation a great Etruscan army including many Umbrian and Daunian auxiliaries – our Greek account cheerfully puts the total at 18,000 (or 28,000) horse and 500,000 foot – marched against it.[73]

In this very year, according to some Greek chronography, a Samian band of exiled enemies of the tyrant Polykrates settled at Puteoli (Pozzuoli), which Cumae also used as a naval station. They called their colony Dikaiarchia, 'Just Government' (cf. modern Concord or Philadelphia); a monument to their feelings about the despotism from which they had escaped.[74] But Samians, no less than Phokaians, had a reputation for piracy. It may well have been the prospect of seeing the Greeks

[73] D.H. vii, 3f (whence the following account). Etruscan Capua was founded, according to Cato (in Velleius, i, 7), '260 years before it fell to the Romans', which, if it refers to the capture in 211 B.C., so 471, must refer to 'incorporation' rather than first occupation. Etruria and Rome, see Fell, *op. cit.* pp. 39ff; Pallottino, *op. cit.* pp. 89ff. Rome a '*Tyrrhēnis polis*', D.H. i, 29, 2.

[74] *Kymaiōn epineion*, Str. v, 245; Samians, Steph. Byz.; Jerome *sub anno* 524 (with *vv. ll.* 528, 521).

on the Bay reinforced by such men that precipitated the attempt, just at this juncture, to eliminate them altogether.

But Cumae weathered the storm. Her own resources were not inconsiderable; according to our detailed tradition (from a local historian of the following century, the first age of prose in the west?), after detaching troops (probably the 'oldest and youngest', in the usual manner) to guard the city (against a sea-borne landing) and others to guard 'the ships' (at Puteoli, against attack from the east?), 4500 infantry and 600 horse were left to give battle, on a narrow-fronted position 'between mountains and lakes, or rather sea-lagoons; such a position as may readily be found, between the rough, volcanic Campi Flegrei and the beaches of La Pineta, astride the main road into Cumae from the north. Here, we are told, the enemy infantry, undisciplined hillmen, attacked in disorder and were thrown back, many trampling each other under foot on the marshy shore. Here, as in his outrageous estimate of numbers, Dionysios' source is perhaps challenging comparison with Herodotos' account of Thermopylai. The Etruscan cavalry fought longer and gave the Greeks a hard struggle; but, being unable to find a flank to turn, they too were driven back from the line of pikes; and the horsemen of Cumae, who highly distinguished themselves, completed the rout.

Cumae was saved; but the battle was at once followed by a dispute about the *aristeia*, the Prize of Valour which Greeks awarded after a victory, sometimes to an individual and sometimes to a contingent or regiment; but only one prize on one occasion, and therefore frequently to the accompaniment of violent partisan feeling.[75] The aristocratic senate which controlled the government wished to award it to Hippomedon the cavalry commander, but 'unbiassed judges' (here the historian reveals *his* bias) to Aristodemos, of the middle-class infantry, who had borne the brunt of the attack; he is said to have killed the enemy commander with his own hand. Feeling ran so high that finally the older men persuaded the people that the prize should be, exceptionally, shared. 'And thereafter Aristodemos became the political leader of the commons.' The story is entirely in accordance with the political conditions common in Greece at this time.

The Etruscan defeat was shortly followed by a movement against

[75] Cf. H. viii, 93 (Salamis; p. 490 below; also D.S. xi, 27, Plut. *Mal. Hdt.* 40, which while unhistorical illustrate the possibilities of partisanship); Plato, *Symp.* 220; etc.

their overlordship among the Latins. The expulsion of the Tarquins from Rome (509 tr.) may in reality have been later; but in any case, Rome remained an Etruscan bridgehead. Lars Porsena (or Porsinna) of Clusium, according to the legend, was induced by the desperation of the Roman resistance to desist from an attempt to restore the Tarquins; but he established his own overlordship, and troops under his son Arruns advanced into Latium. Aricia, at the foot of the Alban Mount (the seat of a famous and primitive type of priest-king), under siege by Arruns, appealed for help both to the other Latins and to Cumae. The government of Cumae sent Aristodemos with 2000 men, as the story says, 'of the lowest of the people', embarking them for the voyage up the coast on 'ten old and poorly-found ships, commanded by the poorest of the Kymaians'. At this point the partisan story, or Dionysios' version of it, sinks into nonsense; skippers could not be among 'the poorest'; but it is not incredible either that Aristodemos and his supporters formed a war party, or that the aristocrats may have hoped to see him killed or discredited.[76] Joining the Latins, among whom the chief contingents came from Tusculum and the port of Antium (the whole army outnumbering Arruns' force), Aristodemos advanced to Aricia, and a battle took place in which Arruns is said, after breaking through the Latins, to have been taken in flank by the men of Cumae and defeated and killed. The remnants of his army fled back to Rome.[77]

The sequel to this was that Aristodemos carried through a revolution at Cumae with the support of his soldiers, massacring the senate, carrying out a redistribution of the land and cancellation of debts (the usual revolutionary programme), and being appointed General-in-Chief by the acclamation of the Assembly. Thenceforth his career, recorded at length by Dionysios, continues on the lines that became conventional for the Story of a Tyrant. He disarms the people and carries out house-to-house searches for concealed arms; he relies on paid guards; but an original touch is that he had three kinds of guards:

[76] Cf. Thk. iv, 28, 5!

[77] D.H. v, 36; vii, 5f; Livy ii, 14. It will be noticed that if Rome was still under her Etruscan dynasty at the time of the siege of Aricia, and so in stable alliance with Etruria (cf. Gjerstad in *Opuscula Romana* III (Lund, 1960), pp. 69ff), this story runs more smoothly rather than otherwise. It runs even better if, as Alföldi has recently argued, it was Lars Porsinna himself who expelled the Tarquins. The Battle of Lake Regillus, 496, will then really have been fought by the Latins as allies of the Tarquins, as well as of Aristodemos and the Greeks; see A. Alföldi, *Early Rome and the Latins* (T. S. Jerome Lectures, Univ. of Michigan, 1961; publication forthcoming, Ann Arbor Press, Michigan (1963?)).

one recruited from among 'the dirtiest and meanest of the citizens' (i.e. political supporters); one from among slaves who had killed their masters in the revolution (for his more menial tasks?); and finally a regular military force of 2000 Italian 'barbarians'. It is not *only* the conventional tyrant-story; for instance, there admittedly *are* crimes which he might have committed and did not. Disregarding the epic maxim 'Folly it is to leave the sons after killing the father' – an established tenet of Greek machiavellianism[78] – he did not put to death the children of the senators killed in the revolution; but he sent them to the country to work on farms, and systematically broke up the schools and gymnasium-organization through which the young aristocrats had received their education and learned the use of arms and *esprit-de-corps* (or class solidarity). He is said meanwhile (but this may have been interpolated from Roman tradition) to have given asylum to the exiled Tarquins whom the Lord of Clusium had 'let down'; and certainly we need not suppose his policy to have been either racialist or doctrinaire. It was, rather, like that of most Greek tyrants, the satisfaction of personal ambition, using the revolutionary trend of the time as a means to personal power; and, in the usual manner, his rule ultimately fell.

Refugees increased in number abroad, many of them at Etruscan Capua, where they were headed by sons of the aristocratic general Hippomedon (p. 162). When Aristodemos was past his prime (probably, after 490), refugees and malcontents opened a guerrilla resistance in the inland districts. A pretended betrayal of their 'hide-out' led to the despatch of the tyrant's army, without its master, on a wild-goose chase; and in their absence a 'commando' slipped into the city at dusk in the guise of woodmen bringing in fuel, and made an end of the tyrant and all his family. The 'ancestral constitution', *patrios politeia*, was then restored; but we may infer that, as in most Greek cities after a *tyrannis*, it was no such narrow oligarchy as before; not, at least, if we may judge by the sympathies of the unnamed historian, who relates these events in a manner hostile both to the old regime and to the strong-handed soldier who had led the revolution.[79]

Cumae (it may be mentioned here) survived at least one more Etruscan attack as late as 474, when it was menaced by sea and saved by the Battle of Cumae, a great defeat of the Etruscan navy by that of Syracuse

[78] From the *Kypria*; cf. Clem. Alex., *Strōm.* vii, 2, 19.

[79] D.H. vii, 6–11; Tarquin at Cumae, Livy ii, 21; A. still flourishing *c.* 492, *ib.* 34.

under the admirals of the tyrant Hieron; an event of which a concrete relic survives in the shape of a bronze helmet with dedicatory inscription, presented among other spoils at Olympia and now in the British Museum.[80] Etruria, like Carthage, had taught the Greeks to fear her power; but both Cumae and, in spite of much mutual piracy, the Greek trade survived, though archaeology seems to show a marked diminution in it, especially after the Syracusan raids of 455–3.

In the meantime the Etruscan cities kept up close ties with Carthage, with agreements both for political alliance and for the regulation of trade; agreements as to what goods might be imported, and for the orderly settlement of disputes, so close that Aristotle remarks that, if economic regulations alone were the criterion, they would form one state.[81] Of such agreements between Carthage and Italian cities we have some examples in the early treaties, recorded by Polybios, between Carthage and Rome.

The earliest of these treaties Polybios, who deciphered it after a struggle, as he tells us, with the archaic Latin, assigns to the year 509–8;[82] though, as the consuls for the year are *not* mentioned in the text, nor yet any other dating evidence, it is not clear whether this date is more than a conjecture. The following, he says, was the sense, so far as the archaic Latin could be made out by the best authorities:

> On the following conditions there shall be friendship between the Romans and their allies and the Carthaginians and their allies:
>
> The Romans and their allies shall not sail beyond the Fair Cape, unless constrained by storm or by enemies; and anyone making land there perforce shall not buy or obtain any goods except what may be required for repairs to the ship or for sacrifice ['and', Polybios adds, not here but in the commentary, 'shall depart within five days'].
>
> Those who come to trade shall conclude no business except in the present of a herald or town-clerk; and the price of goods sold in the presence of these shall be assured to the seller on the credit of the state, both in Libya and in Sardinia. If a Roman come to the part of Sicily which is Carthaginian territory, he shall enjoy equal rights.
>
> The Carthaginians shall do no harm to the peoples of Ardea, Antium, Laurentum, Circeii, Terracina, or any other of the Latins

[80] Pindar, *Pyth.* i, 72ff; D.S. xi, 51; *GHI* (1969), no. 28.

[81] *Politics*, 1280a.

[82] iii, 22ff. But Alföldi (see n. 77) has now joined those earlier authorities who would date the first treaty 348 and the second very soon after it; both on the eve of Rome's last reckoning with her fellow-Latins.

who are subject to Rome. In the case of any who are not subject, they shall not occupy their cities; and if they take a city, they shall deliver it up to the Romans intact. They shall build no fort in Latin territory; and if they enter that territory in the course of military operations, they shall not camp there overnight.

The Fair Cape is explained by Polybios as that 'lying before Carthage to the north' (Cape Bon?), and the limit set as debarring Romans from trade east thereof, with the 'Emporia', the trading stations in the Syrtes; though if so, it is curious that no westward limit is set.[83] The implied Roman claim to dominate Latium is hardly compatible with the earliest years of the republic, when her territory seems to have been hardly twenty miles across. Under the Tarquins Rome may have been the capital of a larger area; and it is therefore tempting to suppose that the 'First Treaty' really may date from the time of these Romanised Etruscan kings.

'Later', Polybios continues, 'they made another treaty, in which the Carthaginians include on their own side Tyre and the Republic of Utica' [the most ancient Phoenician city in Tunisia, which kept some such religious prestige as the Romans for a time accorded to Alba]; 'and they add to the Fair Promontory the names of Mastia and Tarsēion' [Massia in Spain and a Tarseion near 'Tarshish'? If so, the Romans retain the right of trading along the coast of Europe as far as the limit of the area conceded to their allies, the men of Marseilles]. The Romans this time are, however, entirely excluded from 'trading or settling' in Sardinia or Africa though not from Carthaginian Sicily. The power of Carthage to preserve her local monopolies has increased in the mean time.[84]

In the late sixth century, however, the Greeks had not yet abandoned all ideas of aggression against Carthage. We have noted above (p. 151) the existence of prophecies that Spartans were to colonise on a great scale in the furthest western corner of the Gulf of Syrtes. Barka, as we have seen (p. 150), had already sent a fleet westward, which fought against Carthaginians in these waters;[85] and it was probably while Barka still stood, that a Spartan prince duly appeared to claim his inheritance. This was Dorieus, son of King Anaxandridas of Sparta;

[83] Polyb. iii, 22. But the identification of the cape is much debated; see F. W. Walbank, *Commentary on Polyb.*, I (1957) *ad loc.*
[84] *ib.* 25.
[85] Servius, *ad Aen.* iv, 42.

moreover, the eldest son of Anaxandridas' first wife, and in the eyes of many the Man Who Should Have Been King. But the birth of a son to Anaxandridas had been long delayed; so long that, after resisting pressure from the representatives of the people to put away his wife and marry another, he had at last married another *without* putting away the first, 'and kept two households; which was quite contrary to Spartan custom'.[86] And the second wife bore one son, Anaxandridas' eldest; and after that, the first wife bore three in succession. But it was ruled that Kleomenes, the eldest son, was even so the legitimate successor; and he came to the throne, probably not later than 520 B.C. (p. 171).

So 'Dorieus, bitterly disappointed and disdaining to live under Kleomenes, asked the Spartans for men and led them out to found a colony, without consulting the Delphic Oracle or fulfilling any of the usual customs; but he went in anger, and took his ships to Libya, conducted by men of Thera'.[87] The aristocracy of Thera, themselves descended from migrants from Lakonia, also claimed descent from Jason the Minyan, captain of the *Argo*; so it was in their interest also, and in that of their colonists in Cyrenaica, that the above-mentioned prophecies had been issued, that Greeks should settle in mass hard up against the home territory of Carthage.[88]

Dorieus came to the river Kinyps, in later Tripolitania, and there 'settled in the fairest land of the Libyans beside a river. But he was driven out after two years by the Libyan Makai and the Carthaginians, and returned to the Peloponnese. There he was advised by one Antichares of Eleōn, out of the Oracles of Laïos, to found a city at the Sicilian Herakleia; for he said that all the land of Eryx belonged to the Herakleidai, since Herakles himself had won it. At this Dorieus went to Delphi to ask the oracle whether he would hold the land for which he was bound; and the prophetess said that he would hold it. So Dorieus took the same expedition which he had led to Libya, and sailed along the coast of Italy.' Here he was said to have taken part in the great war that had just broken out between Sybaris and Kroton, and assisted the Krotonians in the destruction of their rivals; though the Krotonian

[86] H. v, 40.

[87] H. v, 42. – But D. did not sail to the west until about 514 at earliest, if his adventures there, which occupy only four or five years at most, really ended in the year after the fall of Sybaris, *c.* 510. – cf. p. 173; M. Miller in *Historia*, forthcoming.

[88] pp. 150f, above; cf. H. iv, 145ff; Pindar, *Pyth.* iv; *Lyric Age*, pp. 136ff.

patriotic saga denied all knowledge of such aid. Then he proceeded to the 'land of Eryx' in north-west Sicily, and was defeated and killed by the Phoenicians and the men of Egesta. Thus, in accordance with the oracle, he 'occupied that land permanently'. Some said that it was a judgment on him for disobeying the God's command by carrying out another task on the way.

Only one of his four chief Spartiate officers or 'fellow-founders' survived the disaster. This man, Euryleon by name, now led the remnant of the colonists back from the city which they had founded (it may mean no more than the dedication of an altar) under Mount Eryx, to take land in a less exposed position at Minoa, which he renamed Herakleia, in the eastern territories of Selinous, 'and helped to liberate the Selinuntines from their tyrant Peithagoras'. If Selinous under its tyrant was at this time already in alliance with Carthage, Euryleon was thus still continuing the 'patriotic war'. 'Afterwards, however, having overthrown him, he tried to make himself tyrant of Selinous, and did rule it, but not for long; for the Selinuntines rose against him and slew him, though he fled for sanctuary to the altar of Zeus of the Market Place.' [89]

The Carthaginians proceeded, now if not before the intrusion of Dorieus, and certainly before the destruction of Barka by Aryandes' troops 'about the time of Darius' Scythian expedition' (513±), to push their frontier in Africa far to the east. That there was some fighting against the Greeks (probably of Barka) is stated by late authors; but finally the frontier was fixed near El Agheila, at the Altars of the Philainoi. The Philainoi ('lovers of praise') were said to have been two brothers who, when serving as ambassadors of Carthage, volunteered, apparently as a pledge in fulfilment of an oath that they had acted honestly, to be buried alive there.[90] The story of self-immolation is at least thoroughly Semitic.

Carthage had no small reason to be proud of her achievement. In

[89] H. v, 43–6, to which D.S. iv, 23, Paus. iii, 16, add only the detail (in D.) that Dorieus did 'found' his city. On the Sybarite War, see *Lyric Age*, pp. 384f. If Sybaris fell 58 years before its refoundation as Thouria by Athens, i.e. in 511 (D.S. xi, 90), his years on the Kinyps should be about 514–12 (Dunbabin, *WG*, p. 349).

[90] Sallust, *Jugurtha* 79 (S. had access to some Punic sources in translation, *ib.* 17); Mela, i, 7; Val. Max. vi, 6, ext. 4; the name first appears in ps.-Skylax, 109. Meyer, *GdA* III, pp. 749nn (who needlessly doubts the story of war between Carthage and the Greeks of Cyrenaica), points out that the story of parties starting out from each 'capital', under oath not to cheat by starting too soon, to fix the frontier where they met, reappears in the story of Lampsakos and Parion (Polyainos, vi, 24, etc.).

Spain, in Africa and in the islands, she had checked the Greeks and driven them back some distance. By about 510, the political map of the western Mediterranean had been drawn, which was to last, little altered, until the rise of Rome.

Chapter IX

Sparta and Athens, 520–500

Phoibos Apollo, Lord, who hast fenced our city with towers
  Granting grace to the prince, Pelopid Alkathöos,
Save from the ravaging host of the Medes this city of ours
  Gladly to praise thy name, saved from disaster and loss;
Hundreds of beasts, in the coming of spring, to thy festival bringing
  (Joy in the bountiful feast! Joy in the lyre and the psalm!)
Shouting 'Paian' around thine altar, with dancing and singing;
  Oh! – for I tremble to see how they neglect the alarm,
While Greek faction and strife into ruin the people are flinging.
  Lord, have mercy upon us, and save our city from harm.

Thus prays Theognis, or, if his name be over-sceptically doubted, certainly a poet of Megara, since he honours the memory of Alkathöos, the Megarian hero, who slew the lion of Mount Kithairon.[1] Another poem (ll. 757–68), possibly a little earlier, says 'Let us drink and be merry together, not fearing the host of the Medes'. Now (was it after Darius had begun to use his sea-power and, by taking the Bosporos cities, Megara's colonies, gained a stranglehold on her trade with the Black Sea?) anxiety in old Greece is beginning. The poet deplores, as well he might, the attitude of those who did not share it and were more interested in the internal *stasis*, the neighbourly feuds and envies, which were the curse of Greek life.

Theognis fears for Greece; for the Greek way of life, which he loved, and of which the high tides were marked by those communal festivals of worship, dancing and song, athletics and feasting with the god, on the flesh of the sacrifices; very good to men who had well exercised themselves in dancing or running or wrestling while the huge barbecue was being prepared, and who rarely ate meat on ordinary days. Every human interest was included, from worship to eating (wine was less

[1] Ll. 773–82. On Theognis, see *Lyric Age*, pp. 247–64; Alkathöos, Paus. i, 41, 4; 43, 4.

of a rarity than meat); and all under the brilliant blue sky and among the flowers of an Aegean spring. How long would it all last?

In manpower and skill in arms, both in their use and manufacture, Greece was potentially strong – if she had been united; but Greece was never united; not even the individual cities were that, as our poet grieves to say. Megara, a middling Greek town both in her Isthmian position and in strength (she could raise 3000 armoured soldiers and twenty of the new triremes in 480[2]), had through most of the poet's lifetime been paralysed by class-struggles, in which the old families, the poet and his friends, lost their lands and had to flee for their lives, returning later in a counter-revolution, when the democracy had fallen into confusion, in a mood for revenge.

At this time beyond Kithairon the little city of Plataia, where elements of a pre-Boiotian population held out with their backs to the hills, was surviving with difficulty under pressure from Thebes. Land-hungry like any normal Greek city, Thebes doubtless regarded pre-Boiotian remnants as fair game. In 519, as we hear, the Plataians threw themselves on the mercy of the young king of Sparta, Kleomenes, who 'happened to be in the vicinity'.[3] The question what he was doing there can be answered with a confident conjecture: he was enrolling Megara, under her restored aristocratic government – a government such as Sparta approved – in the confederacy of 'the Lakedaimonians and their allies', called by modern writers the Peloponnesian League.

Sparta, since her defeat of Argos in the Battle of Thyrea (546 tr.), had been beyond dispute the leading power in the Peloponnese. With Messenia conquered and its rebellious helots tamed after a bloody revolt, her own territory embraced two-fifths of the peninsula; though the unquenchable spirit of disaffection in Messenia made that land at times a serious military liability. Failing unexpectedly to conquer her Arcadian neighbour Tegea, Sparta had then wisely turned away from a policy of yet more annexations. Tegea was constrained at last to accept permanent alliance and control of her foreign policy: 'to have the same friends and allies as the Lakedaimonians', i.e. especially, to take her side against Argos. The same policy was applied to the other cities and highland cantons of Arcadia, among which many neighbourly

[2] H. ix, 28; viii, 1.

[3] H. vi, 108; date from Thk. iii, 68. P. not included in the original Boiotian conquest, Thk. iii, 61, 2; 'aboriginal' population, Paus. ix, 1, 2 (cf. the Theban *ex parte* statement in Thk., *ib.*).

enmities made it easy to apply a policy of 'divide and rule'. Elis, with conquered borderlands of her own to hold down, became a faithful ally; so did Corinth and Sikyōn, glad to be protected by a distant suzerain against their powerful neighbour, Argos; so, for the same reasons, did inland Phlious and the cities of the Argolic peninsula, Epidauros, Troizēn and Hermione. And the aristocrats of Megara, 'squeezed' from without by Athens and Corinth, and with disgruntled democrats within, were no doubt glad to accept the same powerful protection.[4] The only Peloponnesian states outside the League were now Argos, whose sulky hostility kept her neighbours loyal, and Achaia, embracing a dozen small cities along the Corinthian Gulf, cut off from Arcadia by rugged mountains and with their own best communications by sea. Close relations with them would have meant northern contacts, which Sparta, a 'sated power', had no reason to desire.

How easily an extension of Spartan protection might lead to new problems was shown conspicuously by the case of Plataia. Sparta had no desire to incur the resentment of distant and powerful Thebes, nor to become involved beyond the Isthmus at all. She was on excellent terms with Athens, now ruled by the able and pacific Hippias, son of Peisistratos. But Athens, already the largest town on the Greek mainland, was growing fast and was potentially very powerful indeed. It probably would have gone against the grain for Kleomenes, brought up in the Greek heroic tradition, to reject a suppliant in any case; but he was also not without a streak of machiavellian cunning. He answered the Plataians, saying that Sparta was really too far off to give effective protection; 'you might all have been taken as slaves several times over before we ever heard of it. But our advice to you is to place yourselves under the Athenians; they are your neighbours, and no mean protectors either.' And this advice the Spartans gave, says Herodotos, not so much for any love of the Plataians as from a desire to embroil Athens and Boiotia.

Athens and Thebes, the leading city of the Boiotian League, as neighbours, could easily become enemies; but it was not a foregone conclusion that they would. They had a good mountain frontier, and if Sparta had shown signs of expanding her sphere of influence still further, they might quite easily have joined forces against her. Later,

[4] For this earlier history see *Lyric Age*, pp. 88, 220, 250, 276ff.

in fact, in the early fourth century, they did. Kleomenes' diplomatic stroke averted that particular danger for 120 years.

The Plataians now formally 'offered themselves to Athens; and the Thebans, hearing of this, marched on Plataia. The Athenians marched to the rescue; but when the armies were in presence, the Corinthians intervened in force, making an offer of arbitration, which was accepted by both sides. Corinthians then defined the frontier, and laid down the condition that Thebes should not molest cities which did not wish to join the Boiotian League. Having given their decision the Corinthians departed; and as the Athenians were withdrawing, the Boiotians attacked them, but were defeated. The Athenians then advanced beyond the Plataian frontier laid down by Corinth, and made the Asōpos the Theban frontier with Plataia and Hysiai'[5] (another village, more to the east, not reckoned as part of Attica).

Kleomenes had thus deftly limited Sparta's commitments in central Greece; but some Spartans, not least the king's brother Dorieus, were ready to use her strength even overseas. She was not without sea-power, and she had long-standing connections with Cyrene and with Asia Minor, especially through an old friendship with Samos.[6] Already Croesus of Lydia had sought Spartan assistance for his war with Cyrus, and Sparta had made an unavailing diplomatic *démarche* to Cyrus on behalf of the Ionians (pp. 39, 44). The Spartan attack on Polykrates of Samos had followed his defection from alliance with Egypt to the side of Cambyses, though it was also prompted by a desire to restore to power Sparta's old allies, the aristocrats; and in 517–16, which would be immediately after the fall of Samos to the Persians and the disappearance of Samian sea-power, the Thalassocracy-List records a two-year thalassocracy (i.e. control of the central Aegean) by Sparta herself. (It is only after this, we notice, that Dorieus appears to have found things intolerable at home and sailed to Libya.) There next follows a fifteen-year sea-power of Naxos, which at this time is credited by Herodotos with over-lordship over 'Paros, Andros and the other Cyclades', a considerable 'duchy', capable of raising 8000 armoured soldiers.[7] What had happened is evidently that Sparta, which overthrew the despotism of Lygdamis (an old ally of Peisistratos and of Polykrates) at Naxos,[8] probably at this time, had assisted the Naxian aristocracy to consolidate

[5] H. vi, 108.

[6] Cf. *Lyric Age*, pp. 45, 91f, 180.

[7] H. v, 30f.

[8] Plut. *Mal. Hdt.* 22.

a lordship of the Archipelago, such as had been held in his time by Polykrates. A 'power-vacuum' in the Aegean would be a standing invitation to Persia to engage in further raids like that which had won Samos; an organized Aegean state might, it was hoped, be less tempting. The arrangement broke down when the commons of Naxos, who a generation before had risen under Lygdamis against the arrogance of their nobles, did so again; and the tyrant of Miletos, Persia's lackey, pointed out to Artaphernes at Sardis that this was Persia's opportunity (see below, p. 195).

Hippias of Athens was also considering his position in relation to Persia. His outpost at Sigeion, at the mouth of the Dardanelles, at one time governed by his younger half-brother Hegesistratos, had been within Persia's sphere of influence since the time of Cyrus, though it was not administered or effectively controlled till later. Hegesistratos' defence of his outpost against the islanders of Mytilene, who claimed the whole area, must have come well after the Persian conquest of Lydia; for he was not born till after 561, though old enough to be in command (nominally?) of volunteers from his mother's city of Argos at the time of his father's final re-establishment at Athens.[9] Such minor wars in the far north-west could, then, go on under Cyrus, no less than clan-fights in the Highlands under the Stewart Kings of Scots; it was not till the settlement of 493 that Artaphernes, acting for Darius with his eye to peace and taxable prosperity, insisted that they should stop (p. 221).

However, the Scythian and Balkan expedition had now brought the king in person to the Hellespont, and the Hellespontine tyrants had helped to make and guard his bridge on the Danube. Hippias' governor at Sigeion (no longer Hegesistratos, who had returned to Athens) must have 'done homage' for his principality; and Hippoklos, tyrant of Lampsakos, which city had fought repeated wars against the Athenian outpost in the Chersonese, had won favour with Darius by loyal service. Darius had personally returned through the Chersonese; Persian power was firmly established in Europe; and Miltiades, prince of the Chersonese, whom Hippias and his brothers had sent out in a warship to take over on the death of his brother Stesagoras, was now on the run. Hippias apparently 'wrote off' the Chersonese and decided on friendship with Lampsakos, arranging a marriage between his daughter Archedike and Aiantides, son of Hippoklos, 'an Athenian with a Lampsakene'.

9 H. v, 94; *Ath. P.* 17, 3f.

The point of this remark of Thucydides is not, as some have understood it, that Lampsakos was an insignificant city; it was rich and important; but that it was an old enemy.[10]

In this change of front, Hippias was looking out for a line of retreat, as Thucydides tells us, in case his position at Athens should become untenable. It was already shaken.

Relations between the Peisistratidai and the other leading families of Attica had deteriorated since the 'honeymoon' at the beginning of Hippias' reign, when the heads of all the chief families in succession had held the official headship of state, the annual archonship, beginning with Hippias himself. Kleisthenes of the Alkmeonidai had gone into opposition and into exile, at Delphi, where long ago his grandfathers had met as allies, 'liberating' the oracular sanctuary in the First Sacred War; he was now applying his great practical talents to the rebuilding of the temple, accidentally burned down in 548 tr. Miltiades, 'written off' as an asset, may already have been accusing the Peisistratids of the murder of his father Kimon, thrice Olympic victor in the chariot-race, who had been killed at Athens by 'persons unknown' before 524. Harmodios and Aristogeiton of the Gephyraian family, who claimed descent from the companions of Kadmos, had murdered Hippias' brother Hipparchos and been killed themselves, though admittedly this was in prosecution of a private quarrel. Hippias, in fear for his life, killed men on suspicion, and made more and more enemies. He began the construction of a castle giving the chance of a retreat by sea, on the rock of Mounychia, west of the Bay of Phaleron where Athenians at this time drew up their ships, the first recorded construction on the site where the great port of Piraeus was to arise. But before it was finished he was expelled by Kleomenes of Sparta, in obedience to the command of the Delphic Oracle to 'liberate Athens'.[11]

Later it was commonly believed that Kleisthenes had used his influence at Delphi, not excluding bribery, to procure this oracle; but Kleomenes, who, in the Spartan tradition reported to Herodotos, is never given credit for any prudent or patriotic motives, may have had his own reasons. The Peisistratidai had always kept on good terms with Sparta; but now, Hippias' relations with Persia were at least

[10] Thk. vi, 59; Wade-Gery, *Essays*, p. 166; Hippoklos at the bridge, H. iv, 138; wealth of L., Xen. *Hell.* ii, 1, 19, cf. Ath. Tribute-Lists (usually about 12 talents).

[11] On all this see *Lyric Age*, pp. 320ff. Mounychia, *Ath. P.* 19.

ambiguous, and the Spartan king may have calculated that a restored Athenian republic would be more reliable.

Kleisthenes of Athens came home in triumph; but for all his prestige and his contacts in the business world, the leading position in Athenian politics, to which he aspired, did not prove easy to gain. Already his father before him had been protagonist among the defenders of the economic reforms and modernised constitution of Solon, against both reactionary squires on the one hand and Peisistratos, the revolutionary Friend of the Poor, on the other. Now, with the late dictatorship discredited, surely the path to leadership should be clear for the republican who enjoyed the powerful friendship of the Delphic Apollo?

But among the other aristocratic families, the brilliant House of Alkmeon was not popular; and for two years it seems that, to use eighteenth-century terms, a coalition of tories kept the formidable whig aristocrat out. Under Solon's constitution, real elections by the Assembly of all free adult male Athenians determined which candidates, qualified by the possession of 'equestrian' landed property, should hold the yearly archonships, and thereafter, if their account of their actions was passed by the Assembly, pass into the august Council of Areopagus for life. Earlier, it appears that candidatures had been discussed in advance by the Areopagites, and that, whether or not there was a formal election by the Assembly (we are not told that there was), the nominees of the Areopagus, like those of the committee in many modern voluntary societies, were always chosen.[12] Solon had put a stop to this by putting the preparation of business for the Assembly into the hands of his new People's Council of four hundred citizens (citizens in good standing and prepared to give freely of their time) chosen by lot, a hundred from each of the four ancient Ionic tribes; a committee of good, average citizens, in whose selection family influence and personal prestige played no part. But influence could still play a great part in the canvass for the direct election of the great officers: the Archon or Regent, who was the civil head of state, the sacral King, the War-Chief and the six Judges or Thesmothetai. Groups of political allies, called 'companionships' (*hetaireiai*), among the well-to-do political class, devoted themselves with success to promoting the election of their friends.

[12] *Ath. P.* viii, 2.

Among the voters, the most amenable would naturally be those peasant farmers who were accustomed to look up to the chief families of their districts. Attica was still predominantly a peasant country; but the city and its manufactures (pottery the best known to us) had grown fast under the Peisistratids; and the voters *least* amenable to the persuasion of the aristocracy may be presumed to have been the city workers, some of them prosperous craftsmen, artists and workshop proprietors, whose ties were with their neighbours and fellow-craftsmen, rather than with the squires. This class would tend rather to reinforce the Coast-Dwellers, who had long since followed the lead of the cosmopolitan Alkmeonidai.

But many of these townsmen were immigrants, or immigrants' children. Thus the best hope, for the conservatives, of preventing them from some day electing their own candidates to office, lay in weakening their voting strength by excluding as many as possible of them from citizenship. Solon had provided that masters of a useful craft, who migrated to Athens with their families, might become citizens.[13] Many had so migrated; especially, it is probable, under the Peisistratids and since the Persian domination of Ionia, which many Greeks found irksome from the first. Under the tyrants they passed unchallenged as residents and, in this sense, Athenians; there were no reasons why they *should* be challenged, since the election of archons, though not discontinued, was controlled by the government: 'they saw to it that the offices were always filled by one or other of their own people'.[14] Now they expected to exercise voting rights. But many of them, even if qualified under Solon's law, had evidently failed to fulfil the formalities which would have secured them an unchallenged place on the citizen rolls. Many too had probably turned out to vote by acclamation for the Chief's candidates, who, though not immigrants, were of dubious citizen status; sons of a citizen father and a slave mother, for example. 'Those who were not of pure descent' rallied to Peisistratos, says the Aristotelian writer, perhaps reading back the conditions of 510 into the 550's, through fear [i.e. of being relegated to inferior status]; 'as we may see from the fact that after the fall of the tyrants a revision of the voting lists was held, on the ground that many were exercising political rights who ought not to be'.[15] It was the natural desire of the

[13] Plut. *Solon*, 24.
[14] Thk. vi, 54, 6.
[15] *Ath. P.* 13, 5.

well-organised conservatives to disenfranchise as many as possible of these potentially radical voters.

The first two chief archons elected after Harpaktides (511–10), in whose year Hippias was ejected, are practically unknown to us. Skamandrios, under whom the decree was passed forbidding the use of torture against Athenian citizens, may well have been the first. The decree is likely to have been one of the first popular enactments of liberated Athens; and torture had recently been used on Aristogeiton and others in the investigation into the murder of Hipparchos.[16] The name Skamandrios is itself interesting, suggesting as it does that at the time of his birth his father was engaged in one of Athens' old wars with Mytilene or other kindred activity in connection with her foothold in the Troad. Next seems to have come a Lysagoras, named in the Parian Marble as archon when 'choruses of men first competed'.[17]

Through these two years, Kleisthenes had met with no success in pressing his own candidate; not himself, for he had already been archon in 525, and it was not customary to hold the chief position more than once, but probably a kinsman named Alkmeon (p. 187, below). Meanwhile many of the voters who had passed as citizens under the tyranny had been disenfranchised, and more of them probably feared that they would be. The archon elected to take office at midsummer, 508, was Isagoras,[18] son of Teisandros, 'of a noble family', says Herodotos, 'but I cannot say who his ancestors were'. As Isagoras passed into history with a 'bad press', perhaps his family in the fifth century were not anxious to claim him. It is tempting to connect him with the same family (Miltiades' family, the Philaïdai) as Teisandros the father of Hippokleides, 'related to the Kypselidai of Corinth', who had been the rival of Kleisthenes' father for the hand of the daughter of Kleisthenes of Sikyon,[19] but the name Teisandros is a common one, and one cannot build on it.

[16] T. J. Cadoux, 'The Athenian Archons', in *JHS* LXVIII, p. 113 and T7 (p. 71), = Andok. *On the Mysteries* 43 (the Decree).

[17] Cadoux, *loc. cit.* and T27. (Isagoras, read here by some, after Böckh, is an emendation.)

[18] D.H. i, 74, 6; v, 1, 1, fixing the date by that of Olympiad 68.

[19] H. vi, 128f; v, 66. Wade-Gery (*Essays*, p. 164, n. 3) objects that there is no recorded relationship between the younger Miltiades' father Kimon and uncle the elder Miltiades except through their mother, and that this tie 'did not make Kimon a Philaid', such as his half-brother, Miltiades the son of Kypselos, was (Marcell. *Life of Thucydides*, 3, from Pherekydes, = *FGH* 3 F2). It did, however, as he says, 'bind the half-brothers very closely'. Not only the name Miltiades but also the principality of the Chersonese passed

But at this point Kleisthenes decided on more drastic action. 'Getting the worst of it in the *hetaireiai*', 'he took the people into his party', say our sources;[20] both remarks sound like echoes of the hostile comments of his opponents. He proposed a measure by which all free dwellers in Attica should be placed on the citizen rolls at one stroke, by legislation. There was great enthusiasm; even those who had been struck off could, presumably, demonstrate. The Assembly may even have passed the measure in principle, at once; and Isagoras, alarmed at the prospect of seeing his rival dominating future elections with the backing of thousands of lower-class voters, sent for help to Kleomenes. He could appeal to the sacred bond of hospitality, for Kleomenes had lodged in his house at the time of the recent siege of the Acropolis. 'Kleomenes was also rumoured to have had an affair with Isagoras' wife', adds Herodotos (v, 70), which is a typical piece of Greek scandal. But no doubt he also added the political argument that revolution was imminent; the respectable republic so recently established by Sparta was in danger of breaking down. In the meantime, he set the machinery of law in motion against Kleisthenes himself. Kleisthenes and all the Alkmeonidai, he asserted, should not only be disenfranchised but should not be in Attica at all; they were under a curse and had long ago been legally banished for the sacrilegious massacre of the partisans of Kylon.[21] A message arrived from Sparta indicating that King Kleomenes approved of this purge.

Kleisthenes, in face of the attack, withdrew abroad. Since nothing in his career suggests that he was either scrupulous or faint-hearted, this remarkable move suggests that he had formed a clear judgment of the people's temper and of what was likely to follow. The people, oblivious of what their fathers had owed to Peisistratos, had been glad to see the Spartans come to end the tyranny of Peisistratos' sons; a tyranny grown truly tyrannical in the modern sense, whose guards, supported by Thessalian riders and Scythian archers, the disarmed populace could not have ejected by themselves. But they had not cheered for freedom and the ancestral laws in order to see the ring of patrician families take

---

from the childless Miltiades, son of Kypselos, to his maternal half-brother's family. I would suspect that this means not only that 'her family was important', as Wade-Gery says, *ib.*, but that her two husbands were themselves related in the male line. Was she too a Philaïd heiress?

[20] (*a*) *Ath. P.* 20, 1; (*b*) H. v, 66, 2.

[21] See *Lyric Age*, p. 286f.

back all power into their own hands. Let the reactionaries, with or without a foreign king, try to interfere with the Council's and Assembly's action under the powers clearly granted to them by the Laws of Solon, and let them see what they would stir up.

Meanwhile, Kleisthenes would not risk being the first to cause bloodshed, or remain as a symbol of discord with the stigma of ancestral blood-guilt upon him. His great-grandfather had incurred the family curse through being too impatient. Kleisthenes knew how to wait. He had waited for years.

Sure enough, Isagoras and his friends were encouraged by his withdrawal to overplay their hand. Now was the opportunity, they felt. Their friend Kleomenes came, with a bodyguard, not an army, to support a friendly government in the restoration of good order; and, no doubt by sentence of the Council of Areopagus, always the supreme court in cases of homicide and Protector of the Laws (especially of religion) under the constitution of Solon, they proclaimed the banishment of 700 families, including the whole Alkmeonid faction. The banishment was to be for ever. Alkmeonid graves were dug up, and bones cast out beyond the frontiers. The fine sixth-century tombstone to two children of a Megakles, perhaps a brother and sister of Kleisthenes, in the Metropolitan Museum at New York, may owe its ultimate preservation to having been thrown down at this time. Then the reactionary party took the decisive step. With the support of Kleomenes, they proclaimed the dissolution of the People's Council of Four Hundred, to be replaced by three hundred of Isagoras' partisans.

This meant putting the clock back to the times before Solon. It was the overthrow of a lawfully constituted authority by force; and it was at this point that the Athenian people rose. They had regained control of their arms presumably at the time of the fall of Hippias. The Council refused to go (no mean display of courage by four hundred average citizens, faced by Athenian aristocrats and a king of Sparta). A crowd collected, and Kleomenes and Isagoras with their men fell back on the Acropolis; 'and the rest of the Athenians with one accord besieged them there for two days'.[22]

This is all that our sources actually tell us about the operation, and a blockade of two days might hardly seem to rank among the great sieges of history. Yet it was not least among the achievements of the

[22] H. v, 72; *Ath. P.* 20, which for the most part follows H., but adds a detail or two.

people of Athens. The remarkable fact is that they did this – they not merely rioted, but kept up an effective blockade of a fortress containing several hundred well-armed, trained and desperate men, for forty-eight hours, initially without even organized leadership. They did have, among other stabilising influences on morale, the fact that they were defending established and legal rights; and they had among them the four hundred stalwarts of the Council who had committed the first act of resistance; but the Council had never been an executive body, and its members, chosen by lot, had never even been meant to include, unless by the luck of the draw, any natural leaders. Through the treason of Isagoras and his friends and the banishment of Kleisthenes' party, there must, indeed, have been hardly a single really prominent Athenian left among them; but never did the Greek capacity for concerted action without obvious leadership show to greater advantage.

It is worth while to imagine the situation from the point of view of the besieged. No one had expected this development, and the citadel was presumably unsupplied with food or water. At first, they may have expected to be able to sally out when the mob's enthusiasm had cooled off. But the Athenians proved to be more than a mob. When evening fell, they were still there. In the middle of the night they were still there, sleeping all over the place, but with their weapons handy; Kleomenes was not going to lead his Spartans out into that wasps' nest. In the morning, we may imagine, Kleomenes woke with a question on his lips, to receive the answer 'They are still there'. The thirsty garrison could see the women bringing up food and drink; and probably more contingents from the country were joining the townsmen. And so on through the heat of the day, to the second evening and the second night. When the third day dawned, they were still there, and Kleomenes sent his herald out to negotiate. Isagoras was a badly frightened man; but the position was hopeless. The herald returned. The Council's terms, from which they refused to budge, were that the Spartans must surrender their arms; having done so, they should receive safe conduct out of the country. All others on the Acropolis must surrender at discretion.

Never had a Spartan king been so humiliated; but Kleomenes was a realist. He went, with his men; and with them he succeeded in conveying out his guest-friend, the wretched Isagoras, abandoning his comrades, who in due course were put to death. The Athenians did not flout heaven by a second Kyloneian massacre; they kept them as prisoners for a short time and voted their execution regularly. It was the people's finest hour to date. A century later the chorus of Old Men in Aristophanes' *Lysistrata*, when the women's Stop-the-War movement has seized the citadel, recall, by dramatic licence, their part in the matter:

> Shall women have the laugh of me? – Now, by Our Lady, NO!
> Why, not Kleomenes himself, who seized it long ago
>   Got off so lightly; woe betide
>   The snorting Spartan in his pride;
>   He left his arms with me!
>   And, barely decent in his shirt,
>   Unkempt, unshaved, in six years' dirt
>   Unwashed, we saw him flee.
> So fierce a watch and ward did we upon *that* hero keep,
> With seventeen-deep embattled shields before the doors asleep![23]

So, says Herodotos, 'for Kleomenes the word was fulfilled; for when he went up to the Acropolis intending to seize it, he went towards the sanctuary of the Goddess to address her; and the priestess rose up from her chair before he passed through the door, and said "Stranger from Sparta, go back and do not enter the holy place; for it is unlawful for Dorians to enter here." But he said: "Lady, but I am not a Dorian but an Achaian." So, not availing himself of the omen, he made his attempt, and was driven out together with his Spartans.' [24]

Meanwhile the Athenians had already sent for Kleisthenes and his fellow-exiles; and promptly, still 'in the archonship of Isagoras', now if not before the disturbances, the great reform-bill was voted by the Council and People. In the usual manner for Greek states when it was intended to enfranchise numerous new voters, Athens adopted a new tribal system.[25] Instead of the four ancient Ionic tribes, a system of ten was introduced; no doubt, in the growing population, it was administratively convenient to have a larger number of subdivisions. They were named after ancient kings and other 'heroes' or worthies of Attica.

[23] *Lys.* 271ff; H. v, 72f; 74, 1; the whole play is rich in reminiscences of this heroic age; cf. 630ff (Aristogeiton), 664ff (Leipsydrion), 1150ff (fall of the tyranny), 675, 1250ff (Xerxes' invasion), as well as of later history.

[24] v, 72, 3.

[25] Cf. H. iv, 161 (Cyrene); D.S. xii, 11 (Thouria); these are the most fully described examples.

A list of a hundred names was submitted to the Delphic Oracle, and the names given by its choice were (in an order regularly followed in inscriptions from the fifth century onwards) Erechthēis, Aigēis, Pandīonis, Leontis, Akamantis, Oinēis, Kekropis, Hippothöontis, Aiantis, Antiochis.[26] To these were allotted all free men of Attica, according to their places of residence or *dēmoi*, administrative parishes as they might be called. These were for the most part named after existing villages or townships; Marathon, Eleusis, Acharnai were each a large *dēmos*; but where convenient names did not exist, as in the city or in scattered farming areas, they were allotted; many of these are of patronymic form (e.g. Lakiadai, Skambonidai, the demes of Kimon and Alkibiades), and so are probably derived from the names of local families whose monuments were there. To be a registered member of a *dēmos* was, henceforth, to be an Athenian, of the tribe to which that *dēmos* belonged; and every Athenian's 'official style' consisted of his name, the name of his father and the name of his deme. So there were to be no more pettifogging questions about whether a new citizen or the son of an immigrant was properly affiliated to one of the ancient Athenian families.[27]

This was one aspect of the great reform, and the aspect, no doubt, which aroused the greatest enthusiasm among the democratic voters. No longer could one have one's credentials inspected, at the clan level, if one displeased the squire and his relations.[28] As for eligibility to the higher offices, that continued for fifty years yet to be confined, as in Solon's constitution, to the 'cavalry class'. There is no evidence that the masses even aspired to it. That a poor man could afford the time or possess the skill to cope with the growing administrative work of an archon no doubt appeared impossible; and when, in 457, the archonships *were* thrown open to citizens of the Zeugite or 'smallholder' assessment,[29] it was when not only had 'the people gained confidence',

[26] Cf. e.g., the war-memorial of 440–439, *IG* I², 943 (Tod, *GHI* 48); a possible allusion, H. vi, 111, 1, on Marathon, in the phrase 'as the tribes were numbered'. Aiantis (for Ajax of Salamis, not an Attic hero but 'a neighbour and ally', H. v, 66, 2) proclaimed the definitive incorporation of Ajax' island.

[27] *Ath. P.* 21, 2. For deme-registration see *ib.* 42.

[28] For the kind of thing that could happen at the 'local government level', still under the democracy, if an influential man wanted to get a fellow-citizen struck off the deme-roll, see Demosth. *Against Euboulides* (with a classic case of the mistake of getting a majority vote larger than the total of those present); but at least there was now an appeal to the courts. In 508, the fact that democracy might develop its own forms of corruption was still happily unknown.

[29] *Ath. P.* 26, 2.

as the Aristotelian writer would say, but the archonships themselves had lost their ancient prestige and importance. Ordinary Athenians were never envious that prominent men should monopolise the great offices and their care and danger, so long as Demos could first choose among the candidates and afterwards control them (harry them, sometimes) in the Assembly and in the People's Courts when they gave an account of their actions. Social equality, as between rich and poor citizens, never existed in classical Athens. 'Do you, a poor man, dare to talk like that?' is a thrice-repeated attempt of the Acharnians and the general Lāmachos to snub Aristophanes' hero Dikaiopolis, whose name stands for 'political justice';[30] and the comic extravagance is in the fact that he does dare; not that people try to suppress him, but that he is irrepressible. Only the grossest exhibitions of arrogance based on wealth roused effective opposition, as to Demosthenes enemy Meidias, and, after many years of 'getting away with it', to Alkibiades; and even the fact that a gentleman cannot push a poor man out of his way is ranked as an example of democratic cheekiness by the late fifth-century 'Old Oligarch'.[31]

However, there was another aspect of reform that Kleisthenes had at heart. Like the French revolutionaries on their larger stage, he was concerned for the effective unification of the country; for the ending of those local rivalries and the combination of political and social with local differences, which had emerged in the struggles of Plain, Coast and Upland parties in the generation after Solon, and had rendered political quarrels more liable to lead to civil war. Kleisthenes is always in our sources given the credit for every detail of the great reform; and though this might be an example of a well-known convention in historical traditions, there is in this case no reason to disbelieve it. Certainly the originality and ingenuity of the machinery now devised was the work of a master-hand.

Kleisthenes could most easily and obviously have grouped the local demes into local tribes; but this was exactly what he carefully avoided. Instead, he formed the demes (probably about 170 in number)[32] into *thirty* groups, called Thirds, *trittyes*; sometimes a very large deme, such as Acharnai, may have formed a whole *trittys*. Ten of these were formed

[30] *Ach.* 558, 578, 593.
[31] Ps.-Xen. *Pol. Ath.* i, 10.
[32] Polemon (3rd century) *ap.* Str. ix, 396, says 174.

in the city and the surrounding country, ten in the other coastal districts, and ten in the interior; and to every tribe was allotted a *trittys* from each 'section', so that it contained citizens from each part of the country. The word *trittys* was already familiar; there had been 'thirds' as subdivisions of the four old tribes, though we know nothing of their functions; a consideration which caused Kleisthenes, it was said, to avoid the otherwise convenient number of twelve tribes, in the interests of making his operation of 'mixing up the people' still more radical.[33] The Kleisthenic local *trittyes* were deliberately given no administrative functions; the Tribes were the administrative units, competing in the musical and athletic festivals and raising each a battalion of the army. Thus the work of Theseus of old in the unification of Attica was effectively completed. It will have been noticed that the name of Theseus is conspicuously absent among the Heroes of the Tribes; and this is not, I think, merely 'the luck of the draw'. Theseus, the Unifier, belonged to all Athens.

The organization of the Council was also reformed on the basis of the new tribes. Its numbers were raised from 400 to 500, 50 from each tribe; and the tribes took it in turn to 'preside', *prytaneuein*, for one-tenth of the year, 35 or 36 days, which period was called a prytany. (The year had normally 354 days, with periodic intercalation of a month.) This function was performed not in the fixed tribal order, but in an order determined by casting lots, towards the end of each prytany, among the tribes that had not yet presided during the current civil year; this avoided such inequalities as allowing any one tribe always to preside over the annual elections. During its prytany the Councillors of the presiding tribe, themselves called *prytaneis* or presidents, daily drew lots for the appointment of an *epistates*, the 'man in charge' or duty-officer of the republic. 'He holds office for a night and a day, and may not do so for longer than that, nor do so twice.' (A man might be Councillor twice in his lifetime.) 'He keeps the keys of the temples in which the treasuries and the archives are kept, and the seal of the state, and he must remain in the Round House' [*Tholos*, the prytaneis' clubhouse or mess, next to the council chamber] 'together with one-third [*trittys*] of the prytaneis, whichever he commands. And when the prytaneis convene the Council or the Assembly,' – probably he, in the fifth century, was chairman of the meeting, though at the time of

[33] *Ath. P.* 21, 3f.

writing of the *Politeia* a more complex arrangement had been devised. In the fifth century it appears that the Epistates had the duty of 'putting the question'; no small power and responsibility for this ephemeral President. It is typical of the fourth-century reformers to put even this power into commission.[34]

When it was needful, this democratic machinery could function very fast. Any ambassador or any messenger from abroad knew, or anyone in Athens could tell him, where at any hour of the day or night he would find the responsible officers of the state on duty; and then it rested with the epistates and his committee to decide whether the business demanded an immediate meeting of the full council or the assembly (which could only meet after the council had considered, at least summarily, the business to lay before it), or whether the military authorities, who would act only on instructions from the assembly, should be informed, so that they might be considering their measures. A good example of the democracy in action is Demosthenes' account of what happened when the news came in that Philip of Macedon had passed Thermopylai unopposed and secured the old fortress of Elateia in Phokis:

> Evening had fallen, when a man came in with news to the prytaneis of the occupation of Elateia; and at that, they sprang up at once in the middle of their dinner, and some started clearing the stallholders out of the market-place and setting fire to the wicker-work,[35] and some sent for the generals and summoned the trumpeter; and the whole city was in an uproar. And next morning at first light, while the prytaneis called the council to the council-chamber, you were on your way to the assembly; and before the council had done its business and prepared an agenda-sheet, the whole people was seated up there on the hill. Then the council entered, and the prytaneis reported the news they had received, and introduced the man who

[34] *Ath. P.* 44. For the 5th cent. cf. Thk. vi, 14 (argument that public interest should override the fear of getting into trouble for the formal illegality of re-opening a question that has been decided); Xen. *Mem.* i, 1, 18; iv, 4, 2, where Socrates as Epistates refuses to put the question on the illegal proposal, denying proper trial to the generals in 406. Plato in *Gorgias*, 473–4, makes S., with characteristic irony, refer to this, saying that he was so inexpert in politics that he did not know how to put the question and made a fool of himself. Xen. *Hell.* i, 7, 14f, and Plato in the *Apology*, 32b (passages where both authors are probably being more careful of their history), say only that S. was one of the Prytaneis; but the more colourful story is evidence on the function of the Epistates.

[35] Presumably of the stallholders' huts; there was no time to 'clear the decks' in an orderly way.

had brought it, to tell his story; and finally the Herald asked 'Who wishes to address the meeting?'

– and after a dramatic silence, which he allowed to last long enough to let the city feel its need of him, Demosthenes came forward, the man who in all Athens had probably been least surprised by the news. He proposed that forthwith, forgetting old grievances, an alliance should be offered to Thebes, which was immediately threatened, that the fleet should put to sea, to cut Philip's sea communications, and that, in support of the offer to Thebes, the army, horse and foot, should move out at once as far as Eleusis.[36]

The new system was in being under the next known archon, Alkmeon, probably a kinsman of Kleisthenes. He might well, though we lack definite evidence, be the son of that Alkmeonides, son of the elder Alkmeon, who dedicated in exile in Boiotia a votive thankoffering for a victory in a Panathenaic chariot-race, and father of the man who prosecuted Themistokles in 471.[37] But danger from abroad was not yet over. Kleomenes, smarting under his humiliation, was calling out the levies of the Peloponnesian League; and, realising that he would not accept defeat easily, the Athenians sent envoys to Sardis to seek help from Persia. Artaphernes was very willing to offer protection, on the usual terms: Athens must offer the symbolic earth and water, the tokens of the surrender of the land to the Great King. This the envoys, 'on their own responsibility, promised, in their anxiety to obtain the alliance; when they got home, they were severely censured for it'.[38]

Thus Herodotos, who, receiving information from circles close to Pericles, Kleisthenes' great-nephew, is frankly committed to the view that the Alkmeonidai were always hostile to the Peisistratidai and therefore to their friends in Persia.[39] They never *really* collaborated. Part of this plea we know to be false, and we are therefore bound to question factual statements which support it. Can we really believe that Kleisthenes did not know that Persia gave protection only to those who acknowledged the supremacy of the king? And can we believe that the answer to be given if Artaphernes demanded earth and water, even from west of the Aegean, had not been discussed with them before they

[36] *On the Crown*, 284f.

[37] A. 'under whom the tribes became ten in number', Pollux, viii, 110. Votive inscr. from the Ptöion in Boiotia, *BCH* XLIV; Hiller v. Gärtringen, *Hist. Gr. Epigramme*, 4; Leobotes, s. of A., Plut. *Them.* 23; Cadoux, *op. cit.* p. 114; T. 97.

[38] H. v, 73.

[39] vi, 121.

left home? All that we know of the Alkmeonidai in the sixth century is consistent with the view that they followed a strictly dynastic family policy, with power in Athens as its end, and with any means that would serve. If Kleisthenes himself disowned the ambassadors on their return, it is probably because stirring doings, which may have taken place during their absence, had rendered the danger to his reforms less immediate.

In the spring, probably, of 507 Kleomenes led out all the power of the Spartans and their allies to crush the revolution. His object, we are told, was to install his friend Isagoras as tyrant of Athens; but that is probably Kleisthenic propaganda. It would be more in keeping with current Spartan policy if he intended to restore him to power in an aristocratic republic. In any case, the Peloponnesian levies advanced to Eleusis. Some damage was done, in the normal course of 'ravaging the land' (an operation which served, in Greek warfare, the strategic purpose of trying to bring the defending army to battle); damage, if not to the famous sanctuary itself, then at least to some property belonging to it; Athenian piety delighted to attribute Kleomenes' later misfortunes to the wrath of the Eleusinian Goddesses.[40] In the meantime, to make final and overwhelming victory yet more sure, the Chalkidians and Boiotians invaded Attica, at the prompting of Kleomenes, from the north-east and north-west; the latter, leaving Plataia to be dealt with at their leisure, overran the intermontane villages of Oinoe and Hysiai, covered against any Athenian counterstroke by Kleomenes' army at Eleusis. The Athenians had mustered to face Kleomenes, whose best line of advance was through the wide gap between the north end of the Aigaleos ridge and the forest edge of Mount Parnes. They must have been terribly outnumbered, but it was never their way to concede defeat without fighting. And now, it must have seemed to them, a miracle happened: the enemy did not advance further. There were signs of animated discussion, with comings and goings between the contingents; and presently, contingent after contingent turned and marched off. Without a blow struck, the vast army of the Peloponnese melted away.

The allies, it appears, had not been informed of Kleomenes' intentions; by their treaties, they must have been pledged to follow where they were led; but they were not slaves of Sparta, and when the objective

[40] H. vi, 75, 3.

did become clear, the Corinthians, old friends of Athens against Aigina and Megara, pleaded qualms of conscience and marched away. Then Dāmarātos, the other king of Sparta, 'who had not been opposed to Kleomenes previously', took the lead among the doubters; 'and as a result of this dissension, it was made law at Sparta that both kings should not go out on an expedition; and, as one of them was omitted from the command, that one of the Sons of Tyndareus should be left behind too. Hitherto both of them also used to go with the army, being summoned to its aid.' [41]

Such was, as one might say, the Valmy of the Athenian revolution. Its first great feats of arms followed at once. Having 'seen off' the main enemy, the Athenians turned about and marched against the Chalkidians, of whose depredations they had probably heard more than they had heard from Oinoe and Hysiai. The Boiotians in turn marched east to the rescue of their allies. The Athenians, whose reconnaissance work was evidently entirely adequate, then changed direction suddenly and fell upon the Boiotians first, routing them with great slaughter and the loss of 700 prisoners, who were held for ransom. Meanwhile the Chalkidians had got away home across the water; but the Athenians, so far from being content with what they had done, crossed after them, fought a second battle on the same day, and routed them too. It was a shattering defeat for Chalkis. Once more there were many prisoners for ransom, and the Athenians broke for ever the power of the once formidable horsemen of Chalkis, annexing a vast slice of territory, which the Hippobotai ('horse-pasturers'), 'as the rich men of Chalkis were called', had used probably for ranching, and distributing it in smallholdings to no less than 4000 poor Athenians. These colonists, called *klērouchoi*, literally 'allotment-holders', kept their status as citizens of Athens, though distance must have prevented them from playing much part in politics. The prisoners were kept in irons until ransomed, at the then customary price of 200 drachmas apiece; after which the Athenians dedicated the fetters on the Acropolis as a trophy. 'These fetters', adds Herodotos, 'were still there in my time, hanging on walls marked by fire from the Persian invasion, opposite the west end of the Temple. With a tithe of the ransom-money, they also set up a bronze four-horsed chariot-group', with a verse epigram commemorating the victory, which, as surviving remains show, was to be

[41] H. v, 75.

restored later, in the time of Pericles, to cheer Athenian spirits in a time of more chequered fortune.[42]

The crushing of Chalkis must have been very welcome to Chalkis' south-eastern neighbour, Eretria. That sister city, across the water-meadows by the Lelantine torrent, had colonised long ago in partnership with Chalkis, in the first pioneering ventures on the Bay of Naples, and at Corfu on the way. Then had come rivalry at home and abroad, and defeat in the great Lelantine War; and for two centuries Eretria scarcely figures in our histories. But she remained still a not inconsiderable city, ready to take the lead in Euboia again should anything happen to her rival, and even to play a part on a wider stage. Something had now happened, and it is after the Athenian victories on land that Eretria figures, according to the Thalassocracy-List, as the chief sea-power of the Aegean for a space, beginning in 505; succeeding Naxos, whose power was being disrupted by class-struggles at this time (p. 195). Eretria did not rise to this prominence suddenly from nothing, and it has been plausibly suggested that she was already on friendly terms with Athens, and that her fleet assisted the Athenians in their swift crossing of the strait.[43] But we must not make too much of this. It is surely open to doubt whether Eretria was ever really so powerful as the List suggests. Was she really stronger than Chios, for example, said to have had 100 ships in 495 (p. 210)? And if the 'thalassocrat' had really been on terms of regular alliance with Athens, then Athens' war with Aigina should have taken a different course. It seems more likely that any sea-power of Eretria at this time was strictly local, and that her co-operation with Athens was limited to particular occasions, against particular enemies; against Chalkis very probably, as against Persia later (pp. 199ff).

> So Athens grew [continues Herodotos in a famous passage]; and it shows, not in one incident only but throughout, what a noble thing is democracy [*isēgoriē*, 'equality of speech']; for the Athenians when under the tyrants were no more than a match in war for their neighbours, but when they were quit of the tyrants they were far the best. This shows therefore that when they were under a master they did not do their best, as working for him, but when they were freed every man was zealous to do the best for himself.

[42] H. v, 77; *IG* I², 394+, = *GHI* (1969), no. 15; Hiller, *H. Gr. Ep.* 9 and 51; the standard ransom, cf. H. vi, 79.

[43] Myres, in *JHS* XXVII; and in *Herodotus, Father of History*, pp. 182f.

It might also have been Kleisthenes' finest hour; but in fact he drops out of Herodotos' story, and we hear no more of him. A late and weak tradition[44] says that he was exiled, the very first victim of one of his own ingenious laws, under which any man who was thought a danger to the republic might be banished, without loss of property or status, for ten years (cf. pp. 286f, below). Whether or not this is literally true, it has often been suggested that he fell into disgrace when his policy of submission to Persia was disowned, as it evidently was now that the pressing danger had been averted. One ought not to ignore the possibility that the truth is less sensational, and that he merely fell sick and died about this time; it was now about sixty-four years since the marriage of his parents. But it is still perhaps a little surprising that, after all his adventures and achievements, he passes in silence from the stage.[45]

War with the Boiotian League continued. The Thebans consulted Delphi, and received the vague oracular advice to 'ask aid of those nearest'. Since the cities of Tanagra, Koroneia and Thespiai were already actively taking part in the League's war, this appeared unhelpful, until the suggestion was made that, since in the mythical genealogies Thebe and Aigina were daughters of the river-god Asōpós, Aigina was a 'sister city', and application should be made to her. The Aiginetans took a good deal of rousing. Their first response was to 'send the Aiakidai', presumably the images of those heroes, to be carried into battle as the Spartans carried the Tyndarid Great Twin Brethren; among the famous Aiakidai, incidentally, were Telamon and his son Aias of Salamis, whom the Athenians had just made the eponymous hero of one of their new tribes. This was a polite evasion of a request for active intervention. Finding, however, that this presence brought them no victory, the Thebans returned the images and indicated that human help would be more welcome; and the men of Aigina, strong at sea and having, indeed, an old enmity with Athens, of which Herodotos gives an account much mixed with mythological detail, moved at last, though without formal declaration of war; they

[44] Aelian, *VH* xiii, 24.

[45] A little surprising, I must repeat; not very. When Herodotos mentions the non-violent death of one of his chief characters, it is usually in direct connection with the accession of his successor, as king or head of a family; e.g. i, 25f (Alyattes); v, 39 (Anaxandridas); vi, 38 (Miltiades the elder). He says nothing about the old age and death of Solon, or of Peisistratos. What is perhaps significant is that K. is not 'canonised' in Athenian tradition as Solon was. No personal traditions about him prompted a biography by Plutarch.

raided and burnt the main Athenian port of Phaleron and 'many villages of the coast-land, and did great damage to the Athenians'.[46]

Athens in turn now consulted the Oracle, and received advice to 'wait thirty years, and then dedicate a sacred precinct to Aiakos' (thus formally 'annexing' the enemy's Hero) and so to go to war with Aigina; if they failed to wait, they would have a severe struggle before they won. Undeterred by this, the Athenians, we are told, dedicated the precinct, 'which is still there, in the *Agorá*', but could not bear to wait. But they were given pause by yet one further threat from Sparta.

The story of Kleisthenes' corruption of the Oracle, to influence Sparta against the Peisistratidai, had leaked out; and the Spartans, exasperated that they had been tricked into turning against their good friends and delivering the city to 'an ungrateful democracy', sent for Hippias from Sigeion and convened a congress of their allies, at which they proposed explicitly to restore him by the united action of their League. Kleomenes' *protégé* Isagoras was thus dropped, and Kleomenes is not said to have taken the lead in this episode; he is only mentioned in it incidentally, as having helped to promote it, in that he had brought back from the Acropolis (in 509?) a collection of prophecies left behind by Hippias, the study of which revealed that Sparta would 'suffer much harm from Athens'. However, Sparta's attempt to use her League against Athens was once more foiled by the opposition of the allies, once more headed by Corinth, which, with living memory of the last and worst days of her own tyrants, as well as friendly feelings to Athens, protested, through her delegate Sosikles: 'Now truly shall earth and heaven change places, and men dwell in the sea and fishes where men dwelt, since you, Spartans, propose to suppress republics [*isokratiai*] and restore tyrannies in the cities.'[47]

Hippias, 'of all men knowing best the oracles', protested in answer that the Corinthians would regret their action one day; but it was in vain, and he returned once more to Sigeion. Not long after this, the domestic quarrels of Greece were overshadowed, and the urgent need for Sparta to set things in order if she would keep her proud position was emphasised, by the stirring and tragic clash of arms that broke out in Ionia.

[46] H. v, 79ff. Undeclared war, cf. Myres in *CR* LVII (1943), pp. 66f, criticising E. M. Walker in *CAH* IV, pp. 254ff; on the old war, Dunbabin in *BSA* XXXVII (1936–7).

[47] H. v, 89–93. I consider it certain that the tyranny at Corinth lasted till the middle of the 6th century and that the chronographic date for its end, 581, is too early; cf. *Lyric Age*, pp. 405f.

Chapter X

Revolt in Ionia

INTERNALLY, Athens was still occupied with legislation arising out of the Reform of Kleisthenes. 'Four years after this reform', says the *Constitution*, (*c.* 504), 'they drafted the oath to be taken by the Council of Five Hundred, which they swear to this day. Then they elected the Generals, tribe by tribe, one from each, while the Polemarch commanded the whole army' (*c.* 501).[1] Then, in 499, there arrived in Athens Aristagoras, acting-governor of Miletos for his brother-in-law and cousin Histiaios, whom Darius had carried off to Sousa. He was soliciting support for Ionia, in revolt against Persia.

As causes of the revolt, Herodotos after his manner gives only personal griefs. Histiaios, sick of his gilded captivity and separation from Greece, is said to have sent a message to Aristagoras, which he tattooed on the shaven head of a slave, and then waited for his hair to grow before sending him off; 'the Man with the Tattooed Head', says Herodotos – it was evidently a well-known story. The message proposed that Aristagoras should provoke trouble in Ionia, so that the trusted Histiaios might be sent down to settle it. And the messenger arrived to find Aristagoras himself in a state of desperation, having just got into serious trouble with Artaphernes.[2]

But the question which Herodotos frequently, as here, fails to ask, is not why leaders acted as they did, but why people were ready to follow them. Ionia was evidently seething with discontent, and the reasons for this we are left to conjecture. There was, first, the tribute; 400 talents a year (2,400,000 drachmas) from the Greeks of Asia with Karia, Lykia and Pamphylia, was a burden heavier than that which Athens raised later from a comparable area; and it was made heavier by the fact that not much of it was returned into local circulation. But probably a worse cause of exasperation was the Persian

[1] *Ath. P.* 22. [2] H. v, 30–7.

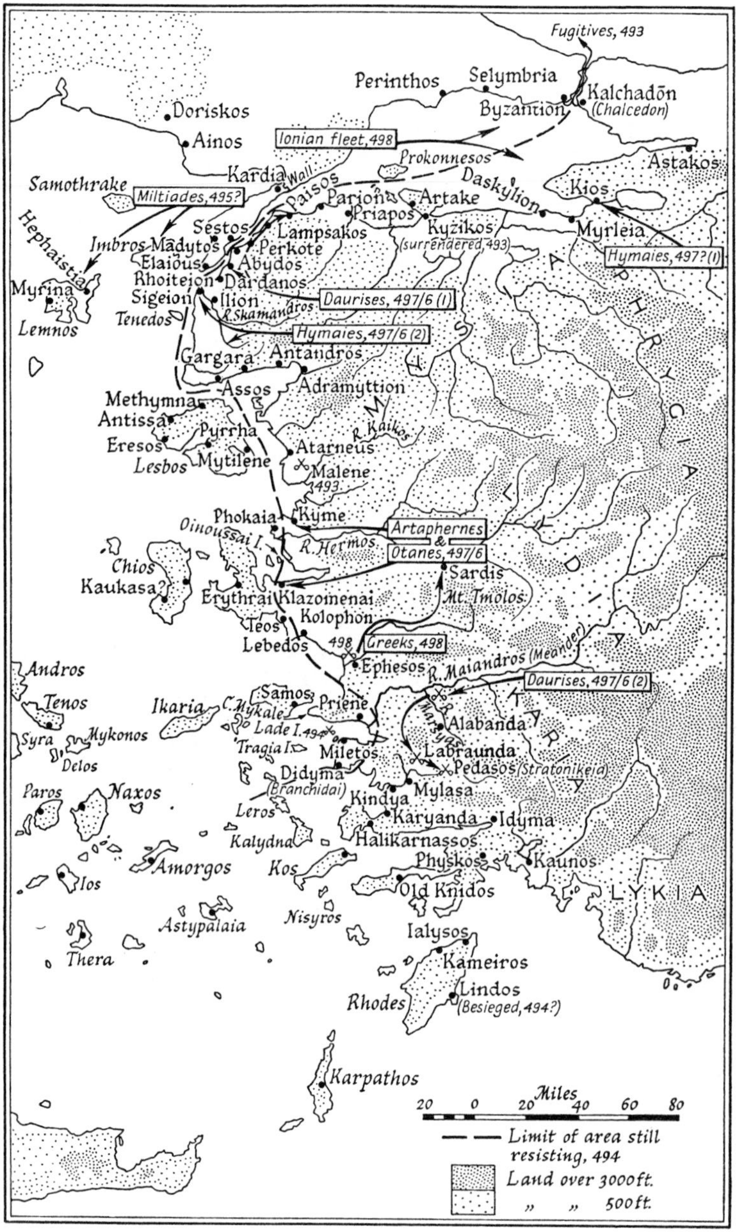

The Ionian Revolt

system of local government through Greek 'tyrants'; it became a commonplace of Greek political philosophy that a despot could not be expected *not* to abuse his power. When Cyrus originally conquered Asia Minor, which was now a long generation ago, tyrants had been flourishing in many independent cities of Greece as the not unpopular leaders of popular revolutions against aristocracies; but a generation or two had usually been enough time for the revolutionary dictatorship to fulfil its function, grow unpopular, and be overthrown in favour of a government either mildly oligarchic, as at Corinth, or democratic, as at Athens. In the forty years since Cyrus' conquest, despotism as a system of government had been in full retreat in Greece; but in Ionia, the city tyrant had the satrap behind him; and behind him the king. It seemed impossible to get rid of the petty monarchy without throwing off the yoke of the greater. The great Ionian revolt appears in perspective as an episode, not only in a national struggle but in a widespread process of revolution. It failed to break the yoke of Persia; but in ending the régime of the city tyrants, at the cost of appalling suffering, and through the remarkable breadth of mind shown thereafter by the Persian government, it did actually succeed.

To return to the story of Aristagoras: To Miletos, in or about 500, came a refugee body of 'the Fat', as they were rudely called, or men of substance, of Naxos, recently expelled by a popular rising. The history of Naxos in the sixth century had generally moved 'in step' with that of Athens, and that the rising had been encouraged by the recent Athenian example is a reasonable conjecture. They had been friends of Histiaios, and appealed to Aristagoras for help to restore their power. Aristagoras, very willing to extend his own influence, said that it might be done, by the help of Persia, and referred the matter to Artaphernes, pointing out that Naxos was the central power of the Cyclades, which were still independent, and the appropriate base for a still further advance to Euboia. Artaphernes, as always, referred the scheme to the king his brother, with an indication that he approved it, and in the spring a large fleet, raised from Artaphernes' satrapy, mustered at Miletos. It was joined by a force of Persian soldiers under Megabates, another Achaemenid and cousin of Artaphernes, who was to command the expedition. For the sake of surprise, the fleet sailed out northward, as though for the Black Sea; but they then lay up at the bay of Kaukasa in Chios island, whence they could sweep down upon Naxos, swiftly and unobserved, across a long stretch of open water, on the wings of the regular summer northerly wind. It was a good plan; but, unfortunately for Aristagoras, surprise was not obtained.

While the fleet was at Kaukasa, Megabates made a round of inspection, and found, on a ship from Myndos in Karia, no guard set. He proceeded to inflict a severe 'field punishment' on the captain, tying him up with his head sticking out through a porthole, unsupported and exposed to the elements. This was reported to Aristagoras, who knew the captain, and he proceeded, after interceding with Megabates in vain, to release him on his own authority. There was a fierce quarrel between the two leaders and, according to Herodotos, Megabates, in order to revenge himself on Aristagoras, sent a pinnace under cover of night to warn the Naxians. It seems incredible that an Achaemenid officer, and one, moreover, whose own credit was involved in the success of the expedition, would do such a thing, though it is possible that Aristagoras, in his subsequent desperation, may have suspected it; perhaps Megabates, later in the campaign, may have made some such remark as 'This is the result of your indiscipline'. Every precaution had been taken to avoid suggesting to the Naxians that the expedition was being mounted against them; but the Naxian exiles knew, and the leakage may very easily have taken place through them.

Anyhow, Naxos had been forewarned and was ready. The open country had been cleared and the walled town provisioned. There was a long blockade. The money provided by the Persians was exhausted; Aristagoras poured in much of his own, and still the siege went on. Finally, after four months, the besiegers installed the exiles in forts on the island, and sailed for Asia. It was a complete fiasco, and Aristagoras was not looking forward to his next interview with Artaphernes.

At this juncture 'the man with the tattooed head' is said to have arrived; and Aristagoras called a meeting of his adherents to discuss the project of rebellion. Hekataios, the geographer and historian, who knew better than most the resources of the Persian Empire, was against it; but finding that he was in a minority, he proposed that, to secure a war-chest for the fleet, since sea-power offered the only hope of survival, they should immediately lay hands on the great treasures, including Croesus' dedications, of the sanctuary of Branchidai. This bold proposal, however, was defeated too. An emissary was sent to proclaim revolt in the fleet from Naxos, which had not yet broken up and was near Miletos, at Myous. The proposal was received with enthusiasm (the sight of Persian soldiers baffled had no doubt had its effect); and the insurgents secured the persons of many of the tyrants, including two who had been prominent in the Scythian expedition, Aristagoras of Kyme and Koes, whom Darius had thereafter made tyrant of Mytilene. All were handed over to their fellow-citizens. Koes was stoned, but the tyrant of Kyme and most of the others were let go free. Aristagoras of Miletos laid down his own tyranny and was elected general; and the wave of revolt swept through Ionia. Everywhere tyrants fled or were turned out and generals were elected; and the Ionian League, which held an annual religious *Panegyris* at the sanctuary of Poseidon on Cape Mykale and had sometimes in the past taken joint political action (e.g., p. 43), returned to active life. The different cities, which had used coins of various weights, now appear to have coined on a common standard (essential for convenience in paying soldiers of a League army on a long or distant campaign); and delegates, *probouloi*, met at the Panionion. We do not know their exact powers or terms of reference; probably they were simply representatives of allied sovereign governments; but through them an authority called the Commonwealth of the Ionians, *koinon tōn Iōnōn*, was able to direct the movements of allied armies and, more especially, fleets throughout the theatre of war.[3]

Herodotos mentions these central organs only in passing, and in general his account of this great struggle is grudging and less than fair. He introduces his narrative of it simply as that of 'a disaster' (v, 28); the Athenians are 'misled' into supporting it, and their support is a 'beginning of disasters for Greeks and barbarians' (v, 97). His native city of Halikarnassos seems to have stood aside from it; Samos, where he had friends, the old enemy of Miletos, betrayed it at the last (p. 213); Periclean Athens, which he admired, was in his time justifying her overlordship over Ionia on the ground that in 'liberating' it from Persia she had done for the Ionians what they could not do for themselves; the Kleisthenic abolition of the Ionic tribes is represented as a

[3] Planning and commencement of the revolt, H. v, 36–8; the *probouloi* as strategic planners, vi, 7; the *Koinon*, v, 109, 3; its history, cf. M. O. B. Caspari (M. Cary) in *JHS* XXXV; early C5 coinage on common standard, presumably that of the Revolt, P. Gardner in *JHS* XXXI, pp. 151ff, pl. 7; C. T. Seltman, *Greek Coins*, pp. 87–8, minted centrally in Chios? – Myres, *Herodotus*, p. 197. E. S. G. Robinson believes that the whole issue is simply the coinage of Chios itself.

repudiation by Athens of her Ionic character (v, 69, 1; cf. i, 143: 'for the Ionians were far the weakest of all the Greeks'). As usual, he is at the mercy of his mostly oral sources, and rarely rejects any views presented to him except in cases where there was flat contradiction. He does tell us, however, that the revolt lasted into its sixth year (vi, 19), and, as we shall see, there were 'mopping-up operations' even after that. It was a much more sustained effort than any that was demanded of Athens and Sparta in the two years of Xerxes' invasion.

Working back in Herodotos' narrative in Book vi from the Battle of Marathon, which the ancients uniformly dated to the year 490, it seems that the extinction of the last embers of the revolt took place in 493 and the end of major operations 'in the sixth year', in 494. The beginning of the revolt will then fall in 499, in early autumn or late summer, when the fleet had returned from its four-months siege of Naxos, but had not yet dispersed. Through the intervening years we have to distribute the campaigns described in his narrative, without being able to date every event precisely, especially in the middle years, 497–5.

It was highly desirable to obtain help, if possible, from Old Greece, and thither went Aristagoras in person (winter, 499–8?), armed with a map, engraved on a bronze tablet, showing 'the whole circle of the earth and the sea and all the rivers';[4] a product of the geographical science of Miletos. Anaximandros (who probably knew of the maps on bronze, made centuries earlier in Babylonia) had produced the first map seen in Greece, and the geographical knowledge collected by Ionian sailors had since been reduced to writing by Hekataios.[5] The Spartans, who had never seen such a thing before, remembered it vividly.

The proverbial 'glance at the map', making the great unknown known and the routes of south-western Asia, in appearance, all too tidy and straightforward, was a powerful 'visual aid' to the Milesian's oratory on the subject of the practicability and profitability of a Greek offensive. Kleomenes, says Herodotos, was not unimpressed. (Herodotos writes here as if it was only the king – and *one* king – whom Aristagoras had to persuade, which is certainly erroneous.) But, with sound common sense, the king wanted to know about the scale of the

[4] H. v, 49.

[5] Eratosthenes, *ap*. Str. i, 7. For Myres' reconstruction of it in *JRGS* VIII (1896), see now his *Herodotus*, pp. 34ff and figs. 1–8.

map: 'How many days is it by the Royal Road, from Ionia to Sousa?' 'Three months,' said Aristagoras incautiously; and Kleomenes ordered him out of Sparta before sundown. Aristagoras, says the story, did not give up so easily. He took the green bough of a suppliant and visited Kleomenes at his home. He found the king with his eight-year-old daughter Gorgo, 'Bright-Eyes', and, wishing to speak confidentially, asked him to send her away; but Kleomenes bade him say what he wished and not hesitate on her account. Aristagoras implored aid, and when it was still refused resorted to monetary inducements. Ten talents? Twenty? Thirty? Fifty? And then the *enfant terrible* broke silence: 'Daddy, if you don't get up and go away, the foreigner will corrupt you.' Kleomenes was pleased with her remark and (as one could not eject a suppliant) broke off the interview by walking out of the room.[6]

But Aristagoras met with better success at Athens and at the seat of the leading sea-power of the Aegean, Eretria. Opinion at Athens was by no means undivided as to the wisdom of provoking Persia further, but finally it was decided to send twenty ships with troops. Eretria added five to the expedition; the number is small, from a city which boasted the best fleet in the western Aegean, had a large territory extending over much of southern Euboia, and (probably at this time) dominated also the islands of Andros, Tenos and Keos;[7] but it was not the whole of Eretria's contribution to the cause. The fear of her power, now united to that of Athens, probably served to keep Aigina quiescent; and Plutarch, on the authority, which it is impossible to evaluate, of (an unknown) 'Lysanias of Mallos and other writers', adds that *before* the land campaign in Asia (more probably simultaneously with it, though before it in the account?) an Eretrian fleet sailed into the Levant, to interfere with the enemy's naval mobilisation, and 'defeated the Cypriotes in the Pamphylian Sea'.[8] The story is inherently quite probable. The Cypriotes in question would be especially the Phoenicians of the island, as well, perhaps, as Greek contingents under the dynasts supported by Persia. Cyprus as well as Phoenicia certainly would have been under Persian orders to mobilise; conversely, it was

[6] H. v, 50f.

[7] Str. ix, 447f; cf. Myres, *op. cit.* p. 195.

[8] Plut. *MH* 24. Lysanias of Mallos (near Tarsus), evidently a Hellenistic writer, was presumably interested in the history of his part of the world. He *may* have had some genuine chronicles to go on; and P. adds that he devoted some part of his work specially to Eretria. He *may*, like most of the later writers who try to supplement or improve on Herodotos' narrative, have been simply romancing. But he does make sense.

only common sense for the insurgents to try to induce these easternmost Greeks, whose power was not negligible, to change sides. An Eretrian (and Ionian?) naval victory in their home waters may well have done more than a land offensive in Ionia to account for the fact that the Greeks of Cyprus did join the revolt in the following year.

In Asia the winter had passed in preparations, the insurgents planning, as sound strategy would dictate, to take the offensive both by land and by sea. Their agents penetrated far inland, in Karia, in Lykia, in Phrygia; down the Hermos, in early spring (498?) came a tribe of refugees: the Paiones, deported twelve years before from Thrace to Phrygia (p. 135). 'Subverted' there by agents of Aristagoras, they made for home. Chian ships took them off in time to escape pursuing cavalry, and subsequently ferried them to Lesbos, and the Lesbians took them on to Thrace.[9] The Persians would get no supplies from *their* labour.

Meanwhile Artaphernes, if we may trust the same passage of Plutarch, had not stood passive. Without waiting for reinforcements, he embarked on a 'spoiling' offensive with what he had, and despatched all the force that he thought he could spare on a direct thrust at Miletos. But Aristagoras too refused to be thrown on the defensive. Melanthios of Athens and Eualkidas of Eretria brought in their ships further north, to Korēsos, the port of Ephesos; and there Aristagoras, remaining himself at Miletos, sent troops to join them under Hermophantos and his own brother Charopīnos. There were, it seems, other Ionians too. 'Leaving their ships at Korēsos, they marched up country in great force, with Ephesians as guides. They went up the Kaÿstros and thence over Mount Tmōlos, and captured Sardis without resistance, with the exception of the citadel, which was held in force by Artaphernes in person.' But their hopes of rich spoils were disappointed (though the loss of supplies to the Persians was no doubt serious); for Sardis was a city of straw huts, with thatched roofs even to the more solid brick houses, and fire, once set to a hut or two by the soldiers, almost immediately got out of control. The whole lower town went up in flames, 'including the temple of the native goddess Kybēbē, which the Persians made a pretext for burning Greek temples later as a reprisal'.

Like Napoleon at Moscow, the Greeks could not stay. Persian forces were reported marching on Sardis from all sides (not least, probably those from Miletos, which Herodotos does not mention); and the burn-

[9] H. v, 98.

ing of their city and temple had made the Lydians hostile. The allies retired to Tmolos, and thence, under cover of night, began their retreat. The Persians were too late to cut them off, but followed hard in their tracks. The Ionians gave battle before Ephesos, but were defeated with heavy loss, including that of the Eretrian general, 'an athlete, whose victories had often been sung by Simonides'.[10]

'The survivors scattered to their cities.' Ephesos, too far from the coast to be supplied by sea, submitted now or not long after. The Athenians and Eretrians went home in chastened mood, and nothing that Aristagoras could say could induce them to send help again. Feeling at Athens was painfully divided, and one reverse with some losses turned enough votes to tip the scale. The growing strength of the peace party was dramatically shown two years later, when they carried their candidate for the archonship for 496–5: Hipparchos, almost certainly Hipparchos the son of Charmos, Peisistratos' general. Hippias the exiled tyrant was married to his sister; but this Hipparchos was one of those 'who had done no harm during the troubles' and been allowed to stay in Athens. Kleisthenes, fearing his family sympathies and his blameless character, against which no charge could be brought with hope of success, was said to have devised, with him personally in mind, the law providing for *ostracism* (p. 286), under which any one citizen might be exiled in any year, by a sufficiently large majority, simply as a political measure. But the climate of opinion in which this law might have been applied against the son of Charmos had not lasted; and now, a frightened Athens elected him head of state: the man who, if anyone could, might obtain forgiveness of what they had done against Hippias and against the Great King.[11]

But in Asia the burning of Sardis made a deeper impression than any subsequent reverses. The revolt spread more widely. The important Karian seaport of Kaunos joined it at the news, having previously stood out, and was accompanied by most of that warlike country. The Ionians 'sailed to the Hellespont and brought under their control Byzantion and all the other cities of that region'. (Byzantion had suffered for its earlier revolt after the Scythian expedition, and Herodotos' words perhaps suggest that pressure was required to 'bring it

[10] *ib.* 99–102.

[11] Archon 496, D.H. vi, 1; Kleisthenes and H. son of Ch., *Ath. P.* 22, 4; relationships, Ath. xiii, 609.

out' again.) And in Cyprus the anti-Persian parties gained control. Onēsilos, brother of Gorgos, the pro-Persian king of Salamis (for in that remote corner of Hellas the ancient kingship survived), closed the gates against his brother when out of town, raised the city in revolt, and was followed by all the other Greek cities. Gorgos took refuge with the Persians, and Onēsilos laid siege to the native city of Amathous on the south coast, which (with Phoenician Kition, we may presume) refused to join a Greek national movement.[12]

These events perhaps occupied the year 497. But by now the resources of Darius' empire were mobilised, and Onēsilos, as he lay before Amathous, was recalled by the news that an enemy fleet and army were mustered in Cilicia. An Ionian fleet came in answer to an appeal for help; but while it lay at Salamis (modern Famagusta) the Persians slipped across, probably on the wings of a north wind, and marched on Salamis over the pass of the Kyrenia (ancient Keryneia) range, while the Phoenician covering fleet rounded 'the cape called the Keys of Salamis', now the Karpass peninsula, in battle array.

'The kings of the Cypriotes' gave battle somewhere in the central plain, with infantry and, in the archaic Cypriote manner, war-chariots; we hear nothing of cavalry. A picked force of the men of Salamis and western Soloi faced the native Persian contingent. They fought well, and Onēsilos and his Karian squire are credited with having killed Artybios, the Persian commander, who charged them on a horse 'trained to rear up against an enemy and fight with hoofs and teeth'. But in another part of the line Stāsānōr, king of Kourion, betrayed the cause; and 'straightway after that, the war-chariots of Salamis followed their example; and so the Persians gained the victory'. Onēsilos fell, and with him the king of Soloi, Aristokypros the son of Philokypros, 'the Philokypros whom Solon of Athens on his visit to Cyprus praised in a poem most of all kings'. The men of Amathous, with a score to pay off, cut off the head of Onēsilos and took it home to hang up over a city gate; but 'when it was hollow' a swarm of bees nested in it, and an oracle bade the Amathousians offer sacrifice to Onēsilos as to a hero.... Meanwhile the Ionians had once more defeated the Phoenicians at sea, the Samians distinguishing themselves; but seeing that Salamis was on the point of making its surrender to Gorgos, they sailed away home.[13]

The war in Cyprus ended with a series of sieges, of which we have

[12] H. v, 103f.

[13] *ib.* 108ff.

a few details. 'When the Medes and Kitians besieged Idalion' (Dali, not far from modern Nicosia), the city under its king Stāsikypros held out long enough (and not too long) to surrender on terms. This we learn from a bronze tablet, solemnly promising rewards to a family of doctors, 'Onāsilos the son of Onāsikypros and his brothers', who during the siege had been 'drafted' to treat the wounded free of charge.[14] At Paphos, Kouklia, the excavations of 1950–3 enabled a most dramatic story to be deduced of the operations in progress. A stony corner of a field, in which fragments of sculpture and of architectural ornament had more than once come to light, proved to contain the remaining lower strata of a siege-mound of just this date (nothing in it was necessarily later than about 500). The mound had filled and covered a deep, V-shaped ditch with bare, red sandstone sides (cut into the soft rock, or deepened, apparently at the last moment, when the siege was imminent) and lay up against a massive wall with heavy stone outer faces, its interior filled with well-laid mud brick. On the verge of the ditch and under and in the mound at all levels were found hundreds of bronze arrowheads, of the three-bladed Near Eastern type (as found also at Thermopylai and at Carchemish; *triglōchīnes oïstoi*, as in Homer), shot from the battlements against the working parties; those shot *at* men on the wall by archers giving covering fire were naturally less in evidence.

It was one part of the mound, piled on when it had already reached the ditch and half filled it, that contained nearly all the statues and architectural fragments. Just at this point, having used up material which came readier to hand, the Persians, with their Hebraic contempt for the images of the heathen, laid hand on that of a sanctuary (or perhaps rather a roadside cemetery, with the elaborate monuments of kings and noblemen) somewhere not far from the walls. It was full of gaily painted statues, cut from the soft and easily worked island limestone; many probably stood in little gabled shelters or shrines, for protection from the weather. There was no single uniform series of architectural ornaments, as though from one large building. For over a century the collection had been accumulating; some of the earliest and roughest monuments were in the style of the Assyrians. In a few days it was cleared; statues of bearded priest-kings wearing the *uraeus* crown, gentlemen in the Egyptian kilt much affected in Cyprus in the

[14] Collitz, *Gr. Dialektinschr.* I, no. 60:

days of Good King Amasis, young athletes in the 'Minoan' bathing-drawers that still survived here; sphinxes and lions, inscriptions in Cypriote script, foliage-capitals and *akroteria*, the luxuriant oriental predecessors of classical Ionic: all alike, the worked with the unworked stone, were hauled up the back ramp of the mound and pushed out under the mantlets that protected the workers on its front. Stone trunks slithered down the scree, heads and arms snapped off and rolled (pieces that fitted together were often found far apart). The besieged might groan at the desecration: 'Now they break down all the carved work thereof with axes and hammers.' But it was no time for mere gazing. The arrows still flew; stone and rubble continually shot out under the screens to pour down the front 'scree' of the mound, and every now and then the great, blind, rawhide-covered mantlets on its crest were pushed forward a few inches.

Presently the mantlets were not many yards away, nor far from level with the battlements. Below them, the great mass of stone and rubble had filled the ditch on a front of thirty or forty yards, and lay. shallow as yet but rapidly deepening, against the foot of the wall, There were limits to what could be done in the way of raising the height of the threatened portion; besides, improvised structures were often flimsy,[15] and would yield to the ram. The besieged tried another plan.

Running under the wall and under part of the mound where it filled the ditch were found two narrow saps. Paphos was rich in copper; there would be men among the defenders who were skilled in mining. At each sap-head were found the remains of a huge, bronze caldron, but flaky and brittle; all that had been left by ancient exposure to intense heat. Above the mines, many cubic yards of the material of the mound had been reduced by the same heat to fine, white dust, while round about these the stones were blackened and cracked, falling apart into small splinters when the pressure of surrounding material was removed. On the edge of these, again, one piece of painted marble (a sphinx's wing-feathers) had kept its bright colours with unusual vividness as the result of having been thus accidentally 'fired'. The roughly compacted mound, it appears, would function like a kiln. One is reminded of how Caesar before Bourges was called at midnight with the news that *his* siege-mound, now 'all but touching the wall', was emitting smoke,

[15] Cf. Thk. iv, 115!

having been similarly fired by means of a mine. The Gauls then, in the midst of the confusion, attempted to rush and burn his siege-towers in a sortie.[16] We do not know what the Paphians did. But it was all in vain. The city fell. All the cities fell, the last to hold out being Soloi in the north-west, which 'the Persians took in the fifth month by undermining its walls' [17] (late summer 496?).

'So Cyprus was subdued again after a year of freedom'; and meanwhile the Persians, reinforced, were also passing to the offensive in Ionia. Daurises, a son-in-law of Darius, took Abydos on the Narrows of the Dardanelles and then, moving 'upstream', Perkōte and Lampsakos and Paisos, 'each of them in one day'; the resistance can hardly have been desperate; these were among the cities which had joined the revolt only under pressure. 'But as Daurises was marching from Paisos upon Parion', he was recalled by orders to turn south and deal with the more serious revolt that had broken out in Karia. Hymaies, also a son-in-law of the king and, like Daurises, 'one of those who had pursued the Ionians who marched to Sardis', operating further east, took Kios on the Sea of Marmara, but was then diverted west to replace Daurises; he subdued the Troad, and died there of sickness. Artaphernes himself with Otanes (the son of Sisamnes, who had served in the west since the Scythian expedition?) struck due west and broke through to the Aegean, taking Kyme in southern Aiolis and Klazomenai in northern Ionia. Phokaia on its peninsula still held out; but from the north, as by the loss of Cyprus, the revolt was being increasingly circumscribed and confined to its original area in Ionia.[18]

But in Karia there took place probably the fiercest land fighting in the course of the war. Giving battle to Daurises on the river Marsyas, a tributary of the Meander, the Karians were bold enough, on the unwise proposal of 'Pixodar the son of Mausōlos of Kindya, who had married a daughter of Syennesis, King of Cilicia', to fight with the river at their backs, 'that, having no retreat, the Karians might surpass themselves'. The result was a disaster; 10,000 Karians are said to have fallen, and 2000 Persians. The survivors rallied at Labraunda ('Place of the Axe'), their national sanctuary of Zeus the Lord of Hosts. While they were wondering whether to give up the struggle, 'the Milesians

[16] Caesar, *Gallic War*, vii, 24. On Kouklia, Illffe and Mitford in *AJ*, 1951.

[17] H. v, 115.

[18] H. v, 117, 122f. – 'League' coins with the badge of Lampsakos indicate that that city was in revolt for longer than H.'s narrative would suggest. (But cf. n. 3 above.)

and their allies' from southern Ionia arrived to reinforce them; thus encouraged, they fought again, to be defeated with even greater carnage, the worst of the loss this time falling upon the Milesians. But now the victorious Daurises overreached himself. Confident in his success, he pressed on into the hill-country. At the threat to their homes, the Karians still rallied again; and Herakleides the son of Ibanōllis of Mylasa (probably brother of the local tyrant, who had been arrested at the beginning of the revolt) proposed a trap. Chastened by defeat, the bold Karians had learned to use cunning. 'They laid an ambush on the road to Pēdasos, into which the Persians fell by night' (it looks as though Herakleides, by a Themistoklean false message, had lured them to attempt a surprise-move) 'and were destroyed, along with their generals . . . and with them, Myrsos the son of Gyges'.[19] (Who was he? Herodotos does not enlighten us, but we may suppose that this Lydian nobleman, perhaps of the old royal house, was commanding a Lydian contingent in the Persian army.) Herakleides of Mylasa is undoubtedly the same as that 'greatest tactician of his time' who proposed naval tactics 'at Artemision', which the Massaliotes remembered in the days of Hannibal (pp. 158f).

Herodotos writes as if all these operations took place within one campaign, an immediate sequel to the Greek reverse on the retreat from Sardis, and contemporary with the fighting in Cyprus. Since, however, this would leave the fourth year (496) of his six-years war completely blank, it seems that this must be an example of his *insouciance* over chronology. These events, and no doubt many other operations and adventures that are nowhere recorded, must surely have occupied at least two summers, 497–6.

Circumscribed and thrown back on the defensive, the revolt was already in a parlous state; so at least thought Aristagoras, who, says the unfriendly Herodotos, was no hero and now found that he had stirred up more than he meant. After the fall of strong Klazomenai, which had once defeated Alyattes, he consulted again with his chief followers. Hekataios thought that the undefeated Ionian sea-power might yet secure a stalemate; he therefore proposed that the island of Leros, with its fine harbours, thirty miles to the south-west and long a Milesian possession, should be transformed into a fortified main base and potential refuge. But Aristagoras was thinking, according to Herodotos at

[19] H. v, 118–21.

least, in terms of flight, to Sardinia or at least to Thrace. Finally he handed over the command at Miletos to one Pythagoras, and sailed with a volunteer force 'to prepare a refuge' at Myrkinos, where Histiaios had begun to colonise years before. The potentialities of that region, later realised by Philip of Macedon, had struck Ionians and Megabazus the Persian as they were to strike fifth-century Athenians. It might, too, have supplied food to Miletos if beleaguered by land. 'And on an expedition from this place Aristagoras was killed and his army destroyed by the Thracians, while besieging a city which the Thracians had offered to evacuate under an armistice.' He had presumably decided that he wanted the Thracians dead rather than lurking hungry in the hills, and thus driven them to desperation.[20]

Histiaios, at long last released by Darius on the plea that he could restore peace in Ionia and would then extend Persian power to the western Mediterranean (Sardinia is again mentioned), arrived at Sardis to find himself the object of well-merited suspicion. He reported to Artaphernes and tried to start a discussion on the causes of the rising. 'I will tell *you* the fact, Histiaios,' said Artaphernes: 'You stitched this shoe, and Aristagoras put it on.' Artaphernes presumably had not any sufficient evidence, on which to clap his royal brother's *protégé* straight into irons, but he did not want him about the place. (Histiaios' next action looks as if Artaphernes was having trouble with some of the other leading Persians, through whom Histiaios may have hoped to secure a peace by negotiation.) Artaphernes, however, succeeded in frightening him, to such purpose that 'on the very next night he made off for the coast'. He crossed over to Chios, where he *was* arrested, on suspicion of playing the part of a 'double agent'; but he talked himself out of it with his usual *aplomb*, alleging that he had urged revolt only because he had inside information that Darius intended to deport the Ionians, interchanging them with Phoenicians.

From Chios, he also wrote treasonable letters to some of 'the Persians at Sardis', sending them by the hand of one Hermippos, of Atarneus in Aiolis (a man whose city was thus already under Persia). It is difficult to imagine Persian officers actually intriguing against their king and country in the middle of a war; but there may have been

[20] H. v, 124ff; dated 496 by Thk. iv, 102 (31 + 28 years before the Athenian colonisation of Amphipolis under Hagnon, which D.S. xii, 32 dates to the archon-year 437–6). For a defence of A.'s last action, cf. Grundy, *GPW* p. 116.

disagreements about policy and some sort of a general-staff intrigue against Artaphernes, especially after the Karian disaster. Hermippos, however, really was a double agent. He took the letters to Artaphernes, who, having read them, badc Hermippos deliver them to the addressees and bring him the answers. 'Artaphernes then put to death many of the Persians, and there was dire confusion at Sardis.' This may perhaps account for some inactivity of the Persian land forces in 495; but Histiaios, says Herodotos, had failed in his main hopes.

Histiaios then went to Miletos, but the people wished to see no more of their old tyrant, and closed their gates; he tried to force his way in by night, and was repulsed, slightly wounded. Chios refused to give him a command; but he induced the Lesbians to entrust him with eight ships, with which he established himself at Byzantion and 'held up the ships sailing out of the Black Sea, except those whose crews promised to obey him'.[21] This sounds like mere privateering, and is often interpreted as such; but the Lesbian ships were surely not obeying Histiaios for no reason at all. With the Persians already on the Sea of Marmara at Kios, it made good sense to have such a guard squadron on the Bosporos, against possible privateering from enemy-held territory, and to see that trading ships bringing foodstuffs from the Black Sea went where they should and not to the enemy. Further west, facing the enemy-held coast of the Dardanelles and Troad, there was also a strong hand on the reins; for it was almost at the same time, according to Herodotos, that Miltiades, recalled once more in a time of trouble by his old subjects the Dolonkoi, settled again in the Gallipoli Peninsula. From this point of vantage he also mastered Lemnos and Imbros, which had been taken by Otanes some fifteen years before. Since the Persian reoccupation of the Troad, they also represented a potential 'menace to shipping'. Lykarētos the brother of Maiandrios, the Samian installed by Otanes as governor of Lemnos (p. 137), was dead, and we hear of no Persian garrison; but Miltiades expelled the 'Pelasgian' inhabitants, one of whose two main villages, the eastern Hēphaistia, was surrendered without a blow by its chief, Hermon. Myrina (modern Kastro) stood a siege unavailingly. Miltiades then, wishing to put the islands into

[21] H. vi, 1–5. Lydians, rather than Persian intriguers, How *ad loc.*; a Persian GHQ intrigue against Artaphernes? – Grundy, *GPW* p. 120. Beloch (*GG* II, i, 12f, 16f) makes Histiaios in this his last phase play the part of a determined patriot who never lost heart; this is not the impression which H. gives, but in view of H.'s low view of the revolt and all its leaders, it cannot be excluded. Black Sea corn trade, H. vii, 147.

reliable hands, invited Athenians to colonise them; many came, and the islands remained closely linked with Athens through the following centuries. Miltiades may have hoped thus to involve the Athenian government again in the war; it was a vain hope, but to pick up two islands, strategically placed and able to absorb many of the poorer peasants, at a time when Phoenician sea-power had never yet threatened the Aegean, was a different matter.[22]

What with the Karian disaster, involving great losses, and a 'purge' at Sardis, the Persians apparently engaged in no sensational operations in 495; but Herodotos' silence is no ground for supposing that they did nothing at all. Lebedos, south of Klazomenai across the peninsula, and the large cities of Ephesos and Kolophon, both of which were slightly inland and could be cut off from the sea by Persian land forces, disappear in silence from the insurgent ranks; and so (a more serious matter) does Karia. Having suffered severely but shown that they were still formidable in their hills, the Karians did nothing; perhaps they were already negotiating. In 493 the men of Pēdasa, in whose land the great ambush had taken place, were on sufficiently good terms with Persia to be allowed to occupy Milesian territory.[23]

It was thus a truncated Ionia that faced the campaign of 494. Teos and Erythrai in the central peninsula; northern Phokaia, lonely on hers; Miletos with her small neighbours, Myous and Priene: in all the mainland, only these six still fought. And now the Persians, mobilising all the fleets of their Levantine vassals, from Phoenicia, Egypt, Cilicia, even newly conquered Cyprus (the Great King had their families as hostages), advanced on the Aegean by sea. They are credited with raising 600 ships, a conventional figure for a Persian fleet (it reappears in the Scythian and the Marathon expeditions), and no doubt exaggerated; but there is no doubt either that it was a formidable array. Meanwhile, the Persian land forces concentrated against Miletos. The sense of this is obvious. If Miletos fell and her sea-power were eliminated, the combined navies of the islands would be outnumbered, and they would fall in turn. In the meantime, the Persians do not seem from their behaviour to have had any overwhelming superiority at sea. When the fleets were in presence, there was no action for some time, and the Persians resorted first to political warfare.

[22] H. vi, 40; 140; D.S. x, 19 and see further n. at end of this chapter.
[23] H. vi, 20. Cf. *ib.* 16, 2 (Ephesos clearly out of the war in 494).

For the three great eastern Aegean islands, with Miletos, could still raise a powerful navy. The Ionian war-council, at its last recorded meeting, decided, we are not surprised to hear, that no land army could be put into the field. The Milesians must see to the defence of their own walls, while every available ship was concentrated against the new threat at sea. Herodotos gives figures for the contingents, from east to west in their order of battle, and no doubt also when encamped before battle; an order corresponding to the geographical position of the cities, so that lines of communication for supply convoys did not cross:

Miletos	80	ships
Priene	12	,,
Myous	3	,,
Teos	17	,,
Chios	100	,,
Erythrai	8	,,
Phokaia	3	,,
Lesbos	70	,,
Samos	60	,,
Total	353	,,

Phokaia, Erythrai and Teos appear as shadows of their former selves; perhaps also, in the existing strategic position, their contingents were weakened by the need of men for defence at home. The main camp was on the island of Lade, off Miletos, today a ridge, long since united to the mainland by the silt of the Meander.[24]

Against these the Levantine fleets came up through the Dorian islands. Their chief admiral was probably Dātis the Mede, famous for his command four years later at Marathon, with, among his subordinates, a rising officer, the young Mardonios. Their advance, or perhaps only that of a squadron detached under Mardonios, was delayed for some time by resistance at Rhodes. Rhodes was not in alliance with the Ionians, and Herodotos says nothing about the episode, which was indeed of only local importance; but it seems that the islanders, hitherto untouched by Persia, reacted to the approach of a foreign fleet in characteristic Greek insular fashion. In the words of the Hellenistic Temple Chronicle of Athena of Lindos:

'When Dareios, King of the Persians, sent great forces to subdue

[24] H. vi, 7ff (the whole campaign, vi, 6 to 17).

Greece, his fleet came to this island first. There was panic in the countryside, and the people fled to all the fortified places, but the greatest number to Lindos' (which was indeed the largest city). 'And the barbarians besieged them there, until the Lindians, oppressed by lack of water, began to think of surrender. But at that very time the Goddess appeared in a dream to one of the chief magistrates, and bade him be of good cheer, for she would pray her father to give the water that they needed.' Rain duly followed, accounted a miracle in the Aegean summer; and the city was enabled to submit on terms. 'Datis set sail for his main objective, making a treaty with the besieged, and saying "The gods protect these men." ' The Persian general no doubt insisted on entering the temple on the citadel; and there he made an offering of his arms and his fine clothing (such an offering as Pharaoh Necoh, who also had dealings with Lindos, had made to Apollo of Branchidai in thanksgiving for a victory a century before). They were treasured in the temple until lost in a fire, probably in the fourth century.[25]

The absence of a squadron, left besieging Lindos, might indeed also account for the delay in giving battle before Miletos. But in any case, neither side was in a hurry. The Ionians had appointed a Supreme Commander at sea, a veteran, Dionysios of Phokaia, and he considered that his fleet needed tactical training. Herodotos says that he talked his way into a precarious leadership by a good speech at a mass-meeting. It seems more likely that he had been appointed by the war-council, and, if so, his selection from among the small contingents is interesting; intended perhaps to avert jealousy among the larger. His terse speech, as reported by the historian, then becomes a manifesto on taking up his command. As such, it could be genuine:

> Ionians:
>
> Our cause is now balanced on 'the razor's edge': whether we are to be free or slaves – and recaptured runaway slaves at that. Now, then, if you are prepared to endure hardship, you will have hard work here and now, but you shall have the power to beat the enemy and be free; but if you give way to slackness and indiscipline, I see no hope of your escaping punishment by the king for your rebellion. So obey me, and put yourselves in my hands; and I undertake that, if the

[25] *Lindische Tempelchronik*, ed. Blinkenberg, pp. 34–8 (the 'epiphany' and miraculous rain), 26f (the offerings), citing an array of Hellenistic historians, some of them otherwise known. – See additional note 1 at end of chapter.

Gods deal fairly with us, either the enemy will not give battle, or, if they do, they will get the worst of it.

Meanwhile the Persians had started their political warfare. They had with them the dethroned tyrants, who had been let go by the insurgents, and they ordered them to get into touch with suitable men in their various cities, promising that they should not be punished if they would submit voluntarily, even now. 'But if they insist on fighting', went on the directive, 'then you must threaten them with what will happen to them: when they have been beaten they will be sold as slaves, and we will make their boys eunuchs and carry off their maidens to Baktra, and we will give their land to other inhabitants.'

At first, however, this persuasion had no effect. The Ionians obeyed Dionysios with a will, and he practised his fleet, 'leading them out in line ahead, to practise the rowers in the manœuvre of "breaking through" against each other, and having the marines under arms' (practising the use of their arms on the moving decks?); 'and for the rest of the day, he kept the ships at anchor' (did not let the men land) 'and kept the Ionians working from morning to night.' Keeping the fleet constantly in instant readiness (like Lysander at the Goat Rivers in 405) he may have hoped for a chance of a surprise if the enemy relaxed their attention. But it was the discipline of his citizen sailors that began to crack first.

We are not called upon to swallow the unfair and ungenerous strictures of Herodotos, imputing softness and inexperience of hard work to these men who had explored the Mediterranean and had beaten the Phoenicians before. But Greek citizens did take unkindly to long-continued discipline; also, in the height of summer, they were very awkwardly placed, with an appallingly cramped base on the little island. Practically every pint of water, as well as all food, had to be brought in boats from a distance. Thucydides, speaking of the deterioration of the Athenian fleet at Syracuse, refers it largely to unhealthy surroundings;[26] and if the Ionians were not so long at Lade, their overcrowding was far worse. The enemy, meanwhile, with their army dominating all the land outside the walls of Miletos, had all the space they needed, and readier access to water and all supplies. Sickness began to weaken the resolution of the Ionians.[27] They rationalised their discontent in resentment at being commanded by a man of a small allied

[26] vii, 47.

[27] H. vi, 12, 3.

city ('Why do we obey this braggart who brings in only three ships?') and presently the men simply refused to continue with his programme of training. It was at this point, too, says Herodotos, that the Samian commanders, foreboding disaster, began to think of saving their city from the worst by listening to the proposals of their ex-tyrant, Aiakes the son of Syloson. This was enough to encourage the Persian commanders. Satisfied that the situation was now favourable, they launched their ships all along the miles of beaches and sailed out to battle.

The Ionians were not caught napping. In their prearranged order they met the attack: Samos and Lesbos on the right, far out to sea, Miletos on the left, before the city, powerful Chios in the centre, with the smaller contingents on either side. But as in the land battle in Cyprus, treachery turned the scale. Without striking a blow, nearly the whole squadron of Samos hoisted sail – the great square sails, useless for manœuvring and always stowed away in battle – and took to flight. Only eleven stout-hearted captains kept their ships in line. This exposed the flank of the Lesbian squadron, and whether in panic or in premeditated treachery, they went too, some of the smaller northern squadrons following. Chios and Miletos fought gallantly; but the odds were now too great. The Chians, with 100 ships and forty marines on each, finding their right flank hopelessly turned, counter-attacked fiercely to clear their line of retreat. Herodotos uses the technical naval word for 'breaking through', *diekpleontes* (cf. p. 158); some moderns have doubted its accuracy, pointing out that it was a manœuvre for ships in light fighting trim; later Athenians reduced their marines. The Chians were equipped for fighting in the old way, boarding when ships became locked; but that they did break through, not as a tactical manœuvre but with the strategic purpose of escape, is clear; there was no escape otherwise. 'After taking many enemy ships and losing most of their own', a remnant finally got clear and made sail for home.

Other Chian ships, crippled and unable to follow, fell back perforce, north-east. Their crews beached them under Mykale, and began to make their way, inland of that mountain, overland. This took them, after nightfall, into the territory of Ephesos, no longer friendly; moreover (it was now autumn) the women of Ephesos were out in the fields, conducting the ancient fertility-ritual of the Thesmophoria, Hearing of the irruption of a large band of men, the men of Ephesos took them for raiders bent on seizing women (or so they said later; had no one from the coast brought news of the battle?). They sallied out in arms, and slew many of the fugitives.

Dionysios of Phokaia saved himself in good order. Having taken three enemy ships in the battle, when he saw that it was lost he broke through and sailed, not to Phokaia, knowing well that there was no refuge there; 'but he sailed, just as he was, straight to Phoenicia, and having sunk merchant ships till he had collected rich spoil, sailed to Sicily; and basing himself there, he became a pirate, plundering no Greeks, but Carthaginians and Etruscans'.[28]

Meanwhile 'the victorious Persians besieged Miletos both by land and sea, and, undermining the walls and bringing up all manner of siege-engines, took it by storm, in the sixth year from the revolt of Aristagoras' (end of 494?), 'and led the people captive. . . . And the holy place of Didyma, both temple and oracle, was plundered and burned', as Hekataios had feared; though possibly some of its treasures had been rescued before the catastrophe and transferred to Apollo's other great seat at Delphi.[29] Many men were killed, many led captive to Sousa. There, however, 'King Darius did them no further harm, but settled them on the Red Sea, as it is called, at Ampē, where the River Tigris flows into the sea.' And of their territory, the Persians themselves occupied the plain and the parts round the city, and the uplands they handed over to the Karians of Pēdasa. A number also escaped, and joined a large band of the Samian upper classes (the party hostile to the tyrant Aiakes and so faithful to the national cause), who fled to Sicily and seized the town of Zankle or Messina.[30] Their adventures will concern us later.

'Thus Miletos was bereft of her people' concludes Herodotos. However, the reports of total annihilation were, as often in history, greatly exaggerated. After the loss of all the killed, the refugees in Sicily and

[28] H. vi, 17.

[29] Bury, in *Klio*, II, pp. 23f, cites a point made by C. Niebuhr (in *Mitt. der Vorderas. Gesellsch.*, 1899), that 'there is something very odd' about Herodotos' account of the offerings of Croesus at Delphi. He says (i, 92) that they were exactly duplicated at Branchidai. But (i, 48ff) many of those at Delphi were presented when Croesus had tested the Greek oracles and Delphi alone had stood the test. Did C. then present similar offerings to the Branchidai, who had failed in it? Or did C. then present to Delphi duplicates of all his earlier offerings at Didyma?! Niebuhr's theory (which Bury treats with reserve) was that some of the treasures seen by H. at Delphi had been transferred from Didyma, and the inscriptions on them erased; this was why they were *anepisēma* (H. i, 51). (Or, one might ask, were the inscriptions at Didyma on bases, which were not moved?)

[30] H. vi, 18–20, 22.

the deportees at Ampe, there were still Milesians who were no Persian settlers, ready to rebel fifteen years later, when the tide flowed the other way. But archaeologists have found that the seaport quarter, whence the fleets had sailed to colonise the Black Sea, was never rebuilt again. It was Miletos' end as a force in history.

Histiaios at Byzantion heard of the naval disaster, and came south, leaving his guardpost to one Bisaltes the son of Apollophanes of Abydos (the names are interesting), to try to save something from the wreck. With his Lesbians he fell upon luckless Chios, 'falling by surprise upon a Chian garrison at a place called the Hollows in the Chian countryside. Of them he slew many, and gained control over the rest of the Chians, shattered as they were by the naval battle.' Possibly, as some have thought, he was trying to secure the island as a base for further resistance. He rallied there a host of Ionians and Aiolians (refugees from the recent fighting, and from places not yet occupied?) and with them went off, leaving Miletos besieged, to attack Thasos; he was evidently still thinking, as in his days at Myrkinos, in terms of establishing a base in the north-west Aegean. If Miletos held out, there might be time to do it. . . . But Miletos, taken by all-out storm and not by blockade, did not outlast the winter, and before Histiaios had bent neutral Thasos to his will, he heard that the Phoenician fleet was moving northward. Back in haste came Histiaios to Lesbos 'with all his army'; but the island, though large and rich (but no doubt crowded with fugitives), was unable to feed them. Histiaios therefore went over to the mainland on a large-scale foraging expedition, 'to reap the corn of Atarneus' (on the adjacent Aiolic coast) 'and that of the Mysians in the plain of the Kaïkos'. This would be in May and, in these sheltered and low-lying areas, probably early May (493). The hungry army wanted its bread soon. 'But in this area was Harpagos, a Persian, with a strong force', and he engaged Histiaios at Malēne in the land of Atarneus. His tactics illustrate what a Persian army with cavalry could do to Greeks if caught in 'cavalry country'. The infantry engaged 'and fought for some time; but the cavalry started later, and fell upon the Greeks'. It looks as though they were deliberately held back, in order to come in on a flank; Greek tactics were primitive at this time, and they had no idea of the use of reserves.

By this action of the cavalry, the Greeks were routed. Histiaios, hoping that the king would not put him to death for his present misdeeds, still made a bid to save his life; as a Persian was just overtaking him and about to run him through, he called out in Persian and declared himself: 'I am Histiaios the Milesian.' Thus he was taken prisoner. Now if he had been taken before King Darius, I believe he would have got off scot-free, and Darius would have forgiven him; but because of this, and that he might not escape thus and recover his influence with the King, the satrap Artaphernes and Harpagos, his captor, as soon as he was brought to Sardis, impaled his body on a pole, and salted down his head and took that to Darius at Sousa. And when Darius heard the story, he rebuked them for doing this and not bringing him alive, and gave orders for the head to be washed and honourably buried, as that of a man who had done good service to him and to the Persians.[31]

There remained only 'mopping up' operations to be completed. 'The Persian fleet, which had wintered at Miletos, set sail in the new year and took with ease the off-shore islands of Chios, Lesbos and Tenedos', carrying out a man-hunt after irreconcilables. Herodotos tells a childish story of cordons of troops, shoulder to shoulder (though we need not actually translate 'holding hands'), stretching from sea to sea, 'combing' the islands; a method which would have been as impracticable among the wooded hills of Chios and Lesbos as on the mainland of Asia. Someone may have recorded seeing cordon operations on a more limited scale.[32] And they took the mainland cities of Ionia in the same way, except for the 'combing' operation, which was impossible. 'Then the Persian generals did not fail to carry out their threats; they chose out the handsomest boys and made eunuchs of them, and the most beautiful girls they sent up to the king; and they burned the cities, including their temples.' [33] Ephesos, which had made timely surrender, saved herself and her Artemision. But the destruction was exaggerated in tradition, and the savage reprisals were selective and soon over; for the cities were soon restored to normal life, paying taxes and furnishing ships for the service of the king. Last to be cleared were the European coasts of the narrow seas, from the Gallipoli Peninsula to the Bosporus. Kardia, near Bolayir, alone survived the Phoenician raid, and presumably made terms afterwards; Kyzikos had already negotiated her submission with the satrap of Daskyleion, a son

[31] H. vi, 26–30.
[32] For a discussion, see G. C. Whittick in *L'Antiquité classique* XXII (1953), pp. 27ff.
[33] H. vi, 32.

of Megabazos. The people of Byzantion and Kalchadon did not await the coming trouble, but fled to their recently founded colony of Mesambria in the Black Sea.[34]

One important rebel escaped by a hair's breadth: Miltiades. He hung on in the Chersonese till he heard the Phoenicians were already at Tenedos; then, with his goods loaded on five ships, he sailed westward from Kardia by the north side of the peninsula. As he cleared Helle's Cape, Phoenician ships sighted him. There was a desperate chase. A ship with his eldest son Mētiochos (not by the daughter of Oloros, but by his Athenian first wife) was captured; the young man was graciously treated, perhaps through the influence of the Peisistratids. Darius 'gave him an estate and a Persian wife, and their children lived as Persians'. Miltiades with four ships escaped to temporary refuge at Imbros; evidently the main Phoenician fleet had not come up yet, and the pursuers would have to draw off for water. Thence, when the coast was clear, he got safe to Athens.[35]

[34] H. vi, 33.

[35] *ib.* 40. – Miltiades' first marriage dated from years when he was on good terms with the Peisistratids, and Wade-Gery guesses that Mētiochos' mother may have been related to Hippias (*Essays*, p. 167).

ADDITIONAL NOTES

1. – *A Siege of Lindos in 494?* (pp. 210f and n. 25)

Scholars have taken widely differing views of the evidence of the Lindian Temple Chronicle and the Hellenistic historians there cited. Wilamowitz (*Jahrb. Arch. Inst.*, 1913) regarded the whole tradition as a 'Schwindel'; Beloch (*GG* II, ii (1916), pp. 81ff) accepted it, assigning the episode reasonably to 494 rather than 490; that is, to the first appearance of a Perso-Phoenician fleet in Rhodian waters, rather than to 490, when Persia was mistress of the sea; and he is followed by Cary (*CAH* IV, p. 225). Meyer (*GdA* IV, i (1916), p. 306, n. 1) follows Blinkenberg (*ad loc.*) in referring it to 490, and mentions no other possibility. (His and Beloch's references to each other's work on the revolt generally resemble a long-range artillery duel.) Xenagoras (Jacoby 240), cited in the Chronicle as sole authority for Mardonios as the besieger, 'sent by Datis', is little known apart from the citations in the Chronicle itself, where he is the most cited authority. He wrote, however, whether within or apart from the *Chronikē Syntaxis* repeatedly cited there, a work cited as *On Islands* (*Et. Mag.*, *s.v.* Sphēkeia, said to have been an old name of Rhodes; Harpokr., *s.v.* Chytroi). His date, 'noch im IV Jahrhundert' according to Beloch, does not seem to be well established. If Mardonios did besiege Lindos, it was not in 490, when he was recovering from wounds, and perhaps under something of a cloud (p. 223). – In the list of offerings, § xxxii (p. 26 Blinkenberg), where the name of someone 'General of the Persians' is obliterated, it would be tempting to restore the name of Mardonios, since Blinkenberg's 'Artaphernes' imports a name not otherwise found in the Chronicle, and A. should surely be rather with the land forces in his Satrapy; while 'Datis', suggested by Beloch, is too short to fill the space. But the eight authorities there cited are almost all the same as those elsewhere cited as naming Datis; and Xenagoras, Mardonios' sponsor, does not here appear.

2. *Miltiades' return to the Chersonese* (pp. 208f)

The date, according to H. vi, 40, 2, is 495, 'in the third year' before his flight in 493, and the year 495 gives time enough for his conquest of the islands, recorded, dateless, in vi, 140. Herodotos may be wrong, but the conquest must surely, in any case, have taken place under cover of the Ionian Revolt. D. Mustili, *L'occupazione ateniese di Lemnos e gli scavi di Hephaistia*, in *Studi . . . offerti a E. Ciaceri* (1940), pp. 149–158, says that 'the contents of the earliest Greek burials at Hephaistia . . . can all be later than 500 B.C., though the deposits of the pre-Greek temple stop perceptibly earlier' (destroyed by Otanes?). (I quote from Wade-Gery, *Miltiades*, in *Essays*, p. 163 and n. 1). For Hermon, see D.S. x, 19, 6; Zenobios iii, 85; Steph. Byz. *s.v.* Hephaistia; 'Hermon's favours' became a proverbial expression. Legends were produced, no doubt in connection with the negotiations with him, to the effect that the natives, identified with descendants of ancient Pelasgians from Attica (mentioned by Hekataios), had promised to cede Lemnos 'when a ship came there from Attic land in one day on a north wind'; Miltiades claimed that the Chersonese was now Attic (H. vi, 137–9). To adduce legends ('ancient history') as justification for a claim to a foreign land was common form (cf. pp. 151, 167). Berve (*Miltiades*, in *Hermes*, Einzelschriften, 1936–7, 2, p. 49) may be right in accounting for Hermon's surrender on the hypothesis that he and his men had killed Lykaretos and were now afraid of Persian vengeance; but his dating of it 'zwischen 510 und 505' (*ib.* 50 and n. 1) on the strength of its place in the order of the excerpts surviving from D.S. Book x is not impressive.

It must be repeated that H., according to the respectable tradition of his mss, says that 'this' (that the raiding Scyths went away and the Dolonkoi of the Chersonese restored him) 'had happened in the third year before the trouble that now faced him'. § 40 of his Book vi certainly is a muddled paragraph, and if we take H. to say that a Scythian raid, in revenge for Darius' invasion, kept M. out of his principality from two years after his first arrival there till two years before his last departure, it looks like a startling example of his chronological carelessness. But I am not at all sure that this is not what H. wrote (hardly 'what H. meant', any more than the careless motorist 'means' to kill the pedestrian). H. tells his story like a saga, with a dash of (mostly second-hand) chronology here and there. I would be very willing to transfer the blame from our Father of History to anonymous 'scribes', if I thought it probable in this case. One differs from Wade-Gery at one's peril (especially when he has the support of Dobree and Mr Enoch Powell (see *CQ* XXIX, p. 160)); but it seems to me an even more perilous procedure to simplify a well-attested text by crossing out the words that give one trouble.

It may be noted that similar 'telescoping', ignoring some twenty years of M.'s life, appears at the same point in the little encyclopaedia-article by Nepos (§§ 3, 6–4, 1; p. 133). What did happen to M. between the Scythian Expedition and the Revolt, we do not know. He may have spent some of the time in the Chersonese, glowering across the water at Hippias and his new Lampsakene relations-in-law; but he may quite possibly have been in exile the whole time (the blank years, forgotten in his saga), e.g. in Thrace at the court of his father-in-law King Oloros, biding his time. Peisistratos had been in Thrace biding *his* time for eleven years at a stretch.

Chapter XI

From Ionia to Old Greece: 494–490

For many Ionians it must have seemed like night without a morrow; but tomorrow dawned as usual, and Darius' officers, in accordance with the best Persian practice, were already concerned with reconstruction. Artaphernes at Sardis sent for delegates from the cities (Diodoros, perhaps from Ephoros, says that Hekataios was among them, and influenced the satrap), and required them, *inter alia* no doubt, to conclude treaties granting each other judicial facilities; what is meant would be, no doubt, access to courts in case of commercial or other disputes, through a *proxenos*, a citizen who undertook to look after the interests of men of another city visiting his home-town. This, Herodotos expressly says, was 'so that they might not raid one another'.[1] He also, Herodotos continues, 'had the land measured out in *parasangs* (a Persian word meaning thirty furlongs), and on this basis assessed the tribute as a land-tax, which they continue to pay, on the assessment of Artaphernes, still in my time. The total assessment came to very much the same as before.' Also, being more methodically assessed and levied on land and not directly on trade, it was presumably less of a disincentive to enterprise. There were thus no direct financial reprisals. though the same tax-burden, levied on cities, many of which had suffered severely, cannot have been light.

Then, 'at the beginning of spring' (492), Darius relieved the existing generals of their commands (probably largely to rest them and their troops; many of the Persian soldiers probably had farms at home to look after); and 'there came down to the sea Mardonios the son of Gobryas' (Gobryas of the Seven conspirators) 'with a large army and fleet; still a young man, and newly married to Darius' daughter Artozōstra'. Through his mother, he was also the king's nephew. If he

[1] H. vi, 42; D.S. x, 25; for such a treaty in western Greece, cf. Tod, *GHI*, no. 34; *Lyric Age*, p. 32 and nn.

had been at Lindos in 494, he had been recalled for honour and promotion. 'Mardonios marched with this army to Cilicia, and there went on shipboard himself and sailed with the fleet, while other officers conducted the army to the Hellespont. And when he came to . . . Ionia, he there took a step which will greatly surprise those Greeks who do not believe that Otanes proposed democratic government for Persia in the meeting of the Seven: he suppressed all the tyrants in Ionia, and introduced democracies in the cities.' [2]

This statement clearly does not apply to every Ionian city in the empire. Strattis of Chios (p. 501) was still ruling in 480.[3] Hippoklos of Lampsakos was succeeded by his sons and grandsons.[4] At Samos, Theomēstor the son of Androdamas was set up as tyrant after Salamis;[5] whether he immediately succeeded Aiakes, who had served Persia effectively, we do not know. However, all the known exceptions are in islands, which might be considered special areas, or outside the old Ionian area; they need not therefore be held to invalidate Herodotos' statement, if we understand it of Ionia in the narrowest sense, the original seat of the revolt. Still less is it invalidated by the existence of dynasts in 480 in Doric Kos and Halikarnassos,[6] which had not revolted, or in Karia, which probably knew nothing of democracy at this epoch.[7] The statement is therefore to be accepted, and shows remarkable breadth of vision on the part of Darius, who must have discussed this policy with his young general before his departure.

'This done, Mardonios pressed on to the Hellespont.' He ordered up Ionian ships and took his army over to Thrace. Doriskos probably became a Persian base in his time;[8] Thasos submitted without resistance; so did Macedonia. The conquest of Europe was being taken up in earnest; and high on the list of priorities is said to have been the punishment of Athens and Eretria for their aid to the rising.

But then Mardonios ran into trouble. The north Aegean can be very stormy; and a north-easterly gale caught the fleet on its way to round Mount Athos, wrecking scores of ships (the Greeks said 300, a conventional 'half the armada') on the rocky coast of the peninsula. Many of the men (Asiatics?) were drowned, being unable to swim, many are

[2] H. vi, 43 (cf. p. 94 above); M.'s mother, vii, 5, 1.
[3] H. viii, 132 (cf. iv, 138).
[4] Thk. vi, 59, 3.
[5] H. ix, 90.
[6] H. vii, 99, 164.
[7] How and Wells *ad loc.* thus quote evidence which is not in its entirety relevant.
[8] Cf. H. vii, 105, for its 'governor appointed by Darius'.

said to have been 'devoured by sea-monsters' (sharks, following the fleet?) and many who got ashore perished from exposure. It was a disaster which the Persians did not forget. On land, the Thracian Brygians hit back fiercely, falling upon the Persian camp by night, killing many men and wounding Mardonios; but in spite of this 'he did not leave their country till he had subdued them'. 'This expedition therefore returned to Asia after a disastrous campaign', says Herodotos. But the reverses are probably exaggerated. Persia's prestige was little affected, for when the Thasians in the following year (491) received a summons to disarm – they had increased their navy and strengthened their fortifications after the attack by Histiaios – they accepted it quietly, 'slighted' their new walls and brought their ships over to surrender at Abdēra.[9]

The occupation of the north Aegean coast was thus completed. The imperial frontier marched with that of Thessaly at Mount Olympos, and the king's psychological-warfare agencies were soon penetrating it (p. 269). Meanwhile, all along the seaboard of the empire, orders had been issued for the construction of additional warships and horse-transports, which, like tank-landing-craft, were specialised craft, and in their time a novelty. The world-state had no intention of stopping at the Mediterranean coast; and Old Greece, divided and chaotic, was clearly marked out to be the next objective. In the same year, 491, Darius sent his heralds to the Greek states to make the formal demand for earth and water in token of surrender. The islands without exception are said to have promised submission, as also many states of the mainland.[10] Sparta and Athens were among those which refused.

Opinion at Athens was painfully divided. Those to whom the world overseas meant anything must have waited in helpless agony while ill news followed ill news as Ionia went down; especially those who felt that, both for honour's and for interest's sake, Old Greece should have helped wholeheartedly in the struggle of the eastern Hellenes. Some, however, well informed and hard-headed practical men, were in favour of accepting Persian lordship as inevitable; among them the Alkmeonidai, who already in the days of Kleisthenes and the archon Alkmeon had tendered submission (p. 187). Probably at the spring Dionysia of 493 the tragic poet Phrynichos staged a performance, not on one of the usual themes from mythology, but on *The Fall of*

[9] H. vi, 44–8, 1. [10] *ib.* 48, 49, 1.

Miletos; such was the title of his piece (at this date a sort of oratorio with the singers in costume). It was perhaps the first time that a subject from contemporary history had been so treated; and the effect was tremendous. 'The whole audience was moved to tears' – tears not only of pity and terror but, for many, of shame. Phrynichos was prosecuted and fined 1000 drachmae 'for reminding the people of troubles that touched them nearly', and an injunction was added that the piece should never be revived.[11] The alleged complaint can hardly have been a legal ground for prosecution, though it may have been that of an appeal to prejudice urged at the trial. Possibly the legal action may have been a prosecution for 'impiety', in introducing current human affairs into a performance on a sacred occasion; but the motive of the prosecution was surely political; it was the protest of those who had opposed intervention, and their determination that the sacred theatre should not be used for political propaganda was not inspired solely by reverence.

To this city, divided as bitterly as was any western democracy by the Spanish Civil War, came Miltiades in the same spring of 493, with his four surviving ships, and was brought to trial by 'his enemies', unnamed, 'for his tyranny in the Chersonese'.[11a] It was a fact that he had held that lordship *as an ally of the Peisistratids*, 'sent out by them in a warship to take over' after the death of his uncle, and that he had there arrested 'the chief men', no doubt including Athenian colonists; and this probably rendered him formally liable to prosecution under the anti-tyrant law.[12] Nor would the fact that he had since committed aggression against Persia by the seizure of Lemnos and Imbros commend him to the peace party. As a chief, even in flight, arriving with four shiploads of his partisans, and with powerful family connections in Attica, he was a rival to the Alkmeonidai themselves. The family rivalry, indeed, was ancient. Their ancestors had been suitors of Agariste, daughter of Kleisthenes the tyrant of Sikyon (Hippokleides, the unsuccessful suitor, was 'related to the Kypselidai' of Corinth; and a Kypselos, a rare name, was father of the elder Miltiades, prince of the Chersonese). It was Xanthippos, married to her grand-daughter the Athenian Agariste, niece of the Athenian Kleisthenes, who was to prosecute

[11] *ib.* 21.
[11a] *ib.* 104.
[12] *ib.* 39; for the law, cf. Andok. i, 96ff (though it is a measure of A.'s reliability as an authority for earlier history that, having appealed to a 'law of Solon', he quotes a decree dated by the prytany of a Kleisthenic tribe).

Miltiades again later (p. 266).[13] Certainly the Alkmeonidai must at least have supported the prosecution of 493.

But Miltiades was acquitted. As it would probably take longer to mount a great political trial than one for impiety, it was probably later in the year than the trial of Phrynichos; and the morale of Athens was rallying. The spring elections brought to the chief archonship Themistokles[14] the son of Neokles, the first radical democrat of Athenian history: a member of the ancient and priestly clan of the Lykomidai, yet always treated by hostile tradition as not a nobleman. (Was his father perhaps one of the Lykomid clan's outer circle of dependent Orgeōnes or Partakers in the Rites, rather than of the Homogalaktes, the family proper?[15] Is the name Neokles, 'New Fame', itself significant of a house rising in the world in the generation after Solon?) In any case, Themistokles himself is said to have been base-born, the son of a slave-woman, perhaps (as the hostile traditions said, contradicting each other in details) not a Greek but Karian or Thracian. In his years of fame he restored the Lykomid family shrine at Phlya, getting the poet Simonides to write a hymn for the occasion; but in his youth he had to exercise at the Gymnasion or sports-club of Herakles at Kynosarges without the walls, which young men marked by the bend-sinister frequented.[16] He was thus one of those who would have been excluded from political life by the stricter regulations either of earlier or of later Athens; he owed his undoubted citizen rights to the reform of Kleisthenes. As archon, Themistokles began the planning and establishment of the great port, with room both for commercial harbour and naval base, at Peiraieus (Piraeus).[17] It was five miles from the city, whereas the open beach at Phaleron was only three; but the shelter to be had in its natural rock harbours was incomparably better; shelter both against bad weather and against men – it was not yet fifteen years since the Aiginetans burnt Phaleron. The rocks of Piraeus could be fortified to such purpose that that could never happen. Hippias had seen the advantages of the site and started to build a castle there already. Later, if not already at this time, Themistokles dreamed of moving the seat of government down there if Athens were threatened by land; twenty years after his archonship, when the great landward wall of the

[13] H. vi, 128, 2; 131, 2; 136, 1.

[14] D.H. vi, 34.

[15] For the distinction, see Philochoros (*FGH* 328 F35; from *Suda*, *s.v.* Orgeōnes); discussion in Wade-Gery, *Essays*, pp. 86ff; Andrewes, in *JHS* LXXXI.

[16] Plut. *Them.* 1.

[17] Thk. i, 93, 3.

port had been completed to his specifications (except that it was never built to the height that he had desired), he even used to propose this publicly.[18] But the Athenians were a conservative people. The idea of separating the seat of government from the historic citadel and its sanctuaries was never entertained. Under Perikles and Kimon, Athens made the best of both worlds, connecting the city with both ports in one great linked fortress by the vast enterprise of the Long Walls.

This, then, was the archon in whose time, probably as chief magistrate, if not, then certainly as archon-designate, the trial of Miltiades ended, against the will both of Alkmeonid and Peisistratid supporters, in an acquittal. Many have speculated as to how much and in what way Themistokles used the archon's extensive judicial powers to influence the course of justice.[19] On this there is no direct evidence, but it seems highly probable that he did use them. Themistokles was far too intelligent to cherish illusions as to how far this colonial 'white rajah's' politics could agree with his own in the long run. In fact, in the long run and when the danger from abroad had passed, the Alkmeonid faction combined with Miltiades' son to break Themistokles.[20] But at the moment, Themistokles' policy was that of Churchill in World War II: 'He who actively opposes our enemy is our friend.' Not long afterwards, Miltiades was elected general of the regiment of his tribe.[21]

Aigina was still hostile, and when the Persian heralds appeared in 491 with their demand for submission she, like other island states, 'gave earth and water'. Her co-operation with Persia and availability as a Persian base would most seriously compromise Athens' defence. The situation was critical, and Athens sent to Sparta, which already, as we shall see, numbered Aigina among her allies, to request intervention.[22] King Kleomenes took the same view as to who were friends and enemies in face of the Persian menace as Themistokles. Forgetful of his

[18] Thk. i, 93, § 7.

[19] e.g. Wade-Gery's charming paraphrase of the saying in Plut. *Aristeides*, 2, in which Th. repudiates the idea of strict impartiality as an ideal for an archon: 'Fair? I'll be better than fair; I'll make certain the right side wins.' (*Essays*, p. 178.)

[20] Plut. *Arist.* 25, *sub fine*.

[21] H. vi, 104. – It is another reasonable speculation, that much of the biographical material about him, especially in H., came into the common fund of Athenian tradition (oral tradition, naturally) after being made widely current by the pleadings at his trial: Munro in *CAH* IV, p. 232; Wade-Gery, *Essays*, 165 and nn.; Hignett, *Ath. Const.* 329; etc. This would account neatly for the mixture of favourable and unfavourable traditions about him, which H., as Wade-Gery says, 'echoes with impartial gusto'.

[22] *ib.* 49.

humiliation by the democracy many years before, he accepted the request; and he was the better able to intervene effectively, for the fact that he had lately smitten the Argives as they had never been smitten before, and firmly consolidated Sparta's hegemony in the Peloponnese.

The dating of Kleomenes' Argive war during the years of the Ionian Revolt is supported especially by the curious 'Double Oracle', issued by Delphi to 'the Argives, when consulting the oracle about the preservation of their city':

> But when the female shall drive out the male
> And glory gain in Argos: In that day
> Shall Argive women rend their cheeks and wail,
> And generations yet unborn shall say
> 'The dreadful, coilèd snake is speared in the mellay.'
> And thou, Miletos, schemer of deceit,
> Shalt be to hordes a glorious spoil and prey.
> Thy wives shall wash a long-haired nation's feet,
> And new folk at My shrine in Didyma shall meet.[23]

The giving of a single response concerning two cities must imply that when the Argives consulted the Oracle, Miletos was somehow intimately concerned; and the most likely hypothesis is that when Aristagoras had appealed for help to Sparta unavailingly, he went next to Sparta's ancient rival, probably on his way from Sparta to Athens.[24] Argos, it would appear, went so far as to consult Delphi; but the Delphic priests, convinced, like their friends the Alkmeonidai, of the futility of resistance, interpreted their medium's utterance in a response obscurely foreboding disaster to Argos, and explicitly predicting the sack of Miletos. The name of Argos existed in the masculine as that of an eponymous hero; and the 'female', whose victory over the 'male' would be Argos' disaster, could be any one of a number of names (Persia, or Media, or Asia, or, nearer home, Sparta or Lakedaimon); though later, in the light of after events, this phrase received a different interpretation. Argos was deterred from helping Miletos, or given an excuse for not so doing; but it is likely that at least a contributory

[23] H. vi, 19, 77 (the two halves separately). Paus. i, 4, 1, puts the war at the beginning of K.'s reign; but his is no high authority, and H., though he gives no precise date, implies that about 490 and even in 481 the war was recent (vi, 92; vii, 148).

[24] Bury, 'The Epicene Oracle concerning Argos and Miletos', in *Klio*, II (1902).

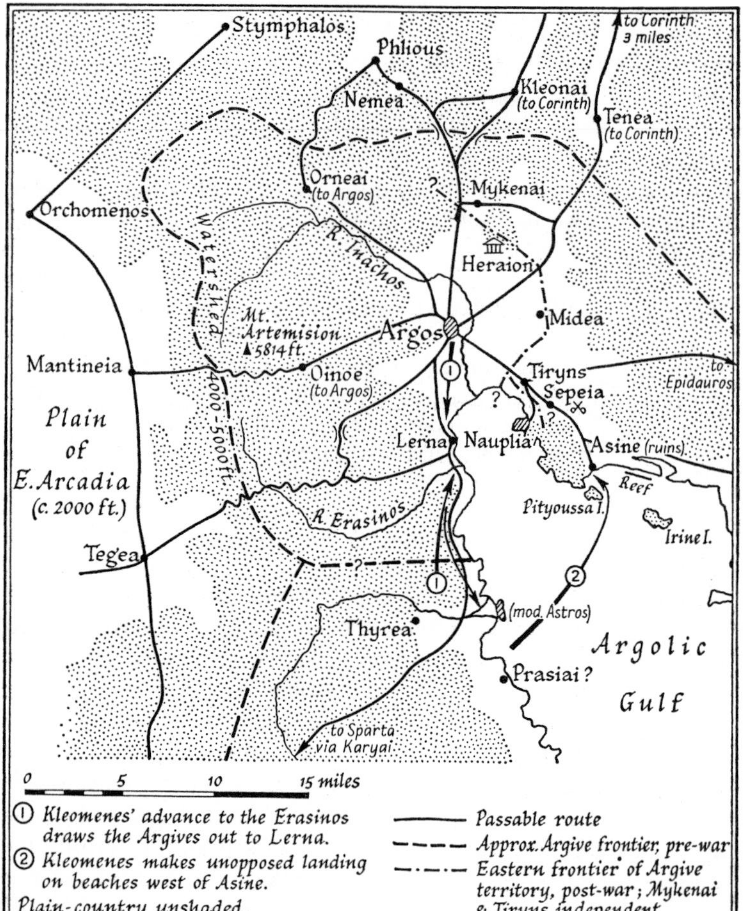

Kleomenes crushes Argos

factor in deterring both Argos and Sparta was that a war was brewing between these Dorian rivals. It was fifty years since, after the unsuccessful attempt at 'limitation of armaments' in the Battle of the Six Hundred Champions, Sparta had defeated Argos and reft from her the coastal borderland of Thyrea. Argos had recovered; Sparta may have had grounds for suspecting her of aggressive intentions;[25] and, probably

[25] Cf. Argos' attitude on the expiry of the treaty of 451, Thk. v, 14, 4; 41, 2f.

soon after the delivery of the Double Oracle, Kleomenes, whose recorded actions in foreign policy are all concerned with the consolidation of Sparta's position in the Greek homeland, consulted Delphi in his turn. This time the answer was lucidity itself: Kleomenes would take Argos.

Kleomenes marched to the Argive frontier river Erasīnos, and offered sacrifice, as was meet and right, before leading his army over. The results, as his diviners reported, were negative; the river-god was unfavourable. 'Very patriotic of him', said Kleomenes, but added that this was not going to save Argos.[26]

There has been too much in some modern books, especially perhaps books of the generation 1880–1920, of a tendency to suggest that all or most fifth-century Greek generals used omens and sacrifices in the furtherance of prearranged policy and strategy, after the manner of a Julius Caesar. So, in this campaign, it is suggested that Kleomenes marched to the Erasinos to draw the Argives thither, intending all along to make his real invasion by sea. He had indeed mobilised a fleet from Sparta's allies, including squadrons from two states which had formerly owned the suzerainty of Argos: Sikyon (brought over the Isthmus 'tramway'?) and Aigina.[27] That Kleomenes really gave his diviners instructions as to what verdict to find on the sacrifices is most improbable; on the superstitions or religious ideas of a classical Greek man of action, one should compare not Caesar but Xenophon. But he had his ships ready, whether for the main invasion or for a diversion, according to circumstances. He now withdrew from the frontier, marched down to Thyrea, and effected an unopposed landing 'in the land of Tiryns and Nauplia'; i.e. probably south-east of Nauplia, well away from Argos, on the beaches near Asine. The Argives, who could not unguard the coast west of Nauplia, were only in time to block his debouchement from the wide strath or elongated plain which runs inland from Asine, between rugged hills, to join the main plain of Argos near Tiryns. An Italian anti-tank-gun position, itself in turn in process of becoming historic, on the rock of Asine, and an anti-tank obstacle half-way up the strath, still indicate, or did in 1957, the fact that this postern-gate still had military significance for those planning coast defence in 1942–4.

For several days the armies, each perhaps of about 8000 armoured men, faced and watched each other. Kleomenes, strategically on the

[26] H. vi, 76. [27] *ib.* 92.

offensive, had no intention of risking disaster by merely charging like a bull. He watched for an opportunity. What further devices or diversions he might have planned, we need not ask; for, probably on the seventh day, the opportunity came.

The Argives were vigilant and determined. Daily at dawn they stood to arms and so stood while the sun grew hot, making it clear that they could play a waiting game as well as any Lycurgean Spartans. Not until the enemy withdrew and fell out for the much needed mid-day meal (Greeks took no early breakfast) did they do the same. But they grew too mechanical. As the story goes, they took to timing their movements by the enemy's trumpet-calls. Kleomenes, like Lysander at the Goat Rivers ninety years after, was waiting for just some such carelessness to develop. When the habit had had time to grow well established, he had the order passed verbally that the trumpet-call for 'Dinners' was to be the signal for attack. (Probably, one fancies, the men were to fall out and, with no further trumpet-call, immediately to re-form line.) The Argives, having settled down to eat in good earnest, had no time to reform theirs; in a matter of minutes the Spartans were upon them, killing many, while 'still more fled to the Grove of Argos', an eponymous hero, where the Spartans surrounded them.

The grove, evidently extensive, was one of those dense patches ot primaeval forest which Greek piety left untouched among the sown land at places deemed sacred. To shed blood within it would have been provoking the wrath of heaven too dangerously to contemplate, if not for Kleomenes, at any rate for his soldiers; and desperate men in a jungle might have been physically dangerous too. But the Spartans' scruples did not extend far beyond that point. Kleomenes got the names of individual Argives from deserters who were with him (no doubt political malcontents) and bade his herald call them out 'saying that he had got their ransom-money'. (So the blockade must have lasted for some time.) Then he killed them. 'The grove was too thick for those within it to see what those without were doing; but presently someone climbed a tree, and saw what was going on.' So this ruse only yielded about fifty victims. Finally in desperation Kleomenes ordered the helots with his army to pile dry brushwood all round the grove, and set it on fire. The guilt of any formal sacrilege would thus, according to the mechanical legalism of Greek thought about guilt, fall on the helots; besides, it could be argued that they did not fire the sacred grove itself, but only brushwood near the grove.[28] Six thousand Argives are said to have perished in the rout or been burned in the grove or butchered as they came out of it. The power of Argos was broken for a generation.[29]

Kleomenes, it was thought, could have taken and destroyed Argos after such a victory; but according to Herodotos he did not attempt it, and, when called to account by the Ephors, answered that when he sacrificed at the Heraion, five miles from the walls, the omens were unfavourable; also that, having discovered too late that the grove itself was called Argos, he saw that he had unwittingly fulfilled the oracle and so could not presume on it further.[30] These are clearly mere excuses, and one may surmise that he reflected that the plain of Argos was in any case going to carry a large population, and since Sparta had not the men to colonise it, an old and now broken city would be less of a trouble to Sparta than a new Argos colonised from round about. (He may even have told the Ephors so; but the tradition is more interested in omens and prophecies than in such things.)

As it was, the Argive territory was dismembered. Tiryns and Mykēnai, with their bronze-age walls and access to plains to the south-east and north-east respectively, became independent cities and allies of Sparta;[31] and in the truncated state of Argos itself, for sheer lack of men, the elders were constrained to admit to citizenship and intermarriage many of their *perioikoi*, the hitherto subject peasants of the plain. These could not now be excluded from citizen rights; it was something of a social revolution, which was partly reversed, after friction between old and new citizen families, 'when the sons of the fallen had grown up'. As Kleomenes must have seen, the land of Argos would not cease to breed men; and such divisions formed as satisfactory a solution of the Argive problem, from the point of view of Spartan power-politics, as could be devised.[32]

Argos later had a tradition, reduced to writing by a local antiquary

[28] For the fact that Greeks really did think, or evade the consequences of thinking, like this, cf. the evasions of guilt by the Ox-Slayers at the sacrifice of the Bouphonia at Athens, Porphyry, *De Abstinentia*, ii, 29f; Farnell, *Cults of the Greek States*, I, pp. 56f, my *World of Hesiod*, 69f; or in connection with accidental homicide, which incurred no less blood-guilt, Antiphon, 1st *Tetralogy*; Plut. *Pericles*, 36. Standard ransom, drs. 200, H. vi, 79.

[29] H. vi, 77–80; 6000 killed, H. vii, 148; 5000 *in the grove*, Paus. iii, 4 (it is not a *variant* tradition). The battle was called that 'of the Seventh Day', Ar. *Politics*, v, 1303a; by moderns that of Sēpeia, from H. vi, 77, 1.

[30] H. vi, 81f.

[31] H. ix, 28; cf. vii, 202.

[32] H. vi, 83; Ar. *Politics*, v, 1303a; Plut. *Brave Deeds of Women*, 4 (= *Mor.* 245).

named Sōkrates, that Kleomenes did attack the city and was repulsed; old men and boys manned the walls (as they undoubtedly would have) and were reinforced by faithful slaves and by women and girls, the whole garrison inspired by the voice and example of the poetess Telesilla. Tombs of women, said to have died in the battle, were shown. Telesilla is an interesting figure in her own right; she is said, after a sickly childhood, to have been advised by an oracle to devote herself to the Muses; which she did – a few words of her poems still survive in quotation – and her health much improved;an interesting case of Greek psychological medicine. One would gladly also accept the tale of the warrior Maid of Argos, and there is nothing impossible in it; but the evidence for it is all late, and it is strange if Herodotos either did not hear of it, if already current, or did not mention a story which so admirably fulfilled the prophecy about 'the female beating the male'. Similar stories are widely reported from mediaeval Europe, often serving as aetiological myths to explain a women's festival or local privilege, and there was indeed such a festival at Argos: the Hybristika or Feast of Outrage, on which the women appeared in arms and men in women's dress.[33] To the Argive tradition may also belong a story which ascribes Kleomenes' victory to treachery, agreeing to an armistice for seven days and attacking on the third *night*.[34] As usual, it is Herodotos' story which alone appears convincing.

To Sparta, then, more completely supreme in the Peloponnese than ever before, came Athenian ambassadors complaining of Aigina's action in giving earth and water to Darius' emissaries. Aigina as an ally of Sparta was presumably pledged to 'have the same friends and enemies as the Spartans'. But as an eastward trading state, it would be economic suicide for her to be an enemy of Persia, even apart from the eventuality of a Persian invasion. To Kleomenes it was evident that Aigina must be coerced; but in this he could not expect the co-operation of his fellow-king Dāmarātos, his open enemy ever since their difference over Kleomenes' attempt to coerce Athens. Damaratos' policy is a puzzle; but assuming that he had a normal man's love of his home and people

[33] Plut. *loc. cit.*; Paus. ii, 20, 8; Polyainos, viii, 33 (with some verbal correspondences with Plut., suggesting a common source). Sokrates of Argos, see D.L. ii, 47. Parallel Amazon-stories, cf. A. H. Krappe, *The Science of Folklore*, p. 77. Scanty 'fragments' of T., Edmonds, *Lyra Graeca*, II, pp. 242ff.

[34] Plut. *Spartan Sayings* (*Mor.* 223).

and was not solely motivated by a desire to thwart Kleomenes at all costs, it would seem that he was at heart a defeatist, who thought that in the last resort it would be better to reign in Sparta under Darius than that there should be no Sparta at all. He was a sufficiently distinguished figure in normal circumstances; he had many friends, and even though later he fled to Persia, they influenced Herodotos, who gives a curiously sympathetic account of him. He could be unscrupulous in personal affairs; he had seized and married Perkalos, daughter of Chilon (and perhaps great-grand-daughter of Chilon the famous Ephor), who was betrothed to his cousin Lātychidas (Leutychides in Ionic), thereby making a dangerous enemy; but his friends remembered him as one 'distinguished for many deeds and wise sayings, and among other things having won for his city an Olympic victory with the four-horsed chariot, the only one of the kings of Sparta who had ever done this'.[35]

So Kleomenes went to Aigina alone, and demanded hostages; but he ran into opposition, prompted as he believed by a secret message from Damaratos. Krios the son of Polykritos, of a distinguished family in the island (cf. p. 465), asked pertinently, where was the other king? And in his absence, where was the evidence that Kleomenes' demand was the demand of the Spartan state? Kleomenes had nothing to say to this; but he asked Krios his name, and hearing it (it means 'Ram') said as a parting shot 'Then gild your horns, Master Ram; you are coming in for trouble'. For a ram had its hour of glory, with gilded horns, when being led out to sacrifice.[36]

Kleomenes determined that Damaratos must go; and he compassed his deposition by casting doubts on his paternity. King Ariston, as the story goes, though he had married two wives, was long childless. He then married a third, the most beautiful woman in Sparta, of whom Herodotos tells a charming fairy-tale of the ugly baby who grew up beautiful after her nurse had prayed over her daily in the shrine of the divine Helen. Ariston had reft her by an unscrupulous trick from one of his friends, to whom she was already married; 'and in less than the usual time . . . she brought forth this Damaratos'. When the birth was reported to Ariston, who was transacting business with the Ephors, he was said to have said 'Then it cannot be mine'; but later he decided

[35] H. vi, 70, 3. Perkalos, *ib.* 65, 2. For 'marriage by capture' at Sparta, cf. Plut. *Lyk.* 15.
[36] H. vi, 50.

that the birth must have been premature, a story later supported on oath by the mother. The child was brought up as his, and was named Dām-arātos, 'prayed for by the people', 'because public prayers had been offered that a son might be born to Ariston as to a man highly distinguished among the Spartan kings'.[37]

Kleomenes now decided to reopen the question. A legal opportunity may have been offered by an archaic custom under which, once in nine years, the Ephors might watch for omens, to see whether heaven still looked with favour upon the reigning kings;[38] and a willing instrument was to hand in the person of Latychidas, who was himself the great-grandson of a king of the Eurypontid line,[39] as well as having a personal grievance. He pressed the investigation of Damaratos' claims to be rightful king. Some of the Ephors of the year of Damaratos' birth were still living, and were called as witnesses; they said they remembered hearing Ariston deny with an oath that the child could be his. Feeling ran high, and the question was referred, as the law on the deposition of kings required, to Delphi; and here Kleomenes had already prepared the ground. Herodotos' informants were prepared to give names: Kleomenes suborned Kobon, a prominent Delphian, and Kobon persuaded the girl medium Periallos to give a response such as Kleomenes desired. 'Later the story leaked out, and Kobon fled into exile from Delphi, and Periallos the medium was deposed.' So Damaratos was declared no king, and Latychidas succeeded him.[40] Later Damaratos,

[37] H. vi, 61–3.

[38] Plut. *Agis*, 11, 3; cf. H. W. Parke, 'The Deposing of Spartan Kings' in *CQ* XXXIX (1945).

[39] H. viii, 131: 'all [L.'s] ancestors except the last two had been kings'. The word 'two' is usually emended to 'seven' in modern texts, in order to square the record with that of Paus. iii, 7, who gives the ancestors of Damaratos as kings, the last seven names being different from the pedigree of L. (H., *ib.*). As Beloch argued (*GG* I, ii, § 68), 'all but seven' is hardly a natural expression to use, when seven is nearly half the pedigree of 16 names, and if L.'s family was so far removed from a reigning king it is also unlikely that, with Damaratos removed, he would have been next in succession. (The line of succession could change at Sparta if an elder son died without reigning and a younger son succeeded to the throne; for then the new king's son would be next in line, and not his elder brother's sons, if any. Thus Leonidas in 480 was succeeded by his son Pleistarchos, though a minor, and the son of his elder brother Dorieus, who had died without coming to the throne, was passed over, though old enough to hold a military command; H. ix, 10.)

[40] H. vi, 65ff. The date 491 is confirmed by Diodoros' figures for lengths of reigns of the 5C Eurypontid kings: L. 22 years, his grandson and successor Archidamos 42, *his* son Agis 27 (D. xi, 48; xii, 35). The last two died in 427–6 and 400–399 respectively, as can be determined from Thucydides (iii, 89) and Xenophon (*Hell.* ii, 3, 1). D. puts both their accessions seven years too early, a mistake which apparently stems from his dating the reign of Archidamos from the exile of L., in 476, instead of from his death, 469; L.'s 22 years are thus 491–469: Beloch, *GG* I, ii, § 70.

stung by the taunts of his successful rival, fled from Sparta and deserted to the Persians (pp. 267f).

So 'the way was paved for Kleomenes; . . . and straightway, taking Leutychides with him' (so the name is rendered in Herodotos' Ionic) 'he proceeded against the men of Aigina.' With the Spartan government united, Aigina did not dare to resist; and the kings arrested Krios and nine other leading citizens as hostages and delivered them to Aigina's bitterest enemies at Athens.[41]

Thus Kleomenes had neutralised the dangerous hostility alike of Argos to Sparta, of Aigina to Athens, and of a rival king. It was done in the nick of time; for in 490 a Persian sea-borne expedition sailed against Athens.

[41] H. vi, 73.

CHAPTER XII

Marathon

THE disaster to the fleet of Mardonios and the contretemps to his army led to no suspension of Persia's westward drive; but with the change of command – for the brilliant young Mardonios was off the stage in 490, recovering from his wound and also somewhat discredited – there was a change of strategy. The fact suggests (like the headquarters intrigue at Sardis, which Artaphernes punished as treason) that Persian high military circles were not less divided on questions of strategy and high policy, even though they might agree about ends, than many other groups of statesmen and generals about whom we know more.

The new commander was Datis the Mede, who, if the Lindos temple-chronicle may be trusted, had probably commanded the imperial fleet on its first entry into the Aegean. He was then senior to Mardonios, who according to one historian had been serving under him (pp. 210, 218). He can hardly have been pleased at being passed over in favour of the young nobleman; and he now obtained the king's agreement to a new plan, that of striking across the central Aegean with a complete army on ship-board, utilising among other transports the new 'horse landing-craft' (p. 223). His object was to secure the Cyclades and then to punish the two mainland cities which had taken part in the raid on Sardis. With him was sent the king's nephew Artaphernes, son of the elder Artaphernes, who probably died about this time; the son later commanded the Lydian and Mysian levies in Xerxes' army. He was probably to succeed his father as satrap of Sardis and political officer with the expedition.[1]

Datis and Artaphernes 'marched to Cilicia with a strong and well-found army'. They embarked it from a base in the Alēïan plain, and 'sailed with six hundred triremes to Ionia'. Thence, from Samos they

[1] H. vi, 94; cf. vii, 74.

sailed due west, 'past Ikaros', the large but harbourless island which can be used to break the force of the summer north winds, that give twenty five miles of choppy water between Ikaros (or Ikaria) and the Cyclades. 'Six hundred ships' is a conventional figure for a Persian fleet, and no doubt much exaggerated; and Datis' subsequent proceedings show that the troops on board were no enormous army, though one believed sufficient for the task in hand. But the armament may well have been far larger than that which had failed to take Naxos nine years before; and when they reached that island, their first objective, they met no resistance. The Naxians, with the example of Miletos before them, fled to the wooded hills of their extensive interior. The Persians hunted down some of them, and burned the town, including its temples; then 'they set sail for the other islands'. Naxian patriotic history later turned this departure into a repulse. The people of the sacred islet of Delos fled in terror, crossing to Tēnos, where the hills might afford hiding-places. But here Datis' policy was different. Delos had committed no offence, and its god Apollo, through his priests at many shrines, had often served Persia well (cf. pp. 114, 227). Datis did not even let his ships put in there, but only across the strait at Rhēneia; he sent after the Delians, protesting that he had the king's orders not to harm the holy place and its people, and having persuaded them to return made a princely burnt-offering of frankincense on the altar.[2]

All the chief Cyclades had now surrendered, presumably, to detachments; the contrasting examples of Naxos and Delos had served their purpose well; and Datis sailed for Euboia, 'taking with him both Ionians and Aiolians', including islanders (p. 223). Karystos, at the south end of Euboia, closed its gates; the Karystians were a proud people; it took force fourteen years later to bring them into Athens' maritime league. But in face of siege operations and the ravaging of their farms, they surrendered in time to save themselves from the worst, and the fleet sailed on, to land its troops at the villages south of Eretria.[3]

In Eretria there was terror. Some were for fleeing to the hills, some for surrender. Messengers had been sent to beg help from Athens, and the Athenians, not desirous to denude their own country, bade the 4000 colonists at Chalkis to reinforce Eretria. They are said to have obeyed, but to have been advised by a prominent Eretrian that the city

[2] H. vi, 95–7. On Naxos, cf. Plut. *MH*, 36.
[3] *ib.* 98f. On the topography, cf. W. Wallace in *Hesperia*, XVI (1947), pp. 130ff.

would not hold out; so 'they crossed over to Orōpos and saved themselves'. The Persians advanced, horse and foot; there could be no resistance in the field, but the final decision was to defend the walls. The Persians 'attacked the walls violently, and for six days the losses were heavy on both sides; but on the seventh' two leading citizens betrayed the town. 'And the Persians entered, and plundered and burned the temples, in revenge for those of Sardis, and led the people captive, according to Darius' orders.' Then, 'after waiting a few days' – during which Datis may have sent Athens a summons to surrender – 'they crossed to Attica, confident after their great victory that they would serve the Athenians as they had served Eretria'.[4]

Datis' army, we notice, was not large enough to tackle Eretria and Athens simultaneously. Herodotos says that the whole force was applied first to the one enterprise and then to the other, and the detail about the 'few days' wait' at Eretria (for rest and reorganization) is explicit.[5]

Even after the fall of Eretria the Persians, embarking on the last and toughest item of the year's assignment, did not sail directly into the Saronic Gulf. Like Kleomenes in his Argive war, they chose their beaches far from the enemy city, and thus secured unopposed landing. The plain of Marathon provided good cavalry country and a short 'carry' from Eretria; and it was recommended by Hippias, who remembered landing there with his father, crossing from Eretria then also, on Peisistratos' return from exile half a century before. Hippias was still in touch with faithful friends in Athens (or enemies of the people; it was all a matter of the point of view). If the republican army did not

[4] H. vi, 100–2; for an embassy at *some* time (not in H.) cf. Ar. *Peace*, 292, with jokes about Datis' bad Greek; Raubitschek, *Das Datis-Lied*, in *Charites* (ed. Schauenburg, Bonn, 1957).

[5] I emphasise this, because it is suggested in *CAH* IV, ch. viii, by J. A. R. Munro, that the Persians did divide their forces: that the Athenians did start to march to join the Eretrians, via Oropos and the Euripos, but were pinned down *en route* by a force which the Persians threw ashore at Marathon, under Datis in person, while Artaphernes (not mentioned again in the Marathon story) prosecuted the siege of Eretria. This accounts neatly for the tradition (which must be true since it represents the memory of thousands), that the armies faced each other at Marathon for several days before the battle; a delay, for which the reason given by (and no doubt to) Herodotos is unconvincing; the young soldiers, who lived until Herodotos' time, did *not* know what went on in the council of war. Munro suggests that the Athenians awaited reinforcements from Sparta until the early fall of Eretria set Artaphernes free to move on Athens by sea, and made it necessary to strike now or never. But not only is this ingenious theory suggested by no source, it is impossible. The Athenians *cannot possibly* have intended to commit their forces in Euboia; for if they had and even if they had won a victory there, they would have left the seaborne enemy free to move on Athens, without a hope of getting back as they did from Marathon.

intervene at Marathon, he might hope for a movement among his father's old supporters in the Uplands. If it did, the aforesaid friends in Athens might be able to do something in the city. Everyone knew that there were divisions in Athens. The Alkmeonidai, jealous of Miltiades, were in touch with Hipparchos. The wedges were in; it should need only blows or pressure from without to drive them home.

Hippias must have been nearly eighty years old by now. It was twenty years since he had left Athens. No doubt he lived much in the past. In fact, he and his Persian allies were to find that, for all the aristocratic factions, the Athenian people in face of invasion was more solid than they thought. The democracy of Kleisthenes had not done badly.

But this was still to be proved. As he looked across to Attica, the old man was full of hope. His political ambitions must have been centred by now on his grandsons; but he felt also a great desire to lay his old bones at home. The night before they crossed, he is said to have dreamed an Oedipodean dream, that he bedded with his mother; and, steeped in the lore of dreams as he was, he took it for an omen that he should indeed be laid in his mother-land. When he hurried ashore, out of breath, he was overtaken by a spasm of sneezing and coughing. 'Aged as he was, his teeth were mostly loose; and he coughed so violently that he lost one. It fell in the sand, and he made a great point of finding it. But he could not; and he gave a great groan.' For the omen was fulfilled; something of Hippias was indeed to remain for ever in Attica, in the shape of that tooth.[6]

Saga-stuff; but very characteristic.

For Athens and for Sparta, pledged to support Athens, the fall of Eretria brought the time for action. So long as there was sea between them and the enemy, it was impossible to intervene; pointless and dangerous even to move large forces forward, in face of the sea-power which enabled the enemy to strike where he chose. Sparta must have been kept informed throughout the summer. Now the dire news of the fall of Eretria was sent by the swiftest means, which meant on the feet of a professional 'all-day-runner', Philippides or Pheidippides. He made good speed; leaving Athens presumably at dawn, he reached Sparta, having covered 140 miles of rough road, on the second evening.[7]

[6] H. vi, 107.

[7] *ib.* 105. – As to the name the mss are evenly divided and if Plut. and Paus. support

(There is nothing superhuman in this. Grote (IV, 460 n. 1) compares the speeds regularly made by modern Persian foot-messengers under parallel conditions; and the John o' Groats to Land's End race of 1960 produced, with good roads and beds, the striking result that several men and two women covered nearly 1000 miles in a fortnight.)

The Spartans professed themselves willing, 'but they said they could not march at once, for they would not break the law; for it was the ninth day of the month, and on the ninth' [once the moon was past its first quarter] 'they would not march until the moon was full.'[8] It was probably, though we are not explicitly told so, the month of the Karneian festival of Apollo, celebrated under the moon in the bright summer evenings of the second month of the year (beginning at the first new moon after the midsummer solstice); a month in which Dorians still, in the late fifth century, normally abstained from warfare. The week leading up to the full moon 'when the moon is high all night', as Euripides says, was naturally the most sacred part of the sacred month.[9]

The crisis came, therefore, in late summer. Athens for centuries commemorated it on the sixth day of the third lunar month, at the Boēdromia, the festival of Run-to-the-Rescue or, more literally, Run-to-the-Shouting, a soldiers' festival, at which the Polemarchos sacrificed to Artemis of the Wilds.[10] The actual crisis probably fell

---

Philippides, Nepos reads Phidippus. But it will not do to say that 'Pheidippides' is excluded because it appears as a comic compromise in Aristophanes' *Clouds*; for the name Pheidippos occurs in the *Iliad* (ii, 678), and, since this existed, 'Pheidippides' is always possible. – '48 hours' (Munro, p. 239) would make him, by Greek usage, reach Sparta 'on the *third* day'. He left *before* the army marched out; H., *ib.*

[8] *ib.* 106.

[9] Thk. v, 54, 75f; Eur. *Alkestis*, 449ff.

[10] *Ath. Pol.* 58, 1. 490 commemorated, Xen. *Anab.* iii, 2, 12. The festival itself was already ancient (founded by Theseus, Plut. *Thes.* 27). Plut. *MH* 26 censures H. for imputing to the Spartans a superstition about the moon, which, he says, they ignored on many other occasions; he does not identify it with the *Karneian* moon. He also claims to catch H. in a gross inaccuracy in that, if the battle was on the 6th Boēdromiōn, there had not been a full moon for three weeks (he repeats the date also in *Glory of Athens*, 7, *Camillus*, 19); it may be noted that he does *not* regard it as possible (as some moderns, from Clinton, *FH* II, p. 28, to W. K. Pritchett in *BCH* LXXXI (1957), pp. 278f, have thought) that the festival-months were grossly out of step with the moon; this phenomenon comes later, with the 'scientific revolution' of Meton's calendar reform in 432; Aristophanes' complaint (*Clouds* 615ff; *Peace* 406ff) that the gods come expecting a feast, punctually by the moon, and have to go home hungry, is typical of his attitude to what is new-fangled. The state was then trying to organise a uniform *solar* year (for purposes of collection of rents, taxes and mining leases, as Pritchett says, *op. cit.* p. 273), and the clash with a lunar religious year was inevitable. Plutarch, no doubt following popular tradition, but also ever ready to score off H., has probably wrongly identified the anniversary of the first commemoration with that of the battle; cf. Meyer, *GdA*³ IV, i, long note on pp. 313f; How

around the previous full moon. Which full moon this was, depends on whether a new moon, observable just at the solstice, was or was not reckoned as beginning the new year; but if it was, the Persians will have reached Euboia by the end of July, which, having met no effective resistance, they should have done. There was time enough for Datis to deal with the more dangerous Athenians, leave the rest under Hippias, and return home with the evidence that the navy could do it.

At Athens there had been keen debate. Many here too were in favour of defending the walls;[11] but the soldier Miltiades carried the day against such passive defence, which would have given the best opportunities for treachery by the disaffected[12] and enabled the enemy to cut off Athens from aid from Sparta. 'Miltiades' decree' was remembered in the fourth century (a point of some importance in connection with the fourth-century inscription, which purports to preserve the text of a later decree of Themistokles, pp. 359f); and its crucial words were [It was resolved by the People] 'to take food and march'.[13] The citizen army was to be ready to move at a moment's notice. Whether men of distant villages were called in from their farms and fed for weeks at Athens is another question. It would have been an economic strain; and until the sea-borne enemy's intentions were known, it was impossible to say where to march. Probably the Decree was passed in good time, empowering the generals (*epimelosthōn hoi stratēgoi*) – at this

and Wells *ad* H. vi, 106, etc. The previous full moon, that of the Karneia and of the Athenian month Metageitnion, is usually taken to be that of the 9th Sept. by our calendar (see tables at end of K. F. Ginzel, *Handbuch der Math. und Techn. Chronologie*, vols. I, II), but an element of uncertainty is introduced by the fact that there was a new moon practically *at* the summer solstice that year. By astronomical reckoning it comes before the solstice, which was then about June 28th (see Ginzel), and so would fall within the old year, which would then have 13 new moons and an intercalary month; but whether it was so reckoned would depend on when it was actually observed (June 29th?) and how Athens and Sparta defined the solstice. If the Karneian moon of 490 was that of August 11th (or 12th–13th by some reckonings), as preferred by Busolt (*GG*² II, pp. 580 n. 3, 596 n. 4) and regarded as possible by Beloch (*GG*² II, ii, pp. 56f), one is the less puzzled by the question how the Persians had managed to spend so much time in reaching Euboia.

The exact date of the Battle of Marathon cannot therefore be given with any certainty. Meritt, in *The Athenian Year* (Sather Lectures, Univ. of California, 1961), p. 239, writes that it is 'a problem of textual and historical interpretation as much as of the calendar'; and historically, a date around the August full moon avoids some difficulties (cf. p. 257).

[11] Walls certainly existed; in 479 the Athenians begin to *re*build them (Thk. i, 89, 3).

[12] Cf. his argument against passivity in the field, H. vi, 109, 5 (perhaps misplaced from this debate?).

[13] Ar. *Rhetoric*, iii, 10 (1411a), reading *episitisamenoi*, 'having provisioned themselves' (Munro, *CAH* IV, p. 238, appears to translate *episitisomenoi*, future, which seems less probable). An allusion also in Demosth. *On the Embassy*, § 303; and cf. Nepos, *Milt.* 5.

time the Polemarch and stratēgoi – to give the necessary orders in the event of a landing.

Then came the news that the enemy's main forces were disembarking at Marathon. It need not have waited on the speed of man or horse, for a beacon, like the beacons that signal the fall of Troy in Aeschylus' *Agamemnon* – by day, a prearranged smoke-signal for 'enemy landing in large numbers' – from the top of Mount Pentélikos could have alerted all Attica. Perhaps the army had already concentrated on the news of the fall of Eretria. In any case it moved fast. Slaves or beasts would carry the heavy meal-bags, 'rations for *x* days', brought along by the individual soldiers, and slaves probably helped also as, literally, armour-bearers. (Some slaves fell in the battle and were buried with honour on the field.) Men of the 'equestrian' class may have ridden to the front, though once there they would dismount to fight in the ranks, after the 'modern' manner. Athens put no cavalry in line. The Athenian regiments on the march were not perhaps a tidy spectacle; but they could move fast. Their words for what they were doing, 'going to the rescue', meant literally to 'run to the battle-cry': *boētheîn, boēdromeîn.*

The road to Marathon runs, in 26 miles, through Pallēne, south of Pentelikos, and east of it, where a strip of alluvium provides cultivable ground between the mountain and the sea. This was the way by which Hippias had ridden in his father's time; it is the only way suitable for cavalry; it is certainly the way by which the Persians would have marched on Athens if the Athenians had hung back, and it is most probably the way by which the Athenians marched to reach the southern end of the plain. The proverbial 'glance at the map' shows that the *shortest* way from Athens, about 22 miles, leads west and north of Pentelikos and descends by the valley of Vrana; but what it does not show is that the last few miles, after leaving the upper Kēphisos drainage basin, are extremely rough; mountain foothill country, although not high, and in antiquity probably forested. Unless there was something resembling a 'made road' – which in pre-classical Greece is most unlikely – it would seem that it must have been a good enough short cut for a messenger or small party, but no way to take a large body of troops to a battle-front. In a defile (any narrow passage) with rough places, as in any other traffic-congestion, the momentary check at each slow place, which matters little to a small party, is multiplied by the number of men in the column, divided by the number who can move abreast, and the delay to the rear thousands becomes appalling.[14]

In any case, the Athenians reached the south end of the Plain of Marathon and secured, presumably, both exits from it, before the Persians did so. If they encountered any Persian advanced troops, it was a small affair and we hear nothing of it. Keeping near the foot of the hills, they encamped in and round a precinct sacred to Herakles, now identified at a Chapel of St Demetrios, where there are ancient foundations, at the foot of the valley where the Vrana track comes in.[15] It would be 'according to form' in Christian Greece, for the soldier-saint to replace a hero like Herakles. Here they would find good water-supplies and a secure defensive position, with its back to the wooded hills; they covered the hill-path, which would serve well for messengers, and they at least denied to the enemy the use of the coast road, between Mt Agrielíki, a foothill of Pentelikos, and the shore. The plain directly in front was 'not completely open; there were scattered trees in several places' (there are olives there now) and they planned 'by means of a line of trees to impede the enemy's cavalry';[16] meaning probably not by a stockade, but by *abattis*; felled trees, hauled into line with their branches toward the enemy, can form a formidable obstacle; a famous modern example of their use was by the French in Canada, at Ticonderoga.

When the Athenians were already in position, a final reinforcement came in: the men of Plataia 'in full force', perhaps 600 strong. 'The Athenians had undertaken many tough actions', says Herodotos, on behalf of the Plataians, since they applied for Athenian protection nearly thirty years before. Nevertheless, in the circumstances (and with Hippias, who had originally extended that protection, among the enemy) they might have hesitated to risk their entire man-power in Athens' quarrel. They too might have stayed behind their walls. But

[14] N. G. L. Hammond (*History of Greece*, p. 216, n. 2) says 'Taking the direct route over Mt. Pentelicus, I walked fast from Athens to the mound at Marathon in 6 hours and returned the same day to Athens in 7 hours. The minimum time for the army's forced march . . . must have been 8 to 9 hours.' This last, by the mountain track, is surely an underestimate. One must wonder whether Col. Hammond, whose distinguished and gallant service in Greece was with guerrilla resistance forces, would really choose to take an infantry division that way.

[15] On all details of topography, see now the careful and detailed survey of W. K. Pritchett (*Univ. of California Publns. in Class. Archaeology*, IV, ii, pp. 137–75 (1960)).

[16] *ut arborum tractu equitatus hostium impediretur*, Nepos, *Milt.* 5. *Arbores rarae* (not *stratae*) Caspari (M. Cary) in *JHS*, XXXI, n. 13.

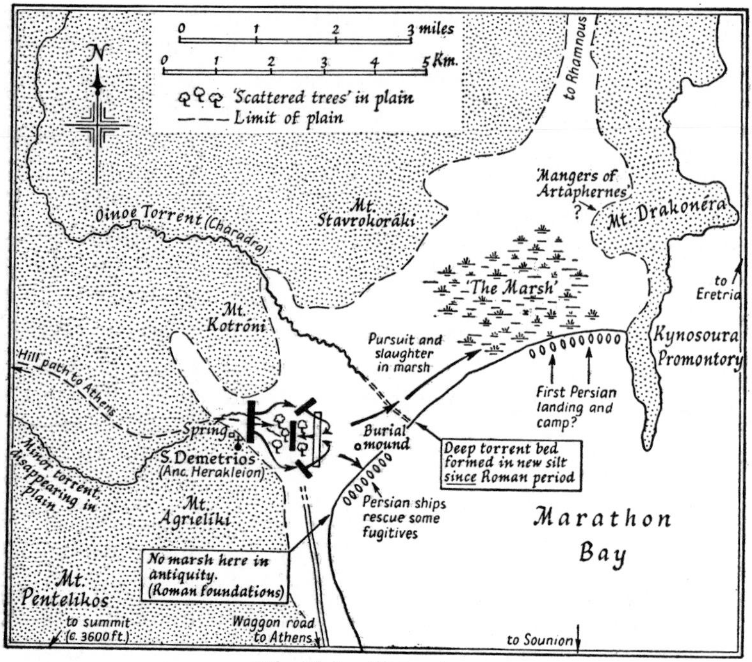

The Plain of Marathon

NOTES: 10,000 hoplites, massed, 8 deep, would have a frontage of about 1250 yards; i.e. such a mass could fill the dip from S. Demetrios across to Mt. Kotroni. When advancing, it is suggested that the Athenians' 'very weak' centre merely showed a front among the 'scattered trees' on the line of the water-course, while the strong wings (4000 men each?) fell *obliquely* upon the Persian wings, intending from the first to converge and meet.

they had taken the longer-sighted and also the brave decision. The Athenians were much touched; and from that day, 'when the Athenians offer sacrifice at their four-yearly festival' (that is the Great Panathenaia) 'the herald of Athens, who leads the prayers for all good things for the Athenians, adds "and for the Plataians" '.[17]

The Athenian 'dash to the rescue' had succeeded, as people say nowadays, in 'containing the enemy within his beach-head'. But we may

[17] H. vi, 108, 1; 111, 2; strength (in 479), ix, 28. The 1000 given by Nepos, *loc. cit.*, Justin ii, 9, 9, is probably a mere guess, like their numbers of Persians (for whom Nepos' '10,000 horse and 100,000 foot' is the most modest estimate!). N. also makes the Plataians join the main body *at Athens*; one of the head-on collisions between our sources which warn us that we cannot simply combine them. Sometimes they are wrong, and attempts to 'save the phenomena' are misguided.

legitimately wonder why the Persians let them. Perhaps they were just too slow. Disastrous though humanly natural failures of advanced troops to push out from a beach-head without support, and of the main body to get landed fast enough and give the support, have not been unknown in modern times (Suvla, Anzio). But they might, with Hippias' and his friends' local guidance, have landed further south, e.g. at Araphēn (Raphína). This was probably ruled out as offering less space for quick disembarkation, and with low but rugged hills close inland; also it was nearer Athens, and the Athenians might have arrived before the landing was completed. Or Datis could have landed at the southern end of the plain; classical remains show that there was no marsh there then. He must have *chosen* not to do this either. We are told that Marathon was chosen because it was 'good cavalry country'. Datis most probably was very willing to let the Athenians get there. If they gave battle in the plain, he reckoned he could beat them. If they did not come, he could march on Athens at leisure, collecting, as Hippias must have hoped, local support. If they came, but stood on the defensive, then he had got them a day's march from the city; he hoped (he tried, finally) with help from Hippias' friends to slip troops into Athens behind their back. With these alternative plans (for he was too experienced a commander to presume what the enemy would do), he probably landed his troops at the north-east end of the plain, where there was good grazing on the shores of a marsh (now the northern or 'greater marsh'; some ancient worked rocks there came to be called 'mangers of Artaphernes' horses')[18] and good anchorage for ships, under the promontory called the 'Dog's Tail', and almost invited the Athenians to occupy the south end.[19]

Then for several days the armies lay facing each other. Datis would not attack the Athenians in position; the Athenians would not expose

[18] Paus. i, 32, 6.

[19] Kynos Oura (Cynosura), Hesychios. At this point it may be convenient to dispose of the torrent-bed, the Charadra, which today divides the plain in two, and has embarrassed all writers attempting to reconstruct the battle. No ancient writer mentions it; yet it is today a significant obstacle. Pritchett (*op. cit.* pp. 156f) with F. J. Turner, Professor of Geology at his university, has now shown that it was not there. The floods of 24 centuries, especially since deforestation, have deposited vast quantities of silt over the plain (e.g. three metres round the base of the soros (see p. 254)), through which the torrent from the valley of modern Marathona has carved this deep channel. Pritchett picked post-classical potsherds out of its banks at a depth of more than a metre. On a British Admiralty chart of 1845, its mouth is labelled 'R. Kenurios', i.e. New River (E. Vanderpool, *ap.* Pritchett, p. 157, n. 144)!

themselves in the plain. Herodotos' narrative echoes the anxieties of young soldiers who lived down to his time, during the days of waiting, and the camp rumours of what was going on in the council of war: five of the ten generals were against giving battle, five were for it, including Miltiades; and Miltiades had gained the ear of the Polemarch, Kallimachos of Aphidna, whose inscription from a dedication, perhaps on entering office, has been discovered at Athens.[20] The Polemarch was *not*, as Herodotos thinks, at this time a mere chairman appointed by lot, but the elected Commander-in-Chief.[21] If he relied much on Miltiades, whom tradition remembered as the architect of victory, that is to his credit.

But though the decision to fight had been taken, says Herodotos' story (at Athens), there was no battle yet. The generals who favoured giving battle each, we are invited to believe, 'when his day of presidency came, transferred it to Miltiades; and he accepted it, but still did not give battle until his own day came round'. This is not only fatuous, but anachronistic; the permanent president of the war-council, until 487 (p. 284), must have been the Polemarch. The Athenians had a very good reason for waiting. They were waiting for the Spartans, who had promised to march as soon as they had kept the sacred Full Moon; and the full moon was at hand. Moreover, the Persians could not stay in their beach-head indefinitely. If they did not choose to attack the Greeks in position, they must re-embark in face of the enemy or make some other move, which might be the Athenians' opportunity.

In the end, Datis did make a move. He and Hippias had their own anxieties; *they* were waiting for a signal from Hippias' friends that the time was ripe for a swoop on Athens; and no signal had come. Datis probably knew all about the Spartans' intentions from the traitors. He waited till the last possible day, the day after the full moon, the very day on which the Spartans were due to march. While they were on the way, there might be just time to win and exploit a victory. The traitors, for their part, had decided to signal – probably to signal 'Ready' – on that same day. Whether they were as ready as they would have liked to be may be doubted; Athens under invasion was proving solider than they had hoped. But even before receiving the signal, the Persian commander had probably already decided to take the last

[20] *IG*, I², 609+; Tod, *GHI*, no. 13.
[21] H. vi, 109; *Ath. Pol.* 22, 2.

opportunity before the Spartans arrived, and try to slip troops into Athens by sea.[22]

To do this meant dividing his army, which he had always hitherto avoided; but time was running out; the risk had to be taken. He embarked some troops, including probably, as we shall see, much of his comparatively small force of cavalry, destined for the dash up from Phaleron. The appropriate place for doing this would be at the north-east end of the plain, and the time at night, by moonlight. The success of the operation depended on obtaining surprise. Surprise was not obtained.

There was later, we are told by the admittedly erratic Byzantine encyclopaedia called *The Suda* (formerly attributed to an otherwise unknown compiler named Suidas), a Greek proverb 'Cavalry apart'; it was used 'of those who break up a formation'; and it was supposed to date from the Marathon campaign.

'When Datis invaded Attica', says the article, 'it is said that the Ionians, when he had left, came up to the trees' [the Athenians' *abattis*?] 'and signified to the Athenians that the cavalry were away; and Miltiades understanding' [*sc.* the significance of?] 'their departure, thus attacked and won the victory.' This is a weak authority, but it does make a factual statement; it is one of the few post-Herodotean texts about Marathon which do give anything but patriotic rhodomontade; and it would have received more respect in our age of *Quellenkritik* if the writer had only quoted, as the book often does elsewhere, the name of his source.[23]

[22] This hypothesis (as old as Munro's article in *JHS* XIX, 1899; Grundy, *GPW*, 1901) is not entirely dependent on an interpretation of the late evidence quoted below; it depends primarily on that of the Athenians' celebrated dash back to Athens 'as fast as their feet could carry them', H. vi, 116. It is argued, e.g. by Caspari, *op. cit.* p. 104, that as the 70 miles by sea would take a good twelve hours (allowing no time for reorganization) there was no need for the Athenians to make special haste over a march of 26 miles – unless some of the Persian ships had already started. That Datis *intended* to divide his force, as it was suggested to Xerxes that he should (cf. p. 402, below), is suggested already by Grote (IV, pp. 474–6, 1847). The notion is rejected by modern German historians (e.g. by Meyer, 1937, IV, i, n. on pp. 312–13, as a 'recht absurde Kombination'); but this throws them back on an account derived from Nepos, which abandons too many of the 'public' facts reported by H., notably the four days' delay. – Meyer, *ib.*, does *not* derive Nepos' account from Ephoros; wrongly, I think, cf. chap. XIII, n. 19, below.

[23] This text, not being assignable as a 'fragment' to a named author, is so seldom quoted that it seems worth while to quote the Greek here:

Χωρὶς ἱππεῖς. Δάτιδος ἐμβαλόντος εἰς Ἀττικὴν τοὺς Ἴωνας φασίν, ἀναχωρήσαντος αὐτοῦ, ἀνελθόντας ἐπὶ τὰ δένδρα σημαίνειν τοῖς Ἀθηναίοις, ὡς εἶεν χωρὶς οἱ ἱππεῖς· καὶ Μιλτιάδην συνίεντα τὴν ἀποχώρησιν αὐτῶν συμβαλεῖν οὕτως καὶ νικῆσαι· ὅθεν καὶ τὴν παροιμίαν λεχθῆναι ἐπὶ τῶν τάξιν διαλυόντων.

translate **ἀναχωρήσαντος** according to Byz. and modern Gk. usage, not 'withdraw',

Meanwhile, the bulk of the Persian forces had, now or earlier, been brought south, to within a mile of the Athenian position. This follows from the accounts of the battle, and from the position of the burial-mound, the *Soros*. Their function was to attract the attention of the Athenians and to make their withdrawal more difficult – scarcely possibly by the coast-road; while if they tried to withdraw by the hill-track through the woods, the Persians could both exert pressure on a rearguard and use the coast-road themselves. In view of the strict defensive observed by the Athenians for four days, and the hopeless inferiority of their light-armed troops to the Persian archers, a demonstration should suffice. The Persians were amazed, says Herodotos (vi, 112, 2), when (probably at first light) the whole Athenian and Plataian armoured force, without cavalry or archers, came out of their lines, spreading out in disciplined order to cover the width of the Persian position, and poured down the plain towards them, moving fast.

Kallimachos, on the advice of Miltiades, and probably with information of the move against Phaleron, had agreed that it was 'now or never'; and the Persian movement up to within a mile (eight *stadia*, H. vi, 112, 1) gave the opportunity to strike a decisive blow. It is not likely that the Athenians had *no* light-armed troops present; some of the slaves who actually fell were probably among them; they might have been useful in defending a barricade with missiles; but for the kind of battle which Miltiades meant to fight, they were useless.[24] Like Bruce at Bannockburn (a battle which, as a successful assault by spearmen on foot against a force potentially more mobile, bears some resemblance

---

as in Homer, but 'leave', 'start', 'depart', as in a modern Greek railway timetable. The *Suad* is a good deal nearer our time than to that of Herodotos. To understand 'coming up to the trees' of a stealthy approach to the Athenian field-works, presumably at night, is a splendid idea of Hammond's (*History of Greece*, p. 215), and incidentally translates the Gk. much more naturally than a much-used rendering, 'climbed trees' to signal, presumably by daylight; which, even if they possessed a prearranged semaphore code, is not what most people would do if they wished to communicate secretly. By daylight, in any case, as Whatley said, the embarkation of the horse should have been at least as visible as an Ionian up a tree. Hammond really makes sense of this phrase for the first time. It may be added that the mention of 'trees' in the extant Marathon sources, only here and in Nep. *Milt.* 5, might suggest a common source; and Nepos' source (I still feel, despite the negative verdict of Meyer) may be Ephoros, whose liking for night operations is notorious.

[24] Slaves at Marathon, Paus. i, 32, 3. Athens in the Peloponnesian War still had no properly organized light infantry (Thk. iv, 94, 1).

to Marathon), Miltiades ordered his 'small folk' to the rear.[25] His whole plan, based on experience of Persian arms and methods, depended on coming to close quarters too quickly for the enemy's archery to be effective. Contrary to the usual practice of his time, he launched his 'armour' without missile preparation. The first reaction of the Persian officers was 'These men are mad'. But meanwhile the 'madmen' were coming on at a quick step,[26] and the Persians, though they had probably bivouacked in their battle positions, had to form up hurriedly.

The Persian front in the plain was too long for the Greek spearmen, perhaps 10,000 strong,[27] to cover in the usual eight-deep formation. Miltiades had taken his measures to deal with this problem too. To smash successfully into the middle of the Persian line would not win the battle. If the Persians were driven outwards from a broken centre, and some on the flanks even left unengaged, the position of the Athenian phalanx, with lighter-armed enemy archers on both its flanks, would not be enviable. His hope of victory depended on the fact that the Persians, between the hills and the sea, were in a limited area initially. They must be constricted further. If victory could not be gained at once along the whole front, it must at all costs be won on the flanks; the heavily armed Greeks could then turn inwards, and the Persians in the centre could not use their superior mobility to escape and come again. By another piece of tactical originality, he extended his line so that 'the centre was thin, and here the line was weakest, but each wing was strong and deep' (H. vi, 111, 3).

Kallimachos of Aphidna led the right wing, with his own tribal regiment, the Aiantis.[28] Then came the other tribes in their tribal order, Arimnēstos of Plataia leading his countrymen on the left. Munro suggests that they advanced in two columns, each of which swung outwards, while the rear regiments came up between the leaders; on the right Aiantis (IX in order, but the Polemarch's tribe), followed by Erechthēis, Aigēis, Pandionis, Leontis (I, II, III, IV); on the left the

[25] For what happened at Bannockburn, see W. M. Mackenzie, *Bannockburn* (Glasgow, 1913); General Sir P. Christison, in *Proc. Soc. Ant. Scotland* XC (1957), reaches the same conclusions independently.

[26] δρόμῳ, H. vi, 112, 3 (opp. to βαδήν, 'slow march', Xen. *Anab.* v, 4, 23; Grundy, *GPW* p. 188n.).

[27] 8000 Athenian hoplites in 479, when there were also some 50 ships, with a considerable force of marines, at sea (H. ix, 28, 6; viii, 131). The '10,000' of Nepos and Justin, *locc. citt.*, are an estimate.

[28] H. vi, 111, 1; as confirmed by Plut. *Table-Talk*, i, 10, 3, citing an elegy of Aeschylus.

Plataians, followed by Akamantis, Oinēis (Miltiades' tribe), Kekropis, Hippothōntis, Antiochis, numbered V to VIII and X. If so, the thin centre was commanded, as a biographical tradition tells, by two Athenians destined to fame: Themistokles and Aristeides, as generals of their tribes, Leontis and Antiochis.[29] If this is how the movement was executed, it would almost inevitably produce the result, with solid wings and an attenuated centre, which Miltiades accepted as the least possible evil. It might also lead to the wings being ahead of the centre, which would suit the over-all plan; and the centre was also probably impeded, or covered, by the 'scattered trees' irrigated by the water (too little to make a torrent) coming from the Vrana valley.

The Persians, according to their usual practice, had their best troops in the centre: native Persians, some of whom had body-armour of scales sewn on to leather jerkins, and Sakai (mounted?) from the eastern frontier; the subject contingents, including Greeks of Asia Minor (p. 237), were on the wings. In the centre 'the barbarians won and broke through and pursued the Athenians inland' (towards their camp? – this may be how some of the Athenian slaves came to be killed); 'but on both wings the Athenians and Plataians were victorious; and then they let the routed enemy flee, while the two wings converged and attacked those who had broken through their centre.' This was an amazing performance, by citizen soldiers in the heat of battle, and must have been premeditated. Were the wing attacks *originally* delivered in converging directions? 'And the Athenians won, and followed up, smiting the Persians, until they came to the sea, and men called for fire' (camp-followers following behind with fire in braziers?) 'and began clutching at the ships. And in this action fell the polemarch Kallimachos, who had fought most gallantly, and Stēsilaos the son of Thrasylaos, one of the generals, and also Kynaigeiros the son of Euphorion' (brother of the poet Aeschylus), 'whose hand was cut off with an axe as he grasped the stern-post of a ship, and many other Athenians of name. The Athenians captured seven ships in this way, but with the rest the barbarians got out to sea.'[30]

[29] *CAH* IV, p. 246; Plut. *Arist.* 5. The hypothesis is brilliant, as a means of getting the IVth and Xth regiments side by side; but this whole story *may* have been invented by someone less interested in Athenian military organization than in 'confronting' Aristeides and Themistokles. It is not mentioned in Plut. *Themistokles*. Oinēis (M.'s son's tribe) Plut. *Kim.* 18, 4.

[30] H. vi, 113–15.

The fighting at Marathon, says Herodotos, 'lasted a long time'. The time of a hand-to-hand mêlée must be counted in minutes rather than hours; but some of the Greeks on the flanks, in the original advance, the turn in against the Persian centre and the final pursuit to the sea, must also have covered some miles of distance. The converging attack on the Persian centre had given the Levantine sailors time in which to take aboard the fleeing Ionians and others, get the loaded ships out to sea, and prepare to do what they could to take off fugitives from the centre under the most difficult conditions. This is why the Homeric battle at the ships yielded the Athenians so few captures at the cost of a number of their bravest men. But of the Persians and Sakai in the centre, few can have got away; 6400 bodies were counted in all, a huge figure to Greeks; but its precision is certain; for, under a vow to the gods made by Kallimachos, every dead enemy had to be paid for.[31] The wall-painting which commemorated Marathon in the Painted Colonnade at Athens showed the fleeing Persians 'pushing each other into the marsh', and 'this is how their greatest loss is said to have been incurred'. Pausanias understood this to refer to the great marsh at the north-east end of the plain, and this, we now know, is the only marsh attested for ancient times. The whole mass of fugitives fled north-east towards their landing place under Kynosoura, to be caught and slaughtered in large numbers at the defile between the sea and the northern marsh.[32]

The fighting and carnage were all over by about nine or ten in the forenoon; but when 'the Persians were already in their ships', some Athenians, as they turned to look round again, saw something that made them catch their breath. From a safe point of vantage, probably some bare crag high up among the forests of Pentelikos, someone was 'showing a shield', probably flashing its polished surface: a signal, as everyone at once concluded, to the enemy. (This gives the hour; for after ten the sun would not be at the right angle for such a primitive heliograph signal.)[33] Hippias' friends, equally aware that the Spartans would by now be marching, had sent their message at last. In haste the Athenian generals reorganized their regiments; and leaving that of Aristeides on guard over the prisoners and the spoil that lay scattered

[31] H. vi, 117; on the vow, see p. 256.

[32] Paus. i, 15, 4 (the painting); 32, 6 (clearly the Great Marsh). Peisianax, dedicator of the Stoa, belonged to Kimon's generation (Plut. *Kim.* 4). Macan (*Herodotus*, II, pp. 228ff) is wrong in denying that the Battle of Oinoe is fifth-century.

[33] H. vi, 115, 124; cf. Hammond, *History*, p. 216 n. 2.

on the plain[34] (Antiochis, if in the centre, had probably suffered severely) they set off 'as fast as their feet could carry them' on the long road home, to encamp once more in a precinct of Herakles, that of Kynosarges without the walls.[35] They had lost only 192 Athenians killed; the shield, vizored helmet and corselet of solid bronze gave good protection to the vital organs; but the number wounded in their unarmoured arms and legs was probably much larger; they may in all have had some ten per cent casualties. Herodotos had no figures for the Plataians and slaves, who also were honoured with burial on the field.[36]

Meanwhile the Persians, detaching some ships to pick up the Eretrian prisoners from their temporary concentration-camps on islets in the channel – so these at least were not 'dashing' for Athens – set off to round Sounion, still hoping to find the city in the hands of those who had gone before them. But when their leading ships arrived off Phaleron, it was only to see the spearmen of Marathon facing them again. The plot had miscarried; no one had taken overt action, and the precise identity of those who had signalled remained a mystery. Many suspected the Alkmeonid faction, whose record of alliances with Peisistratos and his sons, Lydians, Spartans and Persians, as might suit them at any time, gave ample grounds for such suspicion, whatever Herodotos, in the days of Perikles, might say to the contrary.[37] But there was no evidence. The Alkmeonidai remained a powerful force in politics, and bitterly jealous of the position won by Miltiades.

Datis (whom the preposterous Ktesias alleges to have fallen in the battle) drew off his fleet and made sail for Asia. For old Hippias it was the end; he is said to have died at Lemnos, before reaching Sigeion.[38] But Datis and Artaphernes, though, like Mardonios before them, they had suffered a reverse and heavy losses, had conquests to report too. Their retirement was no flight. On the way, they stopped at Mykonos, where Datis, prompted by a dream, it is said, made search in the Phoenician ships for a gold-plated image, which some Phoenicians, on a reconnaissance or foray beyond the narrows of the Euripos, had carried off from the Temple of the Delian Apollo on the coast of Tanagra, contrary to imperial policy. Having found it, he deposited it at Delos, with instructions (which the Delians omitted to carry out) to

34 Plut. *Arist.* 5.
35 H. vi, 116.
36 *ib.* 117; Paus. i, 32, 3.
37 H. vi, 115f, 121ff.
38 Ktes. *Epit.* 18; *Suda, s.v.* Hippias.

return it where it belonged. Then he continued his voyage, and proceeded to Sousa with his large haul of prisoners, especially those from Eretria; 'and Darius, when he saw them at his mercy, did them no harm, but settled them in the Kissian country', about 25 miles from Sousa, among the oil wells which were already being exploited on the borders of Iraq and Iran. Herodotos saw their descendants there, 'still preserving their ancient language'.[39] But it was no light penalty, for Greek seafarers, this deportation, from which the Athenians had saved themselves. Plato appreciated the sadness of it in that famous epigram

> Leaving the rough Aegean's surge and swell,
> Afar in inland Median plains lie we.
> Farewell, Eretria famed, our home; farewell
> Athens, our neighbour there; farewell, dear sea.[40]

Only three days after the full moon, and perhaps on the very day after the Persians had retired, the first Spartan brigade, 2000 strong, reached Athens after a heroic piece of marching. The number is not large; the Spartans are rumoured to have had trouble in the Peloponnese – but if so, why did they not tell Herodotos? – and all was certainly not well at Sparta itself (pp. 271ff). On the other hand, there may have been other troops following (in 479, the ever-ready Spartiates moved first, and an equal force of Perioikoi, who had to be mobilised, followed). If so, they were ordered home again *en route*. Those who had come, 'having arrived too late for the battle, desired nevertheless to see the Medes' (as they called all Iranians) 'and they went to Marathon and saw them' (no doubt studying their armour and weapons). 'And then they congratulated the Athenians on their achievement, and started back.'[41] Even those who had come would have been a most valuable reinforcement. But what has seldom if ever received notice is that Sparta's good will, by forcing the Persians and their secret friends to hurry their operations, probably did exert a real and important influence on the campaign.

The fallen of Marathon were cremated and their ashes buried there on the field; and over their resting-place another battle has raged. A mound marks the spot; it is still nine metres high, after nearly 2500

[39] H. vi, 118f.

[40] *A.P.* vii, 259; Plato 10, Diehl.

[41] H. vi, 120; Plato, *Menexenos*, 240C; *Laws*, 692D–E, 698E. But his other details – 500,000 Persians; 300 ships; siege of Eretria *three* days – do not increase our faith in Plato as an historian, or in oral tradition generally.

years of exposure, with erosion accelerated recently by the after-effects of excavation; but Staïs, who excavated there for the Hellenic Government in 1890, reported that he found its original base three metres below the present ground-level, through the deposit of silt on the plain. It must originally have been well over twelve metres high. At its base the Greek archaeologists found a 'thin pavement' on which the bodies had been cremated, with a thick layer of ashes and burnt bones; thirty early-fifth-century *lekythoi*, as used at funerals; and a great sacrificial pit with animal remains. Near the mound's surface are found fragments of later *lekythoi*, offerings to the Heroes of Marathon. Schliemann, however, who had dug, less thoroughly, in 1884, reported finding in the mound quantities of fragments of Mycenaean pottery (with one Egyptian vase) and other prehistoric ware, an obsidian knife, and numerous flints (arrowheads?); enough to convince him (not the most careful of excavators) that the mound was of earlier *origin*.[42]

It may be, therefore, that for purposes of this burial an already ancient tumulus was dug up, re-used and perhaps enlarged; and it can *not* therefore be confidently said that the Soros shows exactly where 'the Athenian dead lay thickest'. It must, however, have been in a fairly convenient position, and it does tend to indicate that the battle was fought in the southern part of the plain, in the angle between the Athenian camp at the foot of Mount Agrielìki and the sea. On it were set up *stēlai*, tall marble slabs, with 'the names of the fallen, tribe by tribe'. Later a special monument to Miltiades was added, no doubt in the days of the ascendancy of his son.[42a] The place was said to be haunted: 'any night one may hear neighing of horses and noise of battle; no one has ever seen anything definite, who went there for the purpose, but with one who has not heard about it and to whom it happens by chance, the spirits are not angry'.[43] Worship was offered locally to Herakles and to Marathon the eponymous hero, and to 'the hero Echetlos'; this last commemorating 'a man of rustic appearance and apparel, who struck down many of the barbarians with a ploughshare, and then could not be found after the battle'.[44] Echetlos was also shown

[42] Reports of Staïs in *Deltion Archaiologikon*, 1890, 1891, and (summarised) in *Ath. Mitt.* for 1893; of Schliemann in *Zeitschr. für Ethnologie* XVI (1884). I do not feel that Pritchett (*op. cit.* (n. 15, above), pp. 140ff), who summarises fully all that has been done on the mound, entirely disproves Schliemann's conclusion.—But see Hammond in *JHS*, 1968; Burn in *JHS*, 1968. Remains of the prehistoric settlement and cemetery postulated came to light under the silt in February, 1970. [42a] On which see now E. Vanderpool, in *Hesp.* and *AJA*, both 1966. [43] Paus. i, 32, 3. [44] *ib.* § 4.

(no doubt with his name written in, as on a vase-painting) in the fresco in the Painted Colonnade, with Athena and Herakles; and with Theseus, 'rising from the earth' to help his Athenians. There too were Datis and Artaphernes, Kynaigeiros, Miltiades and Kallimachos.[45]

The great victory was also commemorated by the Athenians at Delphi; before the neat Doric shrine or 'treasury' of the Athenians, now re-erected by the French archaeologists, there was added a base bearing a row of statues; here also the figure of the mortal Miltiades stood among the gods and heroes. Pheidias was said to have been the sculptor; even if this attribution was based only on style, it suggests that the monument was completed only long afterwards, perhaps by Miltiades' family. Part of the inscription, re-cut centuries later, is still visible.[46] Olympia received a trophy of Persian arms. Plataia dedicated from her share of the spoils a temple to Athena the War-goddess; here too the cult image was ascribed to Pheidias, and a recumbent figure at its feet was said to be the general Arimnēstos.[47]

These later-completed monuments were not free from a tinge of mid-fifth-century propaganda: Miltiades' family against Perikles, Plataia against Thebes. But there was no lack of earlier artistic celebration. A large marble base at Athens, of which fragments have been found, perhaps supported a *stēlē* with the names of the fallen. Unmentioned by Pausanias, it may, the suggestion has been entertained, have been brought in from Marathon in late Roman times. It bore, exceptionally, *two* verse epigrams, one of which was added later; and it has been suggested that the second was that by Aeschylus, who had fought in the battle, and is said to have been much disappointed that, in public competition, the work of a foreign poet, Simonides of Keos, who had a special genius for short lapidary poems, was preferred to his.[48] The coinage of Athens probably also celebrates the victory in a new issue,

[45] *id.* i, 15, 4; Pliny, *NH* xxxv, 34/57.

[46] Paus. x, 10, 1; cf. 11, 4; Dittenberger, *SIG* 23b +; Tod, *GHI*, no. 14. (Hence the later portrait bust of M., on which see Richter, *Portraits of the Greeks*, vol. I (1965), pp. 94ff.

[47] Paus. ix, 4, 1 (Plataia). At Olympia, the exciting discovery by the Germans, in 1961, of a helmet with the inscription (as it were a museum label) Ἀθηναῖοι Μήδων λαβόντες, 'Athenians took of the Medes' (a scandal to grammarians), makes it more likely that the earlier similar discovery with 'Miltiades dedicated' commemorates Marathon rather than the Chersonese. Both are illustrated in Burn, *Warring States of Greece*, figs 79, 82, (1966).

[48] J. H. Oliver, in *Hesperia* II (1933); cf. *Life* of A. in his mss (in *OCT*, at end). Argument has raged about this monument also; e.g. whether the *upper* epigram refers rather to Salamis, the other being added, from a Marathon monument destroyed in 480. For the present state of the discussion see Meiggs and Lewis in *GHI* (1969), commentary on no. 26.

in which Athena's head is crowned with olive, while the waning moon in the corner probably commemorates the date of the battle.[49] A new epigram of three lines was also added to the dedication set up by Kallimachos in his lifetime, recording his leadership in the campaign.[50] Kallimachos was said to have vowed to Artemis of the Wilds, before the battle, the sacrifice of a kid for every enemy slain. Thereafter, finding that they could scarcely collect so many kids at that season, the Athenians besought the goddess to fund the debt at the rate of 500 a year; 'and', says Xenophon, 'they are sacrificing them still'.[51] This was the vow that was paid, not once but annually, at the festival on the 6th of the month Boēdromiōn, which became for all classical posterity 'Marathon Day'.

One deity, indeed, owed his introduction into Athens to this campaign. 'Goat-footed Pan of Arcady', in the words of a verse inscription ascribed to Simonides, had appeared to Philippides, 'as he himself reported', as he breasted the hills; and indeed, a desperate runner, heavy with news, could hardly be blamed if he saw apparitions. The god reproached him, he said, that Athens neglected him, who had long been her friend; and as the god 'who smote the Medes' (with panic terror in the rout?) and 'who was with Athens', Miltiades himself was said to have dedicated his statue, well known in later times, at a cave under the Acropolis.[52]

So the memory of Marathon early acquired its *mystique*. It was as Bannockburn, as Morgarten, as the defeat of the Armada. And it was like all those great national achievements, in that in cold fact it left the invader weakened only for the moment. The danger would still be there; but the defence would always be buoyed up by a great memory. In fact, the Greeks, with their usual incurable optimism, underestimated the continuing danger. They returned in the following years to the gratification of their internal grudges, while Persia returned to the strategy of an advance round the Aegean, convinced that greater forces would be needed for the conquest of the Greek mainland.

[49] Seltman, *Greek Coins*, p. 91. But C. M. Kracy argues for a date after 479; see 'The Archaic Owls of Athens', in *Numismatic Chronicle*, vol. 16, (1956).

[50] *GHI* (1969), no. 18.

[51] *Anab.* iii, 2, 12 (the story told to cheer Greek troops in a tight corner); K.'s name attached to it, schol. on Aristoph. *Knights*, 658ff.

[52] H. vi, 105; epigram in *Planudean Anth.*, 232, ascr. to Simonides; [Sim.] 143 Diehl, 133 Bgk.

ADDITIONAL NOTE TO CHAPTER XII

THE MARATHON MOON

It has not always been noticed how consistent are the notes of time in Herodotos' Marathon story, for the movements and waits of all the three main participating parties. It *has* often been remarked that the details of his stories are much more convincing than his formal chronology, when he gives it. In this case, he does not seem to have troubled much about synchronisms, but simply let the story tell itself.

Philippides reached Sparta on the 9th of the lunar month. He had left Athens on the 8th; so Eretria had fallen on the 7th, or at earliest on the 6th. The Spartans marched with all speed after the full moon; if they marched on the 16th morning, they reached Athens on the 18th evening, just missing the battle, which probably took place, therefore, on the 16th (or, possibly, 17th).

We thus get the following calendar (assuming the night of the full moon to be that of August 11th–12th, 490 B.C.):

Days of lunar month:	Persians	Athenians	Spartans	Aug.
6 or 7	Fall of Eretria			2
7	Fall of Eretria known at Athens			3
8 }	'A few days' wait' (8th to 10th)	Philippides starts (morning)		4
9 }		Philippides reaches Sparta (evening)		5
10 }			Second week of Karneia (9th to 15th)	6
11	P. disembarkation starts, morning	Ath. army reaches Marathon, evening		7
12 }		No engagement for four days (12th to 15th)		8
13 }				9
14 }				10
15 }				11
Night of 15	P. embark some troops?		KARNEIAN FULL MOON	11
16		BATTLE OF MARATHON	Spartans march out	12
17	Persians off Phaleron; Ath. already there		,, *en route*	13
18	,, sailing east		,, reach Ath.	14
19	Datis at Mykonos		,, visit Marathon	15

Chapter XIII

The Captains and the Kings Depart: 489–6

Miltiades, the architect of victory, was raised by his triumph to a pinnacle of power and glory. Aristocrat as he was, he is sometimes said to have opposed the development of Athenian sea-power as favouring democracy; but this is probably a fable, based on the experience of later Athenian conservatives and on the 'literary' view, standard among later Greeks and Romans, that this was how a gentleman in politics ought to behave.[1] He had fought on land in 490 because Athens was far too weak to fight at sea; but his view of what ought to be done after the retirement of the Persians was exactly the view of Themistokles after Salamis (p. 382): that the Athenian *fleet* should take the offensive and recover as many as possible of the islands which had surrendered to the enemy. Owing to the short range of ancient warships, which, like the fighter aircraft of 1940, were built for speed and not for long endurance without 'refuelling' (filling up, especially with drinking water for a large crew of thirsty rowers[2]), the possession of islands had some of the same significance for galleys in the Aegean as for the forces of World War II in the vast Pacific.

To this end, Miltiades proposed an expedition with the whole fleet of Athens, perhaps brought up from its old establishment of fifty to seventy ships on account of the war with Aigina (p. 275n). If he were given command of the fleet, he said, he did not wish to say where he would lead it; but he would guarantee that it would cost the city nothing; on the contrary, he would show a profit! The Assembly, one imagines, laughed. If the insecurity of the times was to provide an excuse for profitable corsair activities, Miltiades was the man to lead

[1] Stēsimbrotos of Thasos (in Plut. *Them.* 4) said that Themistokles carried his navy bill (pp. 291ff) against M.'s opposition; but it was not carried until years after M. was dead. Plut. himself has drawn attention to S.'s recklessness about dates a page or two earlier (*ib.* 2): S. said Them. was a disciple of Anaxagoras and Melissos!

[2] Cf. A. W. Gomme, *A Forgotten Factor of Greek Naval Strategy*, in *JHS* LIII, and in *Essays in Greek History and Literature*, pp. 190ff.

them. It was common sense not to warn the islanders of one's intentions in detail; but it was contrary to Greek republican principles to give the executive *carte blanche* like this.[3] Politicians who had lived for seventeen years under the constitution of Kleisthenes were alarmed; but they were brushed aside. Miltiades sailed, and did induce a number of islands to return, as Nepos says, 'to their duty', using force where necessary and imposing fines for submission to Persia. Even from Herodotos, who gives only an incomplete and hostile account of this expedition, it appears that, whereas 'all' the islands had submitted in 491 and 490, the western chain, Keos, Kythnos, Seriphos, Siphnos and Melos, with Chalkis and Styra in Euboia, were on the nationalist side in 480.[4]

Having done this (summer, 489?), Miltiades sailed against Paros, which had indeed sent a trireme to join Datis' armament; perforce, but perhaps less unwillingly than some, out of long-standing neighbourly enmity to Naxos. (Paros was forced to pay an indemnity by Themistokles in 480, whereas the Naxian ships then levied by Persia deserted to the Greeks, pp. 468; 440.) But at Paros there was no surprise. The Parians must have been sure from the first that Miltiades would not omit them from his agenda, especially since Lysagoras, a Parian, presumably important, was his personal enemy, 'having reported ill of him to Hydarnes the Persian'. (Which Hydarnes? – if this is the elder one, the friend of Darius, the 'bad report' may have been connected with the Scythian expedition.) Faced with a demand for 100 talents, which at this time would probably have paid seventy ships' crews for half the summer, the men of Paros closed their gates and strengthened their fortifications. 'Where the wall was most assailable, they doubled its height in one night.' Miltiades opened siege operations; but his citizen soldiers were not 'expendable' like the subjects of the Persian king; and for week after week the blockade continued.[5]

This was a serious matter for Miltiades, in view of his unpopularity with the politicians at home. If the Assembly would entrust him with the whole fleet to employ at his discretion, how much longer, they

[3] The usual Greek error was quite the other way; cf., e.g., the assembly's directive (a very bad one!) to a squadron in 429 to reinforce Naupaktos after carrying out another mission *on the way*: Thk. ii, 85, 5.

[4] Eph. fr. 107M; *FGH* 70 F 63, from S.B. on Paros; Nep. *Milt.* 7; H. vi, 132ff; cf. viii, 1, 46, 48.

[5] H. vi, 133.

wondered, would it be before he was above the laws? Themistokles himself is credited with saying at this time that Miltiades' trophies kept him awake at night; the Alkmeonid faction, whom Miltiades' friends accused (clearly with no real evidence) of treachery at the time of Marathon, were only waiting their opportunity; and the new archon, Aristeides, an old partisan of Kleisthenes, was a stern republican.[6]

What happened to Miltiades is commonly quoted as an example of Athenian ingratitude; but it is necessary to remember the nature of Athenian politics in his time.

Political events in early fifth-century Athens were chiefly the expression of the rivalries of prominent men and families. Ambition, in men born to greatness, was a proper feeling: 'Ever to be the noblest *and superior to others*' was a Homeric ideal.[7] It is only after centuries of Christianity, or at least lip-service to Christianity, that this lust after the power and the glory has to be veiled, at least from the public eye, behind a programme of service; even at its most naked, expressed in such a saying as 'I believe that I can save this nation and that no one else can'. To a pagan Greek or Roman, the desire to be the best or noblest (*aristeuein*, a word devoid of moral connotation) was well expressed in the desire to shine in athletics, 'for', to cite Homer again, 'a man has no truer glory than that which he wins with his own feet and hands';[8] and even in Greek feeling about athletics in this age, there is a sense of triumph *over* the defeated rival which is to us repulsive. Pindar twice reminds us of the shame of defeated wrestlers, slinking home, 'avoiding their enemies', as an ingredient in the joy of the victor.[9] Sportsmanship, like humility, is a Christian virtue.

A result of this unblushing ambition and of the hardness of Greek rivalry was that emulation easily became enmity. Greek aristocracies were often deeply divided, and in face of political demands from other classes failed to show a united front.[10] Someone, disgruntled, would 'play the demagogue', as Peisistratos and Kleisthenes in their different ways had done at Athens.

There was a perfectly clear distinction between a tyrant, however popular, and a republican leader, however influential; namely that the

[6] Val. Max. viii, 14, ext. 1; Plut. *Them.* 1 (not with my explanation); Plut. *Ar.* 2; 5.
[7] *Il.* vi, 208; xi, 784; etc.
[8] *Od.* viii, 147f.
[9] *Ol.* viii, 67/89ff, *Pyth.* viii, 81/116ff.
[10] Ar. *Politics*, v, 1305f, *passim.*

former was in a position where, even if he lost his popularity, he could not be unseated unless by force; the tokens of this position were a bodyguard and control of the Citadel. Peisistratos had been a tyrant, Kleisthenes had not; he was probably wise enough not to desire to be. But even his great-nephew Perikles, who could have been voted out of office any year, was compared to a tyrant by unfriendly propaganda, and his partisans called 'the new Peisistratids';[11] and both the tyrant and the powerful republican leader were the object of envy. Even a tyrant might partially placate this envy by dynastic marriages or by promoting members of rival families to positions of honour in the state, as the Peisistratidai had done; and Athenian noblemen had shown themselves delighted to enhance their glory by marrying the daughter of a tyrant of Corinth or Megara or Sikyon.[12] They show not the slightest trace of conscientious objections to despotic rule as a system; what they resented, whether bitterly or mildly, was *being* ruled. They also objected to democracy, as placing their social and cultural inferiors on a level with them; but in fifth-century Athens they became more or less reconciled to it, so long as they could satisfy their sense of dignity by leading the people. Meanwhile, lesser men, who could not aspire to the heights of power, could satisfy their more modest ambitions by supporting a successful leader; if their support was particularly useful, he might reward them, as a leader since Homer's time had been expected to reward his *hetairoi*. It is among these less resplendent people that the word justice (*dikaiosüne*, just-ness) makes its appearance; in extant literature, first in a line of Phokylides of Miletos, a middle-class, 'middle way', moderate man in a city torn by revolution, shortly borrowed by Theognis, a tory but an unsuccessful one: the line 'In being just, all virtue is summed up', ἐν δὲ δικαιοσύνηι συλλήβδην πᾶσ' ἀρετή 'στιν.[13] That *tò kalón*, the beautiful, the honourable, the *fair* (our word has the same double meaning), is largely identical in connotation with the just might seem to later people a thought so obvious as to be hardly worth expressing; but only because men of this age, the age of the beginnings of democracy, had made the identification, making a significant development in the use of words. *Aretē*, 'virtue' in the Greek philosophers, is in the early poets not even exclusively

[11] Plut. *Per.* 16, 1; cf. 7, 1.

[12] H. vi, 128, 2, 131; Thk. i, 126, 3.

[13] Q. as a proverb by Ar. (*Eth. N.* 1129b), whose ethical thought sums up the movement that begins here; ascr. to Ph. *or* Th., schol. *ib*; Theog. 147; cf. *Lyric Age*, pp. 216f.

ethical; a horse could have *arete*; and when it was ethical, it meant excellence, distinction; its root *ar-* appears in *aristos, aristeuein*, aristocratic words by definition. It was the ordinary citizens of democracies who achieved the change.[14] For them, the *best* leader, still a *distinguished* man, was the just man, the reliable man, the man who, having got elected or swayed the Assembly, did not let his supporters down. The difference between seeming *aristos* and really being so, a difference which would scarcely have seemed real to the old aristocrats, appears in Aeschylus' *Seven against Thebes* (l. 592), used of the righteous hero Amphiaraos; and it is said that at the first performance (467, trad.) the audience with one accord turned their heads towards the veteran statesman, Aristeides the Just.[15]

It is not unreasonable to claim that, in ethics as in logic, democracy, especially Athenian democracy, was the parent of a real advance in human thought and practice. At the same time, there was plausibility in the reactionary complaint, put forward unashamedly by 'bad' speakers in Plato, the Nietzschean argument that justice sums up a slave-morality, the morality that suits the many weak, who by uniting on this, the only possible basis, are able to suppress the strong, the superior men.[16]

Now in the early fifth century all this was in its infancy, and while the plain citizens, the majority in the Assembly, philosophically inarticulate, had a conception of the common interest, identified with justice, prominent men and men of the great families were still aspiring to be 'best', *aristoi*, in the old sense; to be superior, to be second to none. If one's own family could dominate the city, that was best; if they could lead it by persuading the Assembly, they would lead the democracy. If rivals gained the ascendancy, one would try to overthrow them; and if driven into exile, one would side even with Persia to obtain one's restoration. The idea that to side with foreigners against one's own city's government was the depth of human villainy was not yet in existence. *Prodotai*, which we translate 'traitors', who conspired to open the gates to foreign invaders, did not think of themselves as

[14] The point has been made that Greek freedom was also the mother of Logic, the set of rules for *proving* one's point, in a society in which no one has power to see that 'What I say, goes' by force (C. F. von Weizsäcker, *The Relevance of Science*, Gifford Lectures, Glasgow, 1960, II, v; publication forthcoming).

[15] Plut. *Arist.* 3. But the man named Dikaios (p. 448) is no democrat!

[16] Kallikles in Plato, *Gorgias*, 482ff; Thrasymachos in *Rep.* i, 338ff.

acting against their own folk; 'one's own' were one's own kindred or friends, *hetairoi*; not, in that ultimately self-destructive aristocratic code, the people, the *demos*, whom even through classical times many aristocrats continued actively to despise and hate. Hatred of the traitor as such, with glorification of the City as such, 'which alone preserves us all', appears in Sophocles, the poet-laureate of classical Athens, who, like his friend the aristocrat Perikles, had drunk in the ideas of democracy. Polyneikes, who has fallen fighting against his city, is to be denied burial; and even here this step, and the arguments with which it is supported, are the acts and arguments of the tyrannical Kreon![17]

In Athens, then, most of the leading factions which competed to sway the Assembly were family factions; factions, united by personal loyalties, *not* political parties united by a programme. The exceptional leader was Themistokles, who, going further than Kleisthenes, might have claimed that the people *were* his faction. With his Lykomid father and his Thracian or Karian or (perhaps more probably) Akarnanian, west Greek, mother, he is said, a tradition reported by late writers, to have been a difficult child and youth;[18] this may be mere guesswork, but it could well be true, and fits in with his radicalism. Leaders of the family factions, of which the most important were the Alkmeonid, Peisistratid (still led by Hipparchos the son of Charmos, archon 496) and Philaïd, the kindred of Miltiades, knew perfectly well that they must persuade the people that what they proposed was best for the people, and that in their own interests they must carry out their promises, or make a convincing show of trying to; but personal and family interests were, I believe, avowedly paramount in their minds; avowedly, that is, among themselves and in their private thoughts; it was naturally not the sort of thing one would emphasise in a public speech. But at least there was no hypocritical self-deception. Mediaeval grandees behaved in the same way; the relations of the houses of Bruce and Balliol with the king of England, when the throne of Scotland was either vacant or occupied by their rivals, form an instructive parallel to those of Athenian aristocrats with Persia.

Family factions, not political parties: the difference is that, while for a 'good party man' the essential thing is that the party's policy should

[17] *Antigone*, 175–210.

[18] Plut. *Them.* 1, 2; Val. Max. vi, 9, ext. 2; Nepos *Them.* 1 (who makes his mother Akarnanian).

be carried out, and by whom is secondary – so that if disappointed of the party leadership he is expected at least to look happy – for the old-time nobleman it was the personal power and glory that was itself the prize, *avowedly*. Best of all, to lead one's city in independence; second best, to rule it under an overlord; third, to be near the throne and intermarry with the ruling house. No Athenian would have called his own attitude 'pro-tyrant'; for a tyrant, by the early fifth century, was by definition a Bad Thing, and the term was therefore one which one would only use of one's enemies. Some, however, were pro-Peisistratid; especially, perhaps, men of moderately prominent families, who might hope for favours in return for service, or at least for protection against the wrath of the Persians if they should come. Likewise, no one was pro-Persian; but there were some, especially among those too prominent to be lost in the crowd, who might think it prudent to agree with so mighty an adversary quickly; and this could best be done through the Peisistratid exiles. No one wanted death, ruin and destruction. But it was not unfair for others to call this attitude pro-tyrannical; for whatever the loyal Hipparchos might say (and what *did* he say? Was it that if the leading Peisistratids were allowed home, they would only want their estates and 'their proper position'?) – it is clear that, if they had been restored as Persia's vassals, tyrants they would have been; for the government of the friends of Persia, under Persia, was certainly a government that could not be unseated without shedding of blood.

Firmest in their resistance to the whole idea of submission to Persia seem to have been some plain, middle-class men of Athens. *They* would not be conspicuous for good or ill; but, apart from a deep-rooted prejudice against barbarians, especially barbarians as masters, they had a pretty clear idea of what Persian rule would mean to them. It would mean tribute, year by year, carried off to Sousa; and it would mean that local government, with Persia behind it, would become arbitrary, even if, as under Mardonios' settlement in Ionia, it used the forms of democracy. It was people like the intelligent and prominent Alkmeonidai, people who might hope to gain a privileged position even under Persia, and might fear that they would be marked for destruction if they led an unsuccessful resistance, who were under the greatest temptation to submit; and it seems that, for a time, they succumbed to it. The clever men were wrong, the plain men were right. What is most to the credit of the Alkmeonidai is that, in the course of the next few years, finding that the people insisted on a resistance policy from its leaders, they not only adopted such a policy but actually became, as it were, convinced whig leaders of the people. In the next generation they produced, in Perikles, the son of a niece of Kleisthenes, the greatest democrat of all.

Thus it was no recommendation of Miltiades, in the eyes of his rivals, that he had done good service at Marathon, if he was going to become so powerful at Athens as to overshadow all others. At the height of his power, his position was like that of Alkibiades in 408, splendid but precarious. His absence through the summer of 489 was dangerous to him as a politician. He had done brilliant service, but he had also aroused great expectations; and the promises by which he had obtained his supreme command could only be redeemed by success. He made great efforts to capture Paros, finally entering into some secret negotiations, as it seems, through a priestess of Demeter and Persephone who had been captured outside the town. These involved a visit, probably by night, to the sanctuary of Demeter Thesmophoros, near the walls, which he entered, 'jumping the wall, as he was unable to get the doors open. He then went towards the temple' – but just for what purpose, Herodotos was unable to find out; he is here citing a Parian story, which was concerned with how Timo was acquitted when brought to trial for abetting a sacrilegious entry, and not primarily with Miltiades. 'But just as he was at the doors a sudden panic came upon him, and he went back the same way, and in jumping the wall,' – fell and suffered a severe injury to his knee or thigh. Ephoros recounted that his negotiations were almost successful (he badly needed that indemnity); but at the last moment they were suspended through a piece of bad luck. A forest caught fire on Mykonos, away to the north, beyond Delos (this is part of the evidence for forests in places where there are none now); and the Parians, seeing the glow in the sky, jumped to the conclusion that it was a signal; the Persians (Ephoros says 'Datis'), to whom they had almost certainly sent an appeal for aid, were coming to relieve them. They called off the negotiations at the last moment (to do this, after 'leading somebody on', was subsequently called by some comedian 'doing a back-paros', *anapariazein*) and Miltiades, with his troops hungry and mutinous, and himself incapacitated by his injury, was unable to hold on even long enough for reconnaissance to expose the false alarm. He returned home, having signally failed to carry out his promise that the expedition would show a profit.[19]

So Miltiades' enemies had their opportunity given to them. Members of the Alkmeonid family did not themselves take the lead; perhaps that would have been invidious; but Xanthippos the son of Ariphon, an aristocrat[20] who had married a niece of Kleisthenes, impeached Miltiades on a charge of 'deceiving the people', probably by the procedure known as *eisangelia,* before the Assembly. All the old charges were no doubt raked up, back to his tyranny in the Chersonese; but on the main count there was no doubt about the fact: Miltiades had promised to enrich the people; he had refused to take them into his confidence (what sort of conduct was this, for a citizen of the republic?) and, so far from carrying out his promise, he had involved the city in grievous expense. Even his choice of Paros to attack was attributed to his long-standing desire to get even with Lysagoras.

If many of his citizen soldiers and oarsmen, after a promise of easy money, were in arrears with their pay it would help to account for the fact that there was a majority against him. Clever men have seldom had much difficulty in turning feeling against the hero of an hour, especially when there has been something feverish about the earlier adulation; and there was no lack of brains on Xanthippos' side. Passionate feeling was aroused, and the death-penalty, demanded by the prosecution, was nearly carried out, it is said, illegally; but the chairman of the day had the courage to stop this[21] (presumably by his power to refuse to 'put the question' if technically illegal or out of order). So the trial was legally concluded, and the death-sentence was rejected, after Miltiades' friends had pleaded the memory of his great services, not least his capture of Lemnos and cession of it to Athens. Instead, a crushing fine of fifty talents was imposed (was it the amount by which the treasury, despite indemnities from the smaller islands, was out of pocket?). But it made little difference to the fallen hero. He was a dying man; for his wound had gangrened, and while his friends

[19] H. vi, 134f; Eph. *ap.* Steph. Byz., *s.v.* Paros (as n. 4 above); Nep. *Mi t.* 7, 2ff, resembling Eph. closely enough to support the view that N. used him.

[20] The name Ariphron (a rare one) figures in the Chronographers' list of archons for life; see Clinton, *FH,* index.

[21] Plato, *Gorgias,* 516E (but Plato is not a good authority on earlier history).

pleaded for him he lay helpless on a stretcher. He died soon after, leaving his young son Kimon financially crippled; the family was not a force in politics again for many years.[22]

Probably almost at the same time as the victor of Marathon, and even more miserably, perished the man who had made the campaign possible, by the coercion of Aigina: Kleomenes of Sparta, rejected by his people, like Miltiades, and essentially for the same reason. He was a leader so formidable as to be felt by other leading men of his city to be a menace to their position. Herodotos puts his death *and its sequel*, a renewal of war between Aigina and Athens, explicitly before Marathon;[23] but this is surely impossible. Even if Aigina had kept quiet during the Marathon campaign through pan-Hellenic patriotism and moral suasion from Sparta (which Herodotos does not mention), it is inconceivable that she would have remained so while Athens extended her influence by a campaign which took her entire fleet half-way across the Aegean. And the events at Sparta, leading from the deposition of Damaratos in 491, after Kleomenes' first, unsuccessful attempt to coerce Aigina, after Aigina's act of submission to Persia, to the death of Kleomenes, though they *can* all be imagined as taking place within twelve months, can only be so compressed with great difficulty.[24]

There is first the flight of Damaratos, on which Herodotos introduces his narrative (vi, 67ff) as follows:

> The above, then, is the story of the deposition of Damaratos; but his flight from Sparta to the Persians was the result of a humiliation, as follows: after his deposition, Damaratos held a magistracy, to which he was elected. The Gymnopaidiai came round, and as Damaratos was watching the festival Latychidas, now king in his stead, sent his servant to ask him in mockery how he liked being an official, after being King?

Damaratos is said to have replied in effect that Latychidas had better wait till *he* had tried both. (Had Latychidas, when *privatus*, not been popular enough to achieve Damaratos' present honour?) Then, feeling that, if he was not to be allowed even to enjoy in peace the position

[22] H. vi, 136; Plut. *Kim.* 4.

[23] H. vi, 94, 1; cf. p. 275, n. 43.

[24] The feat is performed by Hammond, in *Historia*, IV (1955), pp. 406ff, and the resulting very precise dates reproduced in his *History of Greece*, pp. 211f. I agree with Andrewes (*BSA* XXXVII (1937), p. 4) that this involves 'intolerable compression'. This has been the view of most scholars, back at least to Grote (IV (1847), pp. 437–41; V (1849), p. 62), who assumes that the ensuing war began *c.* 488, without even discussing H.'s date.

still open to him, his situation was intolerable, he went to ask his mother, 'on oath, before a burning sacrifice', the truth about his paternity. Herodotos gives, characteristically, as history, a detailed and very touching account of their private interview, in which his mother tells a tale of a mysterious visitor to her bed, and suggests that his father, if not King Ariston himself, was a demigod. Damaratos then left Sparta, giving out that he was going to consult Delphi for himself. He was pursued, on suspicion that he intended to desert, but escaped and reached Asia (cf. p. 277).

Now the Gymnopaidiai took place soon after midsummer, in the Month of the Hekatombs, the great state sacrifices (both at Athens and Sparta) in the first month of the New Year.[25] Much had already happened in the spring of 491, from the arrival of the Persian heralds at Aigina to the deposition. There seems hardly time for Damaratos to be elected to a magistracy for the New Year beginning that same midsummer, unless (as is possible) he was deliberately elected at once as a 'consolation prize', through the influence of his sympathisers. This may even be Herodotos' view, expressed in the words 'who had now become king in his stead' – *if* Herodotos troubled about the chronology at all. It seems more likely that the incident which broke Damaratos' willingness to stay in Sparta took place at the Gymnopaidiai of 490.[26] But surely he would not have fled if the story that Kleomenes had tampered with the Delphic authorities to secure his deposition had already been current.

'But after this', continues Herodotos (vi, 74f), after digressing to deal with the later fortunes of Latychidas, and returning to describe the taking of hostages from Aigina, 'Kleomenes' evil machinations against Damaratos were brought to light; and in fear of the Spartans he slipped away and went to Thessaly.' This account of his motive for going there, retailed by later Spartans to the historian, is no doubt at least incomplete.[27] Mardonios had reasserted Persia's overlordship over Macedonia, and if the Greek peninsula were to be defended, there was reason enough for a king of Sparta to visit what might soon be the northern front.

[25] Xen. *Hell.* vi, 4, 16 (the news of Leuktra arrived then); the battle was fought on the 5th Hekatombaiōn, Plut. *Agesilaos* 28.

[26] As Hammond has it (*HG*, *loc. cit.*), but at the cost of making Damaratos flee after Kleomenes was, on his view, dead and discredited. Grote does have it at the festival of 491 (IV, p. 39).

[27] 'mindestens einseitig', Meyer, *GdA*[3] IV, i, p. 329n.

Thessaly, indeed, was as little solid in face of the prospective invasion as any Greek land. The Aleuadai, supreme at this time among the great families, finding their position shaken by opposition, were prepared to do a deal with Persia in order to hold it. Their emissaries were at the Persian court for the purpose by 486.[28] Later writers also had a tradition, apparently from fifth-century sources, about a colourful character, Persia's Beautiful Woman Agent: Thargēlia the Milesian, consort of the Aleuad 'king' Antiochos, son of Echekratidas, and subsequently, it is alleged, of thirteen other noblemen, all of whom she 'won over to the side of the Persian king'. She is said to have 'reigned' in Thessaly for thirty years, evidently dominating the Aleuad circle by beauty and character.[29] Like her lovers, Thargelia, with the fate of her native city before her eyes, was presumably following a policy of self-preservation.

What Kleomenes tried to effect in Thessaly the hostile tradition does not say, only suggesting that he was in disgrace at Sparta for tampering with the Oracle. Soon, however, he came south again, to Arcadia, where 'he engaged in revolutionary proceedings, working to unite the Arcadians against Sparta and administering oaths to them to follow him wherever he led. He was particularly anxious to assemble the chief men of Arcadia at the city of Nōnakris, to administer an oath to them by the Water of Styx', which there, as Herodotos says, emerges from a precipice, to fall into a chasm in the limestone: the terrible oath by which, Homer said, the very gods were bound.[30] He was clearly aiming at a personal monarchy, and one not confined to

[28] H. vii, 6; called 'Kings of Thessaly', *ib.*; i.e. they had got the position of Tāgos, elective head of state and war-chief of the Thessalian League, 'in the family'. Cf. Pindar, *Pyth.* x, 1ff, where, incidentally, *Sparta* is prominently congratulated on being, like Thessaly under the Sons of Aleuas, ruled by a Herakleid house. Thorax the Aleuad (who was with Mardonios in 479) paid for the Ode (see l. 64), which is dated by the *scholia* to Pythiad 22, = 498. I do not know how secure this date is.

[29] Plut. *Per.* 24 (from Aischines the Socratic, mentioned thereinafter?); Aisch. is named as source for the mention of her by Philostratos, Letter 73 (to Julia Domna), vol. II, p. 364 Kayser (= A., fr. 10); perhaps also source for her '30 years' reign' (anon. *Essay on Famous Women*, in *Parodoxographi Graeci*, ed. Westermann, p. 217; *Suda*, *s.v.* Thargelia). Her 14 marriages, Ath. xiii, 608–9, from Hippias of Elis (= Hip. fr. 3 Jac.). Meyer, *GdA*^{3} IV, i, 344n; Westlake in *JHS* LVI, 15f. Echekratidas, an Aleuad name, not that of a rival family, see Morrison in *CQ*, 1942; hence *Sanguis Aleuae* (Ovid, *Ibis*, 513) also of a Skopas, son of an Echekrateia. (But (1) Roman writers on Greek genealogies are often careless; (2) the *sanguis Aleuae* must have been so widely spread after several generations that different 'septs' may well have appeared.)

[30] H. vi, 74. The oath by Styx, *Il.* xv, 37f; Hes. *Theog.* 395ff, etc.; cf. Paus. viii, 17–18, and Frazer *ad loc.*

the Vale of Lakedaimon. He could offer the Arcadians a position as his personal *hetairoi*, bound by great oaths to follow him, the heir of Achaian Herakles, more attractive to these highland chiefs, who claimed to have held their glens as long as the moon endured, than that of second-class allies to Dorian lowlanders and in-comers, which was theirs under their treaties with Sparta; and if he won the Arcadians, than whom there were potentially no better fighting men in Greece (the bulk of Leonidas' Peloponnesian force at Thermopylai was Arcadian), he might hope to break the exclusiveness of the Spartiate oligarchy and emerge as leader of a united force that could hold any Persian invader at bay for ever. If he had succeeded, his name would have been known to 'every schoolboy' ever since as the saviour of Greece. But to the Spartiates this was revolution, to be averted at all costs. They sent envoys to him, offering immediate concessions. Let him return, to enjoy his full, royal status. To Kleomenes it seemed satisfactory. He returned; and his project of a gathering of Arcadian leaders at the Styx seems to have remained unfulfilled.

'But when he returned', says Herodotos, 'forthwith he went mad; he had been somewhat unstable even before. When he met any Spartiate, he would strike him in the face with his sceptre; and for this behaviour his relatives arrested him and made him fast in stocks as insane.' The leading part in this step must have been taken by his half-brothers. But why, we must ask, if the story of his public behaviour is true, did he become thus unbalanced? Did he suffer from the delusion that his revolution was as good as accomplished, that he was a despot? Or was he driven frantic by finding himself totally isolated, encountering everywhere silent non-coöperation, in effect powerless? There was a story also that he drank heavily of wine undiluted, an un-Greek habit which men said he had learned long since from Scythian ambassadors; it could be true. In any case, his end was near. His body was found in his prison, frightfully mangled with a knife. The official story, transmitted to Herodotos, was that he had intimidated his Helot jailer into giving it to him, and had thereupon proceeded to carve up his own flesh, beginning from his feet, till he reached his stomach, and died. The possibility that he was really murdered is too obvious to need comment.[31]

[31] Madness and suicide, H. vi, 75; drink (the Spartan diagnosis), *ib.* 84. Meyer, *GdA*[3] IV, i, 329, repeats the story with a 'wie man erzählte'; Bury, *HG* p. 259, Hammond,

Kleomenes when in Arcadia had not been working wholly in isolation. There was a spontaneous centralising movement there at the time, of which the concrete evidence is the country's earliest common coinage, with the legend ARKADIKŌN or, abbreviated on small denominations, ARK. They have often been discussed,[32] without final agreement as to their political significance, which is, perhaps, capable of exaggeration. Coinage was spreading through the Greek world, and the earliest issues in Thessaly (from Aleuad Larisa, and, perhaps significantly, on a Persian standard) also date from this generation.[33] To issue coins was a token of modernity in a state, and perhaps, especially in inland or backward states, something of a 'status symbol'. Societies which their members, or some of their members, are trying to modernise are necessarily to some extent in a state of tension, between old and new. It is of interest that the two regions which Kleomenes is recorded to have visited in his last, revolutionary period are both of them attested by their coins to have been in such a state of transition, between archaic and classical Greek ways; but indeed the whole Greek world was in a state of transition. It would be idle to suggest that Kleomenes' visits did more than perhaps to accelerate the process a little in Arcadia; and more probably he really only tried to use for his own ends a process which was already going on. Sparta alone successfully resisted modernisation in the late archaic period, and imposed some delay upon that of the rest of the Peloponnese; thus securing temporary success and the admiration of conservative philosophers, but contributing to the ultimate failure of the world of the Greek cities. Arcadia continued to struggle for independence, or at least a position in which Sparta must treat her with respect; but Sparta, exploiting internal rivalries in Arcadia, especially that between Tegea and Mantineia, succeeded in maintaining her hegemony until the fourth century.[34]

More venturesome is the theory, unsupported by direct literary evidence, that Kleomenes had raised hopes among Sparta's helots of

---

p. 211, without indications of suspicion. Munro, *CAH* IV, p. 261f, Beloch, *GG*² II, i, p. 36, suspect murder.

[32] e.g. R. Weil in *Zeitschr. für Numismatik* IX and XXIX; Hill, *Gk. and Roman Coins*, p. 107; Seltman, *Gk. Coins*, p. 97; W. P. Wallace, 'Kleomenes, Marathon, the Helots and Arkadia', in *JHS* LXXIV.

[33] F. Herrmann in *ZfN* XXXIII (1922); Seltman, *Gk. Coins*, p. 89.

[34] See A. Andrewes, *Sparta and Arkadia in the Early Fifth Century*, in *The Phoenix* VI (1952).

an improvement in their position, and that this was the source of a brief Messenian revolt about the time of Marathon. That there was such trouble, and that it accounted for the smallness and lateness of the force sent to help Athens, is alleged by Plato, whose history is unreliable (p. 253, n. 41) and supported by the statement of Pausanias, whose sources, as he knew, were of the weakest, that refugees from a Messenian revolt were harboured by Anaxilāos, tyrant of Rhēgion about 494–77 and himself of old Messenian descent (pp. 298ff).[35] The silence of Herodotos (and of Diodoros and Justin, so probably of Ephoros) remains a difficulty; yet there is a possible hint of these troubles in Herodotos himself (ix, 37), in the story of Hēgēsistratos the seer, a Telliad of Elis, who had done 'much mischief' to the Spartans before 479, had been captured and condemned to death, escaped from fetters by cutting off part of his own foot, and made his way to Tegea, travelling by night and hiding up in the scrub by day; for 'Tegea was then hostile to Sparta'. Some support is given to the story of a Messenian rebellion at this time by the inscription at Olympia, from the base of a statue of Zeus, certainly that which Pausanias says was the thankoffering of the Spartans for the suppression of 'the second Messenian revolt'; for its lettering is said to be too archaic for the time of the well-known rebellion at the time of the earthquake of 464.[36]

Kleomenes was dead probably by the end of 489,[37] and the rebellion crushed; by 488 the fugitives may have been taking part in Anaxilaos' re-settlement of Zankle, now re-named Messene (p. 301 below). Spartans breathed more freely at being rid of him, no less than the Athenian republicans at being rid of Miltiades. The Persian menace seemed to have receded; if it should come again, Kleomenes' responsibility for leading the defence against it would fall upon his successor,

[35] Paus. iv, 23 – at the cost of dating Anaxilaos *c.* Ol. 29 (664!). Strabo also (barely) mentions *four* wars, viii, 362 (the fourth, *c.* 464?). Kleomenes and the Helots, cf. the brilliant but adventurous article by Guy Dickins in *JHS* XXXII (1912), pp. 31f; Meyer, *GdA*³ IV, i, p. 328ff, and (on Messenians in the west) III, p. 765; cf. p. 500, n. 1; the story rejected, Beloch, *GG*² I, ii, § 103; Jacoby, *FGH* IIIa, pp. 109–81 (on Rhianos and Paus. other sources).

[36] *IG* V, i, 1562, = *Olympia* V, 252; re-studied by L. H. Jeffery, *JHS* LXIX, pp. 26–30, figs. 4, 6. 'The dating of archaic Laconian inscriptions', as she says (p. 28), 'is far from certain; but a lower limit can be set . . .' (before *c.* 475). For the monument, see Paus. v, 24, 3. Implications, W. P. Wallace, *op. cit.* (n. 32); *GHI* (1969), 22.

[37] So, e.g., Meiggs in Bury, *HG*³ (1951), p. 259 margin; 'almost certainly after 490', Andrewes in *BSA* XXXVII, p. 4.

the elder of the half-brothers who were probably privy to his death; the brother's name was Leonidas.

Others too breathed more freely; and none more so than the men of Aigina, still chafing under their impotence while Athens held their chief men as hostages. 'When the Aiginetans heard of the death of Kleomenes, they sent envoys to Sparta to complain of Leutychides [Latychidas] about the hostages held at Athens; and the Spartans convened a court, which found that Aigina had been shamefully treated by Latychidas, and condemned him to extradition to the Aiginetans in return for the men held at Athens.' [38] Sparta returns, it appears, to her attitude of hostility to the recalcitrant democracy, which Kleomenes had suspended in face of the Persian threat. Leonidas certainly would have had no objection to the temporary elimination and humiliation of the rival king; ill-feeling between the two royal houses was normal,[39] and the fact that Latychidas was a creature of Kleomenes and had served his ends was no recommendation. The Aiginetans were deterred from actually carrying off the Spartan king as their hostage by a Spartan, who pointed out to them that Spartan policy would change again, and the insult be resented; but they agreed with Latychidas that he should come with them to Athens and request the return of their leaders. Latychidas made the request, representing the hostages as a deposit made by him, which should be returned at his request after the death of the other depositor. But the Athenians remained obdurate. The Aiginetans now took matters into their own hands, and 'when the Athenians were holding a four-yearly festival at Sounion, they laid wait for the sacred galley and captured it, full of men of the first families of Athens'.[40] Now they had hostages for hostages; but the Athenians were infuriated by this piece of impiety, and forthwith the war was on.

The Athenians now, says Herodotos (vi, 88), found an ally in an Aiginetan democratic leader named Nikodromos, who had returned to the island after a period of exile. They concerted a plan with him that he should raise a rebellion and seize the 'Old Town' on an appointed day, while the Athenians should attack from the sea. But the Athenians, whose fleet was still outnumbered by that of Aigina, determined, as a further surprise move, to increase it, and applied to

[38] H. vi, 85. [39] *ib.* 52, end. [40] *ib.* 86f.

Corinth, 'a close friend of Athens at this time', as she had also shown in 507 and after, and a trade-rival of Aigina, to make twenty ships available. The Corinthians did so, overcoming an objection that it was illegal to deliver warships to a foreign power by 'selling' them at a nominal price of five drachmas apiece. But all this took time, and when the democrats rose in Aigina the Athenians were not ready. The Aiginetan government party attacked Nikodromos and his partisans, and defeated them. Nikodromos and others escaped by sea; but the rest were forced to surrender, to the number of seven hundred, and led out to execution. 'And in this a curse was brought upon Aigina, which they were never able to expiate by any manner of sacrifices. . . . One of the prisoners broke away and fled to the temple portico of Demeter Thesmophoros, and seized the handles of the doors and clung to them. Men tried to drag him away, but could not; and so they cut off his hands, and led him away like that; and those hands were left, clinging fast to the handles of the temple doors.' [41]

Too late, the Athenians arrived with their reinforced navy. They won a victory at sea and effected a landing. Aigina, whose manpower was far less than that of Athens, had probably already appealed for help to her old friend and sometime suzerain, Argos. Herodotos puts the appeal after the defeat at sea, when it would surely have been too late. The Argive government, the government of the 'slaves' or rather the peasant *perioikoi*, which had resulted from the revolution after the disaster of Sepeia, p. 231, refused help; its sympathies would naturally be rather with other democracies; 'but volunteers to the number of a thousand' (the number may well have been exaggerated by the Athenians) came, 'led by one Eurybates, an athlete trained in the *pentathlon*'. Athletes in the age of Pindar were generally aristocratic, and it may well be that his volunteers represented survivors of the old Argive governing class,[42] disgruntled under the democracy and willing to earn a living while striking a blow for class interests abroad. 'Most of these men never returned home, but were killed by the Athenians in Aigina; and their leader Eurybates, who was skilled in single combat, slew three men in this manner but was killed by the fourth, Sōphanes of Dekeleia', long a famous Athenian fighting man.[42a] 'But the

[41] H. vi, 88–91. For the 20 ships which 'gave Athens superiority' (epikratēsis), cf. the Corinthian speaker in Thk. i, 41.

[42] So Andrewes, *BSA* XXXVII, p. 4.

[42a] Distinguished at Plataia, 479; killed in Thrace, 465 (H. ix, 73–5).

Aiginetans attacked the Athenians by sea when in disorder, and captured four ships with all their crews.' The Athenians must have grown careless and let themselves be surprised. Many other ships must have been crippled or damaged, and with several hundred prisoners in the hands of a desperate enemy and their sea communications menaced, they withdrew from the island, probably under an armistice, to obtain the release of their men. They established Nikodromos and his comrades at Sounion, 'and from this base they conducted raids against the Aiginetans on the island'.[43]

Otherwise the war languished. The sea-power of Aigina had shown itself still formidable; the 'Thalassocracy-List' reckons it as 'ruling the waves', 490–481. A state of war still existed as late as 481, but we hear of no more operations. In the meantime the democrat Themistokles had proposed a characteristically radical solution: that Athens should apply her great economic resources to a vast building campaign, more than doubling the size of the fleet, to a strength by which Aigina would be simply overwhelmed. But it took time to 'sell' this idea to the Assembly. It would be very expensive; and while merchants and south-coast fishermen would no doubt have been glad to have an end made of raiders and privateers in the Gulf, the landed voters, from peasants to great landowners, were not deeply interested. A certain amount of raiding on the high seas was something which everyone had lived with, since the days of Odysseus. 'You are in treaty relations with

[43] H. vi, 90, 92f. – In the narrative of this war, I have followed Herodotos' circumstantial account, except that I am sure that the war arising out of Athens' non-return of the hostages must come after Marathon. It is not necessary here to examine the various other rearrangements of Herodotos' Atheno–Aiginetan wars, back to that of Wilamowitz (*Aristotel und Athen* (1893), II, pp. 280ff), who, with characteristic brilliance but somewhat wantonly, transfers the more sober details even of the 'old war' of H. v, 82ff, with its Argive support for Aigina, to the war over the hostages (accepted by Meyer, *GdA*³ IV, i, n. on pp. 331f); or that of Macan (*H. IV–VI*, II, pp. 108ff) who transfers the events assigned to 505 and after to the time of the Ionian Revolt, in an attempt to excuse Athens for failing to support that movement. These drastic reshufflings of the evidence seem insufficiently warranted. But there is a difficulty in the account here given, which must not be ignored: H. says that the Athenians were late in supporting Nikodromos because of the time taken in securing the 20 Corinthian ships. It is usually supposed that these 20, plus the 50 now provided by the Naukraries (Kleidemos, J, 323 F8), brought the Athenian fleet up to 70. But according to H.'s account of Miltiades' last campaign, Athens already had 70 ships in 489. *If* this is right, and *if*, also, the failure to support Nikodromos is rightly connected with the getting of the 20 ships, then this whole episode must be put back into the phase of the war before Marathon, that is before Kleomenes' seizure of the hostages. This may be the right arrangement. If so, we have no details about the operations of the war over the hostages; but the fact is that, however we date the details which we do have, there are long periods in the decades of war between Athens and Aigina about which we know nothing.

us,' says a Corinthian speaker at Athens long after, 'whereas with Kerkyra you have never had so much as an armistice.' [44] The implication is that, except where specific treaty relations put a stop to it, a state of war, implying piracy if nothing more serious, was the natural state of human affairs. A navy of more than 100 galleys, especially of the new and expensive three-banked triremes,[45] was something the Greek world had never yet seen; and Themistokles was talking of 100 new ships to be built in a single programme. It was in vain for some time that Themistokles insisted that the rewards would be enormous, that Athens' future lay on the sea.[46] To many he must have seemed a dreamer; and indeed he, the most practical of men, was that, though also much more. But he was not able to carry his great navy bill until after several years of a fierce and often confused political campaign, not fought on this issue only.

It might indeed have gone ill with Greece, if the Persians had been ready at this juncture to carry out Mardonios' cherished project: an invasion of the peninsula with large forces, by the land route through Macedonia. An immediate threat would no doubt have led, as before 490, to a drawing together of the resistance forces in Greece; a rapprochement between Athens and Sparta, and between the parties within the cities. But Kleomenes and Miltiades were gone, and the great Athenian fleet planned by Themistokles was not yet even voted. But the gods gave a respite. Darius was growing old, and what preoccupations he may have had in the east of his empire we do not know. Herodotos indeed says (vii, 1) that on the news of Marathon, preparations for a greater expedition were at once set on foot, and that 'for three years all Asia was in an uproar' with them. But this probably represents a 'delusion of reference' on the part of the Greeks, imagining that the Persians had no other concern than with them. And then, in

[44] Thk. i, 40, 4.

[45] On the trireme, see J. S. Morrison in *The Mariner's Mirror*, XXVII (1941); J. A. Davison and J. S. Morrison (separate articles) in *CQ* XLI (1947). Thucydides (i, 14) says that 'triremes in large numbers were' [first] 'acquired by the Sicilian tyrants and by Kerkyra, not long before the Persian wars and the death of Darius' [486]; 'these were the last significant navies to arise in Greece before Xerxes' invasion. For the fleets of Aigina and Athens and others were small in numbers, and mostly of fifty-oared galleys at that.' Exactly at what point the simple fifty-oar gave place completely to the trireme as the standard ship of the line, and whether Thucydides can here be completely trusted (he is writing to prove that his was the biggest war ever fought), is a difficult problem. If his statement is completely accurate, there must have been prodigious building activity throughout Greece and the Levant, and not only at Athens, in 490–480.

[46] Thk. i, 93, §§ 3f, 6f (in 478, but also referring back to his archonship in 493).

486, Egypt, chafing under the burden of taxes in cash and kind sent out of the country[47] (including, for instance, rare stones from Sinai for Darius' palace at Persepolis), rose in revolt. A report from an Egyptian official at Elephantine to the satrap Pherendates, dated the 5th October, asks for a guard for grain supplies in transit, in view of the increasing boldness of the rebels, who now even show themselves at mid-day.[48] It is the last dated Persian document from Egypt for some years. It shows the revolt already passing out of its guerrilla stage; and before long the Persians in Egypt were in flight.

Now it is in 'the fourth year after Marathon' (487/6), that Herodotos represents Damaratos the Spartan as having newly arrived at Sousa, to join his solicitations to those of the Peisistratid exiles with their oracle-monger Onomakritos, and the messengers from the Aleuadai of Thessaly (vii, 3 and 6); in the usual manner, he exaggerates the importance of their influence (cf. p. 313). How far his sources could go in this line is shown by the fact that 'it is reported', as he cautiously says, that Damaratos decided Darius' choice of a successor (Xerxes, the son of Cyrus' daughter, born to the purple, rather than Darius' eldest son Artobarzanes, born to an unnamed wife before he was king) by telling him that such was the custom at Sparta! It is not even true that the question of the Persian succession was rendered acute by the necessity of providing for it before Darius set out on a foreign campaign; we hear of no such thing before the invasion of Scythia; and in fact Xerxes, the eldest of at least four sons of Darius by the Queen Atossa,[49] so born probably about 518, had already been represented repeatedly in royal robes, clearly designated as crown prince, standing beside his father's throne, in the reliefs that decorated the walls of Darius' great new palace at Persepolis. In one place, 'on the jamb of the middle palace door, opposite his father's portrait', his identity is made quite clear by an inscription cut on his robe: 'Xerxes, the son of Darius the King, the Achaemenian'. It is impossible to date these monuments within a few years; but as early as 498 we have reference to the building of a palace at Babylon for 'the King's son'.[50] Tall, handsome and dignified, Xerxes appeared a sufficiently imposing occupant for the throne, to which he duly succeeded on the death of

[47] An allusion to this, D.S. i, 46, 4.
[48] Olmstead, *P.E.* pp. 227f, from Spiegelberg in *Sitzb. d. Preuss. Ak.* 1928, pp. 604ff.
[49] H. vii, 2; 64; 82; 97.
[50] Olmstead, *P.E.* pp. 215ff, 227; E. Herzfeld, *Altpers. Inschr.* no. 18.

his father in November 486. One great commendation in Persian eyes was that he was not only Darius' son, but Cyrus' grandson. Xerxes himself confesses and emphasises that he was not only born but chosen to reign; not indeed in a document for the eyes of men, but in a foundation tablet. Even as Ahura-Mazda, the Wise Lord, had chosen Darius to be king when both his father and grandfather were alive [when he was, therefore, far from being the senior male of his house], so, continues the tablet, 'Darius also had other sons, but by the will of Ahuramazda he made me the greatest after himself. When Darius my father passed away, by the will of Ahura-Mazda I became king.' [51]

[51] E. Herzfeld, *A New Inscr. of X. from Persepolis* (Chicago, 1932); *Arch. Mitt. aus Iran*, VII (1932) ['IV', in Olmstead, *P.E.* p. 214 n. 1, is a slip or misprint]; *Altpers. Inschr.* no. 15.

CHAPTER XIV

Themistokles and Athens, 488–1

It would in any case have taken more than the war with Aigina to suspend the excitements of political life in Athens; but in fact, internal conspired with external circumstances in the decade after Marathon, to render that life very lively indeed. The class interests, part complementary, part conflicting, of sections of an increasing voting public – great and small landowners and farmers, great and small traders and merchants, skippers and sailors and many self-employed craftsmen – formed the basis later for what we can recognise without difficulty as the politics of a democratic state; but Kleisthenes' new voters lacked confidence in themselves at first,[1] and indeed, even down to the time of Perikles, continued to listen mostly to aristocratic leaders, men who had learned politics from the conversation of their fathers and their fathers' friends, from boyhood onwards. At first, as we have seen, the result was that the ancient rivalry for power between members of leading families was simply transformed into a struggle to win votes in the Assembly. Gradually, in the process, the aristocratic leaders themselves came more and more to think as 'whig' parliamentarians; and at the same time new leaders appear, who, while not without influential connections (Themistokles a Lykomid, p. 225, Aristeides a cousin of the rich Kallias, hereditary Torch-Bearer of Eleusis[2]), are represented as owing their position to the confidence of the ordinary voters. These men outlive, in the political struggles, such old-style aristocratic politicians as Hipparchos the son of Peisistratos' general, or Megakles the Alkmeonid.

Themistokles, the most brilliant and original leader that Athens ever had, gets a poor 'press' from later Greek writers; even Herodotos, in speaking of him, does more than anywhere else in his work to justify

[1] Cf. the phrase 'the people gaining confidence' (after Marathon), *Ath. P.* 22, 3.
[2] Plut. *Ar.* 25.

the charge of 'malignity' levelled at him by Plutarch. Themistokles even in the midst of the war is lining his own pockets (viii, 4f; cf. 111) and currying favour with the enemy, 'establishing a credit balance with them; preparing himself a refuge in case he should get into trouble at Athens, as did afterwards happen' (*ib.* 109). Even his credit for the victory of Salamis is assigned largely to his *éminence grise*, Mnēsiphilos (viii, 57, rightly censured by Plutarch, *MH* 37; on Mnesiphilos, cf. *Them.* 2). But the 'malice' is not that of the Father of History himself, but rather, as in most of Plutarch's more serious charges against him (cf., e.g., pp. 417f, 444f), that of his Athenian informants. The fact that was held against him was that he was a radical, and, as the founder of Athenian sea-power, also the father of that radical democracy which both Herodotos' informants and the later Greek writers, conservatives almost to a man, disliked. Plutarch, who, like Herodotos himself, discerns the greatness of the man through the mists of prejudiced information, sees the grounds of the prejudice even while (with Plato, whom he so much revered) believing it justified.[3]

Thucydides, the magisterial and impartial, is the ancient writer who best does justice to Themistokles. He tersely notes (i, 135f) that when accused, after the great war was over, of treasonable communication with Persia, Themistokles had already been driven from Athens, politically defeated (defeated, as Thucydides does not have occasion to say, by the united aristocratic leaders of the post-war conservative 'Areopagite reaction'); and he does not commit himself as to whether any accusation of high treason would have been justified. The case did not come to court; Themistokles, whatever the nature of his implication in the doings of the Spartan Pausanias, knew better than to trust himself in the hands of his political enemies, and fled. Thucydides' last word on him is a tribute solely to his intellect, in the famous passage (I, 138, 3):

> Themistokles was a man who most clearly presents the phenomenon of natural genius . . . to a quite extraordinary and exceptional degree. By sheer personal intelligence, without either previous study or special briefing, he showed both the best grasp of an emergency situation at the shortest notice, and the most far-reaching appreciation of probable further developments. He was good at explaining what

[3] Plut. *Them.* 4, quoting Plato, *Laws* 706b (where Them. is not named though probably Plato is thinking of him).

he had in hand; and even of things outside his previous experience he did not fail to form a shrewd judgment. No man so well foresaw the advantages and disadvantages of a course in the still uncertain future. In short, by natural power and speed in reflection, he was the best of all men at determining promptly what had to be done.

Of this genius, first among all the great Greeks except for Miltiades, we are fortunate enough to possess a portrait head, a copy made for a citizen of Ostia under the Roman Empire (and Roman collectors liked their copies faithful) from an original sculpture of, it has been believed after detailed study of anatomical details (ear in relation to skull, for instance), the transitional period, late-archaic to early-classical; that is from the later years of Themistokles' lifetime.[4]

As often, to meet the man thus 'face to face' is a surprise. One might have imagined him, the radical, the brilliant innovator, as 'lean and hungry', a Cassius, hyperthyroid. He is no such thing. Broad-faced, thick-necked, the portrait seems to be that of a stocky man; at least, with such proportions, if he had been also tall he would have been an Ajax, and one would have expected that detail to emerge in the tradition. The beard and hair, which is inclined to be wavy, neither curly nor silky, are cropped short. The mouth is wide and prominent, the lower lip full, sensuous and sensitive; the upper lip is covered by a full, heavy, drooping moustache, the only item of hair, one might imagine, which the owner fancied as an adornment. The mouth and the wide-open eyes, deep-set under a rather heavy and fleshy brow, give the face an expression of eagerness and animation, quite capable of being sardonic (look at the ends of that moustache!) but sympathetic rather than formidable; a face with something Socratic about it;[5] ready to speak, no less ready to learn. Plutarch, who had seen a portrait of him, quite possibly the original of our portrait, in his chapel

[4] Ostia Museum; discovered 1939; discussion (and bibliography up to 1965) by G. M. A. Richter in *The Portraits of the Greeks*, vol. I, pp. 97ff. and figs. It is undoubtedly mere dogma that Greek artists of the early 5th or even late 6th century either could not or never did produce individual likenesses; though, in the time when they were still developing their technique, the result did not always please the sitter, and the attempt was therefore the more sparingly made – except when the displeasure of the subject was intended, as in the famous feud between the sculptor Boupalos and the poet Hipponax, who names Boupalos in more than one extant fragment (Diehl, frags. 1, 13, 15, 20, 70), thereby giving substance to the story in Pliny, xxxvi, 4/11ff, that Boupalos had caricatured him. Between caricature and idealisation lay the perilous channel of portraiture. Cf. Them. himself (in Plut., ch. 5, end) on Simonides' alleged commissioning of portraits of himself, and its unwisdom!

[5] I do not think this is only due to the fact that the herma has lost the tip of its nose.

of Artemis Aristoboule, remarks (*Th.* 22) that he seems heroic not only in spirit, but even in appearance. The current word for what he means is, I think, 'indestructible'.

It almost amounts to an additional argument in favour of the portrait as giving a genuine likeness, that it can send one back to the literary evidence ready to pay attention to some facts that can be neglected, though in a sense they are known to every reader of Plutarch. One may get, through the all-pervading hostile tradition, from Herodotos to some modern schoolbooks, the impression that Themistokles was so untrustworthy that he must always have been more or less mistrusted, valued only for his indispensable brains. This at least is nonsense; no would-be politician's brains were ever thought indispensable unless he was trusted at least by a large body of supporters. Themistokles was popular, affable, approachable, a man's man; he knew 'everybody' by name;[6] he had the great gift that he never forgot a face; and he cultivated a reputation as a fair and incorruptible arbitrator of commercial disputes.[7] He certainly was ambitious, and he certainly did also love money; but not, according to the less hostile accounts known to Plutarch (*loc. cit.*), as a miser; he liked to spend magnificently, in ways that would bring him credit. In his prosperous days after the great war, he paid for a dramatic production by Phrynichos, which won the prize; the group of plays included *The Phoenician Women* (with a chorus of mourners for the Phoenician disaster at Salamis, Themistokles' achievement), to which Aeschylus in *The Persians* is said to have paid the compliment of some imitation.[8] This, indeed, was a civic duty, which fell, in rotation, to every rich citizen; but he is also said to have kept great state when attending the Olympic Games (476?), and he personally paid for the building of a temple to Artemis Aristoboule, the 'giver of good counsel'; this also being quite obviously in honour of himself.[9] 'The people' are said to have resented this display; here we have hostility coming in again. Lavishness at Olympia was all right, we are told, for the young aristocrat Kimon. At this time, when Themistokles' reputation had reached its height, his united opponents were busily exploiting against him that envy which was the bane of Greek life, and which had already been the ruin of

[6] Plut. *Them.* 5.
[7] *ib.*
[8] *ib.*; cf. Aesch. *Pers.*, *Argument.*
[9] Olympia, Plut. *ib.*; temple, *Them.* 22; *MH.* 37.

Miltiades. When he was still on the way up the ladder, it is not impossible that even stories that represent him as financially unscrupulous may have amused his supporters, as examples of how our clever leader overreached the rich and proud.

Themistokles was also a family man; twice married, and no doubt happily (for otherwise, the hostile tradition would have emphasised it; we are told enough about the domestic troubles of Perikles and Socrates). Five sons and five daughters are named by Plutarch, with some account of their marriages or what became of them (ch. 32). With such a start, it is not surprising that his posterity could be traced in Athens down to Roman imperial times. One of them, named Themistokles, was at school with Plutarch. But the family is never again recorded to have produced a man of distinction.

Such was the brilliant, affable, popular, very human man who had led the democrats in Athens at least since 493. It is one of the oddities of Herodotos' story that he only introduces him (vii, 143) on the eve of the great invasion, and then as 'a man who had lately come to the front'. It is probably the result of hostility on the part of Herodotos' sources; we know that he was friendly to the Alkmeonidai, and it was one Leōbotes the son of Alkmeon (Alkmeon the archon of 507?) who formally charged Themistokles with treason at the time of his flight.[10] It is a mistake comparable to his statement that Kleomenes, who reigned *c.* 519–490, 'reigned no long time' (perhaps a confusion with his final brief restoration); both seem to result from the unwillingness of unfriendly witnesses to tell more than was unavoidable about the great man whose importance could not be wholly concealed. However, Herodotos has very little to say about Athens in the seven years after the fall of Miltiades, at all.

It was reserved for the Aristotelian *Athenian Constitution* (*Ath. Pol.*), recovered in papyrus in 1890, to do something to fill this gap, with information, some fragments of which had been previously known from such writers as Plutarch and (notably) Harpokration's valuable *Lexicon of the Attic Orators*. Notably, it is the Aristotelian work which alone tells us the date of a major constitutional change; nothing less than the change from the constitution of Solon, dominated by the archons, whose powers Kleisthenes had left unaltered, to that of classical Athens, in which the chief officers of state, with wide but

[10] Plut. *Them.* 23.

limited powers, were the ten generals. Three years after Marathon, Athens introduced the system of appointing the archons by lot, from among 500 candidates previously elected by the *demes*.[11] The selection of candidates ensured that the archons would be men of respectable character and ability; but they would no longer be the leading men of Athens, and never again would the chief or eponymous archonship be the subject of the intense competition which, as the treatise has earlier remarked (13, 2), had often rent Athens with faction.

Why this drastic and revolutionary change, just then?

It could be presented to the Assembly as a democratic measure; but the candidates still had to be of cavalry census; the archonships were not thrown open by statute to smallholders till 457.[12] The class of voters to whom the measure would appeal *prima facie* was that of the less prominent 'knights', local notables who might hope to appear frequently among the 500 candidates, and thus by the luck of the draw (or by the choice of the gods, as many Athenians probably viewed the matter), some day to occupy the august seats of archons and then for life, if they made no false step while in office, of Areopagites. But the most important immediate effect would be that the archons, these *average* knights, would be more dependent on and amenable to the advice of others. The Polemarch, in particular, would become completely dependent on his staff, the ten *stratēgoi* of the regiments, to whom (especially to Miltiades) Kallimachos had already given ear at the time of Marathon; the *strategoi*, who continued to be directly elected, and could be re-elected, thus gaining experience.

There was also a longer-term consequence, which would not be evident for years. The Areopagus, embodying, like the Roman Senate, the best political and military experience of the city, still possessed enormous prestige. Deprived, by the foresight of Solon, of the all-important task of preparing business for the Assembly, which fell to the People's Council, the Areopagus was still by Solon's law a Supreme Court, trying cases of homicide and, as Guardian of the Laws, empowered to disallow administrative acts which it judged unconstitutional.[13] In a crisis its prestige, like that of the Roman Senate, could give it importance beyond its statutory powers (cf. p. 429); and the influence of a body of ex-magistrates, holding their seats for life (with

[11] *Ath. P.* 22, 5. [12] *id.* 26, 4.
[13] *Ath. P.* 8, 4; 25, 2; *Lyric Age*, pp. 299f.

a majority, therefore, always middle-aged or elderly), must inevitably be a conservative influence.

Now, the new Areopagites would not in future be of the same calibre as the old; and the effect on the prestige of the whole body, especially when it intervened in politics, interpreting its constitutional powers widely, was bound in the long run to be serious. *In the long run;* for some years to come, the leading Areopagites would still be the leading statesmen of the past. In fact, the decisive revolt against wide interpretation of the ancient council's powers came exactly twenty-five years later.[14] Whoever did not foresee this ultimate result, the far-seeing Themistokles must have done so. The reform, among its other effects, was clearly to his advantage. As an ex-archon, he was already an Areopagite. The effect on his position in politics would be to exclude, for the most part, formidable younger men from the ranks of this body, as from the Archonship and Polemarchy. Those appointed by the lot would be easier to steer. There is a story that once, 'when the Persian invasion was approaching and the Athenians were deliberating on the choice of a general', Themistokles bribed a popular candidate named Epiküdes, whom he regarded as unreliable, to withdraw, 'lest, if made general, he might lead Athens to disaster'.[15] Would the decision have been so important, or the danger so great as these two quotations suggest, if Epiküdes had been competing merely for one of the ten generalships? Was he competing against Themistokles for the generalship of his tribe? – This might certainly have been enough to cause Themistokles, in a critical year, to offer him inducements to withdraw his candidature. But the phrases about *the Athenians* deliberating and the danger to *Athens* might suggest that the election is that of a commander-in-chief. There was no elected commander-in-chief after 487. Has Plutarch perhaps mis-dated the story (he clearly thinks of the incident as taking place in 481/0), and does it refer to the danger of a bad choice in the election of a Polemarch? The Persian invasion might be spoken of as 'approaching' at any time after 494; and the danger that, through such an electoral aberration as had led to the

[14] *Ath. P.* 25, 1.

[15] Plut. *Them.* 6, 1; *Mor.* 185A (in the collection of *Sayings of Kings and Generals*, most of which reappear in the *Lives*; a collection, which, like the *Spartan Customs* and some other portions of the *Moralia*, probably represents Plutarch's notebooks; though later, when he was famous, the author polished up and published these notebooks themselves, with a dedication to Trajan, in which the *Lives* are mentioned, *Mor.* 172D).

archonship of Hipparchos, an unreliable hand might be at the helm, might well have contributed to a movement by all who wished to fight for independence, to give less power to individuals. In the interests of unified command, the ten generals could still defer to one of their number, or the Assembly itself could appoint one general to take charge of a particular operation; but in the interests of political reliability, there was a strong tendency in the ancient world to feel that there was safety in numbers; the numbers of a *collegium*.

Hipparchos himself, the blameless brother-in-law of Hippias and friend of the Peisistratid house, against whom no criminal charge could be made to lie (p. 201), had already been eliminated. About this, the *Constitution* says that Kleisthenes, anxious to get rid of Hipparchos, had invented a special expedient for the purpose: the law providing that once a year the people might send into exile for ten years, without loss of status or property, any citizen they chose, merely for the good of the republic (p. 191). But, the treatise says, this law was never applied until 'the people gained in confidence' after the battle of Marathon.[16] It has been endlessly discussed, whether it is credible that this law remained on the statute book for nearly twenty years without being applied, and some scholars have preferred a version quoted by Harpokration from Androtion, a fourth-century writer on Athenian antiquities whom the Aristotelian writer also used, as is shown by echoes of the same phrases. This says that Hipparchos was thus exiled by 'potsherd voting', *ostrakismós*, 'the law being first *introduced* at this time'.[17] If this were so, we might suspect that its real author was Themistokles himself;[18] but no ancient author gives a hint of such a thing, and if it was Themistokles who, in the next few years, finally profited by its repeated application, it was only after bitter struggles and determined efforts by his rivals to make him a victim of it. Why, if the law was on the statute book in 493, it was not used against

[16] 22, 1 and 3 (§ 2 intervening, on other legislation). Honourable exile, Plut. *Them.* 22, *Ar.* 7; general discussion, see J. Carcopino, *L'Ostracisme athénien* (1935).

[17] Harp. *s.v.* Hipparchos (= Andr. fr. 5 M.; 324 F 6 Jac.). Raubitschek in *AJA* LV suggests that Kleisthenes, old but still active, came out of retirement to propose the new law; but, if so, it is the only thing that we hear of him after *c.* 505, and he must have been well over 70.

[18] As does C. A. Robinson jr., in repeated discussions of the subject (*AJP* LX, LXVI, LXVII, and, in reply to Raubitschek, in *AJA* LVI). Certainty is impossible, but personally I would, in the circumstances, tentatively accept the statements of the *Constitution*, in their chronological order, and suppose that Harpokration, briefly summarising, made a mistake in saying that the law was first *passed* at the time at which it was first *applied*.

Miltiades, I do not know; perhaps because, against one who had not figured in Athenian politics in the preceding years, it did not seem a promising weapon. All we can say for certain is that our best, though far from infallible, authority believes this law to have formed part of the main body of the laws of Kleisthenes, and is aware that it is an oddity that, if passed then, it was not applied for so long.

Whenever it was passed, the law was first applied in the years 488–483; then it was applied year after year, in what must have been a furious though constitutionally waged series of political campaigns. Year after year 'in the sixth prytany' (midwinter) the Assembly voted that an *ostrakophoria* should be held this year; and in spring after spring the required minimum of 6000 votes was exceeded, whether as a quorum or as the 'score' against the destined victim, our sources are divided.[19] 'In the very next year' after the ostracism of Hipparchos, the *Constitution* continues, the Athenians introduced the election of archons by lot, 'and Megakles the son of Hippokrates was ostracised. Thus for three years they ostracised the friends of the tyrants.' [20] The name of one victim has evidently been omitted, probably by carelessness on the part of our writer, after introducing his note on the sortition of archons. Guesses can be made at possible names from among 'high-scorers' of early date represented among the large number of ostraka now known (nearly 1500 of all dates down to 415), chiefly from the American excavation of the Agora. Those of our period are mostly found in that area; those from later *ostrakophoriai*, less numerous up to the present, elsewhere, largely from the German excavations in the Keramikos.[21] Far the highest total is of votes cast against Themistokles: no less than 542, many of them found singly (which is statistically important), though one group of 191, much the largest homogeneous group yet found, may represent voting-sherds prepared but not used (p. 290, below). The second highest, built up by the chance of the discovery of one large and two considerable groups, is of 236 sherds with a name previously unknown to history, Kallixenos the son of Aristōnymos of

[19] Winter *procheirotonia*, *Ath. P.* 43, 5; quorum of 6000 required, Plut. *Ar.* 7; 6000 against one man required, Pollux viii, 19, schol. Aristoph. *Knights*, 851ff.

[20] *Ath. P.* 22, 5f.

[21] E. Vanderpool in *Hesperia*, suppl. vol. VIII (enumeration of finds made in all areas up to 1946) and in ordinary vol. XVII, recording a large find from west of the Areopagus in 1947 (pp. 193f, contrib. to Homer Thompson's article on the year's work); on the Keramikos (166 ostraka in all, included by Vanderpool above), W. Peek in *Keramikos*, vol. III, pp. 51ff.

Xypete; while a few aberrant individual sherds reading Kallisthenes Aristonymou, Kleisthenes Aristonymou, and Klalisenos Klestenos (*sic*) may represent either Kallixenos' less important relatives or voters who got the name wrong; the last also gives us a glimpse of the difficulties of the imperfectly literate. The third highest total is of 120 sherds with the name of Hippokrates, son of Alkmeonides of Alōpeke (east of the city, where the main branch of the Alkmeonid house was registered). One large deposit found in 1947 included 145 sherds with the name of Themistokles, 144 with Kallixenos and 36 with Hippokrates. There are also 29 sherds with the name 'Hippokrates, son of Anaxiléos' or simply 'Hippokrates', of the same address; either, probably, a relative, or possibly the father had two names.[22] The fourth-highest early total is that of Aristeides (59); and for no one else of this generation have the chances of discovery yet produced as many as 20. Of Megakles the nephew of Kleisthenes the law-giver, ostracised in spring, 486, we have 13 ostraka[23] and of Hipparchos the son of Charmos, 11.

One of the above high-scorers, then, may have been the unnamed 'friend of the tyrants' ostracised presumably in 487.[24] With the fall of Megakles, we find public opinion turning against the Alkmeonidai, who had triumphed over Miltiades; and if Megakles too was stigmatised as a 'friend of the tyrants', the alleged connection of his family with the shield-signal at Marathon will have figured in the propaganda against him. Megakles did not allow himself to be downcast; he went off to Delphi, where his family had long-standing connections, and there his racehorses won new renown for his house with a victory in the 25th Pythiad, celebrated by Pindar. A scholiast on the ode (the *Seventh Pythian*) adds that Pindar also wrote a dirge for a Hippokrates, perhaps Megakles' father; to it, perhaps, belong the beautiful lines on the consolations of the Eleusinian Mysteries, which he wrote on the death of an initiate.[25] The victory-ode contains a brief expression of the poet's sorrow that 'envy requites the noble deeds' of

[22] Cf., e.g., *Lyric Age*, p. 194, for two cases of this in the tyrant house of Corinth.

[23] H. vi, 131.

[24] The missing name is not that of the elder Alkibiades (for whom we have six well-scattered ostraka, and the literary tradition of Lysias, xiv, 39, [Andok.] iv, 34); they are not from the 480 'fill', like those of all the known pre-480 victims, and one sherd is datable to the second quarter of the century (Vanderpool, *The Ostracism of the Elder Alkibiades*, in *Hesp*. XXI).

[25] Fr. 102 Bergk, from Clem. Alex., *Strom*. iii, 518.

his patron, but bids him take it philosophically. The age of Pindar was, indeed, seeing the sunset of the Greek aristocratic world which he loved; but the poet helped to make the sunset beautiful.

In the fourth year (485), continues the *Politeia*, the people started to banish men other than friends of the tyrants, 'any who seemed over-prominent; and the first man ostracised who was unconnected with the tyranny was Xanthippos the son of Ariphron'. Of votes against him we have 17 examples, including one sherd, *probably* used as a vote, on which a disgruntled citizen has broken into verse:

> Xanthippos, son of Arriphron, is blamed for his rascality;
> Too long he has, the potsherd says, enjoyed our hospitality.[26]

Despite the efforts of scholars, the precise meaning of the gibe remains obscure; but it accuses Xanthippos of being an *aleitēros* (*metri gratia* for *alitērios*, an accursed bringer of famine) 'of the Prytaneion', the town-hall where, *inter alia*, public benefactors were entertained. Xanthippos is thought by some (on late and weak authority) to have belonged to the clan of the Bouzygai,[27] who had some priestly duties. If so, it could be brought up against him the more pointedly (as it was against Perikles) that Xanthippos had married an Alkmeonid, the younger Agariste, of a family still deemed by their enemies to be *aliterioi*, tainted by the Kylonian curse.[28] That he was not compromised with the Peisistratids, if Megakles was, is a curious assertion; the fact remained that he was Megakles' brother-in-law.

Megakles was head of a great family, and Xanthippos, whatever his ancestry (there is an Ariphron – a rare name – in the chronographers' list of the ancient life-archons),[29] was an able man; but was either of them really so powerful as to be a menace to the republic? We know

[26] Tr. O. Broneer, *Notes on the Xanthippos Ostrakon*, in *AJA* LII; cf. also Raubitschek in *AJA* LI.

[27] The rhetorician Aristeides (ed. Dindorf, II, p. 174), after referring to the oratory of Perikles, quotes Eupolis (*probably* the play *Demoi*, cf. Plut. *Per.* 3): two lines of dialogue: 'Is there an orator now, worth speaking of?' – 'The Bouzyges is best, the *aliterios*.' A scholiast on the passage, who could have read the full text of E. but most probably had not, takes the Bouzyges to be Perikles, son of X., himself, but from what we have to go on, it seems rather to be a later orator, perhaps Demostratos, who spoke in favour of the Sicilian expedition (Plut. *Nik.* 12) and receives unfriendly reference in Aristoph. *Lys.* 397 as 'the Cholozyges'; expl. of D. by schol. *ad loc.* The reference to Pericles is rejected by Wilamowitz, *Ar. und Ath.* II, p. 86, n. 25, Kock *ad loc.* (Eup. fr. 96 in *Com. Fr.* I); but accepted by Miltner in *PW*, *Perikles*, and thence by Raubitschek in *AJA* LI, *The Ostracism of X.*

[28] Thk. i, 126, etc.

[29] See Clinton *FH* I, index.

of one man who at this time was rising to unrivalled power; and this was Themistokles. When we notice the enormous proportion of the known ostraka which bear his name, we can see that votes were being cast against him, probably all through the series; and we may wonder whether at least in some of these years the initiative in proposing an ostrakophoria did not come from his enemies, the aristocrats, to whose way of thinking the advance of the democratic spirit was a menace indeed. He was beyond a doubt the most conspicuous figure in the Assembly, on one side; on the other stood all the leaders of noble families. Now the decision to hold an ostrakophoria did not lay down that the decision lay between this leader and that. The question was only, Is there a man whose departure would be for the good of the city? On the appointed day, any citizen might vote against any; and in fact the ostraka do include a considerable number of single specimens, many bearing names entirely unknown; a wasted 'scatter-vote'. If the conservative vote were concentrated against Themistokles on the ground that he was becoming a new Peisistratos (the poor men's leader of his day), while the radical vote was divided between a number of sufficiently imposing targets, Themistokles would go. But things, as we have seen, did not work out like that.

If a politician were in obvious danger of ostracism, there was only one escape for him. He must see to it that those votes which he could influence were well concentrated.[30] It is evident that Themistokles was able to do this; and this implies the presence of a band of willing helpers, a *hetairia* of a new kind, indeed a party organization, which we should not otherwise have suspected. Those against whom his party concentrated were 'shot down' in one salvo apiece, and this helps to account for the small number of ostraka preserved, cast against each of them.

His opponents, for their part, made desperate efforts to get rid of him; and of their labours we have a fascinating relic in the 'record' group of 191 ostraka above mentioned. They are a remarkably homogeneous set; in material – mostly on the round bases of black-glazed cups (evidently 'spoilers' from someone's pottery works); in writing – they were all produced, it seems, by about six hands; even in spelling,

[30] Just what Nikias and Alkibiades did in 416 or 415 (A. G. Woodhead in *Hesp.* XVIII, Raubitschek in *TAPA* LXXIX, 1948), 'concentrating the fire' of their reliable supporters against an essentially less important man, in the scandalous bargain that made this an ostracism to end all ostracisms, Plut. *Nik.* 11, *Alk.* 13.

preferring the form 'Themisthokles'. Surely such 'voting papers', ready-made, a welcome service to those voters who were illiterate or found writing a struggle, would help to 'get the votes out'? – especially, perhaps, those of old-fashioned people who were the conservatives' chief hope. But even such back-room devotion was of no avail. How many of the prepared votes were cast, we do not know; but at least 191 were left on the hands of the party workers, to be dumped, still all together, in a disused well on the north slopes of the Acropolis.[31]

The breaking successively of the Philäid, Peisistratid and Alkmeonid factions by the elimination of their leaders, left two politicians of the new age face to face. Aristeides, the archon of 489, was a less brilliant figure than Themistokles. He set himself to make up for it by being The Man You Can Trust. To the end of his life (and he died old and respected) it was his boast that he had never enriched himself through his political career. Themistokles would have asked, Why not? Later tradition canonised him as the good conservative, over against the clever, unscrupulous radical; Plutarch found in him a Greek counterpart to the Elder Cato. In fact, there was more in common between the two Athenians than the tradition might suggest. On occasions they could work together, as at Salamis.[32] Aristeides, if outshone, was no fool; nor had he any inhibitions about the aggrandizement of his city. After Themistokles had paved the way, Aristeides played a distinguished part in the foundation of the Athenian Empire. And if Aristeides made political capital out of his soubriquet of Aristeides the Just, making himself useful as an arbitrator of disputes, this is exactly what Themistokles, in a less quoted passage of Plutarch (above, p. 282), is also represented as doing.

But on one issue at this time they stood opposed. Themistokles was still agitating for an enormous increase in the navy. With this, and only with this, he was convinced, the inevitable Persian invasion might be defeated; and for those who thought that, after Marathon, the Persians would not come again, he could still point out the desirability of crushing Aigina. Aristeides became the chief hope of the richer citizens, who looked on the prospect of heavy expenditure without enthusiasm; for himself, he may have been honestly convinced (though, if so, it shows his limitations) that what the spears of Marathon had

[31] To be discovered by Dr O. Broneer in 1937; *Hesp.* VII, 228ff.
[32] Cf. the *Apophthegm* of Aristeides (3) in Plut. *Mor.* 186b; it could be genuine.

done once they, with aid from the Spartans and their allies, could do again. In 483–2, in the very nick of time as it proved, came Themistokles' opportunity.

At Marōneia, in the silver-mining district of Laurion near Sounion, the small operators who worked the state-owned mineral, paying a royalty on their holdings, struck an unprecedentedly rich vein.[33] The mines had been in operation 'since time immemorial',[34] but modern survey has confirmed that it was impossible for the rich vein, well below the surface, to be reached until much work had been done. The royalties reached the unheard-of figure of 100 talents, or 600,000 drachmas, at a time when a drachma a day would be a middle-class income. (200, as we have seen, was a ransom for a man-at-arms, pp. 189, 231n.) It was enough to pay for all regular state expenditure, and leave a large surplus even then, which it was proposed to distribute at a flat rate of ten drachmas to every citizen. (How many citizens? If citizens, with every man in service from the Knights down, formed the bulk of the crews of 180 ships in the year 480 at 200 men per ship, in addition to a modest force on shore (pp. 381ff), we get something well over 30,000 men in service; in 479, fifty ships and 8000 men-at-arms with as many light-armed account for 26,000 men; and there are still the older men, home guard, to be reckoned in. A population of 60,000 adult male citizens in all Attica does not seem impossible, though most modern estimates are lower.)[35]

But a speech by Themistokles carried the Assembly. The proposed distribution was called off, and the money devoted to the building of 100 new ships, being entrusted for the purpose to 100 rich men, each of whom was to take charge of one building operation.[36] Herodotos indeed says that 200 ships were *built* under this programme; and in 480 Athens is said to have *had* 200 triremes, 20 of which were manned by her colonists at Chalkis. Since her old navy, according to Thucydides (i, 14, 3), consisted mainly of pentekonters, practically all the triremes

[33] *Ath. P.* 22, 7.
[34] Xen. *Revenues*, iv, 2.
[35] On population, as well as all other aspects of this subject, cf. J. Labarbe, *La loi navale de Thémistocle* (Paris, Les Belles Lettres, for Univ. of Liège, 1957), who likewise regards the figures for Salamis as the best basis for an estimate.
[36] H. vii, 144; *Ath. P.*, *ib.*; disregarding, as one of that treatise's silly stories, the tale that Th. invited the assembly to *lend* the money to the rich men for a purpose undisclosed, and demand it back if they were not pleased with the result. No doubt the ship-builders did have to have their ships inspected and 'passed' when handing them over. The story of a purpose undisclosed might derive from the tradition that Th., though thinking about Persia, talked about Aigina (H. *loc. cit.*). The debate, Plut. *Them.* 4.

must have been of fairly recent construction. We might hazard the guess that there had been a good deal of recent building already, always advocated by Themistokles, to which the emergency programme of the year 483–2 represented a heroic addition.[37]

At the same time, the last *ostrakophoria* of this decade was held, and Aristeides was its victim. Propaganda turned against him even his activities as an unofficial arbitrator. Use of the phrase 'Honest Aristeides' had perhaps been overdone by his supporters, and we hear that Themistokles' campaign-speeches said he was by-passing the peoples' courts and *secretly making himself an uncrowned* (literally 'un-bodyguarded') *king*,[38] which is exactly appropriate for an *ostrakophoria*. Of this ostracism is told also the most famous of all Aristeides-stories, of how 'an illiterate and extremely rustic character passed his potsherd to Aristeides, as to "just anyone", and asked him to write "Aristeides" on it; and when he asked in surprise what harm Aristeides had done him, the countryman said "None – I don't even know him by sight – but I am so sick of hearing him called 'Honest' all over the place." To this Aristeides gave no answer, but wrote his name on the sherd and handed it back.'[39]

So Themistokles himself became for a time the 'uncrowned king of Athens' as his opponents no doubt often complained (the same complaint was often made about Perikles); and the great Athenian navy was ready in time, though only just; when the war came, the Greeks still feared the superior skill of the Phoenicians. Training the thousands of additional oarsmen, many of whom must have been peasants unused to the sea, must have been one of the preoccupations of Athenian naval administration in the last years of peace. And with the process of training should perhaps be connected a mysterious matter: the question, when did Themistokles have his contacts with the west?

Cornelius Nepos has a story (*Them.* 2) that Themistokles' 'first

[37] H. viii, 1, 14, 44, 46; cf. Justin, ii, 12, 12, 'post pugnam Marathoniam, praemonente Themistocle . . . ducentas naves fabricaverant'. The authority is not high, but Pompeius Trogus used some good sources.

[38] Plut. *Ar.* 7.

[39] *ib.* – Though by no means averse to historical anecdotes, which are often revealing, I must confess to doubts about this one, for a reason which seems to have escaped notice: I can hardly imagine that, in a Greek crowd on an election day, one of the protagonists would not have been surrounded by an escort of eager supporters, whose remarks, or at least laughter, would have spoilt the incident. I suspect that the remark was made, but that the story was improved by having it made to A. himself.

public service', in which he employed the fleet built with the surplus from the mines, was in a war in which he defeated Kerkyra and cleared the sea of pirates. This is usually dismissed as nonsense; the name (though it occurs twice) supposed to be a slip for Aigina. Nepos certainly is capable of gross errors; Plutarch has no reference to such a war; and Herodotos (vii, 145) does appear, *prima facie*, to date the peace between Athens and Aigina, promoted by the Greek nationalist Congress, to a time when Xerxes was already on the march. Kerkyra was one of the first naval powers of Greece, a pioneer in rebuilding her whole fleet with the new triremes;[40] and Athens would hardly have embarked on a campaign against this formidable and remote power if the war with Aigina was still actively raging.

But there is a reference in Thucydides (i, 136) to Themistokles having *rendered a service* to Kerkyra; Plutarch (*Them.* 24) expands this, saying that he arbitrated in a quarrel between Kerkyra and Corinth, laying down that Corinth should pay an indemnity of twenty talents (why, he does not say) and that they should share jointly in the privileges of founders at Leukas, a colony which they had jointly founded but which Corinth, when she was able to, treated as a possession. Themistokles certainly was interested in the west, naming two of his daughters Sybaris and Italia;[41] the girls were probably born before 480, and such significant names usually commemorated something in which the father took pride.

Themistokles' visits to the west can be fitted in most easily if the peace with Aigina was concluded a little earlier than its position in Herodotos' narrative would suggest. But this is not really unlikely. Herodotos actually mentions the Congress of 'the loyal Hellenes' (his term, and no doubt their own rallying-cry) only after Xerxes has reached the border of Thessaly; but he makes it clear that it was functioning regularly (e.g. collecting intelligence) much earlier than that, and says that it gave the reconciliation of enemies in Greece the highest priority.[42]

It may be suggested that when Aigina knew that she was about to be outbuilt on a scale to which she could make no reply, she was ready for

[40] Thk. i, 13 ('a little before the Persian War and the death of Darius'). K. manned 60 of them in 480, H. vii, 168, 2.

[41] Plut. *Them.* 32.

[42] H. vii, 145. Greece knew what was coming 'long before', πρὸ πολλοῦ, *ib.* 138. On the League against Persia, cf. P. A. Brunt in *Historia*, 1953, pp. 135ff.

peace; and that Sparta, having no desire to see Aigina's brave and skilful navy destroyed, did not need to wait until Persia was fully mobilised in order to mediate. Persia began work on a canal to by-pass Mount Athos in 483 (p. 318); and with this warning, the movement for peace between the Greek cities, in order to consolidate resistance, must have begun too. In it, we hear, a distinguished part was played by Chileos of Tegea, conspicuous thereafter as *persona grata* with the Spartan government;[43] he had probably started by restoring good relations between Sparta and his native city, recently unfriendly (p. 272).

Themistokles for his own part was probably of the same mind; but if peace was made with Aigina, he had to do something, both to train the thousands of new hands needed for the expanded fleet, and to demonstrate the value of that fleet in a spectacular way, in order to preserve the popular enthusiasm for it, which he had been at such pains to build up. It would be entirely in accordance both with his own policy and with that of Sparta and the panhellenic movement, if in 481 (when Persia's vast preparations were under way, but still far from complete) he set off on a training cruise to the west, incidentally with the mission on behalf of 'the loyal Hellenes', the 'Continental Congress', to use his good offices to effect a reconciliation between Kerkyra and Corinth. The appearance of an imposing fleet would do more than anything else to impress isolationist Kerkyra;[44] and Themistokles won Kerkyra's gratitude by finding for her on some points at issue, against Athens' old ally Corinth, and in accordance with the principles of justice, on which he prided himself no less than Aristeides (cf. p. 282). There was no war, or it could hardly have escaped Plutarch, and no treaty between Athens and Kerkyra (so the Corinthians tell us in Thucydides, i, 40); but the training could include a sweep against pirates (Illyrians in the straits of Otranto?) on the trade-routes that already carried great quantities of Athenian pottery, and doubtless other goods, to the west. Such a cruise could also include a visit, not necessarily by the whole fleet, to south Italy (the Italia of those days), where the cities of Sybaris and Siris had been destroyed in wars with their fellow-Greeks and, though re-colonised by the victors, offered room for more settlers. Here Themistokles could reconnoitre a land

[43] Plut. *Them.* 6; H. ix, 9.
[44] Hence Nepos' *Corcyraeos fregit*, a mistranslation of a source?

which (as he was to remind his Peloponnesian allies, when they were slow to fight outside their peninsula) might afford a refuge for Athenians if, after all, the Persians proved too strong and Athens could not be held.[45]

[45] H. viii, 62; 'Siris in Italy, which is ours from of old'; cf. *Lyric Age*, p. 374.

Chapter XV

Military Monarchy in Sicily

The Greek Congress might well look to the west; help from there would be important, if it could be had. But the western Greeks were no freer from feuds than those of the old country. In Italy, the destruction of Siris and Sybaris had been two major disasters. Since then, in Sicily a major power-bloc had arisen among the Dorians of the south, and the burning question was whether its rulers could extend their sway to the Tyrrhenian Sea.

A new epoch in Sicilian history begins about 505, with the overthrow of the oligarchy at Gela by Kleandros, son of Pantares; very probably that Pantares who had won a chariot victory at Olympia, commemorated by an extant inscription.[1] Gela under him may already have been bursting the bounds of her original narrow though fertile territory in the coastal plain;[2] but it was his brother Hippokrates, after Kleandros had been murdered by a citizen named Sabyllos, who made Gela the basis of a great military power. With his army reinforced by many mercenaries, he set out on a career of conquest, subduing many of the Sikel communities in east-central Sicily, and extending his power,

[1] Ar. *Politics*, v, 1316a; H. vii, 154f; inscr., *Olympia* V, pp. 241ff. The date rests on a combination of evidence: Kleandros ruled seven years, his successor Hippokrates as many (H., *loc. cit.*), and *his* successor Gelon *accessit* Ol. 72, 2, in the archonship of Hybrilides at Athens, = 491–0, D.H. vii, 1, 4. Paus. vi, 9, 2, gives the same indications of date for the accession of Gelon *at Syracuse* (below, p. 305); but this must be wrong, for the tyranny of Gelon and his successors at Syracuse lasted only 18 years in all (Ar. 1315b), ending in 467–6 (D.S. xi, 67), of which Gelon ruled for seven years, dying in 478 (D.S. xi, 36). Hippokrates moreover was already in power and had made extensive conquests when the Samian and Milesian fugitives after Lade arrived in the west, presumably in 493. Against the view that Gelon succeeded at *Gela* in 485 and captured Syracuse almost immediately afterwards (Hackforth in *CAH* IV, p. 371, from Pareti, *Studi Siciliani ed italioti*, 1920, pp. 28ff) see Dunbabin, *WG* 432ff. The chief objection to Pareti's dating is that if Hippokrates accedes seven years before Gelon, in 492, there is not time for him to have extended his power to the straits before the arrival of fugitives from the Ionian revolt. So also Beloch, *GG*² II, ii, pp. 162ff.

[2] See Dunbabin, *WG* 119ff (after Orsi in *Mon. Ant.* XX), for the survival of Sikel natives, with a 'palace', implying a chief of their own, at Monte Bubbonia in the immediate hinterland, down to about 500.

after a series of sieges, over the Chalkidians of 'Kallipolis and Naxos, Zankle and Leontinoi'. If this list (in H. vii, 154, 2) is in chronological order, Hippokrates first breaks through to the east coast at the expense of the small cities under Mount Etna, thus dividing the more important Zankle, on the straits, from populous, inland Leontinoi. By 494, a dynast subordinate to him, perhaps appointed by him, already bore rule in Zankle.[3]

The evidence for this date is Herodotos' statement (vi, 22) that the propertied classes at Samos, repudiating the treason of their captains at Lade, took counsel together when the survivors reached home after that disaster and decided to sail to the west 'before their tyrant Aiakes arrived. . . . For the people of Zankle in Sicily were, at this very time, inviting the Ionians by messengers to come to the Fair Headland (a cape on the coast of Sicily towards Tyrrhenia) and found an Ionian city there.' Since not many weeks, perhaps not many days, can have elapsed between the battle and the Persian occupation of Samos, it is evident that Skythes, the dynast in power at Zankle, had sent the message before the battle. It was general Greek policy in the west, and probably Hippokrates' policy – he was probably behind the invitation, though we are not told so – to consolidate their position against Carthaginian and Tyrrhenian hostility by getting new colonists to occupy vacant areas, such as the north coast of Sicily between the straits and Himera.

In the event a remnant, the nationalist Samians, with some Milesians who had escaped being shut up in their besieged city and 'other Ionians',[4] came in answer to the invitation; but there were enough of them to found a new colony. When they were already in Italian waters, Skythes with the forces of Zankle marched out to besiege a city of the Sikels, presumably in aid of the enterprise. But now a new actor took a hand in the drama.

The people of Rhegion had seen with anxiety a new Dorian power engulfing the cities of their kinsmen up to the straits before their harbour. In this crisis, in 494 a tyrant gained power here too:[5] Anaxilaos the son of Krētines, a descendant of the Messenian exiles who had been influential at Rhegion since its foundation. Anaxilaos took action promptly. He got into touch with the Samians, who had reached Lokroi, and suggested to them that instead of enduring the hardships

[3] H. vi, 23, 4; see below, p. 300. [4] Added by Thk., vi, 4, § 5.

[5] He died in 476–5 according to Diodoros (xi, 48), after a reign of 18 years.

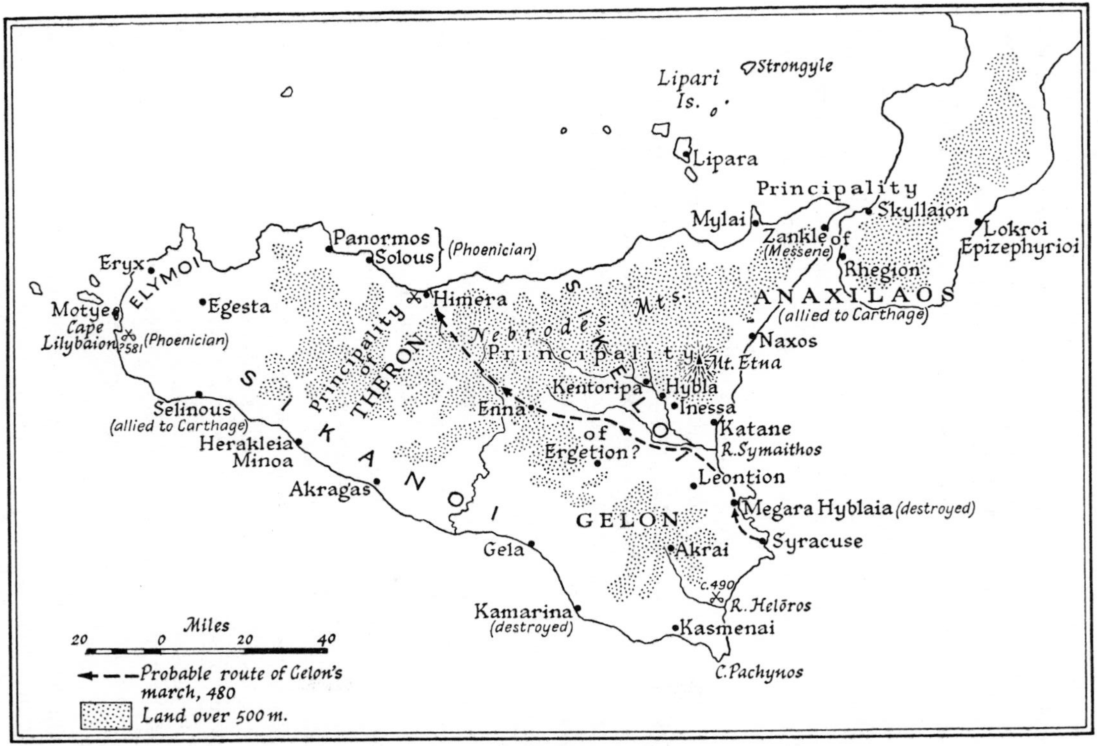
Strongyle
Lipari Is.
Lipara
Principality
Skyllaion
Mylai
Zankle of (Messene)
Lokroi Epizephyrioi
Rhegion
ANAXILAOS
(allied to Carthage)
Panormos
Solous
(Phoenician)
Eryx
ELYMOI
Egesta
Motye
Cape Lilybaion
?581
(Phoenician)
Himera
SIKELOI
Mts.
Nebrodes
Principality
Mt. Etna
Naxos
Principality of THERON
Kentoripa
Hybla
Inessa
Enna
Katane
R. Symaithos
of Ergetion?
Leontion
Megara Hyblaia (destroyed)
Selinous
(allied to Carthage)
Herakleia Minoa
Akragas
SIKANOI
GELON
Syracuse
Akrai
Gela
c.490
R. Helōros
Kamarina
(destroyed)
Kasmenai
C. Pachynos
Miles
20
0
20
40
Probable route of Gelon's march, 480
Land over 500 m.

Sicily

of founders of a new colony, they should take over Zankle itself in the absence of its men. The Samians agreed, and did so. Skythes and the Zanklaians hurried back, to find the walls held against them. They sent for aid to their powerful 'ally' Hippokrates; but he, 'when he arrived with his army, arrested Skythes and put him in irons for losing his city'. Herodotos here (vi, 23, 4) makes it clear that Hippokrates regarded Skythes as his subordinate and the loss of Zankle as a loss affecting himself. Then, concerned, like Anaxilaos and the Samians, solely with the possession of the town and not at all with the welfare of its unfortunate inhabitants, 'he made overtures to the Samians, and after mutual exchange of oaths, betrayed the Zanklaians'. As the price of recognition and of the city, 'the Samians agreed that he should have a half share of all chattels and slaves within the city, and all those in the country without. Hippokrates then arrested and enslaved the majority of the men of Zankle, but 300 of the leading men he delivered to the Samians to be put to death; the Samians, however, did not do that.' These 300, representing the old governing class before Skythes became tyrant and no friends of Hippokrates, 'would have a good deal in common with the Samian oligarchs, who probably admitted them to citizenship. There was still an old Zanklaian element in the citizen body . . . which revived the old name and coin types for a short period after the fall of the Rhegine tyranny.' [6] Hippokrates probably hoped to get rid of them finally, without himself incurring blood-guilt for slaying men with whom he had had treaty relations. With all his ruthlessness, he shared in the superstitions of his time. Skythes, too, shortly afterwards escaped. But most of the population of Zankle, some thousands of people, were sold into slavery; as were myriads of Sicilians in the record of unstable democracies and military despotisms which fills the history of Sicily for the next three hundred years.

There is a series of coins, generally found in the west, and sometimes together with older coins of Zankle bearing her *type parlant*, the sickle (*zanklon* in the native language), which, with a dolphin within it, typified her harbour. The new coins, still on the Chalkidian (Euboic) weight-standard, bear the badge of Samos, a lion's scalp, now shown within a circle, as a badge mounted on a shield; while for reverse they bear a Samian galley (*samaina*, a *type parlant* again), a type found at Samos itself only later. Though they bear no name, these are generally

[6] Dunbabin, *WG* 393f.

recognised as a coinage of the Samians at Zankle. Many of them bear a single letter, A B Δ or E; if gamma has not yet been reported, it is probably by chance. It is suggested that these letters represent a numerical series, 1 2 [3] 4 5, which might be that of issues of successive years, e.g. 493–489. The coinage is in any case of short duration; for 'Anaxilās of Rhegion, not long after, ejected the Samians and himself colonised the city with a mixed multitude, renaming it Messene after his own ancestral fatherland.'[7] There may indeed, as we have seen (p. 272), been Messenians among the 'mixed multitude', belonging to a new wave of fugitives from the Peloponnese; but the romantic story in Pausanias (iv, 23, – in which Anaxilaos is brought into the generation of 664!) provides no foundation for an extensive reconstruction. It is after this that coins with the new types (*not* Samian, as has been thought) introduced by Anaxilaos at Rhegion appear, with the legend MESSENION, to signalise the re-foundation.[8]

Last in our list of Hippokrates' campaigns come the attacks on Leontinoi and Syracuse (with those on 'many of the barbarians', against whom he must have fought both late and early). *If* the order of the list, not being geographical, is chronological, it is asked, why did not Leontinoi cut his communications when he was in the north?[9] To this the answer is (*a*) that we do not know; but (*b*), that (if the question arises) it is not difficult to imagine a variety of answers. Leontinoi *may* have been crippled by a preliminary campaign, but she may equally well have been put off by protestations of friendship, or even granted minor territorial satisfactions. Such methods have been used by astute conquerors from Philip of Macedon to Hitler, and it is not necessary to suppose that Philip invented them. Leontinoi fell, in any case, Hippokrates' greatest prize; an Ainesidemos, tyrant of Leontinoi, is mentioned, and he may be identical with one of Hippokrates' two most distinguished officers, a rival at one time of his great cavalry captain Gelon, destined to fame.[10]

[7] Thk. vi, 4, 6.

[8] See E. S. G. Robinson in *JHS* LXVI. As he argues, some coins with the name of Rhegion and the types of lion's head and calf's head (not the true Samian lion's *scalp* and *bull's* head), which have been thought to show the Samians occupying Rhegion with Anaxilaos for some years before they went to Zankle (C. H. Dodd in *JHS* XXVIII), have nothing to do with the Samians. There is therefore no need for drastic reconstruction of the account given by the ancient historians. Robinson's article appeared too late to be cited by Dunbabin, *op. cit.*, who, however, generally agrees (pp. 388f, 397f).

[9] Dunbabin, *WG* 382.

[10] Paus. v, 22, end; H. vii, 154, 1; cf. Ar. *Rhet.* i, 12, 30, on his sending Gelon a set of

Now Hippokrates attacked the greatest city on the island, Syracuse, thus isolated in the south-east. The Syracusans were defeated on the Helōros river, but Syracuse was saved from capture, partly at least by the intervention of her mother- and sister-cities, Corinth and Kerkyra, for once acting in unison.[11] Their possession of the two best fleets in west Greek waters meant that they could have cut off Hippokrates entirely from Greek trade, curtailing at least his supply of luxuries and taxable wealth. Hippokrates rode up to the city, making a show of virtue in not despoiling the famous temple of Olympian Zeus outside the walls, and accusing of thievish intent the Syracusans whom he caught trying to evacuate its treasures; this, it was thought, with the idea of sowing suspicion among the enemy.[12] He had taken many prisoners, and as the price of their ransom kept part of their territory, including the city of Kamarina, founded by the Syracusans *c.* 599 and destroyed by them 'for rebellion' *c.* 554; the cession was formally confirmed in the peace-treaty mediated by the naval powers. Hippokrates refounded it (thus qualifying for 'heroic' honours) and used it as a source of troops; very likely many of the settlers came from among his mercenaries.[13]

In the last year of his life (491), Hippokrates was campaigning against the Sikels, probably those of the difficult hill-country around and inland from Mount Etna. Earlier he had found them useful as mercenaries; now he decided to break their strength. With characteristic cold treachery he treated with special and lavish favour, in matters of employment and division of spoils, a regiment from the town of Ergetion; thus encouraging more recruitment, until there were few warriors left in the home glen. Then, having set out northward from Syracuse by the coast road, as though for some other objective, one night he sent off his cavalry to seize the town, ordered his herald, with careful religious legalism, to declare war on it, and set his Greek troops from Gela and Kamarina (no doubt already jealous of the 'wild high-

---

kottabos cups (a prize in a party-game) when Gelon had carried out first some piece of aggression which Ainesidemos had been contemplating; Dunbabin, *WG* 410.

[11] H. vii, 154, 3. Distinguished in the battle was Chromios, later to marry a sister of Gelon, to govern the new city of Etna for Gelon's brother Hieron, and to be celebrated by Pindar for a chariot-victory at Sikyon (*Nem.* ix, esp. 40/95ff, and schol., from Timaios x (fr. 85 M, J.)). The long poem assigned to Theognis (*Suda*, *s.v.*) on 'The Syracusans saved in the Siege' may have referred to this episode.

[12] D.S. x, 27 (from the same book of Timaios?).

[13] H., *ib.*; Thk. vi, 5, 3; Polyain. v, 5, 6.

landers') to massacre the Ergetians, whom he had carefully placed, strung out in a column, between the Greeks and the sea.[14] So far, a highly successful machiavellian or rather Caesari–Borgian operation; but such conduct could only render desperate the resistance of other Sikels, and warn them against his blandishments; and in the attack on one of the places called Hybla (probably that south-west of Etna, near Kentoripa) this able and evil 'sacker of cities' was himself killed.[15]

His half-built 'empire' would have fallen to pieces had it not been for Gelon, his cavalry commander, a spectacular and popular person, whom Hippokrates had originally promoted partly 'in order to please the Geloans'. Gelon traced his descent to the earliest colonists of Gela, and before that to a chieftain of the isle of Tēlos, near Rhodes. More remarkably, he was a hereditary hierophant of the Earth Goddesses, that is of the Mother and the Maiden, whose Mysteries had become one of the most popular cults of the Greek world. Gelon owed this honour to his forefather Tēlines, 'a gentle and feminine character', who, before the cult had been officially established at Gela, without violence and purely by the prestige of his private 'holy things', had ended a civil war. Gelon, a strange descendant of this gentle priest, may have been a more attractive character than Hippokrates, but he showed himself equally unscrupulous. He now, proceeds Herodotos, 'took up the cause of Hippokrates' children, Eukleides and Kleandros, against the citizens, who wished to be subjects no longer; but when he had defeated them in battle, he set aside the boys and took power himself'.[16]

As tyrant, Gelon had his 'early struggles'. Carthage was looking dangerous (if there was a justification for military monarchy in Sicily, it was this); and Gelon seems to have conducted a campaign in the north-west, on the pretext of 'avenging Dorieus' on the men of Egesta; he even planned a new offensive in Africa, to 'liberate the Emporia' (the Kinyps country, p. 166),[17] to which end he may have

[14] Polyain. *ib*. The 'Laistrygonian plain', where the massacre took place, is that between Leontinoi and the sea, acc. to Str. i, 20; Pliny iii, 8/14, etc.; so Ergetion was within a night ride from there.

[15] H. vii, 155, 1; for the place (still Sikel in 414) cf. Thk. vi, 94, 1. So, it fits into the same campaign as Ergetion, which is after the refoundation of Kamarina.

[16] H. vii, 153, 155. Dunbabin, to whose great work the present writer owes so much, seems to fall too much under Gelon's spell, p. 410. – Nor do I understand why D. so positively denies (p. 180) that there can have been any native Sicilian element in Telines' Mysteries, in an island in which mother-figures have always been particularly important.

[17] H. vii, 158, 2.

approached 'Leonidas, brother of the King of Sparta' (so, *c.* 490, when Kleomenes was alive but not in Sparta?); but nothing came of this, though there probably was fighting in Sicily.[18] In the meantime, Anaxilaos of Rhegion captured Messina (p. 301).

In the meantime also, a monarchy arose at Akragas, west of Gela and, since the days of Dorieus and the probable fall of Selinous to Carthage (p. 152), more directly threatened. Theron, son of Ainesidamos (not the same as Gelon's old comrade-in-arms, for Theron already had a grown-up nephew), was the richest man in that great city, and renowned for his bounty and 'magnificence'. His family, the Emmenidai, reached the height of human prestige when their chariot, personally driven by Thrasyboulos, son of Theron's brother Xenokrates, was victorious in the 24th Pythiad (490).[19] A hostile story says that he undertook the building of the great temple of Athena on the acropolis of Akragas (which is indeed a temple of the early fifth century); its columns, embodied *in situ* in the walls of the church of S. Maria dei Greci, may still be seen; and that he used the public funds to hire mercenaries.[20] The story, in some detail, is a doublet of one told of Phalaris; but temple-building was indeed an activity undertaken by great noblemen as well as reigning dynasts, as by the Alkmeonidai at Delphi. The great magnifico's rise culminated in monarchical power about 488.[21] His house remained on the best of terms with that of Gelon, who married as his second wife Theron's daughter Dāmaretā; and Theron married a daughter of Gelon's brother Polyzālos.[22]

But in 485 came Gelon's great opportunity. Civil war broke out at Syracuse, where the ruling class of Gāmoroi or Land-owners 'were expelled by their slaves' [rather, serfs?] 'who were called Kyllyrioi'.

[18] Justin xix, 1, 9; before the death of Darius, *ib.* 10; the application is referred *populis Siciliae* here; but *diu varia victoria cum tyrannis dimicatum* (by Carthage, before 480), iv, 3, 6. Discussion by Dunbabin, *WG* 411f.

[19] Pind. *Pyth.* vi; a 'personal tribute' (Sandys, *ad loc.*) to Thrasyboulos from the young poet; the commission for the official victory-ode was secured by the already established laureate, Simonides (schol.). The glory of 'thine uncle' is mentioned (45f); Theron is presumably the head of the family. Pindar had his reward 14 years later, when he wrote the official Odes *Ol.* II, III, for Theron at the height of his power. The magnificence of Theron was also mentioned by D.S. (x, fr. 28, 3, Bekker) about this time, probably as a prelude to his rise to power.

[20] Polyain. vi, 51 (rejected by Dunbabin, p. 413, after Freeman, *Hist. Sic.* II, pp. 145f); cf. *eund.* v, 1 (on Phalaris).

[21] He died in 472–1 acc. to D.S. xi, 53, after a reign of 16 years.

[22] Schol. on Pind. *Ol.* ii (introduction); schol. to l. 29 adds that after Gelon's death Polyzalos married Damareta. Timaios is among the sources.

This brief statement of Herodotos (vii, 155, 2) prompts the question, what part was played by the free but non-land-holding city dwellers, who in a great harbour-town like Syracuse must have been numerous? The answer is given in an excerpt, appropriately placed, from Diodoros,[23] *if* it refers to Syracuse (no city is named), where we read that some ruling class, striving to hold their position, 'preferred to give freedom to their slaves rather than franchise to the free men'. If so, the Gamoroi, under pressure from the free middle and lower classes, freed their serfs, but the serfs threw in their lot with the democratic party. In any case the Gamoroi were driven from the city and took refuge at Kasmenai, on the way to Gela. Here they appealed to Gelon, who marched on Syracuse, found the revolution in too great chaos to organize any resistance,[24] and received its surrender.

Gelon forthwith made Syracuse his capital; if he was already building up his naval power, soon to be formidable, he had probably long coveted its two splendid harbours, the only good harbours in Greek Sicily south of Messina; Gela, like Akragas, had long been content to haul up merchant shipping on an open beach.[25]

> As soon as he had Syracuse, though he remained lord of Gela, he considered it of secondary importance, handing it over to his brother Hieron, while he reinforced Syracuse, and Syracuse was all to him; and it forthwith grew and flourished; for Gelon transferred to it, first of all, the whole population of Kamarina, which he dismantled, granting them citizen rights, and then more than half the population of Gela, on the same terms. The Sicilian Megara surrendered to him under siege; and from here he took the propertied class, who had ventured on resistance to him and expected to be put to death for it, and brought them to Syracuse and made them citizens; while, as for the common people of Megara, who were innocent of any responsibility for the war and expected no harm, he brought them to Syracuse too, and sold them as slaves, to be taken out of Sicily. He made the same distinction also when dealing with the Euboians of Sicily. He did this, in both cases, thinking the common people a most unpleasant living-companion.[26]

[23] x, 26, 3 Bekker; A. Andrewes *ap.* Dunbabin, *WG* 414; but it may refer to Argos after Sepeia (de Sanctis); cf. p. 231 above.

[24] Ar. *Politics*, 1302b.

[25] Dunbabin, *WG* 401f, 415f.

[26] H. vii, 156. Polyainos (i, 27, 3) says that G. *invited* Dorians of Megara (the gentry) to Syracuse, and crushed those who stayed with taxation. (Misrendered by Dunbabin, p. 417.)

He wanted, in fact, a *civilised* population for his great city, and took this ruthless, aristocratic way of securing one.

Gelon was now the most powerful man in the Greek world. Already, while still at Gela, he had reached the summit of glory with a chariot victory at Olympia (488).[27] At Syracuse he continued the building up of his army and navy, against the day when he should make himself lord of all Sicily; the aggressive designs or alleged aggressive designs of Carthage would have provided a *casus belli* if one were wanted. And the day of reckoning could not now be long delayed; for suspicions of Gelon's (and Theron's) own aggressiveness caused the few cities still independent to draw together and to look for help to the barbarian. Selinous, probably harbouring refugees from her mother-city, Megara,[28] must needs feel that, of the two giants, the Greek was the more dangerous. Himera, with previous experience of such a situation between the non-Greek world and a tyrant of Akragas, put forward or fell under a tyrant of her own, Tērillos; and he, seeking allies where he could, visited Carthage, where he was entertained by the Suffete Hamilcar, and gave his daughter Kydippe in marriage to Anaxilaos of Rhegion.[29] Persia, too, was in touch with Carthage through the Phoenicians and, perhaps since before the death of Darius, almost certainly now that Xerxes was preparing to mount a great invasion, proposed concerted operations to prevent the Greeks of east and west from helping each other.[30]

[27] Paus. vi, 9, 4.

[28] Cf. the fragmentary inscription, *Olympia* V, no. 22, which seems to be guaranteeing their status at Selinous; though these exiles might be from some slightly earlier internal *stasis*.

[29] H. vii, 165. (I assume that T.'s *xeinie* with H. must date from before his expulsion from Himera, *ib.*)

[30] This was directly alleged by Ephoros, *ap.* two scholia on Pind. *Pyth.* i, 146 (Eph. fr. 111 M. = J 70 F 186); hence D.S. xi, 1 (not naming E.). No such thing is mentioned by Herodotos, whose account of the war in the west is slight; and Aristotle (1459a, = *Poetics*, 23), on the thesis that a dramatic story should be an organic unity (ὥσπερ ζῷον), cites the occurrence of the decisive battle in each campaign 'about the same time' [not 'on the same day', as early tradition (H. vii, 166) alleged] as an example of a mere coincidence, 'not conducing in any way to a common end'. From this statement many moderns have concluded that Eph. is romancing, as he sometimes does, writing into history what 'ought to have happened'. Pareti (*Stud. sic. ed. it.*, p. 132) thinks that Ar. had Eph.'s assertion in mind. But Ar., not here thinking historically, is really quite wrong; on the stage of history the two campaigns, even if not concerted, *did* conduce to a common end, which was the whole character of the classical age in Greece. Meyer is right: 'Even if Ephoros did have no tradition on the matter (though it should hardly be assumed that, e.g., Antiochos of Syracuse might not have known something about it), he has made the right combination. Modern writers have found it go against the grain to accept this, because they apply a quite wrong standard to the circumstances of the ancient world, and conceive it as far

This was the situation when, probably in 481, a delegation from the Greek congress arrived at Syracuse to seek help. Herodotos gives a long account of the conference (vii, 157–62), with imaginary speeches. The gist of it is that, in reply to the appeal, Gelon first reproaches the mainlanders for having ignored his own appeal for help to 'avenge Dorieus'; however, he offers to be magnanimous and to provide a large armament: 200 triremes, 20,000 armoured infantry, 2000 cavalry, 2000 archers, 2000 slingers and 2000 light-armed men trained to 'run with the cavalry'; and further, to provide grain for the whole Greek army for the duration of the campaign; which is evidence, incidentally, at least for the economic importance of Sicily as a source of grain-supplies.[31] As the provider of such a host, he demands, further, the command in chief. This demand being immediately refused by the Spartan delegate Syagros, he moderates it to a demand for the high command either by land or by sea; but discussion of this proposal is blocked by the Athenian delegate (unnamed), who declares his people's willingness to serve under a Spartan commander, but no other foreigner. Both the Spartan and the Athenian lay emphasis on the *seniority* of their cities, celebrated in ancient poetry, to any mere colony; and that such a feeling existed is no doubt historical.

The account of Gelon's forces is of great interest. Whether the numbers, especially of triremes, are seriously exaggerated, we cannot say; Syracuse, in the death-struggle of 413, had 76, including a few from Corinth;[32] Gelon may have had more. The regular organization of specialist light-armed men marks an advance on Greek citizen armies, characteristic of the military despot. The numbers, from a state including half the population of Sicily, are not unreasonable; though Ephoros, we notice (at least according to the Pindar scholia), reduced the number of hoplites by half.

The negotiations broke down, says Herodotos, over the question of the high command, and Gelon dismissed the ambassadors with the comment that they seemed to be better supplied with generals than with troops; they had better go home, and tell Hellas that 'the spring was gone out of the year'.

Nevertheless, protested some Sicilians later, Gelon really would have

too primitive' (*GdA*[3] IV, i, p. 335n). It would be scarcely conceivable, even with no evidence whatever, that Persia and Carthage were *not* in communication.

[31] Cf. Thk. iii, 86.

[32] Thk. vii, 52, 70.

sent troops if he had not been prevented by the threat from Carthage, which was now imminent. Theron, who must have kept the western marches while Gelon was busy in the south-east, had attained an objective of his own: he captured Himera, and, as perhaps in the days of Phalaris, the power of Akragas reached the northern sea. Terillos fled to his friend Hamilcar, and Anaxilaos, feeling that his turn would come next, supported him with urgent representations, sending his own children to Carthage as hostages in pledge of his loyalty.[33] Diodoros (xi, 2) adds that Carthage prepared, or had been preparing, for three years, but this is probably only in order to match, on behalf of his native Sicily, the three-year preparations of Xerxes. Gelon prepared his own forces for service at home. The expenditure on armaments was heavy and, setting an example, his Queen Damareta herself handed over her jewelry to the war fund.[34]

In the meantime, Gelon, far from certain that the eastern front would hold against the much heavier attack of Xerxes, determined to 're-insure'. To this end he sent to await events at Delphi, where the priests were already prophesying a Persian victory, a man with an Aristeides-like renown for justice: Kadmos, son of Skythes, who 'had inherited from his father the lordship of Kos, on a firm footing; and of his own free will and with no danger impending, but moved by justice, he handed over the government to the people and emigrated to Sicily; and there he took the city of Zankle, which changed its name to Messene, from the Samians' (or 'with the Samians'; for at this point the two main groups of Herodotos' mss. unfortunately give opposite readings) 'and settled there. This was the man whom Gelon chose', and 'sent with three fifty-oared galleys' (escort enough to deal with pirates) 'and a great treasure', to wait at Delphi, see how the fighting went, and if Xerxes prevailed to deliver it to him as a present, with an appropriate oration, and with earth and water from Gelon's dominions; but otherwise, to bring it back. And this, says Herodotos (vii, 164), as not the least of his acts of justice, he actually did.

[33] H. vii, 165.

[34] Pollux, ix, 85; cf. Hesych. *s.v.* Demaretion, 'the coin struck by Gelon . . . when Demarete contributed her jewelry'. – The most famous Damareteia were the magnificent commemorative ten-dr. pieces struck after the war, from the Carthaginian indemnity; but the name could well have been first a slang or propaganda name for the crisis money.

ADDITIONAL NOTE

Two Just Men. – Kadmos' resignation of the tyranny of Kos belongs to the period of the Ionian Revolt (in which Kos played no active part), if he 'took Zankle with the Samians', or perhaps shortly after, if 'from the Samians'. In either case, he acted in sympathy with the democratic movement which, in Ionia, exploded in the revolt, and whose strength was so remarkably recognized by Mardonios. The Justice which was his guide in life is in accordance with the ethics of the Greek 'reformation'; 'all virtue is summed up in justice', as Phokylides of Miletos had said (cf. *Lyric Age*, pp. 216f); justice, whose connection with democracy we have noted in the Athens of Themistokles and Aristeides (pp. 261, 291).

Skythes of Zankle also gained a reputation for justice. When he escaped from captivity 'he fled to Himera and thence made his way to Asia and went up country to Darius; and Darius deemed him the most just of all the men who had come to his court from Greece; for having got leave from the King to go to Sicily, he came back again . . . and finally died in old age and great prosperity among the Persians' (H. vi, 24). Was it, every scholar has inevitably asked, *his son* who was found by Gelon the best available man for a vital diplomatic mission to the son of Darius? Herodotos does not say so. This might be connected with his having, as R. W. Macan thought, first written his story of the Great Invasion (our Books vii-ix) – though, if so, he afterwards added to it (e.g. vii, 137, 3; 233, 2, with references to events as late as 430 and 431) – and afterwards the vast Introduction that made the work we know. A weak point, almost a gap, has often been noticed, between the immediate aftermath of Marathon and the preparations of Xerxes. If so, he omitted to add to the account of Kadmos in vii, 163f, a cross-reference to vi, 23f, *such as he does give sometimes*, e.g. vii, 74, 2, on the younger Artaphernes. Hackforth in *CAH* (IV, p. 368) gives the identification as a fact (after Ciaceri, Pareti and Sitzler, see *ib.* p. 639). Dunbabin (*WG*, 384) writes:

> There are too many things in common between the career of Skythes of Zankle and Kadmos son of Skythes for them not to be father and son. Skythes was in Hippokrates' service, Kadmos in Gelon's. Both ruled at Zankle. Skythes was in high favour with the

Persian king, Kadmos was an acceptable go-between . . . Kadmos was associated with those Samians whom Skythes invited to Sicily. With the agreement of name and the *δικαιοσύνη* which both exhibited, this goes beyond coincidence.

There are difficulties, however. No motive is assigned for Skythes, in middle age and without scruples about personal monarchy, leaving the 'well-established' *tyrannis* of Kos to try his fortune in the west; if he thought the west was likely to provide a fairer field for the exercise of justice he was badly mistaken. If he obtained leave from Darius to leave *Kos* and *on this occasion* (so, Pareti, *Stud. sic. ed it.*, p. 76; but H. does not say so), a just man should not have offered refuge to the King's bitterest enemies. Then, too, we find Kadmos, if he came *with* the Samians, taking part in the betrayal of his own father. (We might still suppose that he was powerless to prevent this turn of events, and that he may have helped to save the lives of the chief men of Zankle.) Macan (*Hdt. VIII–IX*, vol. I, pp. 227f), accepting this reading and the identification, is inspired to suppose a deep-laid plot, Skythes wishing to return to Persia and Hippokrates kindly imprisoning him for the sake of appearances and then letting him escape. This is altogether too ingenious. If, on the other hand, Kadmos 'took Zankle *from* the Samians', i.e. acting for Anaxilaos, he afterwards deserted him for Gelon (though some intrigue against him might have driven him to this course).

On the whole it seems most probable that these are two different men called Skythes (it was not an uncommon name), of whom Kadmos' father died in Kos; that Kadmos came to Zankle with the Samians (we are not told, *pace* Dunbabin, that he *ruled* Zankle); and that when they were driven out by Anaxilaos, he entered the service of Hippokrates' successor. Among other Koans at Zankle who afterwards found refuge at Syracuse were the parents, according to the *Suda*, of the child Epicharmos, born in Kos and destined to fame as the great Syracusan comic dramatist.

Against the identification I am happy also to be able to cite again the authority of Meyer, who dismisses it summarily, *GdA*[2] III, p. 764 n. 3.

PART III

The Great Invasion

Chapter XVI

Xerxes Marches

Xerxes, the eldest of several sons of Darius by Cyrus' daughter Atossa, must have been about thirty-two when his father died; thirty-eight when he invaded Greece. Eight brothers and half-brothers of the king are numbered among his generals; other generals are his cousins, sons of Darius' brothers, or of his sisters, married to Gobryas and Otanes his fellow-conspirators.[1] Herodotos' account of the invasion of Greece opens (vii, 5–18) with keen debate at the Persian court on whether to undertake it; old Artabanos, the king's uncle, deprecates it as a hazardous adventure; Mardonios, his cousin and brother-in-law, is the heart and soul of the enterprise, hoping to be satrap of Greece thereafter (6, 1). The influence of Greeks at the Persian court (Damaratos, representatives of the Aleuadai, the Peisistratidai, reconciled in adversity to their fraudulent oracle-expert Onomakritos) is, as usual, exaggerated; intelligence interrogations were magnified, no doubt by them, into consultations on high policy; but Mardonios could point to them as collaborators whose local knowledge and influence could be very useful. He had been in the west and made a study of Greek conditions; and he is represented, probably rightly, as emphasising the internal divisions of the Greeks and the primitive character of Greek strategy (9, 2). In fact, Xerxes probably took little persuading. The enterprise of Europe was planned and led, carefully but with *élan*, by a band of kinsmen, mostly grandsons of Cyrus, under forty years of age.

Xerxes lives in the Greek tradition as the arch-enemy, presented naturally in an unfavourable light. Herodotos, more generous to the enemy than later writers, alone presents him 'in the round'. His Xerxes has the Persian love of natural beauty; he enjoys being munificent on a princely scale; he can forgive surrendered enemies (even those

[1] See list, p. 94.

surrendered in atonement for a 'war crime'); he weeps for compassion over the mortality of mankind. But he is as easily roused to rage by opposition; he is cruel when crossed, even to those lately favoured; he is uncontrolled in lust, and at heart a coward.[2] It is a well-conceived literary portrait: the Character of an Oriental Prince, born of good stock, brought up to rule, but not to tolerate opposition or endure a setback; there may be much truth in it.

On the other hand, in Persian documents we naturally have Xerxes' own self-portrait, or the official account of the Great King. The great palace at Persepolis ('high reared by Jemshyd in Persepolis' – so completely did the Achaemenid name perish among their own people), first planned by Darius, but completed under Xerxes, is now once more our chief material monument to both of them; the palace, where Darius sits in stone, Xerxes behind him in full stature as crown prince, the people before them somewhat smaller; and up the stairs, in skilful and varied relief, endless troop the peoples of the world to do homage: Median and Persian soldiers, spearmen and bowmen, guardsmen of the Ten Thousand Immortals (so-called because in their ranks there was never a vacancy); and among them the Thousand, whose spear-butts were adorned with golden pomegranates,[3] whose commander, called by the Greeks the Chiliarch, was the praetorian prefect of the empire. It is probably he who, bowing over the incense-braziers, is making his report to the king at the top of the stairs. Then come the tribute bringers of all nations from Arabia to the Caucasus, from the Oxus to the western sea; horses and sheep and camels; as it were a pageant of illustrations to the Second Isaiah (or Third Isaiah), in his hopes for Jerusalem:

> The Lord shall arise upon thee, and his glory shall be seen upon thee; and nations shall come to thy light, and kings to the brightness of thy rising. . . . The abundance of the sea shall be turned unto thee; the wealth of the nations shall come unto thee. The multitude of camels shall cover thee, the dromedaries of Midian and Ephah; they shall come from Sheba, bringing gold and frankincense; the flocks of Kedar, the rams of Nabataea . . .

—but the rams and sheep on the stairway are from Phrygia. There is even a reference to the Mediterranean:

[2] vii, 31; 128 (Tempē); 28ff, cf. 38f; 136; 46; 35; ix, 108ff; viii, 103.
[3] H. vii, 41.

> Who are these that fly as a cloud, and as the doves to their windows? Surely the isles shall wait for me, and the ships of Tarshish.[4]

If we had only the archaeological and epigraphic evidence, indeed, we might well take the reign of Xerxes as the golden age of the dynasty; and even among the conventional phrases of imperial self-praise, there is one detail in an inscription of Xerxes which shows that he took his position seriously. As compared with Darius, he tightened up (far from neglecting) the regulation of religion. An inscription from Persepolis, a proclamation from early in his reign, opens:

> A great god is Ahuramazda, who created this earth, who created man, who created peace for man; who made Xerxes king, one king of many, one lord of many.
>
> I am Xerxes the king, king of kings, king of the lands . . . son of Darius the king, the Achaemenian; a Persian, son of a Persian, an Aryan, of Aryan stock. Thus says Xerxes the King:
>
> By the grace of Ahuramazda, these are the lands over which I am king, outside Persia: –

A list follows (cf. p. 111), in which new names are those of the Dahai (apparently meaning literally 'Hostiles'), in later Dahistan, east of the Caspian,[5] and the Akaufaka or Mountain Men (northern Afghanistan?). Then,

> Says Xerxes the King: When I became king, there was one among these lands which was rebellious. Then Ahuramazda brought me aid. By the favour of Ahuramazda, I smote that land.

The rebellious land is presumably Egypt.[6]

Then comes the most interesting part of the inscription:

> Within these lands there were places where formerly the Daevas had been worshipped. Then by the will of Ahuramazda I uprooted

[4] Is. lx, 3–9. [5] Str. xi, 511.

[6] Olmstead puts here a brief rebellion in Bactria, mentioned only by late western writers (Plut. *Sayings*, *Mor.* 173; Justin, ii, 10), said to have been raised by the satrap Ariamenes, X.'s elder half-brother (not of the blood of Cyrus), who, however, submitted and served X. faithfully until killed at Salamis. If the source is Ktesias, as is likely ('obvious', acc. to O., *P.E.* p. 232 n.6), that is almost a reason for not accepting the story; on Kt., cf. pp. 12, 94 above. Ariamenes, not listed among the numerous brothers of X. mentioned by H., seems to be a conflation of Artobazanes, the eldest half-brother, passed over for the succession before the death of Darius (H. vii, 2) and Ariabignes, Artobazanes' full brother (*ib.* 97), kd. at Salamis (H. viii, 89), where Plut. has Ariamenes. Kt. (if it is he) is once more trying unsuccessfully to improve on H.

that cult of the Daevas, and made proclamation: The Daevas shall not be worshipped. Where formerly the Daevas had been worshipped, there did I worship Ahuramazda according to Truth and with the proper rite. Much else that was ill done did I make good. All that I did, I did by the will of Ahuramazda. Ahuramazda brought me aid until I finished my work. Thou who shalt come after me, if thou shalt think, 'May I be happy while alive and blessed when dead', have respect for the law which Ahuramazda has established, and worship Ahuramazda according to Truth and with the proper rite.[7]

Just what cult(s) of 'false gods' Xerxes suppressed we cannot say; but presumably they would have been ranked among those against which Zoroaster had fulminated. Xerxes is not a fully consistent Zoroastrian, any more than Darius, for he does also mention 'other gods', though he names none of them; and Herodotos describes him and the Magi in his train as sacrificing to foreign gods (e.g. at the 'pergamon' of Troy to Athena and the Heroes [treated as Fravashis?], vii, 43). Gods were perhaps judged partly on their record of service or otherwise to the vice-gerent of Ahura-Mazda, the king himself. The Iranian religion, as reformed by Zoroaster, was developing, as Zaehner puts it, from a 'primitive' to a 'catholic' form, and if Xerxes' religion was 'rather "catholic" than "primitive", as we would expect it to be', he might well identify Athena and Thetis with Anaïtis and the Nereids[8] with the water-spirits, 'wives of Ahura Mazda', who figure in the post-Zoroastrian but still early *Gatha of the Seven Chapters*. 'On the other hand, the command to worship Ahura Mazdā "in accordance with Truth and using the proper rite" must refer to some kind of already existing orthodoxy.' 'In spirit, Xerxes is further removed from Zoroaster than was his father, but he seems to have consciously adhered to the later and admittedly distorted form of the Prophet's religion as interpreted to him by the Magi.'[9]

Xerxes took his royal duties seriously, as one might expect of a son of Darius. He was unable to deal with the Greek question at once, on account of the rebellion of Egypt; but when he went there in person, the rebellion was broken in one campaign (485). It had broken out in

[7] The 'Daeva Inscription'; *ed. princ.* E. Herzfeld in *Arch. Mitt. aus Iran*, VIII (1937); *id. Altpers. Inschrn.* no. 14; now = Xerx. Pers. h, in R. G. Kent *Old Persian* (1953). Trn. here after Olmstead, *P.E.* pp. 231f, and Zaehner, *Zoroastrianism*, p. 159.

[8] H. vii, 191.

[9] Zaehner, *Zor.* pp. 159–61.

486; and in January 484, quarrying on behalf of the king was once more proceeding in the Wadi Hammamat. Xerxes 'reduced Egypt to a condition of much more abject slavery than it had known in the time of Darius, and placed it under the rule of his [full] brother Akhaimenes'.[10] It is a fact, fully borne out by the monuments of Egypt, and especially by some eloquent silences, that no such consideration was paid any more to Egyptian culture and customs as had been paid under the liberal rule of Darius. There are no monuments of Xerxes in Egypt. He refused even to take an Egyptian name as Pharaoh, and was officially named, when he had to be, simply 'Khshayarsha, Pharaoh the Great'. The priests of Buto, who had been among the first to preach rebellion and had lost their lands for it, called him, when they dared again long after, 'that villain Xerxes'.[11]

After that, according to Herodotos (vii, 20), 'for four full years the expedition was in preparation' against Greece; but even they were not wholly uninterrupted, for it appears that Babylon, perhaps offended by a change in the royal title (prefixing 'King of Persia and Media' to 'King of Babylon, King of the Lands', in his *Babylonian* style, which gave a hint of greater centralisation), rebelled in 482, rather than later, as most Greek writers thought. But the revolt was crushed as swiftly as that in Egypt, by Megabyxos, one of the six chief marshals, grandson of Megabyxos of the Seven. Babylon was sacked, its chief temples destroyed, its great golden image of Bel-Marduk carried off, probably to be melted down for bullion, the high priest killed when he protested, and estates confiscated throughout the country; in later documents, wide lands in Babylonia are found to be held by Persians.[12]

Babylon, like Egypt, lost its privileges. The destruction of temples now appears as in accordance with Xerxes' religious intolerance, which may indeed have helped to cause the revolt. Xerxes was clearly no nonentity; he was bigoted, formidable, a centraliser, convinced of his own rightness; a hard master.

[10] H. vii, 7; Olmstead, *P.E.* pp. 235f, citing Couyat and Montet, *Inscrs. du Ouadi H.*, nos. 52, 74, 91, 118.

[11] H. R. Hall in *CAH* VI, p. 138.

[12] 482, Olmstead, *P.E.* pp. 236f, after Parker and Dubberstein, *Bab. Chronology*, p. 15. Ktesias, *epit.* 53, appears to be right here, as against, e.g., Arrian vii, 17 (16, in O. p. 237 n. 23, is a slip), who puts the revolt after the war in Greece; as did H. presumably, as he mentions the seizure of the image of 'Zeus', i, 183, but gives no account of the revolt, i.e. puts it after the close of his narrative. Destruction of temples, Arr. iii, 16, vii, 16. Megabyxos at Babylon, Ktes. *ib.*

Even through these events, the preparations against Greece went on, especially one operation, which alone took three years: the digging of a canal through the sandy isthmus of the Mount Athos peninsula, round which Mardonios' fleet had met with disaster ten years before. The forced labour of the Greek colonists and natives of the region was directed by engineers and reinforced by gangs of other workers, sent in relays from Asia; among them the Phoenicians alone are said to have had the foresight to anticipate the landslips from the sides, which occurred as the canal deepened, and to have worked from the first over a great enough breadth to leave the sides at an 'angle of rest'. Meal already ground, Herodotos notes, was sent from Asia for the workers, and sold at a market in the labour-camp; so presumably the workers were paid in money; a hoard of 300 gold darics, found in the area, probably dates from this time. In charge were Artakhaies, a gigantic Achaemenid, and Boubares, who had served in the region earlier under his father Megabazos, and was married to a sister of Alexander, king of Macedonia. It was a rationally conceived though perhaps extravagant operation; but Herodotos, remarking that it would have been much more economical to have the ships dragged over (as at Corinth; he has not thought out what this would mean in delay, in doing it with a large fleet!), opines that Xerxes preferred to leave the canal as a monument of his power. This view, as part of the picture of Xerxes *hübristes*, the megalomaniac, became a commonplace of the rhetoric of all later antiquity.[13]

At the same time, the river Strymōn (Struma) was bridged near its mouth, and great magazines of grain were established on the Thracian coast, both on the western part of the Sea of Marmara (the White Cape, Tyrodiza 'of the Perinthians') and further west, at Doriskos, Ēiōn at the mouth of the Strymon, and further forward at several points in Macedonia.[14] This food was probably not destined only for the army in transit, for it lived as far as possible on the country (and a heavy burden the local Greeks found it). The labour camp itself was supplied from the straits.[15] The magazines were probably destined to be drawn upon, by land from Macedonia and by sea from the coastal

[13] H. viii, 22–4; on Boubares, cf. v, 21; viii, 136. The rhetorical view, cf. Isokr. *Paneg.* 58e; *Anth. Pal.* ix, 304; Juvenal x, 173ff; etc.

[14] H. vii, 25; position of the White Cape, cf. ps.-Skylax, 68.

[15] *ib.* 118, 22, 1.

depots, for feeding the troops further forward, in hostile country, where local supplies might have been removed or destroyed.

The food probably included large quantities of salt meat as well as grain (*sitia*, Herodotos' word); for the Medes and Persians, great cattle-keepers at home, were not, like the Greeks, principally bread-eaters. We have, from Theopompos, a vivid description of the 'dumps' of a later Persian army, prepared for Artaxerxes III's invasion of Egypt; the writer emphasises the piles of luxury tents and beds and table utensils for the king and his suite, but continues: 'tens of thousands of stand of arms, both Greek and oriental; vast herds of baggage-animals and beasts for slaughter; bushels of condiments, and boxes and sacks, and bales of paper and all the other accessories. And there was so much salt meat of every kind, that it made heaps, so large that people approaching from a distance thought they were coming to a range of hills.' [16] The mention of paper among important stores will be found evocative by anyone who has been initiated into the mysteries of a modern military base. Bureaucracy may have grown more virulent in the 130 years since Xerxes' expedition; but Xerxes' preparations, and the vast quantities of engineers' and quartermaster's stores which had to be handled in the process, not only by Medes and Persians but by Lydians, Babylonians and every nation of the Levant, certainly must have given scope for it. The mounting of this great imperial frontier operation was, indeed, an operation much more 'modern' than anything which the Greeks, with their small states and small armies, had ever yet undertaken or needed to undertake.

Preparations were also being made for the most famous of Xerxes' works: the great twin bridges over the Narrows of the Hellespont, from Abydos to a point near Sestos; a work mocked, like the canal, by later writers, but in fact entirely practical, to eliminate the time-devouring process of embarking and disembarking an army of perhaps 200,000 men, with relatively few wagons but a great number of horses, mules and camels, in the boats of the time. They were floating bridges, supported on hundreds of triremes and pentekonters (the immense building activity of recent years had left plenty available, especially of the latter; for it is probable that the building programme, in the east as

[16] Theopompos (fr. 125 M.; 115 F 263, J), in Longinus, *On Style*, 43, 2; partly also in Ath. ii, p. 67. Cf. de Joinville on St Louis' dumps prepared in Cyprus for his Egyptian crusade, 'looking like large houses' and 'like mountains' (*Mémoires*, Part ii).

at Athens, had been very largely a matter of replacing existing fleets by the latest ships of war). The preparations included the manufacture of huge cables, of *leukolinon* ('white flax'; but would this be strong enough? – perhaps really esparto-grass?) and of papyrus fibre, respectively in Phoenicia and Egypt; 'they were both of equal thickness and beauty, but the linen one was heavier, weighing a talent per cubit'. As this, even in Babylonian talents, equals a hundredweight or 40 Kg. per yard, and as the bridges must have been about a mile long, the total weight of the heavier cables would have been, allowing for securing them at each end, close on 100 tons;[17] probably tradition has exaggerated the weight; probably also they were floated up to the Hellespont on rafts, awash, hoisted up in sections, successively, on to moored ships, and then themselves anchored 'upstream'; for the straits, receiving water from the Black Sea, which receives water from the Danube and the great Russian rivers, and issuing into the sun-evaporated Mediterranean, has a current which, especially in the Narrows, can run at several knots. Other anchors (both series are described as 'of great length' – again perhaps equipment specially manufactured) were dropped on the other side, against the possible south-westerly gales. On each bridge were laid two of the heavy and four papyrus cables; 360 ships formed the north-eastern bridge, which was set at an angle, 'to ease the strain on the cables', and 314 the other; each ship thus carried perhaps 15 cwt. of cable. At certain points sections of the bridge could be towed out and brought back again, to allow small ships to pass; presumably unstepping their masts and slipping through under the cables. A continuous roadway of planks was laid upon the cables, brushwood and earth strewn upon that, and side-screens fitted, so that the thousands of animals which had to cross might not take fright at the change of sound or at sight of the water.

This notable feat of engineering was not completed without mishap. Just when the bridges were to be used, a gale wrecked both of them; on which occasion, Xerxes is said to have executed those chiefly responsible, and ordered the straits to be scourged, branded and 'fettered', the fetters being thrown into them; which, as a symbolic or magical act, does not seem *a priori* impossible. It would not, it has recently been

[17] H. vii, 25, 1; 36, 2. If the cables were made in sections as some commentators have supposed, i.e. if there were not really two main cables but two series of cables, the advantage of special strength would not have been gained.

pointed out, necessarily be contrary to Xerxes' particular brand of Zoroastrianism to treat the 'bitter water' so, since brackish or undrinkable water is actually said (in a later text) to be so, because it has been defiled by the Evil One. An engineer named Harpalos (a Greek name) is recorded as responsible, presumably for the restored and successful bridges.[18]

Xerxes moved out from Sousa, probably in the spring of 481; an eclipse of the sun, said to have occurred just as he was starting (from Sardis in 480, according to Herodotos; but no such eclipse can be computed by astronomers), is perhaps to be identified as that of April 10th, 481; the Magi are said to have cheered him with the explanation that the sun typified the Greeks, and the moon, the Persians (had they learned from Babylon that the moon is the eclipsing body?).[19] He proceeded to Kritalla in Cappadocia, where the army was assembling, presumably to give the mobilisation his personal attention, and moved on in the autumn, to spend the winter in the milder climate of Sardis. From Sardis he also despatched heralds to the states of Greece with his formal summons to surrender; but not to Athens or Sparta; they had placed themselves beyond the pale of diplomatic correspondence, 'for when Darius sent men on the same errand, they had thrown them respectively into the Pit' [for condemned criminals, at Athens] 'and into a well, and told them to get earth and water from there for their king'.[20] The stories are too symmetrical not to arouse suspicion; perhaps the Athenian part is an embellishment; but that the Spartans had slain Darius' heralds is confirmed by the story that later, when in trouble, the Spartans attributed it to the wrath of Talthybios, the herald of Agamemnon and patron hero of the profession, and that two Spartans volunteered to go and surrender themselves to Xerxes, to die in expiation. On the way, says the story, these Spartans lodged with Hydarnes, commander of the Persian Guards in 480, and then General of the Coast Men (cf. p. 136) in Asia Minor. Hydarnes, finding his respect for the Spartans once more reinforced, said to them after dinner, 'Why do you Spartans refuse to be friends of the king? You see from my fortune that he knows how to honour good men.' But the Spartans answered, 'Hydarnes, you know what it is to be a servant, but you do

[18] H. vii, 34–6; Zaehner, *Zoroastrianism*, p. 160; cf. *Teachings of the Magi*, 47 (*Greater Bundahishn*); Harpalos, Diels, *Laterculi Alexandrini* in *Abh. Berl. Akad.*, 1904.

[19] H. vii, 37; Meyer, *GdA*³ IV, i, p. 333 n. 3, after Judeich.

[20] H. vii, 37, 133.

not know freedom; if you did, you would advise us to fight for it, not only with spears but with axes.' So they went on to Sousa, where they refused to bow down before the king, and declared their errand; and Xerxes, in generous mood, said that he would show himself a better man than they, who had offended against the common law of mankind in killing heralds, and let them go free; and the wrath of Talthybios was stayed for the time, although the men, Sperchieus and Boulis, came home alive.[21] At Sardis also, Greek spies were caught in the camp; and Xerxes is said to have ordered that they should be conducted round it and sent home safe, reckoning that the moral effect of a full report on his army would be all in his favour.[22]

After all his preparations, there can be no doubt that Xerxes took to Greece the largest possible army. He knew very well that if Greeks fought they were tough. He knew too, from the exiles, that many Greek states, even many individuals, were in two minds about whether to fight. The more formidable the Persian appeared, the more Greeks would be cowed into early if not immediate surrender; and the less formidable he appeared, the more Greeks would fight. In any case, the mere fact that the king was going in person to extend the boundaries of his empire implies a major expedition. It was important to Xerxes, not only to settle the Greek problem, but to show himself, in the eyes of his people and in his own, a worthy successor of Cyrus, Cambyses and Darius.

To the Greeks, in whose language 'myriads', tens of thousands, stood for 'countless numbers', as we use loosely millions or billions, the host was quite literally innumerable. The contemporary estimates are the largest. A war-memorial inscription in the pass of Thermopylai said, in good Laconic lapidary style:

> Against three million men fought in this place
> Four thousand Peloponnesians, face to face.[23]

Aeschylus, who was present at Salamis, numbers Xerxes' fleet at a round thousand, either inclusive or exclusive of 207 'of special swiftness'.[24] To Herodotos, these figures were sacred, part of the tradition of the heroic story, and he worked hard to get the detailed information, which he had collected, reconciled to them.

Herodotos' detailed information is considerable, and of great interest.

[21] H. vii, 134ff.
[22] *ib.* 146.
[23] Anon., *ap.* H. vii, 228.
[24] *Persians*, 341ff.

He enumerates 46 nations (for the list see Appendix to chap. VI), giving details of their arms, with minor contingents grouped two or more together, under thirty Persian generals, over whom are the six chief marshals, five of them sons of the royal house or of the Seven. They are named (vii, 82):

Mardonios, son of Gobryas [and brother-in-law of the King, vi, 43];
Tritantaikhmes, son of Artabanos who advised against the invasion, and Smerdomenes the son of Otanes; both nephews of Darius;
Masistes, son of Darius and Atossa [Xerxes' full brother];
Gergis, son of Ariazos;
Megabyzos, son of Zopyros.

Megabyzos (or, better, Megabyxos) is thus grandson of Megabyxos of the Seven (cf. above, p. 13). Still active in 454 (p. 560), he is probably the youngest of the marshals (they seem to be in an order of seniority) while his grandfather must have been middle-aged at the time of the Conspiracy. His father Zopyros had held a command under Darius, while his son, another Zopyros, 'who came over from Persia to Athens' (*ib.*) may have been the source of Herodotos' remarkable list of the contingents. Gergis, of whom we know no more, appears as a lone 'commoner' among these grandees (was he the indispensable master of detail, Adjutant- and Quartermaster-General?). It is in any case interesting that one from outside the circle of the Seven Houses can rise so high.

Royal princes and sons of the Seven are also prominent among the thirty infantry generals, especially those commanding the central core of the army, the contingents from Iran. The Persian Guards are under Hydarnes, son of Hydarnes, taking orders directly from the king and not from a marshal.[25] Among the first three 'line' or territorial contingents mentioned, which alone had the Persian 'fish-scale' body-armour, the first (Persian) is under another Otanes, father of Xerxes' formidable queen, Amēstris; the second (Medes) under Tigranes, 'an Achaemenid'; the third, Kissians (Sousiana) under Anaphes, son of Otanes (which Otanes? – the name was evidently common).[26] The

[25] H. vii, 83, 1.
[26] Ktes. (45/14) has an 'Onophas' (Anaphes) among the Seven; he sometimes confuses fathers and sons, cf. p. 12.

sixth, Bactrians and Sakai, the troops from the north-eastern frontier, a very important command, are under the king's full brother Hystaspes; the eighth, the men of Aria, under Sisamnes, son of Hydarnes (brother of Hydarnes II?). Along with these figure two 'commoners'; and both prove to be hand-picked officers, whose subsequent careers show that they justified their promotion: the fourth (Hyrcanian) contingent was under Megapanos, afterwards satrap of Babylon, and the ninth, Parthian and Chorasmian, under Artabazos, son of Pharnakes, who became the empire's chief expert on western affairs and founded a remarkable family. He remained in Greece with Mardonios for the second campaign, extricated his corps from the wreck, and was subsequently sent back to the west, superseding an Achaemenid prince as satrap of Phrygia, to conduct the delicate negotiations with Pausanias of Sparta in 477–6. He even managed to pass on the satrapy to his son, Pharnabazos; and there they stayed, as it were hereditary Margraves, playing a not discreditable part in history in every generation of the fifth and fourth centuries.[27]

Other sons of Darius have outlying commands: Akhaimenes, his second son by Atossa and viceroy of Egypt, joined the expedition at the head of the powerful Egyptian fleet; Ariabignes, one of the older half-brothers, commanded the fleets of Ionia and Karia; Arsamenes the infantry of the Outioi and Mükoi (southern Iran); Gobryas, son of Darius and Artystōne, the younger daughter of Cyrus, 'whom Darius loved most of all his wives, and had a golden statue made of her', the Cappadocians (famous cavalry later, but here they are recorded only as infantry); and Xerxes' full brother Arsāmes, two picturesque contingents from southern frontiers, an Arab camel corps, and 'the Ethiopians from beyond Egypt', with spearheads made of gazelle horn, bows of the midribs of palm leaves and stone-headed arrows, and clubs; 'they painted themselves half white and half red before going into battle'. It has usually been doubted whether Xerxes would really have brought with him such savages, whose military value would hardly be worth their food; but the mention of a young prince of the blood as commanding them sounds rather as if some, at least, of them actually served. Did young Arsames clamour to bring 'my Sudanese'?[28]

[27] H. vii, 61–6; on Artabazos, cf. below, pp. 497f, 539f, 560; Thk. i, 129, 1; and for his descendants, see the family names (esp. Artabazos, Pharnabazos) in *PW* or in Olmstead, *P.E.*

[28] *ib.* 97; 73; 68f.

Ariomardos, son of Darius by Smerdis' daughter, commanded the Moschoi and Tibarēnoi, 'Meshech and Tubal', from the Caucasus, with wooden helmets, targets and short spears 'with large heads'; the Phrygians, with high boots and fairly similar armament, were under a son-in-law of Darius; the Lydians, heavily armed in the manner which the Greeks had adopted, under Artaphernes, the king's cousin, who had been at Marathon. With them were light-armed Mysians, with only targets and sharpened stakes. The Ionians were not under his command, being assigned to the fleet; no people which could provide ships was also represented in the land army.[29]

Cavalry, numbered at the relatively modest figure of 80,000 (not impossible, if an estimate for the whole potential force of the empire), were provided exclusively by Iran and the east, among them the 8000 Sagartians with lassoos, the only people recorded as providing cavalry but no infantry; and we are also told of chariots from India (some drawn by 'wild asses' – jagatais?) and others from Libya west of Egypt. Of three cavalry generals two are 'sons of Datis'; very likely, though we are not told so, the Datis of the Marathon expedition.[30]

Doubts have been expressed, as above mentioned, as to whether some of the more ill-armed and outlandish contingents described would really have been called upon for this carefully prepared expedition; but we can hardly dismiss the possibility. When a prince is described as commanding the stone-age warriors from Africa, we have only three possibilities. Either some Ethiopians served; or the young prince was content to be left behind (which is scarcely credible); or the list of commanders and contingents, so detailed and as a rule so convincing, is unreliable and we really know nothing about the matter. It seems to have been a Persian principle that when the king went, all must go; as under Darius (p. 119), it was death even to apply for exemption;[31] and we hear even of a contingent, 29th and last in the infantry list (the Guards being *extra ordinem*), of the Anaspastoi, the Deportees in the islands of the Persian Gulf. Obviously it would be uneconomic to try to take along the whole man-power of the empire (though this was what the Greeks, accustomed to the *levée-en-masse* of their small states, actually thought).[32] But it would not be surprising if every people was expected to be represented; in what strength would be a matter of

[29] *ib.* 73f, 78.
[30] *ib.* 84–7, 1.
[31] *ib.* 38ff.
[32] Aesch. *Pers.* 117–39.

royal policy, administered by the recruiting officers, who were probably also the commanders. On Trajan's column we see, besides Roman legionaries, some very wild-looking 'allies'; tribesmen, stripped to their trousers, armed only with clubs and stones to throw. (Are they Britons?) Herodotos describes, following the baggage train, which marched first out of Sardis, a horde 'of all manner of nations mixed up', and finally, marching in superb order, the horse and foot of the Persian Immortals.[33] It looks as if here he has described (perhaps been told of) only the best-disciplined and most undisciplined troops, and omitted the Iranian, Assyrian, Cappadocian and Lydian divisions, whose order, if inferior to that of the Guards, was probably more like theirs than like the disorder of the outland tribes; whom, nevertheless, Xerxes may have taken with him in whatever he considered suitable numbers, as light troops, plunderers, expendable without thought, possibly useful in the battle in a plain which (Mardonios had told him) the Greeks regularly fought, instead of 'looking for the most difficult places',[34] and possibly terrifying.

This brings us to the question of numbers. There is an attractive theory, based on the existence of the thirty infantry commanders, of whom Hydarnes commands the 10,000 Immortals, but others, according to Herodotos, army corps of 60,000 each.[35] He explicitly says that he could obtain no figures for the different contingents (perhaps they were, as at Sparta, a well-kept secret); but he does allege that the whole army numbered 1,700,000 infantry ($29 \times 60,000 + 10,000 = 1,750,000$). To this he adds the 80,000 cavalry, 20,000 for the camel-corps and chariots, 300,000 for the Thracians and Greeks picked up in Europe (this might be tolerable as a guess at the whole manpower of the Balkan Peninsula), and figures for the fleet, which he computes as follows (here his estimates of *average crews* are interesting and significant; the number of ships is another matter):

1207 triremes from Asia, at 200 men per crew	241,400
Marines (Persian, Median and Saka), 30 per ship	36,210
3000 (estimate) pentekonters, etc., at 80 per crew	240,000
120 triremes from Greek colonies in Thrace and Black Sea, at 200 per crew	24,000
Total estimated manpower of fleet	541,610

[33] vii, 40f. [34] *ib.* 9. [35] Artabazos (viii, 126); Tigranes (ix, 96).

Adding this to his 2,100,000 for the army, and finding himself still short of the war-memorial's three million, he cheerfully doubles the whole total to allow for non-combatants (cooks, drivers, women – the Guards are recorded to have brought their women along in wagons) and reaches a grand total of 5,283,220. The most remarkable thing, he adds with a descent into realism, is how such a multitude was fed.[36]

But suppose, says the theory, that *all* the 30 named divisional generals were really, like Hydarnes, *myriarchs*; for we are indeed told that the army was organised on a decimal system, up to divisions of 10,000 or *myriads*; the myriarchs being appointed by the commanders of higher formations (whom we shall then identify with the Six; a General Staff?) and the commanders of thousands, hundreds and tens[37] by the myriarchs. Then we get a figure of 300,000 infantry, a number not unreasonable if supposed to be an establishment for the whole army; and if this figure is supposed to be divided into six corps, and to each 50,000 is added a myriad of cavalry, we are provided with a command of 60,000 for each of the six marshals. But Xerxes would not have taken the whole army with him oversea; and in Thrace, we hear of his host moving in three columns, each commanded by two of the Six.[38] It is thus suggested that Xerxes in fact took three of his presumed six army corps, perhaps reinforced with units from all corners of the empire; in all, a force of the order of 200,000 men.[39]

There is one difficulty about this theory, which does not seem to have been recognised; it is that if all the thirty named divisional generals had commands of the same size, then Media, for example, or Bactria *plus* the Saka (Herodotos mentions both their 'pointed caps' and the name Amyrgian, while assigning them to the same people, vii, 64) produce only one contingent apiece, of the same size as that of the Ethiopians and Arabs under Arsames or the 29th contingent, the deportees from the islands; while eight tribes of Kolchis and the Caucasus produce four commands (the 25th to 28th; *ib.* 78f). It does not seem possible that all the thirty commands really were of the same size, and if so, the basis of calculation for this theory collapses. The infantry contingents from

36 vii, 184–7.

37 In Turkish, *bimbáshi, yuzbáshi, onbáshi;* terms still familiar in the succession states of the Turkish Empire.

38 H. vii, 121, 3.

39 The theory worked out by J. A. R. Munro in *JHS* XXII; cf. Macan, *Hdt. VII–IX*, vol. II, pp. 158ff; followed 'with confidence' by How (*Comm.* II, p. 367 n. 1).

Iran, fairly uniformly armed with bow, short spear and large wicker shield, must surely have been much larger, as well as more disciplined, than those from the remoter regions. An analogy once more suggests itself with a Roman imperial army, in which the citizen legions are accompanied by an often roughly equal number of 'allies', more lightly armed, organized only in smaller units, and considered expendable;[40] and the light infantry further includes, in an Antonine army, both cohorts, well drilled and with a century or more of regimental history, and irregular *numeri* like the club-bearers of Trajan's column, little more than savages.

There is, however, an entirely independent consideration which also leads to the conclusion that 200,000 is about the limit for the total man-power of the expedition. Curiously enough, it is derived from that one of all Herodotos' details which, duly exaggerated by the later writers, has been most generally considered fabulous: that the great army 'drank rivers dry'. Herodotos, let it be said in justice to him, does not say this, but merely asks, in one of his rare rhetorical passages (vii, 21), 'What water did not fail them for drinking, except that of the great rivers?' It was left for a professional soldier, General Sir Frederick Maurice, after going, Herodotos in hand, over the little-explored Hellespontine section of Xerxes' route at a time when political conditions for once made free movement possible there, to show how very apposite are Herodotos' comments on the difficulties of water supply for a large army on that route in summer.[41]

Herodotos in fact says that rivers failed to supply the needs of men and animals, i.e. that the expedition suffered seriously from thirst at three points: on the Skamandros in the Troad; at the river Melas (whence the Black Gulf, north of the Gallipoli Peninsula, took its name), and at the river Lisos, between Doriskos and the Thasian colony of Stryme.[42] There is every reason to think that he derived

[40] Cf. Tac. *Agricola*, 35, 2.

[41] F. Maurice, 'The Size of the Army of Xerxes', in *JHS* L (1930). Some of his detailed suggestions on the size and organization of the army are (as he agrees, p. 227, after discussion with Munro) speculative; no conclusions on the subject can avoid this. But his application of British military experience in the moving of armies with animal transport to the narrative of H. added something of permanent value to the evidence. His suggestion of a maximum of 210,000 men with some 75,000 animals, or some 150,000 combatant troops, also marks a reaction from the 19th-cent. German military criticism of Delbrück (*Die Perserkriege und die Burgunderkriege*) which suggested reducing Xerxes' army to 65,000–75,000 combatants.

[42] vii, 43, 58, 108.

these details from a genuine account of the march. Seven days, Maurice considered, would not be an unreasonable time for the crossing of the two bridges by some 210,000 men and 75,000 beasts including the transport; use of the lash, as stated by Herodotos (vii, 56), might well have been necessary, at least on the animals, especially at the exits from the bridges, to keep the column moving and prevent congestion at the beginning of the long and rough defile leading thence past Kallipolis (Gallipoli) to the Melas; and for this stage the army would have to carry water with it. A British army report of 1920 records here 'Water supplies *nil*, except at Gallipoli'. For the same reason – the problem of water supply, even more than of space – it is out of the question that the whole army of 200,000 men, let alone two million, would or could have been concentrated for a review at Abydos (Chanak) before the crossing; though, that Xerxes watched some part of the crossing and some manœuvres by part of the fleet is probable enough.[43]

At Doriskos, on the other hand, the fort founded by Darius in 512 at the mouth of the great river Hebros, there may well have been such a halt as Herodotos describes, to refresh the army after the trying stages – 134 miles, at least seven thirsty marches – from the Skamandros. Here a food depot had been prepared (p. 318), and there would be ample grazing for the animals, spreading out for miles along the river. Herodotos has a childish story that here the infantry were 'counted' and found to number 1,700,000, by herding them successively into an enclosure built to hold 10,000; but that there was numbering, perhaps as the units marched through successively to draw rations for several days at the depot, is not unlikely. They are also said to have been 'divided by nations' here. That there was some reorganization at this point, before the final advance towards enemy country, seems not unreasonable. Maurice suggested a division into 29 commands in addition to the Immortals, as stated by Herodotos, but that these were brigades of 3000 to 5000, rather than myriads as suggested by Munro.[44] It may be tentatively suggested that at this point the Iranian contingents, some of which *may* have been of myriad strength, *may* have had smaller forces of 'expendable' barbarians attached to them, like *auxilia* to Roman legions. In the battles on land, as will be seen hereinafter, we have no trace of any troops but Iranians.

[43] H. vii, 44; Maurice, pp. 229ff. and 223 n. 36.

[44] Maurice, pp. 226f.

The Greek writers were well aware, though they do not say much about it, that the strength of an expedition is limited to the number of troops that can be 'delivered' on a fighting front, and fed there; not the number that can be recruited. Herodotos puts an explicit discussion of the dangers of a commissariat breakdown into a conversation, which he stages at this point, between Xerxes and his uncle Artabanos, who is thereafter sent home; Xerxes answers that the expedition was both carrying food with it and might expect to find more in Greece, since they would be invading cultivated country (vii, 50, 4). And Thucydides makes a speaker say, *à propos* of the Athenian expedition to Sicily: 'It is rare for a large expedition, either Greek or barbarian, to be victorious at a great distance from its own land. They do not outnumber the inhabitants of the invaded country and their neighbours, who are all terrorised into uniting; and if they meet with disaster in a foreign country through failure of supplies, their defeat redounds to the glory of those whom they attacked, even though the breakdown may have been mostly their own fault. This is exactly what has happened to these Athenians, who, because the Persians met with a complete and unexpected failure, have profited from the mere fame of the fact that they were marching on Athens.'[45]

For Xerxes' fleet, unlike the army, Herodotos does give strengths (numbers of triremes) for separate contingents; as follows (vii, 89 ff):

From Phoenicia	300	the largest and finest contingent
,, Egypt	200	with formidable heavy-armed marines
,, Cyprus	150	the equipment mostly Greek
,, Cilicia	100	the men more lightly armed
,, Pamphylia	30	the marines armed as Greeks
,, Lykia	50	the marines wearing feather crowns [like the Philistines of 700 years before] and armour
,, Karia	70	the marines armed as Greeks
Greeks of Asia	290	of whom Ionians 100, Dorians 30, Aiolians 60, Hellespontines 100
From the Cyclades	17	
Total	1207	

[45] Hermokrates of Syracuse, acc. to Thk. vi, 33, 5f. (It would appear that he at least did not believe that the Persian army ran into millions, or even to the 800,000 of D.S. (xi, 3) or Ktesias (23/54).) Cf. also Aesch. *Persians*, 792ff.

– to which are later added (ch. 185, 1) an (estimated) 120 triremes from the Greek colonies in Thrace and adjacent islands. Herodotos tells us when is he merely estimating, or guessing; therefore, for these detailed figures, he believed that he had something to go on, apart from wishing to equal the figures given by Aeschylus, who probably really included the 207 'fast' ships in his total of 1000. It may be suggested that tqe figures are probably genuinely derived from Greek intelligence reports. Numbers of ships, in ports with which the Greeks were familiar (for trade continued with Syria, straight through the war period, without any intermission long enough to interrupt the pottery-series), would not be so easy to keep secret as the numbers of men in contingents; and I would suggest that Greek intelligence probably did collect figures both of the recent naval strengths of the Levant communities, and of their building potential, which had recently been fully employed.

Nevertheless, the figures almost certainly are far too high.[46] It has often been observed that, having built up the fleet to a strength double that of a normal Persian armada (as for Scythia, Lade, Marathon[47]), Herodotos (or, according to Herodotos, God) seems to be at pains to bring it down again by means of storm losses, to 'not many more than the Greeks'.[48] The storm losses may well have been severe, but 400 triremes in a night (not 400 craft of all types, for the victuallers and small craft 'without number' are in the next paragraph)[49] – this is severe indeed! With 200 more 'written off' in another storm (viii, 13), the Grand Fleet is down to about 600 (720 minus losses in battle), and unable to detach a large squadron for independent operations against the Peloponnese without risking losing its superiority at the main point of contact.[50] In short, the Persian fleet, like their army at Marathon, *does not behave as if* it had crushing superiority. As to how the Persian numbers, if based on genuine material, could come to be grossly exaggerated, it may be suggested that raw material was preserved (figures of standing navies, figures of new building), and that, whether or not the Greek high command (or Themistokles) were under the illusion that all these ships could be manned and put into commission at the same time, men of letters after the war, from Aeschylus onward, were delighted to feel justified in saying that they had fought, at sea as

[46] Though accepted by Mr Hammond (*HG*, p. 229), unwilling as always to believe that an ancient source is wrong.

[47] H. iv, 87; vi, 9, 94.

[48] H. viii, 13.

[49] H. vii, 190f.

[50] *ib.* 236.

on land, against overwhelming odds. Adding what they learned of new building to the figures for long-standing Levantine navies, the Greeks may very well have obtained totals, region by region, very much like those of Herodotos; while no allowance was made, probably, for scrapping of old ships, nor was the question asked, or at least examined, how many *crews* could be first raised and trained in Asia and then fed off Greece. In like manner in dealing with the accessions of naval strength from Greek colonies in Thrace, Herodotos' figure of 120 is not impossible; Thasos alone could raise more than 30.[51] What is doubtful is whether anything like that number was actually raised. The figures quoted for the minor contingents on the Greek nationalist side (pp. 383, 385), which are probably accurate, are miserable by comparison. The reason is that the latter are real strengths, whereas the former are *estimates* of what Greek Thrace, Asia Minor, Cyprus, Egypt and Phoenicia could produce if every state made an all-out effort and nothing went wrong. From sheer inexperience, the Greek naval intelligence probably did exaggerate. It is not entirely unknown even nowadays for the same convoy, counted and reported by several sources, to become several convoys; and what could happen in the way of over-estimating enemy forces one hundred years ago in the United States is known to every student of the campaigns of General McClellan.[52]

The figures for naval contingents, then, are not unreasonable, if taken as estimates of the number of triremes which the whole Levant conceivably could have produced; and yet, the Persian fleet in face of the enemy does not behave as if it were 1000 strong, including, in the Phoenicians, the most skilful sailors in the world. A solution to the problem is here suggested; and among other deductions that ought to have been made is probably that of a not inconsiderable number of old triremes (as well as pentekonters) among the 674 old warships required for the Hellespont bridges.

[51] Plut. *Kim.* 14.

[52] E.g., Northern reports as late as July 3, 1862, were still estimating the Confederates before Richmond at 185,000; see *The Times*, 16/7/1862 (reprinted, 16/7/1962).

ADDITIONAL NOTE TO CHAPTER XVI

MEMBERS AND CONNECTIONS OF THE ACHAEMENID FAMILY IN XERXES' ARMY

Eleven sons of Darius took part in the Greek expedition, and three were killed in it.

The relationships of a polygamous and inter-married royal family and aristocracy do not lend themselves to presentation in the form of a *stemma*. E.g. when Mardonios married Darius' daughter, he acquired three brothers-in-law who were also his nephews, but probably older than he was. (Darius' three elder sons by the daughter of Gobryas were born before 522 (H. vii, 2); while M. himself, newly married and young for high command in 493, the son of Gobryas by Darius' sister (H. vi, 43; vii, 5), is probably the offspring of a dynastic marriage contracted about 520.) But a list of known and probable members of the House of Akhaimenes figuring in the military hierarchy gives a vivid picture of the band, largely of kinsmen, that led the expedition.

References are to H. vii, unless otherwise stated.

A. *Sons of Darius by Atossa, daughter of Cyrus:*

XERXES.
AKHAIMENES, Satrap of Egypt, 7; comd. Egyptian fleet, 97.
MASISTES, Marshal, 82; Satrap of Bactria, ix, 107.
HYSTASPES, comd. (6th) Bactrian and Saka inf., 64.

B. *Other sons of Darius:*

(1) by daughter of Gobryas, born before 522

ARTOBAZANES, sometime claimant to the throne, 2; not employed.
ARIABIGNES, comd. Ionian and Karian naval squadrons, 97; killed at Salamis.
(?)ARSAMENES, comd. (14th) Outian and Maka inf., 68. (Mother not stated; but probably the third of this family, see ch. 2.)

(2) by Artystone, younger daughter of Cyrus

ARSAMES, comd. (17th) Arab and Ethiopian inf., 69.
GOBRYAS, comd. (20th) Cappadocian inf., 72.

(3) by Parmys, daughter of Smerdis

ARIOMARDOS, comd. (25th) Tibarenian and Moschian inf., 78.

(4) by Phratagoune, daughter of his brother Artanes (see below)

ABROKOMAS and HYPERANTHES, junior officers, both killed at Thermopylai, 224.

C. *Sons of Darius' brothers:*

TRITANTAIKHMES, 'son of Artabanos who advised against invading Greece', 2nd Marshal, 82; considered faint-hearted, viii, 26.

(?)ARTYPHIOS, son of Artabanos, comd. (10th) Gandara inf., 66.

(?)ARIOMARDOS, 'brother of Artyphios', comd. (11th) Caspian inf., 67.

(?)BASSAKES, son of Artabanos, comd. (23rd) Thracians of Asia Minor, 75. H. does not say that this is the same Artabanos, as he does in 82. The identifications can only be considered 'not unlikely'. Macan accepts them (*ad locc.*) with an 'apparently' at 82.

ARTAPHERNES (or Artaphrenes), son of D.'s half-brother Artaphernes, prominent in H. v, 25 to vi, 42; in Marathon campaign, vi, 94, 119; comd. (22nd) Lydian and Mysian inf., 74.

Another brother of D., Artanes, had died leaving the king his property and his only child, Phratagoune, whom D. married; her two sons (too young for high command?) fell at Thermopylai; cf. B (4) above.

D. *Sons of Darius' sisters by others of the 'Seven':*

MARDONIOS, son of Gobryas, first Marshal, 82; nephew to D., 5; also brother-in-law, cf. B(1), and son-in-law, vi, 42.

SMERDOMENES, son of Otanes, third Marshal, 82.

E. *Son-in-law of Darius:*

ARTOKHMES, comd. (21st) Phrygian and Armenian inf., 73.

F. *Father-in-law of Xerxes:*

OTANES, father of the queen Amestris, comd. (1st) Persian 'line' inf., 61. (Macan says that from the relationship 'it may be argued that he is identical with O. . . . of the Seven'. But this would make him serve in a rank junior to his son, the marshal

Smerdomenes; and equal to that of Ariomardos (B, 3), who could be his great-grandson!

G. *Brother of Amestris* (?)

(?)ANAPHES, comd. (3rd) Kissian (Sousiana) inf., 62; 'son of Otanes', very likely the last Otanes mentioned (cf. the method of referring to the sons of Artabanos, 66–7; (C) above.

H. *Other Achaemenidai:*

TIGRANES, 'an Achaemenid', comd. (2nd) Median inf., 62; comd. land forces at Mykale and fell there, ix, 96, 102. His parents are not specified in any of these places; which is against acceptance of the *v.l.* which makes him (instead of Tritantaikhmes, see (C) above) the son of Artabanos who expressed dismay on hearing of the 'crown of wild olive', viii, 26.

(?)MEGABAZOS, son of Megabates, one of the four admirals, 97; if, as seems likely though it is not stated, his father is the cousin of Darius for whom Artaphernes the elder asked, to command the fleet for Naxos (v, 32). This same Megabates is probably the satrap at Daskyleion *c.* 477, where Pausanias the Spartan asked for the hand of his daughter (H., *ib.*); later he seems to have 'raised his sights' and asked for a daughter of the king (Thk. i, 126); and at this point Megabates, now elderly, was superseded by the sagacious Artabazos (q.v., index). Megabates, it may be noted, does not command the troops of his satrapy (Phrygia).

The same Megabazos might be the king's agent in Greece, *c.* 456 (Thk. i, 109).

(The OCT index to H. is for once in confusion *s.v.* Megabazos. All the references except vii, 67, 97, and perhaps vi, 33, should go to M. the trusted servant of Darius, comd. in Thrace (iv, 143ff; v, 1–26), and his son Boubares (v. 21; vii, 22; viii, 136). They may well have been related, especially if Oibares 'son of M.', satrap at Daskyleion in 494, is son of the only Megabazos so far mentioned (vi, 33).

Pherendates, son of Megabazos, comd. (12th) Sarangian (Drangiana) inf., 67, *may* be a son of M. of Thrace, and *may* also be identical with the general killed at the Eurymedon *c.* 467 (Plut. *Kim.* 12, cf. Ephoros papyrus fr., J 70 F 191). But Macan's 'would seem to be a brother of Boubares' is again too confident.

Similarly, all the following are *probably* Achaemenids, and *perhaps* all more closely related, within one branch of the clan; but Macan's notes *ad locc.* seem over-confident here too:

ARTAKHAIES, son of Artaios, an Achaemenid, supervised construction of the canal, with Boubares, 22, and died there, 117.

(?)AZANES, son of (the same?) Artaios, comd. (10th) Sogdiana inf., 66.

(?)OTASPES, son of (the same?) Artakhaies, comd. (5th) Assyrian inf., 63.

(?)ARTAŸNTES, son of Ithamitres, comd. (13th) Paktyan (Pakhtunistan?) inf., 67.

(?)ARTAŸNTES, son of Artakhaies, previously unrecorded (exceptionally among the officers named in H. viii, ix), is reported in joint command of the fleet at Mykale in 479, and appoints as a third commander his nephew, another ITHAMITRES (viii, 130). Macan, *ad loc.*, makes this Artaÿntes 'no doubt' son of the giant of the canal, and his nephew 'presumably' son of Otaspes. Nothing, indeed, would be easier than to construct a *stemma*, thus:

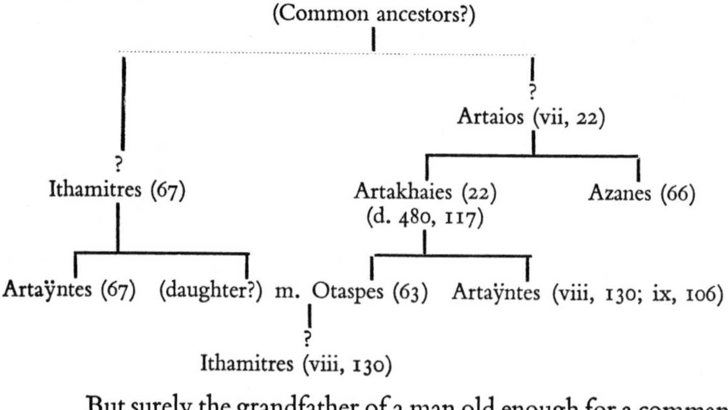

But surely the grandfather of a man old enough for a command in 479, even with the help of nepotism, must have been too old to be roaring at the labour-gangs on the canal in 482–480? If Artaÿntes, who survived at Mykale when the Achaemenid Tigranes (H., above) was killed, was himself an Achaemenid, it helps to account for his daring to draw his sword on the marshal Masistes, the king's brother, when taunted with cowardice. But beyond this we cannot safely go.

Chapter XVII

The Fall of Northern Greece

(Midsummer, 480)

Re-fitted and reorganized in its new divisions or battle-groups, Xerxes' army marched west from Doriskos, able, in the coastal plain east of the Nestos, to reduce its inordinate length by moving in parallel columns. Mardonios and the king's brother Masistes marched by the coast, Tritantaikhmes and Gergis near the foot of the hills; Xerxes himself accompanied a centre column, with Smerdomenes and Megabyxos.[1] Thracian chiefs along the route did homage, and bands of their tribesmen were taken with the army, incidentally serving as hostages.

West of the Nestos, the hills come nearer the sea; both nature and men were wilder. The king of the Bisaltai refused to be Xerxes' subject and fled into the Rhodope mountains; but his six sons, eager for the adventure, defied him and joined the army. When they came back, their father had them blinded.[2] The Satrai north of Mount Pangaion also held aloof, for 'they have never yet been subject to any man. . . . They live in high, forested and snowy mountains, and are tremendous fighters.'[3] Here also lions attacked the baggage train, collecting from far afield (as did African lions, to prey on the workers building the Kenya railway). There were none, says Herodotos (vii, 125), east of the Nestos (i.e. in the lowlands) but they still existed in Macedonia and the mountains as far as the Achelöos. They developed a remarkable taste for camel meat; Herodotos even says that they attacked nothing else. (One reason for this he has himself given; the camels came last, because they frightened the horses; so if ever a column was delayed and unlagered at dusk, the camels would be.) Progress was slow, for a way

[1] H. vii, 121. – In the order in which the marshals are named in ch. 82, these are respectively nos. 1 and 4, 2 and 5, 3 and 6; which looks rather as if the order was an order of seniority, and comprised (as among King David's officers, 2 Sam. xxiii, 8ff; 1 Chron. xi, 11ff) a First Three and a Second Three. [2] H. viii, 116. [3] H. vii, 111.

for the host and its wagons had to be hacked through forests and levelled in rough places. Not till July was Macedonia reached (cf. p. 405); the 300 miles through Thrace may have taken about 45 days. But the way was made. The Thracians, who had never seen anything like it, were much impressed; 'and this road, by which Xerxes marched his army, they neither dig up nor sow, but they look on it with awe, even to my time'.[4] The reference is particularly to the stretch 'round Pangaion', where Xerxes' pioneers probably pushed the road through the wide Symvolon valley, followed by the modern main road, between low coastal hills and the main massif. A coast route and a northern route by later Philippi are both also practicable.

The Strymon was found ready bridged at The Nine Ways, the nodal point between lake and sea, later Amphipolis; probably there were several pontoon bridges. The Magi sacrificed white horses to the river spirit, and when they heard the name of the place, 'they buried alive there that number of boys and maidens of the native people'. Herodotos adds, *à propos* of this barbarity (114), 'I am told that Amestris the wife of Xerxes, when she grew old, also buried alive twice seven Persian boys of good families, as a vicarious offering for herself, to win favour with the "god under earth".'

At Argilos, where the coast bends south to the Chalkidic peninsula, Xerxes turned south from the main route, to visit Akanthos and the Athos canal. He heard good reports of the zeal shown by the Greeks of Akanthos, and 'feasted them and gave them a gift of Median dress', an interesting glimpse of a policy of assimilation for loyal subjects. While he was there, to his great grief, Artakhaies, the Achaemenid giant with the roaring voice, who had been in joint charge of the work, fell sick and died. Xerxes had a huge cairn built over his grave by the troops; 'and the men of Akanthos offer sacrifice to him as a hero, at the bidding of an oracle'.[5] The fleet, ship after ship, passed endlessly through the canal and, under the lee of Mount Athos, rounded the western Chalkidic capes, while the army cut across north of the peninsula to reach the sea again at Therma, by the site of later Thessalonīke.[6]

In the fertile plain of the Vardar, the Greek river Axios, 'the most beautiful water known to man',[7] the army halted again 'for many days', while a third of the infantry was sent forward to clear the next stretch

[4] H. vii, 115.
[5] *ib.* 115–17.
[6] *ib.* 122ff.
[7] Homer, *Il.* ii, 850.

of the route, hacking their way through the forests of 'the Macedonian mountains' [8] towards the passes west of Olympos, up the Haliakmon valley, the Petra and the Servia or Volustána passes, the scene of sharp fighting in 1912 and 1941. Other men and animals rested, and the rear formations straggled in; they must have been several days behind the vanguard, even with the use of parallel routes. The bivouacs (there were no tents, except for Xerxes[9]) spread for twenty miles along the coast, 'from Therma to the Haliakmon', until those to the east (the last arrivals?), using the water of the smaller river Echeidōros, suffered from thirst even here. Here also, Xerxes was awaiting the return and reports of his heralds, sent long before from Sardis with the summons to surrender.[10]

From Therma, too, Xerxes saw the famous view, no doubt at dawn (it fades in the haze of a summer noon), of 'the Thessalian mountains, high Olympos and Ossa; and hearing that there was a narrow gorge between them, through which the Pēneios flows, and that this was one way to Thessaly, he conceived the desire to go and see the mouth of the Peneios; for he intended to advance by the up-country road through inland Macedonia'. Herodotos uses the occasion to give an account of the place (128): Tempē, a beauty-spot famous both in ancient and modern times; but there seems to be no reason to suppose on that account, as some have, that he invented the episode. He writes as though he had been (sticking always to the coast) along the line of Xerxes' route, but also as though he had received, orally or from a written document, a Persian 'log' of the march. Zōpyros (p. 109), son of the marshal Megabyxos, might have provided one. Xerxes had time on his hands at this point; so he paid the visit, embarking on the special Sidonian galley which he always used, with a squadron for escort. It is in accord with Herodotos' account of his Persian love of natural beauty. He has already described how Xerxes had admired and taken steps to preserve a beautiful plane-tree in Lydia.[11] Among other traits of character, Xerxes was an aesthete.

The visit to Tempe was in any case not a military reconnaissance. The pass was not held. Indeed, the whole Mount Olympos line, as Persia's good servant, Alexander of Macedonia, was in a position to report, was clear of the enemy. The pass had been occupied by a considerable Greek army, but it had withdrawn without even waiting for

[8] H. vii, 131. [9] *ib.* 119, 3. [10] *ib.* 127. [11] *ib.* 31.

Xerxes' Invasion

the enemy to approach. As to how this remarkable state of affairs had developed, Alexander, in the account of the matter which reached Herodotos, bears a great share of the credit or discredit; and it is unlikely that he laid less emphasis on this when reporting to the king.

The Aleuadai of Larisa, as we have seen, whom Herodotos calls 'Kings of Thessaly', had long been in touch with Persia (p. 269); but there were men in Thessaly also who favoured the nationalist cause; men influential enough to send a delegation to the Congress at Corinth, appealing for adequate support to enable them to hold their mountain frontier.[12] That the Aleuadai themselves were actually in exile Herodotos does not say; it was 'messengers from them' who had appeared at Sousa. It seems most likely that, as often in Thessaly, different factions based on the great families held different strongholds. The Aleuadai certainly enjoyed considerable support. However, in the spring of 480, 'when Xerxes was about to cross into Europe', an appeal from Thessaly was received at Corinth, and the Congress, now passing from the consideration of political questions and intelligence to strategic planning, determined to send 10,000 armoured infantry. It was in accordance with the most elementary common sense, to fight 'as far forward in Greece as possible'[13] and to assist the immediately threatened north; but it went against the grain for Greek citizen soldiers to go, for defensive purposes, so far from their homes.[14] The decision, or at least its execution, was morally something of an achievement.

The Spartan contingent was probably not large (perhaps a battalion); for its commander, automatically the commander of the whole force, was 'selected from among the Polemarchs, but not a member of the royal family'. His name was Euainetos, son of Karānos.[15] Themistokles himself commanded the Athenians, perhaps more numerous; 'to fight as far forward as possible' was the essence of his strategy. Athens must also have provided many of the ships in which they sailed to Halos in northern Achaia, which had ties with Pharsalos (were the more convenient Pagasai and its overlord, Pherai, unfriendly?). Thebes, says the

[12] *ib.* 172.

[13] Cf. Plut. *Them.* 7 (Th.'s strategy). *Τῆς Ἑλλάδος* is to be read as a partitive gen.; 'as far forward *in* G.', not 'from G'.

[14] And not only Greeks; as was seen, e.g., both in the English Civil War and in the American War of Independence.

[15] 'A lordly name' (Macan, *ad loc.* H. vii, 173). But I cannot think why Macan says he 'was not a Spartan Herakleid'. Polemarchs command battalions, *lochoi*, in 418 (Thk. v, 66), in the 4th-cent. *morai* (Xen. *Hell.* v, 4, 46).

patriotic Boiotian Plutarch, sent 500 men. Probably many cities contributed contingents; and 'the cavalry of the Thessalians', gentlemen and their retainers, joined them before Tempe.[16] It was a force which could have held both the gorge and the adjacent steep path to Gonnos (which Herodotos, here and at 128, confuses with the passes west of Olympos) indefinitely.

This force was in position in good time, early in the campaigning season, while the Persians were still 'about to cross into Europe'.[17] Its commanders naturally concerned themselves with reconnaissance and political intelligence: with the topography of the mountains, with possible routes to and from Macedonia, with the state of feeling among the mountain peoples, especially the Perrhaiboi, in the frontier range from Olympos westward, and with conditions in Macedonia, where they made contact with Alexander.

What they found out was not cheering. Alexander (whom Herodotos never calls king in this episode; he was Persia's vassal) was a person evidently of spectacular and attractive personality. He was full of protestations of good will towards Athens, Sparta and the Greeks generally; he *was* a Greek, he had established his pedigree, derived (heraldically) from the kings of Argos; he had run at Olympia and all but won an Olympic crown. If he was also brother-in-law to the Persian general at Akanthos, in charge of the canal, he had a circumstantial though highly unconvincing story (Herodotos believed it, but we may doubt whether Themistokles did) to tell about that (p. 134).

Had he, if so well disposed, any positive military intelligence, about routes, about Xerxes' army? He had. There were several routes from Macedonia, especially from upper Macedonia, by way of the Haliakmon and Perrhaibia; as to Xerxes' army, he had ample information (either from popular report, running ahead with the speed of the 'bush telegraph', or passed to him by his brother-in-law; for, as the story of the spies shows (p. 322), Xerxes' policy on such information was to use it for propaganda). All this confirmed what the Greek advanced headquarters was finding out from other sources, especially about the passes. Forests would impose delay on the use of them by a large force (as has been seen, they did delay Xerxes, even without any human resistance); but if the approaches from the Haliakmon were to be

[16] H., *ib.*; Plut. *MH*, 31; Westlake, *The Medism of Thessaly*, in *JHS* LVI.
[17] H. vii, 174.

defended, the best method would be not only to block and defend the trails, but to harass columns and working parties. This was not the kind of warfare for which Greek soldiers were equipped, or to which they were accustomed (as Mardonios is said to have pointed out to Xerxes, p. 326). Something might be done, if armoured infantry, blocking the trails, received determined support from the mountain people. Could such support be expected?

It could not. Xerxes' envoys had entered northern Greece months before, very probably by way of Macedonia; and all the hill-tribes, following the lead of the Aleuadai in the great plain, had promised earth and water. The Persian heralds or envoys, moreover, were still there; for they rejoined Xerxes, as we have seen, only when he reached Macedonia. As heralds were supposed to be sacrosanct, there was nothing that Euainetos could do about them without courting the wrath of heaven. A frontier or sea patrol, if any such had been organized long before, might have tried to turn them back; but as it was, they were in; and, even apart from their sacrosanctity, without the good will of the hillmen who were harbouring them it would have been quite impossible to catch them. So, living unobtrusively but probably by no means in hiding in all parts of mountain Greece, were an unknown number of pairs of Persian agents, ready when necessary to remind chiefs and tribal elders of their undertakings, to dilate on the power of the advancing expedition, and to point to Macedonia as evidence that one could accept the overlordship of the Great King and suffer no harm. One has to admit the courage of these Persian agents. They went into some very wild country, and, while there was no Gestapo looking for them, and the persons of heralds were supposed to be sacred, stories which were reported from civilised Athens and Sparta kept the world reminded that they could be murdered.

So the force at Tempe found itself, far from home, in basically unfriendly country. Neither hillmen nor lowland peasants wanted their land fought over, nor the invaders provoked. The whole north was rotten with enemy propaganda, which had been going on for a long time. Only the Thessalian gentry were in favour of fighting, and their cavalry was useless for defending mountains. At best, they might attack the heads of columns as they debouched on to the plain; but how long was that going to delay such a host?

Euainetos liked his assignment less and less. His front was too wide, local support not forthcoming or not such as he wanted, and the courage of his southern allies oozing away. Perhaps one result of their being sent in good time was actually that they were kept there too long; too long for the morale of citizen soldiers, while Xerxes forged ahead slowly through Thrace, the rumour of his power, augmented by deliberate propaganda, flying ahead of him. Even Themistokles was perhaps not heart and soul in favour of the operation; Athens had insisted on sending him with a land army, whereas what he wanted was to put every available man on board his new ships (cf. p. 360). Alexander asked, 'speaking as a friend', was it sensible to stay there at Tempe and be trampled under the feet of the host that was coming, or cut off by troops landed from the fleet? Alexander was a worthy ancestor of Philip; he could out-blandish any Greek. Also, he knew very well what his interest was; it was not to have Xerxes' army delayed in Macedonia, eating up local resources, any longer than could be helped.

So the latter end of it was that, long before Xerxes reached Macedonia, and whether with or without reference to distant Sparta or Corinth we do not know, Euainetos either decided that he could not hold his position or found, willy-nilly, that he could not hold his allies. The whole force marched back to Halos and sailed south; and the Thessalian gentry were left to put the best face they could on a belated submission to Xerxes and the Aleuadai. What reception Euainetos received at Sparta is not recorded. He was never again given an assignment that gains a mention in history; though, in view of the fragmentariness of our sources, that might be a matter of chance. Xerxes' agents, rejoining their own people after the best part of a year in the mountains, were able to report the submission of all Thessaly, with the Perrhaiboi of Olympos, the Magnētes of Ossa and Pēlion, northern Achaia, and even the hill-tribes further south: the Mālians of Othrys, the Ainiānes and Dolopes west of them, and the lowland Lokrians within Thermopylai. A later historian distinguishes these hill-peoples as having decided for submission even while the Greek army was still holding Tempe, the lowlanders after its withdrawal; probably rightly, though very likely also only by 'rationalisation' of Herodotos and not from any independent contemporary evidence.[18] Boiotia itself was wavering, knowing that there was a strong current of opinion among the Peloponnesians in favour of defending only their peninsula. A wave of panic

[18] H. vii, 132; cf. D.S. xi, 3, probably from Ephoros.

swept through Greece, and many, whose cities had not submitted, wished that they would; 'for those who had given earth and water to the Persian were relieved, feeling that they would suffer no harm, while those who had not were in terror, thinking that there were not ships enough in Greece to match the invader's, and the masses had no desire to be involved in the war, but were eager for submission'.[19] Alexander had talked about the invader's fleet. A relatively small number of resolute men saved Greek independence at this hour; among them, Herodotos rightly emphasises the staunchness of Athens, which, however unpopular she might be at the time of writing, alone saved Greece, by making resistance possible at sea. In Athens, he does justice, but only bare justice and on a later page, to the man who led her and had made *her* resistance at sea possible: Themistokles.[20]

In the meantime, all that the nationalist Congress could do was to issue a stern warning to 'Medizers', that any Greeks who took the side of the enemy, or submitted except under extreme pressure, would be treated as enemies themselves (a policy also adopted towards submissive villages by modern Greek guerrilla fighters, Kolokotronis in the War of Independence and the communist-controlled ELAS in World War II). The members of the Congress bound themselves by oath to 'tithe' all such to the God of Delphi.[21] The meaning of this was not to decimate offenders, or to fine them a tenth of their possessions, but to destroy them utterly; for to 'give the tithe' to a god was what Greeks did when they sacked a city, or when a state confiscated the property of a convicted malefactor.[22] The threat was never carried out, both because it would have been inherently difficult to carry fire and sword through the mountain zone in any case, and because the allies, Athens and Sparta, split almost immediately at the end of the war;[23] but at the time when the vow was made it must have rung hollow for quite other reasons. The prospects of victory, even of survival, seemed remote; and Apollo of Delphi himself, now if not earlier, took the side of the enemy.[24] The Cretan cities (mentioned together; perhaps, in answer to the invitation of the Congress, they had held their own local conference

[19] H. vii, 138.

[20] *ib.* 139; Themistokles' part (and first mention of him in Herodotos), 143f.

[21] *ib.* 132, 2.

[22] See H. W. Parke in *Hermathena*, LXXII (1948).

[23] Discussion, e.g., in Busolt, *GG* II², p. 655n; H. Bengtson in *Eranos* XLIX (1951).

[24] I am happy here to register agreement with Hammond (*GH*, 223f). Continental scholars have usually been more sceptical. Bury (it is rather characteristic) at this point makes no mention of the oracles at all.

and sent a joint delegation to consult the god) were encouraged to remain neutral (perhaps already in 481); so was Argos; and Athens and Sparta, committed to resistance, received 'daunting oracles'.[25]

It is easy to blame the Delphic priests, and the Greeks who submitted easily or who chose neutrality, which implied readiness to submit if other men's resistance failed, as it was expected to fail. In the light of subsequent history, they were wrong; and they were held up to scorn in the writings of later antiquity no less than of modern times.[26] The Congress appealed to a wider loyalty than that to the city-state or mountain canton: to Hellas or *tò Hellenikón* (*ethnos*), to 'community of blood and speech and religion and ways of life', as an Athenian was to express it;[27] and the 'epigrams' or verse inscriptions on many war memorials were to honour, in the unsurpassed poetic lapidary style of the early fifth century, those who died for Hellas.[28] But Hellas was no object of the Hellene's primary loyalty, learned from childhood. It had never been to any man the 'dear, dear land' of modern poetry and patriotism. As a concept to which to appeal, it was more like 'the West' or Europe or that Christendom which so signally failed to oppose its united strength either to Mongol or to Turk. Any individuals who, from 1935 to 1938, refused to contemplate war, except in defence of their own *national* interests, are in no position to cast a stone at the insularity of Crete.

The northern Greek peoples who are thus recorded to have surrendered comprised almost the whole membership of the League of Neighbours or Amphiktyony, whose delegates had met from time immemorial at the Hot Gates (or simply Pylai, The Gates) by the hot springs of Thermopylai. For the last hundred years, since Thessalians had led them in the Sacred War or crusade that carried Thessalian arms to the Corinthian Gulf, they had held alternate meetings at Delphi, and the oracular shrine had become their religious capital. All the more reason why they should follow the lead of Delphi, or why Delphi itself should be influenced by the state of feeling in the north, and by the same propaganda. Of all the members, the only ones not recorded

[25] Crete, H. vii, 169f; Argos, 148f; and see below, pp. 355–9, 407, 418.

[26] e.g. D.S. xi, 3 (Ephoros?).

[27] H. viii, 144, 2; below, p. 494.

[28] *Anth. Pal.* vii, 253 (said to be Simonides on Spartans); anon. (Simonides??) *ap.* Plut. *MH* on Corinthians; inscr. from Megara, Tod, *GHI*, no. 20, Hiller, *Hist. Gr. Ep.* 30; inscr. from Opoeis of Lokris *ap.* Str. ix, 425.

to have given earth and water to the Persians are the Phokians, who had lately thrown off the yoke of Thessaly, the Dorians and Ionians; the original members bearing these latter names being the Dorians of Doris north of Parnassos and the Ionians of Euboia. More recently it had been found politically convenient to admit, alongside them, the great Ionian and Dorian powers of the south, Athens receiving one of the two Ionian votes, Sparta and Argos by turns one of the Dorian.[29]

The gloomy oracles addressed to Athens and Sparta have suffered much recent discussion; many scholars have found difficulty in accepting them as genuine. Some, indeed, have denied that any of the extant hexameter verse oracles are genuine. (The earliest source reporting these is Herodotos himself.) 'La réponse oraculaire est un genre littéraire.'[30] This is certainly true, taken as a simple statement; we have scores of entertaining faked oracles, some legendary (many of them probably made up at Delphi *ad maiorem Apollinis gloriam*), some, of later date, perhaps more disinterestedly romantic. But Herodotos quotes *these* oracles from well within living memory; and, moreover, they are not brilliant examples of oracular success. They were *not* what the consulting governments wanted; nor do they predict victory, though they do, in the best Delphic manner, leave a loophole. But a forger *post eventum* ought to have done better. If the oracles of H. vii, 140f, 148, 169 (paraphrased) and 220 were invented after the war, one might suspect them of having been invented to discredit Delphi, if it were not that there is no sign of any movement to do so. On the contrary, the Greeks swarm back with their offerings as if their first thought was to appease Apollo's wrath.[31] The mutually jealous states of Greece competed for the favour of Delphi, and the oracle, in an age of dawning scepticism, kept its prestige remarkably, not least in the circle of Socrates.[32] Like many undoubted facts in history, it is very odd, and not at all what one might have expected. That the oracular responses,

[29] For the League, cf. *World of Hesiod*, p. 224 and n. 3; Sacred War, *Lyric Age*, pp. 200ff.

[30] P. Amandry in *Rev. Phil.* XXX (1956), reviewing, somewhat damagingly, R. Crahay, *La littérature oraculaire chez Hérodote*, in which this view is taken. Equally sceptical is M. Delcourt, *L'oracle de Delphes* (1955). For a common-sense point of view (as it seems to the present writer) cf. Amandry in *Rev. des Ét. anc.* LXI (1959); 'Oracles, littérature et politique', an important review-article.

[31] The suggestion of H. Bengtson in *Eranos* XLIX (1951), reviewing M. P. Nilsson, *Cults, Myths, Oracles and Politics* (Lund, 1951). The present writer is happy to be in agreement with Nilsson, see his pp. 123ff.

[32] Cf., e.g., Thk. i, 112, 5; 118, 3; Plut. *Per.* 21 (Delphi in politics); Plato, *Apol.* 20e (Chairephon); Xen. *Anab.* iii, 1, 5; v, 3, 6; vi, 1, 22.

and the stories attached to them, may have been 'improved' in transmission certainly cannot be excluded;[33] that they were asked for and given, it seems unreasonable to disbelieve.

No better fares a somewhat touching attempt to procure the oracle's acquittal on the charge of defeatism, by arguing that it never had a policy of its own; but that Apollo, as the Healer-god, simply advised the faithful as to what it was best and 'healthiest' to do.[34] On this principle, it is argued that the Athenians were given, in good faith, what was considered the best advice *for them* (not for Greek civilisation – that was not the question), in the advice to 'flee to the ends of the earth'; i.e. to 'go west' like the Phokaians. The fact remains that if the Athenians had taken this advice, all Greece would have become a Persian satrapy. As Herodotos courageously said (vii, 139) in a world in which Athens was the greatest and the most hated of cities, 'At this point I cannot refrain from expressing an opinion which will be widely unpopular, but must tell the truth as I see it: if the Athenians . . . had either fled . . . or surrendered to Xerxes, no resistance by sea would even have been attempted.' And in that case, he continues, Persian sea-power would have made nonsense of any number of walls across the Isthmus. Neither a man nor a corporation, like Delphi, possessing great influence, can evade political responsibility.

The Delphic priesthood was an ecclesiastical corporation, grown very influential and very rich. Of such it is not always vain to expect heroic courses; but the temptation to 'play safe' is severe. Delphi used its influence now for peace, which meant for surrender. The priests knew that Apollo in some of his other sanctuaries, in Asia (p. 114), at Delos at the time of Datis' expedition, had won the favour of the Persians. Miletos, on the other hand, had courted disaster, and Branchidai had suffered. Now, in the response given to the Athenians (p. 355) we find an extraordinarily vivid and, to the questioners, strictly *irrelevant* prophecy of the destruction of 'many castellated walls – not only thine – and many temples of the immortals . . . who now stand sweating and trembling for terror'. Is not this a remarkable way for Apollo to speak of his fellow-Olympians? Or were the priests, for they were well informed about affairs abroad, preparing for Xerxes to treat

[33] As is accepted, e.g., by Meyer, *GdA*³ IV, i, p. 348n.; Parke and Wormell, *The Delphic Oracle* (1956), I, pp. 167f.

[34] H. Berve, in *Gestaltende Kräfte der Antike*, ch. i, esp. pp. 22ff, cf. 19.

the Greek gods as accurséd *daevas*? As intelligent and, surely at least some of them, genuinely religious men, in that age of the dawn of philosophies and higher religions, they must have known something of the Persian religion. Did they realise that, if Apollo was to continue to 'speak all truth to the Persians' he must dissociate himself from *daevas* and find a place, perhaps as an expression and mouthpiece of Good Thought (Vohumana, the Ōmānos of Cappadocia, p. 77) within the 'Catholic Zoroastrianism' favoured by Xerxes?

Herodotos does not precisely date either the oracular responses or the overtures made by the Congress to hesitant Greek states. He treats the whole Greek reaction to the threat of invasion as timeless, a single dramatic act. Xerxes is before Tempe at vii, 128; the Greek embassies to uncommitted states are described in 148–71 (and said to have been sent out *after* the sending of spies to Sardis, where Xerxes was in winter 481–0; that to Sicily, at least, must surely have gone much earlier); and the oracles foretelling the fall of Athens are given, without indication of date, at 140–1. Athens' preparations were really spread over a long time; the oracular responses given to her come, probably, near the end of it (pp. 360f).

One important question which the Congress had settled 'even before the embassy to Sicily'[35] was that of the high command; and here Athens, for the sake of unity, made a noteworthy sacrifice. Other negotiations had broken down over this question (at least nominally; for it is an evident fact that when questions of control, or safeguard against control, or of the 'edge' – 51 per cent – or even of precedence, cause the failure of any negotiations, the real reason is lack of goodwill). Gelon had demanded, if he brought his main forces to Greece, the command-in-chief on both elements, or at least on land *or* sea; but Spartan kings would not serve under a tyrant of Syracuse, nor would Athens place her navy under him. Argos, still shattered by the disaster of Sepeia, with Tiryns and Mykēnai independent on the very edge of her own plain, demanded an equal share in the command of the army; as Plutarch (*MH* 28) says, making a valid point, it was too much to expect them to place their forces at the disposal of their victorious enemies. But it was too much also to expect Sparta to concede equality now to her old rival. There was indeed good reason to believe that

[35] H. viii, 3.

Argos had an understanding with Xerxes; Xerxes' heralds had been to Argos, as they had been almost everywhere; and that there was such an understanding (which must mean that Argos had given earth and water) appeared to be confirmed when Kallias, Athens' most trusted negotiator of the mid-fifth century, was himself at Sousa and heard reports of the conversations of an Argive embassy which he encountered there.[36] The Delphic Oracle's advice to Argos is reported as follows:

> Hated of neighbours around, but dear to the gods, the immortals:
> Keep thy spear in the home, and sit there safely defended;
> Safely defend thy head; and the head shall deliver the members.

So Argos remained quiescent, and did not, for example, molest Mykēnai and Tiryns, which took part in the war. Herodotos finds her conduct 'not entirely dishonourable', adding the famous *gnōmē* that if all men could have a good look at other people's troubles, they would be content not to exchange them but to keep their own; but in a later passage he adds, 'to speak candidly, Argive neutrality was friendly to Persia'.[37]

Athens for her part was content that Sparta should take the command-in-chief; that, indeed, went almost without saying; but she might well have hoped, seeing that her navy now outnumbered the united fleets of all the Peloponnese, for the command at sea. But the Peloponnesians would not have it. Perhaps they did not trust an Athenian not to give their ships the most dangerous assignments and save his own. Aigina, indeed, might well hesitate to place her ships under the orders of her most dangerous enemy. But there was also the matter of prestige. No Greek city really liked placing its forces under the command of an ally; indeed, no Greek really liked placing himself under another's orders at all; Athenian discipline, it has been said, was 'such as one might expect in a place where "to obey" was the same as "to be persuaded"'. Corinth, if she had to depend on a powerful ally, preferred the Spartans, who were not like other men. ('We could never find others so congenial' says a Corinthian speaker later, even in the act of threatening to resign from the alliance if Sparta will not support her.[38])

Athens swallowed her pride and agreed that her fleet too should take

[36] H. vii, 150–2. (Kallias also negotiated the Thirty Years' Peace with Sparta in 445, D.S., xii, 7.)

[37] vii, 148, 3; 152; viii, 73, 3.

[38] Thk. i, 71, 6.

orders from a Spartan, an officer of a minor naval power, 'realising that if they quarrelled about the command, Greece would be lost'. Herodotos does not name Themistokles at this point.[39] Later writers do; and there can be no doubt that they are right. A recent discovery has shown that in kindred matters they followed a tradition current in Athens, at least in the fourth century.[40] Themistokles deserves his credit. It was he who would have held that high command, if Dorian pride and mistrust had allowed it; and he had better reasons than mere vanity for desiring to hold it. Not only had he been responsible for the creation of the big Athenian navy, but he had been studying, for years past, probably with far more thoroughness than any other man, the geographical and other strategic conditions for the defence of Greece.

Another question, to which the Athenians, under Themistokles' leadership, gave earnest attention 'in the archonship of Hypsichides', the civil year which ended at midsummer, 480, was that of the exiles, especially those 'banished for the Ten Year Period', as official language appears to have had it; in the vernacular, 'ostracised'. 'All who had been ostracised' were 'received back', says *The Athenian Constitution* (22, 8); but the Hellenistic inscription from Troizēn, which purports to give the text of the actual Decree proposed by Themistokles,[41] as preserved or reconstructed at Athens in the fourth century, puts a rather different complexion on the matter. According to the Troizen text (ll. 44ff), the ostracised were not simply invited home and their exile cancelled; they were *ordered* home, and bidden to 'go to Salamis and remain there' until the Assembly should have time to consider their status (it was thus left open for different views to be taken on the merits of their individual cases). It was common for Greek exiles to join the enemies of their native cities, in the hope of restoration to their homes (Dāmarātos of Sparta was with Xerxes now); and Plutarch (*Them.* 11) says that Themistokles had this danger in mind. He introduced the clause, according to the inscription 'so that all Athenians may with one mind

[39] viii, 3; cf. vii, 139.

[40] Plutarch, *Them.* 7; Aelius Aristides (A.D. 129–189), ed. Dindorf, II, p. 252; Oration xlvi, *Against Plato, in Defence of the Four* (to give it its full title), i.e. in defence of Miltiades, Themistokles, Kimon and Perikles, whom Plato's Socrates criticises in the Gorgias as having led the city to prefer power to virtue, and suffered the ingratitude of the citizens not undeservedly. For the 'Decree of Themistokles', which both these writers quote on other decisions of 480, see below, pp. 359f, 364–77.

[41] M. H. Jameson in *Hesperia*, XXIX (1960), and in *Greece and Rome*, VIII (1961); below, pp. 364ff.

join in the defence'. But it was not simply an offer. Athens asserted her rights over her citizens temporarily exiled, as she did over those at home and liable for service. Also, according to the *Constitution*, in the same year, 'they directed that all who were ostracised' (present tense this time; not referring only to the past) 'should live within the limits of Geraistos and Skyllaion, on pain of losing all civil rights for good'. Geraistos is the south-east cape of Euboia; Skyllaion, in Troizenia, is the easternmost point of the Peloponnese. The purpose of the regulation, in the circumstances of 481–0, is clearly to prohibit the ostracised from living in Persian territory.[42]

Not all the ostracised responded alike. Xanthippos and Aristeides came home, to render distinguished service. Hipparchos the son of Charmos did not. He had probably already joined the Peisistratidai with Xerxes. Probably to the relief of the nationalists, he stood convicted of high treason at last. He is said to have been condemned to death in his absence. 'His statue on the Acropolis' was taken down (not a statue erected in his honour, for there were none such at Athens till long after; but perhaps an *ex voto* set up by himself for his archonship) and the bronze used (clearly after the war) to make a plaque, on which were the names of *aliterioi* and proscribed traitors. Hipparchos' own name was on it. Thucydides adds that it bore the names of five sons of Hippias.[43] Far better united than at the time of Marathon, Athens turned to face her military problems.

The strategy which the Greeks adopted, and which we have grounds for thinking that Themistokles thought out, aimed, like all good strategy, at exploiting the enemy's difficulties and the possibilities afforded by the terrain. Greeks knew very well that logistics are basic to operations, though they did not (especially the later rhetorical historians) find the subject interesting. Herodotos (vii, 48) makes old Artabanos sum up Xerxes' problems: his two worst enemies would be 'land and sea; for there is not a harbour anywhere, as I guess, that could shelter and protect this fleet if a storm arose; . . . and, even if there were no opposition, still, the further you advance, the more resistance the land will offer. . . . Even assuming no human opposition, more space, in more time, will bring forth famine.'

[42] As was seen long ago by Wilamowitz, *Ar. und Ath.*, I, pp. 26, 114. Some scholars have proposed needlessly to emend the text; see app. crit. to editions.

[43] Lykourgos, *Against Leokrates*, 117; Thk. vi, 55; cf. Wilamowitz *loc. cit.*

Likewise, a Corinthian speaker in Thucydides (i, 69, 5) expresses the judgment that in this war 'the barbarian's troubles were mostly of his own making'. The Corinthian's point of view is anti-Athenian; and Thucydides is not unwilling to remind his fellow-Athenians that the Persians *had* their difficulties. But if there had been no effective resistance, there would have been nothing to prevent the Persians from building up a new forward base in Greece itself.

The general lines for the defence of Greece were determined by the mountain ranges, more especially those whose feet were washed by the Aegean. It seems to have been agreed that there was no hope of defeating Xerxes in a pitched battle on land; not only perhaps because of his mere numbers, for the Greek peninsula could probably have produced as many fighting men as the king had brought with him, and as many good armoured men as Xerxes had of good Iranian troops; but that would have given Greeks their own logistic problems. But Greece was completely outclassed in cavalry and archers, and there was little hope that heavy pikemen alone could successfully take the offensive against the more mobile enemy. Marathon had shown what good hoplites could do against Persians who had put themselves in a bad position because they were in a hurry; but against that victory had to be placed a series of defeats, from that of the mercenaries in Egypt to those in Karia and at Malene. The defence of mountain positions, or (best of all, thought the Peloponnesians) of a wall across the Isthmus of Corinth, seemed more promising; and though such passive defence would not commend itself to modern military thought, it is not unlikely that it did commend itself to Greeks, whose successful method of survival for centuries, when threatened by an invader, had been to shut themselves up within their walls and wait for the enemy's supply difficulties to force him to go away. ('The fox knows many tricks,' said Archilochos, in a line already becoming proverbial; 'the hedgehog, one good one.') But there was still the sea, by way of which the Persians hoped to turn all mountain or isthmus defence lines; and here, though narrow-fronted positions might still be occupied, in view of the enemy's superior numbers and the formidable skill of the Phoenicians, passive defence was not applicable in the same way as on land. Battles would have to be fought out on equal terms; and how and where the greatest losses might be inflicted on the enemy, so as to exhaust his strength (*en venir à bout*, as the French say) before that of the defenders, was the essence of the problem which Themistokles had been studying for so many years.

It was a geographical question; and the answer, at the theoretical level, was simple.

From Mount Olympos to Cape Sēpias, some eighty miles, the mountains of the Magnesians, Ossa and Pēlion, stretch like a wall, steep and harbourless save for a few small coves and beaches. Then comes the first breach, the strait about six miles wide between Sepias and the northern tip of Euboia, where a temple of Artemis Facing the East, *Prosēōia*,[44] held no doubt the votive offerings of many sailors east-bound; and then Euboia, its eastern coast almost as inhospitable as that of Thessaly, stretching for over 100 miles before the next breach is reached, between Euboia and Andros. If the straits of Artemision were held in force, the enemy fleet coming from the Gulf of Therma would face an unpleasant prospect. The distance from the Gulf of Therma to Aphetai on the Gulf of Pagasai (now of Volos) was too long to be done in a day; if covered in that time, as it might be by a special effort, it would deliver the crews in an exhausted condition into the hands of their enemies; but to ride out the night at anchor off the Magnesian coast, where only a small proportion of such a large fleet could be beached, might be disastrous if the weather turned bad; and to come south by squadrons would invite defeat in detail. The straits of Artemision were the key position for the whole defence of Greece. At the same time, the approach by Andros to the Saronic Gulf could not be entirely denuded of defence, since the Persians, with their superior numbers, might detach a fleet to create a diversion or to cut the communications of the Greeks in the Euboian channel.

The ideal station for land forces would have been at Tempe and on the Olympos line, securing Thessaly and giving the enemy fleet a hostile as well as physically inhospitable lee-shore; so Themistokles himself led the Athenian contingent that marched to Tempe. If the orator Isokrates' mention of Athens sending sixty ships (only) to Artemision[45] is a reminiscence of any tradition, it perhaps refers to this abortive expedition. But in any case, by the time Hypsichides laid down his office at midsummer (perhaps at the end of the lunar month, whose moon was full on June the 22nd by our calendar), the Greeks had withdrawn from Thessaly, and Xerxes' army was pouring into

[44] Plut. *Them.* 8.

[45] Isokr. xii, 49.

Macedonia. It was a dark hour indeed and, with the Peloponnesians showing no sign of haste or even willingness to come to the rescue of central Greece, some might well feel that the only hope of safety was in flight to the west, where Athens had staked a claim to the lands of devastated Siris.[46] Others, stout-hearted but perhaps even now not fully appreciating the power of the invader, were in favour of a fight to the death for their homes and temples, and an appeal to Sparta, as in the year of Marathon, to come to their aid.

It was perhaps at this point that Athenian consultants were sent to Delphi; it does not follow that no others had been sent in the previous twelve months, but, if they had, what happened now eclipsed the memory of them. The story of this consultation appears to bear the marks of genuine tradition; which is not to say that it cannot have been 'improved' in details. But it *has* details, including the names of minor characters and other non-essentials.

'The Athenians sent *theopropoi* to Delphi' (two of them – they are addressed in the dual in one line), 'and were ready to consult; and when they had carried out the usual rites in the precincts, and went into the temple and were taking their seats, the Pythia, whose name was Aristonike, spoke as follows:

> Alas, why sit there? Fly, far, far away;
> Leave home and town and castle; do not stay;
> For neither head nor body nor, below,
> Stand fast the feet, nor hand nor heart; they go
> In smoke; he burns, he smites it; from afar
> Fierce Ares rides the Syrian battle-car.
> And many another fort, not only thine
> He shall destroy, and burn with fire the shrine
> Of many a god, where gods now stand and sweat
> And shake and, dripping down the roof-trees wet,
> Dark blood portends inexorable woe.
> Prepare for trouble. Leave the shrine and go!'[47]

It seems as if the medium spoke her daunting words as soon as ever the two Athenians entered the *adyton* or sanctuary, and without waiting for the *prophētes*, the priest who also reduced the medium's utterances to

[46] H. viii, 62.

[47] H. vii, 140. 'Riding the Syrian car' is echoed in Aesch. *Persai*, 84 (472 B.C.); sceptics would no doubt maintain that the oracle echoes Aeschylus.

intelligible and metrical order, to put their question. This was something which her predecessors were said to have done on many legendary occasions.[48] It was obviously an impressive procedure, if to create a special impression was what was desired. The 'usual rites' of sacrifice, etcetera, would give plenty of time for the priests to find out the consultant's business, before the question was handed in (perhaps at this time written on a tablet, which was read out by the *prophetes* before the medium, seated on her tripod).[49] Often the priests may genuinely have waited on the mediumistic utterances of the Pythia; but the Persian War utterances seem all to be clear products of ecclesiastical policy, for the good, as it were, of Holy Church and of this House; and when a state delegation arrived from Athens in 480, it was not difficult to tell what their business was.

'When the Athenian consultants heard these words,' we are not surprised to read further, 'they were much dismayed'. But they were not to be so easily put off. Also, they probably had with them a carefully formulated question prepared by the Athenian leaders, and they had not been given a chance to put it. If they returned without having fulfilled their mission as instructed, they would have at least a very awkward task in explaining things to the Ekklesia.

However, Athens had friends at Delphi. 'While they were consulting between themselves about this prophecy of disaster, Timon the son of Androboulos, one of the most prominent men of Delphi, gave them the advice to take suppliants' boughs' (boughs of olive or laurel, bound with woollen fillets) 'and approach the oracle again, as suppliants. This the Athenians did, and said "Lord, grant us some better oracle about our country, and have compassion on these suppliant boughs that we bear; otherwise, we will not leave the sanctuary, but stay here till we die." And the medium gave a second oracle, as follows:'

(The most literal translation is here required.)

'Pallas cannot appease Olympian Zeus, though entreating him with many words and deep wisdom. But I will speak this second word to thee, having drawn near to adamant.[50] When the other places are

[48] e.g. the cases of Lykourgos, H. i, 65; Battos, H. iv, 155. On the Athenian consultation, cf. Parke and Wormell, *The Delphic Oracle*, I, pp. 169ff.

[49] Rites, cf., e.g., Eur. *Ion*, 226f; question in writing, schol. on Aristoph. *Ploutos*, 39; see further Parke and Wormell, I, pp. 30ff and n. 67; Amandry, *La mantique apollinienne à D.*, chaps. viii, ix.

[50] Difficult. 'Having made it sure as adamant' makes sense, but is hardly translation.

taken, as many as the boundary of Kekrops and the secret place of divine Kithairon enclose, Zeus of the broad heaven grants to the Triton-born a wooden wall alone to remain unsacked, that shall help thee and thy children. Do not thou await the cavalry and the host of foot that come from the mainland, but withdraw, turning thy back; even yet shalt thou face him again, O divine Salamis, but thou shalt destroy the children of women, either, I think, when Demeter is scattered or when she comes together.'

'As these lines were, both really and on the face of it, milder than the foregoing, they wrote them down and departed to Athens.'

The mention of Salamis has been widely taken as evidence that the oracle is *post eventum*, or at best as an addition, dating from a time immediately before the operations round that island; but it need not be, if this time the suppliant *theopropoi* obtained an answer to their formulated question, and if that question was, or included, the question whether it would be well for the Athenians, if they gave battle around Salamis. It is an obvious question, how could anyone, even Themistokles, know that the Persian fleet would approach Salamis and not, for instance, by-pass it and go for the Peloponnese? The answer is that the Persian *land* forces, if they advanced to Athens, their most long-standing and most advertised objective,[51] would find Salamis before them, held in force, protected by its 'silver streak' and crowded with refugees. Not merely the fleet at Salamis, but the island itself would become an important objective; to take it would be to make an end of Athenian resistance, and Xerxes' fleet would certainly be drawn in, in order to attack it. Then, Themistokles thought, if his new navy had an opportunity to fight in the narrow channel for all that they held dear, there might be a chance.

'When Demeter is scattered or when she comes together' is usually taken to mean 'at seed-time or harvest', fall or spring, the corn-goddess being equated with the grain itself (a point not without interest for the history of Greek religious concepts).[52] It was, as has often been observed, a safe prediction that major operations would not take place in midwinter. That midsummer is also excluded is probably an indication that it was already too late in the year for that to be

[51] H. v, 105; vi, 43f, 94.

[52] Macan, *ad loc.* (vii, 141), finds the interpretation 'strained'. But not too much so for an oracle?

possible; which is a reason for dating the oracle about midsummer, after the withdrawal of the force from Tempe.

'The *theopropoi* returned to Athens and reported to the people; and many opinions were put forward as they examined the prophecy, but the prevailing ones were these. Some of the senior men said they thought the god prophesied that the Acropolis would survive; for in former times the Athenian Acropolis was protected by a wattle fence. . . . Others, however, said that he meant the ships, and advocated mobilising the fleet at the expense of all else. Now, those who said that the ships were the Wooden Wall were baffled by the last two lines (with their reference to Salamis); 'for the oracle-experts interpreted them to mean that they must be defeated in a naval battle before Salamis.' It is at this point that Themistokles makes his first entry in Herodotos' story (vii, 143); unfairly late, as we have seen, probably through the hostility of the historian's sources, but certainly at one of his finest hours; with the argument – a weak one, but he was desperate – that the god would have said not 'O divine Salamis' but rather 'O cruel Salamis', if it were really her own people who were to be slain there. No, he said, the oracle referred to the enemies who were to be destroyed there; so his counsel was to give battle at sea. 'As the result of his speech, the Athenians decided that this interpretation was preferable to that of the oracle-experts, who were against fighting at sea, and, to tell the truth, against making any resistance at all, but in favour of abandoning Attica and founding a new city abroad.'

That Themistokles was able to turn the debate is to the credit of his audience, as well as to his own. Apollo had quite clearly advised flight to the west; and the expert 'chrēsmologists' were on his side. The desperate threat to 'fast unto death', which had extorted the second oracle, came from plain men who loved their native land and demanded 'some better oracle *about our country*'; and the majority which voted for Themistokles must have consisted of men who wanted to be persuaded. Not for the first time, the plain men were right, the experts wrong, and the arguments and propaganda, which Themistokles and all who thought with him had conducted for many years, bore fruit now. He would appeal to anything, including superstition (his technique of oracle-interpretation was formally perfect). Is it to him that we owe the preservation of the significant names in the Delphi-story? – For the name of the Pythia herself, who uttered the daunting oracle, meant

'Noble Victory', and that of the friendly Delphian adviser meant 'Honor, son of Manly Counsel'. But he had educated the Athenians, too.[53] He had weaned them away from the 'hedgehog reaction'. Only a minority, and those largely, as we read, 'the older men', still clung to it. So the Athenians 'resolved in the debate after the response of the Oracle, to meet the barbarian invader of Hellas with their entire man-power on shipboard, in obedience to the God and in company with those of the Hellenes who chose'.[54]

Thus ended the most momentous debate ever held on the Athenian Parliament Hill; the Pnyx not yet arranged as we see it now, with the stone-cut platform at the top and a retaining-wall supporting the auditorium; that belongs to a later day.[55] In Themistokles' time, as still in that of Aristophanes, the audience, those courageous, anxious men of 480, sat facing downhill towards the city, and across it to the hills; Lykabettos and far Pentelikos, behind which lay Marathon; facing downhill to the platform where reasoned and pleaded, appealing to their courage, their intelligence and their deepest superstitions, that sturdy, indestructible figure, whose bull neck and broad shoulders seemed to support the falling sky.

The Resolution which Herodotos summarises was called by later Greeks the Decree of Themistokles. It was what purported to be the full text of this that the orator Aischines, himself at that time Secretary to the Council, read out to the Assembly along with the 'Decree of Miltiades' (p. 241), in the course of a patriotic speech, before, according to Demosthenes, Philip of Macedonia bought him.[56] The text which Aischines read out, in aid of an appeal to all good men to rally against the new barbarian menace, may well have been basically the same as that which was restored to our knowledge in 1959, when Mr M. H. Jameson identified it in a modest, battered and neglected inscription from a somewhat later, probably third-century, commemorative monument at Troizēn. Discussion of this interesting text, which remains the subject of keen debate, must be left to a separate note; but it may here be noted as a curious fact about it, that Themistokles according to the Troizēn text proposes on the same day (1) the commitment of the city to the care of the Gods (a euphemism for evacuation)[57]

[53] Aristeides, xlvi, p. 256. Dindorf puts this well.
[54] H. vii, 144, 3.
[55] See K. Kourouniotis and Homer Thompson in *Hesperia*, I; cf. Plut. *Them.* 19; Aristoph. *Acharnians* (the opening scene).
[56] Dem. *On the Embassy*, 303.
[57] As was noticed by Quintilian, ix, 2, 92.

and the removal of non-combatants (children and their mothers, the city's future, to the comparative safety of Troizen, old people and goods (second priority) to Salamis); the mobilisation of every available man for the fleet, half of which (100 ships) is to take station forthwith at the Euboian Artemision; and the recall of exiles, especially the ostracised, who are, however, to 'depart to Salamis and remain there, until the people decide about them'. It is a curious collection of proposals, especially the last; for the proper time for the recall of exiles in the interests of national solidarity (as the text says) was surely at the very beginning of the crisis, and not after it had become acute; and the instruction to the returned exiles to wait at Salamis till the people could decide about them is hardly appropriate to a time when all Athens was setting off on a campaign, so that the Assembly stood adjourned *sine die*,[58] and when every man was wanted at once. Moreover, though the chief resolution in the Troizen text is that summarised by Herodotos at the end of the Oracle debate, 'to meet the invader at sea, in company with those of the Hellenes who chose' – the inscription, interestingly and perhaps authentically, has 'with the Lakedaimonians and Corinthians and Aiginetans and the others who choose to share the danger' – there is no mention of 'obeying the god', or of the oracle at all. The inscription seems to assemble together resolutions which almost certainly (and scarcely any details in history are quite certain) must have been taken at different times. Both its general tenor and some details of style give rise to the suspicion that it is not an authentic copy of a document, preserved since the time of Themistokles, but a 'restoration' of what some later Athenian(s) thought Themistokles ought to have said, on the basis of stories and quoted phrases[59] handed down in the Athenian tradition of the Great War. In this folk-memory, as in Herodotos, but to an even greater extent, what happened in Athens when the invasion was impending is thought of as happening 'all at the same time' (one *kairós*), and anything that Themistokles was believed to have proposed or said, or might have proposed or said, could be imagined as being said on one occasion without arousing uneasiness.

However, to sum up the problem of chronology, which is thus left

[58] As is pointed out by L. Moretti in *Riv. di Filologia*, LXXXVIII, p. 398.

[59] For memorable phrases, quoted from speeches which were not written down, cf. Plut. *Kim.* 16, *Per.* 8.

to us: it is probable that the mission to Delphi and the debate on the oracle's response took place after the collapse of northern Greece; hence the atmosphere of gloom and something like panic which prevailed, and which Themistokles stoutly combated; but it is not likely that the mission and the debate took place after the first clash of arms, which followed, in August (see p. 405, below), for the reason that after that clash there was not time, before the Persians reached Attica. It is possible that a decision was also then taken for the removal of non-combatants, since Themistokles had foreseen the probable necessity of a retreat from the mainland. The Assembly might have voted for placing their women and children in relative safety, since the men were themselves taking the decision *to leave the city*, though not yet leaving it to the enemy.

About this time, too, will have taken place an incident, said to have done much to raise morale. Through the market-place, from the residential area up to the Acropolis, marched a band of young men of the 'knightly' class; young aristocrats, whose pride was in their horses and who at least affected to despise the sailor. They were carrying their bridles. At their head, gaily and proudly, went Kimon, aged about 28, the son of Miltiades. Up on the citadel, Kimon 'dedicated' his bridle, in the Temple of Athena, as men used to dedicate things with which they had done. His friends did the same. Having done this, and said his prayers to the goddess, Kimon helped himself to an infantry shield that hung on the wall, a trophy of some old war, and went, a symbol of the solidarity of Athens, to join his ship as a marine.[60]

It may be noticed that Themistokles' strategy was the same as that which Hekataios, over fifteen years before, had urged in vain upon Miletos: to transfer themselves in a body to the island of Leros, in the hope of being able thence to return to the mainland when the war was won. Hekataios failed to carry his motion, and his strategy was not tried; nor in any case would it have saved the Milesians, since the trial of strength at sea ended in defeat. Themistokles' strategy staked all on another trial of strength at sea, with his new navy.

Themistokles never wavered in the belief that victory was possible. Against all voices raised in pessimism, he stuck to the thesis that there *were* enough ships in nationalist Greece, if they were properly used. That meant, if they were concentrated and not kept in separate

[60] Plut. *Kim.* 5.

detachments, near the cities to which they belonged, as Greek instinct or ingrown habit would have dictated. They must fight pitched battles, and fight in a body; and they must begin fighting as far forward as possible.[61] To inflict losses on the enemy, the best position was still that at the Euboian Artemision. It would have been better if the Mount Olympos line had been held, and Thessaly denied to the enemy; but the north end of Euboia, since it was an island, was still tenable. There the enemy would have to come to them after a voyage along a harbourless lee shore; and Themistokles did not need an inland Delphian to tell him what some Delphians are said to have told the Greeks: that the oracle, when the Delphians themselves consulted it, had given the advice: Pray to the Winds.[62]

It was also at least desirable that an attempt should be made to hold the Persians by land from entering central Greece. There, they could not perhaps have forced the Greek fleet away from Euboia, but they could have made its supply difficult, and the knowledge that the enemy army was south of them would have been bad for morale. Before or after his triumph in the Athenian assembly, Themistokles must have visited general headquarters at Corinth, or sent trusted emissaries; for, at the eleventh hour, he obtained the support of Sparta, and therefore of the League, for his strategy.

It went against the grain for Spartans to campaign at this season; for the Karneian festival, culminating at the second full moon after midsummer, in this year on August the 20th, was now approaching. Also it was an Olympic year, and the sacred Games, held at that same full moon, would attract the attention of all Peloponnesians. These religious scruples, let it be repeated, must be taken seriously. A great Athenian armament was destroyed in 413, and the hopes of Athens with it, because its general would not make an urgently necessary move immediately after an eclipse of the moon. If an Athenian general thought like that then, we have no call to doubt that Spartans regulated their campaigns by the religious calendar in 480. But the views of Themistokles and considerations of military urgency carried the day, to the extent that the naval states sent the greater part of their fleets, 113 Peloponnesian triremes,[63] to join the Athenians at Artemision. The Spartans also agreed that, despite the religious season, support must be given by land; an advanced guard at least, of a few thousand men,

[61] Plut. *Them.* 7, 1.

[62] H. vii, 178.

[63] H. viii, 1.

sufficient to hold a narrow-fronted position until reinforcements could be sent later. To show that Sparta was in earnest, one of the kings and a royal bodyguard of 300 Spartiates would go at once, even though it meant failing to be in their places at the Karneia. Picking up troops from the states along his route (for the decision had been left late, and he had 200 miles to cover – the Persians in Pieria were actually nearer to the chosen position than Sparta was) Leonidas, the brother and successor of Kleomenes, marched for Thermopylai. If Kleomenes had been alive, it would have been his business. But then, if Kleomenes had been alive, and successful, the Persians would perhaps never have reached Thermopylai at all.

THE TROIZEN INSCRIPTION

I.–*Translation*

The following is a literal translation of this famous text, made chiefly from Professor Jameson's *editio princeps* in *Hesperia*, vol. XXIX, but with a few improved readings, which I owe chiefly to the kindness of Professor Meritt. The lettering is thought by most authorities to be of the third century B.C.,[1] though the discoverer prefers the late fourth; the marble is agreed by experts to be Pentelic; obtained, like the text, from Athens. Both in the late fourth and first half of the third century, Troizen was again linked with Athens in a patriotic struggle, now against Macedonia, and this will have provided the occasion for the erection of a monument commemorating Troizen's services in the heroic days of 480. The monument was seen and described by Pausanias in the Antonine age (Paus. ii, 31, 7; above, p. 359). The surface is defaced in its left centre, especially at the top; but most of what is lost can be restored with confidence, with the help of the quotations of the beginning of the text given especially by Aelius Aristides and his scholiast (vol. II, p. 256, III, p. 606, Dindorf), and of the fact that the inscription is cut, in the classical manner, *stoichēdon*, each letter below a letter of the preceding line (after the heading), with 42 letters to a line, except for an accidental additional *stoichos* at the ends of lines 38–41. For convenience of reference the lines of the Greek, which usually divide in the middle of a word, are kept so far as possible.

G O D S[2]

It was Resolved by the Council and People:
Themistokles, son of Neokles of Phrearroi, proposed:
To deliver the City in trust to Athena the Mistress
of Athens and all the other gods to guard
and ward off the barbarian from the land; and that the Athenians themselves and the foreigners who dwell in Athens
shall deposit their children and wives in Troizen
. . . . . . the patron of the land,[3]

[1] G. Daux in *BCH* LXXXIV (1960); M. Guarducci in *Riv. di Fil.* LXXXIX (1961); D. M. Lewis (tentatively) in *CQ* N.S. XI; and cf. *SEG* (forthcoming).

[2] The heading to all decree inscrs.; standing for a list of gods invoked in the Assembly?

[3] Reference to Pittheus of Troizen, grandfather of Theseus?

and old people and goods in Salamis. That the treasurers and priestesses on the Acropolis remain guarding the things of the gods; and the other Athenians all, and the foreigners of military age, embark on the 200 ships which have been made ready and defend against the barbarian their freedom and that of the other Hellenes, with the Lakedaimonians and Corinthians and Aiginetans[4] and the others who choose to share the danger. That there be appointed trierarchs two hundred, one for each ship, by the Generals, beginning tomorrow, from among those who have land and house in Athens and sons born in wedlock and are not over fifty years old, and that they[5] assign the ships to them by lot. That they enrol marines ten[6] to each[6] ship from among those over twenty years of age and under thirty, and four archers; and that they allot[7] the petty officers to the ships at the same time when they allot[8] the trierarchs. That the generals also write up lists of the crews of the ships on notice-boards, the Athenians from the service registers and foreigners from those registered with Polemarch. That they write them up dividing them into 200 companies, by hundreds,[8a] writing over each company the name of the ship and of the trierarch and those of the petty officers, so that men may know in which ship each company is to embark. And when all the companies are made up and allotted to the triremes, the Council shall complete the manning of all the 200 ships with the Generals, after sacrificing a propitiatory offering to Zeus Almighty and Athena and Victory and Poseidon the Preserver. And when the ships are fully manned, with one hundred of them to meet[9] the enemy at the Artemision in Euboia and with the other hundred of them off Salamis and the rest of Attica to lie and guard the land. And that all Athenians may be of one mind

[4] Cf. H. vii, 144, 3. 'Aiginetans' is conjectural, but virtually certain.

[5] *Sc.* the Generals.

[6] This reading now confirmed.

[7] διακληρῶσαι.

[8] ἐπικληρῶσι.

[8a] Meritt now believes this reading to be indicated, on the defaced part of the stone, although not easy to understand; perhaps filling up one hundred for each ship first?

[9] *boetheîn* (cf. p. 242 above).

in the defence against the barbarian, those banished for the ten years shall depart[10] to Salamis and remain there until the People come to a decision about them; and the . . .

Six letters at the end of 47 and an unknown number of lines below are lost. The text may have continued with a reference to the *atīmoi*, those deprived of citizen rights and banished by the courts; since the orator Andokides (i, 107) refers to a decision to re-admit them also in this crisis (no doubt with specified exceptions, as was usual in such an amnesty; cf. Jameson, pp. 221f). 'Depart', in 46, is an odd word if this is supposed to be the first proposal for the recall of the exiles, and suggests the question whether the difficulty of supposing that this had not been done earlier can be avoided. Are the exiled leaders (Xanthippos and Aristeides) to be supposed to have come home, and is their political activity causing embarrassment? But the question still remains unanswered, how and when the People could be expected to 'decide about them' now that all able-bodied men were about to set out on service with the fleet.

II.–*The Question of Authenticity*

The *prima facie* obvious conclusion, that we have here the text of the original mobilisation-orders, proposed by Themistokles and voted by the Ekklesia in 480, is so exciting as to be almost intoxicating; but study of the text and historical context gives rise to uneasiness – not least, the detailed measures proposed for manning the fleet. On the eve of Artemision, were there no ships at sea already, and no ships' companies which had served together, and which it would have been folly to break up? Had the new navy, or any part of it, never been to sea together? Herodotos indeed mentions one crew (viii, 17) distinguished for skill and valour, that of Kleinias the son of Alkibiades, 'who served with 200 men paid at his own expense and with his own ship'. This was perhaps, as Herodotos' language suggests, exceptional; but, taking the Decree as it stands, with its emphasis on distributing the petty officers (helmsmen, boatswains, look-out men, deckhands who managed the sail, called collectively the *hypēresia* or 'service') *by lot*, it appears that it would have required either a special clause in the bill or a separate 'act of parliament' to license Kleinias' patriotic individual action. One would expect better of Themistokles' Athens than this last-minute, deliberately fortuitous assembly of ships' companies which are to meet for the first time at the point of embarkation; and in fact,

[10] ἀπιέναι.

from the little that we know of fifth-century and early fourth-century trierarchs, it seems that trierarchs then personally collected their crews, being appointed in good time so that they could do so, and that 'crowns', *stephanoi*, were awarded for those who produced the best ship and crew. And in Themistokles' navy bill of 483, in which individual rich men were given responsibility for the building of single ships, this system of 'personal trierarchy' seems to be at least adumbrated.[11]

The number of ten men-at-arms (only) as marines also prompts, at least, surprise. It was this number that the swift Athenian ships of the Peloponnesian War, which manœuvred for an attack with the ram, carried;[12] but it seems that this number must have represented a reduction since earlier times. Plutarch (*Them.* 14), we do not know from what source, gives the Athenians eighteen marines per ship in 480; four archers and fourteen men-at-arms. This could derive, through an intermediary, from the same original, with a misunderstanding, at some point in the transmission, as to whether the four were included in the fourteen. (As we shall see, neither Plutarch nor Aristides, though they both quote the memorable opening words of the text, seems to have had the whole text of our inscription, just as we have it, before him.) More telling is the fact that Thucydides (i, 49, 1), on the sea-fight between Corinth and Kerkyra, speaks of 'many hoplites, javelin-men and archers on the decks' as characteristic of 'the old, unscientific way'. We are reminded of the forty men-at-arms carried by each Chian ship at Lade (p. 213). Kimon, on his great foray into the Levant about 467, carried 'many men-at-arms' on deck, and had his ships 'made broader' (says Plutarch, *Kim.* 12, 2) than when they were 'designed by Themistokles for speed and manœuvrability'. It is difficult to see what Plutarch understood by 'made broader'. It looks as if he was trying to reconcile a presumably genuine tradition about Kimon's numerous marines (a 'public fact') with another tradition, irreconcilable with Herodotos, which ascribed the tactics of the later Athenian navy to Themistokles as its founder. For Herodotos, in two important and often forgotten pasages, speaks of the Greek ships of 480 as 'heavier' than their antagonists (wherefore, says Themistokles in a speech (viii, 60a), it is expedient for them not to give battle in open waters), and of the enemy ships as 'better sailing' (viii, 10). The later 'vulgate' reverses this, in its anxiety to make the Greek victory one of skill over mere brute force and numbers. It seems certain that, in the ships of his

[11] Amandry, in *Bulletin de la Faculté des Lettres de Strasbourg*, XXXIX (1961), No. 8, pp. 413ff (esp. 420–2); cf. Demosth. *On the Trierarchic Crown* and, for the individual efforts made by trierarchs, *Against Polykles* (for Apollodoros); Thk. vi, 31, 3 (the fleet for Sicily).

[12] Thk. iii, 95, 2; c.f. 93, 1.

young, mass-produced navy, with all Athens on board and not only sailors by profession, the navy with which he was so anxious to give battle in narrow waters, Themistokles must have planned to carry many more men-at-arms than ten per ship. In this detail, then, as well as in leaving no room for the personal collection of crews by trierarchs, the Troizen text is redolent of the fourth century.

These appear to be the most stubborn obstacles to our believing that the inscription reproduces essentially the words of Themistokles. There are many others, but most can be explained away, or are inconclusive. It is difficult, as has been observed above (p. 360), to imagine that the evacuation of Athens was decided so early, or the recall of exiles so late, as the day before general mobilisation; but we can, at a pinch, accept the former as a possibility and explain the reference to the exiles as *not* the original motion for their recall. Plutarch and Aelius Aristides, in the passages where they quote its opening words (Plut. *Them.* 10, *Ar.* xlvi, p. 256 of vol. II, Dindorf), both put the evacuation-decree explicitly *after* Artemision, in flagrant contradiction of our text, lines 41f. This can be explained on the hypothesis that they knew only the opening lines of the decree, through some literary intermediary; but Plutarch does elsewhere claim (*Ar.* 26, *Kim.* 13), though not in *Them.* 10, to have used the collection of decrees made by Krateros the Macedonian (Jacoby, *FGH* no. 342), which should have contained the whole of it. This, as well as the questions whether and if so why our text envisages the fourth-century organization of the trierarchy, is a point to which we must return when trying to formulate conclusions.

It is the same with many details of style and vocabulary. Thus, it has struck every scholar as an anomaly that Themistokles' name, as proposer, is followed by those of his father and deme, whereas in fifth-century inscriptions recording decrees these are not given. This is fourth-century practice. The few known early Athenian decrees, moreover, begin simply 'Resolved by the People'; 'Resolved by the Council and the People' appears first in the mid-fifth century 'Phaselis Decree', perhaps as a result of the reform of 461.[13] These anomalies might however be the result of later editing, not necessarily of forgery.

In the body of the text, scholars have objected to its 'rhetoric', to phrases such as 'sharing the danger' and 'defence of freedom against the barbarian', which are reminiscent of fourth-century patriotic oratory.[14]

[13] Early practice, see Tod, *GHI* no. 11 (on the cleruchy in Salamis), = *IG* I², 1; cf. 3, l. 16, 4, l. 26. Phaselis Decree, Tod no. 32, *IG* I², 16. Cf. D. M. Lewis, 'Notes on the Decree of Themistocles' in *CQ* N.S. XI, p. 61; Wade-Gery, *Essays*, 180ff.

[14] Amandry (see n. 11), p. 416; C. Habicht, 'Falsche Urkunden zur Geschichte Athens im Zeitalter der Perserkriege', in *Hermes* LXXXIX (1961), p. 8.

Here, one might reply with Lewis (*op. cit.*, p. 62), 'I should be sorry to think that Themistokles was incapable of a little rhetoric on this occasion.' The Decree, if genuine, certainly would have come at the end of a major oratorical effort; moreover, it was not intended for inscription on stone. Executive decrees of passing importance, as opposed to laws and treaties, never were so inscribed in the fifth century, except when they pertained to the handling of *sacred* funds; even the celebrated Athenian Tribute-Lists are lists of the *quotas* paid to Athena. If the Decree or any part of it is a copy of a document, it was a document preserved somehow in archives. Early stone inscriptions are kept short because Demos counted the cost of inscribing them (when imperial Athens set up an inscription making any promise to one of her subject allies, she made the ally pay for it, as in the Phaselis Decree (cf. n. 13) or in *IG* I² 108, = Tod 84, l. 35, etc.); and there is no need to expect Themistokles on a very abnormal occasion, and in a proposal not intended for inscription on stone, to be limited to the dry, normal, lapidary forms of a *Dekretstil*.

In dealing with details the discussion runs into great difficulties; nearly all the arguments are double-edged. If a detail is consistent with Herodotos, it can be used (*a*) as evidence of genuineness or (*b*) as ground for suspicion that a forger has used the current tradition; if it is awkward and anomalous, it can nevertheless be used as an argument for genuineness, on the ground that no forger would have done *that*. If a detail of usage can be shown to be known in the early fifth century by a parallel usage in Aeschylus, it can be suggested that the forger used Aeschylus.

The names and epithets of gods in this text provide, as might have been expected, particularly rich food for controversy. Of the epithet of Athena, 'Mistress of Athens' (*Athēnōn Medeousa*), Jameson writes (p. 210) 'of epic origin . . . it is the most emphatically national of her epithets, . . . and it is this quality which accounts for its use here'. Even Lewis, basically favourable to accepting the decree as genuine though perhaps edited, however looks askance at this: 'The title is basically East Greek . . . Athena Polias looked at from outside Athens' (e.g. by Athenian colonists in Samos, or in an exchange of civilities with the island of Karpathos, Tod II, no. 110). Precisely this phrase had, in fact, aroused doubts as to the genuineness of the decree quoted by Plutarch and Aristides, even before the discovery of the inscription.[15]

[15] E. Preuner in *Ath. Mitt.* XLIX (1924); Lewis, p. 62; Habicht, p. 6; Amandry (independently of Preuner?), p. 418.

On the gods listed in lines 38ff, Lewis comments (p. 64): 'An extremely odd collection, and, I would have thought, beyond the imagination of any fourth-century forger.' Habicht, on the other hand (p. 6), says 'Die Liste ist ganz konventionell, indem sie gerade die und nur die Götter enthält, die man zu jeder Zeit in Athen bei einem solchen Anlass erwarten würde.' I must confess to surprise at this judgment of Habicht's. 'Almighty' (*Pankrates*) as an epithet of Zeus rouses the suspicion of Amandry (418) for quite other reasons: that (like *Athenon Medeousa*), 'L'épithète ne se rencontre que chez les poètes. . . . L'existence d'un culte officiel rendu à Zeus Pancratès n'est attestée nulle part dans le monde grec' (except) 'dans une glose d'Hésychius, citée par Jameson' (Jameson, p. 220). Amandry pertinently wonders whether the Troizenian copyist has not omitted an 'and' between 'Zeus' and 'Pankrates' and inserted one between 'Athena' and 'Victory'; since a small shrine of two heroes, Pankrates and Palaimon, has been discovered on the Ilissos, near the temple of Olympian Zeus (but with no trace of an identification with Zeus);[16] and a cult of Athena Nike is well attested in the fifth century,[17] whereas Nike alone seems to be a later development. Jameson and Lewis (*locc. citt.*) find comfort in the repeated use of *pankrates* as an epithet of Zeus in Aeschylus (especially its use in *Eumenides* 917ff, with a reference to 'the gods who saved Greece'); L. Moretti, on the other hand, suggests that 'the forger' derived it, as a piece of period colour, from his reading of Aeschylus.[18]

It may be observed that, if this was his way of working, the composer showed remarkable restraint in *not* using the later technical and legal word for 'the foreigners resident in Athens', registered with the Polemarch: the word *metoikoi*, which also occurs repeatedly in Aeschylus, and notably, in an Athenian context, in the same play, less than 100 lines later.[19]

The divine names, in fact (a phrase, in itself, ominously reminiscent of the most famous pseudepigrapha in European literature), are not the most promising touchstone for use in the present test. Do we really know that Athenians in a crisis were limited to a list of epithets for the gods known to us from (mostly later) religious inscriptions, and could not offer sacrifice or worship to Zeus or Athena at any of their temples, using epithets familiar from poetry? We are perhaps on somewhat firmer ground in examining more concrete terms; and having noticed

[16] Miliadis in *Praktika t. Arch. Etairias* (Athens), 1953; *BCH* 1954, 1955.

[17] And even the 6th; cf. Raubitschek, *Dedications from the Ath. Acropolis*, no. 329.

[18] L. Moretti in *Riv. di Fil.* LXXXVIII (1960), p. 397.

[19] *Eum.* 1011; cf. *Suppl.* 994, *Seven* 548; less apposite for present purposes, *Pers.* 319, etc. Later official use, cf. *IG* I^2, 188, 52; Thk. ii, 13; Andok. i, 15, etc.

the inscription's avoidance of *metoikoi* in lines 7, 13 and 30, although it occurs repeatedly in Aeschylus, we may well feel more kindly than does Moretti (*loc. cit.*) towards the word *taxis*, used of ships' companies in Greek literature only here (31f, 36) and in Aesch. *Persians*, 380, of the *taxeis* calling to one another as Xerxes' fleet puts out to sea by night.

Another word conspicuously avoided by the inscription is the verb *exostrakizo*, used by Herodotos (viii, 79, 1) and Theopompos (*FGH* 115 F 96b) of 'those banished for the ten years' (45f), or simple *ostrakizo* (*Ath. P.* 22, etc.). This term, 'to potsherd', presumably originally slang, not official language, is avoided in favour of the colourless *methistēmi*, meaning simply 'to remove'. Lewis, having tried to collect all known uses of this word with reference to *ostrakismos*, finds only eight; five explaining the institution and three referring to this episode, if not actually to our text; all, he suggests, deriving directly or indirectly from documents.[20]

Akropolis on the other hand (l. 11) looks like a clear anachronism (so, even Lewis thinks). The word does not appear in Attic inscriptions before the late fifth century; earlier inscriptions regularly refer to the Acropolis as *polis*, 'the City' (cf. the City of London); Thucydides (ii, 15) remarks on this use. But I am not sure that even this cannot be defended. It is noteworthy that when *akropolis* does first appear in a document, the second Decree of Kallias (*IG* I^2 92, = Tod, *GHI* 51B), it is in a topographical context (the fencing of the citadel); and that Kallias in the preceding decree, passed on the same day, referring to the treasury, regularly (four times) uses *polis* in the ancient way. In like manner here, the author has just used the word *polis* for the city in the wider sense (l. 4), which is to be 'entrusted to the gods'; he therefore prefers a different word for 'the City' in the narrower sense, where some people are to remain. The word *akropolis* was both of respectable literary antiquity (e.g., *Od.* viii, 494; Theognis, 233) and in current use (if we may judge by Herodotos) for the citadel of Athens; and if we had earlier inscriptions in which the distinction between city and City (or citadel) was required, we have no grounds for asserting that we should not find it there.

On the whole, therefore, the inscription stands up well to linguistic examination. The forger, if forgery it is, has worked with some skill to give his language a fifth-century colour; an achievement very remarkable, one might almost have said incredible before the age of scholarship; but there is a man, as we shall see, known to have handled a text like ours,

[20] Ar. *Politics*, 1284a; Philochoros (*FGH* 328 F 30, *FHG* fr. 79); D.S. xi, 55; Plut. *Ar.* 7, 6; Poll. viii, 19; and Plut. *Them.* 11. 1, *Ar.* 8, 1; Ael. Ar. xlvi, p. 248 (Dind.); Lewis, pp. 65f.

who seems to have all the necessary qualifications. The most suspicious feature of the language, in fact, is an Isokrateian tendency to the avoidance of *hiatus*. Vowels clash, at the end of one word and the beginning of the next, only nine times in 350 words, an average of 1 in 39, as compared with 1 in 26, 1 in under 22, 1 in 18, in three well-preserved Athenian inscriptions of the years 445 and after, which provide comparable passages of continuous prose.[21] Such avoidance, whenever possible without straining, would be second nature to an orator of the generation after Isokrates.

As to external evidence, it is reasonable to suppose that it was our text or something like it that Aischines read to the Assembly, not long before 346, when making what Demosthenes remembers as 'those long and eloquent speeches' against Philip (cf. p. 359 n. 56, above). But before that, as evidence on how a genuine Decree of Themistokles might have been transmitted to the mid-fourth century, we have nothing. More than that, it seems as certain as such things ever can be that it was not known, at the beginning of that century, to Lysias or Isokrates.[22] For both of them, telling over (already for the how-many-thousandth time at Athens, in public or private?) the glorious story of Athens' 'finest hour', give the usual picture of the decision to evacuate Athens as taken at the last moment, after Thermopylai fell. The modern version of the story, based on the acceptance of the Troizen text as a copy of an 'original document', according to which Artemision was fought merely as a delaying action to give time for the evacuation,[23] is as clearly unknown to them as it is to our one and only near-contemporary historian.

The inscription is not, therefore, a copy of one set up in public at Athens on stone or bronze in the fifth century, or it would have coloured the tradition as transmitted both by Herodotos and by the orators. It was not, as we have seen, customary to set up such permanent records of merely executive decisions, and at the moment, in any case, there was not time. Nor was the Decree of Themistokles probably set up within living memory as part of a memorial (as now suggested by H. Berve in *Sitzb. d. Bayer. Akad.*, 1961, 3); if there was ever any likelihood that it would be, the disgrace of Themistokles and his flight to the Persians would have militated against it; and while we possess

[21] The observation of Mr Lewis (p. 66); well worth making, though, as he says, the samples are small. The three 5C. texts are in Tod, nos. 42, 51A, 61.

[22] Lys. *Epitaphios* 27–47 (esp. 32); Is. *Paneg.* 88–98 (esp. 96).

[23] Jameson in *The Scientific American*, March 1961; S. E. P. Atherley in a B.B.C. broadcast (*The Listener*, 29 June 1961); a reconstruction which I find unconvincing, see further below, p. 377.

many fragments of Persian War memorial inscriptions, we have among them no fragments of any similar voluminous text in prose.

If, then, our text was preserved through the fifth century, it must have been preserved in archives, probably on papyrus; and we have to examine the likelihood of that. *A priori*, the likelihood seems slim, since it would have had to survive the evacuation – two evacuations. In the first, Themistokles could be imagined to have kept the master-copy, as his justification for actions under the mobilisation orders; but in the second year, it was a 'dead file'. That there were Athenian archives, other than public inscriptions, containing the texts of laws among other documents, is certain, from the story of the republication of the criminal law-code ascribed to Drakon and Solon, after the fall of the revolutionary government of the Four Hundred. An inscription exists, bidding the commissioners appointed 'obtain the required texts'; and a long task it proved, so that Nikomachos, presumably head or secretary of the commission, was later accused of corruptly spinning out the time of his salaried employment, in a post to which he was first appointed for four months, to six years; and moreover (though whether there is anything more in this than spite, we do not know), of 'setting himself up in the place of Solon', making his own cancellations and additions, to oblige individuals, for a consideration. This shows both that the archives were fairly voluminous, and that their contents were a mystery to the plain man.[24] But arguments derived from this evidence, here again, can cut both ways. No one knew what there was in the archives, and if a searcher claimed to have found a document which, in the time of Aischines as today, everyone was delighted to see discovered, the chances of his claim being scientifically checked were slight.

The mid-fourth century was, in fact, a time at which numerous documents of the Persian War period, of which nothing is heard earlier even in patriotic oratory, were alleged to have been preserved; and their genuineness was promptly denied by a learned historian who was not an Athenian, Theopompos the Chian. Theopompos denied the genuineness of 'the Oath of the Greeks, which the Athenians say that the Greeks swore before the Battle of Plataia, . . . and the Athenian treaty with the King' (i.e. the Peace of Kallias, 449, which he denied

[24] *IG* I², 111 (Tod, no. 87), first para.; cf. Lysias xxx, 2 (in Tod, *ad loc.*). Mr A. G. Woodhead, whom I would thank for much help in this section, points out that the language, e.g. of the Decree of Kallias (Tod, *GHI* 51), suggests that archives were scattered in many offices in the 5th cent., before the foundation of the Mētrōön as a central record-office; and wonders whether thereafter, in an increasingly historically-minded age, an effort was made to 'restore' texts of some of the famous decrees, which earlier orators, whose speeches were not preserved in writing, had quoted from memory.

because the text published was in the Ionic alphabet, not in the Attic alphabet used in official documents down to 403), also the traditionally embellished account of the Battle of Marathon, and (his words are quoted) 'all the other boasts with which the city of Athens deceives the Greeks'.[25] The quotation was from Theopompos' *Philippika* ('History of Philip'), Book xxv, which is shown by adjacent fragments to have included events of 348–7, just about the time when Aischines was making his patriotic speeches. The documents were being produced and quoted in aid of Athens' new great patriotic struggle, against Philip; and Theopompos had his own bias, since in his view Philip, though by no means above criticism, was the hero of his history, and the leaders of the Athenian war-party were in the wrong. Some have argued, in favour of the genuineness of our Decree, that if what Aischines read out was a forgery, Demosthenes would have said so; but this rests on a false premise; for when Aischines read the Decrees, he was speaking on the side of the war-party, and Demosthenes will have applauded. He later attacks Aischines for changing sides; it would not have helped to attack his earlier pronouncements.

Some, also, have suggested the historian Ephoros, an admirer of Athens, as the researcher who discovered these documents. This would indeed be consistent with the date of their appearance; but against it is the fact that Diodoros, who relied heavily upon Ephoros, quotes only one of them, the Oath. Greek historians, in fact, rarely quote documents; even Thucydides, in a famous case when he does quote a treaty, of which the text is also preserved on stone (v, 47; cf. *IG* I^2, 86+; Tod no. 73), quotes it with some verbal differences. In general, Greek writers do not quote meticulously; they paraphrase;[26] a practice descended perhaps from that of the pre-literate stage of society from which Greece had not long emerged.[27] Greek historical writing seems to bear the marks of its descent from the epic; and one of the most unhappy results of this was the practice of inserting imaginary or at best 'reconstructed' speeches. Thucydides did not invent this practice; on the contrary, he is the only Greek historian to make any apology for it. But in a world in which it was familiar practice to 'reconstruct' speeches, it would not have seemed particularly reprehensible, if it was convenient, to reconstruct Themistokles' Decree.

But the literary men who *were* accustomed to quote documents were

[25] Theop. in *FGH* 115 FF 153–4; on which cf. Habicht (cf. n. 14 above), pp. 11ff; R. Sealey in *JHS* LXXX, 'Theopompos on Athenian Lies'; against Theop., A. E. Raubitschek, 'Herodotus and the Inscriptions' in London Inst. of Classical Studies *Bulletin*, No. 8. See further p. 513, n. 8, below.

[26] Cf. Amandry, *op. cit.*, p. 417.

[27] Cf. my *Lyric Age*, pp. 216o5,9f.

the orators; accustomed first to do so by the practice of producing laws, wills, contracts and the written depositions of witnesses in the courts of law. From this it was a short step to the use of quotations in political oratory; for instance, the quotation of long passages of patriotic poetry, a practice which seems to increase during the middle third of the fourth century. And it seems to have been in the circle of Euboulos, the leading politician and public financier of Athens before 350, that the documents, to which Theopompos objected, made their appearance.[28] It is Aischines, a leading orator of Euboulos' party, who is recorded to have read the decrees of Themistokles and Miltiades; and in fact, if we are to ask, was there a man in fourth-century Athens who was well placed and well qualified either to invent them or to discover them, we need look no further.

During the two years before that unhappy embassy of 347–6, Aischines, as Demosthenes tells us (xix, 249), was himself Secretary of the Council, 'taking his meals in the Tholos', the official Mess of the councillors on duty as prytaneis. As Secretary, he had every opportunity of familiarising himself with the archives. If there were old documents there that might be of use to him as an orator, he had every opportunity of directing a search for them; he had also every opportunity of making himself familiar with official language, both past and present. And it seems by no means impossible, even if at first sight surprising, that his sense of style might have been sensitive to differences between fourth- and fifth-century usage and vocabulary; for he was not only a great orator; he had also been a tragic actor; Demosthenes describes him (*ib.* 247) declaiming the famous opening speech of Kreon from Sophokles' *Antigone*, on man's duty to the city, on the public platform as he had on the stage. Aischines had a sense of the dramatic; and, moreover, politics had just then recently taken a turn which might well stimulate that sense, and direct his attention to the Persian Wars. It was in 352 that Euboulos' government had felt constrained by Philip's activities to take unwontedly vigorous action, and that Philip was bloodlessly checked by an Athenian fleet and army holding Thermopylai. Thousands of Athenians, and not improbably Aischines himself, had recently had the stimulus of serving in a successful and painless campaign off northern Euboia and under that historic mountain wall. It is small wonder if, in 349–7, Aischines searched in the old archives; but whether he really found what he wanted, or was stimulated to supply the deficiency – that remains the question.

It is, as has been observed above, the major more than the minor

[28] Habicht's suggestion (p. 30, and foregoing pp.)

details of our inscription that arouse supicion; most clearly, the ten epibatai to a ship; most far-reachingly, the details of the proposed mobilisation, which would make better sense if the chance-selected crews were to have several weeks together before meeting the enemy, rather than, as before Artemision, a matter of days. The question presents itself, would there be any reason why a fourth-century forger should invent this detailed picture of the distribution of crews by lot? There would. In Aischines' time, and precisely in 357, Euboulos' government had overhauled the system of naval finance and administration. Before the reform, rich trierarchs had been able to secure the best crews by paying extra; and the less rich, as may be seen from Demosthenes' speech, written in the law-suit of Polykles *vs* Apollodoros, had resented it. The suggestion that Themistokles' organization was such as might commend itself to a good fourth-century democrat would not have been unwelcome in the Assembly.

The vigorous argument still current about the genuineness of our Decree leaves one not entirely without hope that scholars may attain some measure of agreement. Jameson and Lewis, believers, agree that there has probably been some 'editing'; Habicht, the sceptic, agrees, *à propos* of the case of Arthmios of Zeleia (on whom Demosthenes quotes what Habicht believes to be another forged document), that there exists a 'Probleme der gewiss historischen Affäre'.[29] Moreover, he believes, 'Unglücklicherweise, existierte wohl eine Überlieferung, die von solchen Urkunden der frühen Zeit sprach'; and 'man durch die Überlieferung ihren wesentlichen Inhalt kannte oder zu kennen glaubte' (pp. 30, 31). This is obviously highly speculative. However, it is something that it is common ground that, whatever was preserved in writing, there has been some editing, and that, however active the fourth-century editor or author, he did have something to go on. Personally, the present writer inclines to the sceptical side, for the reasons given, but does not believe that the case can be positively proved; suspecting, without proof, that an attempt was made, in patriotic circles, to 'restore' lost but famous Persian War decrees. The material available may well have included much more than we have, with Herodotos only; even if it was mainly a more-or-less oral tradition, handed down from schoolmaster to pupil and from one speaker to another of funeral orations, it may well have been to some extent

[29] Dem. *Phil.* iii, 41ff, *Embassy* 270ff, etc., etc. (including Ael. Ar. xlvi, p. 287 D.; schol. *ad loc.* quotes Krateros, cf. *FGH* 342 F 14); Habicht, 16f, 24f. – I must register the opinion that this is by no means on the same footing with the Themistokles Decree, however; for Arthmios was an otherwise obscure person, and unless there had existed a genuine inscription about him there would have been no need to invent him.

complementary to Herodotos, in that it comprised a kind of Themistokles-saga handed down in democratic circles (whence Thucydides drew), doing more justice to the great leader than was done by Herodotos' upper-class informants at a time when Themistokles' death in Persian territory was still recent.

Having been produced in writing, our text was presumably included in Krateros the Macedonian's *Collection of Decrees*, through which, directly or indirectly, it, or at least the knowledge of it, will have reached Plutarch, Aristides (cf. n. 19) and other writers (cf. Jameson, p. 202, n. 6); though Krateros is not actually quoted as a source for this document. But one important fact about its tradition must be re-emphasised (cf. p. 368) before leaving the matter: neither Plutarch nor Aristides, when weaving it into their stories, believed that the mobilisation, the decision to evacuate Athens and the recall of the exiles were voted all in one day. Both explicitly put the decision to 'entrust the city to the gods' after the retirement from Artemision. They therefore did not have before them and accept as a single decree *all* that we have on the inscription from Troizen. Those who believe that the inscription preserves an original document believe therefore that Plutarch and Aristides knew, presumably at second hand, only the spirited early lines. But it seems possible also that, if all that we have was in Krateros, it may not have been set down as one decree, but as what was preserved (by Aischines?) of more than one; and that on the Troizen inscription (a modest little slab, though of Pentelic marble, to which Miss Alison Frantz' fine photography has done more than justice) these were, for the purposes of a memorial, run together.

The Troizen inscription is a third-century manuscript of a text mentioned as existing in the fourth century, but not earlier. It is valuable at least as carrying back Plutarch's sources to that date. But if taken *au pied de la lettre* it gives an unconvincing picture of the planning of the campaign. In particular, it seems incredible that a Spartan king – not merely a polemarch, some Euainetos or Anchimolios – went to Thermopylai merely to give Athens a few more days for the evacuation; and nobody in antiquity did believe it, either before the publication of this document or thereafter.[30]

[30] If Herodotos had been deceived by an 'Athenian lie', in accordance with what one may call the Jameson–Atherley reconstruction, the place where one would expect to find some awareness of it is in Thucydides, who enjoyed correcting both popular tradition and Herodotos; yet in Thk. i, 73–4, we find Athenians repeating the old story that Sparta let Athens down, without protest from either Spartan or Corinthian hearers or from the historian! (Mr Jameson comments (*a*) that Sparta did need time to fortify the Isthmus; and (*b*) that for Aischines to invent this text would be pointless, since Athens was not being evacuated in his time.)

Chapter XVIII

Pray to the Winds

Thermopylai and Artemision, August, 480

Leonidas' famous Three Hundred Spartiatai represented a unit-strength frequently mentioned.[1] He varied the procedure of selection only in one particular; he concerned himself to take men who had sons living, so that the losses which he expected should not extinguish any Spartan line. On his way north he picked up allied contingents. Arcadia provided most of them. Herodotos (vii, 205) gives the muster-roll:

Tegea	500
Mantineia	500
Arcadian Orchomenos	120
The rest of Arcadia	1000
Total from Arcadia	2120

To these, Corinth added 400; she alone of Sparta's allies was represented both on land and sea; inland Phleious sent 200; Mykenai, of old renown, liberated from Argos since Sepeia, made almost her last, and not least gallant mark in history with 80 men. The total, with the 300 Spartiates, is thus 3100. Since, however, the war-memorial inscription seen by Herodotos at Thermopylai (vii, 228) spoke of 4000 Peloponnesians, and since the bias in Greek tradition was all against exaggerating the size of this force, it would appear that the historian has omitted something.

Now later tradition, early enough to be respectable, speaks of 1000 Lakedaimonians in all; others of 1000 in addition to the Spartiates. But the only other Lakonians mentioned by Herodotos, and these merely

[1] H. vii, 205, 2 ('the usual 300'); cf. i, 82; ix, 64; the '300 Knights', viii, 124. But in vi, 56, H. makes the royal bodyguard in the field consist of 100 (100 always on duty?).

in passing (viii, 25), are 'the helots', of whom a considerable number, it transpires, took part in the last stand and fell on the field. In short, probably the missing 900 (out of 4000), whom Herodotos does not mention, *were* emancipated helots, armed as hoplites, such as Sparta more than once employed later for campaigns outside the Peloponnese.[2]

In Boiotia, Leonidas was joined by 700 men-at-arms, the striking force of Thespiai, which, like her neighbour Plataia, was struggling to retain her independence of Thebes, and may have hoped that Athens and Sparta would help her. The men of Plataia were helping Athens, whose manpower was at full stretch, to man her great fleet. Thebes, according to the hostile Athenian testimony that reached Herodotos, was under deep suspicion of disloyalty; but when challenged by Leonidas to send troops with him, the government sent a modest 400. According to Diodoros (Ephoros?), they were the nationalists of the divided city. Their commander was, according to Herodotos, Leontiades the son of Eurymachos and father of another Eurymachos, who was killed in the commando attack on Plataia in 431; but, according to a later but local historian, Aristophanes of Boiotia, a certain Anaxandros. (For calling him A*le*xandros I can find no authority earlier than Jacoby!) – Other Boiotians receive no mention at all, but it cannot on that account be considered impossible or unlikely that there were more. Phokis produced 1000 men-at-arms (there may not have been many more in that upland country who possessed full armour), and the Lokrians of Opous (Opoeis) their 'full force' (a few hundred?), with seven fifty-oared galleys. Some accounts say that they had already promised surrender;

[2] 1000 Lak. in all, Isok. *Paneg.* 90, *Archidāmos* (written for a Spartan king!), 99. 300 + 1000, D.S. xi, 4, 5 (Ephoros?). It is customary here to quote also Ktes. (epit-Phot. 25) who assigns 300 + 1000 to Pausanias at Plataia, which he dates between Ther; mopylai and Salamis; though whether a passage of such confusion is worth quoting seems doubtful.

For helot hoplites, cf. Thk. iv, 80 (Brasidas); vii, 19 (Sicily); etc. The former case, directly after the frightful 'liquidation' of some 2000 of the best men among the helots, shows that the often-asked question 'Were not the helots disaffected?' is, like 'Were the Greeks superstitious?', a question involving an unjustified assumption: that what is true of some for some of the time is true of all, all the time. The helots were an underprivileged, at times even an oppressed, class; but they had not read Karl Marx. The evidence shows that while at times the dominant minority had reason to fear them, at other times, like other serfs or villeins, they could be recruited (selectively, and, as is said above, for campaigns abroad), or promoted into the class of *Neodāmodeis*, 'new members of the People', of whom we hear as a source of additional soldiers, along with helot hoplites, but not identical with them (Thk. vii, 19 and 58; cf. v. 67; Myron, *ap.* Ath. vi, 271, = *FGH* 106 F 1). It is sad that Herodotos' Spartan friends did not apparently give the helots their due; but before he visited Sparta there had been the earthquake of 464 and the helot rebellion, and internal relations had grown much worse.

but they were won back by a spirited manifesto, saying that this army was only an advanced guard; that 'the rest of the allies were expected any day, the sea was secured by the Athenians and Aiginetans and the other naval contingents, and there was no reason for fear; for the invader was no god, but a man, and no mortal man ever lived without some ill-fortune; the greater the man, the greater the disaster; so it was to be expected that he too would be cast down from his pride'. To these Diodoros, who numbers the Lokrians at 1000 and the Phokians at 'nearly 1000', adds 1000 Malians, who may have been omitted by Herodotos' source as not forming part of the main army; but they may well have been important, as local allies, holding strongholds on the rugged hills, west of the main position.[3] They can hardly have included the lowlanders of the Spercheios valley, whose land was not covered by the defence line; but that local hillmen were induced by the presence of a Spartan army to hold their ground is not unlikely.

Leonidas' army was finally in position in good time. Xerxes, when his columns at last advanced by the newly cleared roads, heard 'in Thessaly' that Thermopylai was held.[4] The Greeks had time to repair an ancient wall, built long ago by the Phokians for defence against the Thessalians, but now ruinous.[5] Its foundations have been cleared and may be seen today (though reconstructed later, facing south, with stairs on the north side), following the crest of a small spur, running obliquely down to the seashore, then close to its foot, and with its back, as it were, to the great cliffs that here forbid any easy turning movement. It was the place called 'the Middle Gate'. Herodotos, who had clearly been through the pass, making careful notes, but lacking either the time or the inclination to leave the road, remarks that there were even narrower passages before and after it, with barely room for the wagon-road; he does not say, and probably could not see for trees, why the main defensive positions were not there; but the reason is that behind these places the lower slopes rise relatively gently, so that the inland

[3] H. vii, 202f; 205, 2 and 233, 2 (Thebans); viii, 1 (Plataians); D.S. xi, 4, 6f; Ar. Boi. *ap* Plut. *MH*, 31, 33 (*FGH* 379 FF 5, 6; Jacoby dates him before 370 B.C.; his fragments, mostly on mythology, are not impressive; nor are those of Nikandros of Kolophon, qd. by Plut. *ib.*; perhaps identical with the writer on *Snake-Bites*; see *FGH* nos. 271–2). On the Malians, cf. Munro in *JHS* XXII, p. 313; *CAH* IV, p. 283. There are remains of ancient walls at at least two points west of the Asopos gorge; see map. D.S. mss. actually read *Milēsiōn* (*chilioi*), for which *Mēlieōn* is an emendation.

[4] H. vii, 208.

[5] *ib.* 176; excavated by Marinatos in 1939, see *JHS* LIX, p. 199; *AJA* XLIII, p. 700; Pritchett in *AJA* LXII, pp. 211ff.

flank could be turned. Since he consistently refers (*ibid.*) to the coast-road as running north and south, with the sea 'east' and the mountains 'west' of it, it seems that he must have passed only during the middle hours of a day's journey, with the sun high enough overhead to give him no reminder of his bearings.

Leonidas also had time to make a show of strength in an aggressive movement, reminding the people in front of his position that those who surrendered to Xerxes would be regarded as enemies. A late writer represents him (without geographical indications) as leading his troops forward on a night foray, in which he ordered them to spread out over the country and at a given signal to set fire to farm-buildings and cut down trees (a noisy operation) in order to give an exaggerated impression of their numbers. The people kept inside 'the city' (Lamia??) and left Leonidas to drive off 'the spoil' at leisure; presumably cattle and foodstuffs, thus secured for the defenders of the pass and denied to the enemy.[6] Herodotos also knew a story (vii, 232) that he sent forward Pantites, one of his Spartiates, 'as a messenger' (i.e. on a diplomatic and intelligence mission?) into Thessaly. There Pantites found himself cut off by the Persian advance, and incurred censure at Sparta as having failed to make an effort to rejoin his unit before the battle.

Meanwhile the fleet had reached Artemision in force; though not in the full force which it deployed later, since the likelihood that the Persian fleet would strike south of Euboia could not be ignored. If the 'Decree of Themistokles' may be taken as preserving genuine tradition on this point, the Athenians originally planned to send only half their navy north at once, keeping the other 100 ships in reserve 'round Salamis and Attica' (p. 360); and we find other forces of the allies likewise instructed to muster at Pōgōn, the harbour of Troizen.[7] It is the modern Poros Sound, with anchorage well sheltered by the island of Poros (ancient Kalauria), which has served the modern Greek navy too; a situation well chosen with a view to subsequent movement, as might be required. Here a considerable number of ships is recorded to have gathered; and while some of those which missed the first encounter may be simply late-comers (eleven ships from the west, for example), *most* are from Athens, Aigina and the south-west Aegean;

[6] Polyainos, *Stratagems* I, 32, 3; poor evidence; but the story has little point, if an invented anecdote. J. Labarbe, in *BCH*, 1954, takes it of a raid on the city of Trachis.

[7] H. viii, 42.

from the places, that is, most exposed to a raid through the Andros Channel. The Persians did later attempt such an operation (p. 395); and the threat had to be taken the more seriously since both sides of that channel, at Andros and Karystos, were held by states which had made their submission.[8] They were the first objectives of a Greek counter-offensive in the Aegean when the allied Greeks were in a position to launch one (p. 468).

The detailed figures in Herodotos are consistent with the Troizen inscription in indicating the formation of a reserve fleet. From it, it seems, the northern fleet at Artemision was gradually reinforced as the situation developed.

The cities providing ships, as mentioned by Herodotos (viii, 1 and 43–47, with minor details in chaps. 11, 14 and 82), fall, according to their geography and recent history, into two major and four minor groups. His figures may be presented in tabular form as follows:[9]

Cities providing triremes:	In original fleet at Artemision (H. viii, 1):		Joining later (H. viii, 11, 14, 43–47, 82):		Totals, first and last	
		Group totals:		Group totals:	Cities:	Groups:
1. Athens, with Chalkis						
Athens	127		53		180	
Chalkis	20		–		20	
	—	147	—	53	—	200
2. Peloponnesian League (old members)						
Lakedaimon	10		6		16	
Corinth	40		–		40	
Megara	20		–		20	
*Aigina	18		12*		30*	
Sikyon	12		3		15	
	—	100	—	21	—	121

[8] H. viii, 66; Obst, *Feldzug des X.*, p. 119, sees this point well; though I cannot take seriously *all* his ingenuities.

[9] Cf. also the detailed study of J. Labarbe, in *BCH* LXXVI (1952, pp. 384–441, *Chiffres et modes de repartition de la flotte grecque à l'Artémision et à Salamine*). I am not always entirely happy about Professor Labarbe's conclusions; he seems to me at times to rely too implicitly upon the ancient figures as being precisely accurate, exact and complete, e.g. adding one ship lost in the first skirmish (p. 386, below) to the 200 ships mentioned thereafter by Herodotos, he gives the Athenian navy a strength of *exactly* 201 (his pp. 387f); and he concludes from Herodotos' figures for Salamis that the allies of Athens had lost surprisingly few at Artemision. Personally I think that H. had some official figures for numbers of ships contributed, but not for losses; and that hence, while telling stories which imply losses, sometimes heavy, he simply ignores them when he comes to give his strength for the fleet at Salamis.

Cities providing triremes:	In original fleet at Artemision (H. viii, 1):	Group totals:	Joining later (H. viii, 11, 14, 43–47, 82):	Group totals:	Totals, first and last — Cities:	Groups:
3. Argolic Peninsula (allies of Sparta since defeat of Argos)						
Epidauros	8		2		10	
Troizen	5		–		5	
Hermione	–		3		3	
	—	13	—	5	—	18
4. Western Aegean Islands (exclusive of Chalkis in Euboia)						
Eretria in Euboia	7		–		7	
Styra ,, ,,	2		–		2	
Keos	2		–		2	
Kythnos	–		1		1	
	—	11	—	1	—	12
Total of groups 1 to 4:		271		80		351

The remaining two groups – the ships manned by the gallant people who came furthest or made special efforts to 'share the danger' in a last stand, which they could easily have avoided – do not figure in our first column. They are:

	Cities	Groups
5. Western Colonies		
Ships manned by Corinthian colonists of Ambrakia	7	
,, ,, ,, ,, ,, ,, Leukas	3	
Ship ,, ,, volunteers from Kroton in Italy	1	
	—	11
6. Islands under Persian sway; ships deserting: from Naxos	4	
,, Tenos	1	
,, Lemnos	1	
	—	6
TOTAL, according to Herodotos, 380. But the total of his figures is		368

* Aigina is recorded to have 'had other ships manned' at the time of the decisive battle, but to have been keeping them for home defence; i.e. probably for the defence, if need arose, of her harbour-mouth, a point where decisive struggles could take place (cf. D.S. xiii, 76 (Mytilene, 406); xvi, 7; Nep. *Chab.* 4 (Chios, 357)), and where a *few* ships might be badly needed.

Now Herodotos gives the grand total as 380 triremes; and although he makes a mistake in long division in a much more difficult sum than this (calculating the rations necessary for feeding Xerxes' alleged multitudes) – it seems most likely that his addition was correct, and that a figure (12) has dropped out in 46, 1, where he mentions the Aiginetan home squadron.

For completeness, it must be mentioned that a few island cities produced fifty-oared galleys, the small, old-fashioned ships of war that were already obsolete. They were not used as scouts, being slower than triremes, nor could they be put in the line; but they may have had their uses in 'mopping up' operations. The Lokrians produced seven, at Artemision only; Keos two and Kythnos one, in addition to their battleships; Melos two, and Siphnos and Seriphos one each (viii, 1, 2; 46, 4; 48).

To one studying the figures in the Table, it will appear at once that some of the numbers are conspicuously 'round', as one would expect if they represent an establishment or the fulfilment of a treaty-obligation; others are, equally conspicuously, *not* round, as one would expect when the only object is to muster every available ship and crew. The conspicuously round numbers are, first, that of the Athenian total (Athens had succeeded in manning her new Grand Fleet, using the manpower not only of coastal but of inland demes, and even – showing how Athens was 'scraping the barrel' – that of gallant and faithful Plataia, 'though the Plataians knew nothing of sea-faring', and allotting 20 ships to the men of Chalkis (presumably, therefore, still Athenian colonists[10])); and second, that of the original Peloponnesian League contribution to the fleet for Artemision, totalling 100, to which Epidauros and Troizen add 13. Now Demosthenes, at about the same time at which Aischines was producing Themistokles' Decree, refers to a Persian War fleet of 200 ships, 'of which we produced 100', and again, many years later, to '300 ships, of which Athens produced 200'.[11] One is reminded at once of the 'Decree' 's tradition of two Athenian fleets of 100 ships each; and it looks as if the original Peloponnesian 100 represent the keeping of an agreement made at Corinth, by 'the Lakedaimonians and Corinthians and Aiginetans', as the inscription says, to match ship for ship in the fleet sent to Artemision.

The most conspicuously odd figures in Herodotos' list are the 127 (or 147, including the Chalkidians) and 53 for the divisions of the Athenian fleet a little later. Clearly the northern fleet is being reinforced from the southern; but why the odd numbers? Isolating the geographical groups (2, 3 and 4 in the table) suggests an answer: the odd 27 is exactly the number of ships recorded as manned by Athens' allies (not counting western colonies, volunteers and deserters) but *not* sent to Artemision. As the need to reinforce Artemision becomes more and more pressing and apparent, Athens agrees to transfer more of her ships north; first, perhaps, to strengthen her fleet there by 20 (including those manned by the Chalkidians), leaving 80 in the Saronic Gulf; then to send more ships, on the condition that every ship transferred was replaced by an allied ship at Pōgōn. Meanwhile Argolis, Euboia and Keos

[10] Unconvincingly denied by Labarbe, *Loi navale*, pp. 178f, after Swoboda.

[11] *On the Navy Boards*, 29 (xiv, 186); *On the Crown*, 238 (xviii, 306). The '200' of the best mss. in the former passage ('corrected' by later hands to 300) is confirmed by the figure there of only 100 for Athens. (Cf. also Labarbe, *op. cit.* pp. 384–6.)

produce another 24 ships for Artemision (the Spartan high command still making a sincere attempt to match Athens ship for ship?); but the Saronic Gulf fleet, now also an allied fleet, is kept at a strength of at least 80 as long as the danger of a thrust through the Andros Channel remains in being. Probably, indeed, it was kept at a full 100, or restored to that strength as soon as the ships from the Corinthian colonies arrived; for we may also count here the ships of Aigina which did not join the main fleet at Salamis, as well as the extra twelve which did. If we reckon 10 or 12 of these, as well as the 10 (or 11) ships from the west, we find a total of 47 to 50 allied ships in the southern fleet, with the 53 Athenian. Athens had built and manned 200 ships by her own efforts; she had perhaps contributed not a little to the raising of nearly another 200 by her example. In command was Eurybiadas, a Spartan.

We have still a little more significant evidence on the Greek naval strength; that of the contemporary Aeschylus, and the sage Thucydides; but this will be best taken on a later page, when we come to consider the matter of losses in battle (p. 443).

Moving, as it would, much faster than the army, the fleet, or at least its first nucleus (the 100 ships from Athens and 100 of the Peloponnesian League?), may have been at Artemision before the army reached Thermopylai. It too had plenty of time to make its dispositions. A reliable Athenian, Habrōnichos the son of Lysikles, later ambassador to Sparta with Aristeides and Themistokles, was sent as liaison officer to Leonidas, with a thirty-oared cutter; Leonidas sent a local skipper, Polyas of Antikyra, to the fleet to perform the like service.[12] Look-out posts were placed on headlands of Euboia,[13] and another on the island of Skiathos, off Sēpias, the south-east cape of Thessaly, with arrangements for signalling. Three ships, respectively from Athens, Aigina and Troizen, were also posted at Skiathos to keep a look-out;[14] but in this task they failed. Perhaps by a night approach and an attack at dawn, but somehow or other, they let themselves be surprised.

It was now probably early August; the nights were dark, lit only by the brilliance of Aegean stars, before the coming of the fateful Karneian moon (it would be full on August 20th by our calendar). Xerxes' officers reported to him that the ways to Thessaly over the mountains had been made practicable for his columns. Before he himself left Macedonia, he sent a naval fighting patrol, to reconnoitre the approaches

[12] H. viii, 21; cf. Thk. i, 91. [13] H. vii, 183, 192. [14] *ib.* 179.

to the Bay of Pagasai. Ten fast ships – one, we know, was of Sidon, and probably all were, for theirs was the crack squadron of the king's fleet[15] – were entrusted with this mission. Either making a circle by the South, or coming in at first light, they swooped upon Skiathos, and the three guardships there were caught without room to get away. Praxīnos of Troizen's ship was rushed and captured in a moment; and its captors

> forthwith took the handsomest of the marines on board, and led him to the bows and cut his throat, making an offering of the handsomest of these first Greek prisoners whom they took. (The name of this man who was sacrificed was Leon; perhaps in part he would also have his name to thank for it.)[16] The ship of Aigina, whose captain was Asonides, gave them some trouble, through the presence on board of a marine, Pytheas the son of Ischenöos, who made a great fight that day; when the ship was boarded, he fought on till he was almost cut to pieces; and when he fell, and still did not die, the Persians serving as marines made every effort to save his life, putting myrrh into his wounds and binding them up with strips of fine cloth; and when they returned to their base they displayed him to the troops with admiration, and treated him well; but the other prisoners they took in that ship, they treated as slaves. Thus two of the ships were captured; but the third, the ship of Phormos of Athens, fled [cutting through *northward*, since its retreat was cut off] and finally ran itself aground at the mouth of the Peneios, where the barbarians captured the ship but not the men; for as soon as they grounded, the Athenians sprang ashore, and made their way through Thessaly and reached Athens.

The last detail confirms that this reconnaissance took place before the Persians occupied Thessaly. They had so far even omitted to secure Tempe. Probably they never chose to. They may never have used the Tempe gorge, where the path between cliffs and river was very narrow, at all (cf. p. 339). The whole passage (H. vii, 179–82) is very revealing, showing both the chivalry of the Persians, when their feelings were touched, and their barbarism; while the treatment of the common run of prisoners 'as slaves' is such as they might have received, if not ran-

[15] H. viii, 92; cf. vii, 44, 96.

[16] H. (vii, 180) perhaps means that 'Lion' suggested an acceptable sacrifice. – The trn. is after How; commentators have found the meaning obscure, and made various suggestions.

somed, from fellow-Greeks. In particular, the presence on this Sidonian ship, as it appears, of a medicine-chest and surgical bandages, which Herodotos describes as though he had never heard of such a thing, is a reminder of how much more primitive the Greeks still were, in some of the material amenities of life, than their oriental antagonists.

> Of this incident [continues Herodotos (183)] the Greeks at Artemision were informed by fire signals from Skiathos;[17] and in their alarm at the news, they transferred their station to Chalkis, to guard the Euripos, still however leaving their watchers on the headlands of Euboia. Of the ten barbarian ships, three ran aground on the shoal between Skiathos and Magnesia, called the Ant; and the barbarians then set a stone pillar on the shoal . . . Pammon of Skyros gave them full information about the shoal, which is right in the fairway.

The detail about the Greeks retiring to Chalkis (ninety miles!) in fright is one of the more remarkable pieces of nonsense that from time to time disfigure Herodotos' military narrative; it would have meant uncovering the flank of Thermopylai before their main forces had even been seriously threatened. Perhaps they may have withdrawn somewhat into the narrows of the Oreos channel, a few miles west of the temple of Artemis, drawing in their outposts and evacuating Skiathos; and Herodotos has misunderstood which narrows his source meant. Even so, they were somewhat supine; they appear to have made no effort to chase away the Phoenician scouts; even when three had run aground and been at least damaged, while at least two must have been chasing Phormos of Athens north towards the Persian main body, the Greeks made no effort to interfere with them while reconnoitring the strait, fetching stone for a seamark and building it upon the obstruction. Skyros, inhabited by piratical Dolopes who were on no very friendly

[17] Greek military signalling was capable of sending simple tactical messages, more elaborate than merely 'enemy in sight' or 'attacking'. In Thk. iii, 22, 7f, the besiegers of Plataia signal to Thebes (by night) 'enemy moving'; 'and the Plataians in the city lit many beacons on the walls, which they had prepared for the purpose, in order to confuse the enemy signals and prevent the dispatch of reinforcements'. So there was more in the Theban signal code than merely that fire-signals meant 'Send help'; otherwise the additional flares would only have emphasised them. In the same book, 80, 2, the approach of sixty Athenian ships is signalled from Leukas 'by fire, at dusk' to the Peloponnesians at Kerkyra. The chief refinement which Greek signallers did *not* have was an alphabetic code, by which the unpremeditated could be spelt out; it was left for Polybios (x, 43ff) to suggest such a system. – The Persians had not 'suppressed' the signal station on Skiathos, as Munro 'presumes' they did (*CAH* IV, p. 286), nor would this have been as easy to do as it looks on the map; Skiathos is several miles across, hilly (up to over 1400 feet) and probably then carried a good deal of wood.

terms with the mainland Greeks,[18] will have been among the islands that had long since submitted to Persia; and Pammon, who assisted with the detailed reconnaissance, may have been serving with a Skyriote ship. The seamark is another notable Phoenician refinement.

When Xerxes marched from Therma, he expected to reach Thermopylai in about a fortnight. For the fleet to sail from the Gulf of Therma (or some of its squadrons perhaps from Chalkidike, though Herodotos does not say so) to the Gulf of Pagasai would, on the other hand, take two days. He therefore ordered the fleet to wait for eleven days after his departure.[19] In order to arrive in a body and in good order in the straits where the Greek fleet was posted, it would be necessary to risk waiting for one night off the mountainous Magnesian coast. The weather had for some time been set fair, Aegean summer weather, the surface merely ruffled, no doubt, in the afternoons, by the northerly 'seasonal wind' which modern Greek sailors call the *Meltém*. The risk that it would break then seemed negligible.

In fact, it was not negligible, and should not have been neglected. The season of reliable weather was drawing to a close. Late August is not reliable; it has been a notorious fact in Greek weather-lore, from old Hesiod, who would limit the sailing season for prudent men to fifty days after the summer solstice, to the modern Greek folk-saying that the weather is set fair up to the feast of the Dormition (mid-August), or that *meltém* storms are liable to set in between the Transfiguration (Metamorphosis) and the Dormition;[20] and the Persians, whose

[18] Cf. Plut. *Kim.* 8, 3ff.

[19] H. vii, 183.

[20] Hes. *WD* 663ff (note 670, 'then the breezes are easy to judge [*eukrineẽs*] and the sea is not vicious' (*apēmōn*)). For the modern sayings, cf. A. Daskalakis, *Thermopylai – Artemision: Questions of Chronology and Synchronisms* (in *Annual of the Philosophical School of the Univ. of Athens*, 1957; in Greek), p. 47, n. 1. Professor Daskalakis' studies on Thermopylai (with very full references to the extensive literature in western languages) are about to appear in French, in book-form, as *Problèmes historiques autour de la bataille des Thermopyles* (École française d'Athènes). He says: 'The Greek popular belief still exists that the violent and dreaded *voriádhes*' (Boreas!) '. . . which are connected with various stories and superstitions, occur around the Feast of the 15th August' or 'between the 6th and 15th'. But, as he points out, the stories date from the 19th century at latest, when the unreformed calendar was still in use; so the '6th and 15th' would be our 18th and 27th. I have myself heard the saying only in a modernised form: that the weather *can* brake *after* the Dormition. It does not always; but I have seen some pretty violent late-August storms in the Aegean. – It must be added here that I am not convinced by the argument of Labarbe in *BCH* LXXVIII (1954), on the basis of an alleged saying of Leonidas given by Polyainos, i, 32, 3, that the operations at Thermopylai took place about the time of the heliacal rising of Sirius (end of July); see further note, pp. 403ff. – A charming piece of

political and topographical intelligence appears to have been good would have done well to pay more attention to popular meteorology. If they could have advanced by a week their occupation of Thessaly and the Gulf of Pagasai, it would have made a great and probably an essential difference to the course of the campaign. What physically happens is that the summer heat builds up, in Hesiod's fifty days, to its maximum intensity (temperatures of 40° C. (104° F.) are often reached in Athens, and the maxima in mountain-girdled Thessaly usually run slightly higher), until masses of the warm air lift bodily, and cool air from the north or, in the north Aegean especially, from the north-east, the Black Sea, comes in with violence. The *mistral* of Provence and the Greek sailors' *maïstro*, the 'master wind', are names of common Latin origin for the same north wind.

Now 'the barbarians sailed from Therma', says the historian (vii, 183), 'after the danger in the fairway had been clearly marked;[21] . . . and after a full day's voyage, they reached the part of the Magnesian country over against Sepias and the shore between the Sepiad promontory and the city of Kasthanaia.' After a few paragraphs devoted to computing the numbers of the entire expedition at this point, before the beginning of its troubles, he takes up his tale, repeating the last couple of lines, in c. 188. Here the first ships to arrive drew up on the beach,

> but others coming after them rode at anchor; for since the beach is not a large one, they moored in *échelon*[22] formation up to as many as eight ranks deep. So, they passed the night; but early in the morning, under a clear sky and from a windless calm, suddenly the sea broke in foam, and a furious storm fell upon them, with a strong wind from the east, which the local Greeks call the 'Hellesponter'. Those who realised that the wind was going to get stronger, and whose positions at anchor gave them a chance, hauled their ships up the beach quickly, and saved themselves and their ships; but the ships that were caught afloat were driven, some upon the [rocks] called

modern Greek mythology associates the first rain (often about the beginning of September) with the tears of the Virgin at leaving a world which, in spite of everything, she still loved.

[21] Grundy (*GPW*, p. 322n) has not thought things out with his usual clarity, when he says that 'As far as can be seen from the narrative' (!) 'the ten Persian scouting vessels started . . . on the same day as the main body'.

[22] Literally, 'in the manner of ladders', according to Aristarchos on *Il.* xiv, 35, where the word first appears; used there too of the 'quincunx' formation appropriate to the 'packing' of ships along a beach too short to take them in a single row; a passage which H. may have had in mind. But others take it to mean 'facing outwards', which fits its use by H. in iv, 152, of griffin-heads on a bronze bowl.

> the Ovens, under Pelion, and some upon the beach; some went aground round Cape Sepias itself [trying and failing to get round it?] and some were washed ashore at the city of Meliboia, and some at Kasthanaia. It was a storm beyond all enduring. The story goes that the Athenians prayed to the North Wind, as the result of an oracle, another response having been given to them 'to call upon their Son-in-Law as an ally'; and Boreas has to wife, according to Greek mythology, . . . Oreithyia the daughter of Erechtheus.[23] So the Athenians . . . in the fleet off Euboia . . . when they saw the wind getting up if not before, sacrificed and prayed to Boreas and Oreithyia to avenge them and destroy the barbarians' ships, as before round Athos. Whether this is the reason why Boreas fell upon the barbarians at anchor, I cannot say; but the Athenians say so, . . . and when they went home they set up a shrine to Boreas by the Ilissos. In this catastrophe, the most modest accounts say that at least 400 ships were destroyed.

The estimate was exaggerated in proportion to the original exaggeration of the size of the fleet. Wreckage, and ships drawn up at every available beach, were scattered along fifty miles of coast, from the cape to the south-eastern foot of Ossa. Men of the mountain villages grew rich on the spoils, and storm-bound crews built barricades of wreckage for defence in case of an attack from the hills.

'The storm raged for three days; but finally the Magi, by sacrificing and howling spells to the wind and to Thetis and the Nēreïds, got it to stop; or perhaps it stopped of its own accord.' Herodotos' gentle scepticism has much charm. He adds (191) that they learned from the Ionians that these goddesses were at home here. 'Anyhow, it stopped.' There was, in fact, a proverbial hexameter line which said that such a storm never lasts three days.[24] Both in its violence and in its coming, so promptly at the end of Hesiod's fifty days, the invaders were unlucky.

The Greek fleet had ridden out the storm in shelter, under the lee of Euboia; though hardly at Chalkis, as Herodotos repeatedly says (183, 189); that would be a long day's voyage away. (Herodotos never seems to realise the length of Euboia, as will appear again (p. 395). He must have known that it was in sight from Attica as well as from Pelion; but it is not in sight from the main road south through Phokis and Boiotia,

[23] H. vii, 189; Oreithyia, the 'Mountain-Rager' must originally have been the Storm-Goddess herself; cf. Thyia ('the Rager') in the corresponding Delphian story, 178.

[24] Ar. *Problems*, 26 (941a); cf. How on H. vii, 191.

which he must have travelled; and since he was vague about compass-points, as his description of Thermopylai shows, he may have thought that its long-continuing visibility was due to the shape of the mainland coast, as happens with Lesbos and with Thasos.) By the second day of the storm they were receiving the glad tidings, from their watchers on the heights, of heavy damage to the enemy; presumably enough wreckage was coming down past Sepias to confirm this; and 'they gave thanks and poured wine-offerings to Poseidon the Saviour, and hastened back to Artemision, hoping that they had now not many enemies left to face'. Their spirits were somewhat damped to see the number of ships that had survived (most of them probably had been drawn up on the beaches round Kasthanaia, where the coast is less fierce), and which were now rounding Sepias to reach safety in the Pagasaian Gulf. Here once more the invasion-fleet spread over many miles of beaches;[25] headquarters were at Aphetai, just inside the mouth of the Gulf. Here, says Herodotos (viii, 6), 'they' (meaning the leading ships?) were arriving late in the forenoon (Day 5 since the fleet and Day 16 since the land-army started from Therma). The Greeks, whether from dismay at their numbers, or through having barely got back from their storm-harbours themselves, perhaps missed a good opportunity of attacking them as they rounded Sepias. They were in time to catch only one belated squadron of fifteen ships, survivors of some of those that had suffered worst; fifteen ships collected from various squadrons, under Sandokes, Governor of Aiolis, whom Darius had once had crucified for taking bribes, but then, reflecting more coolly that Sandokes was on balance a good official, had him taken down in time. These, seeing the Greek fleet (presumably at sea, rather than beached at the Artemision, as Herodotos implies (194, 3)), took them for friends and sailed straight into them. Sandokes was apparently killed; and 'in one of the ships was captured Aridōlis, tyrant of Alabanda in Karia, and in another Penthylos, commander of the contingent from Paphos, who had lost eleven out of his twelve ships in the storm, and now, with the one that remained, sailed in and was captured off Artemision. These the Greeks interrogated and, having got such information as they wanted about Xerxes' forces, sent them bound to

[25] As is obvious, and as the source of D.S. xi, 12, 5 (Ephoros?) rightly sees, H. imagines the whole fleet getting into Aphetai (193, end); just as he also imagines the whole fleet arriving at one time (viii, 6).

the Isthmus of Corinth';[26] evidence, incidentally, that the allied 'rear headquarters' there were still functioning.

Meanwhile 'Xerxes and the land army', or rather its leading elements (for a large army in column cannot, as historians sometimes forget, be 'at a point'), 'after marching through Thessaly and Achaia, had arrived in Malis two days before'[27] (D. 14; a point of synchronism for the movements of army and fleet). But there was no assault on Thermopylai for four days. Greek tradition liked to imagine the oriental monarch sitting for those four days, idle and fuming, waiting for his antagonists to run away.[28] The real reason is probably very simple: that the first Persians to arrive were a cavalry advanced guard, and that it took three days after that for the infantry, strung out along the tracks after their fortnight's march from Macedonia, to come up in force. The gales of those days, moreover, so disastrous to the fleet, were probably a not inconsiderable nuisance to the army, moving in at least two columns, along the devious coast and by the shorter but higher route over Othrys.[29] Actually, at the last battle of Thermopylai, the rear-guard action of the British Imperial forces in 1941, a similar interval elapsed between the appearance of the first German motor-cycle scouts and the development of an attack; and that, although the invaders' advance from Macedonia was being speeded by a few Junkers 52 transport aircraft, which picked up troops in rear and put them down on Lamia airfield, in full view from above the pass but beyond effective field-gun range. If the main troop movements were quicker than in 480 B.C., those of the scouts were faster still, in proportion.[30] The first Persian who saw the Spartans at short range was, in fact, a mounted scout (one presumes that there was a squadron behind him, but that they held back, not to provoke counter-action), who, as we read in a famous passage (H. vii, 208f), 'surveyed and saw, not all the army' (who were covered by the Phokian Wall), but those who were on outpost duty in front of it;

[26] H. vii, 195.

[27] *Ξ. . . . πορευθεὶς διὰ Θεσσαλίης καὶ 'Αχαίης ἐσβεβληκὼς ἦν καὶ δὴ τριταῖος ἐ's Μηλιέας*, H. vii, 196. 'Had arrived from Thessaly after two days' march through Achaia is not a translation of the Greek (*pace* Macan, II, p. 274). It would require *ἐκ* (not *διὰ*) *Θ.*, and, preferably, *ἐσέβαλε* or *ἐγένετο* (cf. vi, 120) rather than the analytic plupf. *ἐσβεβληκὼς ἦν*.

[28] *ib.* 210.

[29] Daskalakis (*op. cit.* (n. 20 above), p. 46, n. 1) remarks on the effects *at Thermopylai* of a three-day *meltém*, which also kept steamers in port, at this same season of the year, around August 20, 1956.

[30] See Christopher Buckley, *Greece and Crete*, 1941, pp. 99–113, esp. 111f.

> and it happened that at that juncture the Spartans were on outpost duty. So he saw them, some of the men exercising and some combing their hair. The horseman gazed at them with amazement, and counted them; and having taken in every detail, he rode back at his leisure; for no one pursued him, and indeed nobody took the slightest notice.

Whether Xerxes himself was yet on the spot, we may perhaps doubt; but Herodotos takes the opportunity to stage one of his effective dialogues between Xerxes and the exiled Damaratos, who explains to him: 'This is their custom: when they are going to put their lives in peril, they make their heads tidy.'

('They die with their boots clean.')

Xerxes had had time for a leisurely progress through Thessaly, while the bulk of his forces moved at a foot-pace; among other things, he had time to order a gymkhana for selected Thessalian and Iranian cavalry, since the Thessalian was reported to be the best in Greece, and made the cheering discovery that his own completely outclassed it.[31] That Damaratos was at his side is likely enough. He could be useful in helping to interpret intelligence; also the time was coming when important Greek exiles would, it was hoped, be able to play their part in arranging the details of Greek submission. Later Boiotian tradition maintained that Damaratos did, through his acquaintance with the leading citizens, help to arrange that of Thebes.[32] The Medizing Delphic oracle, moreover, if we may take its advice to Sparta as well as to Athens (p. 356) to be a product of conscious composition and not of mediumism, had hinted the same thing. Either Sparta would perish, the Pythia had said (the composers had provided for all possibilities), or, at the least, she would mourn a Herakleid king; but resistance was, in any case, useless; 'not even the strength of lions or bulls shall stay him' (Xerxes) 'for he has the power of Zeus'.[33] And yet Sparta *might* survive. How could that be possible? Surely the meaning, at the time, is evident, though after the event a different interpretation was given, which has coloured all later tradition. Sparta might survive under King Dāmarātos, once wrongly deposed, through the agency of a Delphic medium since found out and ejected; Damaratos, now Xerxes' friend. But, to

[31] H. vii, 196.
[32] Plut. *MH* 31; on whose sources, see n. 3 above.
[33] H. vii, 220, 4.

that end, there was one man who could not live: Damaratos' kinsman and bitter enemy, King Lātychidas.

Damaratos, evidently a likeable man (he is mentioned by many later writers,[34] and, deserter though he was, there is a curious absence of rancour in the tradition), must have been hoping, like all Greek exiles, for restoration to his home. He did not want that home destroyed. Like many 'collaborators', he told himself that he could save his people from the worst. Keeping a foot in each camp, he is said even to have sent a secret message of warning when the invasion was imminent: a blank, waxed tablet, the bearer of which was able to pass innocently through the Persian control-posts. At Sparta, it was the woman's wit of Gorgo, the 'bright-eyed' and bright-witted daughter of Kleomenes and now wife of Leonidas, who found the key: the message was written on the wood under the wax.[35] Damaratos had no quarrel with Leonidas; Leonidas had always been on bad terms with his half-brother Kleomenes, Damaratos' enemy, and finally had taken the lead in locking him up as mad, and perhaps in his murder (pp. 270–2). Damaratos must have heard with mixed feelings the reports that reached Xerxes in Thessaly[36] of the presence of a Spartan force at Thermopylai and of the name of its commander.

Both in the Greek army and fleet hearts beat faster when the massive Persian forces, now coming into position, could actually be seen; and men on both elements are said to have counselled retreat. There is no reason to disbelieve this; every Greek private soldier would, in the course of nature, have his private opinion and make no secret of it; and there were Peloponnesians in both forces, whose private opinion had never changed, that the proper place to fight was the Isthmus of Corinth (Athenian gossip here had some preposterous stories of Corinthian cowardice and Themistokleian slickness). But the commanders had their orders and a strategic plan to carry out, and they stood firm. Leonidas did, however, send messages south, to warn headquarters that the enemy was now in sight, and that the promised reinforcements should make haste.[37]

Inside the gulf of Pagasai, the disorganized Persian armament was sorting itself out and re-numbering. This must clearly have been more

[34] e.g. Xenophon (*Anab.* ii, 1, 3; vii, 8, 17; *Hell.* iii, 1, 6), who knew his descendants, living as minor barons under Persia in the Troad; Damaratos' son or grandson had given *his* sons the ancient, historic names, Eurysthenes and Prokles!

[35] H. vii, 239. [36] *ib.* 208, 1. [37] *ib.* 207; viii, 4.

than the work of one afternoon; yet Herodotos (viii, 6f) appears to put into one day (D. 16) their arrival at Aphetai 'late in the morning'; eagerness to engage the Greeks, 'seeing that they were few', checked only by the reflection that it would be better to cut off their retreat first, lest any escape; the dispatch, with this end in view, of 200 ships to cut off their retreat in the Euripos by way of capes Kaphereus and Geraistos (the south end of Euboia), which ships leave, sailing 'outside Skiathos, in order not to be seen by the enemy'; the reorganization of the remainder, and finally a battle, late in the day, brought on by a forward move of the Greeks, in which the invaders are represented (viii, 12) as dismayed at being involved in 'a tough naval battle, before they had drawn breath after the shipwrecks and the storm off Mount Pelion'. Clearly all this is too much for a day, and in part internally inconsistent; it is inconsistent too with the statement in ch. 15 that the three days of serious fighting at sea coincided with the three days fighting at Thermopylai (DD. 18–20); and it does not leave time for the detached squadron to reach southern Euboia, as it is reported to have done.

Scholars have dealt variously with the discrepancy, which here appears, between the 'parallel diaries' of Xerxes' army and fleet.[38] To the present writer it seems certain that the root of the trouble is in this passage, where Herodotos has failed to 'square' the count of days with that of his 'diary' for the land army. His 'parallel diaries' are here summarised (p. 396). We cannot be sure of the precise accuracy of any reconstruction; but the events of the next days may have been as follows:

On D. 16, the capture of the 15 stragglers in the afternoon was probably the limit of the Greek success; they had already rowed some distance from their storm-station, and it was late in the day. It was probably under cover of darkness that a swimmer crossed the strait to desert to the Greeks, with important information: Skyllias of Skione, the most famous diver of his day, a man around whom 'tall stories' clustered; 'but some of them', says Herodotos, 'are true'. One

[38] See, e.g., Macan, II, pp. 274ff; Grundy, *GPW*, chap. viii and table, pp. 342f; Busolt, *GG* II, pp. 681f; Beloch *GG*[2] II, ii, pp. 87ff; How and Wells, II, pp. 371ff; Munro in *CAH* IV, pp. 284ff and synchronistic table, p. 316; Daskalakis and Labarbe, *opp. citt.* nn. 20 and 9, above. My views are nearest to those of Grundy and Busolt; and I would also agree with Labarbe (p. 398) in 'tenant pour simplement partielle la simultanéité qu'il (H.) déclare totale, sans doute sur la foi d'une tradition enjoliveuse'.

HERODOTUS' ‘PARALLEL DIARIES’ OF THE THERMOPYLAI–ARTEMISION OPERATIONS

(References in brackets are to chapters of H. vii, 183–223, and viii, 6–21.)

	Day	
Persian land forces move from Therma	1	
	12	Fleet sails, mrn; moors off-shore south of Kasthanaia at dusk (183, 188)
	13	Storm blows up at first light (188, 2). Fleet storm-bound for three days; heavy damage (188–191)
Persian land forces before Thermopylai, ‘two days before’ fleet reaches Aphetai, 196, 1. No assault for four days (210, 1)	14	Disaster to P. fleet reported to Greeks by look-outs (192)
All quiet at Thermopylai (2nd day)	15	Third day of storm
” ” ” ” (3rd ”)	16	Storm ceases. Fleet (leading ships?) reaches Aphetai by late forenoon (6). Squadron sent off to round Euboia; remainder reorganizing (7). Fifteen stragglers caught by Greeks (194f). Skyllias of Skione escapes to Artemision (8).
” ” ” ” (4th ”)	17	*TWO DAYS OMITTED HERE BY H.; FOR:–
First assault on Thermopylai (210f)	18*	*On the same day as arrival* (*day 16*; viii, 12, 2), but *on same day as first assault on Thermopylai* (15), Greeks raid enemy anchorages, late afternoon. Heavy rain and thunder at night (12). H. puts here destruction by storm of detached fleet off Hollows of Euboia (13)
Second assault on Thermopylai (212) Flank march of Hydarnes after nightfall (215ff). Windless night (218, 1)	19	Arrival of 53 Athenian ships, and news of destruction of P. detachment at the Hollows; second raid (on Cilician squadron), late afternoon (14)
Final battle at Thermopylai, beginning mid-morning (223ff)	20	Pitched battle before Greek anchorage, beginning about noon (15, 1). News of fall of Thermopylai arrives (21). Greeks withdraw in the night

* The discrepancy is clearly due to H. having failed to distinguish the days, in his narrative of the sea operations, between the arrival at Aphetai and the first battle at sea. The reorganization (‘numbering’) after the catastrophe of the storm may well have occupied the whole of D. 17; and the destruction of the detached squadron off the Hollows (of *southern* Euboia, Ptol. *Geog.* iii, 14, 22; cf. Labarbe in *BCH* LXXVI (1952), p. 402, n. 1) must have taken place before the night of DD. 18–19, to give time for news of it to reach the 53 Athenian ships and then for the ships to reach Artemision within the forenoon of D. 19. It *may* even have taken place, as many scholars have thought, in the first storm; and the last échelon of the Athenian reserve fleet, after confirming the reports and perhaps dealing with any survivors who escaped to leeward of Euboia (cf. Munro in *JHS* XXII, p. 311), would then be free to come north.

of the tallest was that he dived into the sea off Aphetai and came up at Artemision, ten miles away; 'but I think', says the Father of History, 'that he came in a boat'. Here Herodotos seems to err in a direction for which he has received little credit, that of excessive scepticism; for the distance (*not* all under water) would not be formidable for a good swimmer; and to swim, as much under water as possible in the initial stages, by night, would seem a more promising way of attempting escape from a naval station than hoping to escape notice in a stolen rowing-boat.

Skyllias, like all escapers who have been working for the occupation forces, 'had been meditating escape before, but had not an opportunity'. He had been employed on salvage operations among the wrecks off Pelion, and 'had saved much money for the Persians, but also secured much for himself' (left in convenient places to collect later?). Perhaps his employers were beginning to get suspicious. He gave the Greeks additional information on the extent of the damage, and also the serious news that the enemy had sent a squadron to round Euboia. News of this was presumably sent south; for (as had occurred to many writers before new light was shed on the matter by the Troizen inscription), the 53 Athenian ships which had not yet appeared at Artemision seem to have been on the look-out for this squadron.

It may have been on Day 17 that the Greeks carried out their next offensive move; late in the day they raided the enemy anchorages, where repair-work and reorganization was presumably still in progress, inflicting damage before the enemy – who, as Ephoros rightly pointed out, must have been spread over many anchorages – could rally to drive them off; the strategy (probably rightly again, even if it is Ephoros' guess) is ascribed to Themistokles.[39] 'There they captured thirty ships, and also an important prisoner, Philaon . . . brother of Gorgos King of Salamis' (cf. p. 202), in Cyprus. The enemy swarmed out against them, but the Greeks, keeping in close order against the enemy's *better sailing* ships (says Herodotos, viii, 10, a much neglected passage) and engaging with their own *heavier* ships (cf. viii, 60) prow to prow, did reasonably well, and withdrew to Artemision under cover of darkness 'having fared much better than they expected'. The battle-practice, which, we are told, the Greek command (Themistokles?) had been desirous to give their crews, had produced a great

[39] D.S. xi, 12, 5f.

moral and a not inconsiderable material success. With them as they sailed back came one (but only one) Greek ship deserting from the enemy; its captain was Antidōros of Lemnos, the son, no doubt, of one of Miltiades' Athenian colonists); 'and the Athenians for this action gave him an estate in Salamis'.[40]

The night set in wet and stormy. 'It was the middle of summer' (i.e. well within the normally dry season, as opposed to Thucydidean 'winter', the non-sailing and non-campaigning season; we cannot press the words, to mean 'about the summer solstice'); 'and it came on to rain torrentially all night, with loud thunder from Pelion; and the corpses and wrecks came drifting into Aphetai, and wrapped themselves round the prows of the ships and got in the way of the oars; and the soldiers here' (marines?) 'as they heard it were in deep dismay and thought they were doomed.' This is a different kind of storm from the earlier 'Hellesponter'; a violent thunderstorm, with rain, such as *can* occur, infrequently but usually catastrophic when it happens at all, at any time in the Greek hot weather, especially towards its end; noisy and alarming, especially to simple people, even though they have known it happen before. Thucydides notes (vii, 79) how, when the Athenian army in Sicily was nearing collapse, 'there was thunder and rain, such as often happens towards the beginning of autumn; and the Athenians were still more depressed, and thought that all this too was happening to signalise their destruction'. That was in September, about a fortnight after the eclipse of the 27th August, 413. And, Herodotos continues (ch. 13), 'for those who had been sent to round Euboia, that same night was still wilder, for it found them in the open sea; and grim was their end; for the storm and rain caught them as they were sailing off the Hollows of Euboia, and driven by the wind, and unable to see where they were making, they ran upon the rocks; and heaven was leaving nothing undone, that the Persian fleet might be reduced to the same numbers as the Greek, or not greatly superior'.

The two storms are of different character, and should not be reduced to one.[41] It remains possible, as some of the modern reconstructions have it, that the destruction of the Euboia squadron was due to the nor'-easters which wrought the havoc off Sepias, and that Herodotos, or even the Greeks off Artemision, attributed it to the second storm

[40] H. viii, 9–11.
[41] So, R. Lattimore in *CR*, 1939; Daskalakis, *op. cit.*, pp. 48ff.

because they heard of it after that. If the 'Hollows of Euboia' are to be taken to be the bays of its *south-west* coast,[42] then the ships had actually passed through the Andros strait and were off the coast of friendly Karystos, where some of them may have found refuge; for it is, as Beloch says (see n. 38), hard to imagine the whole fleet perishing, 'Mann und Maus'. But the destruction may have happened on the east coast, in which case survivors will have straggled back to the main fleet. In any case, they made no further impact on the course of the campaign.

'At Aphetai, glad were the barbarians to see the light of day; and they kept their ships where they were, and were content, in their miserable condition, to remain passive.' As there is still a day to be accounted for in Herodotos' naval narrative, it may be that there was still some sea running, and that the Greeks on this day (D. 18 since the army left Macedonia) were content to rest too. But the storm was over; and on land it was on this day that heavy fighting started at Thermopylai.

On the morning of D. 19, the Greek fleet was reinforced. Fifty-three more Athenian ships, the remainder of their 200, came up from the south, simultaneously with, if not actually bearing, news of the total elimination of the outflanking squadron. (This, it will be seen, is where Herodotos' arrangement, unrevised, leaves barely 24 hours for the voyage of the outflanking squadron along the whole length of Euboia, its destruction at 'the Hollows', the confirmation by Greek reconnaissance that it was no longer a danger, and the arrival of the news and the Athenian reserve squadron at Artemision.)

In the evening, the Greeks struck again, falling upon the Cilician squadron (reckoned at 100 ships before the storm), inflicting heavy losses and getting away under cover of the swift southern nightfall. But by now the Persian command also must have heard the news that the outflanking movement had failed; also, messages had probably come from Xerxes, bidding them do something, and urgently; for the army, in two days of heavy fighting, had completely failed to clear Thermopylai. The whole invasion force was held up in Malis, and unless the fleet could break through to them and bring in supplies they would soon be hungry.

[42] So, Str. x, 445; Grundy, p. 335, etc.; but the name may have meant the 'concave' part of southern Euboia generally, cf. Ptol. *Geog.* iii, 14, 22; Labarbe in *BCH* LXXVI, p. 402, n. 1. But it must have been a south wind that blew the wreckage in the north into Aphetai.

So, on Day 20, the whole surviving strength of the Levantine navies, refitted and reorganized, swarmed out from the Gulf of Pagasai, formed in a vast crescent with enveloping wings thrown forward, and about mid-day advanced in frontal attack. The Greeks stood on the defensive, 'by the Artemision', according to Herodotos (viii, 16); but as he adds (in 15) that the object of the attack was to force the straits (which he calls the Eurīpos, a term usually confined to the narrows at Chalkis; here again he seems to have his idea of Euboia foreshortened), it seems more probable that they were really blocking the straits further west. They awaited attack, probably in their own half-moon formation (as in Herodotos' account of the first battle, viii, 10–11) with wings thrown *back*, but ready, with their heavier, solidly built ships, to engage head-on. The two great fleets of galleys, low on the water, with masts unstepped and the great, square sails stowed as useless in manœuvre, met front to front with crashing of broken oars and splintering timbers, and there was stern and bloody fighting by the soldiers on deck, through hours of the long, hot summer afternoon. Wounded ships drew back if they could, while others from behind passed through to replace them; those that could not get back and received the *coup de grâce* from an enemy's ram, sank waterlogged; being of wood, they did not go to the bottom. Many oarsmen probably escaped; for neither side had much leisure for knocking swimmers on the head, and many (but one wonders about those recruited from inland Attica) could swim. Crippled ships impeded those behind which, after the initial stages, were still trying to get forward.

The sea-fights of 480 were largely marines' battles, for the press of ships rendered impossible much manœuvring for favourable position to use the ram. The Persian ships, in particular, became overcrowded and fouled each other, as they converged against the smaller Greek half-moon; but they pressed doggedly on, 'thinking it ignoble to be forced to retreat by so few'; also, we may perhaps guess, to be put to the worse by the raw, mass-produced Athenian navy; 'for there was much talk of the Athenians in their camps'.[43] The Persian ships carried each, we are told, thirty marines of the Persians, Medes and Sakai, the fighting peoples of Iran, 'in addition to native marines'; and the Greeks, to confront them, must surely have carried a not disproportionate

[43] H. viii, 16, 2; cf. 10, 3.

number; something much more like the 'many' of Kimon's time than the small number which fourth-century tradition, known to Plutarch, fathered on Themistokles (p. 365, cf. 475). The standard crew of a trireme long remained at 200; but in the late fifth century, while the number of marines was reduced, ingenuity had probably found ways of fitting in a few more upper-bank oars at bow and stern. The early triremes probably had only the standard 25 oars a side in each bank, 150 in all, leaving 50 as the total number of officers, petty officers, skilled sailors and marines; the trierarch himself would carry arms in case it came to fighting on board.[44] At Artemision, the fewer but heavier Greek ships and their armoured marines held their own well, on the whole. Their most formidable antagonists were the Egyptians under Akhaimenes, whose marines were also heavily armed; they had 'plaited helmets' (of wicker-work?), 'convex shields with prominent rims, boarding-pikes and pole-axes; and most of them also had corselets and heavy, short swords'. By the end of the day they had carried five Greek ships by boarding and taken them 'with their crews';[45] for when the marines were beaten down, the packed and almost naked rowers were helpless.

As the sun sank, exhausted crews backed water and the fleets fell apart; and 'both sides were glad to make for their anchorage. The Greeks kept control of the dead and wreckage; but they had suffered severely, especially the Athenians, half of whose ships were damaged; and they began to meditate retreat.' In the meantime, by order of the generals, the hungry men built up their strength with a full meat meal on the sheep of the Euboians, who had driven them to the shore too late, with a view to evacuation. Themistokles urged that 'everyone should sacrifice as many as he pleased, for it was better that the men of the fleet should have them than the enemy'. Polyas of Antikyra with his cutter was presumably ordered away to warn Leonidas; but Leonidas was beyond reach of warning. 'While the men were so employed, their observer came in from Trachis'; Habronichos the Athenian (p. 385), with the news that Thermopylai had fallen, and Leonidas and all the rearguard had been cut off and killed. 'At this they delayed no longer.' Leaving many fires burning, to suggest to the enemy that they were

[44] Labarbe, *Loi navale*, pp. 175–7. Totals of 200 in 480, H. viii, 17; vii, 184 (where the *Iranian* marines are extra). Total of 174 *oars* in the 4C naval inventories, *IG* II^2, pp. 1604ff.
[45] H. viii, 17; Egn. armament, vii, 89.

still in position, all that could still be rowed of the battered fleet streamed off, under cover of night, down the Euripos channel.[46]

Themistokles, indomitable as ever, brought up the rear with a squadron of his best ships, and found time, as they passed the water-points, to scratch propaganda messages on the rocks, urging the Greeks in Xerxes' armament to desert. Even if the messages did not have that effect, he thought (and in fact they did not), they might at least sow suspicion among the enemy.[47]

The holding of the Artemision position by the fleet, Themistokles' plan, was decisive of the whole course of the war. The difficulties imposed upon the enemy in bringing a large fleet up to that position, and the losses which they sustained in the process, less at the hands of the Greeks than by stress of weather, in storms for which there was good reason to hope, determined the course of the subsequent operations. After the last battle on that position, the Greeks were indeed no longer in a condition to renew the fight; but they fell back on their bases and towards their reserves. The enemy followed them at leisure, and still, the Greeks said and we may believe, in superior numbers; but the numbers were diminished to a point at which, as a Persian council of war decided, they were no longer in a position to detach a strategic raiding force against the Peloponnese; for instance, to seize Kythēra and create diversions in the south, as Damaratos is said to have proposed. To do this now would be to risk defeat of the main fleet, and of the whole expedition. So argued Akhaimenes, the king's brother and admiral of the Egyptians, at this point in the operations; and henceforth the fleet was kept together, considered capable of applying decisive force at one point only.[48]

[46] H. viii, 18–21.

[47] *ib.* 22; though we are not called upon to believe that the Athenians took time off in a retreat to inscribe on stone the whole chatty and argumentative paragraph given there by H.

[48] H. vii, 235f. – Beloch (GG² II, ii, p. 88) argues from the fact that A. in this speech does not mention the Euboia squadron to the conclusion that 'A. knows nothing of' such a squadron and therefore that no such squadron was sent; a form of the argument *ex silentio* of which scholarship has seen too much. In fact, though the council takes place after Thermopylai, and after X. has regained contact with his fleet, it is *described by H.*, whose arrangement of his material here is not of the happiest, *before* the operations off Artemision, and therefore before he has mentioned the loss of that squadron. It is not necessary to mention it here, and this, surely, is why he omits it, saving himself some anticipatory explanation. I take this discussion of strategy to be historical; H. could have heard of it at Halikarnassos, ultimately from circles near Artemisia, who as a contingent-commander would hear of decisions taken.

POLYAINOS AND THE DATE OF THERMOPYLAI

Polyainos, *Strategemata* i, 32, 2, runs as follows:

Λεωνίδας μάχην συνάπτειν μέλλων ὁρῶν νεφέλας χειμερίους ἁλιζομένας πρὸς τοὺς ἡγεμόνας ἔφη, ὡς οὐ χρὴ θαυμάζειν ἀστραπῶν καὶ βροντῶν γιγνομένων· ἀνάγκη γὰρ αὐτὰ συμβαίνειν, ἄστρου κινουμένου. πολλῶν οὖν διοσημειῶν γιγνομένων οἱ μὲν τοῦ Λεωνίδου προιδόντες τὸ μέλλον θαρροῦντες ἠπείγοντο. οἱ πολέμιοι δὲ ἐκπλαγέντες ἄθυμοι πρὸς τὸν κίνδυνον ἐγένοντο καὶ παρὰ τοῦτο ἡττήθησαν.

'Leonidas when about to join battle, seeing storm-clouds gathering, said to the commanders that they must not be surprised at the occurrence of thunder and lightning; for these things must needs happen when a star moves. So when many signs in the heavens took place, Leonidas' men, having foreseen what was going to happen, went forward cheerfully; but the enemy, being dismayed, had no heart for the battle and therefore were worsted.'

M. Jules Labarbe, in a most ingenious article in *BCH* LXXVIII, argues (*a*) that this is the famous Leonidas (and, as he says, in view of Polyainos' capacity for confusing homonymous persons, this does need to be argued); (*b*) that the place is Thermopylai; we know virtually nothing about Leonidas' life except the occasion of his leaving it, but there is no positive reason for supposing that any likely source of Polyainos knew more; (*c*) that the 'star' is the Dog-Star, 'the Star' *par excellence*, e.g. in Alkaios, fr. 94 Diehl, where the identification is certain; cf. Hesiod *WD* 582ff, on the 'dog days', which Alkaios is paraphrasing. Here L.'s case would be strengthened if Polyainos, like Alkaios, had the definite article; but it is quite possible that the article is omitted when speaking of 'l'Astre par excellence', as it can be with the words 'sun' and 'moon'. He further argues (*d*) that its 'movement' must be its heliacal rising, which, astronomically, would have taken place on the 29th July, though it might not have been actually observed for a day or two after that. This step in the argument is more dubious; for when Alkaios says 'the Star comes round' he is merely referring to the dog-days in general, and actually the visible heliacal rising of Sirius was a sign that the dog-days were now numbered; the worst of the heat was when the Dog-Star was aloft, though invisible, by day; as Hesiod says, it was breaking and 'men move more lightly' later, 'for' (note the word 'for') 'then Seirios goes but little over the heads of mortal men by day, but has a greater share of the night' (*WD* 414–19).

Nor, if Leonidas ever used such words referring to the heliacal rising of the Dog-Star, was he either showing superior scientific knowledge, or even talking sense; for, as M. Labarbe admits, 'la littérature conservée ne fournit aucun texte, semble-t-il, qui reconnaisse à Sirius une influence orageuse nécessaire'. This is not surprising, for it would have been nonsense to suggest it. The rising of the Dog-Star usually takes place in a period of settled, hot weather.

It will be seen that no single step of M. Labarbe's argument is proved for certain, while the last one is very dubious indeed. He suggests that the point is that Leonidas 'doit avoir tiré de sa belle invention' this alleged necessity, and that his stratagem 'comportait un élément de ruse'. Whether his 'commanders' (those of the allied contingents?) would have been disposed to accept, on the authority of a king of Sparta, a piece of pseudo-science which was entirely baseless and contrary to their own experience, is a question into which M. Labarbe does not enter.

Polyainos' story is probably completely apocryphal; for naturally the Greek public was not unwilling to hear more about the hero of Thermopylai, about whom authentic history tells us so little; and there was a tendency, from the age of the first sophists on, to invent stories which illustrated the advantages of Science over Superstition. A better-known example is that of Perikles telling his helmsman not to be dismayed by an eclipse at the start of the expedition to Epidauros (Plut. *Per.* 35); a story which is demonstrably untrue, since the nearly-total eclipse, to which the story certainly refers, and which is mentioned by Thucydides, took place in the preceding year. But whoever invented the saying – even if it were Leonidas himself – is, even so, less likely to have intended a reference to the rising of the Dog-Star, which is manifest nonsense, than some other astronomical-meteorological fancy, which the brevity and vagueness of Polyainos' expression does not enable us to identify.

M. Labarbe develops his argument, it should be said, with caution equal to his ingenuity; but the same cannot be said for the adoption of his thesis by Mr Pritchett, who in his otherwise excellent article, 'New Light on Thermopylai' in *AJA* LXII (1958; chiefly on the topography), states categorically, on the authority of Labarbe, that 'the battle . . . was concluded on August 3 or 4, one of the few Julian dates which we would be willing to accept for an ancient event'. A little later (pp. 203f) he adds 'the facts are now clear from the researches of Labarbe, on the basis of a fragment [*sic*] of Polyainos referring to the movement of the star Syrius' [*sic*]. The fact that *is* clear is that Mr Pritchett, having demonstrated that in later times Greek calendars, based on more scientific approximations to the length of the solar year, frequently had their months out of step with the moon (see his *Calendars of Athens* (1947) and article in *BCH* LXXXI (1957)), is disposed to believe that, in the pre-sophistic period also, religious festivals (such as the Karneia and Olympia, which took place about the time of Thermopylai), though supposed to take place at the full moon, did not really do so. I believe that they did, both because Aristophanes grumbles at festivals being out of step with the moon, as he grumbles at anything new-fangled (see p. 240, n. 10, above), and because revelling by the light of the moon was part of the festivity (see Euripides on the Karneia, *ibidem*, above; Pindar, *Ol.* x, 73f, on Olympia). These festivals, at least, must have been as firmly linked to the moon as is Easter; and the date of the second new moon after midsummer in 480 (unlike 490) is not in doubt; it was on the 3rd–4th August (full on the 19th–20th). Around the 19th–20th fell the operations at Thermopylai; if, that is, we still, with Meritt, 'assume the first day of the festival year to have fallen on the first day after the summer solstice on which the crescent of the new moon was visible' (*The Athenian Year*, p. 241).

Chapter XIX

Too Few and Too Late

(*The Fall of Thermopylai*)

LEONIDAS, we are assured (p. 363), had been promised reinforcements; and when the enemy vanguards began to appear he sent messages south to bid them hurry; but no reinforcements came. For this the government of Sparta cannot escape blame, at least for being too leisurely and for an error of judgment. 'They had never expected the fighting at Thermopylai to be over so quickly.'

The scruples of Sparta about the Karneian month must, it has been argued above, be considered genuine; but religious scruples could also be a handy excuse for delaying doing something that one did not really want to do at all. Many Spartans, we may suspect, were still hedgehog-minded, even if on a Peloponnesian and not a city-wall scale; they had never really liked the northern strategy of Themistokles; and even military excuses were not hard to find. Leonidas' 7000 men should be enough to hold a pass; moreover, if the fleet were defeated – and many Spartiates probably cherished a deep suspicion of the naval arm – to extricate the army might be difficult. The fewer sent, the fewer would be endangered. Nevertheless, a general Peloponnesian mobilisation was ordered, to take effect as soon as the Olympia and the Karneia were over; and it did take effect, for, though such a mobilisation was a slow business (in 431 – certainly this was after no previous warning – several months' notice was given[1]), a League army was actually at the Isthmus, under Leonidas' brother Kleombrotos, early in September; it must therefore have been preparing *before* Thermopylai fell.[2] More Spartiates could have been sent north more quickly, as in the days of Marathon; but Sparta presumably did not wish to endanger more of her precious and limited manpower without her allies. Leonidas had

[1] Thk. i, 125.

[2] H. viii, 40; 71; the inference is drawn by Beloch, *GG*[2] II, ii, p. 92.

known that he was going on a dangerous mission, when he took with him only men who had sons living. Later tradition took up this point, and represented him as taking fewer than he was offered because he was sure none would return.[3] Already in Herodotos he is represented as bearing in mind the thought that by his death the prophecy might be fulfilled, that Sparta might be saved at the cost of a Spartan king (vii, 220). The story of the royal sacrifice, appealing to something deep-seated in human nature, became very popular. It was also useful immediately after the event, in shedding an aura of glory over a military disaster. The cold fact was that Leonidas was left too long, insufficiently supported.

Herodotos' story of the battle (vii, 210–26) lies, in point of literary form, somewhere between sober history and the *Chanson de Roland*; nearer to history, admittedly, in that the principal facts are probably accurate; but 'fictionalised', not only in the accounts of the enemy's losses, but in the picture of that enemy, a cruder and more childish picture than is given elsewhere: Xerxes, the foolish tyrant, who waits four days for the enemy to run away, who has no plan except to hurl his troops against a fortified pass, until a countryman offers to show him a way round; who 'leaps from his throne in terror for his army', and whose troops are no better than he deserves; slaves who have to be driven with whips to the slaughter; 'many bodies, but few men'. On the Greek side, the allies, except the Thespians, are fainthearted or worse. Only the Spartans shine. Nevertheless, it is a fine story, and deserves to be translated, though some comments are necessary.

To begin with, it is most improbable that the commanders of the Persians, a great military people and a mountain people too, when confronted with a mountain defence-line, spent two days in dashing their heads against it before using them for any other purpose. It may be safely assumed that reconnaissance began on the day of the arrival of the first Persian cavalry, and was not confined to the solitary horseman recorded to have ridden through the 'west Gate' and counted the numbers of the Spartan picket.

In the mountain wall that shuts off the view as one looks south from Lamia, one feature that is conspicuous is the oblique line of the Asopos ravine. It is clear in the sketch by Edward Lear, reproduced by Grundy

[3] D.S. xi, 4, 3ff; Ael. Arist. xlvi, pp. 254f Dind.; Plut. *Spartan Sayings*, Leonidas, 3; etc.

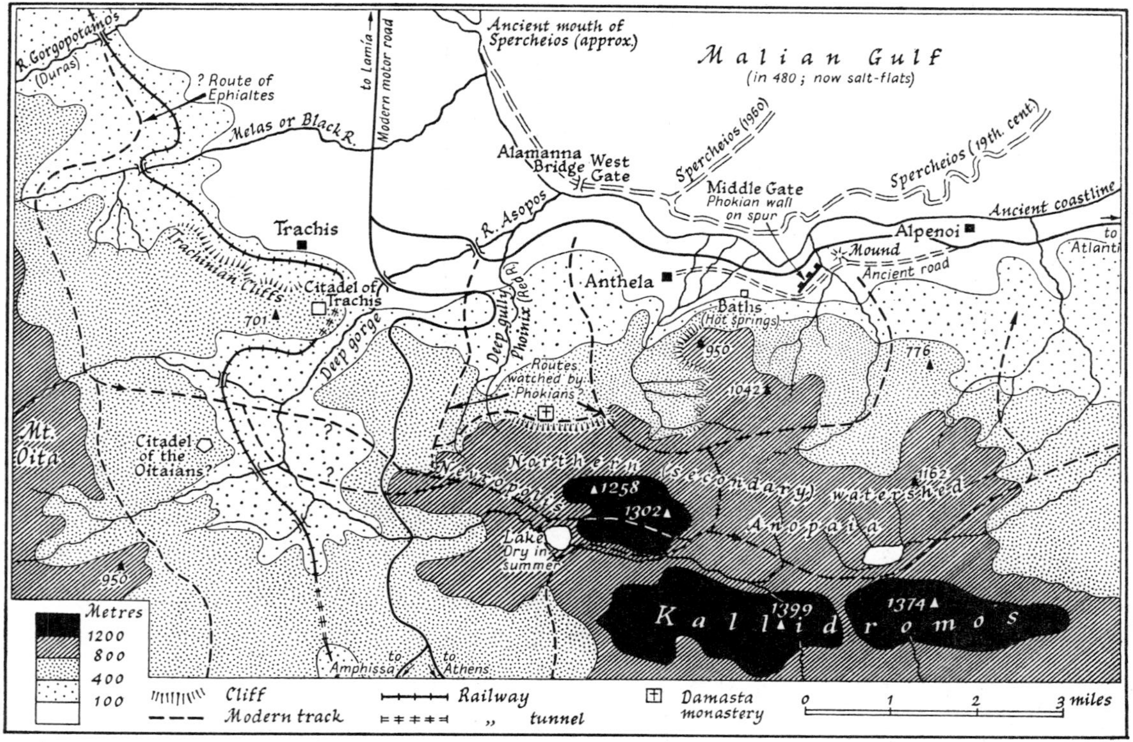

Thermopylai and Kallidromos

(*GPW*, facing p. 257); an illustration which also brings out the relatively gentle general gradient of the mountainside (though at close quarters it will prove still to have rugged passages) east of the ravine, on the side towards Thermopylai. The route to Phokis across a projecting corner of Doris, which some of Xerxes' troops followed after the opposition was broken, may actually have gone through the ravine; it is quite easy in dry weather, though quite impossible (filled by a roaring torrent) after any considerable amount of rain. It is, however, from its roughness, with many water-borne boulders, and narrowness (only twelve feet for considerable stretches, between walls, often vertical or overhanging, several hundred feet high) unsuitable for a large army even without opposition, and the most recent study is perhaps right in denying that it was used at all.[4] What is quite certain is that no invader ever attempted to use this route against opposition; the obvious opening is also an obvious trap. It is completely commanded by an ancient Greek hill-town on the flat top of the cliffs on the left bank,[5] and from these cliffs artificial avalanches could be conveniently discharged.

If any route fit for tactical exploitation were to be found alternative to the coast road blocked by 6000 Greeks and the Phokian Wall, it must be by way of the gentler slopes, clear of the ends of the Trachinian Cliffs. The wide loops and stone embankments of the modern road rather obscure the natural lie of the land along its course; but clear of it, a track in use in Turkish and no doubt in earlier times, using the lie of the land with little engineering, remains traceable from the foot of the mountain, and continues, *à peine carrossable*, as the French guidebook would say, right *along its spine*, as Herodotos was told, and tells us (vii, 216). It rises from the right bank of the Asopos torrent where it emerges from the gorge, and rises, skilfully avoiding minor torrent-beds, up the gentler slopes, clear of the cliffs. It was up these same slopes

[4] The former view is that of Grundy (*GPW*, 261), interpreting H. viii, 31; followed by How *ad loc.*, Munro in *CAH* IV, and the present writer in *Studies pres. to D. M. Robinson*; criticised by W. K. Pritchett in *AJA* LXII, n. 39, I think rightly. Pritchett's exploration of the whole area, made more accessible by modern conditions, is not only the latest but the most thorough ever made; much more thorough than my own, on visits in 1939, 1946 and 1951, which were impeded by two arrests on suspicion of espionage; and where he differs from my conclusions I would accept his, while gratefully acknowledging his kind references to my work. For views of the ravine, see Grundy, and Pritchett, *locc. citt.*; Burn: *Warring States of Greece*, fig. 88.

[5] Cf. Y. Béquignon, *La Vallée du Spercheios*, pp. 243ff; Pritchett, *op. cit.*, pp. 204–6, n. 25.

that the attack of a German mountain division, without succeeding in breaking through, developed the most serious threat to the defence in the rearguard action of 1941; and it was along the top of the mountain, with some cover from trees, that British motor transport withdrew in the same action, evading the German air attacks on the main road.

This was the secret of Thermopylai; the un-obvious fact that made the famous position less strong than it appeared, and which also gained for the mountain south of the pass its ancient names: in Herodotos' time Anopaia 'the same as the name of the Path', as he says (vii, 216); in later days (or at least, Herodotos does not use the name), Kallidromos, the Beautiful Running Track.[6] The crest of the east–west ridge is not a single 'bristly ridge' of rock, as one might expect; there are two parallel ridges, both rounded, earthy and still carrying some remains of forest, and between them a narrow, elongated, intermontane plain, carpeted in spring with crocuses, along which the uppermost course of the Asopos flows slowly in meanders between grassy banks.

Xerxes' officers could see from afar that the hill-slopes were gentler between the Asopos and the fierce precipice which guards the inland flank of the Middle Gate; but it needed someone with local knowledge to tell them the strange facts about the 'corridor' along the top of the mountain. Without such knowledge, the prospect of an outflanking movement that way did not look very promising. As to a general invasion of Greece over the wooded mountains by hunters' or animal trails, such as some modern writers have suggested, that need not be considered. The stringing out of men in single file on rough tracks

[6] e.g. Strabo (ix, 428), who uses the topographical sections of H. (vii, 176, 198–200, 216) and supplements them at a few points; e.g. (*ib.* 427) on the extension of the territory of the Ainiānes of Mt Oita to touch that of the Lokrians, along the range of these hills; a point which elucidates, as will be seen below, Herodotos' and Pausanias' accounts of the Anopaia path, and which I overlooked in *op. cit.* (n. 4); see Pritchett's p. 208. Pritchett traversed the whole length of the ridge in a jeep, driven by E. Vanderpool (see his p. 211), and descended north to the coast road east of the narrows; as he says, 'This was a route by which an army of 10,000 men could have proceeded.'

It must, I fear, be added that Grundy's exploration was woefully incomplete. He did not go to the top of the mountain, for fear of being murdered by Vlachs (his p. 302); admittedly the Turkish frontier was then near, and the country disturbed after the war of 1897. He consequently worked out a much inferior route, meandering along the northern slopes well below the top, which has been reproduced on maps in a distressing number of modern works, including the *CAH.* The real modern pioneer of exploration here was Major-General Gordon (the Philhellene), whose *Account of Two Visits to the Anopaea* (Athens, 1838) remained little known; he was guided by Greeks in 1835 to Nevropolis (Slav *polye*, 'field'), as the *kalós dromos* is now called; but his account remained unknown to Grundy.

would be such that leaders could be killed off by any 'hostile natives' whom they might encounter, before their supports came up in any significant force; and men trying to move uphill, through the woods, with shield, spear, bow and quiver, on a wide front, with no path, would simply move so slowly that they would have to come back for more food before they had arrived anywhere. In short, as in Napoleon's Spain, any large number of men would starve, and a small number would be beaten.

And, as Persian reconnaissance probably did not take long to discover, this part of the mountain was held by the enemy. Leonidas had been informed about the mountain 'corridor' by the Trachinians soon after his arrival; earlier strategic reconnaissance, which had decided on the suitability of the position, had failed to collect this information.[7] Now, his 1000 Phokians volunteered to hold it;[8] a suitable position for them, from the rear of which tracks running due south formed a supply-route direct to their own country.

The Persians, we have seen, waited for four days; waiting for their main forces to come up; probably delayed by the break in the weather; and perhaps hoping that the fleet would break through to make contact with them and force the evacuation of the pass. But the fleet was still repairing storm damage at Aphetai, and the problem of feeding a large host in the valley of the Spercheios, fertile as it was (but probably scoured for foodstuffs by Leonidas before their arrival, cf. p. 381), would soon become serious. On the 18th day since leaving Therma, Xerxes, saving his own Persians for the present, ordered Tigranes the Akhaimenid and Anaphes the son of Otanes (brother of the Queen Amestris?) to take their (2nd and 3rd) Median and Sousiana divisions,[9] and clear the pass; 'Capture those men and bring them to me', he is said to have ordered; but that is probably part of the over-coloured Greek saga. So, with the Medes leading, for there would be little room for two columns side by side, the attack began:

> The Medes swept forward; but when they clashed with the Hellenes, they fell fast; but more came on after them, and they did not draw off, though they were losing heavily; and they made it

[7] H. vii, 175, 2; cf. 177.
[8] *ib.* 217, end.
[9] *ib.* 210; cf. 61f; Ktesias (epit. 20) makes 'Onophas' father of Amestris, the same confusion as in his list of the Seven; cf. p. 323, n. 26.

> clear to all, and more especially to the King, that there were not many *men* in all that mass of humanity.

This unfair and unworthy sneer is unlike Herodotos; but probably it was already in the saga, and popular, and he liked the play on the two words for 'man', and so repeated it. He continues (211):

> The battle went on through the day. At last the Medes, sorely handled, withdrew; and in their place advanced the Persians, whom the king called 'The Immortals', Hydarnes' command; surely these at least would easily overcome the opposition? But when they in their turn came to close quarters with the Hellenes they fared no better than the Median division, but exactly as they had, fighting as they were in a narrow pass, and with shorter spears than the Greeks, and having no opportunity to use their superior numbers.
>
> The Spartans gave a memorable account of themselves, displaying their skill as past masters in the art of war among amateurs. Among other manœuvres, they would make pretended flights, all at once; and the barbarians, seeing them fleeing would pursue with shouting and noise; and then, when just being overtaken, they would turn and face them; and in these about-turns they cut down Persians beyond counting. Some few of the Spartiates themselves also got killed doing this. At last, since they could make no progress towards winning the pass, whether they attacked by companies or whatever they did, the Persians drew off. During these attacks it is said that the king, as he watched, three times sprang up from his throne in fear for his army.
>
> Next day the barbarians strove with no better success. They hoped, since their opponents were few, that they would be worn down with their wounds and too exhausted to resist longer; but the Hellenes were organized in regiments according to their states, and relieved each other in the line (except for the Phokians, who were stationed on the mountain to guard the path). So, when the Persians found themselves doing no better than on the previous day, they drew off again.
>
> The king was in despair. But while he was wondering what to do next, there came to him a man of Malis named Ephialtes . . . asking for an audience in the hope of getting a great reward; and he told him about the path over the mountain that led to Thermopylai.

The path that led *to Thermopylai*; that was the secret; the path, so unexpectedly easy, along the top of the mountain, and not merely the fact that small bodies of active men could ascend the mountain, a piece of useless knowledge, which the Persians could find out for themselves and no doubt had.

It may be doubted whether Ephialtes' appearance was quite such an unexpected windfall as Herodotos suggests; Persian topographical intelligence must surely have been catechising any likely native, and offering rewards, ever since the vanguard arrived in Malis. The fact that there was a path up there may have reached them almost as easily as it reached Leonidas. But it still remained to find a man prepared to follow its curves, and take the right course at forks, in the dark. It has been doubted whether Xerxes would have committed his guards to the certainty of heavy losses in the frontal attack on a prepared position, where their skill in more open warfare could not be used; but that depends on just how desperate Xerxes was. Certainly they were still in good fettle on the second evening for a night march in which everything depended on perfect march discipline, keeping the column closed up in case a fight did develop, on a mountain path – a good one, but still a mountain path – in the dark. For it was evidently judged unlikely that the path could be forced if determined opposition were encountered. In the meantime, it may be noted that the losses incurred by the Persians in the heavy and fruitless assaults along the coast road had not been entirely wasted. Leonidas' dispositions were uneven: 6000 men on the coast road, and only 1000 on the mountain; dispositions which were reasonable on the assumption that the enemy had no detailed knowledge about the path, and that, if they attempted to cross the mountain, their initial exploratory flounderings would give ample notice.

As for Ephialtes, he lived for a short time after the war, 'on the run' and with a price on his head; and when he judged it safe to come home to Antikyra, he was killed there by a personal enemy, and the reward duly claimed from the Amphiktyonic Assembly; an assembly of influential men, most of whom had led their states unresisting into Xerxes' camp, and, thanks to the immediate post-war split between the allies, succeeded in retaining both life and position. If Dante had heard of him, Ephialtes would have been in his lowest hell with Judas and Brutus. Such are the judgments of tendentious history. And yet, he did no more than was done for the Gauls in the third century, in the same place, by a large enough section of the local population to find safety in numbers; and that, 'not out of ill-will towards Greece, but from anxiety to get the Kelts out of their country and not have them sitting there and devouring it'.[10] Hellas was an ethnological concept, not a patriotic slogan; and other names were named in 480 (one of them that of a man of Karystos) as having something to do with the matter, though they escaped being proscribed.[11]

The Anopaia path, says Herodotos, 'begins from the River Asopos (the river which flows through the gorge)'.[12] Later he adds (217) that they crossed that river at the beginning of their all-night march. This would admirably suit the starting-place proposed by Pritchett (see n. 6, above, after Gordon), just west of the Damasta spur, where the Asopos, after leaving its ravine, flows near the foot of the hills. But on the other hand, Herodotos also says that their 'way round and up' was much longer than their way down from the top, which is not true of this route; that the way up took them all night; and that during it they had on their left 'the mountains of the Trachinians'. But it was the great cliffs west of the Asopos gorge which were known as the 'Trachinian Cliffs.' Also Pausanias, no mean topographer, believed a tradition that the Persians went not by the steep way up but by an easier way round 'through the land of the Ainianes' (as did also the Gauls later, concealed by a mountain mist as were the Persians by darkness);[13] and the Ainianes included the 'Oitaians' at the top of those cliffs.[14] It really looks as though Herodotos, who, as we have seen, seems only to have visited Thermopylai in the middle of one day, and not had time to explore the mountain, is here internally inconsistent, though, as usual, reporting his sources faithfully, and mentions *both* the foot of a way up (Pritchett's), east of the gorge, which had no doubt been pointed out to him, and a report, probably from another informant, that the Persians went a longer way round.[15]

Herodotos continues (215ff):

> Xerxes joyfully approved Ephialtes' undertaking, and forthwith

[10] Paus. x, 22, 9. [11] H. vii, 213f.

[12] Grundy (*GPW* 299) mistranslates 'that part of the Asopos river which flows', etc., and even defends his translation in the interests of his theory. He also has to interpret H. on the Persians crossing the river as meaning that they went a mile up the gorge before leaving by the right bank.

[13] Paus. x, 22, 8. [14] Str. ix, 427; 'Tr. Cliffs', cf. H. vii, 198, 1.

[15] Cf. J. L. Myres' letter to the present writer, quoted at the end of my article (see n. 4 above). Myres suggested that it was the high part of this route, over Kallidromos, which alone bore the name of Anopaia, beginning at the right bank of the Asopos.

ordered away Hydarnes and his division. They left camp about lamp-lighting [as soon as it was too dark for the movement to be observed by watchers on the hills].

This path was first discovered by the local Malians; and they used their discovery to guide the Thessalians over it against the Phokians, in the days when the Phokians had walled up the pass and thought they were safe; the Malians' knowledge of its sinister possibilities was thus of long standing.

The path runs as follows: it starts from the River Asopos (the one that runs through the gorge); and both the mountain and the path bear the same name, Anopaia.[16] This Anopaia stretches along the spine of the mountain, and ends at Alpēnos, the first city of Lokris on the side towards Malis,[17] and at the Black-Buttock Rock and the seats of the Kerkōpes,[18] where the road is narrowest.

By this path, then, the Persians, having crossed the Asopos, marched all night, having on their right the mountains of the Oitaians and on their left those of the Trachinians;[19] and dawn was just breaking as they reached the top of the mountain.

At this point on the mountain, as I explained above, were keeping guard 1000 Phokian hoplites, both protecting their own country [down the Kephisos valley to the south] and watching the path. . . . The first warning that the Phokians had that the Persians were up was as follows (for during their ascent the Persians were hidden, the whole mountain being covered by oak forest). It was a windless night; and there was, naturally, a great rustling of the leaves that lay thickly under their feet.[20] The Phokians sprang up and buckled on

[16] Meaning something like 'the upper way'? Cf. *Odyssey* i, 328.

[17] Also called Alpēnoi; the supply-base of the defenders of the Pass, ch. 176.

[18] For identification, see Pritchett (n. 4 above), p. 211, pl. 55, 11; Marinatos, *Thermopylai*, pl. 14. For the legend of the Kerkōpes, the mischievous dwarfs (with tails?) who teased Herakles (whose legends cluster thickly in this region, from the Hot Springs to Mt Oita), cf. How *ad loc.* It was often figured in archaic art; e.g. on one of the early metopes from Selinous.

[19] This sentence crystallises the difficulties about where Hydarnes started up. Starting the night march by crossing the Asopos suggests the short way up (Pritchett's view). Taking all night, with the moon (*pace* Pritchett) in its second or third quarter, and the other considerations mentioned above, suggest the long way round (the better to surprise the Phokian outposts?). Pritchett however explains away Myres' point about the mountains by pointing out that Oitaians lived on top of the Trachinian Cliffs, and that Thermopylai itself is included by H. in Trachis (viii, 21, 1). Identifying suitable places on Kallidromos for Hydarnes' brush with the Phokians remains an occupation for a holiday, which may be recommended to any seasoned hill-walkers.

[20] If these are to be supposed to be freshly fallen leaves detached by the recent gales (as suggested by Labarbe in *BCH*, 1954), it is an argument (against his view) for a relatively late date in the summer; by late August, the leaves are much less tenacious than three weeks earlier (Daskalakis, *op. cit.* (p. 388n), p. 56).

> their armour; and almost at once the Persians came in sight. When they saw before them men taking up their arms they were astonished; for they had hoped to meet no opposition, and had run into an army. Hydarnes, nervous lest the Phokians might be Spartans, asked Ephialtes of what people these troops were; and when he heard the truth, he drew up the Persians to fight. The Phokians, as the arrows began to fall thick and fast, fled to the peak of the mountain, thinking themselves the primary object of attack, and prepared to die. That was what they thought; but the Persians with Ephialtes and Hydarnes took no further notice of the Phokians, but started their descent of the mountain, going fast.

'Started down' is in fact wrong; the Persians would have a good deal further to go, more or less on the level, 'along the spine of the mountain' before beginning the descent. Probably wrong, too, is the detail about expecting no opposition; if Ephialtes knew what troops these were, he had presumably known before the march started; and anyhow it seems incredible that the Persians had not done enough scouting to find out that there *were* enemy troops on the mountain. But the contrast between the citizen soldiers who imagine that the enemy's primary purpose is to kill *them*, and the disciplined Immortals, who scare the citizen troops out of their way and then at once proceed to the main objective, is good and sounds true.

> To the Hellenes at Thermopylai, first their prophet Megistias, when taking the omens, foretold the death that was coming with the morning; and then some deserters also reported the Persian flank march. These did so while it was still night; and then thirdly it was confirmed by the men from the observation-posts on the heights, who ran down when it was already growing light.

Diodoros (xi, 8, 5) names one of these deserters, or rather courageous escapers (all no doubt Greeks); Tyrrhastiadas of Kyme. This is probably historical, the proud memory of the Man who Warned Leonidas being handed down in his family for a century, to reach Ephoros, also of Kyme, Diodoros' source. But Diodoros' account of the rest of the operation represents Ephoros at his worst. The mountain path, in the interests of romance, has to be made 'narrow and precipitous' (8, 4), which is just what it is not, and the Spartans' reaction to the news is (as also in Plutarch, *MH* 32) to raid the Persian camp before dawn, where they reach Xerxes' tent, causing him to flee in a hurry, while the barbarians slaughter each other on all sides, taking friends for foes. The Persians apparently have no sentries, no outposts and no passwords. To read the passage is to be warned against accepting, without careful consideration, anything suspected of being derived from Ephoros. The best parts of Diodoros' history of Xerxes' campaign are rationalised Herodotos; though we may also perhaps thank Ephoros for preserving the 'Laconic' saying of Leonidas – probably apocryphal, but *ben trovato* – 'Have a good breakfast, men; we shall dine in Hades!' [21] The way in which Greek historical story-telling developed, and the caution indicated in its use as historical material, is well exemplified in the same context. Herodotos himself gives one of the earliest of these Spartan soldier-sayings, attributed to Diēnekes, one of the 300, who had a reputation for them. A man of Trachis (presumably unfriendly to the Spartans for choosing his country to fight in) told him the report that when the Persians shot their arrows they darkened the sun; to receive the celebrated reply, 'Very good, we shall fight in the shade.' But in Plutarch, in spite of his knowledge of Herodotos, we find the remark transferred to Leonidas himself.[22]

Leonidas sent away most of his troops, and stayed himself, with a rearguard; an event of which many fanciful explanations have been given both in ancient and modern times. Popular in our century has been the theory that the main body was sent to try to prevent Hydarnes' column from debouching from the Anopaia, a view which the character of the north-eastern slopes does not support.[23] Herodotos says simply 'It is said that Leonidas himself sent them away, being concerned to save their lives';[24] the lives of good spearmen, who had fought well and successfully, and learned to know their enemy. They could fight another day. He kept with him his Spartans and the Helots, and also the Boiotians; the latter, perhaps on the cool calculation that, as their cities were shortly going to be open to the enemy, *they* might as well be treated as expendable. Herodotos' Athenian friends told him that, while the gallant Thespians volunteered to fight and die, Leonidas kept the Thebans against their will, 'as hostages'; on which Boiotian Plutarch

[21] D.S. xi, 9, 4; also in Plut. *Spartan Sayings*; Leonidas no. 13; Cicero *Tusc.* i, 42/101; Val. Max. iii, 2, e. 3.

[22] H. vii, 226; Plut. *op. cit.* Leon. 6.

[23] Cf. Pritchett (*op. cit.* p. 211, n. 68).

[24] vii, 220, 1. – The addition of *καί*, giving 'It is *also* said' and making H. countenance the view that they simply ran away, is an emendation, and not an improvement. Cf. the opening words of 222.

comments, making for once a sound point against his bugbear, that if that was the idea he would have done better to deliver them to the departing Peloponnesians to take south under escort.[25]

Leonidas had not, perhaps, shown the highest qualities of generalship; in face of the heavy Persian frontal attacks, he had kept 6000 men on the main road and sent only 1000 to guard the hill route; if he had sent 2000 to the hills, and a few Spartans to see that they kept a good look-out, the pass might not have fallen so quickly; though, in view of what happened at Artemision, this would have made little difference to the strategic situation. But there was a very good reason why he should stay with a rearguard. Probably no rearguard would have stood its ground without him; and it was necessary that a strong rearguard should stay. For otherwise the enemy, strong in cavalry, would have rounded up the whole army in the open within the day. If he had desired to save his own life as valuable to the cause, he could have left by sea on the dispatch-boat; but such a course, in the words of the marching-song,[26] was 'not the Spartan way'; life saved by deserting comrades would be valuable no longer. Probably he did, when he saw his flank hopelessly turned, remember the words of the oracle, that either Sparta or a Spartan king must fall, and believe, like Balin, that 'that horn was blowen for me'; one may believe that, without accepting therewith all the fulsome details of the later legend, such as that he celebrated his funeral games before leaving home.[27] He stayed, with his own regiment, so that others might live to fight another day; he keeps his place among the heroes, with all who have given their lives for a good reason when they might have lived longer.

> At the rising of the sun, Xerxes poured a drink-offering. Then he waited till mid-morning[28] before launching his attack. This had been recommended by Ephialtes; for the descent from the mountain is much steeper and shorter than the way round and up. Then Xerxes' barbarians advanced; and Leonidas and the Hellenes, as men going out to die, now came out much further to meet them, in the wider part of the pass; for the wall was their defence-line, and on the previous days they had made small sallies, to fight in the narrow part. But now they gave battle outside the narrows, and the barbarians fell in great

[25] H. vii, 222; Plut. *MH* 31.

[26] Tyrtaios (?), acc. to schol. on Dion Chrys. (*On Kingship*, ii, 59), who q. the lines only as Spartan.

[27] Plut. *MH* 32.

[28] H. vii, 223; in the pleasant Greek idiom, 'the hour when the market is full'.

numbers; for their regimental officers came behind them, using their whips indiscriminately and urging them on. Many were driven into the sea and drowned, and still more trampled under foot by their own comrades, and none took thought for the dying. For knowing well that their death was approaching at the hands of those who were turning their flank by way of the mountain [the Greeks] now put out all the strength they had, fighting like men desperate and possessed. By now the spears of most of them were broken, and they slaughtered the Persians with their swords. Leonidas was killed in this part of the action, having shown great prowess, and with him other Spartiates of good name; and I have learned their names, as those of men who deserve to be remembered; in fact, I have found out those of all the Three Hundred. And there, too, fell many Persians of good name, including two sons of Darius, Abrokomes and Hyperanthes, born to him by Phratagoune the daughter of Artānes. Artānes was brother to King Darius, and son of Hystaspes; and he left his daughter to Darius along with all his possessions, for she was his only child.

Herodotos here shakes his head over the vanity of human wishes. For all Artanes' care, his line ended on the beach at Thermopylai.

Two brothers of Xerxes, then, fell there fighting over the body of Leonidas; and there was great press of battle there between the Persians and Lakedaimonians, until the Hellenes by their valour dragged out the body and made their opponents to turn and flee four times. And so things stood until the column with Ephialtes arrived. When the Hellenes knew that they had come, they drew back again into the narrow part of the way, and took up their position at the Mound, all together, except the Thebans. The mound is in the entrance, where now the stone lion stands as a monument to the Lion's Son (Leonidas). In this place they defended themselves with their daggers (those who had them still serviceable) and with hands and teeth, until the barbarians almost smothered them with missiles, those from in front following up and piling stuff against the wall, while those who had gone round enclosed them on every side.

So perished the Spartans and their helot fellow-warriors and, according to the story, all the Thespians, with their leader who bore the Dionysiac name of Dithyrambos; while the Thebans, when the others fell back, surrendered.[29] This story, as we have seen, is deeply marked by Athenian prejudice; but it may well be that there was a certain

[29] H. vii, 226f, 233.

amount of surrendering among the Boiotians, when the order was given to fall back for the last stand – or of attempting to surrender; for in the heat of the battle, not all who dropped their weapons and 'went forward with outstretched hands' were spared. They had done valiantly up till then, and they were in no condition to inflict much more damage; but the Spartans, like Japanese, would rather die.

The mound or hillock of the last stand was identified for certain by Marinatos in 1939, just where Herodotos said it was (contrary to some nineteenth-century views), close to the road and inside the Phokian Wall. It had houses on it in Roman and Byzantine times, and the stone lion has long since vanished. But in the sandy soil, among later foundations, Marinatos found large numbers of arrowheads, mostly of the same oriental, three-edged type as those from Carchemish, dating from 605; one spearhead, probably Persian; and one spike from a spear-butt (the last weapon of someone whose spear had broken?) described as 'probably Greek'.[30]

It was all over by mid-afternoon; though the last agony must have been somewhat prolonged by the victors' wariness of the 'hands and teeth' of doomed men. The news reached Artemision after sunset (p. 401). In the meantime, there were a few barbarities incidental to clearing up the battlefield. The Great King promenaded among the corpses of his enemies; the body of Leonidas was identified, and the head cut off and stuck on a pole; and the prisoners were branded with 'the king's mark', which, as Plutarch remarks, was if anything an honourable scar to bear.[31] Then he set his men to burying their own dead; most were out of sight before a swarm of visitors from the fleet arrived, by gracious leave of His Majesty, to view the place where the king had triumphed over his enemies. The fleet had by that time occupied northern Euboia, overrunning 'all the coastal villages'; and Herodotos' east-Greek informants vividly remembered the intense competition for a place in a boat to visit the land battlefield.[32]

For the Greek cause, the fact that a disaster had been suffered was only too clear. Thanks to the slowness of the Peloponnesians in sending reinforcements, the strongest position north of the Isthmus had fallen

[30] S. Marinatos, *Thermopylae* (an illustrated pamphlet), Athens, 1951. Summary report on the excavations of 1939 in *JHS* LIX, pp. 199f (C. M. Robertson) and in *AJA* XLIII (Mrs Blegen). The arrowheads are in the Nat. Mus. Athens; cf. those from Carchemish in BM, and from Paphos (p. 203, above). Illust., Burn, *Warring States of Greece*, f. 89.

[31] H. vii, 233, 238; Plat. *MH* 33.

[32] viii, 23, 2–25.

after only three days' fighting, and a king of Sparta had been defeated and killed. The best that propaganda could do was to emphasise the courage of Leonidas and his rearguard. After the war, much was also made of the Delphic oracle's pronouncement; but at least part of it, the lines which explicitly said that resistance was useless, was unsuitable at the moment. So the Thermopylai legend, the legend of a glorious defeat, was not slow to be born. As the memory mellowed, it became clearer that the propaganda-line was truer than many such; the last stand of Leonidas and his men deserved its glory. The battle was commemorated both at Sparta and on the spot. Herodotos' concern to 'ascertain the names of the Three Hundred' involved no tedious research; he could read them on the Thermopylai Memorial at Sparta, near the (much later) theatre, as Pausanias tells us, adding that there were there, too, statues of Leonidas and of Pausanias, the hero of 479 (iii, 14, 1). It was in this quarter that the British excavators found the head and torso of an early fifth-century statue of a warrior, now at Athens, which from its attitude, 'gardant' rather than triumphant, is generally conjectured to be the Leonidas. A speech commemorating the battle was delivered there annually (another glimpse of Greek oral tradition); and there were games 'at which only Spartiates are allowed to compete'.[33] The embittering of relations with the Helots after the earthquake of 464, when even the Lakonian helots rebelled, had given rise to a conspiracy of silence over the part played by the helot contingent among the Four Thousand.

More famous have been the monuments at the Pass itself, with the three famous verse inscriptions. The stones have long perished, though it is not impossible that fragments may remain, under later foundations and the hard stony deposits from the hot springs; but Herodotos copied them, and the works of his pen have been more lasting than stone. One we have already seen:

> Against three million men fought, in this place,
> Four thousand Peloponnesians face to face.

Most famous and most often translated of all these anonymous, lapidary poems is that on the Spartans:

> Tell them in Lakedaimon, passer by:
> Carrying out their orders, here we lie.

[33] Paus. iii, 14, 1.

The genius of this couplet is in the fact it is so simple that any soldier might have said it, and it might have happened to be an elegiac couplet by accident. It was later assigned to Simonides of Keos;[34] but Herodotos' words (ch. 228) are: 'It was the Amphiktyons who set up in their honour the plaques and their inscriptions, except that on the prophet Megistias; but the inscription on him was written by Simonides the son of Leoprepes, from personal friendship.'

Herodotos has earlier mentioned (221) that Leonidas tried to send Megistias (an Akarnanian, like many seers, and 'said to be of the line of Melampous') south with the retreating column, but he declined to leave Leonidas; 'but he sent away his only son, who was serving with the army.' Simonides' contemporary, written evidence is the best that we could ask, for the attitude of the men of 480 to prophecies. It is difficult to imagine that Leonidas and his seer did not, in their last hours, have some discussion on the subject of the oracles of Delphi.

Simonides' lines on the Seer, his friend, may be rendered:

> Here great Megistias lies, whom Median men
> Killed when they crossed Spercheios; who that day,
> Seer as he was, with Sparta's captains then
> Knew what was coming, and preferred to stay.

[34] e.g. *Anth. Pal.* vii, 249. Lykourges. *Againrt Leokrates* (who has just quoted Tyrtaios by name, 107), names however no author for this couplet (109).

Chapter XX

The Razor's Edge

THE retreat of the Greek fleet was unmolested; fortunately; for it was a battered fleet that streamed southward down the Euripos channel. Many ships still capable of bringing their crews to port were no longer battle-worthy, at least without repairs: ships with damaged rams, ships limping, short of oars, ships with holes temporarily plugged and bloody patches on deck; crews willing to fight again for homes and families, but in a desperate rather than hopeful mood. Their commanders might tell them, especially the ever-sanguine Themistokles, that to fight at Artemision had been fully justified; that the enemy's losses had been enormous, and that they themselves would find reinforcements awaiting them. The men needed all the cheer they could be given.

However, as often in the history of war, the force that had been fought to a standstill was allowed to fall back on its reserves, while an invader could not or at least did not pursue without pausing to reorganize. Most of the Persian army had probably not been engaged, though some divisions had had heavy losses; but it was probably necessary to wait while the flotillas of victuallers brought in food from the depots in Thrace, to supplement the insufficient local resources, and meanwhile the fleet did not venture ahead. Once more, it appears, it was given orders to wait until the army secured the coast for it.[1]

Before dawn on the day after the battle (D. 21 from Therma?)

> a man of Histiaia came over in a boat to the barbarians, to tell them that the Greeks had slipped away from Artemision. They mistrusted the report and detained the messenger, while they sent some fast ships to reconnoitre. Then, when these had reported the facts and when the sun was rising, the whole fleet sailed over to the Artemision. They stayed there till mid-day, and then sailed on to

[1] Cf. H. viii, 66, 1.

Histiaia, occupied the city, and overran all the coast villages of the Hellopian region, which is the territory of Histiaia.[2]

Next day Xerxes, whose troops had meanwhile cleared up the battlefield at Thermopylai and buried most of their own dead (estimated by the Greeks, no doubt with much exaggeration, at 20,000), invited men of the fleet to come over and see the bodies of 'the foolish men who thought to withstand the power of the King'. There were some 4000 of them, including helots.[3] In the meantime, some Greek deserters came in:

> some Arcadians – not many of them – lacking the means of life and desiring employment. They were led before the King, and the Persians interrogated them as to what the Greeks were doing; one Persian conducted the interrogation on behalf of them all.[4]

Once more, Greeks are surprised at Persian methods; among the Greeks everyone within earshot would have wanted to join in. But we are left wondering who these Arcadians were, and how they reached Xerxes. Had they crossed the Corinthian Gulf and come all that way through the mountains simply to 'seek employment', when they could have had it at the Isthmus? Were they adherents of the fallen Kleomenes, hostile to the present government of Sparta? Or were they (it seems far from impossible) some of the Arcadian highlanders who had fought under Leonidas? – hill-men, to whom, as to Ephialtes the Malian, the concept 'Hellas' meant nothing, and a victorious king might seem better than a dead one. It is admitted in later Greek tradition that Leonidas' disaster had a serious moral effect;[5] and in Herodotos too, there hangs together with this story a striking negative fact. 'The rest of Arcadia', west of Tegea, Mantineia and Orchomenos, ever a home of good fighting men, had supplied a quarter of Leonidas' Peloponnesian brigade; but in the following year, when all the Peloponnesian League was called to arms and Herodotos gives a list of the contingents, from all this area not a regiment came.[6]

[2] H. viii, 23. D.S. xi, 13, 5, says they 'stormed and sacked' Histiaia, but this may only represent Ephoros heightening the effect. – For the name Hellopia (Ellopia in Hdt.), probably connected with that of the Hellenes and Homer's Helloi or Selloi (*Il.* xvi, 233), cf. the *loc. class.*, Str. vii, 328 (q. Homer, Hesiod, Pindar and Philochoros) and ix, 445; Macan (on *-op-* names) on H., *ad loc.*

[3] H. viii, 24f. – H. had been told a story that X., by the burial of the Persian dead, tried to deceive the sight-seers into thinking that very few had fallen, and rightly brands this as a silly idea; his 'public facts' are, as usual, probably true.

[4] *ib.* 26.

[5] D.S. xi, 16, 2.

[6] A point made by Beloch, *GG*[2] II, ii, p. 105.

Herodotos includes this significant story because it contained one detail which pleased him. In answer to the question what the Greeks were doing, the Arcadians were said to have answered that they were at Olympia, watching a festival of athletics and horse-racing; and it was added that, when the Persians heard what Greeks would do for a 'corruptible crown', one at least, Tritantaikhmes the son of Artabanos (or, some mss. say, Tigranes), was not unimpressed.

On the third day (D. 23) 'the army with Xerxes took the road', using, as usual, all routes. Wagons would have to go by the coast road through Lokris; but the statement that the army entered Phokis *via* Doris[7] seems to imply that the infantry took the shorter hill routes, practicable now that there was no opposition, including perhaps the way through the Asopos ravine. Lokris, though it is said to have sent earth and water to Xerxes and then reverted to the Greek side, is not said to have been devastated; the Dorians in their valley-head, who had sent no troops to Thermopylai, were protected. The Thessalians, whose chiefs were now helping the Persian intelligence, took credit to themselves for this. Phokis, on the other hand, against which the Thessalians had a grudge for its successful and recent rebellion against them,[8] was singled out to be made an example of the consequences of resistance, and the Persians let loose their young barbarians to rape and murder and devastate.

Every village in Phokis, the wide and beautiful vale by the upper waters of the Boiotian Kēphisos, was systematically burned: Elateia of the fir forests under Parnassos, Parapotamioi 'beside the river', Hyampolis where they beat the Thessalians and Abai with its oracular shrine, which yielded rich plunder; Panopé and Daulis and Aiolidai; Herodotos enumerates fifteen 'cities' in all. The Phokians fled for their lives, westward, most of them, to Amphissa, beyond Parnassos, whither the invasion did not extend. Some 'took to the hills' in the great Parnassos massif itself, the high intermontane plains between its peaks, which modern Phokians cultivate in summer; 'the height called Tithoréa', says Herodotos truly, 'is well adapted to receive a multitude'. Some of them were overtaken, and received no mercy.[9]

Through Daulis and Panopé a column, it is said, turned west for Delphi; but Delphi, which had been so useful to the Persian cause, was not sacked. The Delphians, Phokians themselves, though since they

[7] H. viii, 31f. [8] Cf. *Lyric Age*, pp. 203f. [9] H. viii, 31ff.

had grown rich they never made common cause with their country cousins, might well be afraid; they might hope for Xerxes' favour, but still fear plunder and massacre by troops out of hand. 'They sent their women and children across the water to Achaia, while most of the men took refuge in the heights of Parnassos and the Korykian Cave', a refuge that has done duty down to World War II; a vast cave with a slit-like entrance from a small terrace above a steep place. It is quite hard to find now, and must have been doubly so when the forest was thicker. 'Some also retired to Amphissa in western Lokris', where they would meet the earlier stream of refugees, fleeing from northern Phokis over the Gravia Pass. There remained only, to protect the sanctuary against casual looting, sixty men and the Prophētes, whose name was Akēratos. The treasures, it is said, were not moved; the God had said that he was able to protect his own. And sure enough, the Persians, after pushing their devastating raid to the nearest corner of Phokis short of Delphi itself, turned back. To men who knew no other reason why they should, it seemed a miracle; surely Apollo and the Delphian heroes had intervened. It is a reasonable guess that Xerxes, who according to Herodotos (viii, 35) knew all about the treasures of Delphi, had given his orders, and that the column which ravaged Daulis obeyed them; but if any leading Delphians knew this, the fewer men were in the secret the better; and fugitives watching the smoke of burning villages from Parnassos, or among the sixty in the sanctuary, who had prayed desperately and found their prayers answered, were ready for a more marvellous explanation. A legend duly arose, of thunder from heaven, of two huge rocks that broke off from Parnassos and crushed many (and the rocks, at least, were there to be shown to visitors thereafter, lying by the Temple of Athena Pronaia, near the road); a legend of a mighty voice shouting a battle-cry from that temple; of sacred arms, that no man might touch, that came out of the Temple of Apollo of their own accord (Akeratos vouched that he himself had seen them lying outside), and of two warriors in armour, of more than human size, who followed the Persians slaying them as they fled in panic all the way to Boiotia.[10] And such was the prestige of Delphi that no extant literary source questions this story.

So the invaders came to Boiotia; and here discipline was reasserted,

[10] H. viii, 35ff; D.S. xi, 14, 2ff, quoting inscr. in commemoration (which has been found; cf. Meritt in *Hesperia* XVI, 1947).

and the devastation stopped. More numerous and powerful than the Phokians, the Boiotians could be useful allies. They were no more kindly regarded by the Thessalians than the Phokians were; Boiotia too had been overrun by the Thessalians in the sixth century, and had delivered itself by fighting (see n. 8). But they had got into touch, in good time, with Alexander the Macedonian, that ambiguous Philhellene (and, according to Plutarch, *MH* 31, with Damaratos), and while we may guess that the cities kept their gates shut until they could open them to responsible Persian officers, Macedonian liaison officers, sent by Alexander, mediated their surrender.[11] Two cities only were marked out for destruction; Plataia and Thespiai. The Athenian ships which had Plataians among their crews had stopped, in their retreat, opposite Chalkis and landed them, to make their way home across country and see to the evacuation of their families; they and the Thespians fled to the Peloponnese.[12]

In central Euboia, the people of Chalkis, Eretria and Styra may have fled to the extensive and wooded mountains. What is striking is that, like Athens, they did not surrender. Their ships were to fight again, all the same 29 ships, according to Herodotos, who takes no account of losses at Artemision, and 1000 armoured men on land later.[13] With the strategically important Karystos already in friendly hands, the Persians did not divert troops to occupy central Euboia, and even their fleet cannot have had time for more than perfunctory raiding; for, after waiting for three days to let the army secure the land ahead (D. 24–26), it is said to have sailed directly south from Histiaia, and in three more days (D. 27–29) joined up with the land forces in Attica.[14] The Persian advance by land was rapid; it appears that, while some troops (miscellaneous barbarians?) were let loose in Phokis, cavalry advanced guards were probably opposite Chalkis, where a main route south once more comes close to the sea, in four days from Thermopylai (D. 27).

Meanwhile Athens was in the throes of an evacuation.

Themistokles, as we have seen (p. 361), may have got a vote passed

[11] *ib.* 34. [12] *ib.* 44.

[13] *ib.* 46; ix, 28, 5.

[14] *ib.* 66, 1. The devastation of Euboia by the Persian fleet alleged by Diodoros (xi, 14, 5) is therefore probably mythical and at least greatly exaggerated, though possibly some rear squadrons may have been given this task. The story probably represents Ephoros writing history in terms of what he thinks *should* have happened.

by the Assembly at the time when all Athens' man-power first took to the sea, to entrust the city to the gods and to send children and their mothers to Troizen and old people and goods to Salamis.[15] The hundred ships of the reserve fleet may (though no ancient writer actually says this) have been expected to cover and help with this evacuation. Some enlightened and provident people, perhaps mostly the more educated and well-to-do, may have acted on the decree, and removed their families in good time. Troizen responded nobly, and in later days treasured the memory of a decree moved by one Nikagoras, voting money for the maintenance of the refugees at the rate of two obols (one-third of a drachma; probably per day, per family), fees to schoolmasters who taught Athenian children, and permission for the children to pick fruit in the country.[16] It was the season when grapes and figs would be ripening, as every traveller knows, in abundance for all. But little Troizen can hardly have been in a position to extend such generosity to all or even half of the children of Athens.

Most ordinary Athenians, it is clear, sanguine as ever and unwilling of leave their homes, had done nothing about it. Even when the news to disaster flashed through the land (probably very quickly, by beacons soon followed by runners) they still looked for the great Peloponnesian army, which was to have reinforced Thermopylai, to meet the enemy in Boiotia.[17] It was not until the fleet rounded Sounion and, at the Athenians' request, bore up into Salamis Sound so that they might evacuate their women and children, that most non-combatants awoke to the stark reality, with a proclamation by their own authorities that they should 'save their children and households where they could': *sauve qui peut*. Then, says Herodotos (viii, 41), 'most sent them to Troizen, but some to Aigina and some to Salamis'; but it was a long 'carry' to Troizen, when the enemy fleet might be arriving any day, and the accuracy of this detail *at this time* may be doubted. The appear-

[15] That the evacuation was begun after the retreat from Tempe, the view now definitely implied if we accept the evidence of the Troizen inscription, was already suggested by Munro in 1902 (*JHS* XXII, p. 320); though it is conspicuous, and must be repeated, that the later ancient writers who cite the Decree of Themistokles all put this part of its provisions after Artemision.

[16] Plut. *Them.* 10. – The theory that N. was not the Troizenian mover, but in reality the Athenian mover of the evacuation-decree, was always more clever than well founded. This decree of Troizen probably was genuinely remembered (not necessarily its *text preserved*); an occasion when it may have been cited by orators and so transmitted to historians being well known, namely in the mid-fifth century, when Troizen left Sparta's alliance for that of Athens, and was no doubt a democracy.

[17] H. viii, 40.

ance of Aigina, old enemy turned new friend, is, on the other hand, unexpected and of great interest.

It was a grim awakening. It was too late now for a 'tidy' evacuation; what had not been done in good time must be done in a hurry, and in the last stages there was a certain amount of panic. Boats of every kind, loaded almost to sinking, ferried the refugees to Salamis. Later Greek rhetoricians (i.e. popular lecturers, who often treated historical subjects) often pictured the scene; for instance, our friend Aelius Aristides (xlvi, p. 257 D.), describing Themistokles, alone cool and undismayed 'while women and children shrieked' (as unsophisticated Greek women suddenly called upon to leave home certainly would),

> and some people had to be left behind, and the whole situation was almost as if the city had been taken by storm; for no one could foresee the future, and hope was faint and uncertain, and what was actual was the loss of their city and possessions and all familiar things; and they were not even all going the same way to the same exile, but there was separation of fathers from children, and husbands from wives, and every circumstance that is terrible even to hear of, and how much more to live through! And there are stories of how the dogs howled at being left behind, and, with other pet animals, followed people down to the shore, causing great distress.

Plutarch (*Them.* 10), in a generally similar picture, says that the very old had to be left; and adds the story of one dog (remembered because it belonged to the boy Perikles' family). Xanthippos, back from exile, embarked on a ship of war; and his dog plunged into the sea and swam across the strait to Salamis, only to die exhausted after dragging itself ashore; a landmark on a headland of Salamis was said to be a memorial to it: *Kynos-sēma*, the Dog's Monument.

Many poor men ran out of money; a serious matter, for in Greek fleets the men were usually paid in coin, and had to buy their food from stores in private hands; and the treasury itself was empty, too. But patriotism triumphed over that. The well-to-do ex-archons of the Areopagite Council raised a subscription, and provided the generals with enough money to pay eight drachmas to each man;[18] enough to buy food for a month, if there was food to buy. (Drs. 8 for, say, 45,000 needy sailors and soldiers, a sum of 60 talents, would be a sum

[18] *Ath. Pol.* 23.

not impossible for 200 wealthy citizens to raise out of their strong-boxes in a crisis.) Another story was told, that Themistokles, on the pretext of looking for the Gorgon ornament (of gold?) from the breast of Athena's cult statue, which was said to have been stolen in the confusion, had baggage searched, and impounded large sums of money for the public use;[19] presumably, if the story is true, only suspiciously heavy baggage, and sums in excess of what the individual was considered to need, or to have been likely to come by honourably.

Herodotos adds (viii, 41) that the evacuation was accelerated (perhaps the earlier and more orderly evacuation, not in the final panic), both by reference to the (Wooden Walls) Oracle,

> and by the following circumstance: the Athenians say that a great Snake is guardian of the Acropolis, and dwells in the Sanctuary; and they not only say this, but put out rations for it, month by month, in the form of a honey-cake. This honey-cake, which in time past had always been consumed, was on this occasion left untouched; and when the Priestess reported this, the Athenians were much readier to leave the city, in the belief that the Goddess herself had left the Acropolis.

Plutarch (*loc. cit.*) says that Themistokles suggested this explanation; and it is a reasonable modern guess that he knew more about the 'portent' than he said. The story is of interest, both for the primitive character of the belief, which links classical Athena with the Snake-Goddess of the Bronze Age, and for the fact that it shocks Herodotos; not what 'they say' – he was accustomed to mythology – but the fact that they put out food for the Snake, as for a real, physical Presence. It does not appear that there was a real snake (as in later Asklēpieia) for people to see.[20]

Even so, in spite of all persuasion, the evacuation was incomplete. Apart from the old and helpless, who presumably either perished from neglect or were killed by the invaders, we find later (p. 548) that the Persians had collected over 500 prisoners in Attica; and these must have been able-bodied people worth preserving as slaves. Probably they were largely the remoter country people, who (any men among them

[19] Kleidemos, *ap.* Plut. *Th.* 10.

[20] The old woman in Aristophanes (*Lys.* 710) who is afraid to sleep on the Acropolis because she once 'saw the Snake' has presumably been seeing visions. On sacred snakes, and rations for them (as in the O.T. apocryphal *Bel and the Dragon*), see further Macan on H., *ad loc.*

having already ignored and evaded the call to come down and man the fleet) drove their sheep and cattle up into Parnes; it is unlikely that the Persians caught a high proportion of them. And in the city itself there were still the die-hards who refused to leave the temples and citadel, insisting that its palisades were the Oracle's Wooden Wall. The Rock, with its precipitous sides, assailable without climbing only at its west end (where there was probably also covered access to the Klepsydra spring), was indeed a very strong position; and it was left garrisoned. 'The Treasurers of the Sanctuary' stayed on it, says Herodotos (viii, 51); and with them 'some few poor men, who for lack of means of subsistence had not withdrawn to Salamis'; they 'barricaded the Acropolis with planks and timbers, thinking that they had understood the Oracle'.

The phrase 'not withdrawing for lack of subsistence' is an odd one, and even odder the fact that it passes unnoticed by the commentators; for if these men had joined the fleet, they would have been no worse off than their comrades; but it clearly made sense to Greeks. Probably they understood that, to set off on a campaign, one had to be able to lay hands on the sack of meal that was the commissariat of the Greek soldier and was normally carried by a trusted slave.[21] According to the Troizen inscription (11f; p. 365), Themistokles himself sponsored the decision that 'the priests and priestesses' should remain on the Acropolis to look after sacred property (like the Sixty at Delphi); but that was earlier, at the time of the mobilisation. However, it seems rather probable that the Acropolis was now regularly garrisoned, perhaps as a concession to die-hard opinion, and that it was only after the event that this step was discounted by propaganda as the enterprise of a few poor fanatics.

The Athenians were, in the end, granted about six days in which to clear the city, removing to Salamis such valuables and, in particular, as much grain as possible; but much, it appears, was lost, since later it is stated that Athens lost 'two harvests'[22] (those of 480 and 479). The corn must have been reaped by the end of May, when Xerxes was still at Doriskos; but the general mobilisation would have interrupted the prolonged process of threshing, which normally goes on through July and much of August, and there was little time for removing, with pack-animals and ox-wagons, the high proportion of the grain that

[21] Cf, Thk. vii, 75, 5.

[22] H. viii, 142, 3.

would usually have been consumed in the villages. Greek cities when all went well clearly used to accumulate large stocks, in private hands, an insurance against war or a bad harvest; many passages of Thucydides and Xenophon show that a city could hold out for a year before people went seriously hungry, and that even a modest-sized city could easily 'provide a market' for a passing army or fleet. In 480, it is reasonable to suppose that governmental and private foresight had accumulated considerable stocks in Salamis; but with the island crowded with the men of over 300 ships and perhaps a considerably larger number of refugees, the Persians, when they gave thought to the matter, had good reason to think that its supplies would soon be exhausted.[23]

Meanwhile the Peloponnesian army, duly mobilised when 'the Karneia and the Olympic Games were over',[24] was mustering at Corinth under Kleombrotos, the youngest and now last survivor of the sons of Anaxandridas; and when the news of disaster at Thermopylai flashed through the land, belated contingents hurried. There may well have been 30,000 armoured troops there, as well as light-armed 'small folk' and soldiers' servants, armour-bearers and food-carriers. But Kleombrotos had no intention of advancing into open country. He had indeed some excuse. There are narrow places on the way through Boiotia, where the battle-names cluster, between Lake Kōpaïs and the slopes of Helikon; but there is no Thermopylai, and the enemy would have been able to use his cavalry and archers. The Kithairon–Parnes line, the northern frontier of Attica, has passes near Plataia, and is also passable at its eastern end, and to try to hold that would have necessitated dividing the army in face of a more mobile enemy; it would have courted the danger which Sparta was above all things anxious to avoid: that of compromising the defence of the Peloponnese itself by a disaster beyond its gates. So Kleombrotos sent forward troops only to the Geraneia range, south of Megara, to demolish the road that wound sinuously under the sea-cliffs, the road 'made by Skiron when he was war-chief of Megara';[25] the Skiron whom malicious Athenian legend turned into a highway-robber. This would leave the enemy only the hill paths through Tripodiskos, by which Brasidas marched his few thousand men in 424. The main body proceeded to throw up an embankment across the Isthmus between

[23] H. viii, 68, 2, b2. [24] *ib.* 72.
[25] Paus. i, 44, 6; on Skiron, cf. 39, 6; 44, 8; demolitions, H. viii, 71.

Lechaion and Kenchreai, just south of the narrowest part, where the slipway for ship-transporters ran, for the sake of better protected flanks; 'and as there were many myriads of men there, and every man worked' (men-at-arms alongside the light-armed and slaves), 'the work went fast; stones and bricks and timber baskets full of sand' (for mortar) 'were brought up continuously, and the work went on ceaselessly, day and night'. The result was no Great Wall of China; by the fourth century, it had crumbled into a state in which it was apparently no longer a military obstacle; but its remains probably underlie those of later works, from the days of Valerian, Justinian and the Venetian-Turkish wars, which may still be seen crossing the modern road some distance south of the Canal.[26]

So far had things gone, when the last Athenian observers from the hills fell back, to report that 'the barbarians had entered Attica and were burning all the land'. Their fleet, rounding Sounion and burning the coastal villages *en route*, was reaching Phaleron Bay by the ninth day after the fall of Thermopylai (about the end of August) and about the same time Xerxes' advanced guards entered deserted Athens. 'From the beginning of their march from the Hellespont, where they had spent a month while crossing into Europe' (including everything up to the reorganization at Doriskos?) 'in three further months they had reached Athens.'[27] It was no mean achievement.

Now the Persians assaulted the Acropolis. They took up their position on the Areopagus rock, facing the way up, and shot flaming arrows into the palisades, which were soon on fire;

> but the Athenian garrison still held out, though in desperate case, and though their palisade had betrayed them. They refused overtures, communicated to them by the Peisistratidai, for a surrender on terms, and defended themselves resourcefully. When the enemy advanced towards the gates, they sent rolling stones down upon them

(sweeping them off the *glacis*, perhaps with pillar-drums from some unfinished building project)

[26] H., *ib.*; How, *ad loc.*; D.S. xi, 16, 3; Frazer, *Pausanias* III, pp. 5ff. Unmentioned by D.S. on the campaign of 369, xv, 68. Brasidas, Thk. iv, 70.—On the Tripodiskos road, cf. Hammond in *BSA* LIV. But the towers protecting its northern continuation (see Hammond's illustrations) look C4 or later. Unmentioned by Hdt., was it still only a rough track at this time?

[27] H. viii, 50f; 66.

and for a long time Xerxes was completely baffled by his inability to capture them. However, the barbarians found a way in, after their perplexity; for it was destined, according to the Oracle, that all continental Attica was to fall to the Persians. In the front part of the Acropolis, but in rear of the gates and the approach-way, at a point which was unguarded, since no one would ever have anticipated that any man could scale it – there some of them got up, climbing the sheer rock, by the sanctuary of Aglauros the daughter of Kekrops. And when the Athenians saw that they were up, some threw themselves down from the walls and perished, and others fled to the temple; but the Persians who had got up turned their attention first to the gates, and opened them, and then slaughtered those who had taken sanctuary; and having killed them all, they plundered the temple, and burned everything on the Acropolis.

Then Xerxes, having completed his capture of Athens, sent off a dispatch-rider to Artabanos to announce his victory. But the next day . . . he called together the Athenian exiles who were with him, and bade them go up to the Acropolis and offer sacrifice after their own manner; whether it was that he had seen some vision in a dream, or whether he was uneasy at heart, after he had burnt the holy place.

Herodotos continues (viii, 55):

Now there is on the Acropolis a temple of Erechtheus, the Earth-born as he is called, in which there is an olive-tree and a Sea [apparently a well of salt water] which, according to the legend of the Athenians, were set there by Poseidon and Athena for a testimony when they contended for the land. This olive had been burnt by the barbarians along with the whole place; but on the next day after the fire, the Athenians who were bidden by the King to offer sacrifice, when they went up to the temple, saw that the stump had put out a shoot, already half a yard long; such was their statement.

This story includes some of the earliest extant testimony on the topography of the Acropolis and on its legends.

It was in this sack that there were thrown down and smashed all the archaic sculptures of the Acropolis, including the charming series of the Maidens (thank-offerings set up by girl acolytes or their parents, at the end of their service?) which are now among the most loved treasures of Athenian sculpture; statues which owe their desecration then their preservation to this day; for the Athenians after the war, rather than restore sculptures which, to a fifth-century eye, were already quaint and old-fashioned, put them reverently away in a hollow of the rock, to be rediscovered by German archaeologists only in the nineteenth century. Similar was the fate of the eleven-foot early sixth-century Youth from the temple at Sounion, no doubt pushed over by men of the Persian fleet at this time, and of other *kouroi* of Attica; different, that of the bronze statues of the tyrannicides, Harmodios and Aristogeiton, which (pointed out to Xerxes by the Peisistratids as those of the slayers of a friend of Persia and heroes of the democracy?) were carried off as spoils of war and stood for 150 years at Persepolis. Restored to Athens by Alexander, they are known only through copies, the originals having been melted down at some unknown date in the wreck of later antiquity.

For courage, the defence of the Acropolis ranks with that of Thermopylai; but it did no like service to the cause. Unlike Thermopylai, the Acropolis did not deny any essential ground to the enemy. The rock is not large enough for more than a small portion of the Persian forces even to be able to attack it at one time; its importance was purely moral. Its defence can have done nothing to delay any operations against Salamis and the Greek fleet there; and on the contrary, the fall of yet another strong position to Persian drive, enterprise and daring – perhaps after the attack, kept up for a few days, had reduced the defenders' vigilance by sheer exhaustion – is said to have had a daunting effect upon Greek morale.[28]

Estimates (which are mere guesses) of the duration of Xerxes' 'bafflement' before the Acropolis at as much as two or three weeks[29] have, in fact, been based chiefly on a desire to answer the question, what the two sides were doing during the whole first half of the month of September. Herodotos' count of days for the Persian advance from Therma ends with the occupation of Athens (less the Acropolis), possibly because his Persian source depends ultimately on Xerxes' despatch; and the next firm date which he gives us (at ix, 10, 3) is that of a solar eclipse, some days after the decisive battle, which astronomers

[28] H. viii, 56.

[29] A fortnight, Bury in *CR* X (1896), Busolt, *GG* II, p. 695; questioned by Munro in *HS* XXII, p. 321, n. 39, as 'hard to reconcile' with Hdt. viii, 66–70, but accepted as 'right in the main'; cf. How on H. viii, 53; Munro later (*CAH* IV, p. 304) proposed three weeks. But, as is said above, it seems unlikely that the defence of the Acropolis can really have delayed the sea-battle at all.

have dated to October the 2nd. Plutarch says that the battle was fought on the 19th Boedromion (c. September 20th, the full moon having been on September 17th), which would be acceptable; and Herodotos indicates that it was at the season when, in time of peace, the Eleusinian Mysteries would have been celebrated; an agrarian feast in origin, falling in Boedromion at this epoch, at the time of the first rain and before the autumn ploughing.[30] But what the opposing forces were doing in the meantime is a question still to be faced. Herodotos, clearly without a calendar for the operations, gives the impression that the battle followed within a few days of Xerxes' arrival in Attica.

The delay of some three weeks in joining battle at Salamis was perhaps occupied largely by a trial of patience; each side hoping that the other's logistic difficulties would force it to move. Each side, it is clear, was ready to accept battle in waters of its own choosing. The Persians might hope that lack of supplies and the fears of the Peloponnesians for their own country would force the Greeks out of the straits into open waters, where their still superior numbers and Phoenician seamanship might achieve another Lade. The Greeks – especially Themistokles, but surely not he alone, as the Greek saga has it – were very willing to fight in the narrow waters, where their heavier ships (Herodotos puts the phrase into the mouth of Themistokles exactly at this juncture[31]) and the prowess of their armoured marines might be expected to inflict more loss than they would sustain. Themistokles must, as has been seen, have envisaged for years the possibility of a 'last act' in the drama of a Persian invasion, in which Salamis would be Athens' island citadel and the Salamis Strait quite literally the 'last ditch'; and the naming of Salamis in the 'Wooden Walls' Oracle suggests that Athens, at his prompting, had put that name into the question.

For Xerxes, meanwhile, the island (the fact is not always realised) crowded with Athenians, including Athenian troops and the magistrates and councils, represented an important military objective, the capture of which might end the resistance of Athens and bring within sight the end of the war. The Persians had their own anxieties. Their navy,

[30] Plut. *Camillus*, 19; accepted, e.g., by Bury, *HG*³ p. 281; Hdt. viii, 65. – Plutarch's remarkable alternative date for the battle, 16th Mounychion (in spring! – *Glory of Athens*, 7), is probably, like his date for Marathon, that of the festival at which it was commemorated (Goodwin in *Harvard Studies* XVII, p. 88).

[31] viii, 60. – Plutarch' evidence to the contrary (*Them.* 14) is from a worthless source; see p. 475.

reduced by tempest, was no longer strong enough to divide in face of the enemy (p. 402); hence they dared not attack the Peloponnese by sea while the Greek fleet was in being; and a decision was urgently wanted within a few weeks, before the gales of autumn made it impossible to move supplies by sea. There was still one thing that they could do, to get at the Greeks in their island fastness: one of those great military engineering works, which had been part of the Persian repertory since Cyrus diverted the Tigris. Like Alexander before Tyre, but on a much larger scale, Xerxes ordered his army to throw rocks into the sea in the narrowest part of the strait to form a mole, and 'began lashing Phoenician merchant-ships together, to serve both as a floating bridge and as a protection'. Thus Herodotos (viii, 97); but he says that it was done only after Xerxes had been defeated at sea, and as a 'cover-plan' to conceal his real intention to retreat. Since it is added that he began to retreat after only a few days, the cover-plan seems improbably cumbrous; and this is one reason (and good reason, it must be emphasised, is needed) for following here the inferior sources, who say that Xerxes' *first* plan was to reach Salamis by means of a mole.[32] How Herodotos may have come to make this mistake (if it is a mistake) will appear shortly.

[32] Strabo ix, 1, 13 (p. 395 Casaubon); Ktes. epit. 26; Aristodemos (*FGH* 104 F1; *FHG* V, pp. 1ff). It is necessary to emphasise how inferior these sources normally are, since Mr Hammond (in *JHS* LXXVI, 1956; the sole modern treatment of these operations to which reference is made in his *History of Greece*, 1959, with a brief warning that there are other opinions, p. 239, n. 3) gives countenance to the view that 'the ancient evidence is sound'; a state of affairs to which he mentions no exceptions. Now the only reputable author among the three here cited is Strabo; and even he, a learned but armchair geographer, in his description of the Salamis strait from NW to SE, on Mr Hammond's own interpretation describes the mainland coast as far as the narrowest point, and then goes back without warning to mention the Pharmakoussai or Enchantress Islands, at the north end of the strait (*if* these are to be identified with the modern Kyrádhes or 'Bad Ladies'), before resuming; a point slurred over in Hammond's article (pp. 34f) with the statement 'Strabo continues, rather vaguely'; Strabo here is not vague, he is positively misleading, if Hammond's identification of these islands is right; a point of some importance when we later come (p. 473, below) to try to identify the island of Psyttáleia. Strabo also describes the narrows as about 400 yards wide, which would be less than half the real width even if the ancient sea-level (certainly lower than at present) were as low as the two-fathom line; the shores are steep.

On Ktesias, comment has been made above (e.g. pp. 12, 94,). Aristodemos, here resurrected from his deserved obscurity, is the author of a Greek History (for schools?), of which a long extract, dealing with the fifth century, is preserved. It contains nothing which is both otherwise unknown and also sense, and no blunder seems too childish for him to make. e.g., after describing the peace of 445 between Athens and Sparta, he continues 'and in the fourteenth year the Athenians besieged and took Samos . . . and in the same year, in this way, the Thirty Years Peace was broken and the Peloponnesian War began'. (Any scholar accustomed to reading the examination papers of beginners

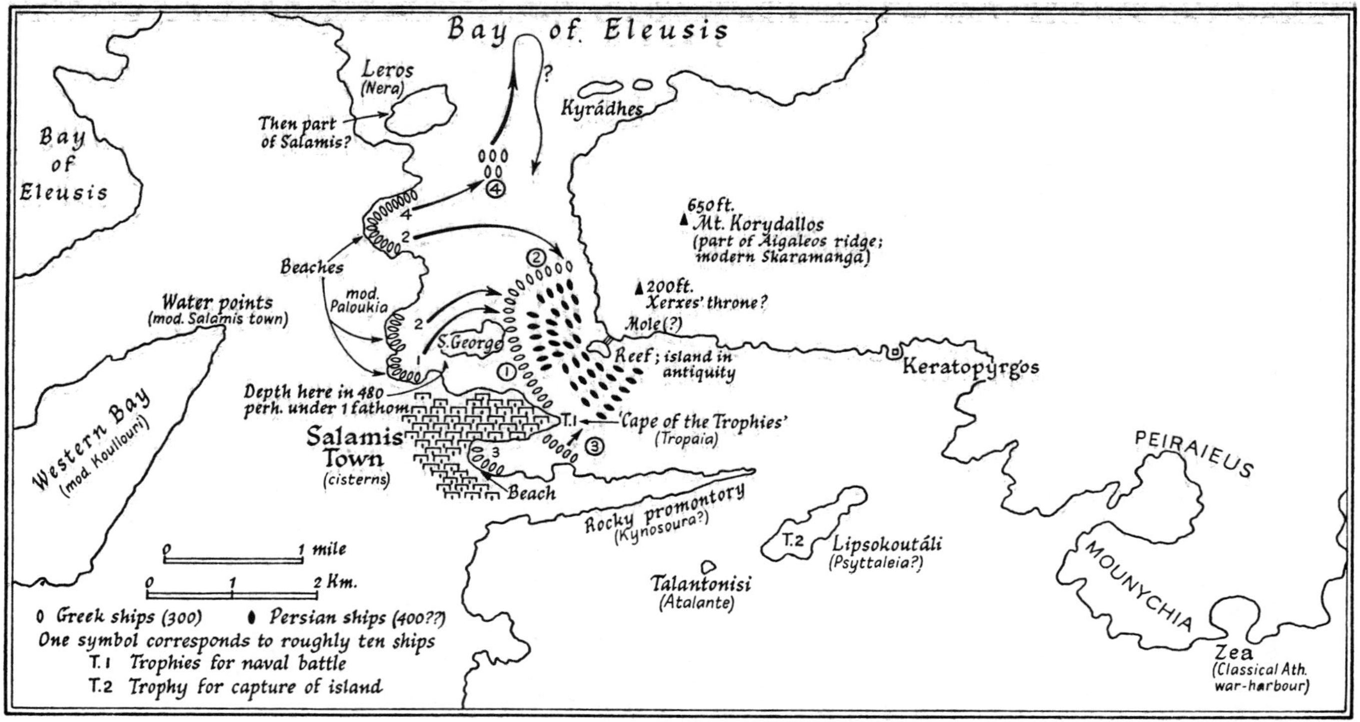

The Battle of Salamis (for notes see opposite)

The mole was a vast but entirely typical Persian siege-operation. Getting ships up into the Narrows (presumably opposite St George Island, which was then probably within wading distance of Salamis,[33] and an obvious outpost of the Greek defence) must have been difficult in face of the undefeated Greek fleet, but could be done, for instance with the aid of towing, along the mainland shore, under cover of the vastly superior Persian archery. But the Persians' real difficulties, like Alexander's at Tyre, would begin as the mole reached deep water, and as its flanks became longer. Archery was clearly going to be of vital importance if the mole ever got near enough to Salamis to be dangerous. (Actually, the stone jetty built out from the mainland cannot ever have got far; otherwise, in a battle fought *inside the Strait*, as all our sources say,[34] it would have been a conspicuous feature and impediment to movement; but it must have been intended to use the 'rafts' of merchant-ships lashed together as assault-bridges over the later section.) Athens had already, unlike any of her allies, and probably since Marathon, organised a small but efficient archer regiment;[35] we do not know how strong their bows were. Ktesias (26) says that, on the initiative of Themistokles and Aristeides they got archers from Crete.

---

in Greek history can analyse both his sources and the nature of his errors, but it is needless to do so here.) In dealing with Salamis, he makes Xerxes throw 'several myriads' of troops on to the island of Psyttáleia, which is, to say the least, excessive.

From the above it may be concluded that when A. makes Xerxes sit on Parnes to watch the battle of Salamis, he means exactly what he says; it is waste of time to try to save his face by saying that he is 'regarding Mt Aegaleos as an extension of Parnes' (Hammond in *JHS*, n. 1), and worse to use him as evidence for topography.

[33] W. K. Pritchett in *AJA* LXIII (1959), p. 257; and see that whole article, important for the detailed criticism of Hammond's methods.

[34] e.g. Thk. i, 74, 1.

[35] H. ix, 22; contrast vi, 112, 2.

NOTES ON MAP:

The Strait north of the promontory is a mile wide, and allowing 60 triremes per mile abreast or 20 in line ahead, 1200 could occupy one square mile without congestion. There was ample room for both fleets within the Strait, but the Persians suffered congestion on reaching the Narrows (1000 yards).

1–(1). Greek leading (right) wing heads down channel along friendly shore before engaging.

2–(2). Athenians hang back to let Phoenicians pass the Narrows.

3–(3). Ships of Aigina and Megara (50 at most; from Bay of Ampelaki?) 'lying in wait in the channel' emerge to attack flank and rear of the Ionians.

4–(4). Corinthians (50?) 'flee' north under sail in sight of leading enemy and return to intervene at their admiral's discretion. The extended Greek line would be thin enough to need them.

This makes excellent sense, but it *may* only be one of Ktesias' attempts to improve on Herodotos. Cretan mercenary archers were famous in his time.[36] (We note that, if present at Salamis, they must have been hired well in advance, and if by Aristeides, then he must have been back from exile well before Artemision.)

The Persians – it is a point little emphasised by our Hellenic or phil-Hellenic historians – were indeed at full stretch, badly needing a victory before winter, and not at all sure that they were going to win it. They were calling in their last reserves, ships which had not joined previously from 'Karystos, Andros, Tenos and the other islands', places which had perhaps hitherto pleaded that their ships were needed for defence against the Greek Saronic Gulf fleet; scrapings of the barrel, which Herodotos fantastically suggests might compensate for all their losses hitherto.[37] Moreover the islanders, shrewd men of small states, whose fate often depended on judging accurately the balance of power between the fleets of the great, were, to judge by their behaviour, not at all convinced that Xerxes had a won game. Little Paros, like great Kerkyra on the other side, arranged for her squadron to arrive too late, after hanging about at Kythnos, which in the meantime had sent one trireme to join the nationalists; one may wonder whether these two islands 'paired', arranging a mock war between themselves. Demokritos of Naxos, more gloriously, persuading his fellow-captains, brought his city's four, five or six galleys into the Greeks' base at Troizen before the enemy reached the Gulf;[38] Panaitios of Tenos deserted with his ship, crew and vital intelligence in the night before the battle. All honour to these men for their courage and patriotism; but it would have shown something more than courage for them to involve their cities in the fate of a cause which appeared hopeless.

But if the Greek cause, in the opinion of shrewd observers, was not lost, it was certainly not yet won. The fate of all Greece (in the words later inscribed on the tomb of Corinthian sailors buried in Salamis)

[36] Cf., e.g., Thk. vi, 43; vii, 57, 9.

[37] viii, 66; earlier (vii, 95, 1) he has given the total of all 'island' contingents (*sc.* Cycladic contingents; Lesbos, Chios and Samos would be reckoned to Aiolis and Ionia) at just 17 ships, which is quite likely. Munro (*CAH* IV, pp. 302–5) suggests that they also called in the Hellespontine and Pontic fleets, hitherto on guard duty at the Hellespont; but H. (vii, 96) says explicitly that only Abydos was given this duty of (evidently purely local) care-taking.

[38] Four, H. viii, 46; five, Hellanikos *ap.* Plut. *MH* 36; six, Ephoros, *ib.* (a caution against reposing quite so much confidence in the precise accuracy of our figures as, for instance, Labarbe does (cf. p. 382, n. 9) even though they may be worth something).

was balanced on a razor's edge. It was a situation in which, as was said of Admiral Jellicoe's responsibilities in 1916, an error by an admiral could lose the war in an afternoon.

This is the significance of those protracted conferences of the Greek admirals, of which Herodotos tells us, alleging that the sole subject of discussion was whether to keep the fleet at Salamis at all. That their council was in almost continuous session during the critical days we may well believe; but what went on there was not public. With thousands of Greeks in the enemy camp, just across the water, and with many allied contingents, whose men did not know each other, on the nationalist side, the Greek camp cannot *not* have been riddled with espionage. What happened at Lade shows that the Persians knew all about subversion and psychological warfare; and they had not brought the Peisistratidai and ex-king Damaratos with them for nothing. Anything rumoured in the camp would have been reported to the enemy by next morning. In the circumstances, the council must have met within a guarded perimeter. Also the Greek generals, middle-aged men (Adeimantos of Corinth, whose children were born after the war, was perhaps one of the youngest), were all dead before Herodotos began to write; and what he picked up at Athens (he would have got some very different impressions at Corinth) consisted of the thirty-year-old memories of men who were young in 480, 'strategists of the lower deck',[39] not unaffected by the prejudices born of later quarrels, and smoothed down, dramatised and reduced to saga by much retelling through the years.

It may be true that Themistokles got the whole fleet into Salamis, instead of going to the Isthmus, initially in order to help with the evacuation of Athens; and there the reinforcements and late-comers from Troizen joined them.[40] For all the well publicised fact that there would be 'many more ships, and from more cities', the numbers of those that actually came in were, to the admirals, probably a disappointment. The Peloponnese produced its own scrapings of the barrel: six more triremes from Laconia, three more from Sikyon, two more from Epidauros; three more from little Hermiōn and one from the island of Kythnos, which had sent none to Artemision. Aigina sent twelve more, making 30, while still keeping her older ships (probably

[39] Munro in *CAH* IV, p. 302.
[40] H. viii, 40, 42.

12 in number; a lost numeral, making up the sum of Herodotos' contingents, which is 368, to his announced grand total of 380) for the defence of her harbour-mouth; and, more exciting, there came the little squadron from Naxos, to revive the hope, never realised, that the Ionians would desert Xerxes. Then there were eleven ships, also no doubt well publicised, from the west; ten from the Corinthian colonies (Ambrakia, 7; Leukas, 3), and one provided at his own cost by the young Phaÿllos of Kroton, 'thrice victor at Pytho'. But not a ship came actually from Italy; and Sicily was being kept engaged by an invasion from Carthage. Phaÿllos' crew were 'Krotonians staying in Greece'.[41] Some may have been visitors to that year's Olympic Games; most, if not all, were probably exiles; brave men, but probably not unmoved by hopes of interesting Sparta or Athens in doing something for their recall.

Small islands in the Aegean were probably temporising – those on the Greek side of the water no less than the others; pleading that they must keep men for home defence; hoping that token contributions might save them from reprisal-raids if the Greeks won, while they could perhaps be disowned if the Persians did so. Melos, Seriphos and Siphnos, anyhow, produced four pentekonters between them.[42] These islands might be small, but they could have done more than that.

Most disappointing of all, the 60 ships of Kerkyra, which would have exceeded in numbers any contingent except that of Athens, had not come. They were still in the Laconian Gulf, where at least they might deter the enemy from attempting to occupy Kythera. Their commanders alleged that they were unable to round the notorious Cape Malea; and we know that the weather had been fierce; but everyone suspected that they had not tried very hard.[43]

Altogether the reinforcements, 42 ships of the line including the Naxians, did not even fully replace losses in the late battles; for, while Herodotos gives the total of the fleet at Salamis as 380 triremes, Aeschylus gives a round 300, plus a separate ten,[44] probably the defence squadron at Aigina. Herodotos' totals, it is generally agreed, are 'campaign totals',[45] and the difference of 70 represents net, unreplaced losses in the battles in the north. *Unreplaced* losses; for if the

[41] With H. viii, 47, cf. Paus. x, 9, 2.
[42] H. viii, 48.
[43] H. vii. 168.
[44] *Pers.* 338ff.
[45] Tarn in *JHS* XXVIII, p. 219.

Athenians had 'half their ships' sunk, taken or damaged at Artemision, that figure alone is at least 90, some of which must have been replaced or quickly repaired, and also makes no allowance for losses among the allies.[46] According to one restoration of the Troizen Inscription, the generals at Athens were instructed to divide the available man-power into 212 (not 200) crews[47] (implying the possession of remarkably accurate population-figures), and Athens had 200 triremes 'ready'. Thucydides' Athenian speaker at Sparta puts the 'campaign total' for Athens still higher, claiming that, 'of the 400 ships, we provided nearly two-thirds'[48] (say 250? – this may be a boast, but can hardly be an entirely reckless one); but if so, he allows *less* for the allies than the sum of Herodotos' itemised figures. Probably, therefore, Thucydides or his speaker, wittingly or unwittingly, treats the numbers supplied by Athens and by the allies differently, giving a liberally-estimated campaign total for the former and a battle total for the latter. It is surely possible that such old-established naval powers as Corinth and Megara, credited by Herodotos with having 'the same' 60 ships between them at Salamis as at Artemision, produced some replacements for ships which came home damaged, and that their crews went home to get them and bring them to Salamis.

In any case, the commanders had to plan on the basis of a total fleet of about 300, and Themistokles is credited with persuading Eurybiadas that the best chance of a victory lay in holding Salamis, in the hope that the enemy could be induced to enter the straits and attack them there. In favour of remaining there, he had the support of Megara and Aigina, which a move to the Isthmus would leave exposed. Athens, Megara and Aigina supplied three-quarters of the fleet; but if votes were taken, it seems that each contingent-commander had one; and the commander-in-chief was a Spartan. However, finally the fleet did stay; and the enemy did not venture to by-pass them and sail for the Peloponnese. When we remember the need of a fleet of galleys for frequent access to water-supplies, it is understandable that they might hesitate to place themselves between a hostile coast and a Greek fleet in being.

[46] Accordingly, Labarbe in *BCH* LXXVI, p. 418, concludes that the losses of the allies had been very light; this follows from the axiom, mistaken in my opinion, that our figures are complete and allow for such losses.

[47] I am informed by the kindness of Professor Meritt (but see p. 365, n. 8*a*).

[48] Thk. I, 74.

That the *details* of Herodotos' accounts of meetings of the Greek admirals are unauthentic and represent an Athenian tradition, often unfair to the allies, is shown especially by his treatment of Adeimantos of Corinth. This begins by representing him as 'panting to retreat' from the Artemision before battle was joined, and bribed by Themistokles to stay, and ends with him leading a panic-stricken flight of his city's fleet from Salamis; the last a particularly poisonous slander, which Herodotos says no other Greeks accepted.[49] In fact, Corinth had a very fine war-record; alone of Sparta's allies she was represented in every battle of the war, both on land and sea; her colonists at Poteidaia were the first Greeks to rebel in the enemy's rear (pp. 497–9); and the bones of her men, buried in Salamis (necessarily with Athens' permission!), give the lie to the slander. Part of their tombstone, with its classically simple epitaph, long known from literary tradition, has been recovered:

> O passer-by: we dwelt in well-watered Corinth; but now we lie in Salamis, Ajax' isle.[50]

Plutarch devotes one of the best chapters (ch. 39) of his attack on Herodotos to the vindication of Corinth, quoting in evidence this and other war-memorial inscriptions: for instance, from a cenotaph at the Isthmus:

> When all Greece balanced on a razor, we,
> At cost of our own lives, preserved her free.

The list of names no doubt followed.

Plutarch also quotes an inscription-poem by Simonides, commemorating the Corinthian temple-courtesans of Aphrodite, who at this time offered their prayers together, that Kypris would cause their men to be in love with battle. And concerning Adeimantos, he tells us that he named his daughters, born after the war, Nausinīke and Akrothīnia and Alexibia (Sea-Victory, Firstfruits of Spoil, Repulse of Violence) and his son Aristeus. It was this Aristeus who was the daring and resourceful general in another revolt of Poteidaia, this time against Athens; when the Athenians later captured him, they put him to death.[51] It is the same bitter hatred, which prompted this evil deed, which has also poisoned Herodotos' sources at this point.

[49] H. viii, 5; 21, 94.
[50] *GHI* (1969), no. 28.
[51] Thk. i, 60–5; ii, 67; cf. Hdt. vii, 137.

Now when Adeimantos himself died, they set on his tomb an elegiac couplet, which may be rendered:

> Here Adeimantos rests, whose counsel wise
> Gained for all Hellas Freedom's crown and prize.[52]

Adeimantos clearly was proud of his services, and Corinth was proud of him. It is unthinkable that his contribution to the deliberations at Salamis was confined to proposing an adjournment to the Isthmus, which was not accepted, and which, if it had been accepted, would have lost the war. But what were the 'counsels' of Adeimantos, which, as his epitaph claims in two versions out of three, contributed to winning the war and saving Greek liberties? In part, perhaps, speeches to his own men, to convince them of the fact, far from obvious to any plain Corinthian sailor, that the best place in which to fight for Corinth was at Salamis; for even if Themistokles convinced his colleagues of this, it did not follow that Adeimantos might not have hard work in holding his men. But we shall also find that Adeimantos and his men, on the day of battle and in face of the enemy, carried out a very peculiar manœuvre, which probably not only deceived the enemy to his ruin, but was open to misunderstanding by the Athenian rank and file. If this, as is surely probable, was carried out by pre-arrangement with his colleagues, we may conclude that what Athenian saga represented as a trick of Themistokles, on the spur of the moment, and deceiving his colleagues as well as the enemy, was actually played in combination with them; though naturally the rank and file were not in the secret, and post-war jealousies led to an anti-Corinthian and anti-Spartan version prevailing at Athens. There was probably more fruitful work being done in those long meetings of the commanders of which Herodotos tells (viii, 49; 56–63; 78–81) than merely an endless discussion as to whether to stay at Salamis at all.

It does not follow that Themistokles did not have to persuade his colleagues first; nor that, in the discussions both of where to fight and of how to induce the enemy to give battle where the Greeks wanted him, all was harmony throughout; and it is very likely that there was some jealousy between the admirals of Athens and Corinth, the one the most powerful, the other the oldest and most faithful of Sparta's

[52] *Anth. Pal.* vii, 347; Dion. Chrys. xxxvii, 19; Plut.'s version (*loc. cit.*) omits the word 'counsel' and has only 'through whom all Hellas', etc.

naval allies. If, under conditions of acute strain, there were some bitter words spoken between allies, it would not be unparalleled from the histories of later wars.

Some of the anecdotes about those meetings *may* go back to personal reminiscences; for instance, the saying, not in the Council, of one Mnēsiphilos, an elder statesman 'in the Solonian tradition' according to Plutarch: 'If they once move from here, you won't fight for any one country anywhere; each contingent will go off, city by city, and neither Eurybiadas nor anyone else will be able to stop them.'[53] ('Gentlemen, if we don't hang together, we shall hang separately.') The phrase 'city by city' in this context runs through Greek literature to the end of antiquity.[54] If we had Eurybiadas' reminiscences, they would no doubt contain some observations on the problems of a supreme commander steering a team of sensitive and difficult allies. We hear of Themistokles getting a question re-opened against points of order; Themistokles putting his case to individuals before the chairman has opened a session; the protest from Adeimantos, 'Themistokles, in the Games those who start too soon are beaten', and the swift rejoinder 'Yes, and those who are left at the post don't win'. This sounds good-natured enough, and is undoubtedly more authentic than the later versions, which make the rebuke come from the Chair, and Eurybiades even raise his staff to threaten Themistokles, to be answered, in good philosophic style, 'Hit me then; but listen!'[55] If Adeimantos, after the fall of Athens, in his jealousy of Themistokles' influence, bade him be quiet, as a man who no longer had a city to represent, and urged Eurybiades to rule his motion out of order, it was an unworthy jibe, and deserved the retort that the commander of the Athenian navy could found a city where he chose, and that if the Peloponnesians would not defend the Athenians' families on Salamis, he would take them on board and sail for Italy. The Persians would no doubt have been delighted to grant an armistice and see them go. And elsewhere, we hear of Themistokles turning with great savagery upon the commodore of poor Eretria, for some unknown reason, and comparing him to a cuttlefish 'with a sword but no heart'.[56]

Two points stand out conspicuously: first, that contemporary evi-

[53] H. viii, 57; Plut. *Them.* 2.
[54] e.g. Thk. i, 73, 4; Ael. Ar. xlvi, p. 249 D.
[55] H. viii, 59; 'improved' version, Plut. *Th.* 11; Ael. Ar. xlvi, p. 258 D.
[56] H. viii, 61; Plut. *loc. cit.*

dence exposes as libellous the Athenian legend, which represented Adeimantos, the third in precedence among the Greek commanders, as both a coward and a fool; second, that Herodotos' account of the Peloponnesian contingents as still eager to escape from Salamis on the eve of the battle contrasts oddly with his account of the battle itself, in which all fight gallantly. It is a reasonable conclusion that the generals, once persuaded by Themistokles, stood loyally by their decision and united in the detailed planning; and that, in a camp which must have been riddled with agents and double-agents, if the impression reached not only the Persians but many Greeks that the generals were almost coming to blows, it was probably a well-concerted, 'calculated leak'.

During these days, we are told, Xerxes also held a conference of his naval allied commanders (a different thing from a council of war with his Persian admirals). 'They took their seats in their order of precedence at court': Tetramnēstos (a Hellenised form of his Phoenician name), king of Sidon, Mattan the son of Hiram, king of Tyre, Maharbal of Arvad, Syennesis of Cilicia, Gorgos of Cyprian Salamis, and so on down to the Karian dynasts; hard-bitten commanders, many of them, whose opinions on whether to force a battle at sea might well be worth obtaining. Mardonios conducted the interrogation, while His Majesty listened. Most spoke in favour, for it was known that Xerxes wanted a quick decision; but Artemisia, queen of Halikarnassos, Cretan on her mother's side, who was commanding the five ships of her city and of Kos, Nisyros and Kalydna (Kálymnos), after claiming that her conduct in the earlier battles sufficiently vouched for her courage, urged delay, till lack of supplies and moral pressure, which could be applied by a move by land towards the Isthmus, should force the Greeks out of the Salamis Strait. Her proposal was not accepted, and 'those who envied her prestige' hoped she would get into trouble for opposing the majority and the king's evident inclination. The story also makes her express herself in an improbably undiplomatic manner about 'Egyptians and Cypriotes and Cilicians and Pamphylians'. But Xerxes was pleased with her, though he rejected her minority opinion, and forthwith commanded the fleet to close in on Salamis, while the army, that very night, started for the Peloponnese.[57]

There seems to be no reason to doubt that such a conference was held, though the story is told in such a manner as to reflect the greatest

[57] H. viii, 67ff; the personalities, vii, 98f.

credit upon Artemisia. In fact, it seems clear that it must have been from Halikarnassian sources, who owed it ultimately to the queen herself, that Herodotos heard it; probably in early life, as his first 'inside story' of the great war. He was ready to make a heroine of the Amazon queen, even though, later, members of his family and hers may have been at enmity.[58] But such a story was not concerned with the question whether the battle was fought three weeks after Xerxes' arrival in Athens or three days; and in fact it puts the conference immediately after that arrival, with the battle following shortly after the conference. It may be suggested that it was this story, familiar to the historian from boyhood, so that it never occurred to him to doubt it, which led him wrongly to ignore the earlier and time-consuming operations on Xerxes' mole.

About the time when the Eleusinian Mysteries should have been celebrated (that is, about the full moon, so a fortnight before the eclipse of October 2nd by our calendar) two Greek exiles, Dikaios, an Athenian, and Damaratos of Sparta, were out in the devastated countryside (sick of what they saw around them, and escaping from the company of Persians awhile?). They were 'in the Thriasian Plain; and they saw a cloud of dust moving from Eleusis, as of some 30,000 men; and they marvelled at the dust, as to what men it could be; and forthwith they heard singing, and it seemed to Dikaios to be the mystic Iakchos'. He told Damaratos about the annual pilgrimage, and expressed the opinion that the voice was that of a divine power, coming from Eleusis to avenge the Athenians and their allies. The way the dust went would show where it would strike. 'Say nothing about it, then,' said Damaratos: 'if the king hears that, you will lose your head.' And the dust rose high in the air, and blew towards Salamis.[59]

It has been suggested that this story, which Herodotos heard from Dikaios, adding that Damaratos could confirm it, is true, and that the dust was raised by Persian troops on the road to Megara.[60] They did not go far; for the Persians' 'furthest west in Europe' was marked by a raid into the Megarid in the following year.[61] But as a demonstration

[58] Cf. the late stories (*Suda, s.vv.* Herodotos, Panyasis) that P., the epic poet and uncle of H., was put to death by Lygdamis, her second successor, and that H. migrated to Samos as a result.

[59] H. viii, 65.

[60] Munro in *CAH* IV, p. 306; Myres, H., *Father of History*, pp. 265f.

[61] H. ix, 14.

(the road runs close to the coast between Eleusis and Megara) it was, in its way, a success. There was increased nervousness among the Peloponnesians, 'fearing not so much for themselves as for the Peloponnese'. 'For a time, the men stood in silent groups, worrying inwardly and amazed at the folly of Eurybiades; but at last it burst out publicly, and they held a meeting and made speeches about the same subject as before.'[62] A meeting of the generals was held (Herodotos seems to identify it with the indignation meeting, presumably misled by what his sources told him about what 'we' did); but what he says about the feeling among the men will have been reported to him at first hand. Adeimantos, in particular, will have been having difficulty in holding his troops. It was decided (our sources say, by Themistokles alone; but perhaps rather by the commanders as a whole) to encourage the Persians, representing Greek morale as worse than it was. Detailed plans were perfected, allotting their stations and tasks to the different contingents; and a well-conceived plan for the deception of the enemy was put into operation.

[62] H. viii, 74; cf. 70, 2.

Chapter XXI

The Battle of Salamis

Themistokles slipped out of the meeting, which had gone on for hours, leaving his colleagues in session. He sent for his most trusted slave, Sikinnos, who looked after his children, and gave him a detailed message. (We notice two things: the choice of an agent, a devoted man, like the servants in Greek tragedy, who would stick at nothing to save the children; and the fact that the children themselves were probably on Salamis and not at Troizen.) Themistokles then 'sent him over in a boat into the Persian lines'.

We would dearly like to know more about how this was organized. Greek ships and men must have been thick on the ground near all convenient embarkation points. Themistokles was presumably able to order Athenians who trusted him, to let Sikinnos take a boat and go; a secret mission would not surprise them. Even so, it could hardly be done in broad daylight, or the Persians might be suspicious; and by night, there would be other difficulties. If an essential messenger in a deception operation is held up by patrols or killed by sentries, it is no comfort if they are those of one's own side. Aeschylus (quoted below) says that the message was that the Greeks intended to leave Salamis under cover of night, and that the Persians, accepting this, had time to order their sailors to take their evening meal and be ready to set out after sunset to intercept them; Herodotos (viii, 76, 1) that the Persians moved 'in the middle of the night', an expression which may no doubt be understood vaguely. But it seems that, if Sikinnos crossed under cover of darkness, it must have been that of the *previous* night, perhaps not long before dawn; purporting to give the decision of a council of war, which it would take time to put into effect. It would not be surprising if the whole performance was somewhat longer premeditated, whether by Themistokles alone or with his colleagues, and less of a mere happy thought on the spur of the moment, than the oral tradition made it.

Herodotos' account adds to the message a refinement: that not only were the Greeks intending flight, but their internal tensions had reached such a pass that, if boldly attacked, half of them would change sides. It thus cunningly suggested to the Persians not only one move, but two: that they should send ships to block the western strait, which is even more sinuous than the eastern, and less than half the width, and that they could enter the eastern strait with impunity. Both were moves which the Persians were probably already disposed to make; if they were already attempting to bridge the eastern narrows opposite St George Island, they had reason to try to infiltrate ships along the mainland shore, to engage Greek ships which would try to interfere. But Themistokles' plan aimed at getting them to do more than infiltrate; to enter the strait in force, confidently and impetuously, so that when they were attacked, their leading squadrons would not be able to get out again. It might also (since the Persians would prefer, if possible, to fight outside the straits) lead them to give their sailors a night at sea, instead of a night's rest, waiting for an enemy who would not come.

Our fifth-century sources describe the Persian movements as follows: first Aeschylus (*Persians*, 353ff). The Messenger answers the question of the Queen-Mother Atossa: 'Who began the fight?'

> Madam, the whole disaster first began,
> surely, some demon or malevolent god.
>
> A Greek came over from the Athenian lines,
> and brought this message to the king your son:
> that, come the darkness of the murky night,
> the Greeks would stay no longer, but would board
> their ships in haste and go, this way and that,
> flying in secret, scattering for their lives.
> Then he, not comprehending all the guile
> of that Greek, nor how heaven was turned against him,
> orders his admirals immediately
> to marshal their main body in three fleets[1]
> and guard the exits and the sea-ways well,
> while other ships encircled Ajax' isle.

(Not a mere cordon, which might be broken through, but three strong squadrons, with 'other ships' forming a cordon, for observation only.)

[1] *στοίχοις τρισίν*: strictly 'lines ahead', but not always strictly used.

And should the Greeks escape complete destruction,
finding some way for ships to fly unseen,
'Your heads,' he said, 'shall answer, all of you.'
– So said he, full of joy and confidence,
not knowing what heaven held in store for him.

Then they, with order and good discipline,
prepared the evening meal, and rowing men
settled in rowlocks neatly each his oar;
and when the brilliant sun was fully set
and night came on, each master of the oar
went to his ship, and every skilled marine,
and crew hailed crew as the long galleys moved,
and so they sailed, each in his ordered place.

Then all night long the captains kept their crews
patrolling in the fairway, up and down;
and night wore on, and still the Grecian fleet
had made no move to slip out stealthily;
but when the white horses of day at last
came over all the earth, lovely to see –

But before continuing to the day of battle, the historian must unfortunately interrupt Aeschylus, while he considers what others have to say.

Sikinnos delivered his message and 'made himself scarce'.[2] He was lucky not to be held. He lived to see better times:

> Themistokles got him made a citizen of Thespiai, when the Thespians were enrolling additional citizens, and made him a rich man. And they [the Persian generals] deciding that his message was trustworthy, did two things: they landed a large body of troops on the small island of Psyttáleia, which lies between Salamis and the mainland; and when midnight came[3] they put out to sea with their

[2] ἐκποδὼν ἀπαλλάσσετο, H. viii, 75, end. – Note that the imperfect tense is often, as here and, e.g., in Thk. i, 105, 1 – 2 (the word ἐνίκων), simply narrative, and not always either inceptive (etc.) or descriptive of continued action, as per Hammond in *JHS* LVI n. 43.

[3] *ib.*, 75, 1. This sounds very precise; but what if the Greeks had been ready to break out at nightfall? Probably Aeschylus is right, and the report reaching H. either was not very clear (the informant whom he reproduces having only meant 'when it was quite dark') or emanated from Ionians, at the tail of the column, among the last to be given the order to move; for the fleet (in column of squadrons?) stretched, we note, all the way to Mounychia, beyond the main harbour of Peiraieus. For the place-names, see note at end of chapter. pp. 472–4.

western wing making an encircling movement towards Salamis, while those stationed around Keos and Kynosoura also put out, occupying with their ships all the channel as far as Mounychia. The point of their sailing was that the Greeks might not be able to escape, but be cut off in Salamis and give the Persians their revenge for Artemision; and they landed troops on the islet of Psyttáleia, for the reason that, when fighting took place, men and wrecks were likely to come ashore there; for the island was right in the channel of the battle that was to be; so that they might save the men of one side and destroy the others. They did this in silence, in order to escape enemy observation.

Engaged in these preparations, they got no sleep that night.

Diodoros, whose account of the last battle at Thermopylai is clearly a romance, is much better, or at least makes good sense, on Salamis.[4] He adds (xi, 17, from Ephoros?) that Xerxes sent the Egyptian fleet to block the western passage, while his main body moved directly upon Salamis with orders to engage the enemy and fight a battle that should end the war at sea. The Egyptians, highly distinguished at Artemision, with their boarding-pikes, pole-axes and big shields, were well fitted to hold their own if it came to a head-on collision in the western narrows, where only a few ships could advance in line abreast, with the whole Greek navy; and in Herodotos we note that there is no mention of the Egyptians in the main battle. However, the statement *may* have been based only on inference from this silence of Herodotos. Diodoros adds that 'the Ionian leaders' sent a Samian over to the Greeks to warn them of the Persian movement, and to promise that they would desert during the battle; this also could be true, but if such a promise was made (necessarily by only a handful of Ionians), the main body of their countrymen, and not least the Samians (p. 464), conspicuously failed to keep it.

Pausanias (i, 36, 2) gives the number of men landed on Psyttáleia as 400; we do not know what his source was. He describes the islet as lying 'in front of Salamis'; and since the name Salamis (like other island-names), when used by ancient writers, normally means the island as a whole, and not the town unless this is made explicit, this statement is consistent with the view that the island is that now called

[4] Cf. Polybios' judgment (referring to several later battles) that Ephoros was bad as a military but better as a naval historian; see Introduction, p. 10.

Lipsokoutáli, 'the Defective Spoon'; a name which is probably an example of the often engaging results of Greek demotic philology attempting to turn ancient names into something significant. It is noticeable that the smaller, adjacent islet called Talantonísi also still preserves the ancient name of an island 'near by' Psyttáleia, Atalántē (with the addition of *nēsíon*, 'islet'). Psyttáleia can hardly be St George Island, which was too close to the Greek lines and probably held.[5]

Hitherto the Greeks at Salamis had been able to communicate by sea with the Isthmus and with Aigina, by the western channel or from the western bay; and when they first determined to give battle in defence of the island, they had decided to muster to their aid the island heroes, the Aiakidai; Aias (Ajax) and his father Telamon from Salamis itself, while 'they sent a ship to Aigina to fetch Aiakos and the other Aiakidai'.[6] By the same route came, in the night when the Persians were moving, Aristeides the Just, also from Aigina, with the news that Salamis was surrounded, and that he himself had barely escaped the leading enemy ships. It was probably not his first return from exile, for on the following day he was commanding Athenian troops; probably he had been recalled in the spring and elected a *strategós*. He may have been to Aigina on the mission to fetch the sacred images;[7] if so, the ship, a trireme of Aigina,[8] will have put him ashore in the western bay. It was an hour out of her way, but the matter was urgent. Thence it was three miles by road to the Greek headquarters; while the ship proceeded round the island, to join the fleet in the morning.[9]

Herodotos (79ff) reproduces the tradition, which here as elsewhere seems to foreshorten the course of events: Aristeides (who here first appears in Herodotos) *is* probably imagined as just back from exile, and the generals are again discussing their only topic in his account, which is whether to retire to the Isthmus. But men enjoyed dramatising Aristeides' meeting with Themistokles, and the historian gives here a good piece of fifth-century dialogue: Aristeides coming by night to headquarters, asking for his old enemy, and saying, when he comes out:

> 'Now let us be rivals – especially now – as to which of us can best serve our country! . . . I am reporting what I have seen with my own

[5] Str. ix, 1, 14 (p. 395 Casaubon); see further, note at end of chapter, p. 473.
[6] H. viii, 64 (and cf. p. 191 above).
[7] First suggested by Bury in *CR* X (1896), p. 414; cf. How, *ad* H. viii, 79.
[8] H. viii, 84, 2.
[9] *ib.* 83, 2.

eyes; though the Corinthians or even Eurybiades himself may wish to sail out, they cannot do it; we are completely surrounded. So go in and tell them that.'

Themistokles said 'This is splendid; just what I prayed for; in fact I may tell you that I prompted this move of the Persians. . . . But as you have come with the good news, you had better report it yourself. If I tell them, they won't believe me. . . . So you come along in and tell them.' [10]

The news was shortly afterwards confirmed, and details added, by the gallant crew under Panaitios of Tēnos, who in the midst of this crisis deserted to the Greeks with a full account of what was happening; 'and by this exploit the Tenians won their place in the inscription on the tripod at Delphi, among those who broke the power of the barbarian'.[11]

'And now the Greeks prepared for battle. Dawn was breaking, and they called an assembly of the marines', no doubt while the rowers were getting the ships afloat and themselves embarking. Themistokles delivered a magnificent address, as men remembered, on the theme 'All is at stake': as Herodotos says (83, 1) 'all that is better contrasted with all that is worse in the condition of men; and of these things he urged them to choose the better'. *Sancta simplicitas*; if it had been some of the later historians, we should have had a 'restoration' of the speech in *oratio recta*, which would leave us in doubt as to whether Themistokles really made a speech at all.

The fact shows that the Greek commanders knew they had plenty of time. The Persians had not closed up on the hostile coast nor entered the enemy anchorages in the night, although, if the date was about September 20th, there would have been a moon rising before midnight. There may have been some infiltration, such as we have imagined, along the mainland coast; but the main body was still, probably, in two deep masses (two of the three 'fleets' of Aeschylus), on either side of their island stronghold on Lipsokoutáli; three miles from the main Greek anchorage, if this was, as is probable, on the beaches at modern Paloúkia, north of the narrows. Here there are two

[10] Contrast the much more ornate and less realistic account of the same conversation in Plut. *Ar.* 8; a splendid example of the liberties taken by Greek rhetorical historians.

[11] H. viii, 82, 1; the inscription was not strictly on the tripod, but on the triple Serpent-Column which bore it, the trunk of which still stands in Constantine's Hippodrome (Tod, *GHI*, no. 19).

miles of beach and the shortest 'carry' for water from the only plentiful sources of supply, round Koullouria on the western bay.[12] Out at sea, often resting on their oars or only paddling gently, but, as both Aeschylus and Herodotos show us, not sleeping, the eastern sailors lay in wait for the 'fleeing' foe. Long before dawn the Persian admirals must have had an uneasy suspicion that they had been fooled; but it was impossible now to call off the operation. It was impossible to communicate new orders to a fleet of several hundred ships in the dark; and impossible, when day dawned, to return to Mounychia and Phaleron and give the men a rest before returning to the pre-Sikinnos plan for a direct assault. Eighty thousand or more men, once ashore and asleep, could not be driven on board again quickly; and in the meantime, the Greeks might sail anywhere. Better be killed in battle than have to explain that to Xerxes. There was no other possibility at this stage, but to go through with it: to advance at dawn, seek out the enemy in his anchorages, and destroy him, or try to.

What is quite certain is that the Persians did not, as was thought by scholars before Bury and Goodwin, infiltrate the bulk of their fleet into the strait unobserved by the Greeks less than a mile away until Aristeides and the Tenians told them.[13] If they could have done that, as Goodwin observes, they could have destroyed the Greeks in the act of embarking, as Lysander destroyed the Athenians at Aigos Potamoi; and, we may

[12] Hammond, *op. cit.* p. 42. Mr Hammond's treatment of the ancient literary evidence does not affect the interest of his personal topographical observations. He points out (*ib.*, n. 37) that Munro (*CAH* IV, Map 9) has the Greeks 'beached' on some highly unsuitable rocks. (So too does Bury, *HG*³ p. 280, fig. 82.)

[13] The view, e.g., of Grote (1849), V, p. 172, disseminated through most histories of Greece for the rest of the century; though Löschke, in *Jahrb. d. Philologie*, 1877, for one, pointed out that it was inconsistent with the evidence of Aeschylus (see below, p. 463), that when the Greeks rowed forward they *came in sight* of their opponents. Grote's view is based on the identification of the Persian 'western wing' of H. viii, 76 (above, p. 453), describing the night movement, with the 'wing towards Eleusis and the west' during the battle (*id.*, ch. 85) which certainly is well up the straits. Modern studies, with careful attention to topography and to physical possibilities and probabilities, take a new turn with the work of W. W. Goodwin in *Papers of the American School at Athens*, I (1885); see also his article in *Harvard Studies in Cl. Phil.* XVII (1906), replying to B. I. Wheeler in *TAPA* XXXIII (1902), who argued the old view against him; Grundy in *JHS* XVII (1897), a preliminary study for his *GPW*, ch. ix; and Lieut. Perikles Rhediádes, RHN, who wrote his *Battle of Salamis* (in Greek; Athens, 1902) in the light of topographical knowledge gained during a long tour of duty at the Salamis naval base. Beloch, in his narrative in GG II², i, pp. 48ff, and discussion in II, ii, 106ff (reproducing his article in *Klio* VIII (1908) which he himself curiously mis-cites as from IX, 1909) and rejoinders to critics in *Klio* XI and XIII, sticks to the view that the Persians entered the strait during the night. For further bibliography, see Hammond in *JHS* LXXVI (1956), p. 32.

add, Aeschylus is talking nonsense, and there would certainly have been no leisure for an address by Themistokles.

Herodotos continues (83, 2): 'Then the Greeks put out to sea with all their ships; and forthwith, as they were putting out, the barbarians fell upon them.' But Aeschylus, as we shall see, speaks of the Persians first *hearing* the Greeks chanting their battle-hymn, and then of the Greeks *coming into sight*, with their right wing leading (and surely he means the Greek right wing, not the right wing as the Persians saw it?).

'What really happened' must have been such as to give rise to both these statements.

There is only one place in the Salamis Strait where the Greeks would come into sight with their right wing leading, and that is at the bend north of St George Island and the narrows. The Greek object was to envelop in a net formed of an ordered line the head of a column coming up the straits.[14] This could well be done as the enemy cleared the narrows, where they would have been congested. But the Greeks needed space in which to form their line. A trireme, as can be seen from the foundations of the ship-sheds of the Athenian navy at Zea, was only 15 feet wide, by over 100 (110?) feet long; but we must allow 10 feet on each side for the oars, and at least 35 feet, one 'breadth', for the interval between ships in line.[15] Seventy-five triremes in line abreast would then occupy at least a mile, as would 25 triremes in line ahead with one length interval; and in turning from parallel lines ahead into line abreast ready to engage, ships of a second and third line would have to come up into the intervals of that nearest the enemy.

If the Greek main body (not much over 200 ships, for the fleets of Corinth, Aigina and Megara had special assignments) putting out from the Paloukia beaches formed for its advance in nine lines-ahead, destined to become a triple line of battle with a front of 66 to 70 triremes, it required a space of at least (and probably well over) one

[14] As Aeschylus (*Pers.* 418, translated below) says they successfully did. The prevailing modern view, since Goodwin (Munro in *CAH* IV; How (App. xxi); Myres, *Hdt. Father of History*, pp. 261ff; Bury, *HG* pp. 280f, etc.), which has the battle fought off the easternmost point of Salamis (Kynosoura?) does not really have it fought *in the Straits* (as stated by Thk. i, 74, 1, and all Greek tradition), and has to resort to the awkward explanation that what Aesch. calls the right wing was the right wing as they lay drawn up on shore; it becomes the *left* wing when they turn to face the enemy.

[15] Ancient authors say nothing about what 'close order' for triremes meant in terms of distance, but 35 feet seems to be a minimum, and is probably too little. Hammond (see *op. cit.* p. 50 and nn., for different scholars' estimates) suggests 50-foot intervals, which would give 63 ships per mile.

mile by 250 yards; and to find this space it would be appropriate to move north, clear of St George Island, and form up, out of sight of the enemy fleet now entering the straits, beyond the point of Aigaleos. If this looked to leading enemy ships, or to observers on Aigaleos, who might signal to their fleet, like the beginning of a retreat, so much the better.[16] But there was one remarkable movement which one would like to think was carried out with all due publicity. 'At the very beginning, when the fleets were just coming together' (so said a malicious Athenian story), 'Adeimantos the Corinthian admiral fell into a complete panic and hoisted his sail and fled; and the Corinthians, seeing their flagship in flight, fled in like manner.'[17] No trireme ever moved under sail in battle, since the one square sail gave too little manœuvrability. Many or most of the Phoenician captains, now leading the advance of their fleet perhaps a mile away, must, as young men, have seen the Samians do this, to start the Ionian débacle at Lade fourteen years before.

Other Greek tradition, as Herodotos says, borne out by the Corinthian war-memorials (p. 444) said that the Corinthians fought bravely; but that they headed north under sail – a 'public fact' – must be accepted. Perhaps, as some have thought, they went on to the west and engaged the Egyptians;[18] but it is a long way to the straits by Phaneroméni; perhaps rather they were detailed to guard the rear, at the north end of the eastern straits, in case the Egyptians intervened; sailed into the Bay of Eleusis, where they saw no enemy; and were there met by a pinnace (of no known human origin, according to the legend, but that need mean no more than unknown to the narrator), which turned them back to join, a useful reserve, in the main battle, probably by the news that the Egyptians had not ventured past the western narrows.[19]

The fleet of Corinth (50 ships, including ten from her colonies) was indeed probably, from the first, berthed at the west end of the allied lines, for convenience of communication with Corinth.[20] The

[16] But I find no justification in Aeschylus (translated below) for Hammond's statement that A. 'mentions the *dis*appearance and *re*appearance of the Greek fleet' (*op. cit.* p. 46, n. 51); he mentions only its one appearance.

[17] H. viii, 94, 1.

[18] e.g. Grundy, *GPW*, p. 405; Munro in *JHS* XXII, 329, and in *CAH* IV, p. 306 (where he admits that, if so, they probably went on orders 'long before'; which is not what H. says).

[19] Myres, *Hdt. Father of History*, p. 270.

[20] Cf. the order of contingents at Lade, above, p. 213; Myres, *op. cit.* p. 267.

élite squadron of 30 ships of Aigina may, on a similar plan, have berthed at the east end, i.e. in the small bay (perhaps much smaller before the rise in sea-level) of Ambeláki, south of the fifth-century Salamis town. They appear, at a late stage in the action, as getting between a large part of the enemy fleet and the east end of the strait;[21] and Diodoros (xi, 18) says that they, with the fleet of Megara (20 ships, the next in size and prestige among the contingents), were stationed on the extreme right from the first, while 'the Athenians and Lakedaimonians held *the left part of the line*' (*not* 'left wing') 'opposed to the Phoenicians'. This is not, as has usually been thought, totally irreconcilable with Herodotos,[22] who says that the Lakedaimonians opposed the Ionians; the fact is probably that Eurybiades held, as the prestige of the Lord High Admiral and of his city demanded, the right of the line *in the main fleet*, while the desirability of having the best squadrons on the right was achieved by making a special detachment of them. When the main fleet emerged from its forming-up position in line ahead, by the right, its right wing, led by Eurybiades' squadron, followed by Sikyon and the smaller contingents, probably sailed down channel, overlapping the Phoenicians and ultimately making contact with the right-wing detachment. Megara, on purely geographical grounds, should have had a western station during the days of waiting; but political as well as tactical considerations would support her transfer to the right before the battle, for Megara and Corinth were old enemies, as were Corinth and Aigina. It will be seen that the detailed disposition of the fleet, taking all these considerations into account, affords plenty of work for those long meetings of the commanders, acting as a planning staff, at which the young Athenians, who lived to talk to Herodotos, said they were discussing only whether to give battle at all; and for sage advice from an Adeimantos as well as a Themistokles.

The main fleet, then, formed up where there was room for it, and (while the last ships got into position?) sang in unison the ancient hymn – Doric, like most Greek choral song, but known to all the mainland – called *Paian* (O Saving Lord . . .). Singing, as every Greek commander knew, was good for morale. Evidently there was still time, while the enemy, moving slowly in the 'defile', with the leading ships not anxious to get too far ahead, came up the channel; waiting, till the throng behind should make it impossible for those leading ships

[21] H. viii, 91. [22] H. viii, 85, 1.

to draw back. (So did Cromwell at Dunbar, halting to reorganize, let his men 'sing the 118th Psalm and breathe the horses'.) Then they advanced, Eurybiades leading the foremost line; then the smaller contingents; last of all, but filling the whole centre and left of the main division, the still massive navy of Athens.

The Phoenicians, leading the Persian armada, were followed by the other Levant contingents, some of which (Cyprus, Cilicia) had suffered severely at Artemision; last, the Greeks of Asia;[23] but for all Themistokles' propaganda, they showed no lack of spirit. Xerxes had had a throne set up 'at the foot of the mountain over against Salamis, which is called Aigaleos',[24] no doubt on the 'rocky brow' above the narrows, the site of his abortive mole; and here he took his seat, early in the day, surrounded by his guards, and with a staff of secretaries, prepared to write down the names of captains and their conduct. He had not been satisfied with the performance of his fleet at Artemision; but here, with his eye upon them, Xerxes expected every man to do his duty.[25]

With both sides desirous to deploy their lines, and each moreover keeping nearer the friendly and away from the enemy-held shore, the two columns did not meet head-on. The leading ships shot past each other, the Greeks probably passing east of St George Island, an obvious bastion of their coast defence, until the Laconian ships came opposite the Ionians; and *vis-à-vis* the Phoenicians at the head of the enemy column, the Greeks secured the outside station.

Passing below Xerxes' throne, the Phoenicians saw before them a sagging, wavering line, the Athenian front. They themselves were not in the best of order; for 'as they came into the narrows, they were compelled to take some ships out of line, and this caused much confusion'.[26] But their supports were pressing forward, and the head of the column, in short lines of a few ships abreast, was probably spreading out to try to make room for more – a difficult move to execute

[23] Order of battle from D.S. xi, 17, 3; 19, 1; consistent with H. viii, 85, 1.

[24] H. viii, 90, 4. Akestodoros (a mythographer of Megalopolis, cf. Steph. Byz. on that city), *ap.* Plut. *Them.* 13, puts it 'above' (!) the Kerata ('Horns'; a mountain of that name, unmistakable when seen from Eleusis) 'on the Megarian border'. *Pace* Plut. (and Mr Hammond, *op. cit.*, n. 83) this is almost certainly simply a mistake; confusing place-names, that of the well-known mountain with one which gave its name to a Keratopyrgo and perhaps also to modern Keratsini, on the Salamis strait.

[25] H. viii, 69, 2.

[26] D.S. xi, 18, 4; a detail which sounds convincing.

unrehearsed – when something happened, for which, it is said, Themistokles had been waiting. The south wind, that had filled the sails of the Corinthians, would, as is known to men familiar with those waters, have raised a swell out at sea, which would presently come up the straits,[27] naturally giving very broken water when the wave-systems are broken up and thrown back upon each other from the opposing coasts. Plutarch (*Th.* 14) says that Themistokles refrained from engaging until 'the usual hour arrived, which brings the wind fresh off the sea, and a swell running up the straits'. Plutarch's account of Salamis is in general romantic and thoroughly unreliable, and even here he seems to confuse the *sirocco* off the sea, a well-known but not a regular phenomenon, with the *normal* early morning breeze off the land. Nevertheless, he may here be describing something which really happened, since Herodotos' story of the Corinthians hoisting sail also indicates a south wind. The broken water would be particularly trying to the invasion-fleet, trying to form a front after passing through the narrows; a difficult operation in face of the enemy, since ships cannot move sideways, and to turn broadside on was dangerous; but the Athenians' backing water encouraged them to try. Then came a cry, running along the Greek front 'so that the whole fleet heard it: "Men, how much further are you going to back water?" ' Men said afterwards that the voice came from 'an apparition as of a woman' – one of the many apparitions of Salamis; no doubt many Athenians said outright that it was their own Goddess. In any case, the time was come, and from front and flank, from north-west round to south-west, the Greeks swarmed in. The sagging line of Athens was suddenly a menacing noose, contracting round the head of the Phoenician column. Themistokles had his wish; there should be no chance this time for the Phoenicians to use their speed and seamanly tricks. Simultaneously, so that it was disputed which end of the line struck first, the ships of Aigina, late queen of the sea, supported by Megara and by Eurybiades with his Lakedaimonians, struck hard into the flank of the Ionians, preventing them from forcing their way westward on the left of the Phoenicians and relieving the pressure on them.[28] The fact that the Ionians, in rear, were heavily engaged shows that the whole Persian

[27] Cf. the interesting information collected by Hammond (*op. cit.* pp. 49f) from Mr Vasïlis Deleyannis, professional seaman at the Greek Yacht Club; Deleyannis added that an expert can forecast the coming of such a swell from cloud formations.

[28] H. viii, 84f; cf. 90.

fleet had got into the battle area; and however densely they were packed (too densely, as all accounts agree, to deploy properly in face of the sudden Greek offensive), this in turn shows that the imperial fleet, without the Egyptians, was at the most no longer greatly superior in numbers.

Ameinias of Pallene, a trierarch from an inland deme, was the first Athenian to ram. 'His ship became entangled and could not get clear; and so others engaged in support of him, and that, according to the Athenians, was how the battle began; but the men of Aigina say that it was the ship that had gone to Aigina for the Aiakidai, which led the attack.'[29] Herodotos' account of the battle resolves itself thereafter into a series of tales of individual exploits, interesting in themselves (see below) but giving no overall picture; the best such picture is that of Aeschylus, although we note that, 'stream-lining' his story for dramatic purposes, he goes straight from dawn to the moment just before engagement; just as he later (480ff) gives the retreat of both Xerxes' fleet and army as following immediately after the battle. We take up his narrative again (386ff):

> . . . But when the fair, white horses of the day
> came over all the land, lovely to see,
> first from the Greeks a sound of voices rose,
> —voices of men singing; and loud and strong
> rang back again out of the island rocks
> Echo; and fear fell on our eastern host.
> Something was wrong. These were no men in flight,
> these Greeks who sang the awful Paian then,
> but going out with valiant hearts to war.
> Then trumpets over there set all on fire,
> and the sea foamed, as oars together swinging
> beat on the salt surface in ordered time,

[29] H. viii, 84. The inferior sources (D.S. xi, 27, 2; Aelian, *VH* v, 19, Aristodemos, 3, the *Life of Aeschylus*, 3) make Ameinias a brother of Aeschylus; but Aesch. is also said to have been of Eleusis (*Life*, 1; schol. Arist. *Frogs*, 886; Ael. Ar. xix, p. 421 Dind., etc.), a deme which was not even of the same Kleisthenic tribe. The silence of H. is also significant, in view of his mention of Kynaigeiros. Another fifth-century Aischylos Eleusinios, Hellenotamias in 440 (*CIA* I, p. 240), may be the poet's kinsman; but both Ameinias and Aischylos (and his father's name Euphorion) are quite common names. Probably the embellishment began with a confusion between homonyms, eagerly taken up by the romantic historians. D.S. also (after Ephoros?) makes Ameinias' victim the Persian flagship, as does Plut. *Them.* 14, assigning Am., for good measure, to yet another deme, Dekeleia. The chief importance of the matter is that it shows how very unreliable the details given by late writers are.

and quickly, clear before us, there they were!
The right wing first, in ordered line ahead,
led forth, and after it the whole array
came following on; and now was to be heard
a mighty shouting: 'On, sons of the Greeks!
Set free your country, set your children free,
your wives, the temples of your fathers' gods
and ancient tombs; now they are all at stake.'
And from our side indeed the Persian shout
in answer rose; and now, the hour was come.
  At once, ship against ship with beak of bronze
crashed; but it was a Greek that was the first
to strike, and smashed in a Phoenician's poop;
and so the battle joined along the line.
  First, then, the torrent of our Persian fleet
bore up; but when the press of shipping jammed
there in the strait, then none could help another,
but our ships fouled each other with their rams.
and sheared away each other's banks of oars.
But the Greek ships, skilfully handled, kept
the outer station, and struck in; till hulls
rolled over, and the sea itself was hidden,
strewn with their wreckage, dyed with blood of men.
The dead lay thick on all the reefs and beaches,
and flight broke out, all order lost; and all
our eastern ships rowed hard to get away.
But they – as men gaff tunnies or some shoal
of fish – with broken oars and bits of wreckage
smote and split heads; and shrieks and lamentations
spread with their doleful sound over the sea
till night came down, and darkness hid the sight.

Greeks, presumably shore-defence details now launching out in small boats, were 'clearing up the battlefield', killing the helpless non-swimmers[30] who clung to wreckage.

Herodotos adds details. The enemy fought well, 'much better than off Euboia';[31] even the Ionians, or most of them; 'I could tell the names of many captains who captured Greek ships' (*How* many? – Diodoros gives the total Greek losses as 40 ships;[32] but probably some of those captured were recaptured before the end) 'but I will mention only

[30] Cf. H viii, 89, 2. [31] *ib.* 86. [32] D.S. xi, 19, 3.

Theomēstor the son of Androdamas and Phylakos the son of Histiaios, both Samians; for Theomestor, for this service, was made tyrant of Samos by the Persians, and Phylakos was enrolled on the list of "Benefactors of the King" and rewarded with a large estate. . . . But the bulk of their fleet was cut to pieces in Salamis, by the Athenians on the one side and the Aiginetans on the other; for, as the Greeks were fighting their battle in an ordered formation, but the barbarians had lost their formation and were no longer fighting according to any plan, the result was inevitable.'[33] The reference is probably to the normal naval tactics, in which it must have been the first duty of ships in the second line to cover those obliquely in front of them, if any became entangled after ramming (like Ameinias), so that they should not be rammed themselves while helpless. The 'outside station' obtained by the Greeks, converging upon the head of the Persian column, was decisive. If a Phoenician ship advanced out of the mass, she was at once exposed on one flank or both; if all tried to keep station, or drew back, they were increasingly and fatally crowded by those behind, who, unable to see the disaster that was beginning in front, and aware of the king's eye upon them, were still pressing forward; and for this reason 'when the leading ships turned to flee, that was when the greatest destruction took place'.[34]

Unable to escape down-channel, many of the Phoenician ships and of the Cypriotes, next to them, are said to have run themselves ashore on the Attic coast,[35] under the protection of their land forces. Some Phoenician captains, who had lost their ships, went up to Xerxes' throne and complained that they had been left unsupported by the Ionians, whom they had probably expected to come up on their left; unaware that the Ionians had been prevented from helping them by the attack of the Dorian squadrons. But Xerxes, seeing that the Ionians (who had so far had only one front to face) were still fighting stoutly, 'turned upon the Phoenicians, as one in bitterness of heart and ready to blame everyone, and ordered them to be beheaded, to put an end to their playing the coward themselves and then blaming their betters'.

An incident which is said to have contributed to this royal reaction was the prowess of some Ionian islanders: 'While the Phoenicians were still speaking, a Samothracian ship rammed an Athenian. As the Athenian began to sink, a ship of Aigina bore down and sank the

[33] H. viii, 85f. [34] *ib.* 89, 2. [35] D.S. xi, 19, 2.

Samothracian; but the Samothracians, javelin-men as they were, swept the marines from the deck of the ship that had sunk them, and boarded and captured her.'[36] It is a typical incident of an ancient naval mêlée; and it also gives a glimpse of the later stages of the battle. With most of the Phoenician and Cypriote ships sunk or run aground, the Cilicians and Pamphylians in the centre took to flight,[37] and some Athenians, pursuing down the strait, met the Aiginetans, who had played their essential part by preventing the enemy's rear from supporting the van. With the collapse of all resistance further up the channel, the Ionians in turn gave way. Their admiral, Xerxes' brother Ariabignes, was killed;[38] and the Aiginetans (they were awarded the prize for the best fighting among all the Greek contingents) crowned their service by breaking right through and turning to 'waylay in the channel the barbarians who had taken to flight and were sailing out towards Phaleron'.[39]

There were some dramatic encounters in this part of the battle. Demokritos of Naxos' sailors, who, as deserters, were more particularly fighting for their lives, claimed both to have captured five enemy ships and rescued a Dorian, which was being overpowered.[40] Polykritos the son of Krios of Aigina (that Krios who had once been arrested as a hostage by Kleomenes) rammed a Phoenician ship in flight, a Sidonian. As his men boarded her, Polykritos cast a watchful eye round. Sure enough, there was another enemy ship bearing down – but she was harmless. She was intent only on flight; and after her – Polykritos saw the blazon of the admiral of Athens – came Themistokles himself in his flagship under full press of oars. The ships passed within easy hail, and Polykritos yelled a comradely gibe at his ally, on the theme 'Who said Aigina was pro-Persian?' In the meantime, his men rescued from the sinking Sidonian ship a Greek prisoner: none other than Pytheas of Aigina, who had been captured 'almost cut to pieces' off Skiathos a few weeks before, and whom the Phoenicians had so carefully nursed back to life 'because of his valour'.[40a] One would like to know if Pytheas was able to return the service in favour of any of his late captors.

Ameinias, the Athenian captain who had led the attack, got clear of his first victim, undamaged; he fought through the entire action, early

[36] H. viii,90. [37] D.S. xi, 19, 1. [38] H. viii, 89, 1.
[39] *ib.* 91. [40] Simonides (?) *ap.* Plut. *MH*, 36. [40a] *ib.* 92.

and late, and was one of two Athenians decorated for especially distinguished service, next after Polykritos of Aigina. Late in the afternoon he found himself amid the dissolving ranks of what had been the enemy's left, facing a group of enemy Greek ships that were trying to get clear. Singling out the nearest he prepared to charge, when suddenly his destined victim rammed another of the group. Supposing himself mistaken, and that this was perhaps an enemy that had changed sides, Ameinias went after other game; but later, to his chagrin, he was told that it had been that captain whom the Athenians most wished to capture, and had offered a reward of 10,000 drachmas for her: none other than Artemisia. She was said to have saved herself by running down Damasithümos of Kalynda (Kálymnos), who, as Munro says, 'perhaps stood in her way dynastically as well as physically'. The anecdote added that she had a double escape; for the observers round Xerxes recognised Artemisia's flagship but not that of her victim, and gave the Amazon credit for sinking an enemy; while the king groaned 'My men have become women and my women men'.[41]

A fresh west wind rose in the afternoon (such as is said often to follow a sirocco in the morning);[42] fleeing ships may have spread their sails to it.[43] It also floated the wrecks out of the more easterly part of the strait far down the coast of Attica. The Greeks towed into Salamis such as they could secure, and prepared for another battle, for the surviving enemy ships were still numerous.[44]

But there was one act of the day's drama still to be played. The Persians on Psyttáleia, who were to have killed Greeks and rescued their own men wrecked on the island in a battle fought when the Greeks tried to escape, had been irrelevant when the battle took place inside the strait; and they were 'stranded' indeed when the routed fleet streamed past them making for safety at Phaleron. When the Greeks

[41] H. viii, 87f; 93; Munro in *CAH* IV, p. 312. – Whether we should believe this piece of saga in every detail is questionable; it sounds as if it had been at least embellished. But it may be noticed that its presence in H. serves to cast much graver doubts upon another piece of Artemisia-saga which is *not* in H.: Plutarch's story (in *Them.* 14) that it was she who recognised, rescued and brought to Xerxes the body of the admiral, his brother (here called Ariamenes) who had been driven into the sea when boarding the galley of 'Ameinias of Dekeleia'. If such an interesting story had existed in the time of Herodotos, it seems impossible that he either should not have known it or should not have told it. The matter is of some importance as evidence for the fact that Plutarch used, for his story of Salamis, a source or sources at once fond of romance and generally unreliable.

[42] Hammond, *op. cit.* pp. 48ff, n. 70; the Bounendis or (better, in the Greek of the islands) Ponendis (the opposite to Levandis, 'easterly').

[43] Hammond compares Aesch. *Pers.* 480.

[44] H. viii, 108.

had won the day, says Aeschylus (454ff), and 'amid the confusion', according to Herodotos (ch. 95), Aristeides collected a force of the Athenian hoplites stationed for coast defence on Salamis – no doubt eager for action, which had all day been denied to them – led them to an opposed landing, and cut to pieces the whole force. Aeschylus makes of this a Persian disaster second only to the naval battle, claiming that they were picked men and Persian aristocrats (441ff); men, at the sight of whose destruction Xerxes cried aloud and set his army in motion in full retreat forthwith. The last detail is certainly unhistorical,[45] and the former unlikely; but the action was remembered by Aeschylus and, perhaps chiefly through him, by posterity. He may perhaps personally have taken part in it; probably, too, he desired to glorify Aristeides (naturally, without naming him) and the Athenian hoplites, as well as the sailors. But, politics apart, it was indeed a memorable though small action. For the first time in Xerxes' war, Greek soldiers had taken the offensive and destroyed a Persian unit, and within sight of the king. Truly, the tide had turned.

The Greeks had very efficiently trapped the advancing column entering the straits, and cut off its head; but, as often after a severe battle, the victors did not appreciate immediately what they had done. They themselves had lost forty ships totally wrecked if we may trust Ephoros; as well as, no doubt, many damaged; the Persians, according to the same author, had lost over 200 sunk 'as well as those captured' (no number given); at best, an estimate, and probably exaggerated, but all we have.[46] Herodotos, once more, gives no figures for battle-casualties. Xerxes resumed (Herodotos says, began) preparations for bridging the strait, and ordered his fleet to reorganize as for a new battle;[47] but the heart was out of his sailors. The disaster to the Phoenicians had been decisive; it was not for over ten years that a Phoenician fleet again gave battle to Greeks, in the Levant. According to Ephoros (*ib.*) the surviving Phoenicians, angered by the execution of some of their captains, deserted and went home; a dubious story, unmentioned by Herodotos; but there were probably not many of them left. In any case, within a few days (Herodotos says, under cover of the second night after the battle) Xerxes gave orders to his fleet to withdraw to

[45] Cf. H. viii, 97; 113.
[46] D.S. xi, 19, 3.
[47] H. viii, 97.

Asia and take up positions covering the Hellespont.[48] They wintered around Kyme,[49] where they could be supplied from the Hermos valley. Their morale was said to have been so shattered that, on the night of the retreat, they took the low rocks of the Zōstēr promontory (by Vouliagméni) for a massed fleet lying in wait for them, 'and fled a long way'.

In the morning 'the Greeks, seeing the land forces still in position, thought the fleet too was still at Phaleron and would give battle'; but presently their scouts reported that the roadstead was empty. They then followed as far as Andros, which they besieged, demanding a heavy indemnity. The Andrians, protesting sheer inability to pay, kept their gates closed; they are said to have answered Themistokles, who said that he had come with the backing of two great gods, Persuasion and Necessity, with the humorous parable that *they* had two even more implacable gods, who dwelt in their country and would not leave it, called Poverty and Inability, and in virtue of them, their weakness would be too much for all the power of Athens. However, the fleet levied fines on Paros and Karystos and other island cities which had submitted to Persia, and ravaged the lands of Karystos and no doubt of Andros also. Many islanders were believed also to have made secret payments to Themistokles personally, to secure his good offices.[50]

It is also said that Themistokles, at this point, urged that the whole fleet should sail to the Hellespont and destroy the bridges (which would have been a risky enterprise at best, so late in the year); but Eurybiadas declined, arguing sagely against provoking a still dangerous enemy to desperation. It was in the regular Spartan tradition, not to pursue a retreating foe *à outrance*, but to 'thank God they were rid of a knave'. Themistokles is then said to have sent a second private message to Xerxes, by the hand of men 'whom, he trusted, no torture would induce to reveal his message to the King', claiming the credit for *dissuading* the Greeks from assailing his line of retreat. Sikinnos was said to have been an emissary once more; though later writers substitute the name of one Arnakes, a eunuch who had been taken prisoner.[51] It

[48] H. viii, 107.
[49] *ib.* 130.
[50] *ib.* 108; 112; 121. These stories go back to strictly contemporary allegations; e.g. those of a disappointed man, Timokreon of Rhodes (*ap.* Plut. *Them.* 21, referring to the years 479–8?).
[51] H. viii, 108ff; contrast Plut. *Them.* 16, *Ar.* 9; Polyainos i, 30, 4. D.S. xi, 19, 5, Justin ii, 13, follow H.

certainly would have been more than rash for Sikinnos to put his head into the lion's mouth again, after his first message had turned out to offer mere bait for a trap; and if Themistokles wished to send such a second message, to send it by a prisoner released for the purpose would have been the obvious thing to do. The later version is a great improvement on that of Herodotos; but it does not follow that it is more authentic. Rather, it is a literary improvement, a rationalisation. In public, says Herodotos (*ib.* 109), Themistokles himself addressed the Athenians, deprecating a step that would make the enemy desperate: 'For not we but the gods and heroes have achieved this.... Now therefore, let men patch up their houses and attend to the sowing ... and in the spring let us sail for the Hellespont and Ionia.' When we contrast the report of this public speech with the great emphasis on the secrecy of the message to Xerxes (the unnamed men, from whom wild horses would not drag the truth, although their errand, if it accelerated Xerxes' retreat, had done good rather than harm to Athens, and the absurd afterthought of naming Sikinnos among them), we are constrained to believe that this part of the story of Themistokles' communications with the enemy is an invention of his enemies, dating from the time, a few years later, when his aristocratic political opponents combined together to drive him out of public life. That a supposed leakage of a project to cut him off in Europe was allowed to reach Xerxes, with the object of accelerating his retreat, is not unlikely; but it would have been poor planning to let it come from the same ostensible source as the previous deception. It may be noted that, if such a new deception was practised, it would be desirable to support it by letting the Greek fleet, less a squadron sufficient to guard Salamis against attack by the land forces, disappear from Xerxes' sight in an easterly direction; and if some of the men, in the elation of victory, indulged in loose talk on the theme 'on to the Hellespont' – and Herodotos says that the Athenians did do so; we may remember that Athens had had Hellespontine dependencies for two generations – there was no reason for the generals to 'play down' the idea until it had served its turn.[52]

[52] It is misplaced cleverness to argue, with some moderns, that the fleet cannot have left Salamis until the Persian land-army left Attica. Did it require the whole fleet, which had sufficed against the Persian army *and* fleet, to deter or repel invasion by the land-forces with rafts and small boats?

On the above stories, J. E. Powell says rightly (*Herodotus, Book viii*, p. 135) that

The public speech, rejecting the idea of further offensive operations that autumn, and urging the Athenians to get a roof over their heads and do some sowing, must belong to a time when the Persians had withdrawn from Attica, or at least when they were visibly preparing to do so, though mentioned by Herodotos at an earlier point in his narrative, in connection with the talk of a raid on the Hellespont; but there need be no difficulty about that. The most advanced units of the fleet did not at this time go further afield than Paros; and returning to the Saronic Gulf, they found Xerxes gone.[53]

It was obviously desirable for Xerxes not to prolong his absence from Asia needlessly; he could still represent his march to Athens as a victorious campaign, though it is said that the report of a defeat at sea caused anxiety at Susa; and in handing over the command to Mardonios, as he now did, and returning to his base, he did only what Cyrus had done, leaving Harpagos in the west, after the capture of Sardis, and Darius, leaving Megabazos in Thrace, after the Scythian expedition. Mardonios, who is said to have proposed the king's withdrawal, 'stream-lined' the army, retaining, in cantonments in Thessaly, the good Iranian troops, and some other picked men,[54] but dismissing the mass of '*auxilia*' which, as we suggested, considerations of royal prestige had brought along. One Iranian division under Artabazos, commander of the Parthians and Chorasmians (p. 324), escorted Xerxes to the Hellespont,[55] together with Hydarnes, whose place was at the

---

'Themistocles' subsequent disgrace doubtless promoted their invention and dissemination'. Macan, *ad loc.* (better than his treatment in App. vi, 8 (not vii, 2!), Vol. II), suggests the ugly but only too present possibility that the reference to 'men whom no torture would induce to reveal his message to the King' may have reference to some of the domestics of Themistokles having really been put to the question at the time of his flight, in the effort to prove his 'medism'.

The best evidence for the view that *some* such trick was played is that of Thk. i, 137, 4, the alleged letter of Them. to Artaxerxes, in which he claims credit for delaying the destruction of the bridges; falsely, as Thk. believes; but exactly in the terms of his *public* speech as reported by H. viii, 109. It must have appealed to Them.'s sense of humour, if he was assisted to establish himself in prosperity in Persian-controlled Magnesia, precisely by the 'facts' concocted by his enemies.

Plutarch's account, which may be taken as representing the final, literary version of the saga, is an excellent story, adorned by good sayings: Themistokles' proposal to Aristeides for a raid on the bridges so as to 'capture Asia in Europe', and A.'s reply (characteristically, A. is brought in to represent the higher sagacity, instead of Eurybiades) that one should not force a defeated enemy to desperation, but, rather than destroy his bridge, 'build him another, if it were possible, to retreat by'. But these sayings (like 'Hit me, but listen!') belong to Greek literature, not to the history of 'what really happened'.

[53] H. viii, 113; cf. 121. [54] *ib.* 113; ix, 32. [55] *ib.* 126.

king's side, before returning to join Mardonios. Both Aeschylus (with poetic licence) and Herodotos make much of the horrors of the retreat; Aeschylus in particular introducing a Beresina-episode at the Strymon, where an early frost is said to have tempted troops to cross on unreliable ice.[56] Commissariat is said to have broken down; and no doubt many of the little-regarded and no longer needed auxiliary troops did suffer acutely, and many may have died, as we are told, from hunger and dysentery. But it is probable that all this is much exaggerated; and the time said to have been taken by Xerxes to reach the Hellespont (45 days[57] for some 550 miles, or half the time taken by the advance; not surprising, since his troops did not have to fell forests or to cope with opposition) is not suggestive either of headlong haste or of a total breakdown. We read of Xerxes being entertained at Abdēra and presenting gifts to the city;[58] there were strong Persian fortresses, meant to be permanent, at Eion on the Strymon, Doriskos and other places; and under their protection the sick, 'left in the cities' from Thessaly to Paionia, with orders that they be cared for,[59] were by no means simply abandoned to massacre.

Salamis was a very notable achievement; it had saved Greece from a prolonged occupation and from the horrors of inevitable rebellions; but it had by no means made an end of Xerxes, nor yet of Mardonios and his army.

56 *Pers.* 495ff.
57 H. viii, 115, 1.
58 *ib.* 120.
59 *ib.* 115, 3.

ADDITIONAL NOTES ON SALAMIS

1. *Keos, Kynosoura and Psyttáleia* (H. viii, 76)

We have no ancient topographical evidence for the location of the first two of these anywhere near Salamis; the only Keos in our ancient geographical texts is the famous island, south-east of Sounion, and the only Kynosoura or 'Dog's-Tail' is the promontory sheltering Marathon Bay on the north. Myres (*H., Father of History*, p. 265) says 'there is no need to duplicate these places' (a view with which Munro in *CAH* agrees), and supposes that the Persian fleet was spread out so far, in search of safe beaches, 'after experience of Aegean weather'. But if the harbours of Peiraieus and the whole beach of Phaleron Bay did not suffice, there are other beaches between Phaleron and Sounion, and harbours south of Marathon; moreover, if Persian ships had been called in from Marathon just before the battle, I think any ancient author would have called them 'those around Marathon' rather than 'around Kynosoura'. Most scholars have accordingly sought for a location near Salamis, and have supposed that the long eastern promontory of Salamis was also called 'the Dog's Tail'; which it may well have been, though it is necessary to remind readers, since the name is placed here, without query, on several modern maps, that it is a view supported by no ancient authority. Keos still remains to be identified. Hammond identifies it with the island, modern Talantonisi, next to Lipsokoutáli, which he identifies with the ancient Atalante (Str. ix, 395); but there is no sufficient reason, as will be seen below, for other identifications of these than Lipsokoutáli = Psyttáleia and Talantonisi = Atalante, both still keeping forms of their ancient names. One might hazard the guess (but admittedly it is a long shot) that 'Keos' is an ancient error for Zea (well known from classical sources, including the fourth-century naval inscriptions), the Athenian naval harbour, modern Pasha-Limani; or even an archaic form of the name (it is an odd fact that the name of the well-known Keos has become Zea or Dziá in modern Greek). If that were so, the Persian 'ships around Keos and Kynosoura', which 'fill the whole passage as far as Mounychia', are precisely the main fleet, extending, in column, from Peiraieus to the entry into the Salamis Strait.

J. E. Powell, it should be added, obelizes the whole sentence containing these names, as interpolated, along with the oracle of Bakis in ch. 77. Ch. 77 certainly is a curiosity; but Mr Powell's confidence that he knows just what to excise from and insert in H.'s text is itself too oracular to command confidence.

On the identification of Psyttáleia, where the Persians landed troops in anticipation of a battle when the Greeks attempted to break out (which they never did), the best evidence, though not very satisfactory, is that of Strabo, *loc. cit.*, also reprinted by Beloch and Hammond (see above, n. 13). Strabo enumerates in order along the mainland coast Eleusis, the Thriasian Plain, Cape Amphiale and 'the quarry above it'; not certainly identified, but, best, by Lolling, just above the narrows and the modern ferry; see Pritchett in *AJA* LXIII, pp. 254f. This suits Strabo's text well, for the next feature he mentions is 'the passage to Salamis, where Xerxes tried to bridge the strait with a mole, but was interrupted by the naval battle and retreated. And *here*' (the word is explicit and emphatic) 'are the Enchantresses, two small islands, on the larger of which the Tomb of Circe is shown.' On the face of it, these should be two islands in the Narrows, and the obvious candidates are St George and a reef near the other side of the ferry passage, which would have been an island if, as has been proved at several other Aegean sites, the sea-level in antiquity was between one and two fathoms lower. It is here that Hammond is most unconvincing, in supposing that Strabo suddenly goes back a couple of miles, to mention islands (the modern Kyrádhes) at the north end of the straits.

Strabo continues 'Above this shore is a mountain called Korydallos' (the seaward end of Aigaleos, mod. Skaramanga, which fills the whole immediate hinterland) 'and then the Thieves' Harbour and Psyttalía' (a variant spelling) 'an uninhabited and rocky island, which some have called the Harbour' (*liména*; Koraïs conjectured *lēmēn*, 'eyesore') 'of Peiraieus; and by it is Atalante, bearing the same name as the one by Euboia and Lokris, and another island, this one also, like Psyttalia; and then Peiraieus.'

On the face of it, Psyttalía (Psyttáleia in classical Greek) should be just off, and facing, Peiraieus; hardly St George, up in the narrows, though Mr Hammond (p. 36) makes it so, by an explanation which I do not find convincing (why *eye*-sore?). As to the names, I suspect that Lipsokoutáli is derived from a mediaeval Frankish 'Le Psouttáli', or the like; the *lingua franca* did many curious things to Greek place-names, including both the attachment and fancied detachment of the Frankish article ('Lakédémonie' becoming La Crémonie); and modern Greek popular etymology has often tried to assimilate foreign names to something with a meaning, however far-fetched; as when Italians called Hymettos 'Mont' Imetto' and then Monte Matto, literally meaning 'the Mad Mountain', and this has actually been translated into the vernacular, as Trello Vounó. A similar active fancy, I suspect, turned 'Le Psouttáli' into Lipsokoutáli so that it might mean something.

There remains the question of the 'other island like Psyttalia', and of why it is not named. There is a small rock in the vicinity, but, even with a lower sea-level, it does not seem that it would have been large enough for notice. Here I suspect that what Strabo meant, though if so he did not express himself well, is 'Atalante, with the same name as the one off . . . Lokris, and 'an island *too*' (as is the Lokrian Atalante); and that the search for yet another island next to Lipsokoutáli and Talantonisi, nameless, yet worthy of mention and comparable to the former, may be discontinued.

2. *Plutarch on Salamis*

That Plutarch, one of the most lovable but not most critical of ancient writers, preserves *some* information of doubtful authenticity is common ground; but it will here be suggested, not without regret, that in his account of Salamis in particular he used some peculiarly bad source or sources, to such an extent that, even where he is not demonstrably wrong, no statement, for which he is our sole source, can be regarded as having any authority.

As we have seen, there are places where, in details, if P. is right, Herodotos is wrong; cf. nn. 10, 51, 52, above; but this is a small matter. We also find that P.'s source in *Th.* 14 claims to know that the corpse of the Persian admiral Ariamenes (Ariabignes, H.), driven overboard at push of pike by 'Ameinias of Dekeleia', was picked up by Artemisia, recognised and conveyed to Xerxes. With all due respect to the customary solemn warnings on the *argumentum ex silentio*, I do not believe that, if Herodotos had heard of this, he would have failed to mention it; nor that, if Herodotos did not know of such an event, any other Greek author did.

An important point, on which P.'s source must be wrong, is the point in the proceedings at which the Greeks recaptured Psyttáleia. Aeschylus and Herodotos both put it after the defeat of the Persian fleet; and they can hardly be wrong. But P.'s source, most explicitly, puts it before the naval battle; for it was here, according to the detailed story in *Arist.* 9, that Aristeides captured the three noble Persian youths (sons of the king's sister Sandauke), whom Themistokles, at the instance of his seer Euphrantidas, is said to have sacrificed, before the battle, to

Dionysos Ōmēstes; a story repeated in *Them.* 13 and in *Pelopidas*, 21 In the *Themistokles*, Plutarch names his source: Phanias (better Phainias, as in some other writers) of Eresos in Lesbos, 'a philosopher and not unlearned in history'. Curiously enough, Mr Hammond, rejecting Tarn's proposal in *JHS* XXVIII, p. 226, to accept this order of events, overlooks the fact that Plutarch is Tarn's authority for this view, and not Aristodemos, who in fact says nothing explicit about this: Hammond, *op. cit.* n. 28.

Now Phainias, whose fragments will be found in *FHG* II, pp. 293ff, but not in Jacoby, who reserved them for his unpublished Part IV, was a peripatetic; a learned man, but not one to whom history was an end in itself; rather it was a handmaid to ethics; and so he, like Plutarch, was perhaps somewhat at the mercy of his sources. The *Quellenkritik* of an author, himself lost, is a task from which angels might shrink; but we do find, from the later chapters of the *Themistokles*, on Th. in Persia, that Phainias professed to have a remarkably, even suspiciously detailed knowledge of what transpired there. And at this point it is of interest to find that R. Laqueur, in PW, *s.v.* Phainias (Vol. XIX, ii, columns 1565-1591, a most exhaustive article) comes to the conclusion that Phainias made extensive use of Ktesias.

If this is the source of Plutarch's curious information on Salamis and kindred matters, the fact interestingly increases our fund of knowledge on Ktesias, without modifying our opinion of him. But it does remove any ground for believing the story (which evidently pained and surprised P.; he is at pains to say that his source is respectable) of human sacrifice by Themistokles at Salamis, a story which, through the renown of P., has been widely believed.

These, then, are the grounds for saying that P. on Salamis and on the Persian wars generally has to be treated with more than usual reserve. It may be noted that P. is the sole source for the statements that the Persian ships were larger than the Greek (especially Ariamenes' huge flagship, which if not from Ktesias might well be from a Hellenistic source) and that the Athenians had already reduced the number of their marines to 18. In the *Kimon*, where he had a better source, which spoke of Kimon's ships as broad and robust and carrying many men-at-arms, P., it will be remembered, shows signs of puzzlement at the discrepancy between this and what he had read about Themistokles' ships (*Kim.* 12, 2). It was the source on Themistokles which was anachronistic.

Chapter XXII

Victory in the West

Greek tradition, within living memory of the events, had it that on the very day of Salamis the Sicilian Greeks beat their own Phoenician antagonists.[1] Sophisticated people, such as Aristotle, said that it was only 'about the same time', and Aristotle, as we have seen, cited this as an example of pure temporal coincidence, without dramatic significance.[2] The campaigns were strategically separate; it does not follow that they were unsynchronized at the political level (ch. xv, n. 31, above). Diodoros, however, who in his history of his native Sicily is often at his best, and who may here be following Timaios, synchronizes the decisive battle with Thermopylai; victory with defeat, which is more likely to have been changed by tradition into victory with victory than *vice versa*. Also, since the campaign in Sicily does not seem to have been prolonged, and the invaders did not, like Xerxes, have to undertake a long approach-march through uncleared country, it seems unlikely that the decision was deferred till September. If in August, it was already quite late; but the months since the spring had probably been occupied, for the Carthaginians, with the mustering of their great army of western barbarians, even if recruiting or arrangements for recruiting had been set on foot in the preceding years.

It was a vast horde, we are assured: 300,000 Phoenicians and North Africans, Spaniards and Ligurians, Helisykians (also a Ligurian tribe according to Hekataios' *Geography*;[3] presumably from the Etruscan rather than the Massaliote end of the Riviera) and Corsicans and Sardinians, those tough islanders, whom in their interior castles the Carthaginians had never been able to conquer, transported in a huge flotilla convoyed by 200 ships of war.[4] The last figure, if taken as the

[1] H. vii, 166.

[2] *Poetics*, 23 (1459a).

[3] *ap.* Steph. Byz. *s.v.*

[4] H. vii, 165; ships, D.S. xi 1, 5.

total to which Carthage, like Athens and like Gelon of Syracuse, may have built up her navy, is not incredible. Like the Persians before Marathon, too, Carthage had constructed horse-transports; and like the Greeks of Cyprus, she still relied on chariots, an archaic arm, as well as on cavalry. North Africa is a 'cavalry country'; the Sicilian Greeks were strong in cavalry, at least by Greek standards; and there seems to be no reason to doubt the tradition that the Carthaginian commander (the Suffete Hamilcar, son of Hanno, and himself of Syracusan descent on his mother's side[5] – striking evidence on the absence of merely racial hostility) desired to take as strong as possible a mounted force of his own. But disaster attended the enterprise of moving a vast fleet, as it did that of Mardonios in 493, that of Xerxes in 480, and those of the Roman Republic repeatedly later in Sicilian waters. A storm almost entirely destroyed the cumbersome horse-transports,[6] which, perhaps slower than the ordinary shipping, may have lagged behind or have been despatched separately.

The main fleet got safely, though not unscathed, into the Bay of Palermo (Panormos), whose spacious beaches gave room for all; like Datis and like Kleomenes, Hamilcar had selected a disembarkation-point distant from the enemy. On arrival he is said to have said (as he may, to encourage his troops, if not in so many words) that he considered the war as good as won; the sea had been the main danger. Thence, after three days 'to refresh the troops and to repair storm damage', he moved by land and sea upon Himera, the city whose capture by Theron of Akragas from Hamilcar's friend Tērillos had provided the *casus belli*. Its capture would clear the way by which to join hands with the allies of Carthage on the Straits of Messina, Anaxilaos of Rhegion and his son Leophron,[7] governor of Zankle.

There was good reason for adopting this course, rather than sailing direct to the Straits to join these allies; for first, every day at sea was dangerous; second, Hamilcar had other allies in the Phoenicians and

[5] H., *ib.*; which is evidence on fifth-century feeling, even if H. is by any chance misinformed about the detail. Justin (xix, 1) makes Hamilcar son of (the famous) Mago; substitution of the more famous name for the less famous is more probable than the opposite; he may well have been of the same great family.

[6] D.S. xi, 20, 2; doubted by Pareti (*Studi Sic. ed It.*, pp. 140ff).

[7] Or Kleophron; see schol. on Pind. *Pyth.* ii, 18/34; Leo-, D.H. xx, 7; Justin xxi, 3; surely identical with the Leophron of Ath. i, c. 5, p. 3e (against Obst in PW, *s.v.* Leophron); cf. Her. Pont. 25; Ar. *Rhet.* iii, 2, 14 (q. Simonides, fr. 7 Bgk); Beloch (*GG* II, ii, 175) makes L. governor of Rhegion when A. goes to Zankle; but the schol. could mean either.

Elymites of western Sicily, whom he desired to cover, and from whom he drew some supplies and reinforcements; and third, Messina is divided from the heart of Sicily by difficult hill country (the scene of stiff fighting in 1943) from which it might have been difficult for the invading army to force its way out.

Meanwhile the Dorian tyrants, like the Athenians in 490, were unable to move to the scene of action until the intentions of the sea-borne enemy were revealed; but they were ready. Theron crossed the island with reinforcements for Himera and threw himself into the city, sending messengers at the same time to bring the news to his son-in-law at Syracuse; and before Himera the first fighting took place. Hamilcar beached his war-galleys west of the town, protecting them by a stockade, and ordered his army to protect itself similarly by a line of works extending from the naval camp to the foot of the hills; while the supply-ships unloaded their freight and were sent off immediately to bring more provisions. The defenders attempted a sortie (to interfere with the works?) but were driven back with loss; there was some depression of spirits, but the resolute Theron gave orders to wall up the gates facing the enemy, and assured the citizens that help would not be long in coming.[8]

In the south-east, the forces under the sons of Deinomenes mobilised fast; their mercenary components will have been already on a war footing. We have heard already of the expeditionary force which the tyrant of Syracuse is said to have boasted that he could send to Greece: 20,000 hoplites, 2000 archers, 2000 slingers, 2000 cavalry and 2000 mobile light infantry, *hamippoi*, trained to run with the cavalry or perhaps on occasion to ride on the horses' cruppers. (Two men to a horse on the march was a not uncommon spectacle in crusading and other mediaeval armies.) To these, for a campaign in Sicily with 'all at stake', he could add more of the citizen soldiers of his enlarged Syracuse, those of the east-coast cities that he had not depopulated, and many Sikels. Hieron will have joined him en route with the men of Gela. It was an imposing array. Five thousand of the formidable Sicilian cavalry rode ahead of the foot, passing the enemy's flank and rounding up foragers and plunderers by the hundred. Fifty thousand strong the columns poured over the hills south-east of Himera and joined hands with the defence; and jubilantly the men of Himera tore

[8] D.S. xi, 20, 3–5.

down the rough walls, with which they had so lately blocked their western gates.

Gelon in turn, if we may trust the Sicilian tradition, caused his men to run out a long ditch and stockade on the landward side of the town, making a secure camp of the whole area up to the walls.[9] Greek armies were frequently slack about entrenching, but Gelon's discipline was no doubt stricter than that of an elected, citizen general. Meanwhile his cavalry continued their raids, dominating the open country and confining the enemy to their lines, as Syracusan cavalry were to confine the Athenians in 414–13. The loss of Hamilcar's mounted troops dominates the whole campaign. Hamilcar had already written to Selinous, his ally (cf. p. 152), to send all available cavalry; but now came a crowning stroke of good fortune for Gelon. His cavalry intercepted the return message, saying that cavalry would be sent on an appointed day.

Gelon, experienced general that he was, had been surveying the enemy's lines warily, and had no intention of risking a headlong assault. He is said already to have been considering a raid on the enemy's ships, to cause alarm and confusion, before launching his main army to the attack. This raid would presumably have been conducted by mobile troops, passing right round the enemy's landward flank, out of sight, but might be, as it finally was, supported by a sally from the town. This stood on the west bank of the Himeras torrent, whose bed, almost dry in the late summer, separated the lines of the two armies along the rest of the front. Now his course was clear. It should be a regiment of his own cavalry that should arrive, and gain entry to the enemy's stockaded lines as friends. It seems to have transpired from the captured message, that Hamilcar intended to celebrate a great sacrifice to the sea-god on the appointed day; he may have desired the presence of Greeks to help him in sacrificing duly to the Greek Poseidon. Gelon stationed observers on the hills inland, who were to signal to him when they saw that the cavalry had arrived.[10] Then, at first light on the appointed day, he drew up his main line outside the palisades; and Theron, who had given orders for the preparation of additional sally-ports, made ready with the men of Akragas and Himera for his sortie.

The cavalry from the west arrived. The watchers on the hills saw them shortly accepted as friends and let in through the palisades. They signalled; and forthwith the battle began.

[9] *ib.* 21, 2. [10] *ib.* 21, 3–5.

The detached cavalry killed Hamilcar among his altars, and set fire to tents, ships, anything that would burn and cause conspicuous disarray; and forthwith Theron launched his attack on the naval camp from the east. With the defenders dismayed by indications of panic and some disaster in their rear, the men of Akragas and Himera swept over the barricades; but the citizen troops fell into confusion in the camp, and some, thinking the battle already won, fell to plundering. The battle was far from being won, and there was a moment of serious danger when a force of Iberians sent from the main army, which was not yet disorganized, faced about and swept down, parallel to the original front,[11] in counter-attack. But Theron saved the situation by ordering those with him to 'go round behind' (i.e. up into the landward part of the camp?) and set fire to tents there; both, presumably, to drive plunderers out into the open, where they would be forced to fight for their lives, and to dismay the enemy's main body, now locked in furious combat with Gelon's army, and to create a barrier of fire between that main body and the Greeks in the camp. The stratagem worked. The main body of the barbarians, who had charged fiercely to meet the main Sicilian line, were now in turn dismayed by indications of disaster in their rear; Gelon and his officers cheered on their men, pointing to the flaming camp; and the Carthaginian line broke in flight. There was, as usual in hand-to-hand battles, great slaughter as the flight began; all the more since Gelon had strictly forbidden taking prisoners (a saleable commodity). Nevertheless, a great mass of the barbarians, vaguely estimated at half the army, fell back together to a hill position (perhaps Mt Calogero, five miles west of the city[12]) and stood at bay. The first pursuers were repulsed; but Gelon, when he had re-formed his line facing and surrounding the hill, ordered no assault. There was no water there; and in a matter of hours the enemy main body was compelled to surrender.[13] The campaign ended with a great man-hunt after those who had scattered over the Himeraian and Akragantine hills.[14]

On the fate of Hamilcar there were various stories. One, told by the Carthaginians, according to Herodotos (vii, 167), who gives no details

[11] *παραβοηθούντων*, Polyainos, i, 28. This is the only evidence on Theron's part in the battle; it is not mentioned by Diodoros; indeed, it cannot be *proved* that this episode belongs to the Battle of Himera at all. But Himera was the only famous battle against Carthaginians in which Th. was engaged; and the story fits in with D. xi, 21, 4, on the project of an attack on the naval camp. P. is a most uncritical writer, but he seems to have some genuine information here.

[12] Suggested by Holm, *Gesch. Sik.* I, p. 207. [13] D.S. xi, 22. [14] *ib.* 25, 2.

of the fighting, was that while the battle raged all day 'from dawn till late afternoon', the Suffete, standing back, like Moses or Samuel, prayed and offered sacrifice 'burning whole carcases of victims on a great pyre', in the Phoenician manner. 'And when he saw his army beginning to break, as he was pouring a wine-offering over the sacrifice, he threw himself into the fire; and so he was burned, and disappeared' – though Gelon made diligent search for his body, and would no doubt have surrendered it under a peace settlement. Another Greek story was that Gelon bade Pediarchos, the commander of his archers, impersonate him and offer sacrifice between the lines, confident that this would draw out Hamilcar to do likewise; and that Hamilcar was then shot by archers who had concealed bows under their sacrificial vestments.[15] This, it may be suggested, is a piece of Greek embroidery of a bald tradition that Hamilcar was killed while sacrificing, by a stratagem of Gelon's. The variation is, like the Ephoros-Diodoros-Plutarch story of the last fight at Thermopylai, an object-lesson in the lengths to which Greek embroidery of a tradition could go. The common element in all the stories is that Hamilcar was killed while sacrificing; and the most probable version is clearly that of Diodoros, that he was cut down by the 'long range group' of cavalry. If they then threw him into his own fire, they might have concealed the fact when they found that Gelon wanted the body. The Carthaginian story, on the other hand, that Hamilcar immolated himself as the crowning sacrifice, might well have been invented by his family and their partisans, to save his and their prestige. Since he had been defeated, he could at least be provided with the glory of a noble death; as, more literally than Leonidas, a royal sacrifice. In any case, Herodotos concludes, he disappeared, and was honoured; though the detail (*ib.*) that 'they sacrifice to him, and set up monuments to him in all their colonial cities, and the greatest in Carthage' is reminiscent of a Greek hero-cult and is not Semitic. It is probably based on a Greek misunderstanding of the legend of Melcarth, the sea-god and wanderer, who would have temples in 'all the colonies', and after whom the Suffete, Abd-Melcarth or Servant of Melcarth, had been named.[16]

Another problem arising out of the scanty records of this campaign is that of what Gelon's great fleet was doing. It was not unhonoured

[15] Polyain. i, 27, 2.
[16] Macan *ad loc.*; on 'The Burning of Melcarth', cf. Frazer, *GB*^{3}, Part IV, ch. v.

when the victors came to make their thank-offerings to the gods. Pausanias, 600 years later, saw those at Olympia: 'a great statue of Zeus, and three corselets of linen', housed in a shrine called, from its contents, 'the Treasury of the Carthaginians', with a dedicatory inscription 'from Gelon and the Syracusans, for their defeat of the Phoenicians both with triremes and on land'; and the somewhat stilted expression used for 'both . . . and' sounds as if he were quoting the words of the inscription.[17] Yet we have no account of any naval battle. We might expect the Sicilian fleet to have lain in readiness at Syracuse (since Selinous was hostile, and the rest of the south coast harbourless and no place for a fleet to loiter). If so, Hamilcar evaded it by keeping west and heading north, though suffering a partial disaster on his detour.

Dunbabin most ingeniously proposed to combine this and two other remarkable silences of our sources. First, nothing is heard of Anaxilaos, 'for all his zeal in Terillos' cause'; and second, when Pindar wrote an ode, after 476, for Chromios, the husband of Gelon's sister, a soldier distinguished in many battles, alike 'amid shouting of footmen and horses and hollow ships', he mentions indeed his youthful prowess at the Helōros, long ago, in Hippokrates' time, but has not a word about Himera.[18] Dunbabin's suggestion was that Gelon's fleet under Chromios, approaching the straits, neutralised the forces of Zankle and Rhegion, while 'Anaxilas could hold the Straits with many fewer than 200 ships'.[19] Phoenician ships from Hamilcar's fleet may, moreover, have helped to bar the Straits; it would be rash to feel sure, on our evidence, that they all stayed on the beach to be burned.

There was a reason for the silence of Pindar and the other court-poets of Syracuse as to Anaxilaos' position in 480; for Anaxilaos, far from being treated with any ideological severity for having, as Herodotos expressly says, vii, 165, 'brought in' the barbarian, was allowed to make his peace, and even admitted to the family circle of the House of Deinomenes when Gelon's brother Hieron married, as his third wife, Anaxilaos' daughter.[20] He kept Rhegion and Zankle, handing them on at his death to his servant Mikythos in trust for his

[17] ἤτοι τριήρεσιν ἢ καὶ πεζῇ μάχῃ κρατησάντων. Cf. also schol. Pind. *Pyth.* i, 146 (a), for some naval action in 480 (though P.'s text refers to Cumae, 474).

[18] *Ninth Nemean* (actually for a chariot-race at Sikyon); esp. ll. 34/78 to 43/105.

[19] *WG* 425f; a notable example of three minuses making a plus.

[20] Schol. Pind, *Pyth.* i, 112.

younger children; Leophron must have died before him.[21] But Anaxilaos must have given up support of his father-in-law's claims to Himera. He went over to the Athenian weight-standard for his coins,[22] already adopted at Syracuse; and when he engaged in a war with Lokroi, on his northern border, about 477, it appears that a mere message from his formidable son-in-law was enough to stop him.[23]

Towards the main enemy Gelon showed a similar mildness. The loss of the expedition was a sore blow to Carthage, comparable perhaps to the loss of her Sicilian expedition to Athens; there is no reason to doubt that, in effect, the whole expedition *was* lost, even though Greek romance did palpably 'improve' the story. (Twenty ships got away from the beaches at Himera, crowded with fugitives, so that they all sank in a gale, and exactly one small boatload were all that survived to tell the tale.)[24] Carthage feared that Gelon would carry the war to Africa, we are assured; she manned her walls by night, and sent ambassadors to sue for peace, who came as suppliants and begged for the intercessions of Gelon's wife and Theron's daughter, Dāmarete. Gelon granted them peace at the cost of an indemnity of 2000 talents, enough to pay the whole cost of the war, and of the erection of two temples (one at Carthage and one at Syracuse?) in which the terms of the peace were to be recorded; and the Carthaginians expressed their appreciation by the further gift to Damarete of a golden crown worth 100 talents. From the indemnity were struck some of the noblest coins ever minted, the splendid ten-drachma or, in Sicilian terms, fifty-litra Damareteia, with the four-horse chariot advancing at slow pace, while a winged Victory flies above and a lion (the lion of defeated Carthage?) is shown in the *exergue* below. On the obverse is the head of a goddess, Demeter of Sicily or Arethousa of Syracuse, surrounded by dolphins, denoting sea-power; and it is a tempting guess that the face is that of Damarete.[25] In such coin, Gelon was able to fulfill his promise to repay

[21] H. vii, 170, 4. When A.'s sons grew up and became restive, M. retired and ended his days in prosperity at Tegea; cf. D.S. xi, 66, also Paus. v, 26, 2ff, on his offerings at Olympia; part of the inscr. on these has been found, cf. Kaibel in *Hermes*, XXVIII, p. 60. D.H. (xx, 7; cf. Beloch, *GG* II, ii, 176f), who says L. succeeded A., must surely be simply mistaken

[22] E. S. G. Robinson in *JHS* LXVI, p. 18.

[23] Pind. *Pyth.* ii, 18/35f; cf. schol. in Berlin pap. 13419 (Wilamowitz in *Sitzb. d. Preuss. Ak.* 1918, 749f).

[24] D.S. xi, 24, 2.

[25] *ib.* 24, 3f; 26, 1ff. On the Damareteion, illustrated in every manual, cf. now the very attractive pamphlet of W. Schwabacher, *Das Demareteion* (Opus Nobile series), W. Dorn, Bremen, 1958.

the sums which he had raised, not without pressure, from the citizens of Syracuse; perhaps the first war-*loan* in history.[26]

Plutarch adds that he seized the opportunity to require Carthage, by a clause in the treaty, to give up human sacrifice.[27] This humanitarian measure is elsewhere ascribed to Darius,[28] claiming overlordship over the Phoenicians. Both stories are probably untrue. It was not the sort of thing about which, among foreign peoples, military monarchs troubled themselves; the moral tales were probably made up by later Greek philosophers. But one may wonder whether, in that age of widespread religious reforms, Carthage did about this time lay aside this bronze-age practice, at least except on occasions when she was badly frightened.

Likewise in western Sicily, there was no destruction of the Phoenician settlements; but Theron may have advanced upon them and forced on them a peace on his terms. There was a dedication at Olympia, set up by the men of Akragas from spoils of Motya, which 'report', endorsed by Pausanias presumably on grounds of style, assigned to Kalamis, the early-mid-fifth century sculptor.[29] Motya was thoroughly penetrated by a rather provincial Greek culture, and a few archaic inscriptions show that Greek was spoken there; not in itself any proof of conquest. But at the same epoch both Motya and the Elymite city of Eryx struck coins with the Akragantine badges of the eagle and crab.[30] Subject cities had coined with the badges of their overlords under the late 6th-century 'empires' of Sybaris and Kroton,[31] and this is some ground for thinking that Theron was recognized after 480 as overlord of western Sicily.

There was a great period of temple-building and public works in the victorious cities. 'Gelon built from the spoils noble temples of Demeter and the Maiden' (Persephone) in the new quarter of his enlarged Syracuse on the mainland;[32] and there was a new, probably commemorative, temple at Himera, on the low ground by the port, known from archaeology (e.g., its fine, marble lion's-head gutter-spouts in the Palermo Museum). But no city was so much adorned as

[26] Plut. *Sayings*: *Gelon*, 3.
[27] *ib.*, 1; cf. schol. Pind. *Pyth.* ii, 2.
[28] Justin, xix, 1, 10.
[29] Paus. v, 25, 5; Dunbabin *WG* 430f. (But the inscription did not give the name of Kalamis nor, apparently, that of Theron; the evidence is not quite as strong as D. suggests.)
[30] Dunbabin, *ib.*, from Head *HN*², 158, 138 respectively; cf. Dunb. 334.
[31] Cf. *Lyric Age*, pp. 384–6.
[32] D.S. xi, 26, 7; Dunbabin, WG, p. 429.

Akragas, with several of the magnificent temples, which still crown its southern ridge within the walls today. Its citizens also provided themselves with sewers to drain the lower ground within the city, north of the temple ridge, known, from the name of their architect Phaiax, as 'phaiakes', and with an artificial lake and fishpond '1400 yards round and 30 feet deep', to which swans resorted. Labour for all these works was provided by the enslaved prisoners of war, who were divided among the cities in proportion to the sizes of their contingents in the campaign; but Akragas obtained the largest number (probably because her share of those who surrendered was augmented by those caught scattered in her hills).[33] Thousands of young Libyans and Europeans, who had set out gaily to sack cities and temples, spent their days in chain-gangs miserably building them, till death ended their unsuccessful Odyssey.

Delphi, whither Gelon had sent Kadmos the Just to make his peace with Xerxes in case the worst occurred (p. 308), received his chief dedication in Old Greece: a statue of Victory by a refugee Ionian artist, and 'a golden tripod of sixteen talents weight', celebrated by Bakchylides, Simonides' nephew, along with a similar tripod set up by Hieron (probably later, for his admirals' victory over the Etruscans in 474). The inscription on its limestone base is extant:

> Gelon the son of Deinomenes of Syracuse dedicated this to Apollo. The tripod and the Victory are the work of Bion the son of Diodoros the Milesian.[34]

It is conspicuous that, here as at Olympia (p. 482), Gelon does not call himself king, or by any other title; though it was as King of the Syracusans that the Athenian ambassador is said to have addressed him in 481.[35] 'Tyrannos' he might be called by enemies; and 'king' by flatterers; but he did not use this title. For this powerful and self-made military leader, his own name (like 'Caesar') carried prestige enough; as did the style 'Hieron, son of Deinomenes and the Syracusans' on the helmet dedicated at Olympia for the Battle of Cumae (p. 165).

[33] D.S. xi, 25.

[34] Tod, *GHI* no. 17 (and cf. comm.); D.S. xi, 26, 7; Bakch, iii, 17ff (an ode for Hieron, addressed as 'General of the Syracusans'. An epigram (*A.P.* vi, 214, attributed to Simonides), probably not ever inscribed on the monument, attributes the dedications to all four brothers, Gelon, Hieron, Polyzalos and Thrasyboulos, 'for their victory over the barbarian nations; whereby they extended a mighty hand in aid for the freedom of the Hellenes'.

[35] *GHI* (1969), no. 28. H. vii, 161, 1.

Gelon may, however, like some other dictators, have appreciated the value of a popular vote of confidence taken at an opportune moment. He may (though we are told on no strong evidence) have been acclaimed by the people as Supreme Commander for the campaign of 480.[36] After it, it is said, he came before the Syracusan army, which he had ordered to parade – the people in arms – himself unarmed and even tunicless, in his 'plaid' only, and gave an account of his actions. Naturally there was immense enthusiasm, and the people hailed their war-leader by titles that were sometimes used of Zeus himself, as Benefactor, Saviour, King.[37] The clearest warning that some caution should be used in dealing with this story is contained in the last words. Benefactor and Saviour (Euergetes, Sōtēr) were popular titles with Hellenistic kings ('they that are great among them are called Benefactors'); and Agathokles, tyrant of Syracuse, at the end of the fourth century, did take the title of King and strike coins in his own name. By that time, the legend of the great and good Gelon was well established at Syracuse, and might well have been used to supply alleged precedents for these Hellenistic titles, as also for that of *Stratēgos Autokrator*, also said to have been used by Gelon, but conspicuously absent from his dedication. The story used by Diodoros and Polyainos may therefore have been embellished, if not invented, in the days of Agathokles or of the third-century Hieron, in whose family the name of Gelon reappears. But it may still be true that Gelon seized the opportunity to strengthen his position by such a 'plebiscite'. There is said to have been a statue of Gelon, unarmed, in the temple of Hera, which, it has been suggested, might have helped to give rise to the story.[38] But the question then remains, if the statue was historical, why unarmed? One would expect Gelon to be portrayed as general; and the statue, if historical, may have preserved an early tradition of the incident.

The day of Himera remained the proudest day in all their history for the Greeks of Sicily; they were proud, from the first, that it should be ranked with the repulse of Xerxes. It, with Hieron's victory over the Etruscan fleet, did indeed, as Pindar prayed, mark the definitive repulse of the 'barbarian reaction' against the western Greeks, and inaugurate an age of great prosperity and comparative peace:

Grant, I beseech thee, son of Kronos, that quiet, at home, the

[36] Polyainos i, 27, 1. [37] D.S. xi, 26, 5f.
[38] Dunbabin, *WG* 427, on Aelian, *VH* vi, 11; xiii, 37.

> Phoenician and the Tyrrhenians' battle-cry may rest, having seen the disaster at sea that attended their violence off Kyme; the loss they sustained in defeat by the Lord of Syracuse, that hurled their young men from the swift ships into the deep, and rescued Hellas from harsh slavery. From Salamis I will win the favour of Athens for my reward, and at Sparta will speak of the battle before Kithairon, where the Median archers fell; but by the banks of Himera's fair river I will make my song of Deinomenes' sons: the praise that they won by their valour, where the foe went down.

The ode, sung about 470,[39] is for Hieron; Gelon was no more. His remarkable mildness towards his enemies after his great triumph was ascribed later to a desire to conserve and free his forces for a still greater struggle; for when Carthage sued for peace and was granted it, Gelon had not yet heard the news of Salamis. That, when he heard those tidings, he was 'about to set sail' to bring aid to Old Greece (in spring, 479, no ships having crossed in the winter?) must be put down to the wishful historical thinking of a patriotic Sicilian.[40] There are other possible explanations which are simpler. After twenty strenuous years as general and ruler, and left with nothing to fear, Gelon may have been simply ready for peace; it is possible indeed, that his health was failing. The campaign of Himera was his last great effort; and before its glory could fade he died, *felix opportunitate*, in 478.

[39] *First Pythian*, 72/137ff.

[40] D.S. xi, 26, 4f.

CHAPTER XXIII

Winter of Discontent

(and Spring, 479)

ATTICA was clear of the enemy; so were the Cyclades. Andros and Karystos, though they had resisted attack – for as usual, no Greek citizen soldier wanted to be first up a ladder, for a cause that could be won otherwise – had paid their indemnities, as had Paros and others; in the following spring the Greek fleet could advance in friendly waters to Delos, on the eastern side of the main Cycladic group. The Athenians returned home (though surely not all the children and old people?), got some temporary shelter over their heads where their houses had been burnt, and on Themistokles' advice got on with the autumn ploughing.[1] They probably hoped that now, at least, the Peloponnesian army would advance, as the fleet had, to force a return to the national side upon the Medizers in Boiotia, which the Persians had evacuated; but in this they were swiftly undeceived. Kleombrotos, it was said, went so far as to 'offer sacrifice against the Persian' (taking the omens), but at that very juncture the sun was eclipsed[2] (2nd Oct., 480). The Spartans took this, according to the usual procedure, as an unfavourable omen; but they were not unhappy to have an excuse for going home. Their allies, too, had the ploughing to think about; and it was an excuse for reverting to their policy of confining themselves to their peninsula. They are said to have salved their consciences by sending a herald after Xerxes, before he left Thessaly, to make a formal demand for 'satisfaction' for the death of their king Leonidas; perhaps hoping for some such acknowledgment of defeat as might, in the code of the Spartans, who never pursued a beaten enemy[3] and were not equipped for such operations, be enough to satisfy honour. If so, they were disappointed. Xerxes replied grimly 'Mardonios here will give you your repayment'.[4]

[1] H. viii, 112; 121, 1; 132, 2; 109, 4.
[2] H. ix, 10, 3.
[3] Plut. *Lyk.* 22; cf. *Lyric Age*, 284.
[4] H. viii, 114.

The war was still to be won.

The autumn and winter, 480–79, were indeed full of incidents which foreshadowed things yet to come. The brilliant fifth-century society of Greece bore within it, from its beginning, the seeds of its own decay; and in this season, between the campaigns, may be seen already the jealousy and fear of Athens, felt, not without reason, by the smaller and older maritime states; and the tensions within Athens itself, and within Sparta itself, which were to weaken both, and to make each appear slippery and unreliable in the eyes of the other. Herodotos is never more revealing than in his choice of anecdotes to represent these tensions: anecdotes sometimes passed over as illustrating the essential childishness of the Father of History, or the childhood of the art, and as unworthy of its grave maturity. This is a mistake. The stories may, like others in Herodotos, have been improved in the telling before ever they reached him; and he himself is certainly not the man to let a story *lose* anything through his fault. But they are so revealing in the light of after events, that a more interesting question is whether he chose them in full consciousness of their significance for later developments, or not. Whether he selected them, out of all the war-reminiscences of a generation, for this significance, or merely because he liked them, is only the question whether they are the conscious or subconscious choices of genius.

When the fleet came back from Andros and Karystos, the first thing to do, at the formal ending of the campaign, was to make thank-offerings to the gods. The allies dedicated three captured Phoenician triremes; two presumably to Poseidon, 'one at the Isthmus, which was still there in my time, and one at Sounion, and one to Ajax, on the spot in Salamis'.[5] (Why had not Athens taken steps to preserve the two that were in her territory? We are not told.) They divided the spoil, and sent first-fruits to Delphi, 'from which was made the figure of a man eighteen feet high, holding the prow of a ship in his hand'; a *kouros*, representing the men of Greece presenting the spoils, or, as later generations understood it, Apollo receiving them. This is the version of Pausanias (x, 14, 5), who adds that they dedicated a bronze Zeus at Olympia. There next follows, in Herodotos, an anti-Aiginetan story (cf. p. 543, n. 83), that the Aiginetans had to be prompted by the god before they dedicated the three golden stars on a bronze mast,

[5] *ib.* 121.

which commemorated their receipt of the Prize of Valour; and in Pausanias, an anti-Themistokles story that the God rejected his offerings, 'either because he questioned the God before he had made his offering, or because the God knew that he would one day fly to the Persians'. Both stories reflect the jealousies of days already not distant. Then 'the Greeks', i.e. presumably the generals of the contingents, repaired to the Isthmus, to select the man most worthy to receive the individual prize; and the famous story follows, that when the generals voted, under the most solemn conditions, laying their votes, a first and a second choice, upon the altar of Poseidon, every man voted for himself first, but most of them for Themistokles second. But in spite of this consensus of second choices, 'through envy, the Greeks would not come to this decision, but sailed away, each to his own land, leaving it undecided'. Whether there really would have been such provision for second choices, clearly in a first vote, may perhaps be doubted; but the story enshrines, in saga form, the sad fact that 'through envy', the besetting sin of a brilliant people, the prize, which clearly should have gone to Themistokles, was not awarded.

'But nevertheless, the name of Themistokles was on all men's lips, and he was celebrated throughout all Hellas as the wisest man by far of all Hellenes'; and when he visited Sparta during that winter, he received unprecedented honours. The Spartans crowned their own Eurybiadas for valour with a crown of olive, which indeed was not unfair, but they also decorated Themistokles in like manner 'for wisdom and adroitness; and they made him a gift of the finest chariot in Sparta; and having highly praised him, when he left they sent with him the 300 chosen men of the Spartiates who are called the Knights, and they escorted him as far as the frontier of Tegea'. [6]

Sparta had indeed good grounds for gratitude to Themistokles; he had loyally fallen in with their essentially Peloponnesian policy, holding Athens loyal in spite of the inactivity of the land forces, while in turn persuading Eurybiades to adopt the strategy that won the victory of Salamis; but for the very same reasons, some Athenians were less enthusiastic. Herodotos' next chapter preserves another famous tale, that when he came home 'Timodēmos of Aphidnai' [near Marathon] 'who was distinguished only for his hostility to Themistokles, in furious envy reproached him with his visit to Sparta, saying that it was

[6] H. viii, 124.

thanks to Athens that he had received these honours from the Spartans, and not through his own achievements.' Themistokles put up with this at first, but when Timodemos went on harping on it, he finally produced the crushing reply, 'The fact is, my friend, that while I would never have won such honour from the Spartans if I had been a citizen of Belbina' [a tiny but independent island twelve miles off Sounion] '*you* never would, Athenian though you are.' [7]

It was, indeed, a brutal geographical fact that whereas Sparta, the peninsular land-power, had been delivered from immediate danger by a victory at sea, Athens, the continentally-based sea-power, needed a victory on land to deliver her from the abiding threat of Mardonios' army.[8] This probably did give grounds for some feeling at Athens, unfair but not unnatural, that Themistokles was too compliant towards Sparta and the continental allies. This feeling was no doubt welcome to Themistokles' conservative opponents; and at the spring elections it produced the striking result, that the Athenians elected as generals the two ablest men among those just returned from exile, Aristeides and Xanthippos; it was these who commanded respectively Athens' land and sea forces in the campaign of 479.[9]

It is possible, and erroneous, to build too high a superstructure of theory on these facts. They do not necessarily imply that Themistokles was out of office; Ephoros, who says so, may himself be theorising. Nor was Aristeides, at least, unwilling to coöperate with him. He did so again, with Themistokles taking the lead, against Sparta, in the matter of the rebuilding of the walls of Athens in 478.[10] Plutarch's statements, that Themistokles was elected commander-in-chief, *strategos autokrator*, in 480 and Aristeides in 479,[11] are probably anachronistic, derived from Hellenistic sources which used their contemporary terminology in dealing with earlier history. It is not certain that any such position was known to fifth-century Athens, even in the time of

[7] *ib.* 125; the story later much spoiled by 'improvement', making the grumbler himself a citizen of a small island (Seriphos); so, already in Plato, *Rep.* 329E; followed by Plut. *Them.* 18. Macan (*Hdt., ad loc.*) asks pertinently 'Had the Athenian aristocratic tradition grown sensitive of the fame of Timodemos?' Cf. Churchill on T. E. Lawrence, when it was said that he could have done nothing without supplies of British gold: 'No one else could have done what he did, *with* the gold.'

[8] Cf. Macan, *op. cit.*, II, p. 343.

[9] H. ix, 28 (the last of only four places where H. names Aristeides); viii, 131; Ephoros (D.S. xi, 273) says explicitly that Th. was defeated as having been 'bribed by Sparta'.

[10] Thk. i, 91, 3; below, pp. 556f.

[11] Respectively, *Sayings* (Them.), *Mor.* 185A; *Ar.* 10.

Perikles.[12] It *may* be, therefore, that Themistokles in the summer of 479 was at Athens or at 'General Headquarters' at Corinth, occupied with political and diplomatic tasks, for which he was of all men best fitted. But however that may be, either the Athenian Assembly or the ten generals elected by it, meeting as something intermediate between a war-cabinet and a general staff, selected other men to command the main forces. It probably was something of a set-back for Themistokles. He is indeed never again recorded to have commanded the fleet which he had built up; and with his triumphal visit to Sparta and his retort to Timodemos, he makes his exit from Herodotos' narrative.[13]

It was to this Athens, united in determination to resist and in bitter hatred of the enemy who had burned Athenians' homes and temples, but divided (as men conducting a war usually are) as to what should be done, that there came, as the spring approached, a familiar go-between (Themistokles had seen him last near Tempe), the Macedonian King Alexander.[14] He was the bearer of a peace-proposal from Mardonios, who, charged with finishing off the war, down-graded from a royal expedition to a frontier operation, was intent on dividing the enemy; preferably by detaching Athens, on which he could put pressure, from the Peloponnesian League and using the Athenian fleet to turn the Isthmus defences. He proposed, in return for Athens' adherence to the King, and on the King's authority, that all should be forgiven, right back to Athens' past aggression in Asia. Athens might have autonomy

[12] P. certainly was repeatedly elected 'from among all Athenians', in distinction from his nine colleagues, elected each by his own tribe (so that there could be two generals from Perikles' tribe, and other good soldiers from that tribe, Akamantis, were not permanently excluded); and he is more than once named, alone, by Thucydides (i, 116, 1; ii, 13, 1) in distinction from 'nine colleagues' who are unnamed; but cf. K. J. Dover, '*ΔΕΚΑΤΟΣ ΑΥΤΟΣ*', in *JHS* LXXIX, 61ff. The evidence is insufficient to prove that P. did *not* have special powers, especially in a crisis like that of 431, cf. his 'autocratic' behaviour in refusing to convene the Assembly, ii, 22, 1; but Dover shows that the evidence for a position of *strategos autokrator* in his time or earlier is weak, and believes that his unrivalled position, like that of Themistokles, was due to influence and prestige; in Roman terms, a matter of *auctoritas*, not of *imperium*. In like manner, Dunbabin believed (cf. p. 486) that the story of Gelon being elected *strategos autokrator* by the Syracusan assembly (Polyain. i, 27, 1) was an anachronism, originating when Dionysios, who *was* elected to such a position (D.S. xiii, 94), appealed to Good King Gelon as a precedent.

[13] One more mention of him (ix, 98) being merely a reference-back to Artemision.

[14] Whom H. actually calls King only at ix, 44, though he refers here (viii, 137ff) to his ancestor Perdikkas, as having 'won the *tyrannis* of the Macedonians' – six generations back, so about 680–650, early in the Greek colonial period – in a charming folk-tale, embodying the northern youngest-son-of-three theme; as in the Scythian story, H. iv, 5.

(local self-government, like Tyre and Sidon); she might keep her territory intact, and annex any more that she might desire; and the King would pay for the restoration of her temples.

> Why then be so mad as to resist the King? You can never beat him, and you cannot hold out for ever. . . . Even if you defeat the force now under my command, (which is beyond any expectation if you look at it sanely), another will be forthcoming, several times greater. As long as you try to be a match for the King, you will be denied the use of your land, and only able by continuous effort to survive at all; you would do better not to try, but to come to terms; and your best opportunity to that is now, while the King is so inclined.

To this message from Mardonios Alexander added his own advice, 'speaking as a friend', to the same effect:

> You cannot keep up this war with Xerxes for ever (if I thought otherwise, I should not have brought this proposition); for the King's power is beyond human resistance, and his arm is long. If, then, you do not come to terms now, while they are prepared to offer such great concessions, I am afraid for you, most exposed as you are of all the allies, that you alone will bear the brunt of total devastation, and your country will be the destined no-man's-land between the two sides.

Sparta duly heard of these proposals, and was alarmed. There is said to have been an oracle current, prophesying that they and the other Dorians should be driven from the Peloponnese by the Medes and Athenians (one of the most explicit of all unfulfilled oracles); and the Athenians, realising that this was an unrivalled opportunity to put pressure upon Sparta, temporised until a Spartan embassy arrived. The Spartan offer was not altogether satisfactory; its chief concrete promise was that of economic support for the duration of the war, and especially of maintenance for the Athenians' wives and children and non-combatants, 'seeing that you have now lost two harvests', a remark, incidentally, which is anachronistic, unless it means that there had *not* been time to do the ploughing and sowing; though it became true later. But there was no promise of the massive military aid which Athens really wanted.

Nevertheless, the Athenians took their decision to make no surrender. They answered Alexander:

> We know quite well that the power of Persia is many times greater than ours, so you need not insult us [by telling us] about this. But we desire to be free; so we will defend ourselves as best we can. . . . Now tell Mardonios that the Athenians say: While the sun goes in his accustomed path, we will make no agreement with Xerxes; we will continue our defence, trusting in the gods who fight for us, and the heroes, whom he has set at nought, and burned their temples and sacred images. And for yourself, you had better not appear in Athens again with such proposals, in the guise of friendship urging us to do wrong; we should be sorry if some unpleasant incident happened to you here, when you are our *proxenos* and friend.

Having thus committed themselves in advance – at least, so Athenian tradition said – they then answered the Spartans in the same proud strain:

> . . . There is no gold on earth, and no land so fair, that for it we would join the Medes to enslave Hellas. There are many great impediments to our doing so, even if we wished; first and greatest, the temples and statues of our gods that have been burned and thrown down, for which we cannot do other than exact revenge to the uttermost, rather than make a treaty with him who has done this; and secondly, there is our Hellenic character: the unity of blood and language and common sanctuaries and festivals of the gods and ways of life; for the Athenians to turn traitors to these things would not be well.

Descending to earth, the Athenians thanked the Spartans for their promise of economic support, but added

> We will endeavour to hold out without troubling you. But now, the situation being what it is, send an army, as quickly as you can; for as we judge, it will not be long before the enemy invades our country. He will march as soon as ever he hears that we have rejected his proposals; so, before he reaches Attica, now is the time for you to meet him in Boiotia.[15]

These fine rhetorical chapters of Herodotos are so exactly in the best Athenian style that one may at least hope they represent something like

[15] H. viii, 140–44.

what was said. After all, when calling upon their own people, already under great strain, for a further supreme effort, how should the Athenian leaders *not* rally them in a strain of the highest idealism? But it is possible that what reached Herodotos is already contaminated with some taint of mid-fifth-century feeling; feeling, from a time when Athens was already feeling constrained to justify herself for 'enslaving Greeks' [16] on the pretext of delivering them from the Persian yoke; a trace, too, of anti-Spartan feeling, in the implication that Athens trusted Sparta once more in vain, when she had quixotically cast away her means of applying pressure.[17] Yet it might be true. Athens could, in fact, apply the same pressure still, the pressure of the inexorable fact that the Peloponnese could not be saved without her. The Athenian error was perhaps that of thinking that Sparta, the mass of the Spartiatai, spearhead of the army that had to be moved, would see the truth quickly.

Plutarch attributes the proud answer to Aristeides, as drafter and mover of the Decree for a reply to Sparta; and as we have seen, he probably was Athens' 'man of the hour'; but the actual words of his alleged decree read like a later literary composition.[18] That he further 'wrote', i.e. proposed a decree, that the priests should formulate curses upon anyone who should make overtures to the 'Medes' or desert the alliance of the Hellenes [19] is in the manner of the time, and could be historical; moreover, such a solemn and *sacred* imprecation was the kind of document which early-fifth-century Greeks did publish in permanent form, on bronze or stone.[20] With or without Aristeides'

[16] Cf. Thk. i, 98, 4: 'This was the first allied city to be wrongfully enslaved'; on the treatment of recalcitrant Naxos about 469.

[17] Cf. the surprisingly 'tough' comment of Macan (*ad loc.*, H. viii, 144): 'If . . . the speeches reported be true, or anywhere near the truth, the Athenians had themselves to thank for the Spartan delay in responding to this demand; they have given away their diplomatic weapons in a fit of pan-Hellenic generosity.'

[18] The words in Plut. *Ar.* 10 are worth studying, having a bearing on the question of the genuineness of such documents: 'In a decree drafted by Aristeides, they gave the splendid answer, that they could pardon the enemy for thinking that anything could be bought with money, since they knew no better; but that they resented the Spartans' attitude in having eyes only for the present poverty and want of the Athenians, forgetting their courage and sense of honour, and calling upon them to fight for Hellas for the sake of food. Having written this' (the word used of drafting a *psephisma*) 'he had the ambassadors brought into the Assembly, and bade them tell the Spartans that there is not so much gold on the earth or under the earth that the Athenians would accept it in exchange for the liberty of the Hellenes.' Plutarch summarises; but it looks as if what he had before him was a 'jazzed up' version of H. viii, 144, 1ff, such as could have been produced in any rhetorical school. Cf. nn. 34, 49, below.

[19] Plut. *ib.*

[20] Cf. the 'Teian curses', Tod, *GHI*, no. 23.

name, such an inscription could have been known to later generations, and so through Krateros to Plutarch, independently of the alleged diplomatic documents, which Krateros almost certainly derived only from a literary tradition.[21] But Herodotos here names no individual. Like Thucydides after him to a great extent, he ascribes the public acts of a free society to the people; who was their mouthpiece or standard-bearer is a secondary question. Often it is something that we should like to know; but it is not unimpressive that the historians of the classical Greeks, those great individualists, while by no means ignoring the great man, rejected any 'great man theory'.

So Athens served the cause that winter by standing fast; and Themistokles, whatever the truth about his secret communications or innermost thoughts, had publicly advised the citizens to go home and get some seed-corn into the ground, and be glad Xerxes had gone. But there were others who counter-attacked more actively. The revolt of the Ionians and other Greeks under Persia had throughout been one of the hopes of the allies. So far, propaganda had produced only the desertion of a handful of ships; but about December, 480, came the first larger movement; a revolt in Chalkidiké.

The cities in this region, close to the Persians' main line of communications, had no doubt suffered from the heavy demands for labour and supplies incidental to the construction of the Athos Canal and the passing of the army; but this had not exhausted the loyalty to Persia of Akanthos, or of Abdēra (pp. 338, 471). It looks as if there had been at least some prompting. Most of Chalkidiké had been colonised from Chalkis and Eretria, which had not surrendered; but the centre of the revolt seems to have been at Poteidaia, a colony of Corinth, which always maintained close relations with her daughter cities; Poteidaia, where Aristeus, son of the admiral Adeimantos, held command in a revolt against Athens forty-seven years later.[22] Now it was, as we have seen, Athens, which now needed a victory on land to save her territory, while the Peloponnesians, secure behind their isthmus, hoped that no such severe effort might be necessary. Latychidas, the senior surviving King of Sparta, in the following summer took command at sea. The

[21] Cf. below, pp. 505f, n. 49. On the other hand, if such an inscription did exist, it is rather surprising that it is not among those quoted in 4th-cent. patriotic oratory.
[22] Thk. i, 56–65.

revolt in Chalkidiké looks like a part, the only part for the present which came to anything, of a Peloponnesian and specifically a Corinthian project to dislodge Mardonios by threatening his communications.[23]

Artabazos, returning with his Iranian division after escorting Xerxes to the Hellespont, found Poteidaia in revolt, and its walls, on their isthmus from sea to sea, blocking access to the interior of Pallene, where Eretrian Mende and Skione had joined the rebellion and sent troops to help in the defence. There were stirrings of revolt further afield too, notably among the half-Hellenized Bottiaioi 'driven from the Thermaic Gulf by the Macedonians', who now held Olynthos, a city in a fine situation, about seven miles north of Poteidaia and within sight from the walls.[24]

This revolt was dangerous, both from its proximity to Mardonios' land communications and for what its example might inspire others to do. Artabazos, already regarded as a promising officer, acted promptly:

> He besieged Poteidaia; and then, becoming suspicious that the people of Olynthos were also meditating rebellion, he laid siege to that too. He captured it, drove out the people to a neighbouring lake and slew them, and then offered the city to Kritoboulos, a man of Torone, as governor, and to the Chalkidians; this is how the Chalkidians got possession of Olynthos.

Playing on the Chalkidians' cupidity and rivalry with the Eretrians and Corinthians of Pallene, Artabazos thus prevented the revolt from spreading further. There may have been among the Chalkidians refugees and sons of refugees from their mother-city, captured by Athens 27 years before, and so ill-disposed to Athens and her allies.

> Artabazos now concentrated against Poteidaia. He applied himself zealously to the task, and got into touch with Timoxenos, the commander of the contingent from Skiōne, who undertook to betray the city. How he got into touch with him in the first instance I cannot say (there is no account of this given); but the end of the matter was as follows. When Timoxenos wanted to send a letter to Artabazos, or *vice versa*, they used to wrap the note round an arrow, near the notches, and then put the feathers on and shoot the arrow

[23] Cf. Macan, cited above, (n. 8); Munro, cited below, n. 34.
[24] H. viii, 126f; for the topography, Thk. i, 63, 2.

into a prearranged place. Timoxenos' intended treachery was discovered, when Artabazos, shooting as arranged, missed his mark and shot a Poteidaian in the shoulder. A crowd gathered round him, as usually happens in war, and they took the arrow out, and when they saw the paper they took it to the generals (there were contingents from the other inhabitants of Pallene present too); but they, having read it and seen who the traitor was, decided not to charge Timoxenos with treason for the sake of the city of Skiōne, that the Skionaians might not bear the name of traitors for ever after.[25]

The message presumably was not addressed to Timoxenos by name, and for the alleged remarkable piece of charity we may understand: 'The other generals felt pretty sure that they knew who the traitor was, but decided to hush the matter up for diplomatic reasons.' The small piece of papyrus, buff in colour, and fairly inconspicuous, was apparently wrapped round the shaft near the notch (why plural is not known), and the feathers then stuck in through holes pierced in the papyrus. Aineias, the fourth-century writer on siege-methods, who is particularly interested in matters of secret communication and security, comments when quoting this passage that Artabazos' bad shot must have been due to 'wind and faulty feathering'. The comment that a crowd gathered round the wounded man 'as happens in war' (O rare Herodotos!) is reproduced by Aineias without comment,[26] thus confirming that it is a true and revealing statement about Greek armies.

The wall, strongly held by the united forces of Pallene, survived all Artabazos' attempts to take it, and the siege dragged on for three months (December to March?). Time was running short; soon Mardonios would be needing to call in his detachments for the spring offensive; but it was very desirable to eliminate the rebellion if possible. And then suddenly an opportunity appeared, in the shape of an exceptional low tide (the tidal rise and fall as a rule in the Aegean amounts to only a few inches), which left a wide belt of sea-bottom and shallows exposed at the end of the wall. The sea showed no sign of coming back, and Artabazos with the prompt opportunism of his nation ordered his troops to go through. But when they were nearly half-way, the sea did come back, in an exceptional flood. 'Some were drowned, not knowing how to swim, and some who did know were

[25] H. viii, 128.

[26] Ain. Taktikos, *Siege-Operations*, 31, 25ff. For the method of communication, cf. Caesar, *Gallic Wvr*, v, 48.

killed by the Poteidaians, who launched boats and went after them.' The whole phenomenon was no doubt caused by an undersea earth-tremor; after their fashion, the Poteidaians were perfectly right in attributing it to their patron god, Poseidon the Earth-Shaker; 'for the Persians had desecrated the temple and image of Poseidon, which stood outside the walls.'

After this, Artabazos called off the siege and marched with his remaining troops to join Mardonios in Thessaly.[27] He was not blamed for the unfortunate result of his last enterprise; on the contrary, he was considered to have shown skill in dealing with Greeks. Xerxes probably remembered this when he selected him later to conduct the negotiations with Pausanias of Sparta.

Mardonios himself passed an anxious winter; the measure of his anxiety being the fact, 'public' and to be accepted, that he consulted Greek oracles.[28] The loss of control over the Cyclades and the revolt of Pallene had increased his isolation; though he still kept a chain of signals by beacon, it is said 'through the islands',[29] perhaps really by way of Pelion, Athos and Lemnos or Samothrace (the historical ancestor of Aeschylus' chain of beacons that bring the news of the fall of Troy to Mykenai by that route? [30]). He had one partial success to console him; winter forced the surrender of some of the Phokians in the hills; he had a small Phokian contingent with him in the following summer. But others remained 'out', and harried his communications 'around Parnassos';[31] that is, in the valley of the 'Boiotian' Kēphisos, that wide strath under the wooded steeps; a scene of 'klephtic' exploits, celebrated in song, against the Turks in their time, as well as of train-wrecking in 1943–4. By that route would have to go all supplies from Thessaly for an army further south. The Persians had chosen, as it proved, a bad place in which to commit atrocities during their advance.

The results of diplomatic activity seemed more promising. Thebes was zealous in the cause, against Athens and Sparta, no doubt preferring, on the usual principle, if one could not be first, the greater and more distant overlord to the nearer and too powerful enemy; gold sent to Sparta's enemies in the Peloponnese seemed not to be spent in vain;

[27] H. viii, 129. Once more the campaign of 432 provides an interesting parallel, in the incident when Aristeus, cut off from the city in an engagement before the walls, succeeded in getting his men back to safety by a dash through the shallows: Thk. i, 63, 1.

[28] H. viii, 133ff (with a story of 'polyglot mediumism' at the Ptoïon in Boiotia, 135).

[29] H. ix. 3. [30] *Agamemnon*, 283ff. [31] H. ix, 17f; 31, 5.

and Argos undertook that her hostility would prevent Sparta from sending an army beyond the Isthmus.[32] The effect of Kleomenes' victory was wearing off. This might make it possible to apply overwhelming pressure to recalcitrant Athens.

Spring came, and on both sides the navies moved to positions where they checked one another. The Greeks mobilised 110 ships, about one-third of the fleet they had at sea in 480; these assembled at Aigina, under the command of King Latychidas.[33] We have no figures for contingents, but Aigina, which sent only a token force of 500 men to the land army, was perhaps strongly represented at sea; Corinth, which made a major effort on land, less so, though her contingent, like those of Sikyon and Troizen receives mention. Athens, which mobilised 8000 armoured men on land, about four-fifths of her army, perhaps, though it does not necessarily follow, sent one-fifth of her 200 ships, and among these, under the command of Xanthippos, probably a high proportion of the 20 allotted to Chalkis, which sent only 400 men to the army, a smaller number than that raised by Eretria and Styra. In general, it seems as if the Congress had agreed that the largest naval contingents in proportion to their strength should be raised by the cities in least danger from the enemy army, whose men would therefore be the least uneasy about going oversea.[34]

[32] H. ix, 12. [33] H. viii, 131.

[34] Here must be mentioned the theory of Munro (*Obs. on the Persian Wars*, 3: *the Campaign of Plataea*, in *JHS* XXIV (1904), pp. 145–7), that the Athenian contingent did not, as Herodotos says, join the fleet at Aigina in the spring, and that when it did join it brought up the numbers to 250, the strength given by Diodoros (xi, 34, 2) for the advance to Delos. Munro suggests that it really joined only later, having been previously withheld, perhaps as a bargaining point against Sparta until the Spartan army moved; perhaps also that the presence and voting-power of the sailors might keep Athens firm against any move to accept Persia's terms, which might be fatally attractive to the agrarian hoplite voters; and that it was this accession of strength which emboldened Latychidas to advance *from* Delos (below, pp. 547f). The theory is attractive and may be close to the truth; but it departs far from the sources (from D.S. as well as from H.) and is excessively ingenious in accounting for H.'s precise numbers; his 110 are said to be the result of subtracting *Herodotos*' 200 Athenian (with Chalkidian) ships in the fleet at Salamis from *Aeschylus*' total of 310. Personally I believe that Athens could not at this time (though she could in 431) put her main fleet and main army into action at one time. The fleet at Salamis had drawn even upon 'knights' like Kimon (p. 362); 'the whole city' had gone to sea; and the marines, surely not much less numerous, in battles in which boarding was frequent, than the 30 Medes and Persians *plus* native marines who served on Xerxes' ships, must then have included the bulk of the hoplites of Plataia.

Munro relies for support upon the fact that in the alleged Decree of Aristeides (n. 18, above), no doubt recorded by Krateros, Xanthippos was named as an ambassador to Sparta, after the invasion of Mardonios, which was after Xanthippos sailed with the fleet according to Herodotos; but there are other reasons for doubting the authenticity of this

To this fleet at Aigina came some political refugees from Ionia, sent on from Sparta, with an account of a land ready to revolt as soon as a liberator appeared; their leader, Hērodotos of Chios, son of Basileides, which probably implies descent from the old royal house, had just headed a conspiracy against the tyrant Strattis, but been betrayed by a confederate and had to fly. If this is the same Strattis who had been with Darius in the Black Sea 34 years before, he must now have been an old man. The persuasions of these Ionians 'with difficulty got the Greeks forward as far as Delos', beyond which lay only Mykonos and then the 25 miles of water west of Ikaria. 'Beyond this they would not venture, being short of topographical intelligence, and imagining the whole area full of enemy troops'; Xerxes was, after all, still at Sardis; and Samos, where the enemy fleet was concentrated, 'seemed as far away as the Pillars of Herakles'.[35] This last remark, which has given rise to some excessively solemn expressions of surprise by commentators, presumably reached the historian from some impatient Ionians, such as his Chian namesake.

Equally passive was the attitude of the Persian fleet, the main body of which sailed from Kyme to concentrate at Samos, just east of Ikaria, joining a squadron which had wintered there. It too was only a fraction of the armada of the year before: 300 ships 'including those from Ionia' as against over 1200, according to Herodotos (viii, 130, 2); and the proportion, though hardly the figures, might well be accurate. The Egyptian squadron had landed its well-armed marines for service under Mardonios directly after Salamis, and presumably gone home forthwith; Xerxes and Akhaimenes may have felt that the presence of the royal satrap and the absence of the fighting men, who could serve as hostages, would be expedient in that restive country. The remnant of the Phoenicians was also sent home, later, according to Herodotos, indeed at the last moment, when the admirals decided that they could not give battle at sea; but it is possible that he is mistaken about the time; Diodoros says that they had gone in a state of near mutiny, 'fearing the threats' of Xerxes, after the execution of their captains for failure at Salamis.[36] There remained only what was left of the Asia

---

decree (n. 49, below). I do not exclude the possibility that Herodotos may be wrong; but the balance of probabilities is in favour of following him rather than Plutarch.

[35] H. viii, 132.

[36] Egyptians, see H. ix, 32; Phoenicians, *ib.* 96; contrast D.S. xi, 19, 4, followed by Beloch, *GG* II², i, p. 59, n. 1.

Minor squadrons; and among these, Greeks now formed a dangerously high proportion of the whole, though they would not mutiny as long as each ship was dominated by 30 Persian marines. Their admirals were Persians, newly promoted; Mardontes, from the command of the 29th infantry contingent (Persian Gulf exiles); Artaÿntes the son of Artakhaies, who 'co-opted' his nephew Ithamitres as third in command, possibly from that of the 13th (Paktyes, from Afghanistan), if he is really the same as 'Artaÿntes the son of Ithamitres' (vii, 67) with a mistake in one or the other place about his father's name (cf. p. 336). The other two surviving admirals of the previous year had probably been superseded for their failure. In support, commanding the troops in Ionia, was Tigranes, the tall and handsome Achaemenid, who had commanded the Medes in 480.[37]

With this shaky fleet, then, Mardontes and his colleagues took post at Samos. They did not venture further west,

> nor was any pressure put upon them to do so, but from their position at Samos they mounted guard over Ionia. . . . Nor did they expect the Greeks to sail to Ionia, but rather that they would stay on the defensive, judging by the fact that they had not pressed the pursuit after Salamis, but been glad to see the last of them. At sea, then, they were in a defeatist frame of mind, but on land they expected Mardonios to be victorious. So, at Samos, they consulted as to whether they could do any damage to the enemy, but at the same time waited eagerly for news as to how Mardonios fared.[38]

'So fear kept them apart', sums up Herodotos. Neither fleet is greatly to be blamed for its passivity. Both, with greatly reduced numbers, were destined to play a secondary rôle. They 'marked' each other, while all hung on the prowess of the armies in Greece.

Not until the spring was far advanced and the rains were over did Mardonios march southward. The Theban leaders advised him not to go further than their country, but from that point of vantage to continue his campaign of subversion and bribery; the methods so successfully used later by Philip of Macedon. But Mardonios was eager to occupy Athens again, and to send his pre-arranged message to Xerxes at Sardis 'by beacons through the islands' that he had done so. So to Athens he marched, forcing the Athenians, bitterly disappointed and

[37] H. ix, 96, 2; cf. vii, 62.

[38] H. viii, 130.

angry that, once more, no Peloponnesian army had come to their aid, to a second last-minute evacuation. 'Ten months after the occupation by Xerxes' (so, end of June, 479) Mardonios entered the forsaken city.[39]

Here he refrained from doing damage at first, while, though in no friendly mood towards the stubborn Athenians, he made one more attempt to get them to accept Xerxes' terms, sending over to Salamis a Hellespontine Greek named Mourychides. At this point at last some Athenians wavered. A councillor named Lykides even proposed that the terms be accepted by the Council and laid before the people for ratification; but in an explosion of rage, which can only be extenuated by remembering the extreme strain to which the whole population was being subjected, 'both the members of the Council and those outside, when they heard of it, fell upon Lykides and stoned him to death; but they let the envoy Mourychides go free'. Immediately afterwards, a mob of women went to Lykides' lodging and stoned to death his wife and children.[40] At the same time, delegations from Athens and from Megara, which was now immediately exposed, went to Sparta with a bitter denunciation of the Peloponnesians' failure to move, once they were reassured by Athens' rejection of the terms offered through Alexander.

The Spartans, once more, were keeping a religious festival; this time, the midsummer Hyakinthia,[41] a festival of the Dying God, long since brought under the protection of the Dorian Apollo.[42] To it, still in the fourth century, we find Sparta making arrangements in the midst of a war for the regiment of Amyklai, where the rites took place, to return from a fighting front, with deplorable military results.[43] We may deplore Sparta's superstition, as perhaps Herodotos did, but

[39] H. ix, 2f; 6.

[40] *ib.* 4f. – The story became part of the Athenian national saga, brought forth time and again in patriotic oratory; cf. Demosthenes *On the Crown*, 204, who calls the victim Kyrsilos; Lykourgos *Agst. Leokr.*, 122, who cites a decree condemning him to death, but avoids giving a name. As Habicht says (*Hermes*, LXXXIX, p. 21), what Herodotos describes is a lynching, and it seems unlikely that there was any decree; though it is not absolutely inconceivable that the murder might have been legitimised retrospectively. The different names given suggest that we are dealing with oral tradition; and the text of the decree was probably one of the would-be edifying forgeries of the 4th century.

[41] H. ix, 7, 1.

[42] For the rites, cf. Paus. iii, 19, 3. (Was Hyakinthos, the Adonis-like Young God of the old Aegean world, first identified with the Hellenic Young God, and later, when the incompatibility impressed itself, explained as a youth beloved by him?)

[43] Xen. *Hell.* iv, 5, 11; Paus. iii, 10, 1.

we cannot dismiss as a mere excuse their statement that 'they considered it of the utmost importance to give the god his due'.[44] They undoubtedly believed that things would not go well with them if they failed to do so.

As to the more general reasons for the slowness of the Spartans and their allies to move even earlier, when Mardonios marched and the Athenians expected them, it is clear that we do not know the whole story. Argos, as we have seen (p. 500), is said to have promised Mardonios that she would keep the Spartans from going north of the Isthmus at all; and if many Spartiates were short-sightedly more nervous about the lesser danger within their peninsula than about the greater danger without, they were not nervous about nothing. Even without Persian support for their enemies, they had a major Argive and Arcadian war and probably also a rebellion in Messenia on their hands within ten years.[45] This is the background to the inter-allied negotiations of the preceding months, of which we have only a glimpse from the Athenian side; no doubt they were often tough. The Spartans probably really thought, selfishly perhaps but not unnaturally, that it would be the best strategy to make Mardonios' position untenable by sea-borne expeditions to the coasts of Thrace and Ionia, while the loyal Peloponnesians held the Isthmus, provisioned the displaced Athenians in accordance with their promise, and 'contained' the Medizers within. If to us they seem short-sighted, isolationist, even Maginot-minded ('for their wall across the Isthmus was now being given battlements' [46]), their most deep-seated motive was an intelligible one: the desire not, if it could be avoided, to commit their limited man-power to a severe and bloody campaign.

Nevertheless, it was a short-sighted as well as a selfish policy. It took Athens' threat to withdraw from the war to turn the scale at Sparta; and it may be true that the advice of a more disinterested ally, Sparta's old friend Chileos of Tegea, also contributed to the decision.[47] It is usually commented that it did not take a wise Arcadian to point out that Athens' defection would 'open the back-doors' behind the Isthmus

[44] H. *ib.*; note the (ironic?) δή at the beginning of the sentence.

[45] Isokr. *Archidamos*, 99; cf. H. ix, 35, 2; the approx. date is certain, though no exact date is given. The rebellion in Messenia may also have broken out at this time (nine years before the 'tenth year' of Thk. i, 103, which is before the Egyptian expedition in his narrative, which is usually in chronological order) though it only spread to Laconia after the great earthquake of 464.

[46] H. ix, 7.

[47] H. ix, 35, 2.

defences; but this need not have been the whole of Chileos' advice. Tegea ten years later was in alliance with Argos; and the Arcadian statesman could give needed advice on the state of feeling in his native land now; to assure the Spartans that if they gave a bold lead, Tegea would stand by her old alliance rather than desert it for a new one; perhaps also that western Arcadia would, at worst, stand aloof. Within Sparta too, there must have been already a strong party in favour of a campaign on land; for, once the decision to march was taken, it was carried out with a will, and with an efficiency that indicates preparation well in advance. Prominent among those who had perhaps been straining at the leash were two princes of the house of Anaxandridas: Pausanias the son of Kleombrotos, to whom was committed the command in the campaign, since his cousin King Pleistarchos, the son of Leonidas and Gorgo, was still a boy, and Euryanax the son of Dorieus, whom Pausanias coöpted as his colleague.[48] In any case, the decision once taken, 'the Lakedaimonians and their Allies' swept into action with impressive speed and power.

The Athenian ambassadors, says the story, had asked for one more interview with the Ephors, intending to give notice that in view of Sparta's attitude the Athenians would abandon the struggle and 'make such terms as they could'. They must have noticed that morning that the town seemed quiet; but the ephors surprised them with the news that no less than 5000 Spartiates (perhaps two-thirds of the whole levy, estimated at 8000 by Damaratos, according to Herodotos) had marched overnight, and should by now be at Oresteion on the Arcadian frontier. An equal number of 'chosen men' of the other Lakedaimonian townships marched that same day, with the ambassadors; their mobilisation can*not* have been conducted overnight; and with the Spartiates are said to have gone no less than 35,000 Helots, 'every man armed for war', as light-armed troops, equipped probably with javelins.[49]

[48] *ib.* 10, 3.

[49] H. ix, 10f; Damaratos' 8000, vii, 234, 2; the Helots, ix, 29, 1 (whether the estimated further 5000 light-armed with the *perioikoi* also ranked as helots is uncertain).

It is at this point that Plutarch (*Ar.* 10, end) cites sources which claimed to name the ambassadors: Idomeneus named Aristeides, and quoted his repartee to the Ephors ('This is an ill-timed jest . . .'); 'but in the Decree of Aristeides, not he himself but Kimon and Xanthippos and Myronides are named as ambassadors'. Plut., as often, deserves our gratitude for naming his sources. Idomeneus of Lampsakos (Jacoby no. 338), a friend of Epikouros, is not an impressive authority. He wrote *On the Athenian Demagogues*, a book full of improbable slanders, such as that Themistokles drove into the Athenian Agorá with four courtesans yoked to his chariot (a joke derived from a comedy?) or, in

The secret mobilisation, deceiving even Sparta's friends, and perhaps also the choice of route, all the way up the Eurōtas valley, instead of the shorter way to Tegea by Sellasia and Karyai, may have been calculated to keep Argos in the dark as long as possible; and by the time the columns were necessarily passing close to the Argive frontier further north, it was too late to interfere. All Argos' neighbours, members of Sparta's league since Sepeia where not earlier, were in arms; once they were given the word, in their small territories, mobilisation could be complete in a day. Altogether, the Isthmus region and the north-east Peloponnese mobilised and sent to the front over 17,000 armoured men,[50] a much larger force from a smaller area than Sparta from her broad domains; which is, incidentally, a reflection on the social effects of Sparta's triumphant militarism. With the Spartans in eastern Arcadia, between Argos and the Arcadian highlands, Argos was helpless; and in dismay the Argives sent 'the best long-distance runner they could find' to tell Mardonios at Athens that 'the young men have marched from Lakedaimon, and the Argives are unable to stop them'.[51] How this runner was able to get through, and why he was not stopped at the Isthmus, is a mystery; but Greek security was primitive, and either he must have passed by misrepresenting his errand, or have slipped past in a boat and then taken to the Megarian hills.

Tegea proved loyal to her alliance, as did the little Arcadian Orchomenos; Mantineia, between the two and hostile to Tegea, moved at last, but was slow with her mobilisation and missed the battle, as did the men of Elis, with further to march. Both states, after the event, banished their generals;[52] evidence that their lateness was not unconnected with internal tensions. It is of some interest that the same states, Elis, Mantineia and most of western Arcadia, were those which

another version, *in* his chariot (Ath. xii, 533d; xiii, 576c). However, he did not merely mention Ar. at Sparta in passing, but had a story about him. The alternative version, presumably from Krateros, would be of great interest, if trustworthy; but all three names arouse suspicion; that of Xanthippos because H. says he was at that time with the fleet, and the other two because both men (Kimon, under 20 in 489, Plut. *Kim.* 4, 4; Myronides, who brings Perikles the news from Athens years after his death, i.e. died after him (Eupolis' *Demoi ap.* Plut. *Per.* 24)) seem to be improbably young. Ambassadors (*presbeutai*, 'elders') were usually men of ripe age; sometimes decrees specified that they should be over 50, e.g. *IG* I² 57 (*GHI*, no. 65) or the 'Congress Decree', Plut. *Per.* 17 (*ATL* II, D. 12). The names of his companions contribute to making it risky to base any theory about the movements of the Athenian fleet upon these alleged movements of Xanthippos; and the existence of variant traditions probably means simply that in the fourth century the names of these ambassadors were not known.

[50] Details, p. 523. [51] H. ix, 12. [52] *ib.* 77.

combined with Argos against Sparta in 420–18; though on the other hand, when Tegea for once combined with Argos and the rest of Arcadia around 472–69, Mantineia stood aside. In the circumstances of 479, it is clear that the Peloponnese could not be left unguarded by the allies. The Spartans left as home-guard perhaps a third of the Spartiatai (the oldest and youngest?) and probably more of the Lakedaimonian *perioikoi* than the 5000 'picked men' who marched out; and the immediate neighbours of Argos, especially Tiryns and Mykenai, cannot have left their walls so unguarded as to constitute an immediate temptation.

The expeditionary force was, in fact, large enough. That it was provisioned at the front was no small feat of organization; and over 30,000 Greek armoured spearmen, even though the supporting light-armed troops were inferior, could defeat Mardonios' army if only they could get at it. The tactical problem would be how to succeed in closing with the more mobile enemy.

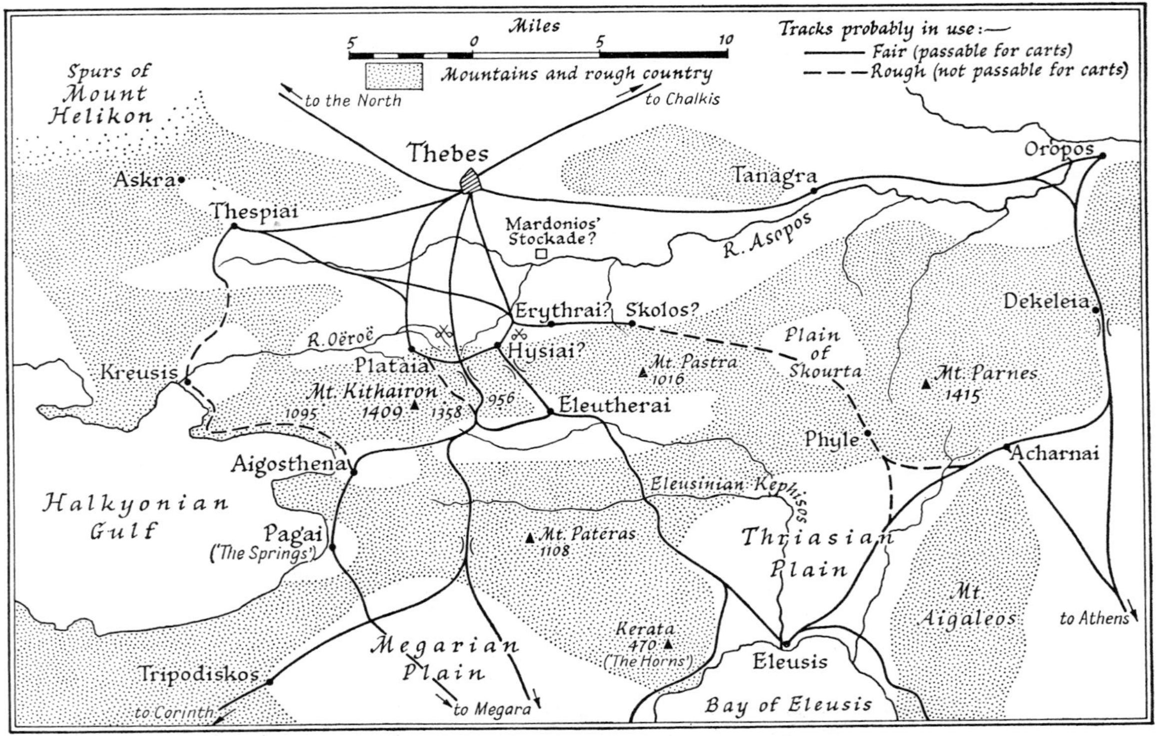

The Boiotian Border

Heights are given in metres

Chapter XXIV

Crowning Mercy

(*Plataia, 479*)

WARNED in good time of the storm that was coming up, Mardonios evacuated Athens. First he destroyed, as thoroughly as possible, the city, thus far held as a hostage. Fire was set to what would burn in the villages too; to holy Eleusis among the rest.[1] The Athenians on Salamis saw the smoke go up, and prayed to the Two Great Goddesses to witness these things.

The Athenians had also been thinking that the Thriasian Plain, inland from Eleusis, would be a good and a likely place for a battle.[2] If Mardonios gave battle there against a Peloponnesian army advancing from Megara, as once the Thessalian cavalry had done when fighting for Hippias, the Athenians might land behind his flank. But Mardonios was too wary to be caught like that. He had advanced, it would appear, by the direct road through Eleutherai, and had seen that the long stretch through the hill country, over two ranges with an intermontane plain between them, provided defiles, where his rear troops might be badly jammed if forced to retreat; while things would be still worse if a Greek force, by way of Pāgai and Aigosthena or the way through the Patéras range, north of Megara, seized a pass in his rear. He got out, says Herodotos (ix, 13ff),

> because Attica was not cavalry country, and if he were defeated there, there was no way out except by a defile which a few men could hold against him; so he determined to retire on Thebes, and there give battle before a friendly city and in cavalry country. So Mardonios began to withdraw; but when he had started, he received a further message that another force – an advanced guard of 1000 Lakedaimonians – had reached Megara. At this he formed the

[1] H. ix, 13; cf. 65.
[2] *ib.* 7, end (where the plan is to *meet* the Persians coming from Boiotia; cf. oracle (if genuine) *ap.* Plut. *Ar.* 11.

project of catching them first, if possible; he turned his army and led it against Megara, and his advanced cavalry overran the whole Megarid. This was the furthest point to the west reached by the Persians in Europe. Then, receiving news that the Greek main body had reached the Isthmos, he retreated by way of Dekeleia; the Boiotarchs [the Boiotian federal executive] sent for local men of the Asopos region, who guided him to Sphendále [in north-east Attica] and thence to Tanagra.

Obviously the whole army did not really turn back for the raid into the Megarid; rather, Mardonios set his baggage-train and infantry in motion, while with a mounted force he conducted what was probably rather a reconnaissance in force, but found no enemy on the road to Aigosthena. Some of his men were cut off by the Megarians; Pausanias (i, 44, 4; cf. 40, 2) was shown a rock-face or rather, perhaps, a sand-stone bluff, near the road to Pagai, with arrows sticking in it, which were said to have been shot into it by these Persians in a panic, in the night before their destruction. The 1000 Lakedaimonians, one may guess, had perhaps been those originally on guard at the Isthmus wall; but Herodotos *includes* them later in the 10,000 of his Spartan total.

From Tanagra, Mardonios turned up the Asopos to the neighbourhood of Skōlos, a hill village up against the foot of the lower, eastward continuation of the Kithairon range. It was in Theban territory,[3] and about 4½ miles east of the Asopos crossing on the road from Plataia to Thebes.[4] Herodotos continues:

> Here he reft of their trees the estates of the Thebans, friendly though they were . . . under stress of necessity, to construct a fort for his army, which might serve as a refuge in case of defeat in the field. His army encamped along the line of the River Asopos, from Erythrai past Hysiai as far as the land of Plataia; the fenced enclosure, however, was not as large as that, but some ten *stadia* to each side.

[3] H. ix, 15, 2; mentioned in Homer's Catalogue, *Il.* ii, 497; a bleak place, Str. ix, 408; but I surmise that the proverbial line, q. by Str. *ib.*, 'To Skōlos nor willingly go, nor follow another', is Athenian, and refers rather to the way thither, by Phyle fort and the plain of (modern) Skourta; a hill track, highly unsuitable for a large hoplite force, though Thrasyboulos and his gallant 70 probably used it in 403. As a pass for Mardonios to guard against in this campaign (as suggested by Munro, *JHS* XXIV, p. 154), it may be ignored.

[4] Paus. ix, 4, 4; the best topographical clue. Skōlos is identified after careful 'potsherding' by Pritchett (*AJA* LXI, 1957, p. 13) at the site of a *metóchi* (farm-priory) of the Monastery of Hosios Meletios (which lies to the south, on the other side of the Pastra ridge), and c. 1150 metres west of Darimári village.

The encampment in the open, holding the river line and extending for some five miles along it, faced the passes on the main routes from the Isthmus and western Attica, by which the Greeks advanced, and this position was presumably taken up when they appeared. The Persians did not occupy the villages named, all of which stood south of the river, in typical positions for Greek *polismata*, along the Kithairon hill-foot; it was their lands which extended down to the river, as well as up the mountain, giving access both to high and low pasture and to wood and water, like the old parishes in many parts of Britain.[5] The fort was somewhat further east, and since there was no need to pay special attention to watching the Phyle–Skolos path, quite the worst of the routes from Attica, we may assume that it was sited so as to keep in touch with Thebes and, if the Greeks, now reported massing in large numbers, tried to out-flank Mardonios by using both the direct route and that by Tanagra, to secure a position between them. The size of the enclosure, an area of some 900 acres, if approximately square, and evidently intended to suffice for the whole army with its horses and baggage, gives some clue to the size of Mardonios' army. The area is 12 to 14 times that of a Roman camp for one legion; and the Romans may have economised space better by superior orderliness. It would thus be consistent with an army of the order of magnitude of 60–70,000 men, of whom 10,000 might be cavalry; if we assume more cavalry, then the infantry would have to be reduced by at least twice as many. This approximation is exclusive of the Boiotians, whose base was the city of Thebes, and probably of other Greek allies. Man for man, the Persians were probably outnumbered by the great Peloponnesian-Athenian army; though the Greek light-armed with their javelins were inferior in armament to the Iranian infantry with bow and short sword, and the Persians had in their cavalry an advantage to set against the Greek advantage in armoured foot. Nevertheless, Mardonios knew that he could win no victory unless the Greeks either exposed themselves rashly or suffered a commissariat breakdown. His refusal to give battle at Eleusis, with defiles behind him, like his fortification, shows that he by no means took victory for granted; and Herodotos heard a story from one Thersandros of Orchomenos, of a conversation with a Persian officer at an inter-allied banquet in Thebes, after the retreat

[5] E.g. those under the Chiltern escarpment, as Myres (*H., Father of History*, p. 286) characteristically observed.

from Attica, which revealed that many Persian officers were pessimistic and doing their duty in a mood of stoical fatalism.[6]

The Greeks, with their whole army on foot, and with their armoured hoplites, stronger in defence than any Iranians, had no similar objection to hills in their rear, and advanced on Thebes by the main road through Eleusis and Eleutherai. Aristeides with 8000 Athenians joined them at Eleusis; among the other Athenian generals are said to have been two younger men destined to fame, Leokrates and Myronides; and at Eleusis the united army renewed the sacrifices and prayers for victory, which the Peloponnesians had already offered at the Isthmus.[7] It will have been here that they took the oath, famous thereafter as the Oath of Plataia; an oath of true comradeship, to fight together against the Men of Unintelligible Speech, which Greeks were to remember, wistfully or bitterly, when the national alliance had almost immediately fallen apart, and when attempts to reconstitute its brief unity always shipwrecked on the rocks of envy and of the desire of local states for temporary advantage. Of it we have versions, differing in detail and not earlier than the fourth century, but one of them cut on stone not later. How faithfully they preserve the phraseology of what was said or chanted in 479, we cannot say; but considering that there certainly must have been an oath taken for this purpose at this time; that our oldest version refers to an original, *written* oath-formula; and that later men would try to remember it and speakers appeal to it, we may judge that there is in the surviving texts enough of archaism and enough that is not Athenian to suggest a significant resemblance to the original.

What follows is, first, a translation of the version inscribed in the fourth century, as an offering by Dion son of Dion of Acharnai, Priest of Ares and of Athena Areia, in the sanctuary of those deities in his native Deme, as the preamble tells us. Words marked by an asterisk are discussed in the text below. Before it stood a text of the oath sworn (we do not know how old it is) by young Athenians in the fourth century, when called up to enter the Corps of Cadets (*ephēboi*) and do their two years' military training (not quoted here); then the heading to the Oath of Plataia:

The Oath, which the Athenians swore, when about to give battle to the barbarians:

[6] H. ix, 16.

[7] *ib.*, 19; Leokrates and Myronides, Plut. *Ar.* 20.

'I will fight to the death, and I will not count my life more precious than freedom. I will not leave my officer*, the commander of my Regiment* or Company*, either alive or dead. I will not withdraw unless my commanders lead me back, and I will do whatsoever the Generals order. I will bury the dead of those who have fought as my allies, on the field, and will not leave one of them unburied. After defeating the barbarians in battle, I will tithe* the city of the Thebans; and I will never destroy Athens or Sparta or Plataia* or any of the cities which have fought as our allies, nor will I consent to their being starved, nor cut them off from running water*, whether we be friends or at war.

'And if I keep well the oath, as it is written, may my city have good health; but if not, may it have sickness; and may my city never be sacked; but if not, may it be sacked; and may my land give increase; but if not, may it be barren; and may the women bring forth children like their fathers; but if not, monsters; and may the cattle bring forth after their kind; but if not, monsters.'

After taking this oath, they covered with their shields the sacrificial offerings and uttered the Imprecation at the call of a trumpet, invoking the curse upon themselves, if after swearing it they should transgress any of that to which they had sworn, and not keep well the oath as it was written.[8]

[8] Trn. from the text of G. Daux in *Studies pres. to D. M. Robinson*, II, p. 777 (from which a few corrections should be made in that in Tod, *GHI* II, no. 204); from a marble stele found at Menídi (the ancient Acharnai), 1932, publ. by L. Robert in *Études épigr. et philologiques*, pp. 296ff, pl. ii.

The orator Lykourgos calls this 'the pledge which they exchanged *at Plataia*'. The version preserved in his speech (*Leokr.* 81) begins at 'I will not count . . .', etc., and differs in other ways. The Athenian and Spartan technical words for battalion and company (or platoon) commanders are replaced by the colourless word 'leaders'; and likewise, no Greek city is named, but the undertaking is given, 'I will not destroy any city of those that have fought for Hellas, but I will "tithe" all those which have taken the part of the barbarian' (cf. H. vii, 132). Finally, it adds the curious undertaking *not* to restore the temples destroyed by the invader, which is discussed below, p. 515. Our third version (in D.S. xi, 29, 3, who ascribes it to the Greeks assembled at the Isthmus) gives almost the same text as Lykourgos; except that it omits the vow of vengeance on the Medizing states altogether.

The existence of the differing versions is of importance, since it shows us in how cavalier a manner Greeks could treat texts, when professing to quote them; simplifying; substituting modernisms for technical words; omitting what was unwelcome to the quoter (the Priest of Ares at Acharnai, where the temple seems to have been built soon after the conclusion of peace with Persia in 449, did not wish to remind his audience of a vow to leave temples lying waste); or singling out names for mention (Athens, Sparta, Plataia, Thebes) out of (I would guess) long lists of loyal and Medizing states, which the Congress must have had, and which may have been read out to the units taking the oath. An alternative method of dealing with the lists was to suppress them and simply say 'all allies' and 'all Medizers', as do Lykourgos, or his editor, and Diodoros; it is perhaps significant that their texts differ verbally just at this point.

Documents were thus treated in exactly the same manner as reported speeches; a method,

* Officer . . . Company: in the Greek, 'Taxiarch or Enōmotarch'; the former an *Athenian* battalion-commander, the latter a *Spartan* 'sworn-unit'-commander of about 50 men. The point is, in each case, 'my Officer', the soldier's immediate leader in battle. The survival of this Spartan word in an Athenian text is one ground for accepting it as more than a mere literary composition; and the fact that the Athenians have no commanders of units smaller than the tribal *taxeis* is characteristic of the difference between the Spartan and all other Greek city-state armies.

* Tithe: i.e. destroy, and dedicate to the gods a tenth of the spoil; cf. p. 345, above.

* Plataia: the mention of this city specially, and alone among the lesser allies, suggests an oath taken immediately before the battle, in Plataian territory; cf. the oath to which the Plataians appeal when besieged by the Peloponnesians in 428–7, Thucydides ii, 71, iii, 59; but the elaborate ritual suggests rather the circumstances mentioned by Herodotos at Eleusis, and the undertaking not to sack Athens (odd, for an Athenian oath!) and Sparta suggests oaths exchanged by the Spartans, as leaders of the Peloponnesian League, and Athens, not represented at the sacrifices at the Isthmus.

* Running water: this undertaking, to mitigate the savagery of war

---

outrageous to modern canons, which nevertheless, in the hands of Thucydides, could give us Perikles' Funeral Oration. It was a method which had been the only one available in the pre-literate past, in which traditions were preserved only by story-telling and poetry, and one which Greek historical writing was slow to outgrow; a disastrous method, as is universally recognized, in the hands of historians whose chief training had been in artistic prose composition (rhetoric), as Polybios complained in his time, and also Theopompos (J 115 F 153), who specifically mentioned this Oath as an example of an 'Athenian fake' (*katapseudetai*). Surely we must take Theopompos seriously, to the effect that the epigraphic text is not an accurate copy of a contemporary document; but it does not follow that it was a cold-blooded forgery *de toutes pièces*. It represents a fallible, but a real, patriotic tradition. Athenians in the 4th century believed that their ancestors in 479 had sworn something like this; and Herodotos tells us the occasion, in the offering of solemn sacrifice, not only at the Isthmus but, when the Athenians joined, at Eleusis. A classical Athenian version of such an allied, military oath is a historical text of real value, though *it is not an original document* of the Persian Wars in any sense that modern historical scholarship would recognize.

The matter has an obvious bearing on the question of the degree of authenticity to be ascribed to the 'Decree of Themistokles' (pp. 366–77ff, above); on which Berve in *Sitzb. d. Bayer. Ak.*, 1961, Heft 3, rightly comments that we are not confronted with 'nur die Alternative von Bewahrung des authentischen Wortlautes und völliger Unechtheit'.

See further Habicht in *Hermes* LXXXIX, 11f, Sealey in *JHS* LXXX (both sceptical); Raubitschek in London Inst. of Cl. Studies *Bulletin* No. 8 (who goes further than I would in accepting the Oath as a document).

between old allies, also appears in the oath of the ancient Amphiktyony of Thermopylai and Delphi,[9] and may have been borrowed from it.

The inscription, with its commemoration of old ties with Sparta and Plataia and old enmity against Thebes, is redolent of the mid-fourth century, when Athens and Sparta were once more allied against Thebes, and Thebes had expelled the Plataians (373).[10]

The two other versions, preserved by the orator Lykourgos (or his editor) and by Diodoros, give texts differing from each other only in a few details, but from the inscription much more (see n. 8); omitting 'I will fight to the death' and the 'Amphiktyonic' clause about starvation and running water; simplifying 'taxiarch or enōmotarch' to the colourless 'my leaders'; omitting the Imprecation with its colourful archaisms, but *adding* at the end, 'and I will restore none of the temples which have been burned and cast down, but will leave them to remain as a memorial to men hereafter, of the impiety of the barbarians'. It is a curious clause. No temples belonging to the Peloponnesians had been destroyed; and one might almost suspect it of having emanated from the Spartans, as unenthusiastic about the rebuilding of Athens, so awkwardly placed outside their peninsula, as they were later about its refortification.[11] Themistokles, who wished that the Athenians would abandon their inland city and migrate to the headland of Peiraieus,[12] might have concurred for his own reasons; but it is a little surprising that Aristeides (if the clause is genuine) consented to it. But it is difficult to see why a forger should have invented such a clause; and it is a fact that when the Athenians, shortly after the war, laid the foundations of a new temple for Athena (though they did not complete it till after the peace of 449) they did not do so on the old site, but on a new one on the highest part, not the centre, of their Acropolis.

The Athenians, as we have seen, had probably expected Mardonios to give battle in the plain of Eleusis, and are said to have obtained an oracle from Delphi (which could easily be reached from the Corinthian Gulf) promising them victory there, 'fighting in their own land, in the Plain of Demeter Eleusinia and of the Maiden'; but it is added that when they advanced into Plataian territory, Arimnēstos the Plataian

[9] Aischines *On the Embassy*, 43; cf. *Lyric Age*, p. 34.

[10] So Daux in *Rev. d'Arch.*, 1941; M. Sordi in *BCH* LXXXI (1957).

[11] Thk. i. 90, 2.

[12] *ib.* 93, 7.

general, inspired by Zeus in a dream, persuaded his fellow-citizens to take up the boundary-stones of his country's frontier with Attica, thus more formally 'giving themselves to Athens' (cf. p. 173) than in the alliance of forty years before.[13] There was, moreover, a temple, said to have been already old, of Demeter of Eleusis in the destined field of operations, near Hysiai, where the road to Thebes descended from the hills.[14]

As the Greek advanced guard topped the Eleutherai Pass, they had on their left and right the steep, northern slopes of the Kithairon-Pastra-Parnes range, descending steeply to the fields along the Asopos. Their view extended over the whole plain of southern Boiotia, to Helikon and distant Parnassos. Thebes was in clear sight, and nearer, just beyond the river, the great, square Persian palisade. They descended the road to Erythrai, and deployed along the lower slopes of the hills, covering the advance of those who descended after them and extended the line to left and right. Mardonios gave them every opportunity to descend further, but finding them too wary he decided to harass them where they were:

> He sent against them the whole of his cavalry, commanded by Masistios, a distinguished officer among the Persians[15] . . . ; he rode a horse of the Nēsaian breed, with a golden bridle and other splendid adornments. The cavalry rode up to the Greek line, discharging their missiles by squadrons, doing much damage and calling them women.[16] It was the Megarians who held the position where the ground was easiest for an attacker, and on them that the brunt of the cavalry attack fell. They were hard pressed, and sent a herald to the Greek commanders,

calling for support. This was given by the Athenians, who were probably now (certainly later) next in line, and possessed what may have been the only regularly organized Greek archer regiment;

[13] Plut. *Ar.* 11; the list of Plataian heroes and local nymphs, to whom the allies are recommended to sacrifice (*ib.*), if really from an oracle of 479, is presumably not from the same one, though that is what Plut. says.

[14] Plut. *ib.*; H. ix, 57, and How, *ad loc.*, 62, 65; Paus, ix, 4, 3, and Frazer, *Paus.* V, pp. 5, 21. Two inscriptions (*IG* VII, nos. 1670, 1671) found at Kriekouki, where the modern main road descends, presumably come from this temple.

[15] H. ix, 20; last mentioned commanding the (28th) Caucasian infantry contingent. Like Artabazos, Tigranes, Mardontes (qq. v., index) and others, he had evidently been promoted in the extensive reshuffle in the Persian command, of which we have evidence between the campaigns of 480 and 479. Cf. p. 542, n. 81.

[16] Is this the first case recorded of badinage between trousered and kilted men?

probably under orders from Pausanias, though Herodotos makes a great story of their heroically volunteering when the other Greeks hung back.[17] The reinforcements consisted of 'the élite unit of 300 men under Olympiodoros, son of Lampon, taking with them the archers'. It looks like a 'task force' specially adapted for advanced-guard action. Since the Athenians, when the army moved westward shortly afterwards, were on the left, furthest from the pass by which they had come, it may well be that they, with their archers and with detailed knowledge of the country, had headed the advance from Eleusis, followed by the Megarians; the cavalry attack, promptly launched, will then have come when the Athenians had deployed westward, off the road, leaving the Megarians astride of it, and when the direction of their movement had shown Mardonios that the Greeks would not come down on to the plain if he waited longer.

Herodotos' account of what followed clearly comes from an eyewitness:

> The fighting went on for some time, but the end of it was this: As the cavalry continued their attack by squadrons, the horse of Masistios, as he rode ahead of the line, received an arrow in the flank, and reared up in agony and threw him. The Athenians swarmed in on him, dismounted as he was, and captured the horse, and killed Masistios, though he fought for his life, and they did not succeed at once; for he was wearing a corselet of golden scales, with a crimson tunic over it. Thrusts on the corselet were ineffective; but finally someone, realising this, hit him in the eye, and he fell and died. The other horsemen did not realise what had happened; they were just turning their horses, and did not see either his fall from his horse or his last moments. Only when they halted did they realise that they were without a commander; and then they shouted to one another and charged all together to recover the body; and the Athenians, seeing them coming, no longer by squadrons but all in a mass, called for the rest of the army. While the main body of infantry was coming, there was a furious fight over the corpse; as long as the Three Hundred were unsupported, they were outmatched, and began to fall back from it; but when the main body intervened, the cavalry in turn gave way. They failed to pick up the body, and suffered additional losses; so they fell back to a distance

[17] *ib.* 21. – Is this a case where the story which reached H. has been affected by oratory, in connection with Athens' later 'rescue' of Megara from the Corinthians (Thk. i, 103, 4)?

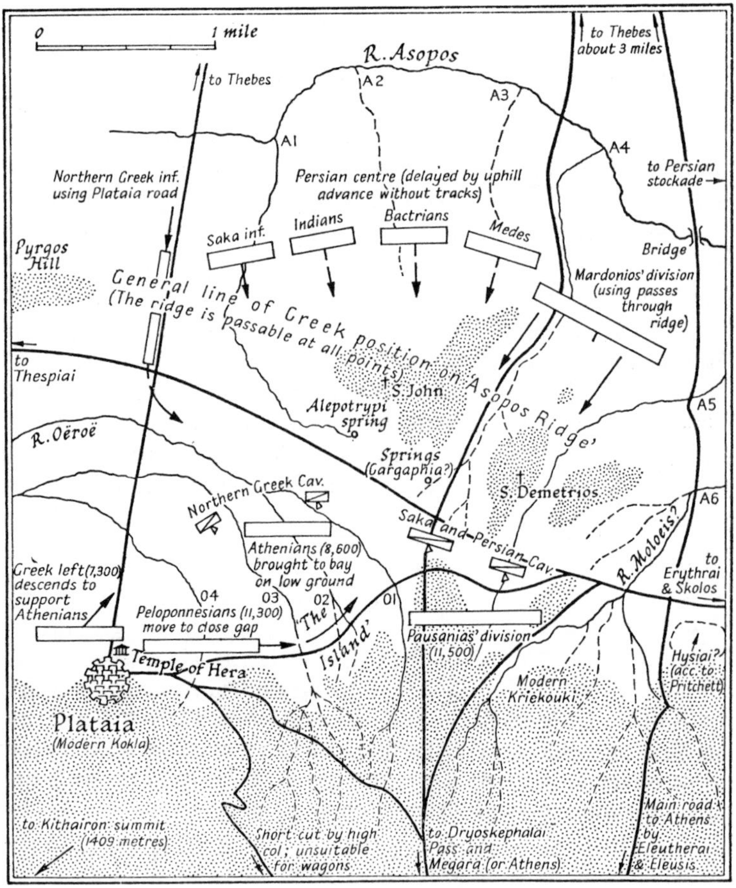

The Battle of Plataia

The gentle undulations of the land north of the Kithairon hill-foot (south of the cart road which I have postulated, from Plataia to Erythrai) are difficult to indicate by contour-lines, unless these are made so numerous as to make map-reading difficult. Here only one is given: Grundy's contour-line '240 feet above the level of the bridge on the Athens–Thebes road', or about 330 *metres* above sea-level. The roads indicated are all, strictly speaking, conjectural; they show the probable lines of ancient routes, all passable for carts, except that to the 'high col' south-east of Plataia.

The lengths of frontage of Greek divisions, in their probable approximate positions on the morning of the battle, are computed in terms of the 'parade strengths' given by Herodotos, reckoning eight men per yard. The amount of space occupied by Mardonios' troops can only be guessed.

Tributaries of the Asopos and Oëroë are numbered, after Grundy; the position of Hysiai is given according to Pritchett, though this identification can only be accepted with reserve; the village may have underlain the modern Kriekouki (now officially, but misleadingly, called Erythrai).

Visitors to the site are warned that the most conspicuous ancient remains of Plataia (modern Kokla) are further north (further into the plain) than the probable fifth-century site of the city.

> of some 400 paces, and after a short consultation, leaderless as they were, decided to ride back to Mardonios. And on their arrival the whole army, and especially Mardonios personally, made a great mourning for Masistios; they cut short their hair and the mane of their horses and baggage-animals, and lifted up their voices in lamentations that echoed all over Boiotia; for they had lost a man who, of all after Mardonios, was of most account with the Persians and their king. Thus the barbarians did honour to the fallen Masistios after their manner.
>
> Meanwhile the Greeks, greatly heartened at having met and repulsed the attack of the cavalry, put the body on a wagon and paraded it along their lines; it was worth seeing for its stature and beauty . . . and men broke ranks to go and see Masistios.[18]

It is a very Greek conclusion to this Homeric episode.

By this time all the Greeks who were present (for several contingents were still far away) had had time to deploy; and Pausanias decided to move into the territory of Plataia, 'for the sake of a better camping-site than at Erythrai', where fear of the cavalry kept them confined to the hillside, 'and better water supplies'. The farthest end of the proposed position was only four miles away, and his trained eye could take it all in from the hillside above the pass. Over there to the left, the upper waters of the Asopos flowed further from the foot of Kithairon; and parallel to its south bank, concealing the river from where he stood, lay a chain of knolls, long enough and not too broken by the cols between them to admit occupation by his whole army in battle array. The chain was about two miles north of the foot of the mountain, on which, on a defensible spur, stood the deserted city of Plataia; and the space between, a shallow saucer, with drainage into the westward-flowing Oëroë,[19] not into the Asopos, gave promise of space where men could move about and food-convoys unload, in safety behind the lines. There were springs there too, as Pausanias' local allies could tell him, and as his own eye could see, indicated by clumps of trees and patches of vegetation still green amid the brown of the late summer fields. Of less

[18] H. ix, 22–5.

[19] The Oëroë, now called Livadhostro stream from a village on its lower course, has, according to Myres (who was a trained geologist), 'cut back' and captured the drainage from Kithairon near Plataia, which in a past geological age flowed north in parallel valleys to the Asopos. Relics of these valleys are the notches in the range of knolls, now for the most part dry, though still carrying a little drainage to the Asopos (tributaries A1 to A5 in Grundy's map); Myres, *H. Father of History*, p. 286.

interest to him, perhaps, but playing a part in what followed, was the fact that a 'long ridge' – nothing more than a strip of comparatively level, comparatively high and dry lowland, between the headwaters of the Oëroë and the streams that flow from the pass to join the Asopos – ran out from the well-marked foot of the mountains towards the nearer and higher of the range of knolls, though not to join them without crossing a perceptible depression, draining to the Asopos. The gently undulating and small-featured lowland to the west of this watershed, between Kithairon and the knolls, contained the home fields of Plataia, and probably gave its name to that city, often written in the plural, Plataiai, 'the Broads' – as compared perhaps with the narrower lowland territories of Erythrai (named for red scars on the hills behind it) and Hysiai.

On these knolls, then, it seemed propitious to Pausanias and Euryanax to await their reinforcements. If Mardonios would attack them there, they were confident that their hoplites could beat him; if not, when all the contingents were in – which would swell their strength to a total, at least 'on paper', of over 40,000 armoured men,[20] it would be time enough to think of a further forward movement; though any such movement in the plain, in face of the enemy's cavalry, would have to be undertaken with circumspection. The present westward move would mean uncovering the foot of the main pass at Erythrai; but there is a second pass, reached from the south by branching from the Eleusis–Thebes road, from the intermontane plain of Eleutherai to modern Villia, just south of the main range, by which ran the customary route from Plataia to Athens. It was called by Athenians the Oak-Heads, Dryoskephalai, and by Boiotians the Three Heads; though the attempt to identify features that would account for the latter name has given varied results.[21] The descent from this pass to

[20] For Herodotos' detailed figures (below) add up to 38,700 without the Eleians and Mantineians, who arrived too late.

[21] Cf. the amusing remarks of Pritchett in *AJA* LXI, p. 21. – It is quite certain that Grundy, to whose work all local topographical studies owe so much, was mistaken in identifying Dryoskephalai with the more easterly (modern main road) pass by Erythrai (*GPW*, 447). The evidence is in Thk. iii, 24, where the escapers from Plataia *avoid* the direct route, and take the road to Thebes, northward. They see the pursuers, with lanterns, taking the mountain road to Dryoskephalai (clearly the obvious route); while they, turning after ¾ of a mile, reach 'the road to Erythrai and Hysiai', where they 'take to the hills'; cf. Myres, *H. Father of History*, 285f; Pritchett, *loc. cit.* On the other hand, the high col (900 metres?) still further west, just south of which, on a path, the present writer in 1946 stepped into a wolf-trap, (indicating perhaps traffic of a sort), may be ignored as

Plataia, the Greek commanders thought, would still be covered, and by it the belated contingents and the large convoys organized to feed their great army could still come in. It is also easier, for wagons and laden beasts, than the steep descent to Erythrai. There must have been a reason why there was no fear of Persian raiders penetrating *over* the Erythrai pass and cutting off convoys near Eleutherai itself, where the roads to the two passes join; and this we may probably find in the supposition that the passes were guarded by some of the numerous light-armed Greeks, of whom we hear nothing in the main operations. Light-armed Greeks could be formidable on their native hills, as Thucydides knew well; and in fact the Persians in this campaign seem never to have attempted to penetrate the mountains.

The Greeks then 'decided to advance down[22] to Plataia; and they took up their equipment and marched, by way of the lower slopes of Kithairon, past Hysiai, into the Plataian territory, where they took up their position by contingents near the spring Gargaphia and the sanctuary of the Hero Androkrates, extending over some low knolls and level ground'.[23] They clearly avoided coming right down into the plain during their flank march, not wishing to be caught there by cavalry.[24] Probably they moved along the hill-foot till they could

---

a means of military communication; though the over-facile Macan (Map VI) marks a Plataia–Megara main road, in red, going apparently over the top of Kithairon. Even a runner from Plataia to Megara would probably find it quicker to go round by Dryoskephalai, forking west south of the col. On these communications, see Hammond in *BSA* LIV; though Pritchett (n. 50) finds him 'unduly hard on Grundy'. On Grundy, Myres (p. 283) rightly says 'The Greek staff-map adds little to his brilliant reconnaissance; but not all his identifications are certain'. His mis-identification of Dryoskephalai is repeated in How's map and in many other publications.

[22] *ἐπικαταβῆναι*, H. *ib.*

[23] I append the more crucial words in the original: . . . *ἤισαν διὰ τῆς ὑπωρέης . . παρὰ Ὑσίας . . . ἀπικόμενοι δὲ ἐτάσσοντο . . . διὰ ὄχθων τε οὐκ ὑψηλῶν καὶ ἀπέδου χώρου*. Hysiai, we note, wherever it was exactly, was between Erythrai, where the main road came down (so Erythrai must be at least *near* modern Kriekouki), and the home fields of Plataia, but off the best through-route; probably further up the hill. In spite of Pritchett's careful 'potsherding', I do not feel quite sure of his identifications (*AJA* LXI, 22f and map).

[24] There were, therefore, tolerable 'made' tracks on the hillside, without which such a sidelong move would have been all but impossible. They may have used the lower part of 'Hammond's road' (see *BSA* XLIX) from modern Kriekouki to Dryoskephalai (whence it continues into the Megarid). A similar route must have been followed by the Boiotarch Neokles, when he surprised Plataia in 373; he led the Thebans 'on the road towards (ἐπὶ) Hysiai, in the direction of Eleutherai and Attica, where the Plataians had not even posted a look-out' (Paus. ix, 1, 6). That, even so, Neokles' movement with a large force of armoured men could achieve a surprise suggests that even the lower slopes then carried a good deal of woodland.

advance in line to the range of knolls. They could have reached the same position more conveniently if they had never gone to Erythrai at all, but advanced in the first instance more to the west by the Dryoskephalai. What they did suggests that the advance to the knolls was a move determined on by Pausanias only after he had seen the ground and the dispositions of his enemy.

The new position on the knolls or Asopos Ridge, as it is usually called, faced rather east of north, still towards Thebes and Mardonios' palisade. Herodotos' description of it was admirably lucid in his time, but with the disappearance of the ancient names and landmarks it has given rise to much discussion. The *temenos* of Androkrates (first in the list of local Heroes, to whom the Greeks were enjoined to sacrifice, according to the oracle in Plutarch, *Ar.* 11) was near the road from Plataia to the 'front' (*wrongly* identified with the Chapel of St John, which stands on one of the knolls);[25] and the spring Gargaphia (really a group of springs; important if large numbers of men were to draw from it) should be the modern Rhetsi, south of the Chapel of St Demetrios on its knoll.[26]

At this point Herodotos puts a long argument, with copious reference to mythological history, between the representatives of Athens and Tegea, both claiming the second-highest post of honour on the left wing, the Spartans, with the high command, having the undisputed claim to the right.[27] If there ever was any such discussion, it must

[25] The escapers from Plataia in Thk. iii, 24 (cf. n. 21 above) 'took the road towards Thebes, having the *Hērōion* of Androkrates on their right'. They follow that road for 'six or seven stades' (1200–1400 yards), and then, after seeing the pursuers, with their lanterns, well away on the Dryoskephalai route, 'turned and took the road leading towards the hills, to Erythrai and Hysiai'. On the face of it Thk. means that they went *round* the *hērōion*, right-handed, as Grundy says (*GPW*, 466ff); though W. J. Woodhouse in *JHS* XVIII (unfortunately followed by Macan, Munro, Bury, How and Wells, in their text and maps) argued that Thk. meant what he does not say, that the Plataians took a *road* which had the shrine on its right (though they turned off it, leaving it on their *left*, when it was still over a mile away). This concurrence in error seems to arise from a human desire to have fixed points. Churches are indeed often built on pre-christian sacred sites; but not always; and the 'precinct' (*temenos*) of *A.* (H. ix, 25, 3) was probably no more than an enclosure round a sepulchral monument, of which all trace has disappeared. It is a not insignificant fact that Pausanias does not mention it. H. says that it was near the Greek position, but not that it was *in* it; and perhaps mentioned it because it was in that direction, seen from Plataia, and because the Greeks sacrificed to the hero (Plut. *Ar.* 11).

[26] So Grundy (465f) after Leake (*Northern Greece*, ii, 332f); Pritchett, n. 78; rather than the less plentiful, more westerly Alepotrypi ('Fox-Hole'; Grundy's 'Alopeki or Apotripi'), though that may have been used too. – The name Apotripi, found in most modern maps, is probably simply a corruption.

[27] *ib.* 26f.

have taken place long before; it was no place to argue about positions in the line of battle, in the presence of the enemy. The fact is that the historian is filling in with a story a break in the action,[28] for there now followed, apparently, a week with 'nothing to report'. For the Greeks, it was not a wasted week, for their contingents were still coming in.[29] But the basic reason for the delay was that neither side (for sound, tactical reasons, expressed to the troops in the form of the statement that 'the omens were propitious only for a defensive action'[30]) wished to take the offensive.

More usefully, Herodotos here (28, 2ff) gives his list of the Greek contingents and their (nominal?) hoplite strengths at the time when battle was actually joined, from right to left as they stood 'in order of battle on the Asopos':[31]

Right wing	Lakedaimon (including 5000 Spartiates)	10,000	
	Tegea	1500	
			Total 11,500
Right centre	Corinth	5000	
	Poteidaia	300	
	Orchomenos in Arcadia	600	
	Sikyon	3000	
	Epidauros	800	
	Troizen	1000	
	Lepreon in Triphylia	200	
	Mykenai and Tiryns	400	
			Total 11,300
Left centre	Phlious	1000	
	Hermione	300	
	Eretria and Styra	600	
	Chalkis	400	
	Ambrakia	500	
	Leukas and Anaktorion	800	
	Pale in Kephallenia	200	
	Aigina	500	
	Megara	3000	
			Total 7,300

[28] As pointed out by Munro in *CAH* IV, p. 332.

[29] H. ix, 28, 2; 38, 2; 41, 4.

[30] *ib.* 36f.

[31] *ib.* 31, 1. Grundy's objection (*GPW*, 470), that the Asopos was 1½ miles in front of them, is pedantic.

Left wing	Plataia	600	
	Athens	8000	
		Total	8,600
		Total armoured strength:	38,700

The arrangement in four divisions (or battle-groups – *ad hoc* and not permanent) appears only in the crisis of the campaign, but may be noticed here, as it draws attention to the principles on which contingents were allotted their stations. All Peloponnesians are to the right, all others (not much over one-third of the army) to the left; the left centre, the smallest and most miscellaneous division, includes the islanders and western colonists, who were, incidentally, probably among the last to come in.[32] To this arrangement there is one solitary exception: the 300 volunteers from gallant Poteidaia, which naturally could not send her main forces, were, by special request of the Corinthians and permission of Pausanias, allowed to stand side by side with them, instead of among 'the rest', as do the 1300 other Corinthian colonials from Leukas, Ambrakia and Anaktorion. The mention of this special exception gives ground for believing that the rest of Herodotos' list also reflects a real order of battle, and is not a mere copy of the list from one of the post-war monuments; a made-up list would surely have dealt with all Corinthian colonials in the same way. There are also other traces of more than chance arrangement. Three cities of Euboia with 1000 men stand together, three western Corinthian colonies, with 1300, together, Epidauros and Troizen, Tiryns and Mykenai; while the curious insertion of Arcadian Orchomenos between Corinth and Sikyon was perhaps intended to separate neighbours who may not have been on the best of terms. Aigina and Megara stand side by side, as, according to Diodoros, in the fleet at Salamis; Tegea next to Sparta, in honour of the old alliance; and Plataia with Athens.

So the Greeks awaited their allies. If Pausanias were to cross the Asopos, he would have to do so initially in hollow square formation, to protect the vulnerable flanks of his phalanx; and if he were ever to deploy from this narrow-fronted and defensive formation into line, there were no anti-cavalry obstacles, for his flanks to rest on, nearer

[32] This geographical arrangement is against Beloch's suggestion (*Bevölkerung der gr.-rom. Welt*, p. 9) that Palians is Herodotos' mistake for Eleians (having read *ϜΑΛΕΙΟΙ* as *ΠΑΛΕΙΟΙ*). But H. does not write παλειοι, but πὰλεες. We remain without an explanation of how the Eleians (and not the Palians), though not recorded in any of the battles, secured a position on the Serpent-Column.

together than the Asopos and the foothills of Helikon, east of Thespiai; an inconveniently long front of fully five miles. If Pausanias ever seriously contemplated crossing the Asopos in face of the enemy, there was no sense in doing so with 30,000 armoured men, when by waiting for a few days he could have 40,000.[33] In the mean time, he had good reason to hope that Mardonios would attack him.

For Mardonios also had his problems. Like Hannibal in Italy after his initial victories, he had to protect his allies. The Greek army at Plataia constituted a threat to them, and most directly to Thebes, which forced the Persians to keep their main army in Boiotia, and feed it there. The period of waiting was a period of sustained effort for the supply services, which succeeded in keeping both armies fed, and a test of endurance for the troops in the front lines. Nor did Mardonios, still hoping to prod the Greeks into a movement, which would give him his opportunity, fail to do what he could to make them uncomfortable. The Athenians and others on the north-western flank, nearer the Asopos, at first drew water from it, rather than from the limited resources of the 'Fox-hole' or from Gargaphia, some three miles away; but the Persian cavalry and archers soon made that impossible, and the whole army was forced to rely on the springs in rear.[34]

It was presumably during these thirsty and tedious days of waiting, while, to the men in the ranks, the stalemate seemed complete and the chance of a victory remote – 'while the fate of Greece hung in the balance and the position of the Athenians was particularly precarious' [35] – that an incident is said to have occurred which, transmitted to us by Plutarch, without naming his source, has been generally doubted: the detection of an oligarchic conspiracy in the Athenian ranks, in dealing with which Aristeides chose to employ extraordinary leniency. Extraordinary indeed it seems to us, at first sight; but we have to remember the character of Greek political life (cf. pp. 260–2, above), in which the boundary between loose talk and treason was vague, and treason itself far from unthinkable. Anti-democratic talk

[33] And therewith we may dismiss all theories suggested earlier in our century, to the effect that P. did intend such an offensive, but was foiled by faint-heartedness or slowness on the part of the Athenians on his leading (left) wing, as the over-imaginative inventions of an over-confident age. Herodotos was not entirely dependent on Athenian sources; he had also been to Sparta, and in the battle which actually occurred, he makes it quite clear that it was essentially a Spartan victory; as does Aeschylus, *Pers.* 817, with his reference to the 'Dorian spear'.

[34] As H. tells us, a little belatedly, in ix, 49, 3.

[35] Plut. *Ar.* 13.

among the young gentry of Athens never ceased, as we may see from Plato's dialogues; and how easily it could pass over into treason we may see, in a better-documented generation, in the proceedings of the Four Hundred in 411. The conspirators, land-owners who had 'lost everything through the war', had no doubt been in favour of the peace-proposals of Lykides, who had been lynched by the democrats; that violent deed had made all overt argument against the policies of the war-party impossible. Now, when off duty behind the line at Plataia where the hoplite class was mobilised in full force, with most of the lower classes, the 'navy crowd', out of the way, they had time to get together.

> Some men of famous families and great wealth, who had been impoverished by the war and saw all their power and glory in the city gone together with their wealth, while others were honoured and held the commands, met secretly in a house in Plataia and swore an oath together to subvert the democracy; or, failing success in that, to obstruct operations and betray the cause to the barbarians.[36] While this was on foot and many in the camp had already been seduced by the conspirators, Aristeides got wind of it. In the existing dangerous situation, he determined neither to ignore the matter [presumably as mere loose talk] nor to expose all its ramifications, not knowing how many men a full inquiry would incriminate. It seemed a time to apply the canons of expediency rather than strict justice. So he arrested eight out of a large number of suspects; and two of these, Aischines of Lamptra and Agesias of Acharnai, whose trial was announced to take place first, and whom the evidence indicated to be the ringleaders, escaped and fled; and he released the others (thus giving those who thought he did not know about them a chance to recover from their fright and come to a better mind) with the admonition that they had the great trial of battle before them, in which to clear their records by true and honest patriotism.

Told as it is *ad Aristidis gloriam*, this story, with the names and *demotika* of the chief conspirators, is circumstantial and in this unlike the general run of Aristeides-stories, which merely lead up to an *apophthegma* illustrating the great man's justice and *gravitas*; here, indeed, the whole point of the story, as a contribution to the sketch of character, which was the main point of an ancient biography, is that

[36] Exactly like the Four Hundred; to capture the government by themselves if possible, but in the last resort to sell out to the city's enemies.

Aristeides, a skilled politician, knew when to temper justice with expediency. A very human man, too, he knew the strain under which these men had been for the last year, and not least for the last few days. He knew that the ice under him was thin; that morale was brittle, and that the schisms in Greek society already ran not only between class and class, but even within the soul. Treason in camp was the same 'rot' which, as Miltiades had warned Kallimachos before Marathon, could set in if action were too long delayed. Aristeides' tact was successful, and the potential traitors of one week fought well in the next. The story did not become famous, since Herodotos did not choose to mention, if he heard of it, an incident that came to nothing; and it was scarcely suitable for quotation in patriotic oratory; but as a source from whom Plutarch *may* have got it, we may notice that Kleidemos, 'eldest of the Atthidographers',[37] is cited by Plutarch later in this biography (ch. 19), and has appeared earlier (p. 430, above) as giving the democrats' rather than the aristocrats' story of how the financial crisis was solved at the time of the evacuation of Athens.

But meanwhile the Persian cavalry, having learned their lesson and had time to regain confidence since their repulse at Erythrai, were growing bolder. There was an interval of two miles between the Greek battle-line on the Asopos ridge and the foot of Kithairon, across which food-supplies for the troops had to come; and if it was supposed to be guarded by the Greek light-armed, these unarmoured javelin-men were no match for cavalry on level ground. Timagenidas of Thebes is said to have advised Mardonios that it would be practicable to raid the outlets from the passes and catch reinforcements on the march; and while it is unlikely that the Persian had anything to learn from the Theban on strategy, Timagenidas may well have advised on topography: 'for the Thebans, having joined the Persians whole-heartedly, took part vigorously in the campaign, and used to act as guides up to the point of action; and from there it was the Persians and Medes who took over and did the best fighting.' [38]

On the eighth night since the occupation of the Asopos ridge, there was a disaster:

Accepting this advice as sound, Mardonios sent his cavalry at

[37] Paus. x, 15, 4. He must therefore have been writing in the generation of 400, and old enough to know old men who, like the poet Sophocles, could remember the war. Other *testimonia* on K. (see Jacoby, no. 323) add little.

[38] H. ix, 40; on Timagenidas, 38, 2.

nightfall to the foot of the pass leading to Plataia, which the Boiotians call the Three Heads and Athenians the Oak-Heads; and their ride was not for nothing. They caught, just coming into the plain, five hundred beasts with wagons,[39] bringing food from the Peloponnese to the camp, with the men escorting them; and falling upon this prey, the Persians slew without mercy, sparing neither man nor beast, till they were glutted with slaughter; and then they rounded up the rest, and drove them off to Mardonios in their own lines.

After this, two further days passed, with neither side wishing to take the offensive; the Persians would advance as far as the Asopos, to tempt the Greeks, but neither side crossed it. But the Persian cavalry kept up its harassing attacks continually.

But Mardonios too is said to have been having difficulty in supplying his troops,[40] reduced as they were largely to local resources; for they were unable to use sea-transport, while convoys from Thessaly, over 100 miles away, had to run the gauntlet of the guerrilla bands in Phokis. Artabazos is said to have advocated a withdrawal to Thebes, where, according to his speech, ample supplies had been built up, both for man and beast; thence they could continue their 'political warfare', with the help of their still plentiful reserve of gold.[41] But Mardonios was growing impatient for a decision by battle. News of this, and of the enemy's shortages, are said to have been brought by night (day 11–12) to the Athenian outposts near the river, by a horseman who finally revealed himself to the generals as Alexander the Macedonian; another chapter in his highly tendentious saga.[42]

At this, it is said, Pausanias, with the goodwill of the Athenians, at first light interchanged the positions of the Athenians and Lakedaimonians at the two ends of his line. If the line was nearly three miles long (reckoning eight men to a yard) the operation of marching two divisions of 8000 and 10,000 men, in column of eights, past each other in rear of the centre, would have taken an hour, and the moment when an attack was expected does not seem the right time at which to do it. The story is usually dismissed as absurd (which it is, if taken to imply that the Spartans were afraid to face the enemy's best troops); but if we take quite literally Herodotos' account of Pausanias' reasons for pro-

[39] ὑποζύγια, ch. 39, and ζεύγεσι, *ib.* 'yoked beasts' implying wagons, cf. Myres, *op. cit.* p. 285; J. E. Powell's translation, p. 650; not pack-animals, as per Grundy, Macan, Hammond (*HG*, p. 248) and others

[40] *ib.* 45, 2. [41] *ib.* 41. [42] *ib.* 41–45.

posing the move, perhaps really carried out earlier, it is not entirely so. The proposal points out that the Athenians had experience of fighting against Persians, while the Spartans' battle-experience was all against other Greeks. Pausanias might surely have been hoping to spring a surprise on the enemy; to demolish the Boiotians and other northern Greeks on Mardonios' right, and then come in on the flank of the Asiatics. But in any case it came to nothing. Mardonios, taking the same view as Epameinondas after him of the importance of having his best troops facing the Spartans, made a corresponding adjustment; after which both sides resumed their original order, and Mardonios taunted the Spartans with cowardice.[43]

On day 12 the enemy infantry still did not cross the stripling Asopos; but their cavalry, now again full of confidence, 'rode up to the Greek line' – standing off carefully, we may guess, from the post of the Athenian archers – 'and harried it from end to end, with their javelins and arrows, horse archers as they were, and impossible to get at'.[44] The mounted archers included a Saka or Scythian regiment from the eastern steppes, which is recorded on the following day to have highly distinguished itself.[45] They rode right round the Greek army, and, as a crowning stroke, seized, fouled and filled with earth and stones the springs of Gargaphia, close in rear of the Spartans' position,[46] the Greeks' last plentiful source of water.

Up on the knolls, the Greek generals met at Pausanias' headquarters in sombre council of war, to discuss 'both this and other matters; for even more serious was the fact that they had come to the end of their food-supplies, and their convoys, which had gone back to the Peloponnese to fill up, were cut off by the cavalry and unable to get through to the camp'. They were, we hear later, halted behind the crest of the pass, where the cavalry were unable to come at them. The Asopos ridge, it was clear, was being made untenable. The council decided to hold on there while the daylight lasted and then to fall back, we are told, 2000 yards, to a line nearer Plataia and between two head-waters of the Oëroë, which, rising near together on the mountain and then diverging to a distance of some 600 yards, formed what was known locally as 'the Island'. This position, too small for the whole army, was perhaps to be that of the Athenians. Half the army, during the same night, would move 'to Kithairon' and enable the food-trains to come

[43] *ib.* 46–48. [44] *ib.* 49, 2. [45] *ib.* 71. [46] *ib.* 49, 3.

down.[47] 'So for all that day they hung on in great distress under the attacks of the cavalry.' The chief factor which limited the effectiveness of such attacks will have been the fact that horse-archers and, still more, mounted javelin-men can only carry a very limited amount of ammunition.

But Pausanias was not thinking only of saving his army from destruction. As the next day showed, he was planning to hit back if, as all the evidence indicated, the enemy wished for battle, and if the Greek retreat, like the feigned flights at Thermopylai, tempted him to follow up. The problem was still, as always, to get the Persians to stand and fight at close quarters, instead of falling back, exhausting the armoured Greeks in pursuit, and using their arrows. If they could have been induced to attack the Asopos ridge, a charge down hill could have driven them over the banks of the torrent-bed. After the retreat, there was another possibility: that they would have behind them the relatively steep slope in rear of the abandoned Greek position, through which the roads from Thebes passed in narrow valleys.[48]

As to what happened in the night, Herodotos gives a picture of confusion, indiscipline and bad morale which, scholars have pointed out, is somewhat belied by the creditable performance of the same troops in the morning. No doubt, among citizen soldiers moving to the rear, or halted for long hours in the dark waiting to retreat after a day in the summer sun,[49] with little water and under a missile attack to which they could make no effective reply, feelings of depression and gloomy suspicions as to what the allies were up to would be only what one might expect. It will be best, here again in our narrative, to pay most attention to the 'public facts' of what the formed bodies of troops

[47] H. ix, 50f. That this move was to be 'sideways along Kithairon' (Pritchett, p. 26) is not stated by H.

[48] Myres, *op. cit.* p. 291.

[49] A precise date cannot be given. The battle was fought 'on the 4th Boëdromion according to the Athenians, but on the 27th Panemos according to the Boiotians, the day on which the Hellenic Synod still meets at Plataia, and the Plataians sacrifice to Zeus the Liberator. The discrepancy in the dates ought not to surprise us, since even now, with greater accuracy in astronomy, different states begin and end their months differently.' So Plut. *Arist.* 19; '3rd. Boëd.', *id. Cam.* 19, where he also tells us that Panemos = Ath. Metageitnion, the month before Boëd., beginning at the second new moon after midsummer. The 27th Pan., 479, is computed to = the 19th Sept., and this *could* be the exact date; but it is quite uncertain, despite Plutarch, whether any attempt was made originally to hold the victory celebrations on the exact anniversary of the battle; cf. pp. 240ff. Meyer, *GdA*³ IV, i, p. 390 n. 3. All we can say for certain is that it must have been several weeks after Mardonios' occupation of Athens about the end of June.

actually did; while recording what Herodotos' informants, mostly Athenians, and young men at the time of the campaign, told him about the motives of their allies, merely as examples of what the soldiers said.

The movement was timed to begin 'in the second watch', about three hours after sundown, when the enemy should have settled down for the night.

> But when the day ended and the cavalry drew off, and it was dark, and the agreed hour for the movement came, the majority of the army got up and went, not giving a thought to the agreed place, but, once they were in motion, taking to flight, glad to escape the cavalry, to the city of Plataia. Their flight ended at the Temple of Hera, which stands before the city, twenty stades [about 2¼ miles] from Gargaphia; and here they halted and piled arms.[50]

In this allegation of 'flight' and near panic on the part of the allies (an allegation which reached Herodotos, we have to remember here again, at a time when Athenian feeling was particularly embittered against Corinth and Megara) we ought to look carefully for what is admitted, against the main tendency. We notice that the move did not start until the appointed hour, and that it ended with an orderly halt in line before the city. It is true that the allies did not stop after 2000 yards, between the headwaters of the Oëroë, as we are told they should have done; but we then have to notice (*a*) that such a position, if that is what is meant by 'the Island', would have offered no better cover against cavalry than that from which they had come; for the headwaters are small and the country gently undulating;[51] (*b*) that, if one of the objects of the night move was to be 'to send half the army to the foot of Kithairon', to cover the descent of the food-train, this is exactly what the centre accomplished. After the movement, which even in the dark must have been completed well before midnight, this half of the army will thus have had several hours in which to obtain food, water (from the wells of Plataia) and some needed rest before dawn.

Meanwhile the Athenians on the left and the Spartans on the right did not yet move. (And what did they eat? We may suppose that any supplies still remaining on the knolls had been left with them.) On the reasons for this, Herodotos tells some still more remarkable stories: that the Spartans were delayed because Amompharetos ('Blameless in

[50] H. ix, 52.

[51] Cf. Grundy on the disadvantages of such an 'island' position, *GPW* 480ff.

Valour'), the commander of the Pitane battalion,[52] refused to compromise his honour by retreating; and the Athenians stayed because they mistrusted the Spartans – surely a very strange reason for remaining longer than had been arranged, in an exposed and isolated position. A despatch-rider, sent by the Athenian generals to Pausanias during the night, found the Spartans still in position, and (it is said) a violent altercation going on between Pausanias, Euryanax and Amompharetos. That there was such an altercation, and still more its details, cannot be regarded as an indubitable 'public fact'; it was not what everyone saw, but rests solely on what the rider said when he returned, or what other people said he said.[53] Since Amompharetos' battalion finally remained as a rearguard, there may well have been some fairly urgent last-hour discussion as to his exact assignment.

The reply given to the despatch-rider (here we are perhaps on safer ground) is said to have been an order for the Athenians to close up on the Spartans and conform to their movements.[54] Dawn was now breaking, and the Spartans together with the Tegeans began their movement southward, keeping along the relatively high ground of the water-shed between the Oëroë and a large tributary-torrent of the Asopos, called the Moloeis.[55] Amompharetos gave them some 2000 yards start, and then led his battalion, with splendid discipline, at the normal parade-ground 'slow pace' to join them.[56] Simultaneously with Pausanias' move, the Athenian generals at last gave the anxious men in their ranks the order to march. Dropping down, at first light, off the ridge which they had been holding (modern Pyrgos?),[57] they were, when the light grew strong enough for the Persians to see that the former Greek position was empty, on low ground near the Oëroë, but *out of sight.*[58]

The position at dawn therefore was that the Greek army, its centre drawn back and its two wings more advanced, but converging to

[52] This was where it came from, but not apparently its official name; hence Thucydides' captious criticism, i, 20, 3; cf. *Lyric Age*, p. 275. It is a tribute to H., if criticism could find nothing worse than this to fasten on.

[53] Palpably wrong is the detail (ix, 55, 2) that A. deposited a large rock at the feet of the generals, and said that that 'pebble' was his vote for not going; for the Spartans did not vote with pebbles, but by acclamation. Cf. Munro in *CAH* IV, p. 335n.

[54] *ib.* 56, 1. [55] For identification of this, see Grundy p. 495.

[56] *ἦγε βάδην*, 57, 1. *Δέκα στάδια* (*ib.* 2) should not be emended to *τέσσερα*, as per Hude (*OCT*). If H. wrote *Δ*, by 5th cent. usage he meant δέκα.

[57] *ib.* 56, 2; Pyrgos, Pritchett in *AJA* LXI, p. 25 (but misplaced in his map).

[58] *ib.* 59, 1.

reduce the distance between them, were on three sides of the square of gently undulating ground between the old Greek position and the city of Plataia. All divisions had reached their positions by disciplined movements, moving and waiting according to their orders; and all except the temporarily concealed Athenians and Plataians faced down gentle slopes, suitable for a charge. It is surely not unreasonable to think that their positions were at least approximately as Pausanias had intended. The movements carried out by each division in the dark, movements of over two miles, back to the foot of Kithairon near Plataia, for the centre, and of over one mile, crossing one branch of the Oëroë, for the Athenians, had the merit of simplicity.

The Athenians were now in the 'Island', between the two streams 600 yards apart. There was probably water there, even in late summer, in the main stream (Grundy's O.1). The next order, to close on the Spartans, given or confirmed only just before dawn, so due to be carried out only when it was possible to see, would involve a change of direction. It would take them up the 'Island' to higher and defensible ground, still within it, between the former centre (half the whole army) and the Spartan division. If the enemy, as was to be expected, advanced in pursuit after getting under arms at dawn, Amompharetos' battalion, retiring on its main body, would draw the Persians on the Greek right on to the Spartan front, astride the watershed ridge with its right on the Moloeis. While the Spartans there took care of the enemy's best troops, the rest of the enemy, if they followed the Athenians as soon as they saw them, would be drawn up against the centre of a concave position, and might be taken in flank by the whole of the former centre, which the Athenians, while in motion, would conceal from view. If this was the plan, however, then owing to the swift movement of the enemy's cavalry and the wariness of Artabazos, who commanded the infantry of Mardonios' centre,[59] it failed. The question so much debated about Plataia, whether it was a mismanaged affair and a soldiers' battle, as Herodotos' narrative suggests, or well planned by Pausanias and his generals, as many scholars have argued, is wrongly put. There are many indications that it was well planned; but

[59] By elimination; for Mardonios commanded the Persian division on his own left wing; Mardonios' Greek allies formed his right wing. There remains for Artabazos, who was second-in-command of the whole army (ch. 41), the command of the centre, consisting of Median and eastern troops (31, 3f), which was not heavily engaged (66).

for a battle to be well planned, and for the plan to be frustrated by the enemy, and for the troops to win it nevertheless, is no rarity in the history of war.

'When Mardonios saw that the Greeks had gone in the night and their position was empty', he is said to have addressed some triumphant remarks on the falsity of Sparta's reputation for valour to the Aleuad princes who were with him.

> And with that, he led on the Persians at full speed across the Asopos, in the track of the Greeks, whom he imagined to be in flight, with a front covering that of the Lakedaimonians and Tegeans only; he did not see the Athenians, who, having marched by the low ground, were concealed by the knolls. And when they saw the Persians set out in pursuit, the commanders of the other barbarian divisions all forthwith raised their battle-standards and followed at their best speed, in disarray and disorder, cheering and yelling, and thinking to make short work of the Greeks.[60]

The cavalry, who had moved at first light without waiting to see if the Greeks were still on the knolls, were already well ahead. They overtook the Spartans within minutes of the rearguard's coming in[61] (Amompharetos had timed it to a hair); and there they started their usual harassing tactics. Pausanias sent a last despatch-rider to the Athenians, to bid them hurry, or if unable all to reach their place in the line, to send the archers.[62] How badly he was going to need those archers will be seen shortly.

But it was already too late. The Athenians, with a longer column than Amompharetos' one battalion, further to come and less than Spartan march discipline, did not succeed in matching his performance of 'clicking' into place at the last moment. They were overtaken by the Medizing Greeks.[63] Initially, this must mean the northern Greek cavalry, the strongest contingent of which was the Thessalian, under the Aleuads, Thorax and his brothers, though the keenest in the cause was the Boiotian, fighting, in the Boiotians' own estimation, for

[60] H. ix, 58–59.
[61] *ib.* 57, 3.
[62] *ib.* 60 (combined in H. with some highly unsuitable rhetoric about the 'liberation-struggle' and complaints that the rest of the army had 'run away in the night', which we must dismiss as later Athenian inventions).
[63] *ib.* 61, 1.

Boiotian soil against the Athenians who had wrongfully seized this corner of it. Athenian tradition drew a kindly veil over the Thessalians' activities; when Herodotos was at Athens, the Thessalians, like Argos, were Athens' friends; Boiotia alone was her enemy both in 479 and a generation later. But behind the cavalry, the strong Boiotian infantry, hot against the invaders of their country, were coming up. It does not seem to have been generally noticed that, moving along the road (a well-beaten cart-track?) from Thebes to Plataia, they had a much easier line of advance than the Persian centre, which had to make its way across the Asopos, nearly dry, perhaps, but with a wide bed full of boulders, without the advantage of any well-used crossing-place, and then to ascend the knolls which the Greeks had just vacated. Moving fast, the Boiotians were probably already well ahead of their allies when they crossed the col between Pyrgos Hill and the hill now crowned by St John's chapel; and there, in full view on their left front, they saw the hated Athenians, already brought to bay by their cavalry; for, in order not to leave citizens in the lurch, Aristeides had felt constrained to halt the column and form order of battle between the streams. There the northern Greek infantry overtook him, and the battle was joined in earnest.

Meanwhile Mardonios' Persian infantry, crossing the Asopos with the help of two regular crossing-places and passing through the valleys on either side of St Demetrios' church (the more westerly of which was used by the Thebes–Dryoskephalai track), had also come up with Pausanias, 'by the River Moloëis', probably Grundy's stream A6, whose steep banks guarded Pausanias' right, 'in the piece of land called Argiopion, where there is a sanctuary of Eleusinian Demeter'. We see once more how clearly Herodotos, for the men of his own time, defined positions on the battlefield; though, with the disappearance of his land-marks, his indications become problems in their turn. The name Argiopion (or Argiopian, adjectivally) no longer means anything; and the Demetrion, mentioned, as we have seen, by Plutarch as 'near Hysiai, under Kithairon', seems to have vanished, stone by stone, into the buildings of modern Kriekouki, where two inscriptions, probably from it, have been found (n. 14, above). The temple is not to be found, though many have sought it, on the hill by modern St Demetrios' church; that is too near Gargaphia, and in the position which had been evacuated. The name might have been a clue;

but the attempt to follow it up produces no corroborative evidence. 'Ayi-Dhimitris' is a very popular saint, and dedications to him are found everywhere.[64]

With his back to Kithairon, then, his right flank protected by the Moloëis and his front, perhaps 1400 yards long (a 'paper-strength' of 11,500, at 8 men to the yard), astride the low watershed, Pausanias awaited the enemy. It is an interesting speculation, but unfortunately cannot be more, whether he had reckoned, when he gave the Athenians the order, so late, to close on him, that the northern Greeks would be drawn eastward in pursuit. If so, and if the Athenians had succeeded in joining him, the effect would have been, as we have seen, to leave the other half of the Greek army, when the Athenians had passed in front of them, to come in on the flank; a design comparable to Hannibal's at Cannae. As it was, the Athenians failed to join him; but the effect of shortening the enemy's front did actually result.

Artabazos with the centre, whose first impetuosity had been curbed, Herodotos says, by his orders,[65] and certainly also by a mile and a half up-hill, halted, probably on the Asopos Ridge, to survey the field. He could see two separate battles going on, with no great interval between them (as on all ancient battlefields, and even at Waterloo or at Gettysburg, the extent of the actual killing-ground seems to the modern eye extraordinarily small). On his left was Mardonios' front line, shooting into the Spartans on the high ground, while other Persians swarmed incautiously up the slope after them; in his front, between the streams of the Oëroë, the Boiotian infantry were advancing to attack the Athenians, while their cavalry took post on the flank. There was no good to be done by merely deepening the mass in either struggle; and lest he might think of advancing between the Spartans and the Athenians, he could see from the ridge, over the heads of the fighters below him, the main body of the Greeks, drawn up before Plataia, now divide into two solid masses and move towards the fighting. The larger, some 11,000 strong, headed by the 5000 men of Corinth, moved east along the hill-foot,[66] to close the gap to left of the Spartans, where the Athenians should have been. Whether they

[64] Against Grundy, *GPW*, p. 496, Myres, *Herodotus*, p. 286, see Pritchett (*AJA* LXI, p. 28), who sought for sherds or other ancient traces round the church without result; Munro in *JHS* XXIV, pp. 162f. Macan (II, p. 362) is here less than fair to Herodotos.

[65] H. ix, 66, 2.

[66] H. ix, 69.

actually came into action is uncertain. What *is* certain is that by moving thus and 'marking' Artabazos' forces, still unengaged, they rendered good service; and as 'holding the centre', the contemporary poet Simonides celebrated the work of the Corinthians in an elegiac poem on this battle.[67]

The Athenians and Boiotians were locked in the stern push-of-pike of a regular hoplite struggle; and the position of the Athenians was grave, since the enemy were supported by a numerous and unopposed cavalry, which might take them in flank or rear. To their aid, with great gallantry, for hoplites on the move in open country were very vulnerable to horsemen, descended the smaller, left-centre division of the main body, a nominal 7300 strong, Megara, from the left, probably leading, followed by all the small non-Peloponnesian contingents, and Peloponnesian Hermione and Phlious.[68] Their advance did not escape the eye of the Theban cavalry-commander Asōpodōros. Perhaps, including, as the division did, so many different small contingents, its advance lacked cohesion. Anyhow, there on the plain of Plataia, they were caught by the northern Greek cavalry and driven back in a bloody repulse, leaving 600 killed. So, says Herodotos (69, end), 'these perished ingloriously'. This miserable slander, dating from the days when Megara had been glad to accept and years later had massacred an Athenian garrison, and when Athens was particularly embittered against her, conceals the fact that, if the Athenian archers had brought relief to the Megarians a fortnight before, on this day of battle the advance of the Megarian and 'miscellaneous' division saved the Athenians. This was something that Athenians did not wish to remember; and they falsified the story by saying that the allies only advanced when the battle was already won.[69] Relief was brought, both to the Athenians and their allies, by evidence of victory on Pausanias' wing; and the Boiotian infantry 'pulled out', undefeated – they lost only 300 killed, out of perhaps 7000, not an undue proportion in a hoplite battle. A phalanx whose line was broken usually lost much more heavily in the retreat; but the Boiotians, efficiently covered

[67] Fr. 84 Bgk., 92 Edmonds; *ap.* Plut. *MH* 42.

[68] H. *ib.*; cf. W. J. Woodhouse in *JHS* XVIII, p. 51.

[69] This is not only a matter of *a priori* probability. When the battle *was* decided, H. says the Boiotian cavalry covered the retreat, 'keeping between their friends and the Hellenes' (68). This is not consistent with devoting their best attention to a column which, on his own showing, had only just started from a position a mile in rear of the Athenians.

by their cavalry, recrossed the Asopos unmolested and retired to Thebes.[70]

Pausanias' division, unsupported by any organized archers, though the helots may have included a few unorganized ones, had been having a trying time. Mardonios' infantry, their cavalry retiring through them, 'made a fence of their wicker shields, and poured in their arrows thick and fast'. The Spartans and Tegeans squatted doggedly behind their shields, while Pausanias sacrificed. But 'the omens would not come right', and even protected as they were, an arrow here and there kept finding its mark. 'Many fell in this time, and many more were wounded'; among others Kallikrates, 'the handsomest man in the whole army', with an arrow in the lungs, through some joint in his harness. Arimnestos of Plataia (pp. 249, 523) visited him, dying painfully, after the battle, and tried to comfort him with the thought that he died for Hellas; but Kallikrates said he had no comfort of that, but grieved that he had not struck a blow or 'done any deed worthy of himself'.[71]

However, the procedure when sacrifices did not produce the right omens for a desired assault was to go on cutting the throats of beasts till a really good heart and entrails were found; and without believing, against the evidence, that all Spartan generals were modern free-thinkers at heart, we can believe that they found sacrificing and taking omens a good way of keeping their men in hand. Pausanias was probably waiting, among more pious considerations, for the Persian line to grow deep enough in front of his position, as the rear closed up, to make sure that when he did charge those in front would not get away. It was a stern trial of Spartan discipline. But at last,

> Pausanias turned his eyes to the temple of Hera before Plataia, and prayed to the Goddess, 'Lady, do not disappoint us of our hope!' While he was yet speaking, the Tegeans broke out of line first, and went for the enemy;[72] and for the Lakedaimonians, at once, after Pausanias' prayer, the omens from sacrifice became good.

[70] H. ix, 67f; 7000, the Boiotian strength at Delion, Thk, iv, 93, 3; engaged also, half-heartedly according to H., may have been the 1000 Phokians (ch. 17, 2) and perhaps other northern infantry (31, 5). His total of 50,000 for the Medizing Greeks is admittedly a guess (32, 2), and, like all his figures for the enemy, fantastic. If there had been even half that number, the battle would have been different.

[71] *ib.* 61; 72.

[72] One is reminded of the victory of Richard Cœur-de-Lion against Turkish archers at Arsuf: there too, the crusaders who first broke out of the line appear to have done so

And now at last they too went for the enemy; and the Persians met them, laying aside their bows. The first clash took place at the shield-wall. Then it went down, and there was furious fighting, right beside the Demetrion, and it went on for a long time, even body to body; for the Persians seized the spears in their hands and broke them. In courage and strength indeed they were not inferior; but they were without defensive armour, and undrilled and no match for their opponents in skill; they rushed on in ones and tens and larger or smaller groups, and hurled themselves upon the Spartans and died.

Still, at the point of the front where Mardonios himself was fighting, mounted on a white horse, and with a thousand picked men of the Persians round him, they pressed their opponents hard. As long as Mardonios lived, they kept up the fight and held the line, and killed many of the Lakedaimonians; but when Mardonios was killed, and the regiment with him, which was their finest, was cut to pieces, then at last they turned and fled, and left the Lakedaimonians victorious. Their ruin was their lack of defensive armour, fighting, as they were, as light infantry against men-at-arms. There, then, the vengeance for Leonidas was rendered to the Spartiates by Mardonios, as the oracle foretold; and the finest victory in all history known to me was won by Pausanias the son of Kleombrotos the son of Anaxandridas; I have given the earlier part of his pedigree when dealing with Leonidas. Mardonios was killed by Aeimnēstos, a famous man in Sparta.[73]

Plutarch adds (*Arist.* 19) that Mardonios fell with his skull broken by a rock, hurled by Aeimnestos. It has been objected that a distinguished Spartiate would scorn to throw stones; but to fell the enemy commander, conspicuous on his horse among the infantry ranks, and defended by his guards, any weapon that was effective would be the best.

Artabazos with the Persian centre waited no longer. He had disliked the offensive against an unbroken enemy from the first, and indeed, we are told, the whole project of leaving Mardonios in Greece. He appears to have remained on the battlefield as long as there might be a possibility of his being useful; but when he saw the disaster to

against orders; but Richard had kept his men in hand just long enough, and at once ordered and led the charge of the whole line.

[73] *ib.* 62ff.

Mardonios' Persians, while the advance of the Peloponnesian division negated any possibility of taking the advancing Spartans in flank, he retired with all speed and took the road to the north. Out-running the rumour of disaster, and giving out that he was bound on an urgent journey to Thrace (which, it may have given him, as a good Persian, some chill satisfaction to think, was perfectly true), he made his way back north and east without more losses on the road than might have been expected; and, as the Greek fleet was by that time already operating in the Hellespont, crossed over to Asia in boats from Byzantion.[74] He has incurred learned censure for his alleged desertion;[75] but Xerxes, who was no easy-going master, and who may be supposed to have made some inquiry into the circumstances of the death of his brother-in-law, considered that he had done well in extricating his command. Of all Persian officers, it was Artabazos especially who emerged from the Greek campaign with a heightened reputation.[76]

The remnants of the Persian left meanwhile fled, covered by their own cavalry, to their stockade, where they had time to man the battlements and dispose themselves for defence as best they could. They repulsed a first attack by the Spartans; but when the Athenians (and, presumably, the rest of the Greek army, ignored as usual) came up, there were perhaps not enough defenders, less casualties and less Artabazos' division, to man fully the whole perimeter.

> At last, after a violent and prolonged assault, the Athenians, fighting with sustained gallantry, mounted part of the palisade and tore it down, and by that breach the Greeks poured in; but the Tegeans were the first to penetrate within, and it was they who plundered the tent of Mardonios. The spoils included the manger of his horses, of bronze throughout, and worth seeing. They dedicated that in the temple of Athena Alea, but the rest they turned in to the common fund of the Greeks.[77]

[74] H. ix, 66; 89.

[75] E.g. Macan, II, pp. 384f, who opines that he may never have crossed the Asopos. This is not the impression that Herodotos gives; but it is a mild departure from his evidence compared to the efforts made by some other scholars to provide A. with an *alibi*, or alternative employment; from Munro, who thinks it 'more probable that he was still several marches in rear' (*JHS* XXIV, p. 165; though he had had several months to make his way from Poteidaia!), to Obst, who suggests that his *Fussvolk* were convoy-raiding *within* the Kithairon *massif* (*Feldzug*, p. 194). All this is indeed what Mr Hammond has described as 'playing tiddleywinks' with the evidence!

[76] H. viii, 126, 1.

[77] H. ix, 70 (trying to reconcile two accounts, Athenian and Tegean?).

All resistance now collapsed, and the Greeks, taking no prisoners, slew wretched fugitives and men trying to hide, until 'of 300,000 troops, less the 40,000 who fled with Artabazos, not 3000 escaped' (*sic*). 'Of the Lakedaimonians of Sparta' (Spartiatai, excluding *perioikoi*?) 'there fell in the shock of battle 91, and of the Tegeans 16, and of the Athenians 52.'

These remarkably low figures were perhaps derived by Herodotos from the count of names on monuments. They are not complete for the whole day's fighting, and almost certainly he did not think they were. They omit the non-Spartiate Lakedaimonians, and they apparently omit the 'many' whom the arrows found while Lakedaimonians and Tegeans were suffering in silence, if we may judge by the comment below (72) 'for Kallikrates died outside the battle'. The Spartans lost several men of high station, noblemen holding priestly positions, who were buried in a special tomb; these included Amompharetos and Kallikrates, and two others, Poseidonios and Philokyon, whom they counted as having shown especial valour.[78] (Was it their duty to stand up, sacrificing, 'under fire'?) Not so did they honour Aristodāmos, who, sick with ophthalmia at Thermopylai, had let his helots take him south, the sole survivor of the Three Hundred, and been in disgrace ever since. Herodotos reckons that no man died fighting with such furious valour (71, 2); 'but, you see,' said his Spartan friends to him, 'Aristodamos wanted to die. Poseidonios and Philokyon wanted to live.' On the 52 Athenians, Kleidemos recorded the curious fact that they all belonged to the same regiment, that of Aiantis, which was judged to have distinguished itself most of all the tribes; 'wherefore the men of Aiantis used to offer the sacrifice to the Sphragitid Nymphs prescribed by the Delphic Oracle for the victory, receiving their expenses for it from the public funds'.[79] Kleidemos probably had this from public records, religious affairs being much more often recorded in inscription in the fifth century than merely political or civil. There will certainly have been some killed in other regiments, if perhaps not many; perhaps Aiantis was on the exposed left flank, in rear during the

[78] H. ix, 71, 2; 85, 1f, where the ms. readings ἱρέας, ἱρέες, 'priests', should not be emended (as in the OCT, after Valckenaer) to ἰρένας,-ες, 'young men' (under 30; yet Amompharetos was commanding a battalion). How and Wells, *ad loc.*, feel the difficulty, yet do not take account of the ms. reading. On special arrangements for the burial of priests killed in war, cf. den Boer, *Laconian Studies*, p. 294, on Plut. *Lykourgos*, 27.

[79] Plut. *Ar.* 19, 6. On these nymphs of Kithairon, mentioned along with the local Heroes Androkrates *et al.*, cf. 11, 3. On Kleidemos, n. 37 above.

movement to the right. Plutarch's total figure of 1360 killed (*ib.*), probably counting hoplites only, is not unreasonable. In addition to the 159 Spartiates, Aiantids and Tegeans enumerated, and some 600 of the left-centre division, it leaves another 600 for other Lakedaimonians, other Athenians, and other contingents; though Herodotos may have been right in believing that the right centre escaped without a scratch. He adds that some of Sparta's helots were killed, and had a separate burial-mound on the field.[80] Among Persians of note who may be presumed killed, we notice Pharandates the son of Teaspes, last mentioned as commander of the (27th) Kolchians. His Greek captive concubine, daughter of a nobleman of Kos, had the wit to look out for Pausanias, emerge from her covered wagon with her maids (or the rest of Pharandates' travelling harem) all wearing their jewellery 'and in the prettiest dress she had at hand', and appeal to Pausanias, with the complimentary title 'King of Sparta', to protect her. It seems an entirely convincing end to this story that Pausanias, having heard who she was, was able to say 'I know your father'.[81]

The victors encamped on the battlefield for ten days. There was a vast spoil to be collected, for the Persians, with the spoils of the east at their disposal, went on campaigns (as still in the days of Xenophon, cf. p. 64) in their most splendid array. Mardonios' gold and silver headquarters-mess equipment was so magnificent that the Greeks thought Xerxes must have left him his own.[82] There were also the dead to be collected and buried, vows to the gods to be made good after this 'greatest victory of all time', and, before thank-offerings could be made with the desired solemnity in the Temple of Hera and others in Plataia, the purification of the shrines, desecrated by the Persians, to be carried out. All fires are said to have been solemnly extinguished, and 'clean'

[80] Plut. *ib.*; H. ix, 85, 2f. The figure of D.S. xi, 33, 1 (over 10,000 Greeks killed) is sometimes quoted as a possible total for killed and wounded; but what D. says is 'killed'; and his whole account of the battle (31f), also sometimes quoted, is a conventional battle-piece in Ephoros' worst literary manner; 100,000 Greeks confront 500,000 barbarians in a narrow-fronted position 'with a high ridge on their right and the Asopos on their left', i.e. in front of the Asopos Ridge? E. perhaps *had* visited the field; and nearly all his details are from H.; but he omits all the details about supply-difficulties and movements not successfully carried out, which make the latter's narrative so much less tidy and so much more convincing. D. has 'over 100,000' barbarians killed; 40,000 escape with Artabazos; and the rest apparently evaporate. There is nothing to be gained by trying to use this stuff.

[81] H. ix, 76; on Ph., cf. vii, 79. It is noteworthy that of five of the contingent-commanders of 480 who are killed in 479, four are the last four on the list of 29. Was there a move, when Xerxes withdrew, to 'give the younger men a chance'?

[82] *ib.* 82, 1.

fire fetched from Delphi, a task which the runner Euchidas carried out within a day, covering about 100 miles. That he then died of his exertions is a story also told of Philippides (p. 239) in post-Herodotean versions, and was not recorded in the inscription at Plataia which Plutarch quotes (*Ar.* 20). Pausanias did his best to see that spoils, including slaves, were collected and distributed to gods and men properly, and in spite of a certain amount of looting this, on the whole, seems to have been satisfactorily done.[83] Pausanias was voted, as his special prize, 'ten of everything – women, horses, talents of the precious metals, camels, and so on with everything else'. Rich offerings went to the pan-Hellenic sanctuaries, from the realisation of which were set up a fifteen-foot-high bronze Zeus at Olympia, a ten-foot bronze Poseidon at the Isthmus, where the Congress had met, and at Delphi 'the golden tripod, which stands upon the three-headed bronze serpent, near the altar'. It was upon this offering (on its base?) that Pausanias caused to be inscribed the couplet 'Pausanias, Captain-General of the Hellenes, having destroyed the host of the Medes, set up to Phoibos this memorial'; an inscription which gave great offence, and marked the beginning of Pausanias' embarkation on that career of pride which led him to ruin.[84] He had behaved with unimpeachable chivalry and simplicity on the field of Plataia, refusing to mutilate the body of Mardonios (which then disappeared in the night, and was supposed to have been secretly buried) and after having Mardonios' slaves set out his dinner-service, laughed and said to his helots 'now put on a Spartan dinner!'[85] But from this time on, we hear no good of him from our sources; Ionians as well as his own people found him arrogant; though Thucydides reveals that his unforgivable sin, in the eyes of the latter, was that he favoured, like Kleomenes, the emancipation of the helots.[86] On the Serpent-Column, of which the mutilated trunk still stands in the Hippodrome of Constantinople, the Spartans substituted the names of one-and-thirty cities – all those represented in the battles of Salamis and Plataia, with the addition of Elis and the omission of Seriphos,

[83] *ib.* 80. H. here adds without suspicion the story that the wealth of Aigina originated (!) in buying stolen gold from helots as bronze.

[84] *ib.* 81; Thk. i, 132, 2.

[85] H. ix, 78–85. Pausanias the traveller was shown a 'tomb of Mardonios'; but by his time local lore had had plenty of time to grow. He himself very soundly goes back, with an 'it is said', to the report mentioned, as one of many, by H. (84, 2), that one Dionysophanes of Ephesos buried the body and was rewarded for it by Mardonios' son.

[86] Thk. i, 132, 4; cf. the whole section, 128–134, and 94–96, 1.

Kroton and Pale, for reasons unknown – and with the truly Laconic inscription

THESE FOUGHT IN THE WAR:
LAKEDAIMON
ATHENS CORINTH
TEGEA SIKYON AIGINA
MEGARA EPIDAUROS ORCHOMENOS
PHLIOUS TROIZEN HERMIONE
TIRYNS PLATAIA THESPIAI
MYKENAI KEOS MELOS TENOS
NAXOS ERETRIA CHALKIS
STYRA ELIS POTEIDAIA
LEUKAS ANAKTORION KYTHNOS SIPHNOS
AMBRAKIA LEPREON[87]

The names, after the first three, are scratched in threes on successive coils of the twined serpents, but in two lines a fourth name has been added later; even so, some small contributions to victory have been, perhaps, simply forgotten by a Lakedaimonian drafter. Pausanias the traveller records from Olympia (v, 23) a similar list, with the further omissions (but whose omissions, we do not know) of Thespiai, Eretria, Leukas and Siphnos.

In this mood of exaltation and thankfulness to the Gods, the allies committed the graves of the honoured dead to the care of the Plataians, with promises of eternal gratitude, to which the Plataians appealed in vain in a later and iron-hearted age.[88] That they also, on the motion of Aristeides, founded a short-lived pan-Hellenic congress, intended to be permanent, with delegates for political and religious affairs (*probouloi* and *theōroi*), who were to meet annually and to celebrate a new festival, the Feast of Liberation, with musical and athletic contests, once in four years; and that they further swore on the same motion, eternal brotherhood in arms against the barbarian, and to raise a permanent League army of 10,000 men-at-arms with 1000 horses and a fleet of 100 ships every year to continue the war[89] – all this must be reckoned romance, derived from some literary piece of historical fiction – one of those

[87] *GHI*, no. 27 (with comm.); Dittenberger, *SIG*³ 31; etc.

[88] Thk. ii, 71, 2ff; iii, 58, 4; 59, 2; 68, 1.

[89] Plut. *Ar.* 21; oath-formulae, D.S. ix, 10, 5, from some philosophic *diatribe* on the Legend of the Seven Sages.

imaginary speeches, of which many were produced in the rhetorical schools;[90] especially since a genuine speech of the fourth century, the *Plataïkos* of Isokrates, pleading at Athens, in the name of old services and alliance, for the restoration of Plataia when its people were expelled by Thebes, makes no mention of this, which should have been the strongest support for his case. Nor does either Herodotos or Thucydides (see note 88) have a hint of such a thing.[91]

The Spartans, whose conception of warfare was *agōnal*[92] – i.e., they fought for admitted victory, as in the games, and not for the total destruction of an enemy – were not interested in pursuit, and declined to countenance it, even when the Eleians and Mantineians, having missed the battle, offered to go after Artabazos.[93] But, after ten days of celebrations, the allied army did march upon Thebes, and besieged it, demanding the surrender of the Medizing leaders, Attagīnos, Timagenidas and others. The allies had sworn to destroy and 'tithe to the gods' states which assisted the invader (p. 345); but it now became evident that to carry out threats of remorseless enmity presented difficulties even more formidable than those which defeated vows of eternal friendship. To 'tithe' all the Medizers would have set every community in northern Greece fighting for its life. No city had helped the enemy more than Thebes; but Thebes was powerful. To destroy it would have cost an effort, and losses, such as none was anxious to face. Also, it was drawing towards autumn; there was rain

[90] E.g. [Andokides] iv, an imaginary *Speech of Phaiax* when in danger of ostracism in 416, with historical errors impossible in a contemporary (cf. Burn in CQ n.s. IV, 1954); or (a parody of the *genre*, with deliberate anachronisms?) the Funeral Orations in Plato's *Menexenos*.

[91] *Pace* Raubitschek in *TAPA* XCI (1960). That the annual commemoration of the Eleutheria was held, there is no reason to doubt; but it was never important enough to be mentioned in history; the only refs, to it which R. (*homo doctissimus*) can collect are one quotation from a late comedy (Poseidippos fr. 29 Kock), a local inscription (*IG* VII, 2509), and the account of it in Plutarch (*l.c.*), which is indeed interesting; but it must be remembered that the feast in his day was not a survival, but a revival, cherished in an antiquarian age. Plataia had twice stood waste for long years after 427 and 373; and it would be remarkable if there was continuity all through the bad years of the Roman conquest and the Mithradatic and civil wars. The foundation of a League against Persia would have been a major political decision, which armies in the field had no authority to take, in the absence of the cities' elders, and of the fleet; the only authority that could have taken it would have been a congress of properly appointed delegates, such as met at the Isthmus. Perhaps the story represents an attempt to find pan-Hellenic precedent for Athens' Delian League. Against it, see further P. A. Brunt in *Historia*, II (1953); Wade-Gery in *ATL* III, 225ff; though Larsen (*Representative Government in G. and R. Hist.*, pp. 48ff, 208ff, nn.) still defends it.

[92] A useful concept; see Pritchett in *AJA* LXI, p. 20, n. 68.

[93] H. ix, 77; on the principle, cf. Plut. *Lyk.* 22.

to be expected, and the ploughing to do. When after three weeks Timagenidas, not without courage, proposed that the wanted men should surrender themselves, there was relief on both sides. Timagenidas asked his fellow-citizens only that, if a heavy ransom was what the allies wanted, the city should pay it. He was not without hope that, if he and the others were allowed a trial, in which they could plead extenuating circumstances and offer a ransom, they would be spared. Attagīnos was not so sanguine, and when the surrender was agreed, he disappeared. His children were handed over; but Pausanias declined either to wreak vengeance on the innocent or to use them as hostages for their father's surrender. But he had no intention of letting the real 'collaborators' try the effects of influence, gold or eloquence on a court of his allies. As soon as he had them, he proclaimed a general demobilisation, took his prisoners with him back to the Isthmus, and there put them to death.[94]

[94] H. ix, 86–88.

Epilogue

The Counter-Offensive and the End of the War (479–449)

The great invasion was at an end, the army of occupation destroyed or in flight, the collaborators in Phokis and Thessaly abandoned to their own devices; the ten days spent by the victors of Plataia upon the battlefield, although Herodotos says little about them and leaves us to depend on a tradition remoter from the facts, seem to indicate consciousness of a great deed done. But the liberation of the north and east remained to be accomplished, and all its problems to be met.

1. *Mykale and Sestos*

While the Greeks still lay at Plataia, before the battle, there came to Latychidas' fleet-headquarters at Delos a boat from Samos, with 'messengers sent by the Samians, secretly from the Persians and Theomestor', their new governor (p. 464). Their leader, Hegesistratos, repeated the appeal of the Chians earlier (p. 501) for an advance to Ionia, giving an eloquent account of the Ionians ready to revolt 'at sight', and of poor morale among the Asian sailors.[1] Latychidas may have had still only his original 110 ships; as has been seen, the figure of 250 rests only upon the authority of Ephoros (D.S. xi, 34, 2); and that the increase was due to his having been powerfully reinforced from Athens after the Peloponnesian advance from the Isthmus is a modern 'combination' (p. 500, n. 34); but he had evidently a strong force of marines; we may wonder also whether at least some of his oarsmen had light infantry weapons, as some did on occasions in the Peloponnesian War. The council of war decided to sail against Samos. Latychidas took up as an omen of success the name of the Samian speaker, which meant

[1] H. ix, 90.

'Army-Leader'; and the Samians, accepted as representatives of their countrymen, 'took the covenant and swore oaths' for admission to the alliance of the Hellenes.[2]

Samos, a large, rugged and populous island, which even produced some guerrilla resistance in the mountains in 1943, was indeed slipping out of enemy control. The Persian commanders decided at once that they could not give battle at sea, and fell back to the mainland; and in the bustle of the evacuation, if not before, the Samians liberated 500 Athenian prisoners, who had failed to join the evacuation of Athens and been captured in Attica (p. 430). There were still some Samians with the Persian forces; but Tigranes the Akhaimenid, commanding the Persian land forces in Ionia, who came down to join in the defence of the fleet on shore, disarmed them as untrustworthy. He also sent his Milesian troops to the rear, to patrol the passes leading out of his position on the mountainous promontory of Mykale. On the south side of this, where alone there are beaches and a narrow strip of plain, 'round the corner' from Samos, Tigranes and Mardontes beached their ships behind an entrenchment of rocks and timber, with *skolopes* (abattis?) in front, 'cutting cultivated trees' for the purpose, and prepared to stand on the defensive.[3]

The Greeks put in 'at Kalamoi, beside the Temple of Hera', in the great sandy bay, west of the ancient capital of Samos. In view of the enemy's passivity, it was suggested that they need not give battle, but might sail at once against the nodal point of Persian communications with Europe, at the Hellespont. But the sounder council of attacking the force before them and trying to destroy the ships prevailed, and they advanced to Mykale. Latychidas sailed his fleet close inshore,[4] shouting exhortations to all Ionians to mutiny, and giving the slogan for the day, 'Hēra!' Then they sailed further, clear of the enemy lines, and landed their fighting men. As they did so, a rumour ran through the host that Mardonios had been defeated in a great battle; 'and when men reckoned, soon after', so it was said, 'they found that it had been so', on the same day, only a few hours earlier, 'for the battle of Plataia took place early in the morning, but that of Mykale in the afternoon'.

[2] H. ix, 91f.

[3] *ib.* 96, 99. For views of Samos and Mykale, cf. the photos in Myres, *Geog. Hist. in Gk Lands*, Pl. ix.

[4] *ib.* 98.

The marines formed up in order: Athens, Corinth, Sikyon, Troizen . . . about half the available force filled the space from the water's edge to the foot of the mountain.[5] The other half, Lakedaimon in the lead, had to take to the hills, up a gully, says Herodotos, and over a ridge, to come down upon the enemy from inland. Since the King of Sparta will have taken the right wing, the Greeks evidently attacked from the east; and since the right wing is said to have been delayed *in coming into contact* by the rough ground, *i.e.* not to have encountered enemy troops on the mountain, it is evident that the army-corps of 60,000 men, which Herodotos' informants assigned to Tigranes,[6] is as gross an exaggeration as Mardonios' 350,000 or Xerxes' millions. The strip of beach and coastal plain was so narrow that half, even of the Greek armoured force, was enough to fill it. Not many thousand fighting men on each side formed the front ranks and decided the battle, 'with the islands and the Hellespont for the prize of victory'.

The battle began early in the afternoon, when the Greek inland column[7] was still struggling over the hills, some distance from its goal. The Persians came out of their entrenchments and formed their shield-wall outside. It looks as if Tigranes determined on an effort to defeat one half of the Greek army in the absence of the other. The account of Ephoros, it may be noticed, also makes the Persians take the offensive;[8] though it is such a conventional battle-piece, with none of Herodotos' tactical and topographical details, that it would be rash to rely heavily on it. The Athenians and their allies, not choosing to stand and be shot at, came swiftly to close quarters:

> As long as the Persians' shield-wall stood, they held their ground successfully. Then the Athenians and their fellows redoubled their efforts, shouting to one another to make it their victory and not the Spartans'; and now the aspect of things changed; they forced their way through the shields and got in among the Persians; and though they met the attack, and fought on still for some time, at last they broke and fled to their defences. But the men of Athens, Corinth, Sikyon and Troizen (this was their order in line) followed them up and burst in along with them; and when their defences were taken, the resistance of the barbarians collapsed, and all took to flight, except the Persians, who rallied in small groups and fought on against

[5] *ib.* 102, 1; important for the size of the forces engaged.
[6] *ib.* 96, 2.
[7] *ib.* 101, 3.
[8] D.S. xi, 36.

> the Greeks as they poured in within the lines. Of the Persian commanders, two fled and two were killed; Artaÿntes and Ithamitres, the commanders of the fleet, fled, but Mardontes and the commander of the land forces, Tigranes, fell fighting. The resistance of the Persians was still continuing when the Lakedaimonians and their fellows arrived and joined in finishing off the work.
>
> The Greek losses were considerable, including the Sikyonian general, Perilaos. The Samians in the camp, who had been disarmed, as soon as they saw the fortune of battle turning, did what they could to help the Greeks; and the other Ionians, when they saw the Samians give a lead, now changed sides themselves, and attacked the barbarians.

The Milesians in the hills also turned against their masters, misleading the fugitives, and 'at last, killing unmercifully. This, then, was the second revolt of Ionia.' [9]

This account of the battle seems convincing, though obviously claiming as much of the credit as possible for the Athenians, who are said, and there is no reason to doubt it, to have been awarded the prize of valour; the individual prize also falling to an Athenian, Hermolykos, the 'all-in wrestler'.[10] The parallelism with Plataia (only one wing of the army fully engaged, battle at the shield-wall, battle at the camp) is not in itself suspicious; though certainly the exhortation to 'make this our victory, not Sparta's' looks rather like the idea of someone who did know about Plataia, and in detail.[11] But in some such form as 'Come on, boys, let's win without them', even this could be a preliminary to the charge, when it appeared that, if the left wing waited for the outflanking column, it would have to do so under fire. The glimpse of the Persians, apparently not very numerous, rallying in groups and fighting to the last, while their allies disintegrate or turn against them, does justice to a brave enemy, and is Herodotos at his best. Ephoros, himself an Aiolian of Kyme, is presumably responsible for the added detail that 'when the battle was already decided, the Aiolians and many others of those in Asia joined in . . . regardless alike of oaths and hostages';[12]

[9] H. ix, 102–4.

[10] *ib.* 105.

[11] There is a good summary of the views of modern scholars down to 1914 (Grote, Hauvette, Grundy, Busolt, Meyer, Macan, Munro, etc.) in Obst, *Feldzug*, pp. 214ff; though I am, as usual, unable to follow Obst in attaching much importance to Diodoros' (Ephoros'?) narrative, nor in his confidence in the importance of the results obtainable by the application of the principles of Quellenkritik. How (*Comm. on H.*, II, pp. 295f) is brief and sensible as usual.

[12] D.S. xi, 36, 5f; for Aiolians, cf. 37, 1f.

Aiolis probably had its own traditions of the war; but in any case Ephoros, it may be suspected, was tired of hearing all the Greeks of Asia indiscriminately called Ionians.

Mykale was a relatively small battle; Thucydides (i, 23, 1), when remarking that the Great Persian War was decided by 'two battles on land and two at sea', does not consider it worthy of mention alongside decisive Salamis or great and long-drawn Artemision.[13] But it was important, in that with it the fruits of victory began to be garnered. By eliminating the Persian fleet from the Aegean coast, it gave Greek fleets complete liberty of action; and it 'triggered' the new Ionian revolt, as Herodotos says, though not all the mainland cities, found among the allies of Athens in the 'tribute-lists' after 454, dared to throw off the Persian yoke at once. Aristogenes, a tyrant of Miletos, was 'driven out by Sparta', probably now; but years later the Persian king could still make grants to Greek collaborators, not only of inland Magnesia, where Themistokles lived as 'tyrant' when driven from Greece, but (also to Themistokles) of rights in Lampsakos on the Propontis and Myous, on the coast near Miletos,[14] and to Gongylos of Eretria of Aiolic Myrina and Gryneion with other small places.[15] And inland, as we have seen, the descendants of Damaratos were still 'lords of manors' in the Troad after eighty years.[16]

The victory was very complete. The Persian and Median marines and any Persian regiments in Tigranes' force had been almost wiped out, and without them the subject nations would not fight. The naval commanders who survived, and were accused of cowardice by the marshal Masistes,[17] had probably been trying in vain to rally their non-Iranian sailors. The Greeks burned all the ships at their leisure, 'after first bringing out the spoils on to the beach; and they found some treasure in money'.[18] But the revolt in Ionia confronted them with a

[13] Olmstead, whose understanding of Greek history was clearly not on a par with his Persian, is very wide of the mark in speaking of a 'check at Salamis' but 'disaster at Mykale', and in saying that 'Mykale and not Plataea was the decisive battle' (*P.E.*, 253, 259).

[14] Thk. i, 138, 5; Aristogenes, Plut. *MH*, 21.

[15] His descendants were still here in 399 B.C., Xen. *Hell.* iii, 1, 6; on G. himself, see Thk. i, 128, 6. Gomme, in *Comm. on Thc.* I, pp. 290ff, followed by Meritt, Wade-Gery and McGregor in *ATL* III, chap. iii, argue (p. 292) that such gifts were 'but empty show'; for the King did not abate his claims even when unable to make them effective. This last is true, as certainly as the fact that these cities paid tribute to Athens. But would it have been good policy for the King to make grants which were ineffective even at the time of granting?

[16] Xen., *ib* [17] H. ix, 107. [18] *ib.*, 106, 1.

new problem. With Xerxes still at Sardis, how were they to protect the newly-liberated? They sailed back to Samos and debated the matter. The Peloponnesians, still thinking in terms of their oath to destroy the Medizing states in Greece, and dismayed at the 'impossible' idea of keeping troops permanently in Ionia, proposed an 'exchange of populations'; let the Ionians migrate back to Old Greece and settle in the trading towns of the Medizers! The proposal was quite impracticable, for there were not trading-towns, above all not sea-ports, sufficient to house a quarter of the Greeks of Ionia and Aiolis; and in any case, proposals for a general evacuation of Ionia (already put forward long ago by Bias of Priene, p. 47) had remained mere words, chiefly no doubt because such an enormous operation was something easier said than carried out. But it was on different lines, and lines characteristic of the time, that 'the Athenians' (i.e. Xanthippos?) chose to answer: that the Ionians were 'colonists from Athens', so it was not for Peloponnesians to decide their fate; nor would Athens consent to Ionia being depopulated.

> In face of this vehement opposition, the Peloponnesians yielded; and then they enrolled the people of Samos, Chios and Lesbos and the other islanders who were on the campaign with the Greeks, in their alliance, binding them by oath and pledge to stand by it and not to leave it. Having done this, they set sail to destroy the bridges, which they believed to be still in place; so they set off for the Hellespont.[19]

The 'exchange of populations' was thus postponed for 2400 years. To destroy Xerxes' bridges had long been in the minds of the Greeks; proposed before Mykale, and even directly after Salamis; the reason being, not only that they enabled the Persians to stop imports of Black Sea foodstuffs, already important to the growing towns,[20] but that Greeks continued to think for a long time that the invasion might be renewed.[21] To demolish the bridging material and not least to capture the precious cables would be a blow at enemy resources well worth striking.

The whole fleet, then reinforced by the new allies, sailed north[22] and, after being checked by the usual north winds off the Troad,

[19] H. ix, 106, 2ff.

[20] And not only to Athens; cf. H. vii, 147, 2.

[21] Cf. the Spartan argument on the walls of Athens, Thk. i, 89.

[22] *ib.* 114, Thk. i, 89.

reached Abydos, only to find the bridges gone. Whether they had again torn loose under stress of weather, we are not told; they may have been deliberately taken down and their shipping released. An officer named Oiobazos had taken the cables (towed them?) to Kardia; but on the news of the Greek approach, the Persians from all round (evidently not many) including Oiobazos, with the cables, collected in the small but strong city of Sestos, at the former bridgehead. Finding the bridges gone, the Peloponnesians went home, but Xanthippos with the Athenians and Ionians, to whom we now find Hellespontine Greeks also rallying,[23] determined to eliminate this centre of resistance. Sestos was ill-provisioned; Artaÿktes, the local governor, former commander of the (26th) Caucasian contingent and 'a terrible and violent man', much hated locally,[24] had been taken by surprise. The defenders held out till they were 'boiling their bed-straps' for soup; autumn came, and the weather broke; the Athenians grew restive, and clamoured for the generals to lead them home; but Xanthippos declined to budge 'till he had taken the place, or the Athenian government recalled him'. (Had he received orders to reëstablish Athenian power in the Chersonese?)

At last the starving Persians slipped out by night, 'down over the wall at the back', on the land side, where there was a gap in the besieging lines; but they did not escape. Oiobazos was captured by the Thracian Apsinthioi, who 'sacrificed him to Pleistōros, their tribal god, in their accustomed manner; but they killed his followers in another way'. Artaÿktes and his party were overtaken by the Greeks at Aigos Potamoi, a few miles up the coast, and overwhelmed after a stern resistance; he himself was one of those taken prisoner, and Xanthippos, refusing an offer of a huge ransom, had him crucified, a piece of savagery accounted for by the complaint that Artaÿktes had plundered and desecrated the temple of the Trojan War hero Protesilaos, on Helle's Cape, keeping his harem in the sanctuary. 'Then they sailed back to Greece, taking with them among other spoils the cables of the bridges, to dedicate in their temples. And this was the end of the operations for that year.' [25]

Artaÿktes is the fifth of the 29 contingent-commanders of 480 to be

[23] Thk., *ib.*

[24] H. vii, 78; ix, 116.

[25] H. ix, 115–120. P. Amandry makes the interesting suggestion that the cables were hung in the Stoa of the Athenians at Delphi (see *Fouilles de Delphes*, II; *Le Portique des Athéniens*, pp. 110f).

named and reported killed in 479, the others being Tigranes (2nd), Pharandates (27th), Masistios (28th) and Mardontes (29th); all, except perhaps Pharandates, are in new posts, presumably promoted between the campaigns. Xerxes had also lost one admiral, Ariabignes; one marshal, Mardonios; and the two younger half-brothers killed at Thermopylai. The list of notables killed need not be complete; but even as it stands, it indicates that the expedition, though by no means destroyed, had been very bloodily repulsed.

2. *Herodotos Ends his History*

It is here, at the end of the campaign of 479, with the liquidation of the great invasion and the return of Xerxes to his amours and their attendant horrors,[26] that Herodotos ends his great work. All later historians, including those who criticised him, followed him here. They agreed that the years 480–79 both witnessed actions and efforts of unprecedented magnitude,[27] and also marked an epoch. Thucydides understands by 'the Persian War' just the events of those two years, and distinguishes it, as a historical 'period', the point at which most of his predecessors had ended their work, from the succeeding fifty years, which so far had never been properly treated;[28] and Diodoros, with the Ephoran 'vulgate' behind him, having recorded the fall of Sestos, likewise marks the epoch: 'This was the end of the so-called Median War, which had lasted for two years', adding that this was where Herodotos ended.

The fact is that Herodotos' choice of a stopping-place is artistic. He stops after a great climax, to which the whole first two-thirds of his work had been building up. It is also not unscientific, in that, with the years after 479, new themes appear: the emergence of Athens as the leading power in Greece, surpassing Sparta for a time, and Athens' dealings with the liberated states which looked to her as a leader; a fit subject for a great history, which unfortunately no one ever wrote. Really, the war with Persia continued, vigorously waged by Athens and her allies; but from 478 onwards it is only one strand in a multicoloured cord of history, together with the dealings of Athens with Sparta, of Athens with her allies and of Sparta with hers, including the upheavals in the Peloponnese which for years rendered Sparta unable

[26] H. ix, 108–113. [27] Thk. i, 23, 1. [28] *ib.* 97, 2.

to exercise any influence without. We could wish that Herodotos had gone on, to tell us of the organization of Athens' new confederacy, and its prosecution of the counter-offensive. But Herodotos had probably also personal reasons for stopping where he did; sheer fatigue, not least, after the prodigious effort of producing his masterpiece under almost primitive conditions in everything from travel to writing materials. But there was also the fact that, if the history of inter-allied relations during the invasion was often controversial, to deal with the rise of the Athenian Empire as a contemporary issue would have been handling dynamite. Herodotos had already felt constrained to apologise for giving his candid opinion that in 480 Athens saved Greece. He felt no call to court martyrdom by writing what he thought about her behaviour since then.

So in the end, the great political and military history of the great Fifty Years never was written; and the actors in its drama died, and now it never can be written. Hellanikos, a learned man but not a Herodotos, wrote down the chief events; Thucydides, dissatisfied with him, wrote but left unfinished a summary of them, for inclusion in the introduction to *his* great contemporary history of the tragic sequel; sketchy and, as he left it, imprecise in chronology; exactly the faults which he found in Hellanikos. Perhaps the first full-length study was that in the general *Greek History* of Ephoros in the next century, an age of political theory and artistic prose, but as little capable of entering into the hopes and heartbreaks of the Fifty Years as the Enlightenment of understanding the Wars of Religion. Plutarch, for his fifth-century *Lives*, was left with these brief chronicles, later histories, contemporary comedy, and for other contemporary prose such things as the pamphlets of Stēsimbrotos of Thasos, a sophist, anti-Athenian and fiercely partisan.[29]

For the history of the Athenian Empire, which developed out of the League of the liberated cities, the most important work done in modern times has been that of the epigraphists, and of the archaeologists who provided them with their raw material; a work which in the course of more than a century has restored to us very nearly as much as ever can be restored of the documents of fifth-century Athens; culminating in the four volumes of *The Athenian Tribute-Lists*, by

[29] *FGH* 107 (with Jacoby's commentary on him). Both on S. and on Plutarch's sources and methods in general, see Gomme's introduction to *Comm. on Thuc.*, I; especially the admirable essay on Plut., *ib.* pp. 54–84.

B. D. Meritt, H. T. Wade-Gery and M. McGregor, and owing much to their former colleague, the late A. B. West. But there is still much that we do not know, and that is probably lost for ever. Among other things, we know scarcely anything beyond what Thucydides tells us in a few lines of his introduction (i, 96) of the initial organization of the League.[30]

3. *The Continuation of the War*, 478–449

There are therefore grounds for ending a history of the Persian Wars where Herodotos ends his; adding only a brief summary of the later campaigns, by way of reminder that the war did *not* end in 479.

Inter-allied differences were not slow to appear with the passing of the acute crisis.

> When the Persians had retired from Europe,[31] having been beaten both by sea and land, . . . the Athenians brought back their women and children and the possessions they had saved, from the places where they had deposited them.[32]

(As far as it goes, this is rather in favour of the presumption that the women and children were *not* brought back immediately after Salamis.)

> They now began to rebuild their city and walls; for not much of the perimeter was left standing, and most of the houses were down, only a few remaining, in which the Persian grandees had lodged.

Sparta, prompted by Corinth and Aigina, now thoroughly afraid of Athens, then demurred, urging that a fortified city could be a base for the Persians if they came again (cf. p. 515 above), and that the Pelopon-

[30] This is fully and brilliantly discussed in *ATL* III (the volume of essays, discussions and conclusions, directed to the general reader and very strongly to be commended); pp. 227ff. On the other hand Mr Hammond's account of it (*HG*, 256f) contains statements for which I know of absolutely no evidence, nor have I met a scholar who does; in particular, that 'The constitution was bicameral, the Athenian state forming one chamber and the Synod of the Allies . . . the other'; and that 'Athens had no vote in the Synod'. The latter was the case in the renewed Athenian naval league of 378; but since the constitution aimed at allaying fears aroused in the allies by memories of Athens' domination of the former ('Delian') league, it is more likely that this provision was a newly invented safeguard. It seems that Mr Hammond, in the effort to be lucid, has fallen into the error of stating as facts things that are at best uncertain.

[31] Thk. i, 89, 2; sc. Artabazos and the remnants of the field army; for, as will be seen, the Persians held fortresses on the north Aegean coast for years.

[32] *ib.*, § 3. 'From Troizen and Salamis', and 'after Plataia', D.S. xi, 39, 1.

nese was the best citadel for all Greece.[33] It looks like a shabby attempt to take advantage of Athens' exhaustion,[34] in order to keep her vulnerable to Peloponnesian pressure; though the extent to which men can believe that what suits themselves is right and proper seems to be unlimited. Mardonios had certainly made no use of any Greek fortifications. But at Athens the fortification was continued and made defensible, under the inspiration of Themistokles, who went himself to Sparta (using his prestige there), blandly denied that any such work was going on, and invited the Spartans to send envoys to see for themselves – who were then held as hostages for the safe return of Themistokles and his fellow-ambassadors, Aristeides and Habronichos.[35] Worked stones out of the ruins, including the archaic bases with the 'hockey-players' and other ball-game and wrestlers reliefs, built into the walls in this emergency, survive as relics of a famous and typically Themistokleian incident.[36]

It was an unpromising beginning to a new era; but the Spartans pocketed their pride and said they had meant well; and the campaign of 478 was planned by the allies, as a direct continuation of that of 479. The commanders on land and sea interchanged their stations. Pausanias, with only twenty ships from the Peloponnese, joined by thirty from Athens under Aristeides and 'a large number of the other allies', among whom the ships of Lesbos, Chios and Samos were prominent, sailed to Cyprus and 'conquered most of it' (winning the somewhat timid adhesion of the Greeks there, but probably not attempting the siege of Phoenician Kition). Then, apparently in the same summer, they sailed all the way round to Byzantion, still held by a Persian garrison, and besieged and took it.[37] Both operations were logical sequels to the campaign of Mykale and Sestos. Meanwhile Latychidas and Themistokles undertook the reoccupation of northern Greece; but the idea of taking fierce vengeance on all who had Medized without 'dire necessity' was dropped as soon as ever the nationalists were faced with the realisation of what it would mean. Even a Spartan proposal to expel from the Amphiktyonic League all states which had not fought on the right side was defeated in its Synod, on the motion, it is said, of Themistokles, fearing that with the exclusion of Argos, Boiotia and all Thessaly,

[33] *ib.* 90, 1f.
[34] Hammond, *HG*, p. 254.
[35] Thk. i, 90f; on H., cf. p. 385 above.
[36] Bearing out the remarks of Thk. i, 93, 1.
[37] Thk. i, 94; cf. Plut. *Ar.* 23.

Sparta and her allies would dominate the League, and arguing that the 31 states, 'mostly quite small', which had actually fought, could not claim to represent Hellas.[38] 'Collaborating' governments were suppressed in Phokis and part of Thessaly; it is to this juncture that we should ascribe the Spartan ejection of 'the tyrants Symmachos of Thasos and Aulis of Phokis... and of the *dynasteia*' [rule of an irresponsible clique] 'of Aristomedes and Angelos in Thessaly by King Leotychides'.[39] But the operations in Thessaly and so far afield as Thasos were prolonged. We hear of a Greek fleet wintering at Pagasai, the port of Pherai, where perhaps Aristomedes and Angelos had held sway, and (a piece of 'secret' and therefore dubious history) of a proposal by Themistokles to destroy the Peloponnesian fleet by arson, rejected by Aristeides (back from Byzantion?) when the Athenian assembly had instructed Themistokles to communicate his mysterious 'secret proposal' to that just man.[40] In the end the crafty Aleuadai kept their position at Larisa, negotiating a peace, and reinforcing their pleas with a 'present' to Latychidas. Latychidas is said to have been 'caught in the act' in his tent, 'sitting on a glove full of money'. After his return to Sparta he was impeached for failure to complete the conquest of Thessaly 'when it was possible', was found guilty of taking bribes (476), and fled to Tegea, where he died seven years later.[41]

The year 477 saw the end of operations by the League of the Hellenes; for in the east, in the mean time, Pausanias had made himself unpopular with the liberated Greeks by tyrannical behaviour, and was removed from the command by his government; and the allies refused to take orders from the officer sent to replace him. They transferred their allegiance to Athens as leader and executive 'managing director' in operations against Persia, and Aristeides was charged, with general approval, with assessing the contributions to be paid permanently to a common war-fund, managed by Athenian 'Treasurers of the Hellenes'.[42] Sparta, with her troubles at home, and uneasy at the repeated cases of her royal commanders 'deteriorating' under the temptations of power abroad, withdrew not unwillingly from oversea operations; and from 476 begin the independent campaigns of 'the

[38] Plut. *Them.* 20; Ael. Arist. xlvi, p. 290 Dind.; discussed by Busolt, GG II², p. 655n; Bengtson in *Eranos* XLIX (1955), pp. 85ff.

[39] Plut. *MH.* 21.

[40] Plut. *Them.* 20.

[41] H. vi, 72; cf. Paus. iii, 7, 9.

[42] Thk. i, 95; Plut. *Ar.* 24f, *Kim.* 6.

Athenians and their allies' organized in the new Confederacy of Delos.[43]

The first task undertaken under the new dispensation was the dislodgment of the Persians from Thrace; and that the Persians were not demoralised is shown by the brave and stubborn resistance of their coastal garrisons. Boges, left by Xerxes at Eion, which guarded the Strymon bridges, was starved out only after a considerable land campaign to cut him off from the Thracians inland, and when things grew desperate 'piled up a great pyre and slew his wife and children and concubines and menservants upon it, and threw all the gold and silver in the city over the wall into the Strymon and finally threw himself into the fire'. Athens commemorated this great victory (476?) by a special monument, and it brought increased prestige to her new, young commander-in-chief, Kimon the son of Miltiades.[44] Maskames at Doriskos held out as bravely and with more success. The Persian power in Europe was firmly rooted. 'Governors had been set up even before Xerxes' expedition, throughout Thrace and the Hellespont region; they were all driven out from both regions by the Greeks thereafter, except him; but Maskames at Doriskos survived all attempts to eject him, though many tried.' [45] His garrison presumably finally withdrew by permission of the King.

In the mean time, Kimon had cleared out the piratical Dolopes of Skyros, and Athens colonised that island (where the 'bones of Theseus' were found and brought home with honour);[46] and proud and isolationist Karystos was forced to join the League; but there was an unhappy foretaste of things to come when Naxos announced her secession (in defiance of oaths sworn; she was already tiring of campaigning under Athens' orders) and had to be coerced by force.[47]

[43] Thk. *ib.*, § 7; 96f; signalising the change by a 'second beginning' to his historical summary, 97, 2.

[44] Thk. i, 98, 1; date presumed from the order in his narrative; Boges, H. vii, 107; more details in Plut. *Kim.* 7, who quotes the 'Eion epigrams' from the monument (on which cf. also Aischines, iii, 183–5); discussion of these, Jacoby in *Hesp.* XIV (1945). This is K.'s first well-authenticated *strategia* (Wade-Gery in same vol.); though Plut. (*ib.* 6, *Ar.* 23) seems to think of him as general with Aristeides already in 478, when he would have been barely 30; if he was elected as soon as ever he was qualified by age, it would be a parallel to the case of another handsome and spectacular young aristocrat, Alkibiades (Thk. v, 52, 2; cf. 43, 2).

[45] H. vii, 106. Thk. (i, 98), mentioning only achievements, omits these operations. For Kimon chasing out Persian remnants in the Chersonese (withdrawing from Thrace?) cf. Plut. *Kim.* 14 (dateless).

[46] Thk. *ib.*; Plut. *Kim.* 8, *Thes.* 36.

[47] Thk. *ib.*

During all these campaigns in the Aegean, moreover, the Persians had reëstablished their control over Cyprus and rebuilt their Levantine sea-power. It was not until after the siege of Naxos that Kimon sailed east of Knidos (467?), bringing Phaselis into the confederacy, not without resistance, and winning the proudest triumph of the Delian League in the destruction of the new Phoenician and Levantine fleets in the mouth of the River Eurymedon; a second and greater Mykale. But then there was again trouble in Greece, with the secession of powerful Thasos, suppressed only after a siege lasting through two winters, and an appeal for help from Sparta against the Helots, ending in open coldness and the fall of pro-Spartan Kimon from favour, when Sparta dismissed her dangerous, democratic allies unthanked.[48]

The triumph at the Eurymedon laid open the Levant, so that (as after Mykale) modest squadrons under Kimon's democratic successors could patrol there unopposed: the young Perikles with 50 ships, and Ephialtes with only 30.[49] But coldness between former allies in Greece developed into open war with Corinth and Aigina. In spite of this, Athens with impressive power and superb self-confidence attempted the conquest or liberation of Cyprus again; and from there, the League fleet of 200 ships, seizing an opportunity which appeared, sailed to support a rebellion in Egypt, in which the royal satrap Akhaimenes was defeated and killed (about 460–59).[50] If this rebellion could have made good the independence of Egypt, it would have been the greatest setback that the Persian Empire had ever suffered; but what followed was to show that Persia was still formidable. The war lasted for six years – as long as the Ionian Revolt – with 'many vicissitudes'. The Athenians cleared Phoenician ships from the Delta; Memphis was taken; but Persian survivors and their Egyptian collaborators held out in the White Castle, the citadel of Memphis, apparently for years, until Megabyxos, the young marshal of 480, with a great army ponderously mobilised, crossed the Sinai desert and broke into Egypt to their aid. A Phoenician fleet trapped the Athenians in turn in the Nile (not, presumably, the same original League fleet, left unrelieved all that time, but certainly a large fleet). The Athenians were besieged in turn, on an island called Prosopitis, somewhere in the western delta, till the

[48] Thk. i, 100ff; Plut. *Kim.* 12–16; D.S. xi, 60–64; 'epigrams' (from contemporary monuments?) *Anth. Pal.* vii, 258 and *ap.* Ael. Ar. xlix (II, p. 512 Dind.); [Simonides] 105, 142, Bgk.; 132, 171 Edmonds.

[49] Plut. *ib.*, 14, 2.

[50] Thk. i, 104; H. vii, 7; cf. iii, 12.

Persians (great as ever in the military use of the spade) dammed and drained the channel in front of them, and assaulted by land (454). 'Few out of many' Greeks, after a retreat across the Western Desert reached Cyrene; Inarōs the Libyan chief, who had led the revolt, was captured, and later put to death; and Egypt was a Persian province again, though parts of the Delta held out for a long time.[51]

It was a terrible disaster to Athens. Some scholars, impressed by the fact that the League and even Athens' dominance in Boiotia, which Myronides had won in 457, did not immediately collapse, have doubted whether it was really so great, and supposed that only a relatively small Athenian and allied relief expedition was involved; but this is not the impression that we get from the ancient authors. 'This was the end of the great expedition of the Athenians and their allies to Egypt', says Thucydides (i, 110, end); and the tradition in the fourth century was that 200 ships and crews were lost.[52] At home, Perikles brought back to the Aegean the 100 ships, which had lately sailed round to Pagai on the Corinthian Gulf.[53] The League treasury was transferred from Delos to Athens, where the lists of Athena's sixtieths now begin. Athens made no more great conquests, and did lose her mainland 'empire' rather easily seven years later. She never again voluntarily fought simultaneously against Persia and the Peloponnesians. She was weakened, though not broken; even the disaster in Sicily in 413 did not break her. But never again was there an *annus mirabilis* like that (459) when the tribe Erechthēis, bleeding from the loss of 177 men including two generals, in a year with no serious reverses, recorded proudly that they had fallen 'in Cyprus, in Egypt, in Phoenicia, at Halieis' [in Argolis], 'at Aigina and Megara, IN THE SAME YEAR'.[54]

Remnants came home; Cyprus 'went lost' again; both in east and west, the wars languished, and for three years Thucydides' sketch has nothing to report. Only when a five-years' truce had been arranged with the Peloponnesians, through Kimon, back from his exile by *ostrakismos*, was another blow struck at the national enemy.

By now only men over thirty could remember Salamis; even

[51] Thk. i, 109f; D.S. xi, 71, 74f, 77; some additional details in Ktesias, 32–34, apparently better here than on Xerxes' expedition, as we get nearer his own time; though it may only be that, with less other information, we are unable to check him.

[52] Isokr. viii, 86. For some modern views, cf. Gomme, *Thucydides* I, pp. 321ff.

[53] Thk. i, 111, 2f.

[54] *IG* I², 929; Tod, *GHI* no. 26.

Perikles, now Athens' leading statesman, was too young to have fought there. Perikles, a realist and ever anxious to husband the city's manpower, was probably already against the view that the war should go on for ever; but he may have agreed that it would be better to make peace after a victory. Probably in 450, once more, as in the year of the Eurymedon, Kimon with 200 ships of the Athenians and their allies sailed for the Levant. It was an attempt to do again what had been done before; like Drake's last expedition.

Greek Cyprus was 'liberated' yet once more; but it does not seem to have shown much enthusiasm. Fought over again and again, the island had suffered much. The classical age, the great age of art in Greece, is in the culture of Cyprus poorer than either the archaic or the Hellenistic. Of the League fleet, 60 ships were detached to support once more the Egyptian resistance, still continuing in the Delta. The rest besieged Kition. But before its walls Kimon died. The besiegers ran short of food, and Megabyxos, the victor of 454, was building up forces in Cilicia for a counterstroke. In face of this threat the Greeks gave up the siege. They recalled the squadron from Egypt, and 'sailing past Cyprian Salamis, gave battle both on land and sea against the Phoenicians and Cilicians and Cypriotes; and, victorious on both elements, they sailed for home'.[55] Kimon's last victory, said to have been planned on his deathbed, had done little more than make good a safe retreat.

Both sides knew by now that no desired objective would be won by continuing the war; at least, no advantage commensurate with the effort required; and there is no reason to doubt Diodoros' statement that at this time (he says, probably by misunderstanding, before the Athenians withdrew from Cyprus) peace was made. Megabyxos and Artabazos, now satrap at Daskyleion, are said to have communicated to Athens the fact that the King, Artaxerxes the son of Xerxes, would deign to negotiate.[56] Kallias, the husband of Kimon's sister and Athens' best diplomatist, headed the delegation that went to Sousa.[57] There were concessions by both sides. Persia agreed not to send warships west of Phaselis and of the Kyaneai (the 'Blue Rocks', just east of the Bosporos), i.e. not into the Aegean or Propontis, and not to station troops within a certain distance of the coasts relinquished to the

[55] Thk. i, 112; Plut. *Kim.* 18; D.S. xii, 3f, who says that Kition was taken; a typical piece of 4th-century 'improvement', by Ephoros or the tradition that he received?

[56] D.S. xii, 4, 4f.

[57] As mentioned first (in passing and without mention of their business) by H. (vii, 151).

Greek League; a distance variously described as three days' march,[58] one day's ride on a horse,[59] or 500 *stadia*, something over 50 miles;[60] all three come to much the same thing, and one would like to know if all represent a distance given in Persian parasangs. Athens for her part abandoned Cyprus and her allies in Egypt; this was no cause for pride, and is not publicised; Kallias is even said to have been impeached and fined. She also appears to have ceased to keep garrisons on the Asian mainland, as she had recently at Erythrai.[61] There appears, in fact, to have been an arrangement for 'disengagement' and the establishment of a 'demilitarised zone'.[62] The peace only became a matter of pride to Athens in retrospect, sixty years after, in contrast with the much worse treaty, surrendering Asia Minor, which Greek dissensions then enabled Artaxerxes II to impose. It is after this that orators begin to glorify the 'Peace of Kallias' [63] and that a version of its terms appears to have been set up at Athens; a propagandist document, which Theopompos promptly pilloried as an Athenian forgery, but which we may perhaps more gently call one of the fourth-century 'reconstructions' of documents from the glorious past (cf. pp. 376ff; 513n). That there was a treaty, though the epigraphic record of it may not have been a contemporary document, seems certain. The silence of Thucydides in the sketch of history in his Introduction counts for nothing; he omits many things; and what is decisive is that in his 'full text' (viii, 56) he mentions Darius II in 412, through Tissaphernes the son of Hydarnes,[64] as demanding, in the course of negotiations, that Athens *recognize his right* to send warships into the Aegean; i.e. negotiating for a revision of a recognized treaty. It had probably been

[58] D.S., *ib.*

[59] Kallisthenes *ap.* Plut. *Kim.* 13, 4 (Plut. with characteristic carelessness over chronology puts it after the Eurymedon); Demosth. *On the Embassy*, 273.

[60] Ael. Arist. *Panathenaic Oration*, pp. 249f, Dindorf; who also defines explicitly the position of the 'Blue Rocks'; *not* to be confused with Chelidoneai or 'Rocks of the Swallows', which he, among other writers, mentions instead of Phaselis; no doubt more authentically, since a city (even a 'frontier city' which Phaselis became) is not a suitable frontier point. Since all the evidence on this treaty is either rhetorical or late (or both) the evidence of this well-read author, much overlooked, is worth noticing, as it is by J. H. Oliver in *Historia* VI (1957), pp. 254f.

[61] *IG* I², 10 + ; Tod *GHI* 29; Kallias fined, Dem. *loc. cit.* (n. 59).

[62] Wade-Gery in *Harvard Studies*, Suppl. Vol. I (1940), still the classic study of this treaty, to which reference is made in *ATL* III, chap. viii.

[63] First explicit extant mention, Isokr. *Paneg.*, 117ff (c. 380).

[64] Patronymic in the Lykian Xanthos Stele; cf. H. Schaefer *s.v.* Tiss., in *PW* Suppl. VII, 1580; probably grandson of the Hydarnes of 480, for whose subsequent command in Asia Minor cf. Hdt. vii, 135.

reaffirmed soon after his accession (423), when one of Athens' representatives was Epilykos, an uncle of the orator Andokides.[65] At the same time, the Great King, who (like many people with less excuse) regarded his rights as on a different plane from other men's, had only recognized the Athenian power to protect Asian Greece *de facto*, as it were, and not *de jure*; and Tissaphernes' negotiations had been prompted by a command from the King that (now that Athens was in difficulties, 413–2) he should collect and forward the revenues of Ionia, which it had been impossible to collect while Athens was powerful.[66]

4. *De Finibus*

With Kimon had passed the last hero of the great years 480–79. Already long before him had passed Aristeides, carrying the banner of Athens into the Black Sea;[67] Xanthippos, not mentioned again after his return from Sestos, perhaps already a sick man; his son Perikles had inherited his estate in time to pay for the production of Aeschylus' *Persians* in spring, 472;[68] Latychidas in exile at Tegea in 469 (p. 558); Themistokles, prosperous in exile, as lord of Magnesia under Artaxerxes, about 465;[69] Pausanias at Sparta, miserably done to death, like Kleomenes before him.

Thucydides devotes a brilliant section of his first book (chapters 128–138, some eight pages of a modern text) to the moral and political decline and fall and death of the victor of Plataia and the escape of Themistokles, involved in his disgrace; it is too long to quote in an epilogue, and much more so to discuss in detail, but it demands mention, epitomising as it does the failure of Sparta; the vanity and luxury

[65] Cf. And. *On the Peace*, 29.

[66] Thk. viii, 5, 4f. – That there was a treaty has long been the verdict of those writers most highly distinguished by common sense, as against hypercritical views based on the silence of Thk. in book i, the exaggerations of its glories by the ever-unreliable tradition reported by C4 orators, and the inauthentic character of the inscription on view in C4 Athens, of which Theopompos complained. It is defended, e.g., by Grote (chap. xlv) against Mitford and Thirlwall; by Busolt (GG III, pp. 346ff), Meyer *GdA*[4], IV, i, 581ff, *Forschungen* II, 71ff; Beloch GG[2] II, i, 177f; How *ad* H. vii, 151; Gomme, *Comm. on Th.* I, 331ff. Wade-Gery, *op. cit.* (n. 62) and, with Meritt and McGregor, in *ATL* III, chap. viii, show how its existence accounts for the ensuing crisis in the fortunes of Athens and her empire. Against it, see now D. Stockton in *Historia* VIII (1959); I am not persuaded.

[67] Plut. *Ar.* 26.

[68] Archon Menon, *Hypothesis* to the play; P. as *chorēgós*, from the *Didaskaliai*, IG[2] II, 2318, *sub anno*.

[69] Thk. i, 138, 4ff; Plut. *Them.* 31.

of a young, princely general, convinced of his own brilliance, in high command in the glittering world outside Lykourgos' invisible walls; the early and apparently spontaneous overtures to Xerxes on the one hand and to the Helots, to support him in a revolution, on the other. The evidence against him sounds damning: that of letters to and from Persia and of his conversation, overheard by prearrangement, with his last messenger to Artabazos, a man of Argilos, whom Pausanias had seduced as a boy; who opened his letter, having noticed that former messengers never came back, and found that indeed it contained a request, 'Please execute bearer'. Thucydides, who did not believe everything he was told, believed that this was genuine. No such explicit evidence is cited against Themistokles, said to be incriminated with him; but his enemies in the aristocratic factions, which had drawn together, with a series of dynastic marriages, had already persuaded the people to 'ostrakize' him, and he did not choose to place himself in their hands for trial. But it must be asked, even if we can give no clear answer, what a man of Themistokles' intellect hoped to gain by communications with the defeated enemy. Was his fault no more than that of seeing too soon that it was folly to think of a war going on for ever, and that something must be done to curb the incessant internal hostilities of Greece? Pausanias sounds both a worse and a more foolish man; but if, instead of failing, he had succeeded in liberating the Helots, breaking the Spartan oligarchy, and bringing an undefeated Hellas into the Persian peace, much futile bloodshed might have been avoided, and historians would have applauded, instead of condemning.

It does not follow that the historians would have been right; and there is no doubt that, if Greece had then lost her freedom, it would have been disastrous. Persian government *was*, in the long run, deadening. Innocent of economic thought, the kings had no better idea of what to do with the vast surplus of their income in gold and silver over peacetime expenditure than to melt it into ingots and store it.[70] In spite of what was mined, taxes at traditional levels became more and more difficult to pay, and subject tax-payers were driven down to the condition of peasants or proletarians at subsistence levels. In Babylonia in particular, where business and legal documents, less numerous than of old, still give some first-hand evidence on economic conditions, it is all too clear that the later Achaemenids ruled an empire of depression and

[70] H. iii, 96; cf. above, p. 109.

decadence.[71] Nor was dominion ultimately good for the master-race itself. More and more land in Babylonia, estates sold off, wholly or in part, by tax-payers in debt to money-lenders, came into the hands of Persians, holding it under the military 'bow-tenure'; but not all families which thus left their native highlands long kept their military qualities. Persian military strength itself was thus dissipated and weakened. One of the reasons for the swift success of Alexander was that the imperial land-system could not produce good infantry;[72] and the kings came to depend for infantry more and more on Greek mercenaries. Herodotos, who travelled in the empire in a time of internal peace, seems to have seen with the insight of genius what was beginning to happen. After recounting the horrible fate of Artaÿktes, that 'violent man' who had enjoyed himself at the expense of his helpless subjects, he finishes his whole work with a Persian tale that the kings would have done well to take to heart. He tells how that same Artaÿktes' forefather Artembāres had taken the lead in proposing to Cyrus that the Persians, with the world at their feet, should migrate to some richer land:

> Cyrus listened, and did not think it a good idea. He said 'Do, if you will; but if so, prepare to be not masters but subjects . . . for it does not happen that the same lands produce splendid crops and good fighting men.' And the Persians were convinced and withdrew . . . and chose to be rulers, living in a poor land, rather than to be farmers in the plains and the subjects of others.[73]

If, then, the Greeks appear, as they so tragically do, to have wasted in wars and quarrelling their freedom so well defended, it certainly does not follow that our tradition is wrong in applauding their victory. It is sad that they so little heeded the teachings of their own wise men on the virtues of justice, moderation and generosity; but before they had squandered their heritage, they gave us what a victorious Persia and a conquered Greece could not have given, in the achievements of the next century. We may regret that we have no great political history of the 'fifty years' – a little less in reality, 478–433 – between the main narratives of Herodotos and Thucydides; but these years, as well

[71] See Olmstead, *P.E.* pp. 297ff, on 'Overtaxation and its Results'. Neugebauer (*The Exact Sciences in Antiquity*) notes, however, considerable progress, under the Achaemenid peace, in Babylonian science and mathematics.

[72] Cf. Tarn in *CAH* VI, 360f, 370, 379 (= *Alexander*, I, 15, 30, 45); etc.

[73] H. ix, 122 (also q. above, p. 61).

as the tragic years that Thucydides recorded, are the age of the Athens that we do know at first hand, in her best achievements: the temples, the sculpture, the poetic drama. We are not wrong if we see Athens as though transfigured, in a golden light. It was, after all, a contemporary and a non-Athenian, Pindar the Theban, who best saluted her:[74]

> O shining city and violet-crowned and famous in song:
> Bulwark of Hellas, glorious Athens, city of godlike men.

[74] Fr. 46 Bgk., 76 Sandys (Loeb), p. 556; itself built up from echoes in Aristoph. *Knights* (1329, cf. *Ach.* 636f) and from scholia on *Ach.* 674, *Clouds* 299, and on Ael. Arist. (III, p. 341 Dindorf).

THE END

Index

Not every proper name occurring in this book has been indexed; e.g. not those of individuals named only once in the text, unless of intrinsic interest or importance; nor, as a rule, of authors cited in the notes. References are given, however, selectively, to some citations of some authors, ancient and modern, whose contributions are particularly important, especially on matters of controversy, or who are themselves criticised, or who, like Aeschylus or Pindar, themselves belong to the period. References to later history are not indexed; nor are passing allusions to matters treated elsewhere; e.g. Panaitios of Tēnos is mentioned three times for one exploit, but indexed once. References to men of a city or country are indexed under its name.

References of the form (e.g.) 288n24, without stops, indicate that the information indexed is in the note.

Vowels long in Greek are indicated below (as in the text, on their first occurrences), with the exceptions of diphthongs, final *-e* and, in men's names, *-as*, *-es* and *-on*, which are always long.

Doric names are given in Doric forms, e.g. Leōnidas, Lātychidas (in Herodotos, Leonides, Leutychides).

The following abbreviations are used in the Index: Ath. = Athens, Athenians. Carth. = Carthage, Carthaginians. D. = Darius. d. = daughter. f. = father. K. = King. Gk = Greek. P. = Persians. s. = son. Sp. = Sparta, -ns. X. = Xerxes.

Postscript 1984

Professional students of ancient history know only too well that twenty-two years is a long time in their operations. Even when there is no new evidence, the old evidence is manipulated in new ways and new questions are asked of it. When we are fortunate, there is new evidence, sometimes provoking new questions. The topics covered in this book have had an active life since its publication in all these ways. However, no apology is needed for its reissue. Although there have been other treatments of its particular subject and of the Persian Empire as a whole in plenty since 1962, the book retains its particular merits. Burn has a thorough knowledge of Herodotos and his text, an intimate knowledge of the most relevant parts of the terrain over which the war was fought, and, above all, a sense of reality which both enlivens and controls his narrative; he hardly ever falls into the most dangerous trap which besets the professional Greek historian, the desire to find a place for all pieces of evidence, regardless of probability.

What is reprinted here is the 1970 text, in which some corrections were made, and he has himself offered a postscript already (Burn 1977), responding with characteristic openmindedness to new evidence and discussion on the battlefields of Marathon, Thermopylai and Plataiai. But he is occupied with other matters, and it has fallen to me to take the opportunity provided by the publishers for including additional material.

The bulk of what follows will be concerned with new evidence on the central themes of the book, and makes no pretence to being comprehensive. Few topics in ancient history, for example, have had more intensive recent study than the reforms of Kleisthenes (pp. 176ff), but the details have no place here; I pass this and other matters over in silence. I have also been sparing in reporting controversy which rests on no evidence other than that available in

1962; the new solutions offered seldom seem preferable to those of the author. This has involved a small amount of self-censorship; I have tried not to forget that this is Burn's book.

The history of the Persians before Cyrus remains obscure (see Cook 1983, 1–10). The views adopted in the text certainly seem to need some modification in the light of two relatively hard new facts. The site of Anshan has now been located well to the east of Elam at Malian, north-north-west of Shiraz, in the heartland of Persis, and a seal still in use in the Persian administrative system at the end of the sixth century bore the legend 'Kurash of Anshan, son of Chishpish'. In contrast, the gold plates from Ecbatana (wrongly described in the text, pp. 26–7) bearing the names of 'Ariaramnes . . . King in Parsa, son of Teispes, grandson of Achaimenes' and 'Arsames . . . King in Parsa, son of Ariaramnes' can no longer be thought of as contemporary documents. They are later Achaemenid pious forgeries, which accord with the genealogy which Darius gives himself at Behistun, but are not independent evidence. It no longer looks at all attractive to distinguish between two royal lines, one in Parsuash and one in Anshan, and it is by no means clear how the royal genealogy and Darius' claim at Behistun to be the ninth Achaemenid king should be reconstructed and evaluated.

On Cyrus himself there is virtually no new written evidence, but his palace and tomb at Pasargadai have now been carefully explored and described (D. Stronach, *Pasargadae* 1978). The most important general consequence is perhaps what may follow for Cyrus' religion from what have been claimed as Zoroastrian fire-holders; for this and all matters concerned with the religion of the dynasty, see now M. Boyce, *A History of Zoroastrianism* II 1982. One central fact even looks rather more doubtful than it did, the date of the fall of Sardis (pp. 40, 43, rather schizophrenic in the 1970 reprint), after re-examination of the crucial entry in the Nabonidus Chronicle (Grayson 1975, 107, 282). There is surely no room for another month name, so that prima facie we are dealing with a place which could be reached within a month after crossing the Tigris, and the reading Lu. . . is more than doubtful, 'suggested by historical probability rather than any clear indication from the traces'. The Chronicle reports no movement of Cyrus for 546/5, and then dissolves into fragments and lacunae for the next six years. To hold to 547 for the fall of Sardis is not impossible, but Herodotos' evidence for an autumn campaign will have to be discounted.

A steady stream of ingenious and learned treatments of the death of Cambyses, the usurpation of the Magi and the accession of Darius (besides the books, see also Bickerman and Tadmor 1978, Gershevitch 1981) have not altered the essentials of the problem; the majority view is still against Darius, despite his own pronouncements on the importance of truth. A good deal of detailed work has been done on the layout and scribal history of the Behistun inscription which need not detain us. It should be noted that Burn's account is almost entirely dependent on the Old Persian version. This and the Elamite (Sousian) version lack the casualty figures which appear in the Bablylonian text (and in Aramaic fragments found at Elephantine in southern Egypt), and which give an additional idea of the scale of the various revolts. Burn's stress on the importance of the Median revolt is justified; the number of those killed is lost, but 108,010 captives are claimed. The only other figure on this scale is, surprisingly, for the Margians, with over 55,000 killed and nearly 7,000 captured; 'the number of dead seems excessive for a tribal engagement. It may have resulted from sack of a city, perhaps Merv'. Rather over 10,000 dead are claimed for the two battles against Vahyazdata, 4,579 casualties in all for the force he sent against Vivana. Hystaspes' two victories in Parthia record about 13,000 dead and over 8,000 prisoners, but for the four successive campaigns in Armenia fewer than 6,000 dead are claimed. The figures for execution are enlightening in a different way: 49 impaled with Nidintu-Bel in Babylon, 47 noble heads hung from the battlements of Ecbatana, 52 (?) nobles impaled with Vahyazdata. The events of the year clearly thinned some local aristocracies a good deal.

There are two new substantial public texts of Darius. There had already been one building inscription from Susa (Kent, *Old Persian*, DSf), in which Darius described the building of his palace there and the various peoples who had brought and worked its various materials; for a very similar text about a different building, see *Revue assyriologique* 64, 1970, 149ff. The more surprising discovery from Susa came in 1972, the first known colossal statue of the Achaemenid period (*Journal asiatique* 260, 1972, 235ff, *Cahiers DAFI* 4, 1974, 73–160). The headless statue, representing Darius himself, is Egyptian in general appearance, but robed as a Persian. On the right hand side of the robe an inscription in the normal three languages, Old Persian, Babylonian, Elamite, reads: 'A great god is Ahuramazda who created this earth, who created the sky above, who created man, who created happiness for man, who made Darius king. This is the stone statue which Darius the King ordered to be made in Egypt so that he who should see it in future may know that the Persian man holds Egypt. I am Darius, great king, king of kings, king of lands, king on this great earth, son of Hystaspes, an Achaemenid. Darius the King says: May Ahuramazda protect me and all that has been made by me.' A much longer Egyptian text on the left hand side of the robe describes Darius, by contrast, in purely Egyptian terms. The simple view would be to suppose that the statue was originally set up in Egypt and removed by Xerxes to Susa after suppressing the Egyptian revolt, but there seems to be strong ground for believing that the stone is local to Susa, which complicates matters considerably.

The base of the statue gives a list of peoples in hieroglyphs, each in a cartouche, visibly the same but better preserved than those of the Canal Stelai (p. 115). It is now clear that these Egyptian texts, besides having variant nomenclature for Saka (Scythians) from that employed on other texts of Darius, did not have any entry for any kind of Greek or Carian at all. The current date offered for Darius' Egyptian texts is 497/6 (Hinz, *Arch. Mitt. Iran* 8, 1975, 115ff), and the explanation has been offered that the Egyptian designer thought it more prudent to avoid mentioning Ionians during their revolt; I doubt whether Darius would have approved of that.

There has been continued discussion of Darius' lists of peoples and complaint against Herodotos that his list of satrapies or financial districts in Book III fails to correspond with them. Since the picture of the Persian lists grows steadily more complex, part of the answer seems clearly to lie in the view put forward by Burn here (pp. 109–11) that the Persian lists are not lists of satrapies at all, but of 'the chief *peoples and lands* over which the Great King ruled'. Due tribute is paid to Burn for saying this in the most sensible treatment of the matter (Cameron 1973). Cameron provides the crucial evidence by pointing out that Elamite, which has determinatives to tell the reader whether he is to expect a human or a geographic name, used the human determinative in these lists. As he says, we can now omit the 'and lands' from Burn's statement. It must be admitted that the abolition of this argument against the authenticity of Herodotos' list does not in itself prove authenticity and some difficulties remain (p. 120, and see Cook 1983, 81–2).

I have referred to the three normal languages of royal inscriptions, Old Persian, Elamite and Babylonian. Since we find them supplemented by hieroglyphic in Egypt, there is no reason to doubt that they might on occasion be supplemented by Greek (p. 129). Our concentration on the Old Persian texts has perhaps obscured our ideas about its nature as a written language. It is now clear that the syllabary in which it was written was an artificial creation and that, with some very minor doubtful exceptions, it was only used for inscriptions of the King himself. There is some reason to think that it was not even created until the first years of Darius, since it seems fairly clear that the Behistun inscription was originally planned without it (Cameron 1973, 51). Moreover, its active life was very short. After the middle of the reign of Xerxes, no one ever writes anything in Old Persian which has not been written before; only the royal names are changed. It looks very much as if Old Persian is a prestige script, devised at Darius' orders, and it is doubtful whether there was ever more than one scribe in the empire at a time who could read or write it (Gershevitch ap. Hallock 1971).

Old Persian was not the, or even a, language of the written administration of the empire, and it is to the written administration which I now turn. It is here that the biggest advances in our knowledge of the empire have been made. In writing this book, Burn was certainly not blind to the possible role of Persian bureaucracy (see p. 319); others have been more prone to assume that, unlike all preceding Near Eastern empires, Persian interests were confined to riding, shooting and telling the truth. But he did not exploit even that evidence available to him. There were clues in Herodotos, not only the royal secretaries present at all satrapal courts (p. 107), but the scribes attending on Xerxes at vii 100.1, viii 90.4, and some significant texts were already available.

I summarise roughly what we now have. Climatic conditions in parts of Egypt are favourable to the survival of papyrus and parchment. Official texts in demotic Egyptian and Aramaic, pen-scripts which used these materials, survive, particularly those concerned with the dealings with the administration of the Jewish garrison at Elephantine and a substantial Aramaic dossier from the late fifth century on the private affairs of the satrap Arsames. Hardly any other place in the empire preserves these materials and, when the satrapal chancery at Daskyleion was found in the 1950s, only the clay sealings survived to tell us what we had lost. Further east, we move into the area of the stylus-scripts, normally written on clay tablets, Babylonian and Elamite. From Babylonia itself we have a little bearing directly on Achaemenid administration and might have more, if there were more assyriologists ready to work on such late and decadent material; there must be several thousand Babylonian tablets of the Achaemenid period lying unpublished in the great museums.

But it is Persepolis itself which has transformed the picture. Here the dominant language for us is Elamite, written on clay in a language easier to read than it is to translate, since the scribal class which produced it was heir to a long tradition which was neither Semitic, like Babylonian or Aramaic, nor Indo-European, like Old Persian. These were the first scribes of the new dominant race, just as, a thousand years or more later, the tide of history made Persians the first instruments of Arab bureaucracy. Fortunately, they did use some loanwords from more intelligible languages. Fortunately, there were other scribes at Persepolis as well, 'Babylonian scribes, writers on parchment'. They wrote in Aramaic; their parchments have not survived, but they have left a few inscriptions on stone objects and a few hundred unpublished clay tablets, and they occasionally scrawled a casual reference word in Aramaic on an Elamite tablet which we would not have otherwise understood. One tablet in Greek and another in Phrygian also survive to make up the picture.

These are the writers, but most of the administrators are Persian, most prominently for us Parnaka (Pharnakes) the son of Arsham (Arsames), who is likely to be Darius' uncle and father of the Artabazos so prominent in this book (see p. 324). Beside him, on a slightly lower level, is Zišsawiš, who long survives him; my guess is that he is Tithaios, hipparch in 480 (Hdt. vii 88.1). Such men do not write. The standard form of a letter from Persepolis is: 'Tell Harrēna the cattle-chief, Parnaka spoke as follows:', the actual message, then a date, then, e.g., 'Karkiš wrote (the text), Maraza communicated its message'. Parnaka's seal is then added. The procedure is clear. Maraza gives Parnaka's instructions to a scribe who commits it to writing. The letter goes to its destination and is read out there by a scribe (cf. Hdt. iii 127 on p. 107). Sound goes in at one end of the system and emerges at the other. No high administrator needs to be able to read, any more than a modern business man needs to understand the electromagnetics of a tape-recorder (Gershevitch ap. Hallock 1971, Gershevitch 1979). Provided that there are scribes with a common language at both ends of the line, the system works.

The Elamite tablets from Persepolis fall into two groups. The smaller group, the Treasury Tablets, was the earlier to be published, but covers a later period. 139 tablets run from 492 to 458. They are all concerned with disbursements of silver from the Persepolis Treasury. At first sight their most interesting feature was the way in which they seemed to show a transition from payments in kind to payments in silver, but later study showed that silver payments in lieu of rations were an emergency measure in winter 467/6, when grain prices seem to have risen very high.

The Fortification Tablets are a much larger body of material; over 2100 have so far been published. Their dates run from 509 to 493, and they are concerned with the transfer of food-products over a wide area responsible to Persepolis (but not Persepolis itself). They introduce us to a wide spectrum over the public sector of the economy, and reveal a picture in which everyone within that sector is drawing rations, on various scales; such scales were already visible in Babylonia and at Elephantine, and there is one Greek source (Polyaenus iv 3.32) which purports to give the allocation for the King himself. The texts vary in their nature: there are letters authorising the issue of rations, receipts for individual transfers, journal plus account texts which, for individual stations, summarise the individual transfers and draw up balances for a given accounting period. The conspicuous gap is any detail of how the foodstuffs arrive in the system in the first place; no doubt much of them come in tribute from the main areas of food production (cf. Hdt. i 192.1; apart from tribute, the whole of Asia is divided up to provide sustenance for the King and his army. Babylonia feeds him for four months, the rest of Asia for eight).

The collection throws light on people at rest and people moving. For those at rest we have extensive information about work-groups, designated rather mysteriously by means of the officials who 'assign' or 'apportion' them, which enables us to build up a remarkable picture of the size of the operations involved. Dandamayev (*Altorientalische Forschungen* II, 1975, 71ff, in English) has calculated that the tablets show over the period 509–494 15,376 people on the ration-rolls attached to 108 villages, and has found 8,728 in 497 alone. His figures do not add up and must be heavily misprinted, but his general scale is right, and so is his observation that men and women are roughly equal in number and that a substantial number of children are fed. These are therefore, broadly speaking, dependent populations, not paid workers, whatever terminology of dependence is used. They have not necessarily been hijacked and branded like those of the satrap Arsames in Egypt (Driver, *Aramaic Documents* VII), but some of them may have been. Some of the very large groups with foreign ethnics, Cappadocians and Thracians among them, are clearly at least transplanted populations.

Sometimes the information about these work-groups is sufficient, with some qualifications about our knowledge of Elamite vocabulary, to build up quite a detailed picture about the range of activities going on in a particular place or area (Hinz, *Zeitschrift für Assyriologie* 61, 1971, 266ff). At Shiraz in 494 we find an establishment of 181 workers: an 'ornament-protector' (the highest paid), six camp-administrators, one metal forger, two artists, ten treasury-guards, four craftsmen, five furniture-makers, five house-servants. All these are male, but the women are also active: one chief-woman, 51 artists and 45 craftsmen, with equal pay to men of the same designation, plus two wetnurses and 11 cooks. Thirty boys and eight girls of various ages complete the establishment. At Rakama in the same year we get a very similar distribution in an establishment of 311. These settlements can almost be described as factories, ten times larger than anything we know of at Athens, except perhaps the shield-factory inherited by the orator Lysias and his brother, but did all their 120 slaves work in the factory? Whether we are translating the trade-designations rightly or not, the general picture is substantiated by texts where skins of slaughtered animals are delivered to at least six 'treasuries' at different places, presumably for processing (the cynical think for parchment, for writing more accounts).

All these workers are on minutely differentiated scales of grain-ration; skill as well as age is clearly relevant. A particularly nice group of texts records extra rations for mothers; they get twice as much for bearing a boy as for a girl.

Not only humans are fed. One establishment had 16,843 goats and sheep, with two male and three female categories for each, and the meticulous nature of the accounting aimed at is most clearly seen from a bird text listing ten different kinds, drawing rations from 1 quart of grain to a fiftieth of a quart a day. Hallock thinks that the biggest rations go to ducks and geese; I am still looking for an ostrich, known from literary sources as a royal delicacy. Greek sources (e.g. Hdt. i 192.3, Plut. *Eumenes* 8.5, Strabo xi 13.7) also gave us some insight into horse-rearing establishments. Media was most famous for this, but Persepolis has one stables where 135 men are looking after the horses and mules of the king and the princes. No stables has more than 90 visible horses, and most of our detail concerns what are clearly detachments of post-horses; doubtless the big horse-farms were in places where there was plenty of grazing. Some, evidently rather special, horses even get wine-rations, one 5 quarts per month (cf. Homer *Iliad* viii 189).

No one so far mentioned receives more than 60 quarts of grain a month, but ration-scales go far higher than this, right to the top of the social pyramid. Parnaka himself is entitled to and gets, no matter where he is, a *daily* ration of two sheep, 90 quarts of wine and 180 quarts of flour, his deputy Ziššawiš one and a half sheep, 30 quarts of wine and 60 quarts of flour, and Parnaka is not the highest. Darius' principal helper Gobryas, father of Mardonios, makes one appearance in the texts, getting 100 quarts of beer; beer and wine are normally equivalent and this is 11 per cent more than Parnaka. It now appears that he was on his way to meet his daughter-in-law, described as 'the wife of Mardonios, daughter of the king'. She gets 90 quarts of flour; the reasonable guess is that Gobryas himself got 200. These high rations mark their recipients as persons of great importance, and have for example made it possible to identify in one Datiya, on 70 quarts of wine, Datis, the commander at Marathon (see below).

The initial suspicion was that these enormous rations were to feed not only the man himself, but his household as well, and this is in fact precisely what is said by Herakleides of Kyme (689 F 2, J), the only Greek author who has the faintest idea about the system: a man's household gets its rations out of his rations. But this view seems to be contradicted by a new tablet: 'Daily by Parnaka together with his boys 480 quarts (of flour) are received. By Parnaka himself 180 quarts are received. By his 300 boys 1 quart each is received.' What actually happens when, as in this case, Parnaka turns up at a way-station on the Royal Road and has to be loaded down with flour, we cannot see clearly; I suspect that he is followed around by agents from the private sector and disposes of it for something more portable.

This last tablet introduces us to the most immediately attractive documents, the travel tablets. Three hundred or so documents record the issue at way-stations along the Royal Road of rations to travellers, in accordance with their entitlement as laid down by a document issued by the King or some official of satrapal status (the Persian word for such a document is linguistically identical with our *viaticum*). The shape of such a document is known from one in Aramaic issued by the satrap Arsames (Driver *Aramaic Documents* VI, quoted by Lewis 1977, 6). Dates of issue and the direction of the journey are often given. We can therefore not only pick out some interesting journeys, but get some precision about the movements of Darius and add to our list of his satraps.

The two most interesting journeys have already been alluded to. Gobryas' meeting with his new daughter-in-law was in February 498; Herodotus (vi 43.1) had been told that Mardonios had recently married the King's daughter Artazostra when he came to Ionia in 493. It had always been likely that Datis the Mede had had some previous experience in the West before he went to Marathon (see pp. 210, 218 here, still not impossible); we now find him returning to the King from Sardis in January–February 494, perhaps from a tour of inspection before the final campaign of the Ionian Revolt (Lewis, *JHS* 100, 1980, 194–5). Another, larger, party had come through from Sardis two months before. Other journeys are less spectacular or more tantalising, that of a mysterious, but evidently important, Indian from India to Susa and back under the guidance of an elite-guide in early summer 499, a party of 32 men taking the 'tax of Udana' (Otanes, but which? and why?) from Parikania to Susa in February 499, a 'treasurer' taking silver from Susa to Matezziš (in Persia) who gets mysteriously stuck for sixteen days in December 500. Sometimes, to diversify our picture of the Road, we get very large parties, 547 Egyptians, 150 Thracians, 1500 'lin-makers', all under elite-guides.

The new information about satraps and other high personages needs to be treated in a wider context. Herodotos' truthfulness, his ability and willingness to seek reliable information, have never lacked critics and sceptics, and they are at the moment a rising tide. In practice, of course, because of the virtually complete lack of Persian narrative sources for anything after the accession of Darius, anyone attempting a task like Burn's in this book has no real alternative to assuming that Herodotus is right except where he can be shown to be wrong; on no other basis can anything be done. I do not think that the reader will have found Burn unduly credulous of Herodotos. There are even traces of an appreciation of Herodotos' proneness to significant patterning and his use of persuasive techniques in his wording. Studies of this kind have been multiplying in recent years. I do not attempt a survey of them here; much is still unpublished. They do produce interesting results, but I tend to wonder whether Herodotos can have expected readers like their authors, equipped with printed texts in books and Powell's *Lexicon to Herodotus*, going over the texts backwards and forwards, and I suspect that some of the patterning detected is unconscious on his part. On a rather different level, there are attempts to see Herodotos as inventor of his facts, hardly travelling or enquiring at all. I select here Detlev Fehling, *Die Quellenangaben bei Herodot* (1971), who claims that, when Herodotos names his source, this is an infallible sign that he had no direct source. For many cases, this is more plausible than may be thought at first sight, and the consequences which may follow for some of Herodotos' travels are well explored by Stephanie West (*CR* 1978, 230–3, reviewing Lloyd's edition of Herodotos ii). A more detailed attack is planned by O. K. Armayor; his discussion of Xerxes' army list (Armayor 1978) is a useful start. In these circumstances, the appearance of a large new body of Persian material offers a welcome opportunity to check Herodotos' information over a wide field. There are more approaches than one, but I shall confine myself here to the prosopography, to the large body of knowledge which Herodotos appears to have about the family and subordinates of Darius and Xerxes.

The Persepolis tablets make one preliminary point. There has always been speculation about Herodotos' sources of Persian information (see pp. 13–14 here), particularly about the three items which look most documentary, the list of Darius' financial districts (iii 90–96), the Royal Road (v 52–54), and Xerxes' army-list (vii 61–99). The search for informants has always proceeded under the influence of a presupposition that there was a political and linguistic iron curtain between Greeks and Persians in the fifth century and that we have to look for specific breaches in it (for a recent survey, see Hegyi, *Acta Antiqua* (Budapest) 1973, 73ff in English). I do not share this presupposition. I have already shown (Lewis 1977, 12–15) that, in the Persepolis tablets, besides Greeks on lower levels, we find them close to high officials, in the same position as Maraza (p. 592), merely designated as Yaunā (the Greek). One was, from December 499 to September 498, the only visible aide of Parnaka himself; another, if he be another, was in the same position with the high official Artatakma early in 481. They only dictate, so they do not need to be literate themselves in Elamite; they do need to have enough spoken Persian and perhaps Elamite to do their job. If we find Greeks in a secretarial position as early as this and as far east as this, there should be no reason to doubt their availability to the King, and to satraps, particularly in the west, in all relevant periods. Certain kinds of information, including general Persian information, would be readily accessible to them, and the demonstration of their existence makes it more likely that Herodotos could have acquired such information. That he could have done is not to say that he did. To estimate the chances of that, we have to look at our new evidence.

The travel tablets, as I have said, provide us with new satraps, as well as confirming old ones. Besides Parnaka, mostly in Persepolis, and his deputy Ziššawiš, we find a Megabanos satrap in Susa (and his deputy Mardunda), an Artabanos satrap in Bactria, Hydarnes in Media, Megabazos in Arachosia/Gandara/Parikania, Artabawa in India, and satraps in Areia and Carmania; a few others are not so easy to locate. That list will illustrate the limitations of our evidence. Persepolis is the furthest east of the empire's capitals, and journeys to it are more likely to originate in the east; even for Babylon we only have one journey to it and none from it. Journeys from the western provinces are much more likely to end up in Susa. Since Herodotos' interests are inevitably fixed on the west, the correlations are likely to be reduced. This is a handicap, but nevertheless I find myself reasonably assured that most of the people in Herodotos must be real people. If one tries to correlate the names in Aeschylus or Ktesias (for this period; he gets better later in the century), one finds a much lower proportion of names directly transposable into Old Persian or Elamite and is left feeling that their names are merely vaguely oriental.

Some pieces of Herodotos' information are directly confirmed. (1) Artaphernes is attested in Sardis, where he should be, in November 495. (2) In iii 88 Darius marries Artystone daughter of Cyrus. In the army-list at vii 69.2 further information is given about her, and her sons Arsames (ibid.) and Gobryas (72.2) are named as commanders. Irtaśduna appears on 25 Elamite texts, as a recipient of rations, as an owner of fairly small numbers of workers, and giving orders for the issue of provisions from her estates, from March 503 to some time in 497. The two earliest texts show the King authorising the issue to her of 100 sheep and, say, 1940 litres of wine, perhaps for a special feast, and at least one more text shows him closely concerned in her affairs. Three texts of 498 associate her with Iršama, who must be her son Arsames. Arsames in his turn orders the supply of a large amount of grain to a woman called Uparmiya. She has been taken for his wife; there is more temptation to identify her with his step-mother, Parmis, daughter of Smerdis, another wife of Darius (iii 88.3, vii 88). (3) The new information about Gobryas and Mardonios I have already sketched. It was already clear that Herodotos had, if anything, underplayed the importance of Gobryas, prominent in the Behistun Inscription and one of the only two Persians to be both portrayed and named on Darius' tomb. Mardonios' rapid promotion is easily explained. (Artobarzanes, Darius' son by Gobryas' daughter (vii 2.2), turns up twice at Persepolis as a satrap whom we cannot place.)

Negative correlations of the type provided by the Behistun Inscription (p. 94) are not to be expected; our texts are not of that type. But it would be fair to say, since I have already mentioned two great ladies and there are two morc, Irdabama and Abbamuš, closely comparable with Artystone, that it has proved distressingly difficult to find Atossa; there is no clear explanation. For clearer contradictions in Herodotos' oriental prosopography, we have to go outside the tablets and outside the Persians. Herodotos appears to think that the King of Sidon in 480 was called Tetramnestos son of Anysos (vii 98, viii 67.2) and may have thought that the Lycian King was Kybernis son of Kossikas (vii 98, with a better word division); substantial doubts are possible about both.

I continue with cases where the tablets provide information consistent with Herodotos, in a way which makes his information sound more plausible. This is of course dangerous ground, since it is hard to conduct the investigation without tacit assumptions that Herodotos is right and that the task is to fit other information round him, but a representative selection may be of interest.

Herodotos reports no reward for the Bagaios who disposed of Oroites (p. 107). The omission can be repaired. Artystone is twice qualified with an Elamite word translated 'princess', a translation recently confirmed by its appearance qualifying ladies named as 'daughters of Hystaspes', who ought to be sisters of Darius; they have enormous beer rations. The only other princess in our texts is one Ištin, who receives two sheep together with Bakeya, presumably her husband; perhaps he is Bagaios son of Artontes. At a guess, since name-elements run in families, their son could be Mardontes son of Bagaios, commander of Red Sea Islanders in 480 and one of three fleet-commanders in 479 (p. 502); there is a suitable identification with Mardunda, deputy satrap in Susa in 499–494.

For most of Darius' commanders in the west, there is no very certain identification, although many of the names turn up in the tablets; the conspicuous exception is Megabates (pp. 195f) who appears at Persepolis itself later in the reign with a title for which 'admiral' seems the most plausible explanation. There is a curious case where Herodotos definitely helps the Elamite. An isolated high personage called Ziššamakka who appears in December 500 was thought by Hallock to be a freak spelling of the well-known Ziššawiš; in view of the Sisimakes (the mss. vary) who gets killed three years later (v 121), this seems untrue. Of the new evidence for Datis I have already spoken.

By the time we get to Xerxes' army, 14 years have elapsed since the last fortification tablet, but it is clearly possible that the senior men might be visible at Persepolis in some capacity. Among the marshals, there is a new possibility for the outsider Gergis who puzzles Burn on p. 323. He may well be the Karkiš who is satrap of Carmania at least from 501 to 494. Hydarnes, commander of the Immortals, is agreed to be the son of Hydarnes, one of the Seven;

Persepolis evidence shows the father as satrap of Media as late as 499. Among the hipparchs, as I have already said, Tithaios son of Datis could certainly be Ziššawiš, deputy to Parnaka and a principal functionary at Persepolis from 504 to 467. Two of the admirals call for comment. First, Prexaspes son of Aspathines. Burn (p. 94) rightly traces the intrusion of Aspathines into Herodotos' Seven to his importance later in the reign. Not only is he named as quiver-bearer on Darius' tomb, but he appears on Persepolis tablets in 494 and 483 as Parnaka's successor in charge of Persepolis. The inscription on his seal has been read as calling him son of Prexaspes. If this is right, this will solidify the connection back to the Prexaspes so prominent in Herodotos iii and forward to this admiral. As for Megabazos son of Megabates, the names are confusing. To Burn's attempt to sort them out (p. 335), I add a Megabazos satrap in Arachosia and Gandara between 501 and 494. A career in Afghanistan and Baluchistan is not a very satisfactory preparation for being an admiral, but perhaps the post is hereditary; see above, p. 600, on Megabates.

It would be tedious to descend to the commanders of contingents in any detail, though the impression of reliability persists. I single out, for his importance in 479 rather than in 480, Artabazos son of Pharnakes. Burn (p. 324) thinks him a rare commoner, but he now falls nicely into place as son of Pharnakes-Parnaka, Darius' uncle, so prominent at Persepolis; he would certainly have the social position to argue with Mardonios.

My general impression of the army list is that its nucleus of posts and commanders is highly plausible, but I do not think that it is a unitary document. It has always been relatively easy to detach the ethnographic notes about the former names of various peoples, particularly those which attempt to tie them into Greek mythology; most of these have close points of contacts with other parts of Herodotos' work, though he does not always tell the same story. As for the weaponry attributed to the national contingents, I agree with Armayor 1978 that there is a strong case for believing that much of it came from the ethnographic work of Hekataios and not from any official list. There are two coincidences with surviving fragments of Hekataios, and there is a further point which I find convincing. At vii 77.1 Herodotos is talking about the Kabelees and says 'they had the same equipment as the Cilicians which I shall describe when I get to the Cilicians as I go through'. I can only explain this by assuming that Herodotos is taking his information from a written source which did describe the Cilicians before the Kabelees and adapting it to his own needs which involve a list which has the Cilicians after the Kabelees.

A closer look at what remains suggests that there is not merely a list, but someone who transmitted it to Herodotos, embroidering it as he went along with a little more extra detail and explanation about, for example, who was married to whom, who was an Achaemenid, if that was not obvious, and scraps about later careers. Of the 29 contingent commanders, we get such extra information for 11. One of these bits, the longest (vii 69.2), is that most amply confirmed by Persepolis.

But to concede that there is a great deal in the list which is not documentary is not to concede that there is no documentary core at all. A very similar list was after all found in the Persian camp after the battle of Arbela (Arrian *Anabasis* iii 11.3–7). In fact, this may be the single case where it is legitimate to try to unwind Herotodos and to disentangle what he gives us into separate strands. It would be gross folly to attempt to extend this in any detail into non-documentary passages where Herodotos has woven his material more closely, but we should not neglect the general indications provided by this case about the way in which he has built up his work and formed first-hand information and the work of his predecessors into a literary narrative.

I turn now to Athens, where there is also new evidence, of a sort, and where there has been much scholarly activity. No one has yet fussed about the word 'recently' (*neôsti*) applied by Herodotos to Mardonios' marriage, which we now know to be of five years' standing; that can be as much a matter of Herodotos' information as of his use of the word. But a great deal of attention has been paid to the same word when Herodotos says of the year 481 that Themistocles had recently come among the first men. Since Burn has had a good deal to say about Themistocles already, he merely notes (p. 358) his late arrival in Herodotos and blames it on Herodotos' sources. There have been several attempts since Burn to support Herodotos, either by denying the archonship of 493/2 altogether, despite the clear evidence for it (p. 225), or by saying that it was unimportant, a young man's post. Consideration of the archonship ties in with another attempt to defend Herodotos, this time in his statement that Kallimachos, the polemarch at Marathon, was appointed by lot. The most ingenious and comprehensive of these studies (Badian 1971) argues that, ever since Kleisthenes' reforms, the nine archons had been elected en bloc and then assigned their particular posts by lot and that the shifting back of the lot one stage in 487/6 (p. 284) was a very minor change; the real heat of an archonship election and the consequent prestige for the winner had been done away with by Kleisthenes, and no long-term planning by Themistocles was involved (a clear survey of the problems by Rhodes 1981, 272–4). Badian's case depends largely on a too strenuous attempt to show that there is no visible difference in the status of the archons known from before and after the reform of 487/6, and he argues too strongly that little is in fact known about Themistocles before 481. It seems to me that what follows from Plutarch's *Themistocles* is that a good deal of anecdotal tradition about Themistocles was available, but that, for stretches of his career where neither Herodotos nor Thucydides had coverage, there was no narrative line to string it on.

The case for supposing Themistocles unimportant until 482 or so would be irretrievably wrecked if we were to acccept the orthodox view of the major relevant Athenian discovery of this period. From 1965 to 1968, Professor Willemsen, directing the German excavations in the Kerameikos, found close to 9,000 new ostraka there. Not many of them have been published so far, and very little about the circumstances of the discovery; since the area was normally waterlogged, the sherds may have moved in any case. But Willemsen has been generous with information and some main features are clear. The most substantial new methodological point is that many of the ostraka have been found to join each other to produce whole pots or parts of them. The natural assumption is that names on joining ostraka were candidates in the same ostracism; this is priceless information.

In what follows, I ignore 150 or so ostraka, mostly for Thucydides son of Melesias and Kleippides (father of the demagogue Kleophon), which clearly belong to the 440s. I take my figures from R. Thomsen, *The Origins of Ostracism* 93–4. My information about joins comes partly from published statements, partly from a lecture given by Willemsen in Athens in 1973. First the numbers. I asterisk names already known from deposits in the Agora which are clearly pre-Persian.

*Megakles Hippokratous Alopekethen	4647
*Themistokles Neokleous Phrearrhios	1696
Kallias Kratiou Alopekethen	760
Menon Menekleidou Gargettios	665
Kimon Miltiadou Lakiades	490
Leagros Glaukonos Cholargeus	83
*Aristeides Lysimachou Alopekethen	53
Agasias Arximachou Lamptreus	43
*Eratyllos Kattariou	36
*Hippokrates Anaxileo	36
*Habronichos Lysikleous Lamptreus	30
Philokydes Pheideleo ek Kolonou	19
Mnesiphilos Phrearrhios	14
(selected names)	
Kallias Hipponikou	12
Myronides Phlyeus	11
Alkibiades Kleiniou Skambonides	6
Alkmeon Aristonymou	6
Xanthippos Ariphronos Cholargeus	6
Dieitrephes Euthoinou	3
*Boutalion Marathonios	3
*Hippokrates Alkmeonidou Alopekethen	2
*Kallixenos Aristonymou Xypetaion	2
*Hipparchos Charmou	1
*Habron Patrokleous Marathonios	0

Of these, joins link Megakles to Themistokles, Kimon, Leagros, Aristeides, Hippokrates Anaxileo, Mnesiphilos and Kallias Hipponikou. No reported joins link Kallias Kratiou to anyone, and Willemsen reports that his ostraka were physically separated from the rest. He was previously virtually unknown; four ostraka describe him as a Mede; one adds a picture of him in Persian dress. It has been widely held that he is the missing pro-tyrant ostracised in 485 (p. 287).

The original assumption was that what we had here was a mixed deposit, covering material from the ostracisms of 486 and 485 together with sherds which might be as late as the late 460s. It was taken for granted that the Megakles ostraka belonged to the ostracism of 486, though there was literary evidence (Lysias xiv 39) for a second ostracism. Various consequences would follow. First, Megakles himself. There are several gossipy ostraka for him, accusing him of adultery, love of money, horse-rearing and the Alcmeonid curse, describing him as son of Koisyra and telling him to go to Eretria. Nothing so far reported suggests treachery; could it be that the story of Alcmeonid treachery in 490 had not yet been invented in 486? Themistokles, with several joins to Megakles ostraka, will certainly have been a prominent candidate in 486. More surprisingly, so will at least four people not known from the Agora to have been candidates in the 480s, above all, Kimon, a mere boy (Plutarch *Cimon* 4) when he paid his father's fine in 489. There are at least three joins between ostraka of his and those of Megakles and Themistokles, and they will take with them a fair proportion of those 490 votes.

With these surprising joins in mind and worried by the slight representation of Hippokrates Alkmeonidou and Kallixenos, prominent in the Agora in 482 (possibly 483 as well; see Meiggs-Lewis, *GHI* p. 44), I suggested another hypothesis (*Zeitschrift für Papyrologie und Epigraphik* 14 1974, 1–4), that the second ostracism of Megakles was a reality, that he had cleared his name of Persian leanings by returning to Athens in 480 (he certainly did), and that the Kerameikos ostraka were a unified deposit from an ostracism in the late 470s at which Megakles was ostracised a second time. To call it a unified deposit was certainly pushing things too far. No one supposes that Hipparchos, ostracised in 487, ever returned to Athens. Even without the complication about the year of Themistokles' ostracism (still not certainly known), there could hardly be a year in which Xanthippos, not heard of after 479 and presumably dead before his son Perikles was choregos for the *Persae* in spring 472, could have been a candidate together with Menon, described on one ostrakon as 'the ex-archon'; he was archon in 473/2. But I still think it likely that the Megakles ostraka, and those of Themistokles and Kimon which go with them, belong to Megakles' second ostracism. A historical reconstruction is not yet possible.

Etiquette prevents me from further discussion of gossipy ostraka; one which describes Themistokles, in curiously Aeschylean language, as 'liable to a curse' is particularly tantalising. Two points about names may be worth making. Themistokles' éminence grise, Mnesiphilos (pp. 280, 446), is revealed as a real figure, from Themistokles' own deme. No trace has yet appeared of the opponent of Themistokles, Epikydes son of Euphemides (Plutarch *Themistocles* 6.1), nor, unless Plutarch has scrambled the demotics, of the traitors of Plataiai (p. 526); late evidence must be treated with caution.

As I said before (p. 587), Burn has had afterthoughts on three of the battlefields. Marathon provides the most new evidence. (1) Vanderpool (*Hesperia* 35, 1966, 93ff) has re-identified the Athenian trophy, or at least a large column from it, near the edge of the Great Marsh and an area where masses of human bones were found in the nineteenth century; this suggests that the chief slaughter of the defeated Persians was a good deal further from the sea than suggested on p. 251. (2) A mound has been discovered in the foothills in the west of the plain. Half of it has so far been excavated, and shows 13 skeletons in separate graves, each with a headstone and a plate consistent with an early fifth-century date. All were males, 11 aged between 20 and 30, a boy of about 10, and a man of about 40, alone with a name on his headstone (ARCHIAS). Archias' grave contained a Boeotian cup. Burn accepts Marinatos' view that this was the grave of the Plataeans who fought at Marathon, on the left wing. (3) Vanderpool also (*Am. Journ. Arch.* 70, 1966, 329ff) stressed the weakness of the case for supposing that the Herakleion was near the Chapel of St. Demetrios where Burn and others had placed it. He urged that the clearest evidence came from an early fifth-century text about the Herakleia (now *IG* i^3 2/3) which had been found in the southern part of the plain, just north of the southern marsh. Burn conceded the force of this and found Vanderpool's placing of the Herakleion more tactically convincing in that the Athenians would be directly blocking, and not merely threatening from a flank, the main track to Athens by Pallene; he remains, reasonably, convinced that this was the way they had come. The argument is now even stronger, since a fifth-century verse dedication to Herakles (*SEG* xxvi 51) has now been found in the same area. It certainly looks as if we have now the approximate location of the Herakleion, and it will follow, despite Herodotos' silence on the point, that the Athenian right wing rested *on* the sea.

'And yet there remain the two phrases of Herodotos, both in vi 113, in which the initially victorious Persian centre pursues "inland", "into the *mesogaia*", and the finally victorious Greeks pursue "until they *came to* the sea". It seems that the battle must have ebbed and flowed at least partly up and down the Vrana valley. If encamped with their backs to Pentelikos, the Athenians might still have swung their left forward across the valley. It must be confessed that, even with the latest additions to our knowledge, many details about Marathon are likely to remain the subject of arguments among scholars for the foreseeable future.'

It is beyond my contrivance to summarise Burn's six new pages on Thermopylai, based on walking the ground of the Persian flank-march in 1974. Much must remain uncertain, though the fact that we are dealing with a body of troops imposes constraint on the choice of routes, the best hardly good. 'The disciplined movement of the Immortals, to get there by any route, remains impressive.' Burn's preferred route is still, roughly, that indicated by the arrows on the map on p. 408.

The note on Plataiai acknowledges a debt to W. K. Pritchett, *Studies in Ancient Greek Topography* I 1965, ch. viii. There was certainly no village under Kriekouki (p. 518), and the most likely sites for Hysiai and Erythrai are off the map, to the east; Burn would now put the first arrival of the Greeks further east as well. On other points he maintains his position; the topographical student will need to read Pritchett and him together.

Herodotos' reliability has been a recurrent theme in these pages and I conclude with an item from last year which is, for me, the worst news yet. It concerns a topic not closely explored in this book, the siege of the Athenian Akropolis. Page 434 gives the text. On it has rested the general inclination of topographers to look somewhere near the west end of the north slope for the sanctuary of Aglauros and for various other points, notably the Prytaneion, put near it by Pausanias (i 18); the difficulty of locating the Prytaneion is particularly notorious. In *Hesperia* 52, 1983, 48–63, George Dontas publishes a complete third-century decree, the text of which orders its erection in the sanctuary of Aglauros; it was found in situ, in its base, tilted slightly out of position by a falling rock, under the great cave at the *east* end of the Akropolis. In my law-abiding view, the area is steep, but not quite impossible; picked men could have got up that way, though it might well have been thought wildly improbable that they should. Burn recalls starting in 1928 from above the Theatre of Dionysos, traversing above the cave with due care and climbing the nineteenth-century walls with the help of a buttress; he warns me that any relevance this might have is weakened by the likelihood that any rock-climb will alter in $2000 + x$ years. The trouble, of course, is to determine how the route could ever have been described as 'in the front part of the Akropolis, but in rear of the gates and the approach-way'. Dontas struggles nobly with the problem, but unconvincingly. 'The most plausible explanation is that the ancients regarded as the official front of the Akropolis not the side where the entrance was situated but that of the front part of their temples, i.e. their eastern part.' 'The Prytaneion was considered the center of the Asty, the city. . . . When Herodotos writes "in front of the Akropolis" he is standing at the Prytaneion, the heart of the city, and looks towards the Akropolis facing its gods. . . .' Since the whole description of the siege has begun by focusing our attention on the Areopagus at the west end, I find this explanation unnatural. I do not think that even Fehling has yet doubted that Herodotos visited Athens and I do not doubt it now. It does seem to me that Herodotos reported this particular episode without getting himself shown the ground.

Thucydides, after getting in two hits at Herodotos without naming him (not perhaps as damaging hits as he thought), remarks: 'So little trouble do most people take in their search for truth, and they turn rather to what lies ready to hand' (i 20.3). The judgment is generally taken to be based only on Herodotos' writing, and little consideration has been given to the fact that, even if Thucydides did not meet Herodotos, he had certainly met people who had and could tell him about him. Thucydides thought Herodotos an amateur, without giving sufficient weight to the range over which he worked. Thucydides' own field of work was narrower, chronologically, geographically, culturally, linguistically. When one considers the body of material which Herodotos acquired and reduced to order, there should be no disposition to make light of his achievement, but no expectation that he should be infallible. It can confidently be predicted that the next twenty-two years will produce as much material to his credit and his discredit.

Some fuller references

Armayor, 'Herodotus' catalogues of the Persian Empire in the light of the monuments and the Greek literary tradition', *Transactions of the American Philological Association* 108, 1978, 1–9.

Badian, 'Archons and *Strategoi*', *Antichthon* 5, 1971, 1–34.

Burn, 'Thermopylai revisited and some topographical notes on Marathon and Plataiai' in K. H. Kinzl (ed.), *Greece and the Eastern Mediterranean in Ancient History and Prehistory* (1977), 89–105.

Cameron, 'The Persian satrapies and related matters', *Journal of Near Eastern Studies* 32, 1973, 47–56.

Cook, J. M., *The Persian Empire* (1983).

Gershevitch, 'The False Smerdis', *Acta Antiqua* 27, 1979 (published 1981), 337–51.

Gershevitch, 'The alloglottography of Old Persian', *Transactions of the Philological Society* 1979, 114–90.

Grayson, A. K., *Assyrian and Babylonian Chronicles* (1975).

Hallock, R. T., *The Evidence of the Persepolis Tablets* (1971). (This was printed, but not fully published, by the Middle East Centre, Cambridge, and will appear in *The Cambridge History of Iran* Vol. II.)

Lewis, D. M., *Sparta and Persia* (1977).

Rhodes, P. J., *A Commentary on the Aristotelian Athenaion Politeia* (1981).

Texts. The Treasury Tablets from Persepolis were published by G. G. Cameron, *Persepolis Treasury Tablets* (1948); there are additional texts in the *Journal of Near Eastern Studies* 17, 1958, 172–6 and 24, 1965, 170–85; Hallock's re-readings and interpretations, ibid. 19, 1960, 90–100, are an essential complement. The major publication of the fortification tablets is by R. T. Hallock, *Persepolis Fortification Tablets* (1969); there are additional texts in *Cahiers de la Délégation archéologique française en Iran* 8, 1978, 109–36. The Babylonian version of the Behistun inscription is republished by E. N. von Voigtlander, *The Bisitun Inscription of Darius the Great: Babylonian Version* (1978); a new edition of the Aramaic fragments is promised. There is a useful supplement to R. G. Kent, *Old Persian: Grammar, Texts, Lexicon* (second edition 1953): M. Mayrhofer, *Supplement zur Sammlung der altpersischen Inschriften* (1978).

Christ Church, Oxford D. M. LEWIS

Index to Postscript